Current Perspectives in
Industrial/Organizational Psychology

Current Perspectives in Industrial/Organizational Psychology

• •

Geula Lowenberg
University of Wisconsin—Parkside

Kelley A. Conrad
Human Resources Development Consulting
Milwaukee, Wisconsin, and Naples, Florida

with

Dan Dowhower
Case Western Reserve University

Christine Harness
University of Wisconsin—Milwaukee

Allyn and Bacon

Boston   London   Toronto   Sydney   Tokyo   Singapore

Editor-in-Chief, Social Sciences: *Sean W. Wakely*
Editorial Assistant: *Jessica Barnard*
Production Administrator: *Joe Sweeney*
Editorial Production Service: *Peggy J. Flanagan*
Composition Buyer: *Linda Cox*
Manufacturing Buyer: *Megan Cochran*
Cover Administrator: *Linda Knowles*
Text Designer: *Glenna Collett*

Copyright © 1998 by Allyn & Bacon
A Viacom Company
160 Gould Street
Needham Heights, MA 02194

Internet: www.abacon.com
America Online: Keyword: College Online

Photo credits appear on p. 618, which constitutes a continuation of the copyright page.

Library of Congress Cataloging-in-Publication Data

Lowenberg, Geula.
    Current perspectives in industrial organizational psychology / by
Geula Lowenberg and Kelley A. Conrad.
        p.   cm.
    Includes bibliographical references and index.
    ISBN 0-205-14252-4
    1. Psychology, Industrial.   2. Personnel management—Psychological
aspects.   3. Industrial sociology.   I. Conrad, Kelley A.
II. Title.
HF5548.8.L664   1997   97-44531
                                                    CIP

Printed in the United States of America
10 9 8 7 6 5 4 3 2 1   02 01 00 99 98 97

Dedicated to our parents:

Hanina and Miriam Grinberg
who gave Geula the courage of her beliefs
and the inspiration to pursue excellence,

Allen and Dorothy Conrad
for their guidance, support,
and unconditional love of Kelley.

And to our spouses:

Benjamin Lowenberg
a loving husband, friend, and colleague,
a symbol to the sanctity of life,

and

Barb Conrad
life is so much easier with your hand to hold,
your love, and your support.

Brief Contents

Contents

Preface

All of us currently working in industrial/organizational psychology—academicians, students, businesspeople, and consultants—are confronted with the challenge of applying this discipline to a rapidly evolving global economy. Today, the mandate of industrial/organizational psychology is to combine theory and practice effectively, in the context of this new reality.

Through the sixteen chapters in this book, we examine a broad range of I/O theories, models, and their applications. In recognition of the expanding worldwide focus of industrial/organizational psychology, we have incorporated a unique feature in our text—numerous uniform resource locators (URLs) delineating resources on the Worldwide Web. To further the goals of theory and practice, we have used an innovative approach of capturing selected historical, scientific, and practical perspectives. Additionally, to bridge theory and practice within the context of current events, we have included "real life" occurrences reported by periodicals such as the *Wall Street Journal*, exercises based on practical application, and subjects such as compensation, human resources management, and international perspectives, often omitted by other industrial/organizational texts.

A good ancillary is a priceless tool, and we have prepared an *Instructor's Resource Manual* to accompany this book. It contains a variety of questions to help test students' knowledge of the subject area. The *Instructor's Manual* also includes a Programmed Review section of fill-in-the-blank questions for students to test their I/O vocabulary.

This book would not have been possible without the help of others who have contributed in many ways. We have found writing a text designed as a comprehensive review of a body of professional knowledge to be a truly humbling experience. We can think of no other activity that has made us more aware of how much of our day-to-day wisdom comes from others. We "stand on the shoulders of giants." To all who have contributed, we extend our heartfelt thanks.

We are especially grateful to our students at the University of Wisconsin—Parkside, Alverno College, Milwaukee School of Engineering, and Mount Mary College. Most have come from the disciplines of psychology, business, or social sciences. Our experiences with these students as well as their encouragement to "write a book," inspired us to commit to this effort. Over the four years we worked on the book, many of our students interacted with us and "the book," providing the feedback we needed. Students whose efforts in support of the book were above what was expected of them include: S. Anderson, C. J. Brey, S. Davis, C. A. Gustafson, C. L. Isetts, P. J. Laupam, D. J. Leemon, K. C. Nilsen, J. Perszyk, J. M. Peterson, K. Simons, J. M. Trimberger,

J. L. Van Horn, L. M. Wiggins, C. Zanin, K. M. Zickus, and J. L. Zurawski.

We are in debt to Perry Margoles, Charlotte Westerhaus, and all our colleagues and consulting clients who read or used chapters or parts of chapters and provided us with constructive input and suggestions. We could not have accomplished this project without the library personnel at the University of Wisconsin—Parkside. We want to specifically thank Sylvia Beardsley, Bruce Johnson, Dina Kaye, Ellen Pedraza, Linda Piele, Judith Pryor, and Teri Weil for their help. This team responded to our most difficult requests with professional acumen.

We want to thank Susan Badger who was our editor through the first three years of writing and revising. We valued her encouragement and support. When she left Allyn and Bacon to pursue opportunities elsewhere, we were fortunate to have our present editor, Sean Wakely. He stepped into the process, doing it so smoothly we hardly noticed our editor had changed. Our editorial assistants, Erika Stuart and Jessica Barnard, cheerfully guided us through our manuscript preparation. Our production editor, Peggy J. Flanagan, and our copy editor, Barbara Willette, have demonstrated how much competent editors can contribute to a writing effort.

Two of our students entered graduate school, but continued to work with us and became our colleagues. Dan Dowhower became a coauthor on three chapters, while Christine Harness became the primary author on one chapter and an editorial advisor. We also owe our gratitude to the following people, who read our manuscript and made suggestions for improvement: Robert Bauer, Valdosta State University; Caran Colvin, San Francisco State University; Diane Davis, Oakton Community College; William P. Gaeddert, State University of New York College at Plattsburgh; Timothy D. Ludwig, Appalachian State University; Beth Martin, John Carroll University; William Roe, Phoenix College; and Allen N. Shub, Northeastern Illinois University.

We know there are many others who have contributed either directly or indirectly—to all of you we extend our warmest appreciation and sincerest thanks. This book is yours. With your help we believe it will be a bridge to greater understanding for many students as they apply the science of psychology to the day-to-day world of work and organizations.

Both of us have often commented that "we wish 'they' would put this or that in a text." Rather than remain "wannabes," we decided to take the bull by the horns and write the book we wanted. Now that we are at the end of the process we have new appreciation for a comment made by President Theodore Roosevelt, who said:

> The key which lifts one to every aspiration while others are caught up in the mire of mediocrity—is not talent, formal education, nor intellectual brightness; it is self-discipline. With self-discipline, all things are possible. Without it, even the simplest goal can seem like the impossible dream.

Current Perspectives in
Industrial/Organizational Psychology

CHAPTER

1

What Is Industrial/ Organizational Psychology?

Chapter Outline

hy am I proud to be an I/O psychologist? I'm proud to be an I/O psychologist because we are idealists who seek perfection and improvement in the world of work. Concerned for the welfare of the worker, as well as the welfare of the organization, we attempt to change things, rather than simply explain them. As pragmatists, we impact organizations by applying nearly 100 years of research in practically useful ways. We attempt to prove that our interventions are worthwhile, increasing the job performance of individuals and groups and enhancing the efficiency and effectiveness of the organization as a whole.

I'm proud to be an I/O psychologist because we design systems that ensure that bias and discrimination are eliminated so that the most capable and motivated people will get the good jobs. We develop programs in training, compensation, performance appraisal, management development, career development, and employee stress management to help develop and transform entire organizations by increasing performance and job satisfaction.

I'm proud to be an I/O psychologist because of the wonderful people in this profession. We are highly educated professionals who combine the free-thinking of liberal arts with the disciplined-thinking of science. In our search for what is of value, we willingly share our knowledge with each other and with those in other organizations and occupations. Motivated by our desire to continually improve our work and our field of study, we are critical of each other's work. Most of us are very hard-working people guided by higher-order principles and standards, yet realistic enough not to take ourselves too seriously.

(Adapted from Campion, 1996, pp. 27–29)

Industrial/organizational psychology studies human behavior as it occurs in business, industrial, and organizational settings. Mike Campion's address as 1995–96 President of the Society for Industrial Organizational Psychologists, which is summarized here, provides insights into what being an industrial/organizational (I/O) psychologist means to many members of the profession. As scientist-practitioners, we often find ourselves with one foot in the world of science, emphasizing empirical evidence, and the other foot in the world of practical reality, applying what we know to solve real problems in organizational and work settings.

The science-practice of I/O psychology values science and practice equally. Each perspective enriches the other; both are vital to finding solutions to industrial and organizational problems. We succeed by improving the fit between the work force and the workplace to improve organizational effectiveness and by contributing our data, analyses, and theories toward furthering the scientific understanding of human behavior.

As *scientists*, I/O psychologists bring research perspectives to the world of work. Using the full range of experimental designs and analyses that are the hallmarks of science, we study human behavior in both laboratory and work settings. As scientists we challenge ourselves and our fellow scientists to think about organizational and work behavior as behavior that is more than simply the sum of its parts. We use our client's interests to direct our investigations. Yet we are on guard against letting practical considerations or client demands bias our science. We advocate a collaborative science in which practical realities and demanding time frames are accepted as meaningful components of the knowledge base we are building and refining.

As *practitioners*, I/O psychologists seek to apply what we have learned from our scientific investigations in ways that directly solve our client's industrial and organizational problems. As professionals we are devoted to our calling: gaining as complete an understanding as possible of the problems and issues that relate to human behavior in work and organizational settings. We use our influence with leaders to enhance the working experience of all employees, to foster individual and organizational development, and to add real-world content to our science. We guard against allowing practical considerations to water down our scientific rigor or to accept less from ourselves than what we are capable of providing.

As **scientist-practitioners,** I/O psychologists are aware of the lessons of the past. Reviewing previous studies in an area is an integral part of our scientific method. We recognize that patterns and trends that are observed across studies have often provided insights that studies in isolation did not. Our definition of I/O psychology summarizes who we are and what we do.

The science-practice of I/O psychology is a psychological profession that involves the study of human behavior as it occurs in business, industrial, and organizational settings. Part science and part applied technology, I/O psychology uses the full range of scientific designs and analyses to study organizational behavior, whether the nature of that behavior is intraindividual (such as job satisfaction and motivation), interindividual (such as ability and performance testing, selection and development assessment, performance appraisal, and cognitive processing), or environmental (such as information displays, environmental stressors, and information processing). This unique combination of interests is directed toward predicting human behavior in work and organizational settings or toward creating a desired, meaningful change in existing behavior.

Because the three perspectives (scientist, practitioner, and scientist-practitioner) are so vital to I/O psychology, we will highlight them throughout the text. Throughout the book you will find practice perspectives, scientific perspectives, and historical perspectives set apart from the text itself. These examples have been chosen to assist you in appreciating the interplay of the major perspectives that affect I/O psychology and to illustrate specific, concrete examples of our unique science-practice.

SCOPE AND APPLICATION OF I/O PSYCHOLOGY

The policies and procedures that govern adults in the workplace must be implemented and managed by some organizational department (Howard, 1991). That department is most often the human resources department. In fact, all employees are influenced by human resources practices, from initially being interviewed for a job to receiving compensation for it.

I/O psychologists have a significant impact on human resources, largely as a result of the scientist-practitioner model. Historical trends and the application in practice of I/O ideas and concepts generate questions; scientific research answers these questions. I/O psychologists use the scientist-practitioner model by (a) conducting research on individual, group, and organizational behavior; (b) applying the principles derived from this research to problems at work; and (c) training others. Although the I/O psychologist's clients are typically organizations, he or she also works with individuals to help match them to their jobs, to enhance their job performance and satisfaction, or to help reduce stress. It is this focus on individuals in work environments and on organizations that distinguishes I/O psychology from other specialties in psychology.

Practice Perspective 1.1 on page 6 illustrates the scientist-practitioner model in a segment of real life.

At this point you might be asking yourself, "How does one prepare for this wide range of activities?" The remainder of this section discusses the training that a person requires to prepare to practice I/O psychology. We also discuss some of the main employment options in the field. As you read, it should become apparent that I/O psychologists have numerous opportunities within their chosen specialty. Their impact ranges from influencing individual lives within the workplace to playing leadership roles in industry and organizations.

Training

The typical I/O psychologist has a Ph.D. This is true for 91.7% of the members who responded to a 1994 survey conducted by the Society for Industrial and Organizational Psychology (SIOP)

PRACTICE PERSPECTIVE 1.1

A Day in the Life of an Industrial/Organizational Psychologist

The question I spend the morning on had kept me awake part of the night. One of my clients, Collections, Inc., is experiencing 100 percent turnover in new hires! How could such a good company be experiencing such high levels of turnover? To find out, I propose a thorough study, beginning with in-depth interviews of key managers in strategic locations. We will also select knowledgeable incumbents and complete a careful job analysis of the positions. Following the job analysis, we will develop and validate new selection and training programs for the company.

My first appointment is for a psychological assessment of a candidate to be a broker for an investment management company. The company has a long history of conservative investment management. Its old selection model sought brokers who would not be unusually competitive or aggressive but who would be very strong in interpersonal relationships and trust. Their new model seeks brokers who can continue to work with individual clients who are used to the firm's former style while also being comfortable approaching the market aggressively. When he finishes his testing, I review the results. After the candidate leaves our office, I spend the next hour outlining my report and dictating it.

I have lunch with Chuck, the human resources manager of a long-time client. Over lunch we discuss Bill, a manager I have been coaching. Bill is a skilled technical person who was promoted to management several years ago. I evaluated Bill shortly after he received poor scores on the company's 360 degree management survey and began

a series of coaching sessions to help him develop his communications skills. He has made progress, but not as quickly as we originally hoped. Chuck and I discuss several opportunities for the manager to work closely with another manager who is a talented communicator. We agree that this is a good plan. Chuck will work with the company's management team to set up the assignments while I will continue to work with Bill.

After lunch, I work for an hour with one of my industrial/organizational psychology externs from the University of Wisconsin–Parkside. This extern, Pat, has been working on a validation of part of our assessment process. She has coded data from all of the tests in our test battery for all candidates from one large machine tool company. I give Pat the assignments to review information about validity studies and to design what she believes would be a good way to proceed. We will review and modify that design the next time we meet.

I leave the office at 2:00 to go to a meeting with a local hospital's management team. We are midway through a series of team-building and strategic planning meetings. For this series we are using a computer-assisted decision-making package to facilitate consensus building. We get started on time, and the session goes well. Although we finish fifteen minutes late, everyone seems pleased that we were able to complete defining and prioritizing the key outcomes for the team. Our next session will move to detailed action planning for the highest-ranked objectives. I log in the time and set off for home.

(Borman & Cox, 1996). The remaining members held master's degrees. Howard's 1990 study found that psychology was the primary area of concentration for about 75% of SIOP's members; the remaining 25% were trained in business, education, or other areas. Only 52% of the SIOP members surveyed had received their degree from graduate programs in I/O psychology. In Howard's survey, the following graduate fields of study were listed, in decreasing order of frequency, as the areas of SIOP members' diplomas: I/O psychology, social psychology, organizational behavior, health sciences, experimental psychology, psychometrics, educational psychology, nonpsychology programs, and general psychology.

Although a number of specialty credentials are available, most I/O psychologists do not obtain such certification. Only 5% of I/O psychologists are American Board of Professional Psychology diplomates (Howard, 1990). However, many states require some kind of licensure for independent practice, and 40% of all I/O psychologists are licensed. In many states this license regulates the use of the title "psychologist," enabling those with a license to work as private practitioners without supervision. This is referred to as a **generic license.** In some states, only clinical psychologists need to be licensed. In Illinois, for example, I/O psychologists used to be licensed, but several years ago this was changed, and now only clinical psychologists are licensed. Some I/O psychologists who were "grandfathered in" under the new law have licenses that read "Clinical Psychologist."

Practice Areas in I/O Psychology

I/O psychologists need to be prepared to deal with almost any problem involving people in organizations. In their survey of SIOP members, Borman and Cox (1996) identified twenty-seven major practice areas in which I/O psychologists work. They grouped these into five categories representing the most active I/O practice areas. These were organizational development and change; individual development; performance evaluation and selection; preparing and presenting results; and compensation, labor relations, and benefits. Examination of these five major practice areas will assist the reader in understanding the nature of many I/O psychologists' daily work.

Organizational Development and Change

I/O psychologists who focus on **organizational development and change** analyze organizational structure and attempt to maximize the satisfaction and effectiveness of individuals and work groups by facilitating organizational change. They address group and organizational issues and managerial roles, such as the delegation of power and decision making. Corporate consultants spend about 38% of their time in this area.

I/O psychologists working with consulting firms spend about 28% of their time in this area. All of the twenty-seven practice specialties that Borman and Cox analyzed were doing some work in the organizational development and change area.

Individual Development

The **individual development** area of practice focuses on career and family issues and includes activities such as stress management and general counseling. Practice groups in which this is a major focus include consulting firms, self-employed I/O psychologists, and all nonacademic I/O psychologists. All of these groups spend between 20% and 25% of their time in this area. In contrast, research and academic I/O psychologists typically spend very little time on individual development work.

Performance Evaluation and Selection

The practice specialty of **performance evaluation and selection** includes developing assessment tools for selection, placement, classification, and promotion of employees. It also entails analyzing job content, validating test instruments, developing and implementing selection programs, and developing and implementing performance appraisal programs. Groups in which this is a major activity area, consuming approximately 33% of their time, included government, research firm, and academic I/O psychologists. All of the major groups that Borman and Cox investigated spent around 20% of their time in this area.

Preparing and Presenting Results

The broadest specialty of *generalists* focuses on research activities such as **preparing and presenting the results** of consulting at professional meetings and writing up results for publication in professional journals. As might be expected from the title of this focus area, it involves a variety of practice areas. Government I/O psychologists constitute the primary group using this focus as part of their practice time (10%).

Surprisingly, academic I/O psychologists are underrepresented in this area.

Compensation and Benefits

The last specialty, **compensation and benefits,** focuses on measuring and compensating job performance. Also important are developing criteria, measuring utility, and evaluating the level of accomplishment achieved by the individual. Employee performance is translated into compensation and benefits through job evaluation. I/O psychologists working in this area focus on the combined effects of effort expenditure, role perceptions, abilities, and traits. The scope of compensation and benefits ranges from ensuring fair and equitable pay to designing benefits programs. This is the smallest specialty cluster identified by Borman and Cox (1996), but practitioners with this focus were present in all specialty areas. The amount of time spent on this focus averages only 5% of total practice time.

Figure 1.1 illustrates the six major practice areas in which I/O psychologists work and the percentage of total practitioner time devoted to work within each practice area (Borman & Cox, 1996).

....
OVERVIEW OF INDUSTRIAL/ ORGANIZATIONAL PSYCHOLOGY

Three areas of psychological research interest have contributed to the development of I/O psychology. They are experimental psychology, differential psychology, and industrial engineering.

Experimental Psychology

Experimental psychology is "the investigation of psychological phenomena by experimental methods [with] the results obtained by experiment, [and] systematically set forth" (English &

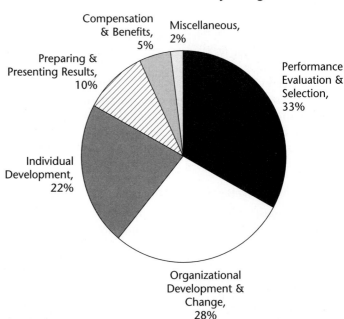

Practice Areas of I/O Psychologists

FIGURE 1.1
Categories representing the most active I/O practice areas.

Source: Based on data in *Who's Doing What: Patterns in the Practice of I/O Psychology* (p. 22), by Walter Borman and Gena Cox, 1996, Arlington Heights, IL: Society for Industrial and Organizational Psychology. Copyright 1996 by Society for Industrial and Organizational Psychology, Inc. Reprinted with permission.

English, 1958, p. 194). Experimental psychology developed from early advances in psychology in which scientific psychologists studied the responses of their subjects to specific environmental conditions. This method became known as **stimulus-response (S-R) psychology.** Its hallmarks were the emphasis on rigorous scientific methodology and on the physiological characteristics and responses of sensory receptors to various stimulus conditions.

Ultimately, however, S-R psychology proved to be too limited because of its extreme scientific rigor. In most situations it is simply impossible to control all variables except the one of primary interest. This issue is still present in I/O psychology. We cannot blindly assume that a result found in a controlled laboratory setting will be generalizable to the working world. However, the rigorous tradition of S-R psychology provides input to all I/O practice areas and is the specific focus of one: the performance evaluation specialty. Experimental psychology is still a key practice area in I/O psychology. It is a focus of many I/O psychologists working in research firms, academia, and the government (Borman & Cox, 1996).

Another early influence on I/O psychology was a direct derivative of S-R experimental psychology. Nothing was more frustrating to the early experimental psychologists than differences in their subjects that affected their results but could not be controlled. This frustration led some investigators to focus on these individual differences.

Differential Psychology

Differential psychology emphasizes the assessment and understanding of individual differences. Its focus is on "the kinds, amounts, causes, and effects of individual or group differences in psychological characteristics" (English & English, 1958, p. 152). Psychologists used the evolving methodology of scientific psychology to study their subjects' abilities, interests, and traits. In this way they created the field of differ-

ential psychology, which focuses on the study of individual differences. One key individual difference was intelligence. At the turn of the century psychologists learned that individuals could be tested and their intelligence described by a score (an intelligence quotient, or IQ). This process was so efficient and easy that it quickly became, and has remained, a popular psychological tool.

Industrial Engineering

Industrial engineering (also referred to as *human engineering*) is "concerned with the design of equipment and the arranging of the physical conditions of work in relation to human sensory capacities, psychomotor abilities, learning capacities, body dimensions, comfort, safety, and satisfactions" (English & English, 1958, p. 243). Industrial engineering emphasizes the design and layout of machinery and its influence on production.

These traditions in I/O psychology provide the intellectual basis for two major I/O practice areas: individual development (which includes individual coaching, executive development, individual assessment, succession planning, and outplacement) and selection (which includes job analysis, personnel selection, assessment centers, performance appraisal, and legal defense of the selection process).

Industrial psychology evolved as a part of the Zeitgeist (the spirit of the time) that existed in the early years of the twentieth century. Researchers were laboring in psychology, engineering, and business, laying the foundations of several fields of inquiry and practice that eventually formed parts of what today we think of as the discipline of I/O psychology. I/O psychology has developed from a narrow field that concentrated mainly on testing candidates for selection and considered only organizational goals to a field that emphasizes both the individual and the organization. As you read this section, you will see how attention has shifted from accomplishing only the organizational ends, to an interest in the interaction between attaining the goals of the employee and the organization.

Brief History of Industrial/ Organizational Psychology

Human beings are curious animals. We are interested in how things work and why we and others like us behave as we do. For much of our history our attempts to understand one another have been speculative. Early psychology was characterized by explanations of personality based on bumps on one's head (phrenology), lines on the palm (palmistry), facial characteristics (physiognomy), and the date and time of one's birth (astrology). The fact that these pseudopsychologies persist demonstrates how difficult it is to disprove and replace existing explanations. Perhaps it is variable reinforcement in operation. When such explanations are correct (reinforced), only rarely and almost at random (with variable intervals between correct and incorrect statements) are behaviors that they generate (and the belief in them) highly persistent and resistant to extinction. Do you doubt that? When did you last check your horoscope? When was the last time it was precisely correct? Do you still check it?

Late in the nineteenth century and early in the twentieth century the scientific study of psychology began to emerge as some daring scientists began to apply the proven principles of the scientific method in their attempts to systematically understand and predict how and why people act as they do. Most historians credit Wilhelm Wundt with establishing the first laboratory for the study of psychology in 1879—just a little over one hundred years ago. Although the field of I/O psychology has a relatively short history (the first Ph.D. in industrial psychology was awarded in 1921), we can identify five main historical periods: the precursor years and the 1910s, the 1920s and 1930s, the 1940s, the 1950s and 1960s, and 1970 to the present.

We now briefly examine the history of I/O psychology through these five historical periods. Notice the development of a professional perspective combining the rigor of science with the challenges of applied practice. This difficult and unique combination of science and practice is the hallmark of I/O psychology.

Precursors and the 1910s

France's greatest psychologist at the turn of the century was Alfred Binet. An experimentalist, he followed the existing French research preferences and stressed individual differences in his research. He founded the first French psychological laboratory at the Sorbonne and in 1903 published his *L'étude expérimentale de L'intelligence*. Shortly afterward, in 1905, he published (with Théodore Simon) the first intelligence scale. The idea of describing people by measuring their intelligence caught on quickly. Binet and Simon accumulated research evidence that helped to improve the measure. Binet used the data to revise his test in 1908 and in 1911. The test was tremendously successful. In 1916, Lewis Terman revised Binet's scale in the United States, creating the Stanford-Binet and with it the very popular concept of intelligence quotient (IQ). The Stanford-Binet and IQ tests became the standard measures of intelligence for the next twenty-five years. Intelligence testing was in such favor that it became a part of the routine selection screening for military service late in World War I. In fact, differential psychology, specifically intelligence testing, became such a dominant force in early psychology that Edwin Boring, the great historian of experimental psychology, called the 1910s "the decade of intelligence testing" (Boring, 1957, p. 574).

Another of the earliest influences on the development of industrial psychology came from advertising and selling. In 1903, Walter D. Scott published the first book applying psychology to industry, entitled *The Theory of Advertising*. In 1913, Hugo Munsterberg wrote *Industrial Efficiency*, which addressed accidents and safety in industry. His book included other topics of applied psychology, such as learning, adjustment to physical conditions, economy of movements, fatigue, and monotony at work.

Time and motion studies, which seek the elimination of waste and inefficiency through cost reduction, work method improvement, and reducing work fatigue, were introduced in F. W. Taylor's book *Scientific Management* (1911). The interest sparked by Taylor's and Munsterberg's books grew into a philosophy of how to study people in the working environment. This philosophy was most successfully elaborated by Frank Gilbreth, an engineer, and his wife Lillian, a psychologist.

The Gilbreths' book, *Applied Motion Study* (1917) brought the strengths of both engineering and psychological perspectives to the study of work. The objective of time and motion studies was to improve work proficiency. Time studies focused on determining a standard time required to complete a task or job. Motion studies focused on the methods, motions, and movements of workers completing a standard task. The balance of mechanical and human emphasis provided a unique combination (see Practice Perspective 1.2 on page 12). The Gilbreths' book was a significant attempt to meld the still young science of psychology with the applied discipline of engineering. A measure of their success is that today's processes for methods analysis (operation charts, person-machine charts, and micromotion studies) are all direct descendants of concepts the Gilbreths created. They did not, however, realize the importance of the repetitive motion syndrome that has become an important part of today's workplace and of effective ergonomic design.

Two main trends were evident in the early history of I/O psychology: attempts to improve productivity and the establishment of selection and employment tests. The first trend consisted of working to discover efficient methods of production, taking into account economic, engineering, and physical conditions. Employees and organizations were considered separate entities; management provided the goals, and psychologists worked with engineers to establish the best way by which the employee could serve the organization. The Gilbreths' purpose in *Ap-*

plied Motion Study, was to devise a method to fit the *average* worker (see Scientific Perspective 1.1 on page 13). Operating within the tenets of experimental psychology, they gave no consideration to individual differences. At this stage in the development of psychology an employee was viewed as a potential variable within the organization. This variable could be measured by using intelligence tests and other measures from differential psychology, and training programs could be used to diminish or banish troublesome individual differences in behavior (Landy, 1989).

As was described earlier, the second trend during this period was the development of selection and employment tests. During World War I, American Psychological Association (APA) president Robert Yerkes suggested that psychology could improve the utilization of soldiers. Another strong advocate of using psychology was Walter Scott, whose views were well known and respected. Their efforts led to the testing of more than a million recruits. The goal was to place them in appropriate jobs in the armed forces, with psychologists assisting in the development and administration of psychometric tests and the prediction of job success. These practitioners assumed that the major difference between individuals who could perform effectively and those who could not was their level of general intelligence. Accordingly, they developed the first group of intelligence tests: the Army Alpha for those who could read English and the Army Beta for those who were illiterate in English. Unfortunately, the program was not fully operational until late in the war. Although it had little effect on the success of the war, it exposed an enormous number of recruits to intelligence tests as a part of placement. This application was the first major success in developing a psychological method to help make a positive change in overall organizational effectiveness. Some people (e.g., Korman, 1977) date the beginnings of organizational psychology to this effort. From this base, testing made its way into general industrial and organizational use for selection.

PRACTICE PERSPECTIVE 1.2

Time and Motion

Time and motion studies are not extremely technical or intricate; they are relatively simple to conduct, provided one recognizes a few basic principles.

A very useful principle is that used in determining the most favored work area, sometimes known as the "semicircular work pit." Regardless of whether the employee is doing office work at a desk or assembling at a workbench, this principle can be applied. By circumscribing an arc with your right hand when your elbow is at the hip, and then with your left hand with elbow at hip, you will define a semicircle in which you can work with a minimum of moving and reaching. Then, keeping your back erect, swing your right arm to the left, and your left arm to the right, and you will define two other semicircles. These two overlapping areas determine a second, and larger semicircle. This is the area wherein you can reach things with the minimum of stretching and body movement. Most work can be done in the first semicircle; but if necessary, it may be extended to the second one. This semicircular work pit is the most favored work area from the point of view of economy of motion and minimum effort.

The prepositioning of tools, another simple principle, is a useful technique in time and motion studies. It avoids much unnecessary delay in looking for tools which have been misplaced. Prepositioning operates effectively for a bank teller, a shipping clerk, a watch assembler, and many other workers.

The prolonged holding of an object is poor motion practice. The introduction of a jig or vise to clamp the work will free the holding hand. Most efficiency concepts encourage the use of both hands. Motion of the two hands is most efficient when they are used in opposite and symmetrical directions. . . .

The introduction of rhythm in work is also an important principle. Experienced carpenters, typists, and painters have rhythm in their work. In fact, a simple but crude manner of judging work performance and ability is to observe the worker on the job and watch for regular, smooth, and even movements. . . .

A drop delivery will prevent the cluttering of the work space and the waste of time involved in transferring the finished product. A hole at the work place leading to a chute which carries the finished product away makes for efficiency and economy. Labor savings of 5 to 10 percent have often been accomplished by introducing a drop delivery system. . . .

The process chart is a desirable and not very technical device. A process chart records exactly what goes on. It may be a *flow chart,* which records the flow of work during the process. Or it may be a *man-and-machine chart,* which records the work of the machine in relation to the work of the man. A third type is the *operator chart,* which is mainly concerned with the separate work done by the left hand and the right hand. The *cost chart,* which establishes the cost of the operation, is a process chart that brings new happiness to the accountants in our society.

Another principle in time and motion study is the reduction of motion. Motions involving only the fingers are considered most efficient because they require least muscular effort. The least efficient motion is one which requires the use of the entire body. It is sometimes claimed that an attempt to reduce motions to such simple levels introduces monotony and related phenomena. Although in some instances this may be true from the point of view of efficiency, it must be conceded that the motion that involves the fewest muscles is the least fatiguing to the individual.

SCIENTIFIC PERSPECTIVE 1.1

Applied Motion

In their book *Applied Motion Study,* Frank and Lillian Gilbreth devised a system of efficiency that included nine principles: (1) individualization, (2) functionalism, (3) measurement, (4) analysis and synthesis, (5) standardization, (6) records and programs, (7) teaching, (8) incentives, (9) welfare.

Their system was all-inclusive and in many respects valid, not only in the production increases obtained but also in the recognition that the individual workman was the unit to be measured. The Gilbreths believed that the details of the work situation should be adjusted to the individual rather than the individual being forced into the pattern of the job. Their writings (1916, 1917) show much more insight and understanding of the individual than Taylor's work, and there is little evidence of the contempt for the workman which Taylor seems to have had.

One of the most interesting of the Gilbreths' contributions was the analysis and breakdown of a task into its basic elements of motion, which they called "therbligs." This word, invented by Frank Gilbreth as the result of a suggestion from his wife, can in some respects be considered as a forerunner of Serutan. Reading therblig backward gives the name Gilbreth except that the t and h are reversed. The therbligs are very useful; each has a name and a symbol. . . .

Every job involves a number of these therbligs. By way of illustration, consider signing one's name. A man usually keeps his fountain pen in his inside coat pocket. In therblig terms he must search, find, select (assuming he has more than one pen), transport . . ., position, disassemble, position, use, assemble, transfer, search, find, position. A lot of work for such a simple task that is done in so short a time.

After all the therbligs involved in the task have been identified, it is then necessary to ask six questions:

1. Is each therblig necessary?
2. Can the task be made simpler by having fewer motions?
3. Can there be less motion in performance or degree?
4. Can the steps be combined?
5. Can the sequence be changed?
6. Can more than one be done at the same time?

To go back to signing one's name, it is immediately obvious that a more efficient system would use a desk-set pen in a fixed position; this requires no assembling and disassembling and no selecting, and many of the other therbligs are not required.

Source: From *Industrial Psychology: Its Theoretical and Social Foundations,* Revised Edition (pp. 578–579), by M. L. Blum and J. C. Naylor (1968), New York: Harper & Row Publishers. Copyright © 1968 by M. L. Blum and J. C. Naylor. Reprinted by permission of HarperCollins Publishers, Inc.

The work that we have described so far was foundational. Psychology was young. Many new approaches were emerging. Some were more scientific, some were more applied, but as yet there was no coherent field of industrial/organizational psychology. Psychologists were developing skill in assessing individual differences and in applying their knowledge to selection processes and to industrial work design situations. One event that demonstrated how important the new science of psychology and its application was becoming was the founding of the *Journal of Applied Psychology.* Begun in 1917, the *Journal of Applied Psychology* was a unique journal that focused on *applications* of psychology rather than simply psychological science. It has continued in existence to the present day and has been the source of many of the important articles that use the science-practice perspective. It has become the primary channel of publication for today's I/O psychologists. Because of its importance and its unique, continuing emphasis on combining science with practice, we believe that it is appropriate to consider the date of the founding of the *Journal of Applied Psychology* as the birth date of I/O psychology.

The 1920s and 1930s

The 1920s brought disenchantment with psychological techniques; psychometric tests did not appear to be as effective as had initially been claimed. As the tests were applied more widely, it appeared that employees who had been hired with the aid of tests were no more effective on the job than were those hired without tests. Additionally, critics of intelligence testing cited the misuse of psychological testing by politicians who argued for discriminatory immigration policies (Snyderman & Herrnstein, 1983) that would impose quotas on immigrants from southern and eastern Europe.

The Immigration Act of 1924 imposed quotas on immigration to the United States that were based on the percentage of immigrants in the United States from each country according to the census of 1890. By using the 1890 census the act excluded many immigrants from southern and eastern Europe (which were the sources of most immigration to America after 1890) in favor of those from northern and western Europe (the sources before 1890). The way in which the quotas were applied and their impact on immigrants attracted a lot of attention.

Unfortunately, it was also discovered that some American psychologists (e.g., Henry H. Goddard, who was the lead psychologist for the Immigration Service) assessed immigrants at Ellis Island using an early version of IQ tests without considering the limitations of the tests. Immigrants whose English was poor were assessed using a verbally weighted instrument written in English. This resulted in a high percentage of these immigrants being labeled as feeble-minded, because of their low test scores.

Many psychologists did not support such labeling and, in fact, were " . . . firmly opposed, to using tests so irreversibly" (Snyderman and Herrnstein, 1983, p. 991). Nevertheless, the damage had been done, and the testing movement lost some of its initial luster. Psychological techniques and intelligence tests, in particular, were no longer seen as easy solutions to organizational problems.

A major development that recognized the importance of individual differences in psychology and industry was the creation of the Minnesota Employment Stabilization Research Institute (MESRI). The institute was established in 1931 to study the psychological and economic effects of unemployment (Tyler, 1965). This focus was expanded by using B. J. Dvorak's (1935) concept of **differential occupational ability patterns,** which compared individual ability profiles to the occupational profiles of effective workers in a variety of jobs to systematically guide individuals toward more satisfying careers. The result was the formulation of two ideas that have significantly affected the field of I/O psychology: (a) the concept that individual differences could be shown by special aptitude tests, not only by general intelligence tests, and (b) the development of aptitude tests such as the Minnesota Clerical Test, the Minnesota Paper Form Board Test, and others. MESRI was successful and expanded. Its success led to the establishment of the University of Minnesota's Industrial Relations Center and Counseling Center and to acceptance of the academic discipline of industrial psychology within the department of psychology.

The development of I/O psychology was further enhanced during this period by the first large-scale systematic analysis of jobs by the U.S. Department of Labor. The first issue of the *Dictionary of Occupational Titles (DOT)* was published in 1939. It moved psychologists further toward realizing the significance of matching individual ability profiles with differential job requirements. A variety of methods were used to accomplish this match, including selection and placement, vocational guidance, and a combination of both processes called **differential job placement** (Dunnette, 1966, p. 184).

At the same time as the controversy about intelligence testing and the disenchantment with its use were taking place, a new emphasis on the individual as an important factor in the achievement of organizational goals was created by the surprising **Hawthorne studies** at the Western Electric Company plant near Chicago. Drawing on experimental methods, the Hawthorne studies began in 1924 as part of an efficiency research project in which the effects of physical or environmental conditions (such as levels of light) on employee performance were to be investigated. The results suggested that changes in physical conditions had no significant relationship to performance. For example, productivity remained constant, or increased, with decreasing levels of light. It *was* discovered that *social factors* such as informal relationships among members of the experimental groups, leadership styles, and employee attitudes had an impact on productivity. One of these social factors was the research study itself. Workers performed better when they knew that their work was the object of the researcher's attentions. The Hawthorne studies' surprising results led to the development of the human relations movement and the recognition that a significant factor in organizational efficacy was treating employees as people. This recognition grew over the next twenty to twenty-five years into classical organizational theory.

These challenges—together with other developments such as the Minnesota Stabilization Employment Research Institute and the Hawthorne studies—led I/O psychologists to consider basic human behavior and individual differences as critical variables in the workplace. One result was the assessment of personality and motivation as predictors of job performance (Korman, 1977). Industrial psychology's primary transformation during this period came from recognition of the impact of social factors on workers' behavior. Industrial field research merged with laboratory human

behavior research. An emphasis on the work group, both informal and formal, together with an emphasis on the individual, led to a wider frame of reference in dealing with practical problems in industry. For example, the employee selection process began to consider not only the requirements of the job, but also factors such as reward systems and the personal needs of the applicant. This emerging theoretical view—the recognition of the interdependence between the individual worker, work groups, management, and the organization as a whole—brought about a revolution in the field. The following decades saw a proliferation of this perspective.

Late in this period there was considerable interest in studying human behavior when workers were using tools and machines. The results of these studies were used to design machines and controls that capitalized on human behavioral capacities, abilities, and motivations. This area of study and practice came to be referred to as human factors engineering and design or, more simply, as **engineering psychology.**

The 1940s

In the 1940s, World War II contributed to the growth of industrial psychology, with practical concerns again dominating the field. Psychologists, building on their experience in World War I, constructed ability tests for the classification of draftees to the armed forces, such as the Army General Classification Test (AGCT). **Situational stress tests** were developed in which candidates for special assignments were observed in situations in which they were required to interact with other candidates to accomplish difficult tasks. Psychologists became involved in the selection and training of pilots, and by 1945, engineering psychology had become a part of industrial psychology.

After the war, the techniques pioneered in military use came into wide industrial use. The techniques of selection and placement were foremost among these. The growth of this specialty was so rapid that it began to develop its own coherent body of practice, which became known as **personnel psychology.** In 1948 the *Journal of Personnel Psychology* began publication.

Time and motion studies influenced the development of engineering psychology into the **person-machine system.** Integrating human factor studies with research on individual differences and group dynamics, this resulted in a system that (a) designed machines, operations, and work environments based on the capacities and limitations of the *average* worker and (b) designed training programs for employees operating these machines. Parallel to this development was a growing interest in organizational characteristics and their influence on individual behaviors, such as employee attitudes, employee morale, communication processes, group interaction, impact of leadership, supervision effects, and others.

The broadening of I/O psychology continued even further through the inclusion of sociological concepts. Organizations used industrial psychology, social psychology, and sociology; and personnel departments applied the knowledge acquired in all areas to the processes of selection, placement, performance appraisal, promotion, and training.

The base had now been laid to support research into complex processes such as motivation, leadership styles, and informal group behavior. During the 1930s and 1940s, Kurt Lewin, who had escaped from Europe and Adolf Hitler, introduced the methodology of controlled laboratory experiments for the investigation of complex group behavior in humans. Lewin's work initiated interest and subsequent research in areas such as group dynamics, effects of leadership styles on individual behavior, the development of management games, sensitivity training, leaderless discussion groups, assessment centers, and group therapy.

The 1950s and 1960s

During the 1950s and 1960s, technological changes and the civil rights movement strongly influenced the development of I/O psychology.

Researchers began to focus on how the organization could best serve the individual, work groups, and ultimately the country as a whole. This period also witnessed the foundation of professional organizations of I/O psychologists such as the Dearborn Conference Group (see Historical Perspective 1.1) for the purpose of discussing and sharing research.

However, "all was not well under the surface, and the decade from 1955 to 1965 saw industrial psychology come under . . . [a] concentrated . . . series of attacks" (Korman, 1977, p. 9). Psychologists were blamed for acting as tools of management without taking the individual employee into account and of not adjusting to the changing social environment emerging from the civil rights movement. Psychologists were charged with using "fashionable thinking," such as assuming that there was a positive, linear relationship between satisfaction and work productivity. They were also accused of not accounting for the presence of ethnic minorities and women in the work force. Finally, they were faulted for applying tests that had not been validated for the purposes for which they were used.

Special congressional hearings held between 1954 and 1955 led to the first publications dealing with standards for testing. These were: Technical Recommendations of Psychological Tests and Diagnostic Techniques (American Psychological Association, 1954), and Ethical Principles of Psychologists (American Psychological Association, 1953). I/O psychologists adjusted to the changing social climate by developing guidelines regulating the application of psychological principles. The goal was consistent with that of the country: to reduce discrimination and bias. The means was to ensure that tests and testing processes were valid and unbiased.

In 1964, Congress passed the Civil Rights Act, under which Title VII forbade discrimination on the basis of race, color, religion, gender, or national origin. This act initiated government intervention in employment practices and led to the creation of the Equal Employment Opportunity Commission (EEOC), which man-

The Dearborn Conference Group

Before World War II, very few organizations pursued any research dealing with personnel issues. Psychologists hired by companies were housed mainly in personnel departments and dealt basically with personnel selection. Interest in other matters dealing with personnel research started to grow rapidly after World War II. The Industrial Relations Research Association (IRRA) estimated that in 1947 there were only twelve special departments in companies dedicated to research in personnel; by 1950 this number had grown to fifty.

In 1951 a group of these managers and professionals doing personnel research decided to organize a special group that would meet regularly to exchange information about their research activities and experiences. The first meeting included fourteen researchers representing such companies as Sears, Esso, and General Motors. All the members of the group came from the personnel staff of these companies. Their discussions of their personnel research were conducted twice a year.

The topics, subjects, and projects that were discussed at these meetings reflect the historical changes that have occurred in I/O psychology: from a focus on organizational issues to one on individual issues, to research dealing with the interaction between the two areas. For example, before World War II the concerns were mainly with personnel selection and an emphasis on productivity. These included discussions about collective bargaining, communication, organizational development, performance appraisal, and other organizational issues. However, the interests and discussions slowly shifted to include areas dealing with benefits to the individual employee. For example, in the 1960s the focus was on civil rights laws, validation issues, discrimination, fairness, and the like. The societal concerns arising in the 1970s were also topics of discussion. These included downsizing, buyouts, mergers and acquisitions, and reorganizations.

Source: Adapted from Meyer (1997).

dated compliance to Title VII on the part of I/O psychologists, employers, labor unions, and employment agencies (Arvey, 1979).

Other developments happened as well. The early 1950s witnessed the development of assessment centers, which have become one of the major approaches in the field of personnel psychology. The American Telephone and Telegraph Company (AT&T) had long pursued efforts to select the very best candidates for new hires for its management development program. Robert Greenleaf, AT&T's director of personnel research, was concerned about the lack of research on adult managers and how they developed. He convinced the Chairman of the Board of AT&T to commit the organization to an extensive study of managerial lives. Douglas Bray was hired to

design and carry out this research, which became known as the Management Progress Study (MPS). The MPS called for assessing young managers when they were hired and then following them through the next eight years. The assessment data, however, were not used in the selection of the managers nor in their development. These decisions made the MPS one of the few large-scale validity studies that were free of initial bias and range restriction in the subject population. At the end of the study period it was clear that the study needed to continue in order to answer the questions it had been initiated to address. It has continued with modifications up to the present (Howard & Bray, 1988).

The mechanism that the MPS used for evaluating the applicants was an assessment center.

An **assessment center** is a comprehensive, standardized procedure in which multiple assessment techniques (such as situational tests and job simulations) are used to evaluate individual employees. Trained management personnel who are not in a direct supervisory capacity over the participants administer the assessment center and make recommendations about the qualifications, developmental needs, and promotional potential of the participants.

The 1960s also saw an expansion of interest in morale, job satisfaction, motivation, leadership styles, communication, and other social effects on work behavior. This research raised many questions. For example, what makes a person work? Under what organizational conditions does a worker perform at his or her best? What types of organizational structures and policies encourage optimal individual performance and satisfaction? Studies investigated questions dealing with peer relationships, group norms, and incentive systems.

This was a prolific period in which several important organizational theories were generated. In their 1979 textbook *Organizational Psychology*, Bass and Ryterband (1979, p. 68) identified nine "theories which dominate efforts to explain what either pushes or pulls people to work and to work hard." The nine most important organizational theories developed in this time frame were those of Vroom (1964), Porter and Lawler (1968), Atkinson (1964), Locke (1968), Herzberg (1966), Maslow (1954), McGregor (1960), Drucker (1954), and Skinner (1953). By the 1960s, organizational psychology had become an integral part of industrial psychology. The discipline was increasingly seen as dealing with psychology in industry and organizations. It combined the methodologies and philosophies of individual differences (e.g., personnel practices, selection) and experimental psychology (e.g., group norms, incentive systems). In 1966 the journal *Organizational Behavior and Human Performance* began publication. In 1973, when the division of the APA that represents I/O psychologists (Division 14)

incorporated, it recognized the growing relationship by formally changing its name to the Society for Industrial and Organizational Psychology, Inc., Division 14 of the American Psychological Association.

1970s to Present

The integration of science and practice that is now the hallmark of I/O psychology is due in large part to developments that have occurred since the 1970s (Dunnette, 1990).

In 1972, Title VII was amended to include state and federal government agencies and educational institutions (Arvey, 1979). This amendment expanded the EEOC's legal authority by allowing the commission to bring action in U.S. courts against these organizations. In 1971 the Supreme Court heard the case of *Griggs* v. *Duke Power Company* (see Historical Perspective 1.2), finding that selection devices (interviews, tests, etc.) must be job related. Arvey (1979, p. 68) noted that this court ruling "opened the door for statistical methods in reviewing the consequential effects of employment practices." It also led to explicit public policy with regard to the use of psychological tests in employment situations (Fincher, 1973). In clarifying and extending Title VII, the 1978 government publication of the *Uniform Guidelines on Employee Selection Procedures* made it clear that employers should not discriminate against members of minorities. In addition, the *Uniform Guidelines* accepted many aspects of current psychological practice as appropriate for proving the validity of any instrument that is used in personnel selection (Novick, 1981).

We believe that the existence of specific legal requirements governing the actions of many I/O psychologists reinforced the use of scientific procedures for addressing practical problems. As a result of these events, I/O psychologists are now liable for their acts and are required to empirically support and document any description, explanation, or prediction of individual behavior at work.

Griggs v. Duke Power Company

The Duke Power Company initially used a high school diploma as a requirement for internal promotion. After Title VII became effective, Duke Power set up a testing procedure for qualifying employees for new jobs. The battery consisted of two tests: the Wonderlic Personnel Test and the Bennett Mechanical Comprehension Test. The company used cutoff scores that were comparable to the national median for high school graduates. The district court and court of appeals found that Title VII had not been violated because Duke Power had not demonstrated discriminatory intent when it designed its new process. The new standards had been equally applied to blacks and whites. The Supreme Court, however, noted that these test standards were more selective than the original high school graduation requirement. The new standards screened out about half of all high school graduates (the effect of using the median for the cutoff score). The court questioned the job relevance of the new standards.

In 1971 the U.S. Supreme Court rendered its decision on the case, ruling against the use of tests in organizations unless the organization could prove that the test was relevant to the job. The decision placed the burden of demonstrating the fairness of a company's testing procedure on the company. This requirement has come to be known as the "Griggs Burden."

Other specific aspects of this landmark decision include the following:

1. The Civil Rights Act applies to overt discrimination and to practices that appear to be neutral but operate in a discriminatory fashion.
2. Employment practice has to be related to job performance.
3. The employer "has the burden of showing that any given requirement must have a manifest relationship to the employment in question" (p. 67).
4. Tests and other measurement devices are useful, but the ones that are used should be used to measure the person for the job and not the person in the abstract.
5. The court strongly endorsed the EEOC testing guidelines.

The *Griggs* v. *Duke Power Company* decision had effects that extended across almost all fair-employment cases. This resulted from its emphasis on the consequences of an employment practice rather than simply the intent of the practice. Companies had to demonstrate that selection devices were job related. *Whether or not discrimination occurred was judged by the results obtained.* These results could be summarized by statistical analyses.

Source: Adapted from Arvey (1979). *Fairness in selecting employees* (pp. 67–71). Reading, MA: Addison-Wesley Publishing Company.

A second major development during this period was the investigations that were conducted to determine the effectiveness and validity of employment selection tests. This research suggested that correlations between selection devices and job effectiveness (validity coefficients) "varied considerably from study to study, even when the jobs and tests appeared to be similar, or the same" (Raju & Burke, 1983, p. 382). Guion (1976) observed that this variability hin-dered the recognition of psychology as a science of behavior, making it difficult to lay the foundation of general principles necessary to move I/O psychology from a mere compilation of assumptions to a true behavioral science (Raju & Burke, 1983).

Responding to these concerns, Glass (1976); Schmidt and Hunter (1977, 1981); Hunter, Schmidt, and Jackson (1982); and Hunter and Schmidt (1990) developed, refined, and extended a statistical technique called **meta-analysis.** This technique enabled practitioners to systematically review large numbers of studies, examining whether results could be generalized across situations, organizations, and so forth. This made it possible to combine practice and theory, transforming previously subjective interpretations into general conclusions based on empirical evidence and statistical analyses. Meta-analysis provided the missing link between theory and application. The process makes possible the meaningful, cumulative, statistical summary of many related studies, and makes the development of theory objective and verifiable. As a result of all these developments, the behavioral and social sciences have finally secured the status of true sciences (Hunter & Schmidt, 1990).

Meta-analysis has become a popular method for summarizing multiple studies conducted in the same topical area. The technique has continued to develop (Hunter & Schmidt, 1990; McDaniel, Whetzel, Schmidt, & Maurer, 1994; Schmidt et al., 1993), though not without some criticism and disagreement as exemplified in Schmidt, Hunter, Pearlman, and Hirsh's 1985 paper "Forty Questions and Answers about Validity Generalization and Meta-Analysis."

A final significant development during this period was the emergence of a multidisciplinary approach, which addressed the numerous areas that were inextricably interconnected in the study of human behavior at work. As an applied discipline, I/O psychology is bound to other disciplines such as law, sociology, communication, and economics. For example, it is impossible to select employees without accounting for the labor and job markets or to predict job behavior without considering physical conditions (both at home and in the workplace), reward systems, performance appraisal methods, and numerous other factors. The multidisciplinary approach suggests that situational diversity and the interaction between individual differences and work roles are key considerations in the explanation and prediction of behavior in the work environment.

Comparing developments in the field between 1980 and 1990, Dunnette (1990, p. 6), concluded that while in the 1980s there was a "heavy emphasis on individual issues, group issues and organizational issues were emerging as critical areas of concern." In contrast, by 1990 the focus was more on the changes occurring in organizations, the work force, and the interactions between the two.

The 1976 and 1990 *Handbooks of Industrial/Organizational Psychology* (Dunnette, 1976; Dunnette & Hough, 1990, 1991, 1992; Triandis, Dunnette, & Hough, 1994) are among the best indicators of the changes that have occurred in the recent development of I/O psychology. The 1990–1994 revision reflects the emergence of a number of new areas of concern in the field (Dunnette & Hough, 1990, 1991, 1992; Triandis, Dunnette, & Hough, 1994). It discusses the development of theories (in areas such as individual differences, cognitive processing, and decision making), the integration of laboratory and field research, a current emphasis on a broader organizational-social framework, and the expansion of international and cross-cultural research.

As a science-practice, I/O psychology continues to develop. Its combination of research, theory, and practice provides a rich, meaningful perspective from which to view and study the world of people at work and the organizations to which they belong. The historical traditions of experimental, differential, and engineering psychology continue to influence and enrich our perspective. I/O psychology has reached a level of maturity at which it is clearly recognized as a specialty within psychology. Its knowledge base is now large enough that it supports, even encourages, theoretical interpretation. Finally, our technology-shrunken world is challenging us to move beyond our own geo-political boundaries and examine the experiences of other nations. Doing so will destroy some of our previous findings but replace them with new, more general explanations of behavioral processes.

To meet the demands of the global marketplace, I/O psychology has expanded its studies of human behavior in business, industrial, and organizational settings to include cultural and cross-cultural perspectives. The growing recognition of the value of I/O contributions has correspondingly increased the demand for trained I/O psychologists with the result that the number of I/O psychologists has doubled during the last twenty years. With that doubling have come increases in the number and composition of professional associations supporting this science-practice.

PROFESSIONAL ORGANIZATIONS

I/O psychologists belong to a variety of professional associations that reflect the current nature of the practice. This final section of Chapter 1 describes the four major professional associations that support I/O psychologists: the American Psychological Society, the American Psychological Association, the Society for Industrial and Organizational Psychology, and the International Association of Applied Psychology. While there are many other, more specialized societies to which I/O psychologists belong, most are members of at least one of these four, which provide the primary professional and scientific forums for I/O psychology.

The American Psychological Society

The newest major psychological association is the American Psychological Society (APS). A nonprofit society, APS promotes the advancement of psychology as a scientific discipline and general human welfare through research and the application of research. A key part of its mission is to encourage free public access to psychology emphasizing scientific research. Founded in Oklahoma in 1988, the society is currently head-

quartered in Washington, D.C. With over 16,000 members the APS also includes a very active psychology student network. There are three classes of members: fellows, members, and affiliates.

For membership information contact The American Psychological Society, 1010 Vermont Avenue, N.W., Suite 1100, Washington, DC 20005–4907; bitnet: APS@APS; e-mail: APS@aps.washington.dc.us; Internet: http://psych.hanover.edu/APS/.

The American Psychological Association

The grandfather of American psychological associations, the American Psychological Association (APA) was founded in 1892. Currently there are over 83,000 members and 57,000 affiliates. APA's purpose is to advance psychology as both a science and a practice and to promote human welfare by supporting psychology in all its branches. The association

- promotes the improvement of research methods and conditions;
- develops and enforces professional qualifications and competence, including high standards for ethical conduct, education, and achievement;
- sets standards for graduate training in clinical, counseling, and school psychology;
- disseminates psychological knowledge via regional meetings, national meetings, conventions, psychological journals, and special reports;
- helps psychologists find employment.

As a democratic organization, governed by a Council of Representatives, the members of the council include representatives from APA's forty-eight divisions and from affiliated state psychological associations. There are three classes of membership in the APA: associate members, members, and fellows.

For membership information contact The American Psychological Association, 750 First

Street, N. E., Washington, DC 20002–4242; Internet: http://www.apa.org/

The Society for Industrial and Organizational Psychology

As the primary home organization for industrial/organizational psychologists, the Society for Industrial and Organizational Psychology (SIOP) is a nonprofit organization with more than 4,000 members and 1,000 affiliates. A division of the APA (Division 14), SIOP is also an organizational affiliate of APS and is incorporated in its own right. The purpose of the society is to promote human welfare through various applications of psychology to organizations. Examples of such applications include employee selection and placement, organizational development, personnel research, design and optimization of work environments, career development, consumer research, product evaluation, and other areas affecting individual performance within organizations.

As a very active organization, SIOP sponsors a number of activities supporting the professional development of its members and the open exchange of information among I/O psychologists. These include the following:

- *The Industrial Organizational Psychologist (TIP),* a quarterly newsletter describing SIOP activities and providing articles of interest;
- Sponsoring symposia, papers, special addresses, and other programs dealing with the application of psychology to organizations at APA, APS, and SIOP annual conventions;
- Sponsoring in-depth professional development workshops for I/O psychologists;
- Sponsoring the publication of the *Frontiers in I/O Psychology Series,* a series of edited books that address topics on the cutting edge of the field;
- Sponsoring a Professional Practice Series of edited books describing the successful practice of I/O psychology in various organizational settings; and,
- Developing policies and principles for sound, ethical practice in the field of I/O psychology.

Membership is open to all fellows, members, and associate members of the APA, as well as fellows and members of the APS. Undergraduate and graduate students are eligible for student affiliate status. We highly recommend membership to serious students of I/O psychology as a way of getting in touch with the field. Individuals who apply for student affiliate status do not have to be majoring in psychology but must have a faculty advisor sign their application to verify that they are in good academic standing. Student members are not required to be student members of the APA or APS but must currently be engaged in formal study related to the purpose of the society as stated above.

For membership information contact The Society for Industrial and Organizational Psychology, Administrative Office, 745 Haskins Rd., Suite A, P.O. Box 87, Bowling Green, OH 43402; Phone: 419-353-0032; e-mail: lhakel@siop.bgsu.edu; Internet: http://cmit.umomaha.edu/TIP/TIP.html.

The International Association of Applied Psychology

The oldest internationally focused association of psychologists is the International Association of Applied Psychology (IAAP). Founded in 1920, the IAAP provides a means of contact and forums for the exchange of information between applied psychologists in different countries. One way this is accomplished is the IAAP World Congress of Applied Psychology held every four years. The congress attracts several thousand member and non-member psychologists from around the world.

In addition, the IAAP and its thirteen divisions host regional conferences, theme-oriented meetings, workshops, and advanced training for psychologists from Third World countries; sponsor a recognition awards program for psychological work done internationally; and publish several journals. One of these, the quarterly *Applied Psychology—An International Review* has been rated as one of the best scientific periodicals in psychology.

The IAAP has its headquarters in Sweden. IAAP conducts its business in the two official languages of French and English. For membership information contact the Secretary General of the IAAP, Michael C. Knowles, Monash Mt. Eliza Business School, Monash University, Clayton, Victoria, Australia, 3168; Internet: htp://www.ucm.es/OTROS/Psyap/iaap/.

SUMMARY

Industrial/organizational psychologists offer advice to industry, academia, and health-related organizations. Because of its focus on the relationships between the individual, organizations, and society, I/O psychology has a broad and diverse impact. Although the discipline is relatively young, its historical roots are important with regard to understanding current areas and processes of application.

I/O psychology developed out of the fields of differential psychology, experimental psychology, and industrial engineering. During the 1910s the field had two primary goals: to improve productivity and to establish employee selection and placement tests. During this period the research differentiated between the organization and the employee and did not concern itself with relationships between the two. A major development of this era was the advent of the *Journal of Applied Psychology.*

A shift in this focus occurred in the 1920s and 1930s, with more attention given to the individual employee within an organizational context. A landmark investigation—the Hawthorne Studies—added to this growing emphasis on individual differences and examined how an employee's behavior could be influenced by societal or environmental factors. Industry's increasing disenchantment with employee tests led to a redefinition of those variables that could predict job performance.

Another shift in focus occurred in the 1940s: The discipline started to become more pragmatic in response to World War II. I/O psychologists were requested to aid in the selection and placement of soldiers, a process that eventually evolved into what is known today as personnel psychology. The time and motion studies of earlier years formed the backbone of the person-machine system, and the discipline found itself expanding to incorporate sociological concepts.

The technological advancements of the 1950s and 1960s created an additional challenge in employee selection, placement, and training. The Equal Employment Opportunity Commission, formed in response to the civil rights movement, added another dimension to the field. The discipline evolved to include issues of importance to both industry and organizations. This was recently recognized when Division 14 renamed itself to become the Division of Industrial and Organizational Psychology.

Since the 1970s the field has been in a state of flux and has been reshaped in accordance with the many societal and industrial changes that have occurred. The 1971 *Griggs* v. *Duke Power Company* Supreme Court decision mandated that the selection instruments that are used in industrial settings must be job related. Statistical advances have allowed researchers to investigate the validity of job selection tests with ease. In addition, researchers have become more aware of the interconnectedness of I/O psychology with other disciplines. Because of their significant impact on human behavior in the work environment, I/O psychologists require comprehensive training. Most practitioners hold a Ph.D., and many are involved in activities such as selection and placement, employee training and development, and the like. Several professional organizations have developed. The four major organizations are the American Psychological Society (APS), the American Psychological Association (APA), the Society for Industrial and Organizational Psychology (SIOP), and the International Association of Applied Psychology (IAAP).

KEY TERMS AND CONCEPTS

assessment center
compensation and benefits
differential job placement
differential occupational ability
   patterns
differential psychology
engineering psychology
experimental psychology
generic license

Hawthorne studies
individual development
industrial engineering
meta-analysis
organizational development
   and change
performance evaluation and
   selection
person-machine system

personnel psychology
preparing and presenting
   results
scientist-practitioners
situational stress tests
Stimulus-response (S-R)
   psychology
time and motion studies

RECOMMENDED READINGS

Bass, B. M., & Ryterband, E. C. (1979). *Organizational psychology* (2nd ed.). Boston: Allyn and Bacon.

Bray, D. W., & Associates (1991). *Working with organizations and their people: A guide to human resources practice.* New York: Guilford Press.

Dunnette, M. D. (1976). Toward fusion. In M. D. Dunnette (Ed.), *Handbook of industrial and organizational psychology* (pp. 9–12). Chicago: Rand McNally.

Dunnette, M. D. (1990). Blending the science and practice of industrial/organizational psychology: Where are we and where are we going? In M. D. Dunnette & L. M. Hough (Eds.), *Hand-book of industrial and organizational psychology* (Vol. 1). Palo Alto, CA: Consulting Psychologists Press.

Dubin, R. (1976). Theory building in applied areas. In M. D. Dunnette (Ed). *Handbook of industrial and organizational psychology* (pp. 17–39). Chicago: Rand McNally.

Landy, F. (Speaker). (1992). *The application of psychological principles to the problems of industry: 1900–1921.* G. Stanley Hall Lectures. Washington, DC: American Psychological Association.

Society for Industrial/Organizational Psychology (1987). *Principles for the validation and use of personnel selection procedures* (3rd ed.). College Park, MD: Author.

INTERNET RESOURCES

APA Membership Categories and Benefits
   This site describes the different types of APA membership and affiliation that are available. It includes information on the dues and fees associated with each type of membership.
   http://www.apa.org/member.html
Divisions of the American Psychological Association
   This site identifies the divisions of the APA. For detailed descriptions of each division and current membership information, contact the APA Division Services office or send e-mail to *division @apa.org*.
   http://www.apa.org/division.html
American Psychological Society (APS)
   This site describes APS, the types of membership and affiliation available, and posts news about current events affecting psychology.
   http://psych.hanover.edu/APS/

Society for Industrial and Organizational Psychology (SIOP)

This site describes the types of SIOP memberships and affiliation available. It also has the latest edition of TIP (The Industrial Organizational Psychologist) several weeks before the printed version becomes available.

http://cmit.unomaha.edu/TIP/TIP.html

Society for Human Resource Management

This site describes classes of membership in the Society for Human Resource Management (SHRM). It also contains the latest news about the society and its programs.

http://www.shrm.org

The Academy of Management On-Line

This site features the latest news and information as well as membership information about the Academy of Management.

http://www.aom.pace.edu/indextext.html

The Academy of Management's Division Groups

This site is a subsection of the Academy of Management page and provides detailed information about the Academy's specialty divisions.

http://hsb.baylor.edu/html/fuller/am/am_div.htm

Psychology UoY

Careers in Psychology. This site reviews some of the options a psychology major has after graduation.

http://www.york.ac.uk/depts/psych/web/etc/careers.html

IOOB-L Industrial Psychology and Organizational Behavior Listserver

This listserver is a publication medium. By subscribing, you get regular e-mail postings of research articles and other items of interest about I/O psychology.

news:bit.listserv.ioob-l

Industrial Psychology Internet Resources

The Industrial Psychology resource page. This site was developed by an I/O graduate student and provides a list of resources that he found useful for his studies in industrial psychology.

http://www.ccnet.com/~bluenote/welcome.html

Warren Bush's PSYCHOLOGY CYBER-SYNAPSE

This psychology-related resources page on the World Wide Web includes David Mahony's Psychology Internet Resources List (PIRL) and links to many other sites contributed by net surfers with an interest in psychology.

http://rdz.stjohns.edu/~warren/psych.html

University at Albany Psychology Department

This site lists other psychology-related Web pages and newsgroups. If your software supports newsgroup access, you can reach these psychology-related discussion groups: Go to NEWSGROUP sci.psychology.

http://www.albany.edu/psy/other.html

Books on Employment and Careers for Psychology Majors

This site lists books and pamphlets that the Kansas State psychology department keeps on hand for loaning to its students. They are well-known publications and should be available at most schools in the United States.

http://www.gasou.edu/psychweb/tipsheet/books.htm

CyberPsychLink

This page is a continuously updated psychology reference page. A brief sampling of what is included can be seen in the table of contents: Search Tools, ListServs, UseNet Groups, Organizations, Electronic Journals & Newsletters, DataBases/Archives, Grant and Job Info, Library Catalogs.

http://cctr.umkc.edu/user/dmartin/psych2.html

Electronic Journals and Periodicals in Psychology and Related Fields

This site is a list of electronic journals and periodicals. Its goal is to maintain a relatively complete index of psychologically related electronic journals, conference proceedings, and the like.

http://psych.hanover.edu/Krantz/journal.html

Suggested Courses to Develop Skills That Prospective Employers Want

The undergraduate psychology major, particularly one who does not plan to attend graduate school, may want to adopt a strategy of strengthening skills that employers seek. This site provides some guidelines.

http://www.gasou.edu/psychweb/tipsheet/suggest.htm

Psych Web List of Psychology Resources Sorted by Topic

This site provides a list of psychology resources on the Internet, sorted by topic. It also contains links to sites that specialize in subtopics within the field of psychology.

http://www.gasou.edu/psychweb/resource/bytopic.htm

EXERCISE

Exercise 1.1

The historical developments of I/O psychology and current societal concerns in the United States have shaped many of the views, theories, and practices in the field of I/O psychology as we know it today. To better understand today's I/O psychology, we suggest the following exercise:

Get together with two other members of your class and review the historical development of I/O psychology. Design a chart describing the five eras discussed in the chapter. For each era, choose a few key words to describe the core trends of the period. Starting with Taylor and World War I, trace the influence of the experimental, individual differences, and industrial engineering ideas on the five key eras described in the chapter. Compare your chart with

that of other groups, making any modifications that will add to your summary.

Consider some of the current issues in I/O psychology. Think about societal concerns in the United States and their impact on I/O psychology. For example, discuss the increase in the percentage of women and members of other minority groups in today's work force, the issue of companies moving to other countries, the takeover of companies, drug testing, the increasing awareness of disabled people, downsizing and layoffs, and other similar subjects. Select two or three of these subjects and discuss the following:

1. The problems and challenges they present to I/O psychologists.
2. The impact that they have (or could have) on the research and practice of I/O psychologists.

REFERENCES

American Psychological Association (1953). *Ethical principles of psychologists.* Washington, DC: Author.

American Psychological Association (1954). *Technical recommendations for psychological tests and diagnostic techniques.* Washington, DC: Author.

Arvey, R. D. (1979). *Fairness in selecting employees* (Chs. 3 and 4). Reading, MA: Addison-Wesley Publishing.

Atkinson, J. W. (1964). *An introduction to motivation.* Princeton, NJ: Van Nostrand.

Bass, B. M., & Ryterband, E. C. (1979). *Organizational psychology* (2nd ed.). Boston: Allyn and Bacon.

Blum, M. L., & Naylor, J. C. (1968). *Industrial psychology: Its theoretical and social foundations* (pp. 578–579; 582–584). New York: Harper & Row.

Boring, E. G. (1957). *A history of experimental psychology* (2nd ed.). New York: Appleton-Century-Crofts.

Borman, W. C., & Cox, G. L. (1996). Who's doing what: Patterns in the practice of I/O psychology. *The Industrial Organizational Psychologist,* 33(4), 21–29.

Campion, M. (1996). Why I'm proud to be an I/O psychologist. *The Industrial Organizational Psychologist,* 34(1), 27–29.

Drucker, P. F. (1954). *The practice of management.* New York: Harper.

Dunnette, M. D. (1966). *Personnel selection and placement.* Belmont, CA: Wadsworth Publishing Company.

Dunnette, M. D. (Ed.)(1976). *Handbook of industrial and organizational psychology.* Chicago: Rand McNally.

Dunnette, M. D. (1990). Blending the science and practice of industrial and organizational psychology: Where are we and where are we going? In M. D. Dunnette & L. M. Hough (Eds). *Handbook of industrial and organizational psychology* (Vol. 1) (pp. 1–27). Palo Alto, CA: Consulting Psychologists Press.

Dunnette, M. D., & Hough, L. M. (Eds.) (1990). *Handbook of industrial and organizational psychology* (Vol. 1). Palo Alto, CA: Consulting Psychologists Press.

Dunnette, M. D., & Hough, L. M. (Eds.) (1991). *Handbook of industrial and organizational psychology* (Vol. 2). Palo Alto, CA: Consulting Psychologists Press.

Dunnette, M. D., & Hough, L. M. (Eds.) (1992). *Handbook of industrial and organizational psychology* (Vol. 3). Palo Alto, CA: Consulting Psychologists Press.

Dvorak, B. J. (1935). Differential occupational ability. Bulletin 8, Employment Stabilization Research Institute, Minneapolis, MN: University of Minnesota.

English, H. P., & English, A. C. (1958). *A comprehensive dictionary of psychological and psychoanalytical terms: A guide to usage.* New York: Longmans, Green & Co.

Fincher, D. P. (1973). Analog and digital descriptions of behavior. *American Psychologist, 28*(6), 489–497.

Gilbreth, F. B., & Gilbreth, L. M. (1916). *Fatigue study.* New York: Sturges and Walton.

Gilbreth, F. B., & Gilbreth, L. M. (1917). *Applied motion study.* New York: Macmillan.

Guion, R. M. (1976). The practice of industrial and organizational psychology. In M. D. Dunnette (Ed.), *Handbook of industrial and organizational psychology* (pp. 645–650). Chicago: Rand McNally.

Herzberg, F. (1966). *Work and the nature of man.* Cleveland: World.

Howard, A. (1990). *The multiple facets of industrial-organizational psychology.* Arlington Heights, IL: Society for Industrial and Organizational Psychology.

Howard, A. (1991). Industrial/organizational psychologists as practitioners. In Bray, D. W. (Ed.), *Working with organizations and their people: A guide to human resources practice.* New York: Guilford Press.

Howard, A., & Bray, D. W. (1988). *Managerial lives in transition: Advancing age and changing times.* New York: Guilford Press.

Hunter, J. E., & Schmidt, F. L. (1990). *Methods of meta-analysis: Correcting error and bias in research findings.* Newbury Park, CA: Sage Publications.

Hunter, J. E., Schmidt, F. L., & Jackson, G. B. (1982). *Meta-analysis: Cumulating research findings across studies.* Beverly Hills, CA: Sage Publications.

Korman, A. K. (1977). *Organizational behavior.* Englewood Cliffs, NJ: Prentice-Hall.

Landy, F. J. (1989). *Psychology of work behavior.* Pacific Grove, CA: Brooks/Cole.

Locke, E. A. (1968). Toward a theory of task motivation and incentives. *Organizational Behavior and Human Performance, 3,* 157–189.

Maslow, A. H. (1954). *Motivation and personality.* New York: Harper.

McDaniel, M. A., Whetzel, D. L., Schmidt, F. L., & Maurer, S. D. (1994). The validity of employment interviews: A comprehensive review and meta-analysis. *Journal of Applied Psychology, 79*(4), 599–616.

McGregor, D. M. (1960). *The human side of enterprise.* New York: McGraw-Hill.

Meyer, H. (1997). An early stimulus to psychology in industry: A history of the Dearborn Conference Group. *The Industrial Organizational Psychologist, 34*(3), 24–27.

Munsterberg, H. (1913). *Psychology and industrial efficiency.* Boston: Houghton Mifflin.

Novick, M. R. (1981). Federal guidelines and professional standards. *American Psychologist, 36*(10), 1035–1046.

Porter, L. W., & Lawler, E. E., III. (1968). What job attitudes tell about motivation. *Harvard Business Review, 46*(1), 118–126.

Raju, N. S., & Burke, M. J. (1983). Two new procedures for studying validity generalization. *Journal of Applied Psychology, 68*(3), 382–395.

Schmidt, F. L., & Hunter, J. E. (1977). Development of a general solution to the problem of validity generalization. *Journal of Applied Psychology, 62*(5), 529–540.

Schmidt, F. L., & Hunter, J. E. (1981). Employment testing: Old theories and new research findings. *American Psychologist, 36,* 1128–1137.

Schmidt, F. L., Hunter, J. E., Pearlman, K., & Hirsh, H. R. (1985). Forty questions and answers about validity generalization and meta-analysis. *Personnel Psychology, 38,* 697–798.

Schmidt, F. L., Law, K., Hunter, J. E., Rothstein, J. R., Pearlman, K., & McDaniel, M. A. (1993). Refinements in validity generalization procedures: Implications for the situational specificity hypothesis. *Journal of Applied Psychology, 78*(1), 3–13.

Skinner, B. F. (1953). *Science and human behavior.* New York: Macmillan.

Snyderman, M., & Herrnstein, R. J. (1983). Intelligence tests and the Immigration Act of 1924. *American Psychologist, 38*(9), 986–995.

Taylor, F. W. (1911). *The principles of scientific management.* New York: Harper.

Triandis, H. C., Dunnette, M. D., & Hough, L. M. (Eds.) (1994). *Handbook of industrial and organizational psychology* (Vol. 4). Palo Alto, CA: Consulting Psychologists Press.

Tyler, L. E. (1965). *The psychology of human differences.* New York: Appleton-Century-Crofts.

Vroom, V. H. (1964). *Work and motivation.* New York: Wiley.

Experimental Design

J ohn Adams just graduated with a master's degree in I/O psychology and has been hired by a medium-sized company as its human resources manager. One of his first assignments is to establish a selection system for the company's management training program for supervisors. All current applicants are supervisors who nominated themselves or were recommended by their managers. A team of managers makes the final selections from a list of qualified candidates that John prepares. John's problem is how to devise a selection system within his time and budget constraints while at the same time (a) complying with the professional and scientific standards of I/O psychology; (b) enabling objective, nondiscriminatory selection decisions by the management training team; (c) developing a process that is quick and easy to apply; and (d) establishing a research design that will allow evaluation of the effects of the new selection program and the managers' performance after training. John Adams is under a great deal of pressure to increase the number of supervisors who are trained and to improve their effectiveness. Can John Adams be a practitioner and a scientist? Or do the operational demands to move quickly and to adhere to budget limitations require him to put together a program that meets immediate needs without his worrying about the science behind it? The discussion in this chapter will help you when you are faced with such questions.

Psychology is the scientific investigation of human behavior and mental processes. Scientific principles underlie the study of human behavior; therefore psychologists must use appropriate methodologies, research designs, statistical analyses, and ethical guidelines when conducting their research. However, they may find it challenging to apply these procedures and rules within the time constraints and complex demands of business situations. Psychologists have difficulty following these principles because real-life problems frequently require immediate solutions.

PSYCHOLOGY AS A SCIENCE

In using the **scientific method,** a psychologist applies specific procedures to the collection and interpretation of data. Some scientific procedures include identifying basic assumptions, applying accepted principles, and objectively measuring outcomes.

Assumptions

1. In psychological research, a major assumption is that behavior is lawful rather than random. This means that each time a particular stimulus is presented in a certain situation, the accompanying response is expected to be the same. For example, when you taste food, you salivate.

2. Another key assumption is that there is a limited number of events that will significantly affect any phenomenon. Human behavior is very complex, so a multitude of variables can interact to influence behavioral responses. When researchers find the few variables that make a difference for a particular behavior, the efforts of future researchers can be focused on those variables.

For example, the area of employee turnover has been the target of much research. This is largely because of the substantial resources that organizations invest in hiring and training employees. When an employee quits, the firm incurs significant costs in terms of personal, work unit, and organizational readjustments. A recent review article by Lee and Mitchell (1994) explored constructs and research findings from the perspectives of decision making, statistics, and social psychology in trying to understand employee turnover. The authors found that the process of employee turnover can be modeled by four distinct decision paths. Each path summarizes how employees interpret their work environments, identify decision options, and then respond. Focusing on seven components (shock, sign of shock, matching frame, evaluation of images, relative job satisfaction, search for job alternatives, and evaluation of job alternatives), Lee and Mitchell discovered the four specific decision strategies that cause employees to leave their jobs. They also found two variables that were very important in these decisions. Those variables were a shock to the system (when a distinguishable event jars employees, causing them to make judgments about their jobs) and whether the shock is easily dealt with by an appropriate response. This example shows how the scientific approach can help to focus on the basic aspects of a problem. Clearly, further research about decision making, shock, and response to shock will help managers and researchers to better understand and predict employee turnover.

Principles

When researchers use the scientific method, they follow the **operational theorem**. This theorem dictates that the procedures that are applied to any true research effort be publicly observed, tested, replicated, and verified. For example, suppose you interview several applicants for the position of bank teller and then select the final candidate on the basis of your own intuition. Because there is no record of how you reached your decision, it would be almost impossible for another personnel director to replicate that decision.

The operational theorem consists of three rules:

1. Research must be objective, or free of experimenter bias or subjectivity. Psychologists try to ensure objectivity by carefully documenting the steps in the process. Each step should be logical and clear enough for others to follow. The data that are collected must support all of the conclusions that the researcher draws.
2. The interpretation of results can be generalized only within the context of the study and the statistics applied. Generalizability

refers to whether the research results can be expected to remain constant over time, in other environments, and with samples composed of different individuals and conceptually related variables. For example, suppose you are conducting a study in which the sample population consists of students attending a private college for women. You can generalize the results only to that specific population, not to the population of college students at large. In applying the results of one study to a new group, it is important to consider the sample population, the statistical interpretation of the results, and the consistency of results produced. This can be a complex process and can lead different people to different conclusions. This is illustrated in Scientific Perspective 2.1 on page 32, in the case of smoking and its relationship to circulatory disease.
3. When describing a scientific inquiry, the researcher describes it in enough detail that other researchers can replicate the study. The description must be available to the professional community through publication, presentation, or another method of communication.

Goals

In defining psychology as a science, the basic assumption exists that it is possible to describe, explain, and predict all behavior. These activities may be part of any scientific undertaking, but for most psychological research efforts, describing, explaining, and predicting behavior are the desired outcomes.

Description

The description of any phenomenon begins with objective observation. Researchers describe a phenomenon by recording *only* the conditions within which it occurs without making interpretations about meaning. This goal requires that psychologists temporarily turn off their analyti-

Principles of Scientific Research

We've all heard the debates regarding the relationship between smoking and cancer, or smoking and circulatory diseases. "Authorities" take various positions about what we know concerning the effects of smoking on health. Some authorities say there is no question about proving the causal relationship: Smoking causes these diseases. Others say the case has yet to be proven, that there is no real evidence that smoking causes cancer, heart disease, or anything else.

Surprisingly, these authorities do not necessarily disagree about the *facts.* Both agree, for example, that the death rate from lung cancer is higher for smokers than for nonsmokers. For one man, this is proof of causality. Another man, however, launches an extensive rebuttal, also based on facts.

He points out that smokers and nonsmokers are different in a thousand ways. They live in different places, work at different occupations, have different backgrounds and life experiences, eat different foods, and so on. He argues that any one of these differences may be the important difference that "really" affects disease and death rates. Finally, he says that smoking may be nothing more than a consequence of the kind of person one is; perhaps nervous people smoke and also have cancer, heart attacks, and the like. According to this line of reasoning, smoking may not be the causal agent at all; rather, it may be the result of some other cause that also happens to produce disease as well.

While these two perspectives are clearly not debating the facts, they are debating what the facts mean, or how they should be interpreted.

Source: From *General psychology: Modeling behavior and experience* (p. 2), by W. N. Dember & J. J. Jenkins, 1970, Englewood Cliffs, NJ: Prentice-Hall. Reprinted with permission.

cal skills and record only what is clearly observable. These observations are like those made with a videocamera, recording without judgment or concern for cause-and-effect relationships.

Explanation

Another goal of scientific research is to explain the occurrence of a particular phenomenon. To reach this goal, the researcher systematically creates and manipulates conditions so that the desired behavior will occur in some circumstances and not in others. The results of such studies enable the scientist to explain why certain differences in behavior occur. Researchers also create theoretical models to organize research findings, increasing the explanatory impact of research. The example of employee turnover explains the complex phenomenon of voluntary employee turnover as the outcome of employee decision-making strategies (Lee and Mitchell, 1994). A factor in the decision-making strategy was whether a shock occurred that caused the employee to reevaluate his or her job. This provided a straightforward explanation of employee turnover.

Prediction

Prediction occurs when the researcher makes inferences based on observations. After recording the observations, the researcher selects factors from the descriptive data and uses them to formulate tentative laws that *may* predict future behavior. In other words, the researcher looks for associations of variables such that one appears predictable from another and then sets up a study to test those assumptions.

A predictive study enables the researcher to forecast future outcomes. The bases for such predictions are the strength and direction of the relationships found between two variables, and the cause-and-effect relationships that the researcher found between variables and behaviors. For instance, suppose you select a group of employees to include in departmental decision making about the methods of production. Shortly afterward, this group begins producing more than does a group of employees who are not involved in the decision-making process. If you hold all other factors influencing production constant, you can draw certain conclusions about the data. In this example you may conclude that the cause is participation in departmental decision making and the effect is improved production.

It is important to note that these goals occur in the order given above. For example, the descriptive stage provides a baseline. You cannot explain or attempt to predict future behavior without first observing and describing the current state of the behavior under review.

It is the procedure that is applied during an investigation that identifies the effort as scientific. Psychologists often talk about behavior. It is important to understand that the psychological definition of behavior encompasses all physical and mental activities of the organism (for example, activities that can be seen, heard, or remembered). Suppose you want to apply this approach to the employee productivity and decision-making scenario. You could measure the increase in employee production (the activities of an organism). You could also use measures that record feelings of job satisfaction or other affective responses to the work environment (reports of subjective conscious experiences).

Industrial/organizational psychologists frequently describe themselves as **scientist-practitioners,** focusing equally on scientific foundations and practical problem solving. These two focuses impelled the field of I/O psychology to develop in a way similar to applied disciplines such as clinical psychology, child psychology, and consumer psychology. The development of I/O psychology was different from that of other research-focused specialties such as comparative psychology and experimental psychology. Rather than being solely concerned with elemental behaviors or theories, I/O psychologists also pursue research directed at solving practical problems in organizations. Over the last ten years, the focus of I/O psychology has been changing. I/O psychologists are increasing their use of theoretical research interpretations as a foundation for applied practice.

Conducting scientific research in organizational settings is a special challenge because more variables exist in the real world than in the typical laboratory. It is harder to test and maintain control over these variables. Industrial/organizational psychologists frequently find themselves wrestling with conflicting perspectives because of the scientist-practitioner emphasis and often must reach a compromise between science and practice. The I/O psychologist's challenge is to combine the best aspects of science and practice. Hoshmand and Polkinghorne believe that there is a need for a new blending of science and practice. They suggest a type of union "in which psychological science as a human practice and psychological practice as a human science inform each other" (Hoshmand & Polkinghorne, 1992, p. 55).

This type of union is not an unrealistic goal in today's practice of human resources. Research in the areas of individual evaluation, training and development, and organizational development can help the organization to adjust to the changing work environment. At the same time, practical experience in these areas can lead to further study of various aspects of each process. The following case study is a good illustration of this.

The client was experiencing an unusually high level of turnover among newly hired employees. A brief but comprehensive research study investigated potential causes for this turnover. The use of in-depth interviews and focus group discussions added depth to the basic research results.

The results of the study made it possible to design and carry out a multiple-hurdle hiring process. In such a process, candidates for employment complete a series of steps, or "hurdles," as they go through the hiring process. To clear each hurdle, the candidate demonstrates a particular ability or provides a critical piece of information. Clearing each hurdle allows the candidate to progress to the next step; failing to clear any hurdle results in disqualification.

The first step in this multiple-hurdle process was a telephone screening interview, during which potential candidates answered key questions about career motives and job history. The next hurdle was an in-person interview that elicited information about areas that were found to be important during the basic descriptive research.

Interviewers used specially constructed scales to rate behaviors that were relevant to specific jobs. The scales were based on earlier research, during which behaviors were observed and then linked to effective job performance. The interviewers rated candidates in nine areas before forming their final judgments.

To clear the next hurdle, successful candidates had to complete two simulation exercises, which were also mini-job models. The design of these exercises and the scoring protocols followed the principles of basic research for evaluating exercise performance. The candidates who were hired were those who cleared all of the hurdles.

These successful candidates then became the subjects of a long-term validation and work performance study. The multiple-hurdle process was a successful one for this company; the turnover in new hires fell by 75 percent. This research also contributed to the scientific development of personnel selection through the publication of several articles. One article is on the role and impact of dysfunctional turnover. Another is on the effectiveness of the multiple-hurdle selection process.

Issues and Definitions

I/O psychology is a part of the tradition of scientific methodology applied to human behavioral issues. Its roots are in anthropology, sociology, education, economics, management, political science, cybernetics, and psychology.

The slight differences among these disciplines are less important than what they share: a clear commitment to the systematic study and evaluation of behavioral phenomena. The following is a summary of this shared methodology.

The first step in objective investigation is to ask a clear question about a behavioral phenomenon in the work environment. This initial question is the **hypothesis,** which is often an educated guess about what is happening or what should be happening. In its simple form, the hypothesis appears as a question. When a hypothesis is presented formally, it appears as a statement, which is used in statistical testing.

For example, Alfred Marcus and Robert Goodman (1991) were interested in corporate announcements made to stockholders during three kinds of crises: accidents, scandals, and product safety incidents. Marcus and Goodman believed that corporate crises often exacerbate shareholder demands, which create conflict between the interests of the shareholders and those of the crisis victims. When crises are created by accidents and product safety incidents, shareholders are likely to suffer if the managers are accommodating to victims. However, in crises created by scandals there is no conflict, and shareholders benefit when managers are accommodating. Marcus and Goodman (1991, pp. 286–289) developed five hypotheses that directed their investigation of the effect of corporate announcements of crises on a company's stock price:

Hypothesis 1: When a company is involved in an accident, its investors will react more positively to defensive signals than to accommodative signals.

Hypothesis 2: When a company is involved in a scandal, its investors will respond more positively to accommodative signals than to defensive signals.

Hypothesis 3: Defensive signals will provide significantly better returns to shareholders in the case of accidents than in the case of scandals.

Hypothesis 4: Accommodative signals will provide significantly better returns to shareholders in the case of scandals than in the case of accidents.

Hypothesis 5: When product safety and health incidents occur, no significant differences will exist between the reactions of a company's investors to accommodative and defensive signals.

Good hypotheses make vital contributions to the research process. They help researchers to clarify their thoughts about the issue and about the variables that are involved.

The second step in objective investigation is for the research design to address the procedures to be used in collecting and analyzing empirical data. A good research design defines the playing field. It tells the researcher what to look for; provides control of independent and dependent variables; and outlines how to measure, analyze, and record results. One of the first steps in choosing a research design is to specify the independent and dependent variables.

Independent Variables

The goal of scientific research is to understand the conditions that shape behavior; therefore it is necessary to define the conditions that precede behavior. Factors that are thought to be responsible for the occurrences of behaviors are the **independent variables.** The researcher decides which variables to hold constant and which to systematically manipulate. The manipulation of independent variables depends on the nature of the phenomenon under review and on the hypothesis. Ideally, the independent variable is under the control of the investigator; this is true more often in laboratory studies than in field research.

Dependent Variables

The next step is to define any variable that changes because of the manipulation of the independent variables. In psychology, **dependent variables** are often specific activities or segments of behavior that the researcher can measure.

For example, Ganster, Williams, and Poppler (1991) investigated the impact of training in problem solving on the quality of group decision making. Individuals were randomly assigned to groups, and the groups were then assigned to either the treatment (experimental) condition or the control condition. Each participant was to complete the NASA moon survival problem (see Practice Perspective 2.1 on page 36), which requires each subject to make an independent decision about the problem.

Individuals in the treatment condition then read training materials about group decision making. Participants in the control condition had an equal amount of time to reconsider their rankings. Each group was then asked to render a group decision about the problem, and this score was compared to an expert rating provided by NASA scientists. The dependent variable was the score on the group decision. Ganster et al. found no improvement in group member resources and no improvement in the quality of the group decisions due to their intervention.

The conclusions that can be drawn from the relationships between the independent and dependent variables are determined by the study's methodology and design. In many situations, only one or a few independent variables serve as predictors. A **predictor** is the event or condition from which researchers make predictions. In some situations the independent variable may be an **antecedent variable,** which is a variable that actually causes a behavior to occur.

Sampling

Another factor to consider is the sample from which the data are collected. For example, if you collect data from a sample of upper-middle-class Caucasian males, the results cannot be generalized to the entire male population. One method for selecting a representative sample of a population is **random sampling.** Random sampling ensures that each individual, and each combination of individuals in the population under review, has an equal chance of being selected for the study. According to Sackett and Larson (1990), the **sampling procedure** determines the extent to which the results can be

---

PRACTICE PERSPECTIVE 2.1

NASA Exercise

Instructions: You are a member of a space crew originally scheduled to rendezvous with a mother ship on the lighted surface of the moon. Due to mechanical difficulties, however, your ship was forced to land on a spot some 200 miles from the rendezvous point. During the landing, much of the equipment aboard was damaged and, since survival depends on reaching the mother ship, the most critical items available must be chosen for the 200 mile trip. Following are listed the 15 items left intact and undamaged after landing. Your task is to rank order them in terms of their importance for your crew in allowing them to reach the rendezvous point. Place the number 1 by the most important item, the number 2 by the second most important, and so on, through number 15, the least important. Since survival is at stake, be as *careful* with the lowest rankings as you are with the highest. You have 10 minutes to complete this phase of the exercise.

_____ Box of matches

_____ Food concentrate

_____ 50 feet of nylon rope

_____ Parachute silk

_____ Portable heating unit

_____ Two .45 caliber pistols

_____ One case of dehydrated milk

_____ Two 100 lb. tanks of oxygen

_____ Stellar map of the moon's constellations

_____ Life raft

_____ Magnetic compass

_____ 5 gallons of water

_____ Signal flares

_____ First aid kit containing injection needles

_____ Solar-powered FM receiver-transmitter

Source: From "Nasa Exercise," by Management Psychologists, Inc., 1980. Chicago, IL. Reprinted with permission.

---

generalized beyond the immediate conditions and environment.

Other factors that influence the ability to generalize results include the sampling procedure used in collecting the data and the extent to which the results of that procedure represent the population from which the sample was selected. In the designs described later in this chapter, it is often impossible or impractical to obtain data from all members of the population. Therefore selection of a sample that satisfactorily represents the population is necessary to enable the researcher to generalize results.

The third step in scientific methodology is to statistically assess the **cause-and-effect** relationships that can be inferred from the study. Inferences drawn from the data relate to past research and to appropriate theoretical models or interpretations. However, as was mentioned ear-

lier, the ability to find cause-and-effect relationships between independent and dependent variables depends on the research design and the degree of variable control. For example, changing the levels of light in a room (*cause*) leads to different degrees of ability to see reading material (*effect*). The researcher can control the level of light (independent variable), which may then lead to different levels of visual discrimination (dependent variable).

Many I/O research efforts are designed to discover **associations** that exist between variables. These associations are often used to predict relationships, rather than to simply identify them. For example, a researcher may discover that level of pay is related to an employee's feeling of job satisfaction. The researcher should then determine whether an increase or decrease in the level of pay causes a change in employee satisfaction.

RESEARCH DESIGN

One prevalent design problem occurs when psychologists conduct research in situations that are removed from the business or organizational context in which they will later apply the results. The farther away the study is from the appropriate context, the more tenuous its application will be. This has raised many questions about the generalizability of research conducted in laboratory settings rather than in a field or natural setting. More sophisticated designs and controls in current use make this issue less problematic than it was in the past.

Researchers can carry out organizational studies in several ways. Certain methods give the researcher more control than others. Some commonly used research designs, listed in order of increasing amounts of control, include naturalistic observation, quasi-experiments, organizational simulations, field experiments, and pure or laboratory experiments.

Naturalistic Observation

Research can sometimes be quite informal, as simple as checking hypotheses through careful observation of the natural environment. A common form of observational study is the survey. Psychologists conduct these studies in the work environment, so this method is also known as **field research.** The researcher uses systematic procedures to observe and record information about the variable of interest when employee data are collected in natural field settings. In designing field observation studies, psychologists must be very careful because there is no control or manipulation of variables. Skillfully conducted field research will be most likely to yield results that can be generalized to a larger population. A description of a survey program that was administered to evaluate the role of supervisor training in constructive confrontation is described in Practice Perspective 2.2 on page 38. Note the care used in constructing items and

selecting the organizations that participate. This attention to detail allowed the investigators to draw general conclusions.

Quasi-Experiments

I/O psychologists attempt to understand how key factors function in the work environment. However, the very acts of observation and measurement may directly influence the factors of interest. In trying to avoid this problem, researchers sometimes use **quasi-experiments,** which attempt to simultaneously increase control and retain realism. In quasi-experiments the researcher unobtrusively observes, controls, and measures some, but not all, of the independent variables. Other variables (both constant and manipulated) may also exist that are under the control of the organization rather than the researcher. Scientific Perspective 2.2 on page 39 offers a detailed examination of a quasi-experiment.

Organizational Simulation Experiments

An **organizational simulation experiment** provides even more control than a quasi-experiment. The psychologist creates a setting that is as much like the real-world setting as possible. This is accomplished by isolating the variables of interest and designing a study that allows careful observation and measurement of the effects of the variations. Because simulation experiments are complicated, expensive, and difficult to conduct, they are rarely used. However, the ones that are conducted often provide valuable insights and can be an excellent bridge between pure experimental studies and field studies. Scientific Perspective 2.3 on page 40 describes one such computer simulation experiment. It allowed researchers to examine the effects that goals with different degrees of difficulty would have on the management performance of 132 simulated companies.

PRACTICE PERSPECTIVE 2.2

Field Research: A Survey

Many companies provide employee assistance programs (EAPs) that offer counseling, referrals to therapy, and medical assistance for employees who have psychological problems that are affecting their performance. A key person in the EAP process is the front-line supervisor. Often, the supervisor is the first person to become aware of a problem or the first person the employee will seek out for help. Schneider, Colan, and Googins (1991) explored training supervisors in constructive confrontation techniques so that employees could approach supervisors and seek help through the company's EAP.

A national telephone survey was conducted. One state was selected at random from each of five geographic sections of the United States (East, South, Central, North, and West). A comprehensive list of EAPs was prepared for each selected state. From this list, a total of 114 EAPs were randomly selected and asked to participate in the survey; 94 did so.

Survey items were generated by a three-member panel of EAP professionals. The items were pretested, and only the items with good clarity and reliability were retained for the questionnaire. Calls were made by four trained research staff members, who asked the same questions in a standardized format of all 94 EAPs surveyed.

The results showed that nearly all the EAPs (92%) held very positive views toward supervisor

training. Eighty-seven percent of the EAPs had conducted such training in the previous year. The average length of a training session was 2.6 hours. Most of the EAPs (97%) included constructive confrontation. The difference between the means of referral rates for trained versus untrained supervisors was statistically significant ($p < .001$).

The authors of the survey concluded that "standard supervisor training," which consisted of a two- to-three-hour presentation on the EAP function and the steps of constructive confrontation, was an improvement over earlier attempts. The results also indicated that the EAPs that were studied were committed to the value of supervisor training. New demands and issues, such as AIDS, wellness, and family and economic instability are putting pressure on EAPs. The authors recommended that EAPs develop more sophisticated training based on the instructional technology model of Goldstein (1986), which emphasizes thorough needs assessment, controlled learning experiences designed to meet objectives, performance criteria, and the use of evaluation data to study effectiveness.

Source: "Supervisor training in employee assistance programs: Current practices and future directions," by R. Schneider, N. B. Colan, & B. Googins, 1991, *Employee-Assistance Quarterly, 6*(2), pp. 41–55. Copyright 1991 by Employee Assistance Quarterly. Adapted with permission.

Field Experiments

Psychologists conduct **field experiments** in natural settings. These settings are not created for experimentation, so the amount of control that the researcher has seldom matches the control available in a laboratory experiment. One key advantage of field experiments is that they take place in the environment in which the psychologist will apply the results. As a result, carefully designed field experiments can be as meaningful as laboratory studies. A field experiment applying behavioral management techniques in order

to improve the quality of teller service in a bank is described in Practice Perspective 2.3 on page 41.

Laboratory Experiments

Laboratory experiments offer the greatest level of control and, as a result, are very popular among researchers. A laboratory study strips a situation down to its barest essentials to identify key cause-and-effect relationships. This allows the researcher to manipulate the independent variables that are believed to cause the

SCIENTIFIC PERSPECTIVE 2.2

A Quasi-Experiment

This study examined the effects of interviewer and interviewee race and age similarity on interview outcomes under two different interview formats: a conventional structured panel interview and a situational panel interview. A total of 2,895 custodial job applicants in a large, West Coast urban school district were interviewed over a two-year period. Each interview was conducted by a panel of two interviewers using either a situationally or a conventionally structured interview format. The interviewers were personnel specialists employed by the school district, and custodial supervisors.

The conventional structured interview: (a) had questions developed on the basis of a job analysis; (b) asked each candidate the same questions; (c) had the panel record and rate answers; (d) was consistently administered to all candidates; and (e) paid special attention to fairness in accordance with testing guidelines. Three dimensions were assessed: willingness to perform custodial duties, work attitudes, and interpersonal skills. The interviewers were all trained for one hour, and were instructed to rate each interviewee on the three dimensions and then arrive at an overall score, ranging from 0 to 100. After interviewers made their independent evaluations they met to discuss any candidates for whom there was a 10-point or greater difference in the overall ratings.

The situational interview used twenty situational questions and corresponding benchmarks generated with the assistance of job experts. The interviewers were trained for three hours. Each applicant was interviewed by a two-person panel. Both interviewers independently rated an applicant's answers by comparing them to benchmarks. A score of 1 (poor), 3 (mediocre), or 5 (good) was assigned to each answer. The applicant's final score was the sum of their scores. Each applicant was interviewed by one of three types of panels: same race as the interviewee, a mixed-race panel, or a different-race panel.

Interviewees were divided into four age groups: under 25, 25–35, 35–45, and over 45. Interviewer panels were classified as same age when both interviewers were in the same age group as the interviewee, and as mixed age when one interviewer was in the same age group as the interviewee and one was from a different age group. The different age group consisted of interviewers from age groups different from the applicant's age group.

Analysis of variance revealed stronger same-race effects with the conventional structured interview than with the situational interview. These same-race effects could be avoided by using mixed-race interview panels. No age similarity effects were found for either interview procedure.

Source: From "A field study of race and age similarity effects on interview ratings in conventional and situational interviews," by T. R. Lin, G. M. Dobbins, & J. L. Farh, 1992, *Journal of Applied Psychology, 77*(3), pp. 363–371. Copyright 1992 by American Psychological Association. Reprinted with permission.

phenomenon under study while simultaneously watching the effects on the dependent variables. Maintaining strict control over the independent variables will allow causal interpretations of the results.

Current Practice

Simply identifying the broad approach used in a research study does not truly answer the ques-

tion of whether or not the research can be generalized. In addition, using this simplistic approach quickly leads to problems of classification. Today there are good examples of highly controlled, well-executed studies that have taken place in field settings. Do these qualify as laboratory studies, as field studies, or as both? The nature of the study is more important in the evaluation of a study than is the laboratory or field distinction. A study will be more generaliz-

```
┌─────────────────────────────────────────────────────────┐
│              SCIENTIFIC PERSPECTIVE 2.3                   │
└─────────────────────────────────────────────────────────┘
```

An Organizational Simulation Experiment

Amelia Chesney and Edwin Locke used a complex, strategic management computer simulation to examine the effect of goal difficulty and business strategies on firm performance. The 132 subjects were graduating seniors enrolled in an upper-level strategic management course. Each student represented one firm, and the firms were further segregated into 16 industry groups. Firms competed against each other to sell a small, generic household appliance. Subjects competed with other members of their group by assuming the role of president and sole decision maker.

Data were presented for the previous eight financial quarters. Each firm started with exactly the same history. In the study, the presidents made decisions for ten quarters. Their objective was to outperform the other firms on a set of financial performance measures: number of markets served, advertising, number of salespeople, product improvements, price, number of products produced, production capacity, number of production workers, raw materials purchased, environmental information, financing, stock issuance, dividends, and short-term investment.

Goals were randomly assigned to the sixteen industries before the start of the game by a letter from the game administrator, who was called the chairman of the board. The easier goal was "Your goal for the next three years is to do your best to run a profitable company; some earnings are expected but your rank with respect to other companies is not important." The harder goal was "Your goal for the next three years is to achieve a performance ranking of one or two in your industry. Outstanding performance is expected."

Strategies were measured in three ways. A strategy questionnaire was developed and administered at the beginning, middle, and end of the simulation. Strategy was scored by using two separate scoring methods for two of the measures, and the third measure was scored by using data collected on the actual decisions made during each of the ten decision periods. The president of each firm made decisions on fourteen issues that represented the performance variables for each of the ten decision periods. These were factor analyzed to yield two factors: sales and income.

Both goals and strategies had significant effects on performance. The authors concluded (a) that the setting of challenging personal goals was positively related to performance; (b) that the setting of challenging personal goals was positively, though weakly, related to the degree of use of an effective strategy; (c) that strategy moderates the goal performance relationship, with the relationship being stronger when an effective strategy was used; and (d) that the effect of strategy on performance was stronger than the effect of goals.

The application of these results to business suggests that having effective task strategies is even more important than having challenging goals for individuals performing complex tasks.

Source: "Relationships among goal difficulty, business strategies, and performance on a complex management simulation task," by A. Chesney & E. A. Locke, 1991, *Academy of Management Journal, 34*(2), pp. 400–424. Copyright 1991 by the Adademy of Management. Reprinted with permission.

able when the researcher carefully identifies and considers all setting-related boundary issues and when the setting is selected so that it is appropriate to those issues. For an in-depth discussion of this perspective, read the chapter "Research Strategies and Tactics in Industrial and Organizational Psychology" by Sackett and Larson (1990) in the second edition of the *Handbook of Industrial and Organizational Psychology*, Volume 1.

A good experiment is one that also identifies and controls extraneous factors. Control can be

PRACTICE PERSPECTIVE 2.3

A Field Experiment

A field experiment conducted by Fred Luthans explored the impact of using behavioral management techniques to improve the quality of teller service to bank customers. Luthans defined "Moments of Truth" (MOTs) as "any contact a customer has with the organization, no matter how remote, that provides the opportunity for that customer to form an impression" (1991, p. 3). These MOTs could be positive or negative. The author hypothesized that behavioral management technique intervention would increase the frequency of positive MOTs.

The study was done in the main location of a medium-sized Midwestern bank. A branch of the same bank served as the control. Ten tellers were studied in the first (experimental) bank; six were studied in the second (control) bank. Customer perceptions were measured on an instrument (developed by Parasuraman et al., 1988) that used a five-point scale to measure five service dimensions: tangibles, reliability, responsiveness, assurance, and empathy.

Baseline data were unobtrusively collected on quality service dimensions for both the control and experimental groups. Observation occurred randomly over a ten-day period. Customers completed questionnaires immediately after interaction with the tellers but out of sight of the tellers. None of the tellers were aware of the data collection. (This was confirmed in postexperiment interviews of the tellers.)

The two independent variables in the field experiment were the use of positive, immediate, graphic, and specific (PIGS) feedback and supervisory social reinforcement.

Differences between the experimental and control groups were compared for the six quality service dimensions on Parasuraman's questionnaire across the three stages of the experiment (baseline, intervention, and postintervention). No significant differences were found in the baseline phase. Significant differences were found for four of the six dimensions in the intervention stage: greeting, speed of service, personal recognition, and appreciation. All were rated significantly higher for the experimental group than for the control group. In the postintervention phase, when the manipulation of the independent variables ceased, the averages for the *experimental* group dropped on all of the six dimensions. One factor, speed of service, dropped low enough that it became statistically significant in a negative direction.

By examining the *control* group means in all conditions, the experimenter was able to see that the means stayed relatively constant across all conditions. This constancy allowed the experimenter to conclude that the selected behavioral management techniques had a positive impact on the quality service behaviors of tellers.

Source: Adapted from "Improving the delivery of quality service: Behavioural management techniques," by F. Luthans, 1991, *Leadership and Organization Development Journal, 12*(2), pp. 3–6. Copyright 1991 by Leadership and Organization Development Journal.

maintained in three ways (Sackett & Larson, 1990, pp. 444–445):

1. By eliminating the extraneous elements from the situation studied
2. By holding the extraneous elements constant for all participants
3. By randomizing the effects of uncontrolled variations to affect all subjects in all categories of study in the same way.

By selecting and limiting the antecedent variables, controlling those that can bring about behavior of interest, and manipulating the conditions under investigation the researcher creates a controlled laboratory-like setting for the experiment. The reason for doing all this is to determine whether there is a cause-and-effect relationship between the antecedent condition and the resulting behavior. One situation in which control becomes very critical is cross-cultural studies, because the number of extraneous variables is so high. Scientific Perspective 2.4 describes an experiment that was carefully controlled in order to make comparative analysis possible for three cultural groups.

I/O psychology scientifically applies psychological principles to the behavior of people at work. Because "sciences and all disciplines within sciences are distinguished not so much by the subject matter they study as by the questions

---

SCIENTIFIC PERSPECTIVE 2.4

Laboratory Experiment

Erez and Earley (1987) examined the effects of participation on individual goal acceptance and performance within a cross-cultural situation. They selected three groups of students from different sociocultural backgrounds: two groups of 60 students from an Israeli university and a group of 60 American students from a Midwestern university.

The designated three goal-setting conditions were assigned, representative, and participative. The three sample conditions were Israel-kibbutz, Israel-urban, and United States. Performance was the repeated factor.

The students were all given a simulated scheduling task in which they had a list of eight university courses with ten different time offerings per course. They were instructed to identify as many nonconflicting class schedules as possible. The assigned goal-setting condition briefly and directly told the students to achieve a specific goal. In the representative condition, groups of five students were asked to elect a representative who negotiated for them with the experimenter for their goal. In the participative condition, the groups were asked to decide as a group what goal would be used for each group member.

Goal acceptance was determined by using two questions: "To what extent do you accept the goal?" and "How committed are you to the goal that has been set?" From the responses to these two questions a composite goal acceptance score was calculated.

The procedure that was used for each sample was identical. Each subject was randomly assigned to one of the three goal-setting conditions. Parallel

groups of five students each made up each condition. Students were seated as a group in a room, instructed on the general purpose of the experiment, and encouraged to express their reactions to the various stages of the experiment. The students then read the task instructions. After a ten-minute practice phase to become comfortable with the scheduling task, the students experienced the goal-setting manipulation. After goal setting, the students were given the questionnaire assessing goal acceptance. The students then performed the task for twenty minutes. Goal-setting manipulations were reenacted before a second performance phase, followed by a questionnaire that checked the manipulations, opinions about the experimenter's characteristics, and personal data. The experiment concluded with a debriefing.

The results indicated that the participative strategy led to higher levels of goal acceptance and performance than the assigned strategy did. Culture did not moderate the effect of goal-setting strategies on goal acceptance, but it did moderate the effect of strategy on performance for extremely difficult goals.

The authors concluded that "the differences between the cultures under study were not so much in terms of the effects of participation as they were in terms of the reaction of individuals to assigned goals" (p. 664).

Source: "Comparative analysis of goal-setting strategies across cultures," by M. Erez & P. C. Earley, 1987, *Journal of Applied Psychology, 73*(4), pp. 658–665. Copyright 1987 by the American Psychological Association. Reprinted with permission.

they ask" (Cascio, 1991, p. 41), it should be clear from this chapter that I/O psychology falls under the domain of a scientific discipline. Specific I/O research designs consider the questions that are asked, the circumstances, and the conditions of the organization and its employees. It is important to remember that any valid and reliable design must follow the scientific principles outlined at the beginning of this chapter. Careful research design ensures that results can be replicated and meaningfully applied to real-world problems.

SUMMARY

Industrial/organizational psychologists often describe themselves as scientist-practitioners. As scientists, I/O psychologists research various work behaviors. As practitioners, they apply these findings to actual work settings.

Because I/O psychology is a behavioral science, it follows the scientific method by using a systematic approach to study behavior in organizations. Scientists adhere to the operational theorem, which states that research should be publicly observed, tested, replicated, and verified. The first step involves stating the hypothesis and selecting the independent and dependent variables. Independent variables are the variables that are manipulated and dependent variables are the behaviors or activities that are measured. The researcher then considers the population under review and draws a sample that is representative of that population. One popular

sampling method is random sampling, which provides a representative sample by ensuring that each person within the population has an equal chance of being selected for study.

Several research approaches are available to the I/O scientist. In naturalistic observation a researcher observes behaviors as they occur in their natural settings. A major drawback to this approach is that the researcher cannot control or manipulate the variables. When using a quasi-experimental design, the researcher attempts to increase control while maintaining a sense of realism. With this design, only some independent variables are measured. Researchers using an organizational simulation approach create a setting that is as close to the actual job setting as possible. This allows for careful observation and measurement of the variables under review. The field experiment approach requires researchers to apply the results of their findings in existing organizational settings. Inherent in this approach is a lack of control. The laboratory experiment provides scientists with the greatest degree of control. Using this approach allows researchers to make causal interpretations about their findings.

In the past it was often possible to base predictions about the generalizability of research results on the design selected for the study. Recently, scientists have become more skilled and careful in their approach. They now believe that it is more important to consider specific elements of the study than merely to consider the design and setting.

KEY TERMS AND CONCEPTS

antecedent variable
association
cause-and-effect
dependent variable
field experiment
field research

hypothesis
independent variable
laboratory experiment
operational theorem
organizational simulation
predictor

quasi-experiment
random sampling
sampling procedure
scientific method
scientist-practitioner

RECOMMENDED READINGS

Chesney, A. A., & Locke, E. A. (1991). Relationships among goal difficulty, business strategies, and performance on a complex management simulation task. *Academy of Management Journal, 34*(2), 400–424.

Luthans, F. (1991). Improving the delivery of quality service: Behavioural management techniques. *Leadership and Organizational Development Journal, 12*(2), 3–6.

INTERNET RESOURCES

Research Methods Resources from ASU COE
These pages are maintained by the Measurement, Statistics, and Methodological Studies program in the Division of Psychology in Education in the College of Education at Arizona State University. **http://seamonkey.ed.asu.edu/~behrens/**

APA Research Methods Page
This site is APA's data base of files on research methods. The abstracts posted here are part of the APA total library of over one million records on-line.
gophers//gopher.apa.org/1

Newsgroups for psychology
One powerful internet tool is newsgroups. By subscribing to a newsgroup you get regular mailings to your e-mail address of the latest information and discussions in that area as they are posted. USENET is the host for some of the most popular newsgroups. Use the following format for addresses: news.sci.psychology.misc. The news choices for sci.psychology are: misc, psychotherapy, research, and theory. For information on how to use the USENET see:
http://sunsite.unc.edu/usenet-i/

EXERCISE

Exercise 2.1

Applying Research Designs

The purpose of this exercise is to learn to apply the research designs described in this chapter.

1. Get together with three or four other students in your class.
2. Review the John Adams story at the beginning of the chapter.
3. Each member in the group should imagine that he or she is John Adams, charged with establishing a selection system for the company's management training program.
4. Decide first on the amount of time and the budget you have to accomplish the project.
5. Each student in the group should select two of the research designs described in the chapter and prepare a list of strengths and weaknesses for the designs selected.
6. Reassemble as a group and review the methodology of each research design, comparing the strengths and weaknesses of each with respect to a selection system for the company's management training program.
7. Compare the effectiveness of the different designs for achieving the goals stated in the John Adams story. These goals are as follows:

   To comply with the professional and scientific standards of I/O psychologists
   To ensure a nondiscriminatory selection program
   To develop a quick, easy-to-apply decision process
   To establish a design that will allow evaluation of the program and the success of the selected candidates both in their training and on the job
8. Determine which of the research designs would be most useful for your purposes within your time and budget constraints.

REFERENCES

Cascio, W. F. (1991). *Applied psychology in personnel management* (4th ed.). Englewood Cliffs, NJ: Prentice-Hall.

Erez, M., & Earley, P. C. (1987). Comparative analysis of goal-setting strategies across cultures. *Journal of Applied Psychology, 73*(4), 658–665.

Ganster, D. C., Williams, S., & Poppler, P. (1991). Does training in problem solving improve the quality of group decisions? *Journal of Applied Psychology, 76*(3), 479–483.

Goldstein, I. L. (1986). *Training in organizations: Needs assessment, development, and evaluation* (2nd ed.). Monterey, CA: Brooks/Cole.

Hoshmand, L. T., & Polkinghorne, D. E. (1992). Redefining the science-practice relationship and professional training. *American Psychologist, 47*(1), 55–66.

Lee, T. W., & Mitchell, T. R. (1994). An alternative approach: The unfolding model of voluntary employee turnover. *The Academy of Management Review, 19*(1), 51–89.

Luthans, F. (1991). Improving the delivery of quality service: Behavioural management techniques. *Leadership and Organization Development Journal, 12* (2), 3–6.

Marcus, A. A., & Goodman, R. S. (1991). Victims and shareholders: The dilemmas of presenting corporate policy during a crisis. *Academy of Management Journal, 34*(2), 281–305.

Parasuraman, A., Zeithaml, V. A., & Berry, L. L. (1988, Spring). SERVQUAL: Multiple-item scale for measuring consumer perceptions of service quality. *Journal of Retailing, 64*(1), 12–40.

Sackett, P. R., & Larson, J. R., Jr. (1990). Research strategies and tactics in industrial and organizational psychology. In M. D. Dunnette & L. M. Hough (Eds.). *Handbook of Industrial and Organizational Psychology* (Vol. 1, pp. 419–489). Palo Alto, CA: Consulting Psychologists Press.

Schneider, R., Colan, N. B., & Googins, B. (1991). Supervisor training in employee assistance programs: Current practices and future directions. *Employee-Assistance Quarterly, 6*(2), 41–55.

• •

Statistical Analysis

Appendix Outline

• •

I/O psychology attempts to describe, predict, and explain human behavior in work situations. In describing behavior, the researcher records and states only what is observable. This is done without making any inferences about the cause or meaning of the behavior under review. To predict behavior, scientists select variables from the descriptive stage to formulate tentative laws that may predict future behavior. To achieve control, the scientist systematically creates and manipulates conditions to secure a desired behavior. Because of the multitude of variables that affect human behavior, we can describe, predict, and deduce only within the limits of probability statements (Nunnally, 1959).

Statistics are primary tools used in the collection, organization, and interpretation of data. Statistical methods ensure that research is objective and scientific. As Pedhazur (1982) stated, "data do not speak for themselves but through the medium of the analytic techniques applied to them" (p. 4). The following review of statistics focuses on (a) descriptive statistics, which summarize and describe data; (b) inferential statistics, which allow researchers to generalize about a large body of observations from a sample; and (c) correlational analyses, which examine the relationships between two or more variables. This discussion of statistical analysis is not comprehensive. It is limited in scope to those statistical analyses that new students of industrial/organizational psychology encounter most frequently. Students who are interested in a more comprehensive discussion of statistical procedures are referred to any of several texts devoted to statistics (see the list in Recommended Readings).

· ·

DESCRIPTIVE STATISTICS

Suppose you are given the scores that fifty-four introductory psychology students received on their last quiz. What can you say about these students? Is it possible to describe these data for the entire class and for each individual?

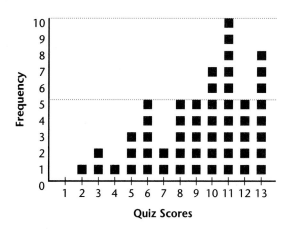

FIGURE 2A.1   Frequency distribution of fifty-four quiz scores in an introductory psychology class.

Graphic Description

One way to describe the data is to draw the shape of the distribution of scores. From this distribution you can learn about the major trends of the group, such as the average class score and the spread of the scores.

Types of Distributions

The first step in plotting the scores is to arrange them from low to high and then show the frequency of each score. This is called a **frequency distribution.** A brief inspection of Figure 2A.1 provides information about the most typical scores and the range of scores. It also allows the comparison of single scores to the class as a whole (see Exercise 2A.1).

· ·

Exercise 2A.1

Practice

The test had twenty questions. What is the most typical score in the distribution of scores as shown in Figure 2A.1? What are the two extreme scores achieved by the students in this class? What is the frequency of each of these scores?

· ·

To create a **frequency polygon,** use a line to connect the points that represent the frequency of scores. A **histogram** or **bar graph** will categorize the scores into class intervals by summarizing the number of scores that correspond to a particular interval. (See Figures 2A.2 and 2A.3 on p. 50 and Practice Perspective 2A.1).

Each of these methods provides the information necessary to describe the group, compare subgroups, and evaluate individual scores. For

---

PRACTICE PERSPECTIVE 2A.1

Inc. 500 Almanac: Descriptive Attributes of *Inc.* Magazine's 1996 Inc. 500

Number of Inc. 500 Companies by State

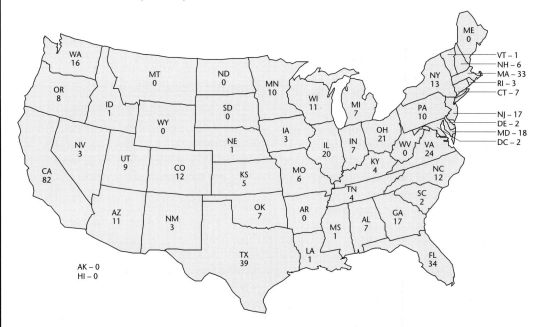

By Business Sector

Service	57%
Manufacturing	27%
Distribution	11%
Retail	5%

By Industry

Computers	30%
Business services	16%
Consumer goods and services	13%
Telecommunications	10%
Health care	7%
Construction	6%
Industrial equipment	5%
Media	4%
Transportation	4%
Financial services	3%
Environmental goods and services	2%

example, Figure 2A.4 on page 50 and Figure 2A.5 on page 51 describe the achievements of classmates by gender. The distribution of scores for the females forms a homogeneous group. Their scores vary between 3 and 13, with an av-

erage score of 10. The lowest actual score is 3, but it is so distant from the bulk of the other scores that it is considered an outlier. (An outlier is a score that lies away from the main clusters of scores.) Because the other scores fall between

Employee Compensation and Benefits
Percentage of companies offering a particular benefit to all employees:

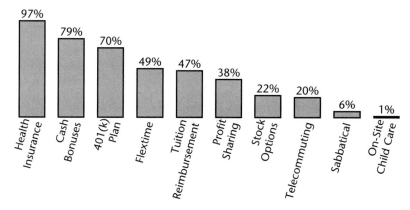

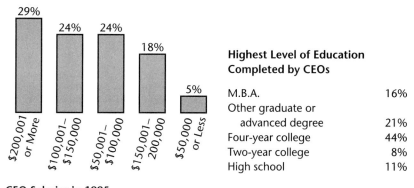

Highest Level of Education Completed by CEOs

M.B.A.	16%
Other graduate or advanced degree	21%
Four-year college	44%
Two-year college	8%
High school	11%

CEO Salaries in 1995

Source: Reprinted with permission, *Inc.* Magazine, Special Edition, October 1996. From "Inc. 500 Almanac" (pp. 22–25). Copyright 1996 by Goldhirsh Group, Inc., 38 Commercial Wharf, Boston, MA 02110.

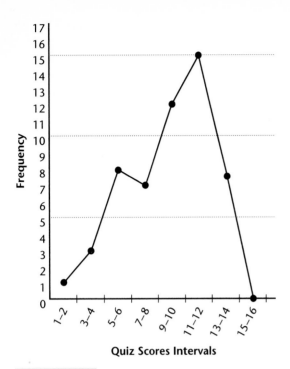

FIGURE 2A.2   Frequency polygon of quiz scores in an introductory psychology class.

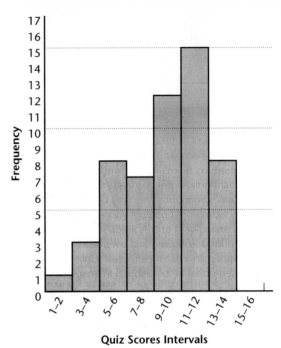

FIGURE 2A.3   Frequency histogram of quiz scores in an introductory psychology class.

6 and 13, the range of this distribution is 7. Males' scores vary between 2 and 13, resulting in a range of 11 points. However, the distribution of scores for the males forms two subgroups. One group has scores that range from 2 to 7, with an average score of 5. The other group has scores that range from 8 to 13, with an average of 11. It appears that the females, as a group, performed better than the males, as a group, on this test. Comparison of the females to each of the male subgroups shows that one group of the males did better than the females.

Shapes of Distributions

Plotting scores often results in distributions of different shapes. Each distribution has specific characteristics that provide the information necessary to make inferences about the group, subgroups, or individuals.

Normal Distributions.   When there are many cases, a frequency distribution approaches the shape of a **normal distribution.** A normal distri-

bution resembles a bell-shaped or **normal curve.** Figure 2A.6 on page 51 shows a normal curve.

In a normal distribution the scores accumulate in the center of the curve and drop off gradually in both directions. For example, suppose you

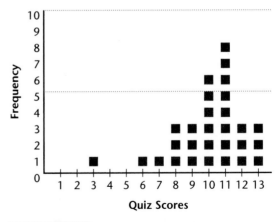

FIGURE 2A.4   Frequency distribution of quiz scores for the female students in an introductory psychology class (*N* = 29).

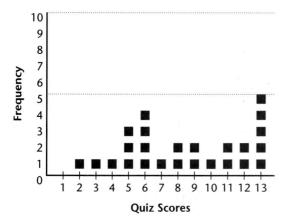

FIGURE 2A.5   Frequency distribution of quiz scores for the male students in an introductory psychology class (N = 25).

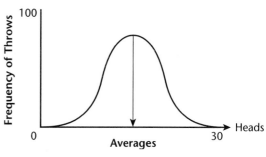

FIGURE 2A.6   Example of a normal distribution curve.

were to drop thirty pennies 100 times and record the number of coins that fell facing heads up each time. According to laws of probability, the shape of the distribution will approximate that of a normal curve. Figure 2A.6 shows that on most of the tosses, the number of coins with heads facing up was near the center of the distribution. Deviations from this pattern lessen in frequency as the distribution moves toward the two extremes. The normal curve is important because (a) in large

number samples, most human traits are distributed approximately normally, and (b) it has quantitative properties that enable us to attach meaning to raw scores and to make inferences.

Skewed Distributions.   Many distributions are skewed, which means that they are asymmetrical and disproportional. This can be due to a nonrepresentative sample, the nature of the data, or both.

An example of a skewed distribution would be the quiz scores for the introductory psychology class. As shown in Figure 2A.7, the distribution of these scores is not the same shape as a normal curve; rather, it is lopsided. This is a

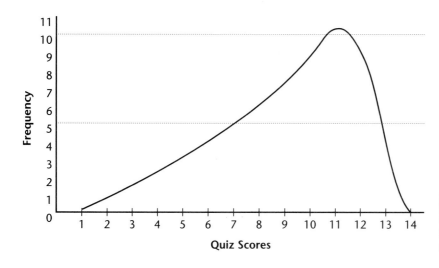

FIGURE 2A.7
Example of a negatively skewed frequency distribution.

negatively skewed distribution because the tail is on the negative end. Another example of this kind of distribution would be the distribution of job performance appraisal rating of experienced welders. Very few of these welders would have low ratings on their welding skills. Plotting their scores would result in a distribution resembling Figure 2A.7.

A **positively skewed distribution** may occur if the introductory psychology class took a very difficult test. With such a test, you would expect many students to have low scores and very few to have high scores. A similar distribution could occur in a factory setting if many untrained, new welders were rated on their performance. For both examples, plotting the results will yield positively skewed distributions (see Figure 2A.8). When a distribution is skewed, it is not appropriate to use the summary statistics that are descriptive of normal distributions.

Multimodal Distribution.   The distribution of scores for male students in the introductory psychology class is a **multimodal distribution** (see Figure 2A.5). Distributions with two or more pronounced humps in them are multimodal distributions. A similar distribution would result if a test were given to a class composed of groups

with different backgrounds. In the business world, for example, a department may employ both skilled and unskilled mechanics. Ratings of the mechanics' job proficiency would create a distribution similar to the one for the male students. The distribution shows that ratings of job performance are high for skilled employees and low for unskilled employees. This type of distribution is a **bimodal distribution;** it has only two pronounced humps.

Numerical Description

It is difficult to interpret data using only graphical descriptions. This difficulty is due to the multitude of scores involved and the need to express those scores in an understandable common language (Tyler, 1965). The process of data reduction involves two statistical measures. One is a measure of the typical score, which describes the central tendency of the distribution. The second is a measure of the variability, which describes the extent of variation.

Central Tendency

Measures of **central tendency,** or averages, describe the performance of subjects in a group. Their values represent a point in the frequency

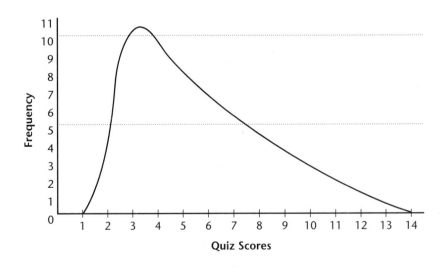

FIGURE 2A.8
Example of a positively skewed frequency distribution.

distribution around which the other values are found. Three of the most common measures are the mode, the median, and the mean.

The **mode** represents the most frequently occurring score in a distribution. It appears as the highest point in the distribution, but it does not necessarily fall in the center of the distribution. The mode may be used as a quick index of the average of the scores.

The **median** is the point in a distribution that occurs above 50% of the cases and below 50% of the cases. When all of the values are ranked from lowest to highest, the median is the middle score or the middle value. Different formulas exist to calculate the value of the median. This is done when the number of cases is large, grouped in intervals, or the middle score is duplicated (as in Figures 2A.1 and 2A.9). The discussion of these formulas is beyond the scope of this text, and the reader is referred to the list of recommended readings at the end of Appendix A (e.g., Jaccard, 1997). For the sake of simplicity we will keep the median as an integer in the following examples. It is often preferable to use the median to describe the average of the scores when the distribution is highly skewed.

The **arithmetic average**, or **mean**, is the most popular measure of central tendency. To calcu-late a sample mean, add all of the scores and then divide the sum by the total number of cases or scores:

$$\overline{X} = \frac{(\Sigma X)}{N}$$

$$\overline{X} = \text{Sample mean}$$

$$(\Sigma X) = \text{Sum of all the scores}$$

$$N = \text{Number of cases in sample}$$

The mode is the least dependable of the three measures of central tendency. For example, suppose three students from the introductory psychology class take the quiz after the rest of the class. Each of these students receives a score of 13. When these scores are added to the other scores in the distribution, the mode will change from 11 to 13. The median is more constant because scores are considered only in terms of rank, rather than value. The mean is based on the values of all scores in the distribution. All three measures have merit, and their use is determined by the type of data under review.

For example, consider the frequency distribution shown in Figure 2A.7. Which of the three measures is the most representative descriptor of the typical score? Figure 2A.9 shows that the mode (Mo) in this negatively skewed distribu-

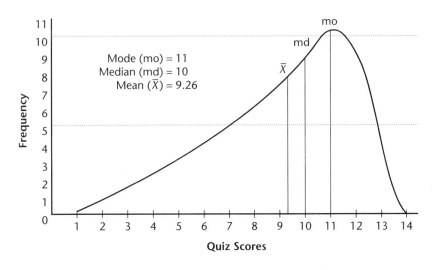

FIGURE 2A.9

Examples of the central tendency scores in a negatively skewed distribution.

tion is 11, the median (Me) is 10, and the mean is 9.26.

This illustration suggests that the median would be the best descriptor because it is unaffected by extreme scores. Adding the three additional scores of 13 would cause only a small change in the median. The three extreme scores pull the mean toward the positive end of the distribution (original mean = 9.26, new mean = 9.45).

In a normal distribution the three values of central tendency are equal to each other (see Figure 2A.6). The normal distribution has certain mathematical advantages that allow the use of other statistics in interpreting data, such as measures of variability. A researcher can manipulate a skewed distribution so that it acquires the properties of a normal curve. The mean and other statistics may then be used to describe the distribution.

Measures of Variability

The shape of the distribution and the measures of central tendency provide only a partial description of the data. For example, suppose two groups complete a test of mechanical comprehension that is worth 150 points. Figure 2A.10 shows the distribution of test results for the two groups. Both of the groups have normal distributions and means of 105.

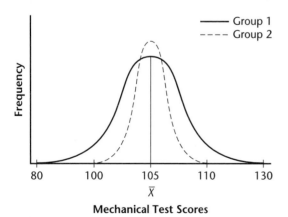

FIGURE 2A.10   Differences in the variability of distributions of mechanical comprehension test scores for two groups.

Suppose you are going to train these groups in skills that require mechanical comprehension. Which of these groups do you think would present the bigger challenge? To answer this question, it is necessary to use a measure of **variability.** These measures allow the psychologist to know how much the members of the two groups differ from each other and from the mean for each distribution.

Figure 2A.10 shows that for Group One the lowest score was 80 and the highest score was 130. For Group Two the lowest score was 100 and the highest score was 110. The scores for Group Two are more homogeneous than the scores for Group One. Group Two will probably take less time to train because its members have similar levels of ability. This example shows why using measures of variability and central tendency *together* would sufficiently describe the group and would enable us to compare individuals in terms of their scores.

Psychologists commonly use two measures of variability: the range and the standard deviation.

The **range** is simply the difference between the lowest and the highest scores in a distribution. In the previous example the scores for Group One vary from 80 to 130, with a range of 50 (130 – 80 = 50). Scores for Group Two vary from 100 to 110, with a range of 10 (110 – 100 = 10). It is important to remember that the range may not represent the diversity that is present in the group.

The **standard deviation** (SD, s, or σ) is a more useful measure of variability than the range. It represents the dispersion of scores around the mean. The formula for determining standard deviation is

$$SD = s = \sqrt{\frac{\Sigma(X - \overline{X})^2}{N}}$$

where Σ = sum of, X = individual score, $\overline{X}$ = the mean of the sample distribution, and N = number of individuals (or scores) in the group. The SD considers the values of all the scores and their deviation around the mean. To calculate the standard deviation, begin by subtracting the group's mean score from each individual score. The resulting deviation score is then squared. Next, compute the average of these squared deviation scores (divide the total by the number of individuals in the group). Finally, take the square root of the average (see Exercise 2A.2).

The standard deviation is "the square root of the average of the squared deviations from the mean" (Willerman, 1979, p. 27). Figure 2A.11 shows three groups that have equal means, but different standard deviations (note that the standard deviations are 10, 5, and 2.5).

The Normal Curve

There is a very exact relationship between standard deviation units and the percentages of scores found in different regions of the **normal curve.** The symmetry of the curve and its mathematical characteristics allow the mean and standard deviation to be used to attach meaning to raw data.

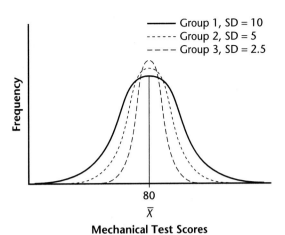

FIGURE 2A.11   Examples of score distributions for three different groups with equal means but different standard deviations.

The total area under the curve includes 100% of the cases. Approximately 68% of the cases fall in the area that extends from one SD below the mean to one SD above the mean. Roughly 95% of the cases are found in the region between two SDs below the mean and two

··

Exercise 2A.2

Calculating Standard Deviations

Suppose the scores achieved by ten trainees on a welding test at the end of their training session are 75, 85, 80, 83, 77, 84, 76, 90, 75, and 75. To compute the standard deviation, we would perform the following steps.

1. Compute the mean:

$$\overline{X} = \frac{(\Sigma X)}{N}$$

$\overline{X}$ = Sample mean

(ΣX) = Sum of all the scores

N = Number of cases in sample

2. Subtract each of the scores from the mean:

$$(X - \overline{X})$$

Because the assumed distribution is normal and scores are distributed evenly on both sides of the mean, the total of these subtracted scores would result in zero. The next step would be to consider the absolute differences by squaring them:

$$(X - \overline{X})^2$$

3. Total the absolute differences and divide by N (10). The result is the variance of the scores, or SD^2 or s^2:

$$SD^2 = s^2 = \frac{\Sigma (X - \overline{X})^2}{N}$$

The standard deviation would be the square root of the variance, or

$$SD = s = \sqrt{\frac{\Sigma(X - \overline{X})^2}{N}}$$

··

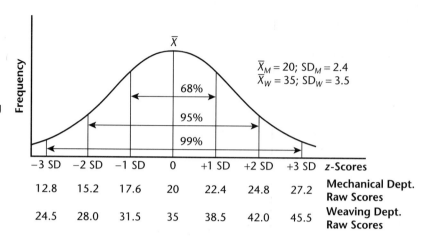

FIGURE 2A.12
An example of a normal distribution curve showing areas defined by z scores and the comparable raw score equivalents for the mechanical department and the weaving department on the pay satisfaction survey.

SDs above the mean. About 99% of the cases lie within the area between three SDs below the mean and three SDs above the mean (see Figures 2A.12 and 2A.13).

This relationship holds true for every normal curve, whatever the mean and standard deviation. This allows the conversion of the scores to standardized scores; which, in turn, allows comparison of scores across various distributions.

Standard Scores

The base line in Figure 2A.12 shows the standard deviation units. It is possible to express scores in terms of deviations from the mean. These scores are z-**scores,** which are shown on the first hori-

zontal line under the distribution. A score of 20 is equal to the mean of the mechanical department and therefore would be expressed as zero. A score of 22.4 deviates from the mean by one SD. The formula to calculate a z-score

$$z = \frac{X - \overline{X}}{SD}$$

transforms individual scores in the distribution so that each score has the standard deviation as a common denominator.

Suppose you conduct a pay satisfaction survey in a textile plant with 1000 employees. One question on the survey might be "How does Joe Doe, in mechanical repair, compare to Bob Dow,

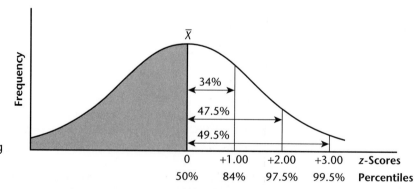

FIGURE 2A.13
An example of a normal distribution curve showing corresponding z scores and percentiles.

in weaving, in level of pay satisfaction?" To make an appropriate comparison, first separate the scores from employees in the mechanical repair department from those in the weaving department. Next, compute the means and standard deviations for both groups. According to Figure 2A.12, employees in the mechanical department have $\overline{X} = 20$ and SD = 2.4. Employees in the weaving department have $\overline{X} = 35$ and SD = 3.5. Joe's score is 23, and Bob's score is 42. Joe's z-score is +1.25 (23 − 20 = 3; 3 divided by 2.4 = 1.25). Bob's z-score is +2.00 (42 − 35 = 7; 7 divided by 3.5 = 2.00). Clearly, Bob's score is higher than Joe's score. This suggests that Bob is more satisfied with his level of pay than Joe is with his.

There is another method that describes an individual's score and then compares that score to other scores. This method involves using the percentage of cases the score is equal to or greater than in the normal distribution. These scores are called **percentiles.** Using the percentages shown in Figure 2A.13, Joe's percentile score on the survey is equal to or greater than 89.5% of the employees scores. Bob's percentile score equals or exceeds 97.5% of the other scores. The shaded area in Figure 2A.13 represents 50% of the cases; 50% plus 47.5%—the area between the mean and $z = +2.00$—equals 50% + 47.5% = 97.5%. These percentages can be identified from the cumulative normal probability table printed in most statistics textbooks.

INFERENTIAL STATISTICS: STATISTICAL SIGNIFICANCE

According to Hays (1981, p. 2), inferential statistics consist of a "theory about uncertainty, the tendency of outcomes to vary when repeated observations are made under identical conditions." An I/O psychologist is an empirical scientist, beginning any research effort with observation and generalization rather than a well-developed theory. This approach is quite different from that of the traditional experimentalist, whose research begins with formal assertions postulated as true, which is a deductive method. This method starts with hypotheses and seeks to derive valid conclusions from systematic tests of those hypotheses. The empirical scientist is a correlationalist by nature, assuming that general conclusions about the phenomenon under study are discovered through induction. The assumption is that any relations among events and/or behaviors have to be "discovered and verified by the actual observation of what happens in the real world of experience" (Hays, 1981, p. 3).

An empirical scientist investigates the nature of relationships among events. Real-world observations can vary according to time or fluctuating circumstances. It is important for the researcher to determine the extent of "errors" that occur in making observations and collecting data. Inferential methods allow psychologists to (a) calculate the probability of making errors in drawing conclusions, and (b) help to determine the extent to which findings from the sample can be generalized to the population under investigation.

It is important for the researcher to determine whether the results of the study would change if it were conducted with different samples drawn from the same population. This refers to **sampling error,** which is the most serious systematic effect on the results of repeated investigations. Inferential statistical tests help the investigator to decide the extent to which the results may be due to chance or systematic effects.

Suppose you want to investigate the relationship between the degree of employee pay satisfaction and job performance. You draw a random sample of 500 employees from 20,000 blue-collar production workers and then collect data on pay satisfaction and job performance. The results show that there is a strong relationship between these two variables. Next, you need to decide whether the results can be generalized to the entire plant population or possibly beyond that to the general population of blue-collar employees.

The first step is to establish a **level of confidence** for the relationship between pay satisfaction and job performance. The level of confidence is used to determine whether the same degree of relationship would exist between pay satisfaction and performance for any two groups randomly drawn from the same population. It also aids in deciding whether this difference has any significant meaning. If the results suggest that there is a significant relationship between the two variables, how much chance is there that the results are wrong?

Statistical significance means that the results of a given study are not due to sampling fluctuations alone. It is the trustworthiness of a statistical measure and is expressed as a level of probability. For example, suppose the probability of accurately determining a relationship between variables is significant at the 5% level (expressed as $p \leq .05$). This means that such results could occur because of chance alone in only 5 out of 100 random samples. Some researchers use more stringent probability levels, such as $p \leq .01$ or $p \leq .001$. At these levels, the risk of being wrong is only once in either 100 or 1000 samples, respectively.

In investigating pay satisfaction and job performance, the psychologist could also make inferences about gender differences in the level of satisfaction. Statistical tests determine the probability of getting, by chance, a difference as large as the one obtained between the male and female groups. Researchers use a *t*-**test,** or *t*-**ratio,** to analyze the difference between the two sample means. When using a *t*-test, the researcher compares the means of samples rather than comparing individual scores to the mean.

There are other statistical tools that a psychologist can use to find the degree of difference between groups, such as chi-square and analysis of variance. Specific descriptions of these statistics are beyond the scope of this book and can be found in most statistics textbooks.

A relationship also exists between significance levels and sample size. A small difference may be statistically significant when the sample size is very large. Conversely, a large difference may not be statistically significant if the sample size is small. In a working environment, investigators need to consider practical significance rather than relying solely on statistical significance. As the number of people in each sample increases, the risk of artificially reaching statistical significance also increases. For example, suppose you are investigating whether a glare reduction feature on video terminals will increase work speed. Each individual in the sample is randomly assigned to one of two large groups. One group works with a glare reduction screen, and the other works with a traditional screen. Because the groups are quite large, even a small difference in the performance between groups could appear to be statistically significant. Practically, you also need to consider whether this degree of improvement in speed will justify the cost of changing all of the terminals.

CORRELATIONAL ANALYSIS

Common techniques that I/O psychologists use include statistics that make it possible to explain the relationship between two or more variables. With most research in industry it is difficult, and often impossible, to manipulate variables in a way that determines whether a causal relationship exists. Many studies take place in natural organizational settings that do not allow the researcher to control the variables under review. Therefore, the psychologist often collects data on as many subjects as possible and then determines the strength of the relationship. For example, suppose a psychologist wants to examine the relationship between income levels of faculty members and the number of articles they have published over the last five years. Knowing the strength of this relationship allows the psychologist to predict changes in income level due to the number of articles published.

Simple Correlation and Regression

Correlation means that two conditions or events vary together, that is, they are "co-related." This is simple correlation, which is also known as Pearson product moment correlation and is represented by the symbol r. As Pedhazur (1982) stated, correlation describes the variance that exists among individuals or groups. This is expressed in terms of the variables and the extent to which they covary. Variance refers to the distribution of a set of scores around their mean and is described by the standard deviation. Covariance refers to the tendency of two sets of scores to vary together around their respective means (Pedhazur, 1982). Correlation measures the degree of linear relationship that exists between the variables, which allows the researcher to predict scores on one variable from the scores on the other variable.

The **correlation coefficient (r)** provides two types of information. It indicates the direction of the relationship and describes the strength or magnitude of the relationship.

Direction of Correlation

The direction of a relationship can be positive or negative. A **positive correlation** is one in which two variables move in the same direction. When the score on one variable increases, the score on the other variable also increases. For example, in a review of the literature, Tett, Jackson, and Rothstein (1991) found that personality characteristics (such as extroversion or agreeableness) have a positive correlation with job performance. That is, people who report high levels of sociability are also rated high on job performance by their supervisors.

A **negative correlation** is one in which the scores on two variables fall in opposite directions. If the scores on one variable increase, the scores on the other variable decrease. For example, the study by Tett, Jackson, and Rothstein (1991) suggests that neuroticism has a negative correlation with job performance. This means that workers who have high scores on neuroticism tend to have low ratings on job performance. Another example of negative correlation would be an individual's weight and speed of running. As a person's weight increases, the speed at which the person runs may decrease.

When two variables have no relationship at all, a **zero correlation** exists. For example, Nicholoson, Brown, and Chadwick-Jones (1976) found no relationship between job satisfaction and absenteeism. Lowenberg, Iverson, and Conrad (1989) conducted a quantitative review of the literature on pay satisfaction. No relationship was found between the level of pay satisfaction and the length of time an individual was employed by an organization (i.e., tenure).

Degree of Correlation

The size of the correlation coefficient expresses the strength or magnitude of the relationship between two variables. Correlations vary from −1.00 to +1.00. When the correlation coefficient is 1.00 (+ or −), it means that there is a perfect relationship between scores individuals receive on the variables. A correlation of +1.00 indicates that the relationship is perfect and positive; a correlation of −1.00 indicates that the relationship is perfect and negative. Because human behavior is so complex, such a perfect relationship is seldom found.

Scatter Plots

A **scatter plot,** or **scatter diagram,** is a graphic representation of the data. Technically, this is called a **bivariate plot.** The correlation coefficient assumes that the relationship between two variables is **linear,** that is, can be described by a straight line. To create a scatter plot, each of the variables is assigned to either the x- or y-axis. The pairs of scores for each member of the group are then plotted on the graph. Figures 2A.14a through 2A.14e on page 60 are examples of scatter plots.

In many studies, the points on the scatter plot tend to cluster along a straight line. When this occurs, the scattered points are described as falling near the **best-fit line,** which is a straight line running through the scatter diagram. Figures 2A.14a and 2A.14b show positive relationships between clerical test scores of secretaries and their job performance as described by supervisors' ratings. In Figure 2A.14a the dots that indicate joint standings show that the distribution is close to the best-

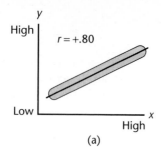

(a)

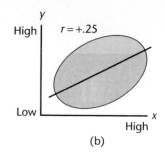

(b)

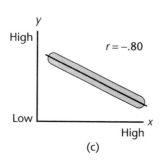

(c)

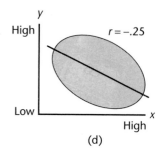

(d)

FIGURE 2A.14
Examples of scatter plots illustrating relationships of different strengths between sets of clerical test scores and on-the-job performance ratings of secretaries.

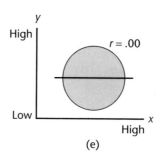

(e)

fit line ($r = +.80$, which is positive and high). Figure 2A.14b shows that the joint scores are loosely distributed around the best-fit line. The slant of this line suggests that a positive relationship exists; however, the association is weak because the correlation is only $r = +.25$. Results in Figures 2A.14c and 2A.14d depict negative relationships of the same strength as the positive relationships in Figures 2A.14a and 2A.14b, respectively. Figure 2A.14e shows that the relationship between clerical test scores for the secretaries and the supervisors' ratings is widely scattered. The best-fit line has no slant at all, so no apparent relationship exists between the two variables. The correlation for these variables is $r = 0.00$ (see Exercise 2A.3).

The formula for the Pearson correlation coefficient in terms of raw scores is

$$r = \frac{N\Sigma XY - (\Sigma X)(\Sigma Y)}{\sqrt{[N\Sigma X^2 - (\Sigma X)^2]\,[N\Sigma Y^2 - (\Sigma Y)^2]}}$$

N = Number of pairs of scores

ΣXY = Sum of products of the paired scores

ΣX and ΣY = Sum of scores on each of the variables

ΣX^2 and ΣY^2 = Sum of the squared scores on the X variable and on the Y variable

Exercise 2A.3

Scatterplot Exercise

The following exercise utilizes Dunnette's (1966b, pp. 18–24) example of validating a clerical test used as an employee selection device. To validate the relationship between the test and performance on the job, a firm hired all fifteen applicants for a clerical position. All were given the clerical test, but their scores were not used at the time of hiring. After six months supervisors rated these employees' performance on a nine-point scale. Following are the two sets of scores achieved by these employees:

Employee	Test score	Supervisors' rating
1	20	7
2	23	8
3	17	4
4	19	6
5	22	7
6	17	2
7	20	5
8	20	1
9	21	6
10	19	3
11	19	1
12	20	6
13	21	5
14	22	4
15	20	4

Draw the scatter plot for these two sets of scores, and answer the following questions:

1. Is the relationship linear?

2. What is the direction of this relationship?

3. What is the estimated strength of the relationship between the clerical test and performance on the job for these employees?

Source: From *Personnel Selection and Placement,* by M. D. Dunnette, 1966, pp. 18–24. Belmont, CA: Wadsworth Publishing. Copyright 1966 by Wadsworth. Reprinted with permission.

Since raw scores are transformed into standard scores (such as z-scores), when we want to compare scores on different distributions, this formula can be expressed as

$$r = \frac{\Sigma Z_x Z_y}{N}$$

or

$$r = \frac{\Sigma \left(\dfrac{X - \overline{X}}{SD_x} \right)\left(\dfrac{Y - \overline{Y}}{SD_y} \right)}{N}$$

The numerator considers the difference between individual scores and the group means for both variables. The product of these differences is summed, and the average is computed. A bivariate distribution results that is the mean of the products of two sets of standard scores (Dunnette, 1966a).

Squaring the correlation coefficient indicates the percentage of variation in the dependent variable that may be predictable from the independent variable. A correlation coefficient of $r = +.59$ means that $r^2 = .35$ (i.e., that 35% of the variability of scores in Y can be predicted from the variability of scores in X).

Simple Regression

A correlation coefficient provides a single statistic that expresses the relationship between two variables. It can also predict the value of one variable from that of the other. The values of the dependent variable can be predicted from the values of the independent variable by using a linear equation:

$$y = a + bx$$

In the equation, x and y are the two variables under review, and a and b are constant values. The predicted score of an individual is y, and x is the predictor value; b is the slope, which represents the changes occurring in y with each value change in x. a is the y-intercept, which determines the value of y when $x = 0$. The correlation coefficient describes the fit that exists between the scores on two variables. Regression can be described as the prediction of scores on variable *y* from the scores on variable *x*.

It is important to remember that these statistics apply only to linear relationships. Within linear relationships, each unit of change in the independent variable has the same effect on the dependent variable (Hedderson, 1987).

In the real world, relationships are more often **nonlinear.** Figure 2A.15 shows the **curvilinear** relationship that Lowenberg, Powaser, and Farkash (1989) found when studying the relationship between levels of income and levels of pay satisfaction of salaried employees. They found that low income (below $15,000) and high income

(above $25,000) were associated with lower pay satisfaction. Employees with moderate incomes ($15,000 to $24,999) expressed the highest level of pay satisfaction. These relationships are not linear and cannot be described by a correlation coefficient or simple regression. Other methods exist to calculate and interpret nonlinear relationships. It is important to study the pattern of the association to ensure selection of the appropriate statistic. Dunnette (1966b) suggests that investigators draw a scatter diagram to view the relationship between the two variables before selecting a statistical technique.

A correlation coefficient provides us with indices of the strength and direction of the relationship between two variables. It does not yield any information about cause and effect between these variables. For example, many studies have examined the relationship between grade point average (GPA) and scores achieved on intelligence tests. These studies have found correlations ranging from $r = +.40$ to $r = +.60$. This information does *not* allow a psychologist to conclude that high intelligence causes a high GPA. Other factors could affect the variables under review. For example, the school the student attends, the amount of coaching and practice the student receives, and similar factors could be responsible for the degree and direction of the relationship found in these studies.

Cherrington, Reitz, and Scott (1971) investigated the relationship between pay satisfaction and level of performance of students. The researchers found no direct relationship between these two variables. They were able to conclude that the covariation between pay satisfaction and performance was caused by a third factor. That factor is the natural relationship that exists between reinforcement and a feeling of satisfaction with the reward. By varying the appropriateness of the reward (amount of pay received), the researchers were able to produce different magnitudes and directions of the correlation between performance and satisfaction. For example, high-level performances rewarded by high pay (an appropriate reward) produced signifi-

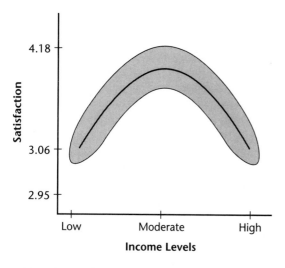

Note: Low income = ≤$14,999
      Moderate income = ≥$15,000 and ≤$24,999
      High income = ≥$25,000

FIGURE 2A.15   Example of a curvilinear relationship between income level and pay satisfaction.

Source: From data presented in Lowenberg, G., Powaser, P. R., & Farkash, A. (1989). Determination of the relationship between pay desire satisfaction and appropriate pay differentials relative to income levels. In B. J. Fallon, H. P. Pfister, & J. Breber (Eds.), *Advances in Industrial/Organizational Psychology* (pp. 201–209). Amsterdam: North-Holland, Elsevier Science Publishers.

cantly greater feelings of satisfaction than high-level performances rewarded by low pay (an inappropriate reward).

The natural relationship between reinforcement and satisfaction led to the correlation between satisfaction and performance. However, neither of these variables causes the other to occur. It is important to remember that a cause-and-effect relationship can be determined only from a carefully designed and controlled experiment.

Multiple Correlation and Regression

Multiple correlation is an extension of the bivariate correlation. It takes into account the degree of relationship between two or more independent variables (x_1 and x_2) used as predictors and a dependent variable (Y = predicted). The multiple correlation coefficient is expressed as R and indicates the strength and direction of the relationships under investigation. The formula for the two predictors is

$$R_{1.23} = \sqrt{\frac{r_{12}^2 + r_{13}^2 - 2r_{12}\,r_{13}\,r_{23}}{1 - r_{23}^2}}$$

where 1 is the dependent variable and 2 and 3 are the independent variables or predictors. Interpretation of the multiple correlation is the same as for simple correlation, except that multiple correlation is based on the interactive effects of several independent variables.

The prediction equation for multiple regression is

$$Y = a + b_1 x_1 + b_2 x_2 + \cdots + b_n x_n$$

As in simple regression, y is the predicted score (dependent variable) and the x's are the predictors (independent variables). The b's are weights assigned to each of the predictors and a is a constant.

Multiple regression predicts the best estimate of scores on the dependent variable based on the combined effects of the independent variables. As in simple regression, the interpretation

for multiple regression assumes that (a) the effects of the independent variables are linear, (b) scores are normally distributed, and (c) the independent variables are not correlated with each other (Hedderson, 1987).

....

OTHER SCIENTIFIC INFERENCE TECHNIQUES

I/O psychologists often apply research methods that include inferences based on more than one study, relationships based on more than one dependent variable, and summaries based on multiple numbers of correlations. Some examples are factor analysis, the multitrait-multimethod matrix, and meta-analysis.

Factor Analysis

Suppose an introductory psychology class were a year-long course and that the students were given twenty tests throughout the year. You might ask whether these tests measured proficiency in different sets of information covered in class. A method that helps to answer that question is **factor analysis.** Cronbach (1970, p. 309) defined factor analysis as "a systematic method for examining the meaning of a test by studying its correlation with other variables." It is a way of summarizing data from multiple tests taken by many people when the scores on each test are correlated with scores on the other tests. The resulting table of intercorrelations among these tests can then be analyzed and explained in terms of fewer factors or components (Fruchter, 1954). Factor analysis would help you find out whether (a) you are testing different categories of information covered in class, and (b) you can reduce the twenty tests to a smaller number and still measure proficiency in all areas covered in class.

The following are the topics covered in five of the tests:

1. Test 1 describes the role of the individual employee and the organizational framework.
2. Test 2 measures statistical techniques.

3. Test 3 covers methods in scientific research.
4. Test 4 consists of class discussions on performance evaluation at work situations.
5. Test 5 brings up issues related to methods of promotion in organizations.

Table 2A.1 presents the intercorrelations among the five tests.

An inspection of Table 2A.1 identifies two clusters of tests that intercorrelate highly among themselves. The first cluster includes tests 1, 2, and 3; the second cluster includes tests 1, 4, and 5. A factor analysis of the intercorrelations (Table 2A.2) shows that there are two underlying components.

The results of the factor analysis are reported in terms of loadings. A **loading** is the correlation between test scores and underlying factors. The higher the loading of the test on the factor, the stronger the relationship that exists between the factor and the test. Tests 2 and 3 covered material about techniques and strategies of investigation in I/O psychology, so the first factor may be identified as "Research." The second factor is related to tests 4 and 5, which cover human performance at work. It may be identified as "Work Outcomes." Test 1 loads on both factors (.54 on Research and .60 on Work Outcomes). This is most likely because the test addresses general issues within an organization. With the help of factor analysis the number of tests that

TABLE 2A.2   Factor analysis results showing the loadings of the five introductory psychology class tests with underlying components of material covered in class

Tests	Factor Loadings	
	Research	Work Outcomes
1	.54	.60
2	.77	.04
3	.80	.29
4	.14	.55
5	.11	.85

are needed to cover all of the material included in the original five tests can be reduced to two.

Factor analysis has been extremely useful in the research on intelligence. Theories of intelligence often define it as a general factor that contributes to all of our mental activities. Other theories explain intelligence as having many factors, each dealing with a different content area or a different mental process and producing a different outcome. All of these theories are based on studies involving factor analysis. In I/O psychology, factor analysis has been used to investigate leadership components, factors underlying job satisfaction, and many other areas. However, a review of 152 studies using factor analysis suggests that this method is poorly applied in I/O psychology (Ford, MacCallum, & Tait, 1986). Guidelines were provided to improve the quality and validity of information gathered from applied factor analytic research.

Multitrait-Multimethod Matrix

Another method that is used to investigate relationships among tests is the Campbell and Fisk (1959) matrix. This matrix consists of a table that includes intercorrelations between tests. Because there are multiple tests, each measuring at least two traits, the table is called a

TABLE 2A.1   Intercorrelations of scores from the five introductory psychology class tests

Class Tests	Class Tests				
	1	2	3	4	5
1	1.00	.80	.50	.50	.60
2		1.00	.75	.40	.02
3			1.00	.15	.30
4				1.00	.75
5					1.00

multitrait-multimethod matrix. Using different measures of the same trait enables the investigator to study the extent to which a specific test measures what it is supposed to measure. This concept is known as **validity**. Also the investigator is able to make inferences from the test scores to the psychological trait underlying a specific behavior. This is known as **construct validity**. An example of this method is a score achieved on an honesty test that correlates with being a dependable, trustworthy teller in a bank.

The multitrait-multimethod matrix is based on the logic that (a) sets of scores on different tests representing the same trait should have positive and high correlations between them, and (b) scores on tests representing different traits should have zero or low correlations (Lowenberg, 1969). For example, assume that you have constructed a questionnaire to measure the traits of honesty and courtesy in bank tellers. To confirm your hypothesis that the questionnaire actually measures these psychological characteristics, the questionnaire is given to a group of tellers. They are also given a psychological test (one that has already been validated) that measures honesty and courtesy. Table 2A.3 presents the matrix of correlations between the scores of the tellers on these two measures.

Researchers use correlations to establish the reliability of a measure. **Reliability** is the extent to which a measure produces consistent results. A reliable measure will produce similar scores for the same individual on different occasions, resulting in a high correlation between the scores. The circled numbers in Table 2A.3 are the correlations between the same measures (the questionnaire or test) and the same characteristics (honesty or courtesy) taken at different times. These correlations are high enough (.75, .80, .85, and .90) to suggest that both the questionnaire and the test are reliable measures of honesty and courtesy. The correlations also indicate that the measures of honesty do not measure courtesy ($r = .25$, .01, and .20). Finally, we can see that the correlations of $r = .52$ and $r = .69$ demonstrate that the questionnaire and the test measure to some extent the *same* underlying traits. The data from this example show that the scales for honesty and courtesy on this instrument have construct validity. Studies (e.g., Neidig & Neidig, 1984) using the multitrait-multimethod matrix often include more than two traits and methods. Researchers frequently use variations on the original format of the multitrait-multimethod matrix. For example, the multiple test measures may be replaced

TABLE 2A.3	Example of a multitrait-multimethod matrix				

		Time 1 Questionnaire		Time 1 Test	
Time 2	*Traits*	*Honesty*	*Courtesy*	*Honesty*	*Courtesy*
Questionnaire	Honesty	.75			
	Courtesy	.25	.80		
Test	Honesty	.52		.85	
	Courtesy	.01	.69	.20	.90

Source: Adapted from *The Psychology of Individual and Group Differences* (p. 45), by L. Willerman, 1979, San Francisco: W. H. Freeman & Company. Copyright © 1979 by W. H. Freeman & Company. Used with permission.

by ratings from multiple raters to examine the validity and reliability of raters in giving performance appraisals (Lawler, 1967). Results from multitrait-multimethod studies are often confirmed by other procedures, such as factor analysis.

Meta-Analysis

In Chapter 1 we mentioned that one of the major developments in I/O psychology in the 1970s was the formation of a quantitative methodology called meta-analysis. Prior to the 1970s, most cumulative reviews of studies dealing with the same subject had been accomplished through a subjective summary by the reviewer. Conversely, **meta-analysis** is a systematic and statistical summary of results of independent studies dealing with a specific subject matter and using the same independent and dependent variables (Hunter, Schmidt, & Jackson, 1982; Hunter & Schmidt, 1990). It is a statistical procedure designed "to cumulate findings from a number of validity studies to estimate the validity of the procedure for the kinds of jobs or groups of jobs and settings included in the studies" (SIOP, 1987, p. 38). The goal is to enable the researcher to review the relevant literature and to reduce the subjectivity often found in traditional reviews.

Meta-analysis uses studies as subjects. The method describes the distribution of actual correlations found in these studies between a specific independent and a dependent variable. It then provides an objective procedure for averaging the desired statistics (e.g., correlation coefficients) across the studies cumulated. Since "studies are never perfect" (Hunter & Schmidt, 1990, p. 43) and the correlations cumulated vary from study to study, the next step is for meta-analysis to correct the methodological and situational errors (artifacts), such as divergent sample sizes. This is the equivalent of conducting an experiment with many times the number of subjects that would be included in each of the individual studies. Because these conclusions are based on many studies corrected for their arti-

facts, meta-analysis is assumed to give a more accurate estimate of the "true relationship" existing between the variables studied.

While meta-analysis has contributed to a significant compilation of I/O research, it also has created some controversy. This arises from the decisions an investigator must make about the types of studies to include, the thoroughness of the search for relevant studies, the quality of the studies included, and the interpretations of the final results. In spite of these issues, many current perspectives in I/O psychology are based, in part, on meta-analytic summaries of research in areas such as validity of employment tests, job satisfaction, training, leadership behavior, and job conflict.

Discussion of the formulas used in meta-analysis is beyond the scope of this book. For further information, refer to the recommended reading in Chapter 8. Inasmuch as most of the applications of meta-analysis explore the validity of personnel procedures, we will discuss this procedure with respect to validity generalization in Chapter 8.

SUMMARY

I/O psychologists describe, predict, and explain human behavior within the work environment. They collect data and attempt to determine associations and cause-and-effect relationships that exist between variables. I/O psychologists use statistical analyses to interpret their data. Some of the analyses that they use include descriptive statistics, inferential statistics, and correlational statistics.

Descriptive statistics allow researchers to summarize and describe data. One way to do this is through graphic description. Frequency distributions, frequency polygons, histograms, and bar graphs are examples of the graphic presentation of data. Graphic distributions occur in different shapes, such as a normal distribution, skewed distributions, and multimodal distributions.

Researchers also use numeric descriptions to understand their data. These descriptions typically use two basic statistics: a measure of the average and a measure of variability. Numerical descriptions of averages are called measures of central tendency and include the mode, median, and mean. The mode is the most frequently occurring score, the median represents the midpoint for a distribution, and the mean is the arithmetic average. The type of data collected will determine which of these measures is the appropriate one to use. Measures of variability tell researchers the extent to which members of a group vary from each other and from the mean. Two commonly used measures of variability are the range and the standard deviation. The range is simply the difference between the lowest and highest scores in the distribution. The standard deviation allows researchers to estimate the distribution of scores around the mean.

Researchers use inferential statistics to generalize findings to a population. A serious problem that can occur is sampling error. Statistical significance refers to the degree to which the results of a study could have been obtained by sampling fluctuations or chance alone.

Correlational analyses determine whether two or more sets of variables are co-related. These measures provide information about the direction and strength of relationships. The direction of the relationship can be positive (i.e., two variables move in the same direction), or negative (i.e., when one variable increases, the other decreases). The strength of the relationship is represented by a number that falls within the range of −1.00 to +1.00. Strong relationships are close to 1.00; weak relationships are close to 0.00. A zero correlation indicates that no relationship exists. These relationships are graphically represented by a scatter plot. A regression equation allows researchers to predict one dependent variable on the basis of measures of other independent variables.

I/O psychologists use additional statistical methods to obtain information and make inferences about the data. Examples are factor analysis, the multitrait-multimethod matrix, and meta-analysis. Factor analysis provides a way of summarizing data that come from multiple measures. The multitrait-multimethod matrix provides the researcher with data based on intercorrelations of at least two traits being measured by at least two different tests. Meta-analysis adds objectivity to summaries of literature reviews.

KEY TERMS AND CONCEPTS

arithmetic average	loadings	positively skewed distribution
bar graph	mean	range
best-fit line	median	regression
bimodal distribution	meta-analysis	reliability
bivariate plot	mode	sampling error
central tendency	multimodal distribution	scatter diagram
construct validity	multiple correlation	scatter plot
correlation	multiple regression	standard deviation
correlation coefficient	multitrait-multimethod matrix	statistical significance
curvilinear	negative correlation	*t*-ratio
factor analysis	negatively skewed distribution	*t*-test
frequency distribution	nonlinear	validity
frequency polygon	normal curve	variability
histogram	normal distribution	zero correlation
level of confidence	percentiles	*z*-scores
linear	positive correlation	

RECOMMENDED READINGS

Alliger, G. M., Tannenbaum, Bennett W., Jr., Traver, H., & Shetland, A. (1997). A meta-analysis of the relations among training criteria. *Personnel Psychology, 50* (2), 341–358.

Freedman, D., Pisani, R., Purves, R., & Adhikani, A. (1991). *Statistics.* New York: W. W. Norton & Company.

Hays, W. L. (1967). *Quantification in psychology.* Belmont, CA: Brooks/Cole.

Hunter, J. E. & Schmidt, F. L. (1990). *Methods of meta-analysis: Correcting error and bias in research findings.* Newbury Park, CA: Sage Publications.

Jaccard, J. (1997). *Statistics for behavioral sciences.* Pacific Grove, CA: Brooks/Cole.

Locke, E. A. (1986). *Generalizing from laboratory to field settings.* Lexington, MA: Lexington Books.

Norusis, M. J. (1986). *The SPSS guide to data analysis.* Chicago: SPSS, Inc.

Schroeder, L. D., Sjoquist, D. L., & Stephan, P. E. (1986). *Understanding regression analysis: An introductory guide.* Sage University Paper Series on Quantitative Applications in the Social Sciences, 07–057. Beverly Hills, CA: Sage.

Suzaki, K. (1993). *The new shop floor management: Empowering people for continuous improvement.* New York: Free Press.

Wanous, J. P., Reichers, A. E., & Hudy, M. J. (1997). Overall satisfaction: How good are single-item measures? *Journal of Applied Psychology, 82* (2), 247–252.

Wolf, F. M. (1986). *Meta-analysis: Quantitative methods for research synthesis.* Sage University Paper Series on Quantitative Applications in the Social Sciences, 07–059. Beverly Hills, CA: Sage.

INTERNET RESOURCES

Statistics Gopher
Gopher servers present text in hierarchical menus and submenus. This one is the statistics section of the United Kingdom's math archives. It accesses a number of good articles about statistics.
gopher://archives.math.utk.edu:70/11/software/msdos/statistics

Institute of Statistics and Decision Sciences, Duke University
This site contains links to statistics servers and many other links. Academic departmental servers in many countries are listed by country.
http://www.isds.duke.edu/stats-sites.html

Guide to Locating Health Statistics
This is a guide to locating health statistics and resources that are available on the World Wide Web and at Falk Library of the Health Sciences.
http://www.hsls.pitt.edu/statcbw.html

A Guide to Statistical Computing Resources on the Internet
The University of Michigan, School of Information and Library Studies, provides this list of general statistical resources.
http://asa.ugl.lib.umich.edu/chdocs/statistics/general.html

The World-Wide Web Virtual Library: Statistics
Sponsored by the University of Florida Department of Statistics, this site contains links to job announcements and special events as well as links to universities and associations around the world.
http://www.stat.ufl.edu/vlib/statistics.html

Pitfalls of Data Analysis (or How to Avoid Lies and Damned Lies)
By Clay Helberg, M. S., at the Research Design and Statistics Unit, University of Wisconsin Schools of Nursing and Medicine, Madison, WI. helberg@maddog.fammed.wisc.edu.
http://www.execpc.com/~helberg/pitfalls

Statistics on the Web
This is a list of statistics resources Clay Helberg has discovered on the World Wide Web.
http://www.execpc.com/~helberg/statistics.html

REFERENCES

Campbell, D. K., & Fisk, D. W. (1959). Convergent and discriminant validation by the multitrait-multimethod matrix. *Psychological Bulletin,* 56, 81–105.

Cherrington, D. J., Reitz, H. J., & Scott, W. E. (1971). Effect of contingent and non-contingent reward on the relationship between satisfaction and task performance. *Journal of Applied Psychology, 55,* 531–536.

Cronbach, L. J. (1970). *Essentials of psychological testing.* New York: Harper & Row.

Dunnette, M. D. (1966a). Fads, fashions, and folderol in psychology. *American Psychologist, 21,* 343–352.

Dunnette, M. D. (1966b). *Personnel selection and placement.* Belmont, CA: Wadsworth.

Ford, L. K., MacCullum, R. C., & Tait, M. (1986). The application of exploratory factor analysis in applied psychology: A critical review. *Personnel Psychology, 39* (2), 291–314.

Fruchter, B. (1954). *Introduction to factor analysis.* New York: D. Van Nostrand Company.

Hays, W. L. (1981). *Statistics* (3rd ed.). New York: Holt, Rinehart and Winston.

Hedderson, J. (1987). *SSPS^X made simple.* Belmont, CA: Wadsworth.

Hunter, J. E., & Schmidt, F. L. (1990). *Methods of meta-analysis: Correcting error and bias in research findings.* Newbury Park: Sage Publications.

Hunter, J. E., Schmidt, F. L., & Jackson, G. B. (1982). *Meta-analysis: Cumulating research findings across studies.* Beverly Hills: Sage Publications.

Lawler, E. E. III. (1967). The multitrait-multirater approach to measuring managerial job performance. *Journal of Applied Psychology, 51,* 369–381.

Lowenberg, G. (1969). *Investigation of convergent and discriminant validity of trait dimensions, defined by a self-descriptive adjective checklist.* Unpublished doctoral dissertation, University of Minnesota, Minneapolis.

Lowenberg, G., Iverson, N. M., & Conrad, K. A. (1989). *Evidence of generalizability for correlates of pay satisfaction.* Paper presented at the Fourth Annual Conference of the Society for Industrial and Organizational Psychology (SIOP), Boston, MA.

Lowenberg, G., Powaser, P. R., & Farkash, A. (1989). Determination of the relationship between pay desire satisfaction and appropriate pay differentials relative to income levels. In B. J. Fallon, H. P. Pfister, & J. Breber (Eds.), *Advances in industrial/organizational psychology* (pp. 201–209). Amsterdam: North-Holland, Elsevier Science Publishers.

Neidig, R. D., & Neidig, P. J. (1984). Multiple assessment center exercises and job relatedness. *Journal of Applied Psychology, 69* (1), 182–186.

Nicholoson, N., Brown, C. A., & Chadwick-Jones, J. K. (1976). Absence from work and job satisfaction. *Journal of Applied Psychology, 61* (6), 728–737.

Nunnally, L. C. (1959). *Tests and measurements: Assessment and prediction.* New York: McGraw-Hill.

Pedhazur, E. J. (1982). *Multiple regression in behavioral research: Explanation and prediction.* New York: Holt, Rinehart and Winston.

Society for Industrial and Organizational Psychology (SIOP), Inc. (1987). *Principles of the validation and use of personnel selection procedures* (3rd ed.). College Park, MD: Author.

Tett, R. P., Jackson, D. N., & Rothstein, M. (1991). Personality measures as predictors of performance: A meta-analysis review. *Personnel Psychology, 44* (4), 703–742.

Tyler, L. E. (1965). *The psychology of human differences.* New York: Appleton-Century-Crofts.

Willerman, L. (1979). *The psychology of individual and group differences.* San Francisco: W. H. Freeman.

Human Resources Management: A Strategic View

Chapter Outline

S uperior Connectors, Inc., a small, highly successful manufacturing firm, found itself facing some new challenges. It was unable to find talented, technically trained people in its hometown, the company was heavily dependent on a single customer, there was internal frustration caused by a broad, unfocused product line that was becoming dated, and the company had no clear sense of direction. Its human resources department consisted of one person, who had a master's degree in personnel management from a local college. A bright, capable person, she had contributed a great deal to the company by updating and standardizing its personnel processes. She was also a motivating force, encouraging the management team to think in broader, longer-term ways. She persuaded top management to hire an industrial psychologist to assist in strategic and personnel planning.

The I/O psychologist met individually with all members of the top management team and with all the other key managers, soliciting their thoughts and developing a feeling for the organization. A four-day top management retreat was held to build the team and develop Superior's vision and strategic plan. The I/O psychologist used group decision support software and a number of process facilitation techniques to guide the group. The session began with guided brainstorming, which generated many ideas about Superior's future. These were honed into a vision, a mission statement, and five key objectives for the next three years. The discussions were lively, and a high level of consensus was reached. Six months later, the team met again to review and refine the plan by adding action items and planning for major contingencies.

One key objective addressed Superior's personnel needs. The company, which had long relied on its local, semirural labor market, realized that this market would no longer support Superior's growth. The objectives that were defined as part of the management team's plan were to increase the knowledge base of new hires and to fill all of the current open positions with experienced people. This required a much larger recruiting area and an entirely different human resources strategy. Work-

ing with the I/O psychologist, the management team designed and implemented a new selection process. The generalized validity for the instruments selected was relatively high, enabling the selection process to be implemented immediately. Documentation procedures ensured that predictive validity could be examined once enough candidates had been processed.

The I/O psychologist also assisted with training Superior's managers in the new selection process, paying special attention to interviewing because in the past the managers had done this on their own, with no guidance. The new process used a structured interview and required ratings from the managers on applicants' abilities and characteristics.

Another part of the long-range personnel plan was a management succession plan. Working as a team, the managers developed a chart listing all incumbents with management responsibility. For each position they also identified the best immediate replacement, employees who could be ready for the responsibilities in two to three years, and employees who might be candidates three to five years in the future. This took several meetings over four months to complete. Another retreat that the I/O psychologist facilitated helped Superior's managers to extend their knowledge of career planning and to develop several major career paths leading to senior management responsibilities. Planning also included the amount and kinds of formal education, on-the-job training, and experience needed to be considered for promotion. Individual managers then communicated the new plans to employees. The next step was to complete individual development plans for all employees as a part of a cooperative effort built into the new performance appraisal process.

All these efforts have proven to be worthwhile. Four years after initiating the new strategic and personnel planning processes, Superior has successfully built a system that allows it to keep up with its personnel needs. All positions are currently filled. The experienced people the company recruited have proved to be vital "fresh blood," providing many new ideas, several of which have led to successful new products. The company has focused its product lines and added a number of new customers, making it a more stable, long-term employer. It recently began negotiations to buy a similar company, a former competitor, in a neighboring town. The I/O psychologist and the management team continue to work together at annual planning retreats and periodic special topical meetings.

This story illustrates how companies' human resources practices, strategic planning, and the applied practice of I/O psychology are interrelated. Human resources management is "the attraction, selection, retention, development, and utilization of human resources in order to achieve both individual and organization objectives" (Cascio & Awad, 1981, p. 3). As the definition shows, many human resources managers focus their efforts in areas that are the same as those of the I/O psychologist but emphasize the day-to-day challenge of finding and preparing people for their organizations. In fact, the interests and goals of industrial/organizational psychologists, strategic planners, and human resource managers often overlap (Boudreau, 1991; Cascio & Awad, 1981). Here are some examples:

1. In general, these professionals work with people. They deal with decisions about people in the workplace and about all types of managers. Personnel managers participate in decision making that affects people, employment relationships, hiring, selecting, developing and utilizing personnel to achieve organizational goals, objectives, and strategic positioning.
2. They participate in decisions affecting staffing in organizations. For example, they deal with training, compensation, and performance appraisal. In today's tight labor market, this also requires long-range strategic planning to ensure

that needed staff will be available or can be developed.
3. They work together addressing issues of motivating employees, preventing conflicts, and planning for staff needs across different positions and jobs. They also work together on the integration of feedback from employees, customers, and clients into definitions of jobs and the desired organizational outcomes.
4. Additional collaboration between these professionals includes issues such as equal employment opportunity, employee rights, participatory decision making, and quality of work life.

To achieve these goals and influence decisions about people in organizations, many industrial/organizational psychologists serve as consultants to industry. Others work as personnel managers, concerned with issues such as those mentioned above. For example, much information that comes directly or indirectly from employees affects the decisions in human resources management. Some information reveals serious discontent or frustration. Employees may claim that their supervisors practice favoritism or discrimination. They may believe that people are discharged or disciplined arbitrarily or unfairly. These feelings may be expressed in high rates of tardiness, absenteeism, complaining on the job, and union organizing. The I/O psychologist works with management to investigate these situations objectively. Data might be collected by administering a morale or attitude survey, and the information collected might be used to develop plans for actions to deal with the complaints or to reduce tardiness and absenteeism. The primary difference between human resource management and I/O psychology arises from the I/O psychologist's scientist-practitioner perspective. In contrast, most human resources managers have business or human resources training rather than scientific training.

In this chapter we will describe some key concerns of human resource managers and I/O psychologists working in human resources areas. These are strategic planning, personnel planning, and succession planning.

....
STRATEGIC PLANNING

I/O psychologists help organizations anticipate future needs. Their efforts may include such tasks as redesigning jobs or reengineering the organization to make it more efficient and participatory. This is a strategic planning role with a strong focus on the human side of the organization.

The **strategic planning process** is a logical, comprehensive approach that helps organizations prepare for the future. Strategic plans determine *what* an organization will do; tactical plans determine *how* something will be done. Traditionally, strategic plans are developed for periods of three to five years. However, in today's business environment a competitive advantage may last only a few days. The most successful organizations work to outdate their own products and approaches before their competitors do so. Strategic planning is an important mechanism for channeling an organization's major efforts into appropriate areas such as developing new products, opening new markets, or improving customer service.

A basic strategic planning process involves eight steps:

1. Establishing a clear business definition
2. Understanding the current business climate
3. Setting appropriate objectives
4. Selecting strategic alternatives
5. Preparing the strategic plans
6. Executing the plans skillfully
7. Providing accurate controls
8. Doing contingency planning

We will review each of these steps to show how the planning process works and the critical information it provides.

Establishing a Clear Business Definition

The **mission statement** is a clearly written definition of the business; it describes its purpose, goals, and aims. Until recently, such ideas as having a higher purpose, broad goals, or commitment to basic values were not considered central to the "real" business issues facing managers. However, John Williamson (1984, p. 193) noted,

> All this has changed dramatically in recent years as managers are faced with increasingly complex and unpredictable situations—situations where a common sense of direction rather than prescribed procedures is a more reliable compass for decision making. In addition, managers find themselves responsible for and to the "new worker" who is educated, sophisticated, and demanding; who has job alternatives; and who insists that work has meaning and significance beyond a paycheck and career ladder.

Many current mission statements define a select set of **superordinate goals.** These goals state the quintessential focus for the business; that is, above and beyond everything else, what the business hopes to achieve through its existence and activities. In their book *The Art of Japanese Management,* Richard Pascale and Anthony Athos (1981) suggested that the superordinate goals that are developed in the mission statement should be significant, durable, and achievable. They identified the following categories of superordinate goals: the company as an entity, the company's external markets, the company's internal operations, the company's employees, the company's relation to society and the state, and the company's relation to culture (including religion).

Understanding the Current Business Climate

The next vital component of strategic planning is **environmental scanning,** the process of understanding the current business climate. When changes occur in the business environment, they can have broad implications for a business. Whether social, economic, technological, legal, or political, external factors need to be identified and examined before realistic goals can be set. Good strategic planning demands that the assumptions that are used in planning take external factors into consideration and be as accurate as possible. To accomplish this, companies often use a tiered approach that has several planning horizons. For example, plans are simultaneously developed for two-, five-, and ten-year horizons. When a tiered approach is used, a different set of assumptions is established for each time horizon (tier).

Companies use several key indicators to determine the current business climate. These include economic indicators such as the Gross National Product (GNP), the Consumer Price Index (CPI), and the prime rate. Other factors are also considered. These include market trends, consumer profiles, buying habits, demographics, lifestyle, competition, trends in market share, market type, numbers, location, pricing, promotion, products, packaging, advertising, industry financial ratios, technological developments, political climate, governmental rules, proposed legislation, consumer environment, foreign trade, international events, and social trends. It is preferable to deal with these factors in quantitative terms, using numerical indexes for measures of historical and projective data.

Setting Appropriate Objectives

Most planners believe that companies are smart to have several scenarios when setting objectives. The most popular approach uses three: the most probable or **realistic scenario,** a **pessimistic scenario** that predicts the worst will happen, and an optimistic scenario anticipating that things will go well. It is important to balance the effort here with the potential results. Because people can get discouraged if too much time is spent in analysis, most companies focus on the realistic scenario.

Establishing objectives requires conceptual long-term thinking. An example of a long-term objective is "To bring about consistently increasing earnings per share, attaining a satisfactory return on stockholder's equity while providing consistently increasing dividends." As can be seen from this example, long-term objectives are often too general to be of much use to the company other than providing a general direction. Because of this, objectives are usually refined into goals that are specific, time-based targets containing built-in measurement, for example, "The wallet assembly cell will be fully functional with all team members cross trained and operating at a daily rate of 1160 units by December 12th." A common test for goals is the **SMART test.** We can evaluate how effective a goal statement is by ascertaining that it is:

Specific
Measurable
Actionable
Realistic
Time specified

Selecting Strategic Alternatives

The next step in strategic planning is to map out the general plan or strategy the company will follow to achieve its objectives. Some key elements included here are establishing new products, research and development, diversifying products, exploring mergers and acquisitions, reorganization, reengineering, realignment of authority, divestment and liquidations, constructing new facilities, executive development, succession planning, and creating new markets. For example, suppose a company's objective were to increase earnings per share by a particular amount. The plan could consist of acquiring a company with special technological expertise. This company could then be used as the basis for developing and introducing several new products, or it could be used for expanding the market by defining a new niche.

Preparing the Strategic Plans

Next, the plans are carefully documented and distributed to all managers. Well-prepared plans have sections that translate overall objectives and goals into specifics for divisions and departments. For example, a product-marketing strategy would specifically address existing markets, existing products, new markets, and new products. These would be described first as a part of the strategic whole and then in terms of each department's goals.

Executing the Plans Skillfully

Once the plan has been developed and distributed, it must be executed well. An effective action plan will specify, in detail, precisely how the company and each operating area will carry out its strategy. The typical time frame for short-term planning is one year unless the situation is changing very rapidly, as it does in some fields such as computer technology. Included will be a specific target for the department, a description of how the objective will be attained, and a list of the resources (such as human, equipment, and financial) that will be needed. The responsibility for the action plan must be clearly delegated. Most managers are given specific objectives for which they will be held accountable.

Providing Accurate Controls

Plans that are not monitored and controlled often get off track. If this happens repeatedly, it may become difficult for the employees to take the planning process seriously. This situation can be avoided by requiring department managers to explain how they plan to accomplish their goals and monitor progress. Timeline planning makes a plan visible, which increases the

ease with which progress can be monitored. As each action is completed, a new program moves into place. In addition, an annual review of the strategic plan is often conducted to evaluate the year-end results for each goal. The company can thereby see how much progress is being made and determine if corrective action is necessary.

Doing Contingency Planning

Any number of outside events can throw a strategic plan off track. Often, these are major economic trends such as a recession, unusually high or low interest rates, a shortage of parts and materials, or technological changes. Because a company cannot foresee and plan for every development, it is important to be prepared with a contingency plan. This can be accomplished in the following ways:

1. By identifying the developments that have the potential for the greatest impact on the company.
2. By estimating the likelihood of each of these occurring.
3. By establishing trigger points for the events that can have great impact and that have high probability of occurring. A trigger point is the level at which a certain indicator or indicators will signal that the event has occurred and that a response is needed.
4. By developing strategies for responding to the disruptive events that are considered most likely to occur. Contingency plans should be brief, focusing on minimizing the negative impact of the event.

Once a company's strategic plan is in place, the planning emphasis shifts to questions of personnel. Through careful personnel planning, an organization ensures that it will have enough people with the right talents to accomplish its objectives.

PERSONNEL PLANNING

Today, when many organizations are experiencing a shortage of skilled workers, it is becoming ever more important to make effective use of employees. There are many programs designed to enable employees to fully utilize their talents in their work. A key objective of these programs is to match employee talents to the demands or needs of their jobs. This matching is accomplished in the **selection process.** It is through the selection process that an organization has the greatest power to remake itself. When properly executed, a well-run selection program identifies people who have the talents the organization needs. It also assists with matching new hires to jobs in which they are most likely to succeed. The selection process structures the development of new employees so that they will quickly become effective on the job. Over time, information from the selection process continues to assist workers in keeping up to date and in building the new skills they will need in the future.

Selection is one part of the broader field of human resource management. As will be discussed in detail in Chapter 8, the selection process can be thought of as a step-by-step approach through which an organization is able to identify the best people to perform a given job. By following a systematic process, an organization can ensure that there is a good match between the candidates who are selected and the jobs they will be completing. Figure 3.1 outlines a typical seven-step selection program (Gatewood & Feild, 1994). Because the selection process is discussed in detail in Chapter 8, we present here only a short preview of the important steps in human resource planning.

Job Analysis

The selection process begins with **job analysis,** or the gathering of information about the job as it exists in the organization. Job analysis is described in detail in Chapter 4. For now, it is sufficient to know that effective job analysis describes the tasks, activities, results, equipment, and environment that define a job. In the selection process, job analysis provides the information necessary to communicate the nature of the job to applicants. This creates appropriate ex-

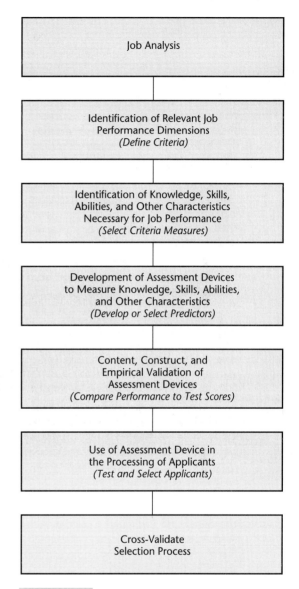

FIGURE 3.1   Steps in a Typical Selection System.

Source: From *Human Resource Selection* (p. 10), by R. D. Gatewood & H. S. Feild, copyright 1987 by The Dryden Press. Reprinted by permission of the publisher.

pectations and enables some potential applicants to remove themselves from consideration. More importantly, job analysis provides the base of job information on which the rest of the selection

HISTORICAL PERSPECTIVE 3.1

25 Common Job Characteristics and Requirements, 1975

1. High school degree: high school diploma required.
2. Technical school or apprenticeship: some form of nondegree post–high school training required.
3. Junior college degree: requires Associate in Arts degree.
4. College degree: requires at least a bachelor's degree.
5. Jobs widely scattered: jobs are located in most areas of the United States.
6. Jobs concentrated in localities: jobs are highly concentrated in one or a few geographical locations.
7. Works with things: job generally requires manual skills.
8. Works with ideas: uses one's intellect to solve problems.
9. Helps people: assists people in a helping relationship.
10. Works with people: job generally requires pleasing personality and ability to get along with others.
11. Able to see physical results of work: work produces a tangible product.
12. Opportunity for self-expression: freedom to use one's own ideas.
13. Works as part of a team: interacts with fellow employees in performing work.
14. Works independently: requires initiative, self-discipline, and the ability to organize.
15. Work is closely supervised: job performance and work standards controlled by supervisor.
16. Directs activities of others: work entails supervisory responsibilities.
17. Generally confined to work area: physically located at one work setting.
18. Overtime or shift work required: works hours other than normal daytime shifts.
19. Exposed to weather conditions: works outside or is subjected to temperature extremes.
20. High level of responsibility: requires making key decisions involving property, finances, or human safety and welfare.
21. Requires physical stamina: must be in physical condition for continued lifting, standing, and walking.
22. Works with details: works with technical data, numbers, or written materials on a continuous basis.
23. Repetitive work: performs the same task on a continuing basis.
24. Motivates others: must be able to influence others.
25. Competitive: competes with other people on the job for recognition and advancement.

Source: From U.S. Department of Labor, Bureau of Labor Statistics, (Spring 1975) "Focus—Toward matching personal and job characteristics." *Occupational Outlook Quarterly 19,* 1.

process depends. Historical Perspective 3.1 summarizes a list of twenty-five common job characteristics and requirements that are representative of those that frequently appear in job analyses.

Define Criteria

The second step in the selection process is to identify the relevant **job performance** dimensions. The organization wants to select people who will be successful on the job. As is discussed in Chapter 6, an underlying assumption is that we can measure differences in performance on the important parts of a job.

Select Criteria Measures

The third step is to identify the knowledge, skills, abilities, and other characteristics a worker must possess to perform the job, as well as the ways by which these attributes can be measured. In Chapter 4 we note the difficulty involved in arriving at a usable list of characteristics. Recently, the preferred focus has been on **knowledge and skills** (KSs) because they represent observable job behaviors. **Abilities and other characteristics** (AOs), in contrast, are more abstract and can be linked only indirectly to job performance (Harvey, 1991).

Develop or Select Predictors

The fourth step in the selection process involves the identification or development of the **selection measures** that will be used to collect information from job applicants. In Chapter 7 we discuss some of the many instruments that can be used to collect information from and about applicants. These include apparatus tests, application blanks, biodata forms, cognitive abilities, computer testing, interviews, job simulations, interest profiles, mental ability tests, personality assessment, projective tests, physical abilities, references, sensorimotor abilities, and special ability tests. Whatever we choose, it must provide a representative measure of the KSs that have been identified as critical to job performance, and the results should differentiate among the applicants. That is, different people should perform differently on the selection measure with their scores being directly related to their later job performance.

The purpose of collecting information about applicants is to predict their future performance on the job. This process of prediction is essential to decision making in personnel management. In Chapter 7 we discuss variations in predictors, which depend on the purpose for which we use them, and their measurement qualities.

Application Blanks

Most job applicants complete some form of **application blank,** which consists of a series of questions about the applicant's background. The questions can cover areas such as education, job experience, physical health, interests, and special skills. There are great variations in the length and effectiveness of application blanks, but the purposes of all are the same: to decide whether the applicant meets the minimum requirements of the position and to assess and compare the relative strengths of the various applicants who apply for a given position.

With the advent of Title VII of the 1964 Civil Rights Act and the Equal Employment Opportunity regulations (a subsequent development of these regulations is known as the Uniform Guidelines), companies have become more careful about the questions they place on application blanks. These issues are discussed in detail in Chapter 8. The essence of effective, legal practice is that the questions on an application blank be job relevant. The only way to ensure this is through a careful job analysis.

Reference Checks

The best predictor of future job performance is past job performance. The most direct way to get information about past job performance is through **reference checks.** To conduct a reference check, the potential employer collects information about the prospect from companies where the person worked previously and from people who have had contact with the person. This is often done through telephone contact, and follows guidelines like those summarized in Practice Perspective 3.1 on page 80. Information from reference checks is used to confirm information that applicants have provided and to assemble additional data that may predict future job performance. Research has shown that references are more often a reason for rejecting applicants than a source of information that identifies new qualifications. Most firms use some kind of reference checking. This is true even though the current legal environment has made many sources reluctant to release critical information. In some cases, simply confirming the applicant's job history can be important.

An important question is: How valuable are reference checks? If they do not yield reliable and valid information, they will not be useful in a selection process. An important component is

PRACTICE PERSPECTIVE 3.1

Telephone Reference Checking

There are three ways in which most reference data are collected: by phone, by mail, and in person. Pyron (1970) found that telephone reference checks were the most popular form. When well-structured, telephone reference checking can yield a lot of information in a short time. Here is a brief example of a structured telephone reference check for a sales applicant:

Hello, I'm _____, of _____. We are in the process of considering Mr. Applicant for a sales position with our firm. It would be helpful if we could review your appraisal of his previous work. We do have a signed release from Mr. Applicant authorizing us to contact you for information about his previous employment with you.

When was Mr. Applicant employed with your firm?

Was he under your direct supervision?

What was your working relationship with him?

How long did you have the opportunity to observe his job performance?

What was his job title and what were his responsibilities with your firm?

Did he supervise any employees? How many?

Can you describe an example of a difficult situation he handled well?

How about one that did not go so well?

How closely do you believe he needs to be supervised?

Can you describe his biggest sales success?

How did he handle customer complaints?

What things caused him the most difficulty?

How would you describe his work habits?

Do you have any other comments?

Thank you for your time and help. I appreciate your cooperation. The information you provided will be helpful to us as we consider Mr. Applicant.

---

the reference source. Has that person had a chance to personally observe the applicant? Is the person competent to make the requested evaluation? Is the person willing to give an honest evaluation? Can the person make what he or she knows understood?

There is not much research on the validity and reliability of reference data. Much of the research that is available shows only low or moderate validity. However, it has been demonstrated that the quality of reference information can be improved by having the applicant's previous supervisor provide the information and by ensuring that there was adequate opportunity to observe the applicant. In addition, it helps if the applicant is of the same sex, race, and nationality as her or his previous supervisor and that the old and new jobs are similar in nature.

Employers who use reference checks are advised to do so systematically to eliminate any

adverse impact and to increase the predictive validity of the data collected. The following steps can help to ensure effective, legal use:

1. Seek only job-related information.
2. Develop a standard form or set of questions for each position.
3. Remember that reference checks are subject to the Uniform Guidelines. They are *not* a method to acquire information one cannot obtain any other way.
4. Be as objective as possible.
5. Have written permission from applicants to contact their references.
6. Train the people who conduct telephone and other interviews used to collect reference information.
7. Be especially careful with negative information. Make sure it is accurate and valid before using it to disqualify applicants.

Biographical Information

Another valuable source of information about applicants is **biographical information,** that is, information about the person's background and life experiences. William Owens summarized the uses of biographical information in the 1976 *Handbook of Industrial and Organizational Psychology.* He described biographical information blanks as providing opportunities for applicants to describe themselves in terms of "demographic, experiential, or attitudinal variables presumed or demonstrated to be related to personality structure, personal adjustment, or success in social, educational, or occupational pursuits" (Owens, 1976, pp. 612–613).

Biographical data (or biodata) have many unique advantages (Stokes, Mumford, & Owens, 1994). These include replacing some information normally collected in selection interviews with more standardized questions, increasing accuracy and reliability, broadening the understanding of what makes a good employee, ensuring that only job-relevant questions are asked, and using information as both a predictor and a criterion. Biodata are often criticized as being fakable by applicants. Another criticism is that people from disadvantaged backgrounds, or backgrounds different from those of most employees, may be excluded for not having had the "right" experiences rather than because they lack potential to do the job. This process is discussed in more detail in Chapter 8.

Selection Interviews

The **selection interview** has long been, and continues to be, the most popular selection procedure. In practice, selection interviews are often misused and criticized. For our present discussion it is helpful to summarize the following common problems that occur in selection interviewing:

- Too much time is spent on non-job-related topics.
- Unfavorable information is a stronger influence on the interviewer than is positive information.

- Inter-rater reliabilities among interviewers are poor unless the interviewers have been carefully trained.
- Interviewers often make early, global judgments.
- Interviewers often talk more than the applicants do.
- Interviews have low predictive validity.

Interviews can be significantly improved by following a few simple guidelines:

- Narrow the scope of the interview by asking only job-related questions about KSs and AOs.
- Limit the use of information obtained before the interview.
- Use a structured or semistructured format.
- Use only job-related questions focused on job-relevant behaviors. Assess each behavior by using several questions.
- Train all interviewers.
- Use more than one interviewer.
- Develop a formal scoring process for the information collected, relating it directly to the KSs and AOs that are critical for job success.

Interviews are the most popular selection tool. As was mentioned above, unstructured interviews have many problems; structured interviews are better. Scientific Perspective 3.1 on page 82 summarizes a study that shows how structured interviewing improves interviewer judgments.

Ability Tests

Our definition of ability tests in Chapter 7 includes the measurement of previous learning, of the potential for learning specific skills, and of the potential to solve problems and profit from experience. The most popular form of ability measures is cognitive ability testing. In spite of their popularity in practice, measures of cognitive abilities such as general intelligence are still the source of many arguments. Some psychologists (e.g., Guion, 1991) argue that cognitive tests are better predictors of success for training

SCIENTIFIC PERSPECTIVE 3.1

How Structured Interviewing Improves Interviewer Judgments

R. L. Dipboye and B. B. Gaugler examined the process of conducting structured interviews and provided a summary of research indicating why such procedures may improve validity by reducing individual interviewer differences in the conduct of interviews. The relationship between the way the interviewer conducts an interview and the applicant's statements and behavior can be described as an information-sampling process (Motowidlo, 1986). The interviewer samples information from the total that is available from the candidate about his or her job-related behavior and skills. What the applicant says and does determines the interviewer's success in predicting future performance. There are six possible outcomes of this sampling process.

Outcome 1: What they say is what you get. Statements sampled in structured interviews are good indicators of what the applicant will do in the future. Situational interviewing (Latham, 1989) proposes that intentions and goals are the best predictors of future job performance. Patterned behavior description interviews (Janz, 1982) sample past behavior as the best predictor of future behavior.

Outcome 2: What they do is what you get. In addition to (and sometimes in contrast to) what they say, applicants exhibit many verbal and nonverbal behaviors during an interview that can reflect important job-related characteristics. For example, poor eye contact and a halting tone of voice could indicate a lack of social skill. This would be a serious limitation for a sales candidate. Work samples included in structured interviews provide an opportunity for objective observation. For example, a sales applicant could be instructed to, "sell me this book." The multimodal employment interview (Schuler, 1989) is another approach that provides for periods of free conversation during which the applicant is assessed.

Outcome 3: What you get is what they want you to see. Some applicants are skilled impression

managers, able to project positive impressions of their ability to perform on the job (Baron, 1989). In fact, some outplacement counseling firms coach their clients on impression management. Structured interviews discourage impression management by limiting the number of opportunities for applicants to manipulate and shape the interviewer's impressions. Caution is necessary, since there are jobs in which impression management is a desired, criterion-related skill.

Outcome 4: What you get is the product of what you have done. In some situations, interviewers can be biased by their general impressions of the applicant with the result that the interviewer's behavior influences the behavior of the applicant (Dipboye, 1982; Dipboye & Macan, 1988; Dougherty, Turban, & Callender, 1992). The interview becomes a self-fulfilling prophecy for the interviewer.

Outcome 5: What you see is not what you get. There is evidence for many biases in information processing and judgment when interviewers rely on broad general categories and neglect specific information. These include causal attributions, inaccurate retrieval of information, rating effects, and bias from irrelevant characteristics such as sex and race.

Outcome 6: What you see is not what I see. Some studies have shown large differences in the predictive validity of judgments among interviewers (Dougherty, Ebert, & Callender, 1986; Dipboye, Gaugler, & Hayes, 1990; Kinicki, Lockwood, Hom, & Griffeth, 1990). These can be reduced through a structured interview process that limits individual differences in how interview information is gathered and processed.

Source: Based on a description in "Cognitive and Behavioral Processes in the Selection Interview," by R. L. Dipboye and B. B. Gaugler. Chapter 5 in *Personnel Selection in Organizations* (pp. 147–155), (1993), N. Schmitt, W. C. Borman, & Associates, San Francisco: Jossey-Bass Inc. Copyright 1993 by Jossey-Bass. Adapted with permission.

and on the job performance than are specific ability tests (e.g., a test of clerical ability). Others argue that organizational conditions and work conditions should be investigated to determine the usefulness of ability tests.

Performance tests are selection devices that closely approximate parts of the job the applicant is being considered to fill. Typically, performance tests require the candidate to complete a job activity under structured testing conditions. The performance tests are a sample of the job tasks required. They provide the opportunity to observe the applicant in action. An important consideration is that the work sample selected be representative of the job. An example of a performance test is a typing test for secretaries. The secretarial applicant is asked to type a document similar to what will be produced on the job. In a law office this might be a brief; in an insurance office, an application for insurance; in an educational institution, a research paper.

Some constraints on performance measures are that they must be representative of the job activities, they must be similar in difficulty to the tasks performed on the job, they are costly to prepare, they can be difficult to administer, and the applicant must already have the skill. These limitations have led psychologists and human resource managers to develop other methods for selection and development. Two of these, psychological assessments and assessment centers, are so popular that they have become practice specialties of some I/O psychologists. They are discussed in detail in Chapter 7.

Compare Performance to Test Scores

The first four steps in the selection process provide the information needed to select applicants who will be able to perform the job. In and of themselves, however, these steps are not sufficient. Robert Guion (1976) described this part of the selection process as being similar to forming hypotheses whereby the practitioner identifies observable behaviors—knowledge and skills

(KSs)—that can be tested to predict future job performance. The rest of the selection process is focused on testing or validating those hypotheses. This demonstrates that the KSs deemed important relate to successful job performance. Recently, Guion (1991, p. 350) noted that

> In any approach to validation, it is important to recognize that validation and validity refer to inferences drawn from data (scores), not to the predictors, except insofar as their nature and use influences the scores. It is not the predictor that is validated in empirical hypothesis testing; if the predictor is a test battery, it is not the battery, either. What is validated is the hypothesis that criterion performance can be inferred from the scores. Levels of one important criterion may be validly inferred from the scores on a given test, but inferences of levels on a different criterion may not be valid.

The fifth step in Figure 3.1, **validation** provides evidence that the results of our selection measures are related to job performance, and that the instruments used are selecting applicants who can perform effectively on the job. As explained in Chapter 8, these are the criterion-related validity strategies. Additional validity strategies: **Content validity** ensures that predictors are representative of the job, that is, that predictors accurately sample the behaviors that are critical to job performance. **Construct validity** tests the degree to which the individuals being tested actually possess the traits or abilities reflected by their test performance. Validation is such an important process that we have devoted a considerable part of Chapter 8 to it.

Test and Select Applicants

The sixth step in a selection program represents our original purpose of processing and selecting applicants. Often, processing applicants becomes a process itself. One example is the **multiple-hurdle program,** in which applicants must successfully pass each hurdle before proceeding to the next hurdle. The hurdles may be a preliminary screening interview; completing an application form, a screening test battery, or an employment interview; having their references and background checked; passing a medical examination and performance tests. An applicant may be rejected at any step, and only those who clear all hurdles are hired. (See Chapter 8 for a fuller description of these methods.)

Cross-Validate the Selection Process

As discussed in Chapter 8 and shown in Figure 3.1, the last step in developing a selection program is to cross-validate our prediction equation. This is the process of applying the prediction equation developed on one group of employees to a new group of employees or applicants. This is necessary because one byproduct of the statistics used on the original group in a prediction selection system is that the calculation process capitalizes on the variations existing in that group. Because new groups of employees and applicants are always slightly different from the original sample, the accuracy of the equation used will fall short. This drop in prediction is due to errors such as using too small a sample for the number of variables in the equation, or having a sample unrepresentative of our population. When the equation developed on the original group is predictive of the criteria of the new group, we have evidence of the accuracy of the prediction process, that is, evidence of cross-validation.

Legal Issues

A thorough understanding of the legal environment and existing legal guidelines is vital to the design and validation of any selection process. An organization that does not follow the legal requirements is open to charges of discrimination; if it is found guilty, the penalties can be very costly. One way to understand this regulatory climate is to use models. One such model of the federal standards of personnel activities covered by the **equal employment opportunity** (EEO) regulations was developed by Ledvinka and Scarpello (1991, as cited in Gatewood & Feild, 1994). This model is presented in Figure 3.2.

By examining the leftmost column of the model, one can see that EEO regulations were created to address broad national issues such as unemployment, segregation, social conflict, and judicial and penal systems. In response to these societal problems, legislators or executives such as the President pass laws or issue executive orders. These empower regulatory agencies. Regulatory actions from the agencies trigger management responses and complaints that are then settled by the courts. More details about the laws, executive orders, and court decisions that affect selection are presented in Chapter 8.

• •

SUCCESSION PLANNING

Succession planning is a systematic method that is used to determine job appointments in a way that addresses the company's growth needs as well as the individual's developmental needs. A typical succession planning approach is one in which data are gathered in an organized way, using paper-and-pencil measures. The applicant receives a test, or set of printed questions, and records his or her responses in writing on the form provided. The data are often entered into a computerized database with other information about the individual. A complete data set includes biographical information, job history information, performance appraisals, appraisals of potential, salary history, and any special needs that may exist. The data contribute to a thorough understanding of the individual, which will indicate readiness and fit with a position in the organization.

The goal of a succession planning system is to provide a continuous flow of competent employees and managers. Ideally, succession planning is done corporatewide, but it is so time consuming that it is often focused on supervi-

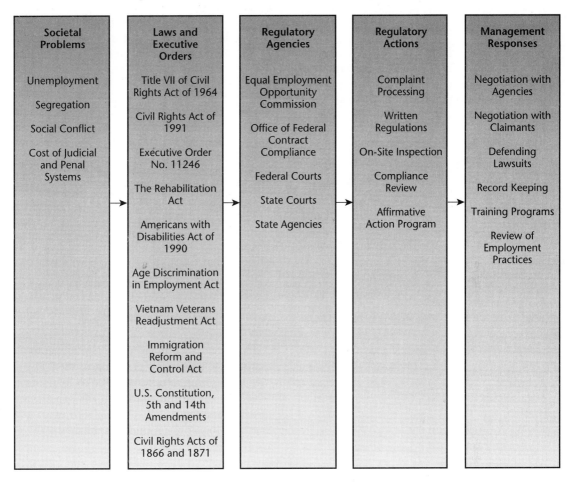

Societal Problems	Laws and Executive Orders	Regulatory Agencies	Regulatory Actions	Management Responses
Unemployment	Title VII of Civil Rights Act of 1964	Equal Employment Opportunity Commission	Complaint Processing	Negotiation with Agencies
Segregation	Civil Rights Act of 1991	Office of Federal Contract Compliance	Written Regulations	Negotiation with Claimants
Social Conflict	Executive Order No. 11246	Federal Courts	On-Site Inspection	Defending Lawsuits
Cost of Judicial and Penal Systems	The Rehabilitation Act	State Courts	Compliance Review	Record Keeping
	Americans with Disabilities Act of 1990	State Agencies	Affirmative Action Program	Training Programs
	Age Discrimination in Employment Act			Review of Employment Practices
	Vietnam Veterans Readjustment Act			
	Immigration Reform and Control Act			
	U.S. Constitution, 5th and 14th Amendments			
	Civil Rights Acts of 1866 and 1871			

FIGURE 3.2   Ledvinka and Scarpello's Regulatory Model of Equal Employment Opportunity.

Source: From *Federal Regulation of Personnel and Human Resource Management* by J. Ledvinka and Scarpello, © 1982 PWS-Kent Publishing, by permission of South-Western College Publishing, a division of International Thomson Publishing Inc., Cincinnati, OH. Adaptation from *Human Resource Selection* (p. 27), by R. D. Gatewood & H. S. Feild, copyright 1987 by The Dryden Press. Reprinted by permission of the publisher.

sory and management positions. Successful organizations frequently develop an internal flow from employee to supervisor and from first-line supervisors through low-level managers.

Succession planning has been found to be most effective when the top executive is personally committed to the system. Managers need to care about preparing employees to perform well in their jobs and to advance in responsibilities. In addition to planning for the development of their employees, managers also need to plan re-

placements for key positions. This is succession planning, which is successful when most promotions are internal and are based on performance.

To be effective, succession planning requires good support. A variety of forms and records must be collected and kept up to date. Some organizations create staff positions to ensure that these tasks are completed. Current positions should be examined periodically to determine their developmental potential. Because most managers develop on the job, a good succession plan provides managers with appropriate on-the-job experiences.

The basic requirements for a succession planning system are straightforward. First, data from employees and management must be gathered and entered on a regular basis. Most organizations update information at least once a year, often as part of an internal inventory. This process requires supervisors and managers to review where they stand in several areas, such as the quality of people in their departments, the future management of their areas, and how to determine employee advancement. They may also be asked to identify the person they believe to be the best candidate for their own immediate replacement.

The minimum amount of information necessary to develop an effective system includes the following:

- The position title
- The job classification level for the position
- The current incumbent
- The date the incumbent was appointed to the position
- The age of the incumbent
- The incumbent's recent performance
- An estimate of the incumbent's management potential
- The best immediate replacement candidate
- A list of possible replacement candidates, including the length of time required for training.

A succession planning system cannot succeed without data on the employee's career objectives, ambitions, and perceived limitations. Performance appraisal information is also necessary and should include the employee's opinions about his or her personal limitations with regard to job performance. Some systems are designed to be guided primarily by this type of information.

Succession planning is directly related to the business plans for the company as a whole and for its units. The same procedure that is used to plan for leadership positions can also be used in filling specific lower-level positions. The planning process requires that each supervisor and manager forecast the future of his or her organizational unit. This forecast describes changes to be addressed by the supervisor or manager.

The result of succession planning is developmental planning. Good faith communication among all parties is necessary for the process to be effective. The process is confidential, but as much information as possible is shared with employees. There must also be a free exchange of information about the quality of talent available so that the most qualified person will be considered in filling job openings.

Succession planning is straightforward, but unfortunately, few companies have complete and effective systems. There are several reasons for this, including the following:

1. The chief executive is not personally committed to succession planning. If the CEO is not willing to take the time to be involved and do the planning, the other senior managers are unlikely to do so either. In addition, once established, the process must be used.
2. The accumulation, evaluation, and distribution of data are monumental administrative tasks. Computerized systems help, but keeping the information up to date and organized is still time consuming. Many companies are unwilling to commit the resources needed to do this job effectively.
3. Many companies are satisfied with a simple **replacement table** of candidates for each key position, which is updated annually. These data are valid only for short periods. When an organization uses this approach, the data are seldom helpful when vacancies occur. Eventually, the organization learns to ignore the replacement table in making decisions.

An organization cannot be assured of continuously having good-quality management without establishing some type of succession planning system. If an organization does not have a planning system, a manager or supervisor can still apply the planning elements. There are even computer programs that can simplify the process of collecting and organizing data. All organizations are experiencing increasing rates of change. With that change comes increasing, possibly health-threatening, levels of job stress.

SUMMARY

This chapter addressed the many facets of human resource management. At a macro level, the strategic planning process is important because it helps organizations to prepare intelligently for the future. A clearly written definition of the business vision and mission provides direction. Strategic planning must be conducted with an understanding of the surrounding environment. Often called "environmental scanning," the process of understanding the current business climate provides this vital part of strategic planning. Most planners believe that when setting objectives, companies are wise to develop several scenarios. Common approaches include having an expected or normal growth scenario, a pessimistic scenario, and an optimistic scenario. Selecting strategic alternatives allows the company to map out the general plan it will use in reaching its objectives. Plans must be carefully documented and distributed to all managers. It is also important that plans be executed skillfully. Failure to monitor and control plans can allow them to get off track. However, because a company cannot predict and plan for every development, it is important to be prepared with contingency plans.

In today's work world, organizations must use their employees effectively. Matching the talents of employees to the needs of the organization is accomplished during the selection process. A thorough understanding of the legal environment guides the design and validation of any selection process. Selection begins with job analysis, or the gathering of information about the job as it exists within the organization. Next, the psychologist identifies the relevant job performance dimensions. This background enables the organization to define the knowledge and skills (KSs) and the abilities and other characteristics (AOs) the employee needs to perform the job. The psychologist then identifies or constructs instruments that will appropriately measure these KSs and AOs. Next, validity studies are conducted. Criterion-related evidence is collected to show that measures are related to future job performance. Content validity ensures that predictors are representative of the job. Construct validity demonstrates that a test measures a particular skill or ability. Cross-validation tests the formulae and weights derived from the original sample to check the accuracy of predictions of success on a second sample. After test results are cross-validated, they can be generalized and used to predict performance of applicants similar to the ones originally sampled. Only after all seven steps in the development of a selection system have been successfully completed can we confidently use the system for the selection and placement of applicants.

Various predictors are used in selection. These include information gathered from application blanks, reference checks, biographical information, interviews, ability tests, and psychological assessments. An application blank consists of a series of questions about the applicant's background. Reference checks provide information about past job performance from previous employers. Biographical data includes information about the person's background and life experiences. This information is often collected through questionnaires. The most popular selection procedure is the selection interview, which can be improved by asking specific questions. Ability tests measure mental or cognitive ability. Another popular tool is the performance test, in which an applicant completes a job simulation. For senior management positions, psychological assessments or assessment centers are often used.

This chapter provides an overview of the ways I/O psychology is applied in human resources management. More details will be presented in several of the chapters that follow. Human resources management is becoming an important and popular area within I/O psychology.

KEY TERMS AND CONCEPTS

abilities and other characteristics
  (AOs)
application blank
biographical information
construct validity
content validity
environmental scanning
equal employment opportunity
job analysis

job performance
knowledge and skills (KSs)
mission statement
multiple-hurdle program
optimistic scenario
performance tests
pessimistic scenario
realistic scenario
reference checks

replacement table
selection interview
selection measures
selection process
SMART test
strategic planning process
succession planning
superordinate goals
validation

RECOMMENDED READINGS

Bray, D. W., & Associates (1991). *Working with organizations and their people: A guide to human resources practice.* New York, NY: Guilford Press.

Cropanzano, R. (1993). *Justice in the workplace.* Hillsdale, NJ: Lawrence Erlbaum Associates.

Greenhaus, J. H. (1987). *Career management.* Chicago, IL: Dryden Press.

Hall, D. T., & Associates (1991). *Career development in organizations.* San Francisco, CA: Jossey-Bass.

Lawler, E. E. (1991). *High-involvement management.* San Francisco, CA: Jossey-Bass.

Plunkett, L. C., & Fournier, R. (1991). *Participative management: Implementing empowerment.* New York, NY: John Wiley & Sons.

Schmitt, N., Borman, W. C., & Associates (1993). *Personnel selection in organizations.* San Francisco, CA: Jossey-Bass.

Zedeck, S. (Ed.). (1992). *Work, families, and organizations.* San Francisco, CA: Jossey-Bass.

INTERNET RESOURCES

Strategic Planning: Vinovich International Consulting Group Case Study: Business Challenge.

This is a report of a national South American education and training organization that tried to improve its profitability by thoroughly reevaluating its strategic business objectives and by reshaping itself to achieve those objectives.
http://www.interlog.com/~vinovich/cases.html

History of the Autodesk Company (A computer-assisted design programming company).

This interesting site documents the development and growth of Autodesk, a successful software company. Many original documents from the company's internal correspondence are used to trace its history. This is a unique and valuable collection of a real company's historical records as they developed and became available for research and study. It is particularly interesting as a case study in organizational restructuring, since it documents several sets of goals, how they were communicated, and the efforts made to achieve them.
http://www.fourmilab.ch/autofile.html

Dun and Bradstreet: Tips to help you create a planning roadmap.

This site describes elements of strategic planning. In business planning, the two most commonly asked questions are: What business are we in? and What business should we be in? The site provides a seven-step approach to help direct a company toward its ultimate goal.

http://www.dbisna.com/dbis/planning/hplannin.htm

Mailing list: HRD-L Mailing List

This reference provides an ongoing mailing list to participants for discussions on topics in the field of human resource development.

mailto:listserv@mizzou1.missouri.edu

Assessment: Nijenrode University—The Netherlands Business School's Business Webserver.

A European leader in assessment for selection and development of employees in businesses, Nijenrode University has developed an extensive Webserver dealing with human resource management and organizational behavior. This includes Human Resource Management & Organizational Behavior at Nijenrode's Gopher, and articles from the Nijenrode Research Centre for Organizational Learning and Change on such topics as employee motivation, employee empowerment, and methods of equity-based compensation.

http://www.nijenrode.nl/nbr/hrm/

Stress and Anxiety: University of New York at Buffalo Counseling Center Self-Help Home Page.

This site provides a number of useful self-help guides to help students cope with the day-to-day stresses and difficult periods in their lives. It includes papers and descriptive documents, internet resources, referrals, and reading lists. Self-help topics addressed under stress and anxiety include: stress management, time management, test anxiety, study habits, overcoming procrastination, preventing perfectionism, a description of typical stress periods for students, and study skills self-help.

http://ub-counseling.buffalo.edu/

Stress Management and Peak Performance by Wesley E. Sime, Ph.D./MPH/Ph.D., Professor, Department of Health and Human Performance, University of Nebraska—Lincoln.

A self-help tutorial describing the core concepts of stress management education, particularly as they relate to performance.

http://www.unl.edu/stress/mgmt/

....

EXERCISE

Exercise 3.1

Developing a Strategic Planning Database for Human Resource Planning

Many companies maintain a database of current employees who are prepared to handle certain positions. Such a database helps a company know where its strengths and weaknesses are with respect to staffing. It is desirable to have a current employee trained as a backup for all critical positions. It is also wise to identify how prepared and ready employees are to take on additional responsibilities. One way this information is collected is to request that employees provide an internal resume summarizing the current state of their training and experience.

Develop a format for an internal resume that could be used as part of an organization's succession planning process.

Design a database for collecting, comparing and using your internal resume information. Include in your design the following functions:

- Training
  Equipment use
  Reports
  Data
- Documentation
  The database elements
  Information on what and why to include data
  Updating schedule
- User support
  Training or other ongoing support
  How to handle queries
  How to assess whether the system is working
- Marketing
  How to sell others on the use of the system
  Demonstrations
  Keeping the data credible
- Security
  Passwords and how to maintain confidentiality
  Data security
  User monitoring: How are data used?

- Technical components
  Typical or regular reports
  Adding new database elements
  Keeping the system and information up to date

Compare your system with those of other students. Modify your resume form and database design to improve their effectiveness.

REFERENCES

Baron, R. A. (1989). Impression management by applicants during employment interviews: The "too much of a good thing" effect. In R. W. Eder & G. R. Ferris (Eds.), *The employment interview: Theory, research and practice.* Newbury Park, CA: Sage.

Boudreau, J. W. (1991). Utility analysis for decisions in human resource management. In Dunnette, M. D., & Hough, L. M. (Eds.), *Handbook of industrial and organizational psychology* (2nd Ed., Vol. 2, pp. 621–746). Palo Alto, CA: Consulting Psychologists Press.

Cascio, W. F., & Awad, E. M. (1981). *Human resources management: An information systems approach.* Reston, VA: Reston Publishing Company.

Dipboye, R. L. (1982). Self-fulfilling prophecies in the selection recruitment interview. *Academy of Management Review, 7,* 579–587.

Dipboye, R. L., Gaugler, B., & Hayes, T. (1990, April). *Individual differences among interviewers in the incremental validity of their judgments.* Paper presented at the meeting of the Society for Industrial and Organizational Psychology, Miami, FL.

Dipboye, R. L., & Macan, T. (1988). A process view of the selection/recruitment interviews. In R. S. Schuler, S. A. Youngblood, & V. L. Huber (Eds.), *Readings in personnel and human resource management.* St. Paul, MN: West.

Dougherty, T. W., Ebert, R. J., & Callender, J. C. (1986). Policy capturing in the employment interview. *Journal of Applied Psychology, 71,* 9–15.

Dougherty, T. W., Turban, D. B., & Callender, J. C. (1992, May). *Expectancy confirmation behavior of employment interviewers.* Paper presented at the meeting of the Society for Industrial and Organizational Psychology, Montreal, Quebec.

Gatewood, R. D., & Feild, H. S. (1994). *Human resource selection.* Fort Worth, TX: Dryden Press, Harcourt Brace College Publishers.

Guion, R. M. (1976). Recruitment, selection, and job placement. In M. D. Dunnette (Ed.), *Handbook of industrial and organizational psychology.* Chicago, IL: Rand McNally College Publishing.

Guion, R. M. (1991). Personnel assessment, selection, and placement. In Dunnette, M. D., & Hough, L. M. (Eds.), *Handbook of industrial and organizational psychology* (2nd Ed., Vol. 2, pp. 327–398). Palo Alto, CA: Consulting Psychologists Press.

Harvey, R. J. (1991). Job analysis. In Dunnette, M. D., & Hough, L. M. (Eds.), *Handbook of industrial and organizational psychology* (2nd Ed., Vol. 2, pp. 71–164). Palo Alto, CA: Consulting Psychologists Press.

Janz, T. (1982). Initial comparisons of patterned behavior description interviews versus unstructured interviews. *Journal of Applied Psychology, 67,* 577–580.

Kinicki, A. J., Lockwood, C. A., Hom, P. W., & Griffeth, R. W. (1990). Interviewer predictions of applicant qualifications and interviewer validity: Aggregate and individual analyses. *Journal of Applied Psychology, 75,* 243–260.

Latham, G. P. (1989). The reliability, validity, and practicality of the situational interview. In R. W. Eder & G. R. Ferris (Eds.), *The employment interview: Theory, research and practice.* Newbury Park, CA: Sage.

Motowidlo, S. J. (1986). Information processing in personnel decisions. In K. M. Rowland & G. R. Ferris (Eds.), *Research in personnel and human resources management* (Vol. 4). Greenwich, CT: JAI Press.

Owens, W. A. (1976). Background data. In M. D. Dunnette (Ed.), *Handbook of industrial and organizational psychology* (pp. 609–644). Chicago, IL: Rand McNally.

Pascale, R. T., & Athos, A. G. (1981). *The art of Japanese management: Great companies make meaning.* New York, NY: Simon and Schuster.

Pyron, H. C. (1970). The use and misuse of previous employer references in hiring. *Management of Personnel Quarterly, 9*(2), 15–22.

Schuler, H. (1989). Construct validity of a multimodal employment interview. In B. J. Fallon, H. P. Pfister, & J. Brebner (Eds.), *Advances in industrial organizational psychology.* Amsterdam: North-Holland.

Stokes, G. S., Mumford, M. D., & Owens, W. A. (Eds.) (1994). *Biodata handbook: Theory, research, and use of biographical information in selection and performance prediction.* Palo Alto, CA: CPP Books.

Williamson, J. (1984). *The leader manager.* Eden Prairie, MN: Wilson Learning Corporation.

Job Analysis

Chapter Outline

DEFINITIONS
- Criterion Development
- Predictor Development
- Job Similarity, Role Difference
- Key Elements
- Terminology

USES OF JOB ANALYSIS
- Job Classification
- Job Description
- Performance Appraisal
- Employee Selection
- Outplacement
- Compensation
- Legal Defense to Adverse Impact
- Strategic Planning

COMPARING METHODS OF JOB ANALYSIS
- Harvey's Taxonomy of Job Analysis Methods
- Sources of Information
- Methods for Collection of Job Analysis Information
- Specific Examples of Job Analysis Instruments

Summary
Key Terms and Concepts
Recommended Readings
Internet Resources
Exercises
References

A medium-sized receivables management firm was faced with a problem that is typical in the business: high turnover among front-line collectors. For several years, turnover of these employees had been above 80%. Given that it takes the firm two full weeks of training to prepare someone to work effectively and legally, the top managers were more than a little discouraged by the fact that many new employees were not staying thirty days. A cross-functional team was formed to investigate. Four probable causes came out at the top of their list: pay, benefits, hours, and management practices. The team also conducted exit interviews. These provided several additional causes for the turnover: lack of feedback, lack of respect, unfair treatment, lack of a career path, and unrealistic prehire descriptions of the job.

The firm hired two industrial psychologists to work with the human resources manager, employment manager, training department, and office managers to develop and implement a selection system to address the problem. The psychologists collected critical incidents, examples of on-the-job behaviors the supervising managers considered to be outstandingly good or bad (see Flanagan, 1954), and performed a thorough job analysis using the Work Profile System. They also interviewed a number of managers and high-performing collectors. This analysis found that several jobs existed for collectors instead of the single job for which the company had been hiring. When the company realized that it was no longer simply hiring "collectors," but hiring people to fill five different jobs, it changed its testing and interviewing process to recognize that fact. The existing process, which consisted of an application blank and a manager interview process, was extended to include a scored application blank, a simple battery of psychological and ability tests, and a structured manager interview. Scoring protocols were developed for all five jobs. Six months after the program was initiated in several branch offices, retention improved in those offices. One year later, turnover rates had dropped to 40% in offices where the program was tested. Plans were then made to implement the program throughout the company.

In the introduction to his book *Job Analysis: Methods and Applications*, Ernest McCormick (1979, pp. 3–4) noted that, historically, there have been two related objectives in planning the involvement of people in the production of goods and services:

> efficiency in the use of human talent and the maintenance or enhancement of certain human values (health, safety, job satisfaction, and the like). . . . Because of the importance of both of these objectives, human work comprises a legitimate area of systematic study and analysis in its own right. . . . In a sense, the phrase *study of human work* is more descriptive of the intended content than *job analysis* in that it is somewhat broader and more encompassing. However, because it is more commonly used and because of its semantic simplicity, *job analysis* is the term generally used.

When I/O psychologists study human work, they usually begin with a job analysis. On the basis of a job analysis, specific behavior criteria can be identified that accurately reflect on-the-job performance. The accuracy of the criteria can be confirmed by studying performance appraisals using objective observers. Once we are clear about our criteria, we can look for ways of predicting that performance using validated predictors. Finally, when all these pieces are in place, they can be assembled and used in personnel. In this and the following four chapters we will examine these components in turn.

DEFINITIONS

Harvey's chapter in the 1991 *Handbook of Industrial and Organizational Psychology* defines job analysis more precisely than has been done in the past. Harvey advocates "that the term job analysis be applied *only* to procedures that collect information describing verifiable job behaviors and activities" (p. 73). His definition specifically excludes procedures that apply job analysis data to solve personnel problems, for example, writing biodata items and identifying personal life history events. He also excludes job analysis methods that make inferences about personality traits, dispositions, and other personal attributes that are required for successful performance of a job.

Harvey (1991, p. 74) defines **job analysis** as

the collection of data describing (a) observable (or otherwise verifiable) job behaviors performed by workers, including both what is accomplished as well as what technologies are employed to accomplish the end results and (b) verifiable characteristics of the job environment with which workers interact, including physical, mechanical, social, and informational elements. Job behaviors or contextual characteristics can be observed both directly (e.g., physical actions performed, tools and machines used, people contacted, materials modified, services provided, or sources of data used as input) as well as indirectly through the use of strong inference from other observable job behaviors.

Harvey's definition emphasizes that job analysis is the description of work behaviors, work products, and job context.

Harvey defined three criteria that are important for any job analysis:

1. Job analysis should describe observables. If the work behavior is not observable, the job analysis should identify and analyze the aspects of the behaviors that can be observed and the observed work products.
2. Job analysis should describe the work itself and how the work is done, not the personal traits or performance effectiveness of people doing the job. The unit of analysis is the job, not the incumbents who do the job.
3. Job analysis data must be verifiable and replicable. The data should be accurate and valid so that every job analysis rating is supported by observable behaviors, ac-

tions, and outputs. In addition, when replicated by independent observers, the job analysis should produce functionally equivalent ratings.

The impact of Harvey's definition and criteria is significant. To see why, let us examine the popular shorthand way of describing the results of job analysis. This describes the **KSAOs**, or job knowledge, skills, abilities, and other characteristics needed to perform the job tasks.

In Harvey's approach, the **KS** portion (job knowledge and skills) is directly observable and can be "unambiguously specified in terms of observable job activities" (Harvey, 1991, p. 76). Psychologists can define and measure job knowledge in a standardized, objective manner. A psychomotor skill that is involved in completing a task can be objectively specified through observable job behaviors.

In contrast, the **AO** portion (abilities and other characteristics) is usually not detailed in the job analysis itself. Instead, it is implied in performance measured by standardized tests of the abilities or traits. Typically, these are paper-and-pencil cognitive skills tests or personality tests. The AO requirements are described as hypothetical traits (e.g., cognitive ability, dominance, introversion, leadership, etc.). They are characteristics on which people differ, not characteristics of jobs per se.

For example, when using job analysis in employee selection, an employer begins by conducting a detailed analysis of the important job activities and their relative importance to successful job performance. This is the KS portion of the process; it yields a description of the job knowledge, specific abilities, and job-related skills an employee needs to perform the job. It is closely tied to the work content. The KS portion is assessed by using work samples, simulations, and specific knowledge tests.

Many job analysis processes yield information about job attributes that goes beyond the specific skills needed to perform the job itself yet is inferred to be job relevant. Examples of this information are abstract thinking abilities, general intelligence level, honesty, leadership and personality traits (like dominance, assertiveness, and need for achievement). Measures of these attributes are seldom job specific. A typical personality test, for example, is validated on the personality constructs in subgroups of the population, *not* with respect to job performance. This lack of job-specific content is the primary reason Harvey believes that the AO portion is distinct and needs to be treated separately in the job analysis process.

For many years, job analysis was viewed as a straightforward, uncomplicated process that was easily accomplished by using a checklist or simple observation and description. Recently, job analysis has become an integral part of the process of demonstrating the validity of selection and promotion decisions. As a result, job analysis is now a factor in legal defense of these decisions. This change has made the process of job analysis more interesting and important.

Today's job analyst needs to be concerned that his or her results can be used, without reservation, along with any other personnel procedures. To stand up in court, the job descriptions and job family groupings resulting from job analysis must have documented reliability and validity. The documentation should substantiate that the job descriptions and job families meet government regulations (such as those of the EEOC), are not discriminatory, and can be linked to other similar data (via validity generalization).

In the validation process, test scores of individuals are compared on the variables that we expect will provide a measure of the characteristic in question. When people who are high performers on the job demonstrate high scores on the measures of these key variables, we have demonstrated the criterion-related validity of the test scores. This form of validity is used extensively in the validation of selection tests and measures. Two basic components are needed in any validity study: the criterion and the predic-

tor. Job analysis plays a role in both. We will discuss these components in Chapters 5 and 7; for now, we will briefly describe the role of job analysis in each of the components.

Criterion Development

The careful specification of the content of the job is a critical part of any validity study. This is because the job analysis provides detailed description of expected job behaviors. An accurate job analysis and thorough job description define the desired target. When selecting experienced people, we are interested in measures of specific job-related knowledge or skills required by the job. For these situations, we want the content of the tests to correspond closely to the content of the jobs. We are defining the criteria against which the tests will be evaluated. For example, achievement tests and job-sample tests often are based directly on the behaviors required for successful job performance.

Predictor Development

In selection, we are interested in predicting applicants' suitability for learning or adapting to the job. Such prediction is usually based on their abilities, personality, and other attributes. Evidence that the tests are relevant for a particular job can come from a criterion-related validity study or a sound job analysis. However, the focus in selection is on the predictors, that is, the abilities, personality, and other attributes that are significantly related to job performance. A thorough job analysis enables us to specify the components of the job precisely enough to have several areas of performance we can attempt to predict using the test battery.

Job Similarity, Role Difference

Ilgen and Hollenbeck (1991) believe that there are important elements beyond those typically captured by a job analysis. That is, there is "an extra set or collection of task elements [that] needs to be added to those that originally constituted the job" (p. 174). They call these elements *emergent task elements,* defining the subjective, personal, and dynamic environment within which jobs exist.

For example, we might have two individuals who have the same job but very different roles. In sales, a rookie and a veteran could have the same job descriptions. The established, defined duties for each would read the same. However, because of the veteran's years of experience, he or she would demonstrate many more emergent task elements (e.g., networking, calling customers and prospects, developing interface teams with customer work groups, partnering on major long-term projects). The rookie salesperson would not demonstrate these behaviors. The cognitive approach in job analysis emphasizes the consideration of job similarity and role difference. This broader perspective is important to developing a full understanding of jobs in order to describe them accurately.

Job analysis is a well-developed discipline within I/O psychology. As such, it has its own specialized terms and methods. The remainder of this chapter will describe and explain this terminology and the major methods used in job analysis.

Key Elements

Job analysis is the *process* of collecting data describing the observable job behaviors that workers perform and the verifiable contextual characteristics of the job environment with which workers interact. Data from a job analysis are summarized formally in a job description.

A **job description** is a *narrative report* of the significant, unique data observed in the job analysis that are characteristic of the target job. An effective job description accurately describes the activities one could observe a skilled worker doing during the process of successfully completing a job. The units of analysis for job description are the job and the job tasks. A job description

can be validated by using content validity. An example is shown in Historical Perspective 4.1 on page 98

In contrast, **job specifications** describe the personal characteristics that have been found to be necessary for effective job performance. The units of analysis are the person and the personal traits or characteristics inferred as necessary for job performance. Showing the validity of job specifications requires construct validity or criterion-related validity.

Terminology

Like other areas of psychological research, job analysis has its own vocabulary. Unfortunately, many terms in the vocabulary of job analysis have their own everyday meanings. These definitions are often in addition (and sometimes in contrast) to their more precise use within job analysis, describing specific job components. Some common job analysis terms and their definitions follow.

Element

Usually considered the smallest practical division of work activity, an **element** consists of very specific motions or movements that are completed in the performance of a task. Elements play an important part when industrial engineers design or redesign a job and its tasks to achieve maximum efficiency. The following are examples of descriptions of elements: Move hand and arm from assembly bench to parts bin; grasp two rivets with right hand; position hands and arms to prepare for typing. See Figure 4.1 on page 99 for an example of analysis of an accountant's job.

Task

A **task** is any discrete unit of work done by an individual. To be considered discrete, a task must have an identifiable beginning and ending. A logical sequence of tasks defines a duty. Tasks are described in brief statements, usually only one sentence, consisting of an action verb describing

HISTORICAL PERSPECTIVE 4.1

Sample Job Description from the *Dictionary Of Occupational Titles*

045.107.030 PSYCHOLOGIST, INDUSTRIAL-ORGANIZATIONAL (profess. & kin.)

Develops and applies psychological techniques to personnel administration, management, and marketing problems: Observes details of work and interviews workers and supervisors to establish physical, mental, educational, and other job requirements. Develops interview techniques, rating scales, and psychological tests to assess skills, abilities, aptitudes, and interests as aids in selection, placement, and promotion. Organizes training programs, applying principles of learning and individual differences, and evaluates and measures effectiveness of training methods by statistical analysis of production rate, reduction of accidents, absenteeism, and turnover. Counsels workers to improve job and personal adjustments. Conducts research studies of organizational structure, communication systems, group interactions, and motivational systems, and recommends changes to improve efficiency and effectiveness of individuals, organizational units, and organization. Investigates problems related to physical environment of work, such as illumination, noise, temperature, and ventilation, and recommends changes to increase efficiency and decrease accident rate. Conducts surveys and research studies to ascertain nature of effective supervision and leadership and to analyze factors affecting morale and motivation. Studies consumer reaction to new prod-ucts and package designs, using surveys and tests, and measures effectiveness of advertising media to aid in sale of goods and services. May advise management on personnel policies and labor-management relations. May adapt machinery, equipment, workspace, and environment to human use. May specialize in development and application of such techniques as job analysis and classification, personnel interviewing, ratings, and vocational tests for use in selection, placement, promotion, and training of workers and be designated Psychologist, Personnel (profess. & kin.). May apply psychological principles and techniques to selection, training, classification, and assignment of military personnel and be designated Psychologist, Military Personnel (profess. & kin.). May conduct surveys and tests to study consumer reaction to new products and package design and to measure effectiveness of advertising media to aid manufacturers in sale of goods and services and be designated Market-Research Analyst (profess. & kin.) II.

GOE:11.03.01 STRENGTH: L. GED:R6 M6 L5 SVP: 8 DLU:77

Source: From U.S. Department of Labor, (1977). *Dictionary of occupational titles* (4th ed.), Vol. 1, p. 51. Washington, DC: U.S. Government Printing Office.

the activity and the object describing what is acted upon. Some examples of task statements are: Type survey results into computer database; write monthly production report; assemble pre-cut pieces to form pocket; respond to customer complaints; instruct employees in new procedures. See Figure 4.1 for an illustration of how tasks relate to elements and other components.

Duty

Duty refers to a collection of tasks that define one of an individual's key work outcomes.

Duties are the major activities involved in the work. Tasks making up a duty may or may not be similar, but they are related. Examples of duties include supervising assembly of machine tools, repairing electronic instruments, and providing administrative support in an office. The relationship among duties, tasks, elements, and other components is illustrated in Figure 4.1.

Position

A **position** is the collection of tasks, activities, responsibilities, and contextual characteristics

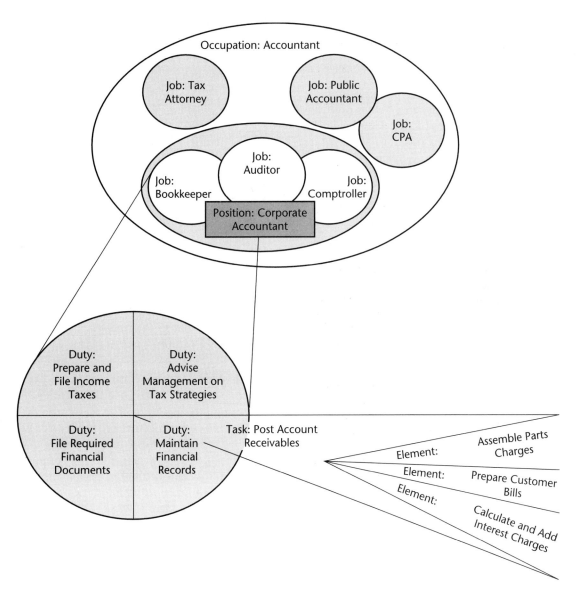

FIGURE 4.1   The relationship among components of a job analysis.

that define the most elemental unit of work in an organization. The collection of tasks and responsibilities that constitutes a position is typically assigned to a single person (termed the **position incumbent**). The collection exists as a basic organizational unit, whether or not the po-

sition is assigned to a person. This makes it possible to complete a job analysis of a position even when that position may not have a current incumbent. Examples of positions include secretary to engineering manager, assembly technician, and computer programmer. The relationship of position to the other elements in a job analysis is illustrated in Figure 4.1.

Job

Jobs are families of closely related positions. It is often convenient to group together positions that have similar responsibilities, describing them as a *single job*. Grouping positions as jobs eliminates the need to have a complete job analysis on every position in an organization. It also makes it easier to use the job analysis data for compensation and other purposes, since we can define procedures that apply to the groups (jobs) rather than defining them for every individual position. This is illustrated in Figure 4.1.

Although the positions grouped as one job are not all alike, they are at least functionally interchangeable with respect to the major work activities. The fact that there are differences, however, can sometimes cause difficulties. It is not always easy to answer the question "Why is this position classified as this kind of job?" When position incumbents are dissatisfied with the results of a job analysis, they often complain, "My responsibilities and tasks are too different from those of this other worker to be considered the same job!"

Job Family

A **job family** is a group of jobs that are related to one another based on key work activities. Examples include billfold assembly cell, machine shop, office staff, exempt employees, and salaried employees. Job families are typically created for personnel purposes. We might combine data from several similar jobs to create a group that is large enough to use the data for test validation or to develop performance appraisal and compensation forms and guidelines.

Occupation

Often, it is useful to group job families with related or common work content by occupation. The Dictionary of Occupational Titles (U.S. Department of Labor, 1977) defines an **occupation** as a group of jobs and job families that require similar skills, efforts, and responsibilities across different businesses. Examples of occupations include taxi driver, nurse, accountant, psychologist, aviator, engineer, research scientist, and university professor. Questions can arise about the level of similarity between the jobs and job families that are included in each occupation.

To reduce the confusion, Harvey (1991) believes that job classification procedures should be considered as separate and essentially different from the basic process of job analysis. He believes that "all higher-level organizational constructs—(jobs, families, occupations)—necessarily involve aggregating across, and thereby ignoring and deeming unimportant, a potentially sizable number of both large and small behavioral differences that exist between positions" (Harvey, 1991, p. 80). His concern is that when the broader classifications are used, there are more chances that abstractions will include nonsignificant behavioral differences. Another concern expressed about the current processes for creating job families is that these processes are not sufficiently objective and replicable. We need job families that can be reliably used in generalizing test validities from position to position, from setting to setting, or from job to job. With this basic understanding of job analysis, we can examine some of the uses that make the process so vital to I/O psychology.

USES OF JOB ANALYSIS

A strong case can be made for the argument that job analysis should provide the basis for many, if not most, personnel decisions (Harvey, 1991). The relationship is a clear one for personnel decisions such as performance appraisal and compensation. It is less clear when job analysis is used to specify ability-based or trait-based requirements for employee selection.

Job Classification

One of the most direct applications of job analysis data is **job classification,** in which a job or a job family is defined. The decisions about which jobs can be classified as being sufficiently alike that they can be considered interchangeable in personnel procedures have become highly important in the last fifteen years because of validity generalization. A small organization can use generalized validity to substantiate that its approach is valid while it is accumulating the data it needs for its own validity study. Because it can take a long time to collect enough data to conduct appropriate statistical studies, it is necessary in the interim to substantiate what the organization is doing.

Job Description

A job description is a narrative description of the work activities performed on a job. Most also describe other aspects such as working conditions, equipment, and tools needed. A standard rule of thumb is that a job description specifies what the job incumbent does, how the work is done, and why it is done. By examining the what, how, and why questions job analysts raise, we can understand the construction of job descriptions.

"What" questions focus on the physical and mental activities performed on the job. Butler (cited by McCormick, 1979, p. 62) suggests the following questions for the job analyst:

What tasks have been observed during the performance of the job?

Are the tasks included for this job performed by all workers designated by the job title?

What is the frequency with which the tasks are performed?

What is the relative difficulty of each task as compared with the rest of the tasks on the job?

Are there additional tasks which have not been observed?

Are there additional tasks customary to all workers on the job?

Have the data obtained by observation been verified?

"How" questions describe the methods or procedures used to complete the job tasks. Physically, this may involve the use of tools or machinery; mentally, it may involve the use of formulas or the exercise of judgment. Butler's questions for examining the "how" aspect of jobs include the following:

How are tools, materials, and equipment used to accomplish all of the tasks of the job?

How are other tools, materials, and equipment (that have not been observed) used?

How have methods or processes been used to accomplish the tasks of the job?

How are other methods or processes used to do the same work?

"Why" statements describe the basic purpose(s) of the job. Some questions for examining the "why" aspect include the following:

Why does this job exist? What is the overall purpose of this job?

What are the specific job elements and why is each performed?

Why does each of the job elements exist and how do they relate specifically to the objectives of the job?

The last consideration in writing the job description is the writing style. In the *Handbook for Analyzing Jobs* (U.S. Department of Labor, 1972, p. 200) the following suggestions are summarized:

a. A terse, direct style should be used.

b. The present tense should be used throughout.

c. Each sentence should begin with an active verb.

d. Each sentence must reflect an objective, either specifically stated or implied in such a manner as to be obvious to the reader. A single verb may sometimes reflect both objective and worker action.

e. All words should impart necessary information; other words should be omitted. Every precaution should be taken to use words that have only one possible connotation and that specifically describe the manner in which the work is accomplished.

f. The description of tasks should reflect the assigned work performed and worker traits ratings.

A sample narrative job description is presented in Figure 4.2.

It is also possible to write job descriptions from a task-oriented frame of reference. Such job descriptions provide a list of job tasks and descriptive statistics derived from current job incumbents. This style of job description has the advantage of being readily updated by using the information stored in the personnel database. In fact, current computer technology makes this style of task-based job description an attractive alternative to the more laborious method of writing narratives. In addition, computer capabilities make it possible to provide updated, job-relevant, task-based job descriptions quickly as jobs change. Figure 4.3 on page 104 illustrates this form of job description.

Performance Appraisal

Since the early 1970s, courts have required that employers be able to substantiate the job related-ness of their performance appraisal systems. One element in this process is to show that a thorough job analysis has been completed. The results of the job analysis can then be linked to the appraisal procedures. Two errors may be made in this linking process. **Criterion contamination** occurs when performance appraisal rates the job incumbent on factors that are not a demonstrable part of the job. For example, rating the incumbent on "maintains a tickler file" is appropriate only if this task

is necessary for effective job performance. The error of **criterion deficiency** occurs when the performance appraisal fails to rate an aspect of performance necessary for effective job performance.

Job analysis data can be tied to performance appraisal by a number of different methods. These currently include holistic, trait-oriented, task-oriented, critical incident, and weighted checklist approaches.

Holistic methods, or whole job approaches (advocated by Schmidt and Hunter, 1981), use a *single* holistic score to describe individual effectiveness on the job. The holistic view is often used in job evaluation. This is because the goal is to come up with a *single number* that expresses the worth of the job in relation to all the other jobs in an organization.

Trait-oriented methods use data that describe human attributes or traits (such as aptitudes, physical abilities, or personality). Trait approaches are effective when the instrument is carefully developed so that the traits included cover the full domain of the job.

Task-oriented methods use task-based job analysis to develop a list of duties based on specific tasks performed on the job. Such performance appraisal forms consist of simple checklists indicating whether performance on a task is acceptable or needs improvement.

The **critical incident** method offers a different approach to performance appraisal. **Weighted checklists** include the entire list of critical incidents identified in the job analysis. Each critical incident is weighted to create scale values that represent the importance of each incident with respect to overall job performance. A final numerical total is calculated. That total represents performance on dimensions, duties, and the overall job.

Employee Selection

Job analysis plays a key role in **employee selection.** Job analysis is the source of behavioral descriptions of job activities. These descriptions provide the base for identifying both the

City Architect I

Nature of Work

This is professional and technical work in the preparation of architectural plans, designs, and specifications for a variety of municipal or public works building projects and facilities.

Minimum Qualifications

Education and Experience—Graduation from an accredited college or university with a specialization in architecture or architectural engineering; or equal.

Knowledge, Abilities, and Skills—Considerable knowledge of the principles and practices of architecture; ability to make structural and related mathematical computations and make recommendations on architectural problems; ability to design moderately difficult architectural projects; ability to interpret local building codes and zoning regulations; ability to secure good working relationships with private contractors and employees; ability to train and supervise the work of technical and other subordinates in a manner conducive to full performance; ability to express ideas clearly and concisely, orally and in writing; skill in the use of architectural instruments and equipment.

Illustration of Duties

Prepares or assists in the preparation of architectural plans and designs all types of building projects constructed by the City, including fire stations, park and recreation buildings, office buildings, warehouses, and similar structures; prepares or supervises the preparation of final working drawings including architectural drawings, such as site plans, foundations, floor plans, elevations, section details, diagrams, and schedules rendering general features and scale details; prepares or supervises some of the engineering calculations, drawings, and plans for mechanical details, such as plumbing, air-conditioning phases, and lighting features; writes construction standards and project specifications; prepares sketches including plans, elevations, site plans, and renderings and makes reports on feasibility and cost for proposed City work; writes specifications for all aspects of architectural projects including structural, mechanical, electrical, and air-conditioning work; confers with engineering personnel engaged in the preparation of structural plans for a building, making recommendations and suggestions as to materials, construction, and necessary adjustments in architectural designs to fit structural requirements; inspects construction in the field by checking for conformity with plans and material specifications; inspects existing structures to determine need for alterations or improvements and prepares drawings for such changes; performs related work as required.

Supervision Received

General and specific assignments are received and work is performed according to prescribed methods and procedures with allowance for some independence in judgment in accomplishing the assignments.

Supervision Exercised

Usually limited to supervision of technical assistants in any phase.

FIGURE 4.2
A sample narrative job description.

Source: From W. Cascio (1991). *Applied Psychology in Personnel Management* 4th ed.), p. 193. Englewood Cliffs, NJ: Prentice-Hall. Copyright 1991, by Prentice-Hall. Reprinted with permission.

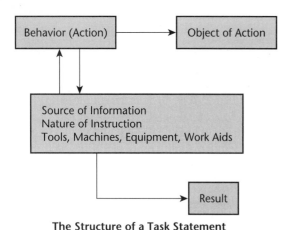

The Structure of a Task Statement

FIGURE 4.3   A sample task-based job description.

Source: From S. A. Fine (1989). *Functional job analysis scales* (Rev. Ed., p. 2). Milwaukee, WI: Sidney A. Fine Associates. Copyright 1989, by Sidney A. Fine. Reprinted with permission.

KS (knowledge and skills) and AO (ability and other) requirements of the job. These requirements, in turn, define the criteria for the selection assessment.

By completing a thorough worker-oriented job analysis, an organization establishes a strong empirical basis for its KS requirements. In validation studies for KSs, the job analysis data can be used as a direct specification of the job criteria. The validation of the assessment instruments is then based on the measurement of these behavioral descriptions.

AOs are descriptions of characteristics and traits that are inferred to be present. This inference is based on personality or other measures that have been constructed and validated as measures of a characteristic or trait rather than as measures of behaviors needed for the job.

Outplacement

Many organizations are offering support for laid-off and terminated employees through out-placement services and support. **Outplacement** provides terminated employees with career and psychological counseling, training in job search skills, moral support, and administrative support during their job search.

Job analysis data are useful when an organization has to downsize. The success of downsizing depends on the quality of the people the company retains. To avoid creating dysfunctional turnover by letting its better employees leave while retaining poorer performers, a company needs to have accurate job descriptions and performance appraisals. When it is carefully planned and uses objective, accurate data, downsizing can provide an opportunity to improve productivity.

Another way in which job analysis data assist in downsizing and outplacement is in counseling laid-off and terminated employees. Many organizations contact other employers and provide detailed information about the qualifications their former employees have and the specific jobs they held. When the new jobs involve relocation, job analysis data can be helpful during the counseling process to employees who are making the decision to move themselves and their families. This can occur when the job analysis data assist the employee in comparing the new job with the former job. Job analysis data also assist in helping the former employee to seek additional training to upgrade his or her skills or to obtain a promotion as a part of relocation.

Compensation

Job analysis data are used most frequently in compensation decisions when there is a desire to demonstrate that the criteria of the Equal Pay Act of 1963 are met. Equal pay means that when a group of jobs involves equal skill, effort, responsibility, and working conditions, those jobs are considered to be of equal value to the organization. Compensation for jobs of equal value should be equal. Job analysis is also used to predict the compensation for a job based on job duties and task structure. When the courts examine the equivalence of jobs under the Equal Pay Act, they often use job analysis data. Because the legal evaluation includes abstract components such as effort and responsibility, there is often difficulty in moving from specific job behaviors, in which the comparison is straightforward, to the abstractions in which it is more complicated. Even when legal considerations are not paramount, job analysis provides information that is useful in compensation decisions.

Standardized, worker-oriented job analysis questionnaires such as the Position Analysis Questionnaire (PAQ) have been used successfully for computing and predicting compensation. The process involves analyzing an organization's jobs using one of the worker-oriented methods, calculating job dimension scores, and then using the scores as multiple-regression predictors of market compensation rates for the jobs being analyzed. Once this has been accomplished, predicted compensation rates can be derived by applying the regression weights to the job dimension scores for any job.

Organizing information from job analyses is a challenging task. One approach is to create a dictionary of job titles that can be used by job analysts. The *Dictionary of Occupational Titles* is such a reference.

The last use for job analysis that we will discuss is to avoid adverse impact and protect the organization from legal action.

Legal Defense to Adverse Impact

An important motivator for organizations to complete job analyses has been the need to limit their legal liabilities from employment discrimination lawsuits. Unfortunately, this has become such an important factor that it is often an end in itself. As we have seen, job analysis data are extremely useful in human resource management. The many applications in which job analysis can accomplish important human resource goals make it one of *the* critical business activities. It is wise for any organization that takes the time,

trouble, and expense of completing a set of thorough job analyses to make full use of the data.

Good science and effective practice are not sufficient guarantees that a job analysis and the decisions based on it are adequate. An I/O psychologist must be alert to potential adverse impact and the legal consequences of discrimination (intended or unintended). There are three major legal influences on job analysis: laws, court decisions, and professional standards documents. We will briefly examine each.

Beginning in 1964 with Title VII of the Civil Rights Act, several laws have been enacted that have directly influenced job analysis. Title VII was the first. It specifically prohibits employment practices that have adverse impact based on race, sex, color, religion, or national origin. These are often referred to as protected groups. Its impact on job analysis comes from the judicial interpretations of the act that require job relatedness (the ability to demonstrate that an employment practice is specifically related to job performance). To substantiate the use of a test or other selection device, an employer must demonstrate that a job analysis has been completed and that the tests or other selection decisions that are employed are based on objective job analysis data. An employer must also demonstrate that the selection decisions do not have adverse impact. In most situations this means that the employer must show that the measures or the cutoff scores for the selection process utilized are not prejudiced toward or against any group. This is accomplished by conducting separate analyses for all protected groups to demonstrate that the selection rates for each group are appropriate (usually this means that the ratio of those selected is representative of the ratio of that group in the geographical region from which applicants are drawn) and based on job relevant criteria.

Another law that affects job analysis is the Age Discrimination in Employment Act of 1967. The act prohibits age-based discrimination in employment. For job analysis this means that it is necessary to use test validation and performance appraisal to demonstrate that the *work activities* of younger workers (age 39 and under) are not significantly different from those of older workers (over age 40). In many jobs there are no differences in work activities that are legitimately related to age. Given these circumstances, the company must not show favoritism in hiring younger rather than older workers (which would be an adverse impact on older workers). When there *are* legitimate differences, these can be used in selection. When an organization needs to hire younger workers for certain jobs, the organization must show that this decision is job-related. An organization substantiates such a decision as legitimate by completing an appropriate and thorough job analysis.

The Equal Pay Act of 1963 bars sex-based discrimination in determining and awarding compensation. Job analysis data are used to develop the compensation systems and to ensure that comparable work is comparably paid regardless of the sex of the worker.

Most laws do not specifically address job analysis or how it should be completed. This is an interpretive issue that is left to the courts. Several landmark decisions have had considerable influence. *Griggs* v. *Duke Power Co.* (1971) established the need for job relatedness. *Albemarle Paper Co.* v. *Moody* (1975) established job analysis as a virtual necessity for the defense of challenged employment practices. It also extended this need to cover both original and new target jobs in which validity generalization was used to establish validity of the selection process. Today, it is understood that the courts expect on-site job analyses be conducted that comprehensively describe the full domain of job behaviors and identify the most important ones. In addition, the courts have consistently used the term *tests* to describe performance appraisals, thereby extending validation standards and, with them, the importance of job analysis to performance evaluation.

Courts often use professional standards documents (most notably the Uniform Guidelines, the APA Standards, and the SIOP Principles, discussed next) to indicate the professional state of the art in validation. Consequently, these docu-ments are significant. They are worth examining in order to understand the three key standards documents.

The *Uniform Guidelines on Employee Selection Procedures* (1978) specify the necessity of conducting a job analysis describing work tasks as a part of all validation strategies. They also require that when validity generalization is used, the job analyses of the positions being compared demonstrate that the jobs in question require incumbents to perform substantially the same work behaviors.

The APA's *Standards for Educational and Psychological Testing* (American Psychological Association, 1985) are less specific than the Uniform Guidelines in describing job analysis requirements. However, they do specify that "critical job content factors are substantially the same (as is determined by a job analysis)" (p. 61). For construct validity the standards specify that "if construct-related evidence is to be the major support of validity for personnel selection . . . there should be evidence for the validity of the construct as a determinant of major factors of job performance." (p. 61).

The SIOP's *Principles for the Validation and Use of Personnel Selection Procedures* (Society for Industrial and Organizational Psychology, 1987, p. 5) specifies that "a less detailed job analysis may be all that is required because of past research . . . concerning predictors and criteria. [This] can be developed with little reference to a specific job analysis in a particular organization." The principles agree with other standards, documents, and court decisions in requiring a detailed task-based analysis of job behaviors for content validation.

Harvey (1991, p. 124) summarized the following general principles, which have emerged from the general regulatory climate that has existed since 1964:

> First, behaviorally specific job analysis
> is the only effective strategy for identify-
> ing and (content) validating KS-based job
> specifications: demonstrable links to such
> data are also vital for developing and defend-

ing criterion measurement and appraisal systems.

Second, the techniques for identifying and validating AO-based job specifications are qualitatively distinct from those used to validate KS-based requirements. Although many types of job analysis data can be used in the process of (construct) validating inferences of general ability and trait requirements, specifications of ability requirements must be based on something more than just the "professional judgment" of the analyst.

Third, a job analysis is needed to justify validity generalization or transportability decisions, although the specificity of this information is open to debate. To the extent that behaviorally specific predictor tests are used (e.g., work samples), it is likely that more specific job analysis data should be used to assess job similarity.

Strategic Planning

With all the areas we have discussed in which job analysis is helpful, it is understandable why it is an important element in the strategic planning process. Driven by the rapid evolution and change occurring in the workplace, companies are finding it more important to anticipate their work force needs in sophisticated ways. Only a few years ago, companies were satisfied with reasonable estimates of the number of people they would need to sustain their growth rates. Today, as skilled workers become increasingly scarce, companies use job analysis data and sophisticated technological modeling to project the number and type of skilled workers they will need. In some cases, strategic planning alerts the organization that the talented people whom it will need may not be available. This realization is pushing some companies into extensive educational efforts to train current employees for future needs. These educational efforts also extend to the public schools. Many companies are forming business–education partnerships to support schools in preparing students for the jobs of the future. Job analysis data are useful in these efforts. Educators use the data to identify the knowledge

and skills that will be needed and to design programs that teach future employees. The job analysis data also provide information that can help in designing internship and apprenticeship programs closely aligned with business needs.

COMPARING METHODS OF JOB ANALYSIS

In a significant article in *Personnel Psychology,* Cornelius, Carron, and Collins (1979) reviewed job analysis models and job classifications. They suggested that the different job analysis philosophies underlying the various techniques provide an effective way of examining and classifying the techniques. Some approaches produce job-specific listings of *job behaviors.* Others construct *descriptions of the consistencies* in task-dissimilar jobs. Following this suggestion and extending the earlier taxonomic work of McCormick (1979) and Cornelius, Carron, and Collins (1979), Harvey (1988, 1991) developed a taxonomy of job analysis methods using two dimensions. These were the behavioral specificity of the job ratings and the rating scale comparability across jobs. For each of these dimensions, Harvey defined three categories that are useful for sorting job analysis methods. In the next section we will describe Harvey's important taxonomy in greater depth.

Harvey's Taxonomy of Job Analysis Methods

The Behavioral Specificity Axis

Harvey's first axis is the **behavioral specificity axis,** which classifies job analysis methods on their behavioral or technological detail. Harvey's taxonomy uses three levels of categorization: low, moderate, and high. At the low level of behavioral specificity, a job analysis method would be very abstract in its descriptions of work. The method would use holistic groupings and have a narrative format. There would be few, if any, descriptions of specific task behaviors or task technologies. At the moderate level of behavioral specificity, a job analysis method would provide descriptions of behaviors and technologies that were meaningful, but not overly specific. There would also be some meaningful categorization on the basis of general job behaviors. At the high level (the most desirable from Harvey's point of view) the job analysis would use items that were closely tailored to the individual jobs. These items would be detailed and specific enough that they could reveal significant differences between jobs that might be perceived as similar (in the same category) in a more holistic or abstract analysis.

The Comparability of Rating Scales Axis

Harvey's second axis, the **comparability of rating scales axis,** classifies job analysis methods on the meaningfulness of cross-job comparisons. That is, a method is judged in terms of the degree to which it would produce job ratings that were directly comparable to each other because they used a common rating scale in their description. This axis sorts job analysis methods in terms of whether they produce descriptions that are relevant only to the job on which they were originally conducted (within-job-relative) or can be meaningfully compared to all the other jobs rated using the method (cross-job-relative). Between these two categories lies a third. Job analysis methods that fall in this category use within-job-relative ratings, but instruct raters to attempt to rate in a consistent way across all jobs.

Harvey's Taxonomy

By combining the two axes just described, Harvey developed a straightforward taxonomy for job analysis methods. Table 4.1 summarizes the nine categories of job analysis methods defined by Harvey's taxonomy.

These categories are helpful in comparing different approaches to job analysis. For example, Harvey observes that there are a number of Type 4 methods. This is because of the popularity of using relative rating scales for task inventories. The only difference between these methods and the much preferred common metric (Type 1) is the scale. Accordingly, he finds it hard to understand why job analysts do not make the effort to develop scales that would allow cross-job comparisons. For more information about the Harvey taxonomy the interested reader is referred to Harvey's chapter in the second edition of the *Handbook of Industrial and Organizational Psychology* (1991).

Sources of Information

In addition to the decision regarding the level of behavioral specificity desired and whether to use within-job-relative or cross-job-relative scales, another critical decision in job analysis is to select the people who will provide the data. In job analysis it has been common to use job incumbents, supervisors, and trained job analysts. Each choice has advantages and disadvantages.

Job Incumbents

The most credible and frequently used sources of information are job incumbents. They know the job by virtue of doing it daily. Unfortunately, many job incumbents lack the verbal skills to complete some job rating and description tasks. They may not understand terms used to describe jobs that are at a higher level than the ones they hold. They may not have the ability to read and comprehend some standard surveys. The Position Analysis Questionnaire, for example, has been criticized (Ash & Edgell, 1975) for its high reading level. In addition, job incumbents may not be motivated to complete job rating, may have conflicting motives, and may exaggerate their duties.

Supervisors

Supervisors usually have better verbal skills than job incumbents and play an important role in what is done on the job. In many cases they are former job incumbents. One key concern about using supervisors is their motivation. Exaggeration of duties (to achieve increased compensation) is a frequent criticism. Another is that supervisors may use old information in their ratings. That is, they describe the job more in terms of what it was like when they did it than in terms of its current content.

TABLE 4.1	Harvey's Taxonomy of Job Analysis Methods, Including Examples of Each Type		
	Behavioral/Technological Specificity		
Kind of Scale Metric	*High*	*Moderate*	*Low*
Cross-job-relative; meaningful level-based comparisons frequency scale	Type 1 Task inventory rated using absolute scale Task inventory rated using "do you perform" checklist	Type 2 CMQ items rated on absolute frequency, frequency data Dichotomous CMQ, JEI item ratings	Type 3 CMQ dimension scores based [on a metric applicable to all jobs] JEI dimension scores based on dichotomized data FJA ratings of Data, People, Things
Within-job-relative; ratings expressed relative to the other activities performed on job or rated on scales that are not anchored in terms of verifiable job behavior	Type 4 Task inventory rated using relative-time, relative-importance, percent-time scales	Type 5 JEI item ratings using relative-time scale Duty ratings on relative-time, relative-importance	Type 6 JEI dimension scores based on relative-time ratings
Qualitative; no numerical ratings, or no quantitative comparisons possible between jobs	Type 7 Job-specific listings of tasks Behaviorally specific critical incidents	Type 8 Long narrative job description Behaviorally abstract critical incidents	Type 9 Holistic job grouping judgments Short narrative job description

Source: Modified and reproduced by special permission of the publisher, Consulting Psychologists Press, Inc., Palo Alto, CA 94303 from *Handbook of Industrial and Organizational Psychology* (2nd Edition, Volume 2, p. 85) by Marvin D. Dunnette and Leaetta M. Hough. Copyright 1991 by Consulting Psychologists Press, Inc. All rights reserved. Further reproduction is prohibited without the publisher's written consent.

Job Analysts

Using trained job analysts is, in many ways, the best approach. Careful training ensures that the analysts can complete good descriptive interviews and reliable ratings. However, job analysts are expensive to train or hire. When the analysts do not know the jobs in question, it takes considerable time to bring them up to speed. If this is not done, the analysts may bias the data by using their preexisting stereotypes about the jobs being rated or about the incumbents. For example, an analyst who has never held a blue-collar job can underestimate the knowledge and skill required to provide sophisticated

control in a complex machining process. If such an analyst uses what he or she thinks is needed instead of carefully observing and recording actual knowledge and behavior, the job analysis will be biased.

Other Sources

In addition to the three major sources just described, other information can provide a basis for job analysis. Some sources that have been used include training manuals, job descriptions, performance evaluations, psychological assessments, job descriptions from similar jobs in other companies, and content analysis of anecdotal records.

Methods for Collection of Job Analysis Information

Another major decision in setting up a job analysis involves how the analyst plans to collect the data that will be used. A number of different methods have been devised, each with its own set of advantages and disadvantages.

Checklist Method

In the **checklist method,** the job incumbent is asked to check off all the job tasks, using a prepared form. A difficulty is that a job analysis is required to construct the list of tasks that is used. The list needs to be representative of the job tasks. For the analyst to be sure this is the case, a preliminary job analysis must collect behavioral descriptions of job-specific behaviors. These behaviors are refined into the set used for the checklist. Advantages of this method include the following: It is easy to give (often it is mailed), it is easy to respond to, and the data are easy to tabulate. Some disadvantages include the following: It requires much preparation (actually, a job analysis needs to be completed to generate the task listing that is then used to complete the final job analysis), the task statements in and of themselves do not provide an integrated picture of the job, and tasks that are shared or that overlap other jobs may not be identified.

Critical Incident Method

Examples that represent outstanding or inferior job performance define the extremes in job performance. When such incidents are captured and carefully defined, the results are called *critical incidents*. A job analyst using the **critical incident method** interviews job incumbents to collect statements about job performance. These statements are based on the incumbent's memory or observations. The goal is to identify and describe examples of good and bad performance. These should include descriptions of situations in which there is no question that the performance was successful, as well as contrasting ones demonstrating failures or problems. The critical incident method is described in greater detail later in this chapter. Advantages of the critical incident method include providing direct information on critical aspects of the job (both positive and negative) and describing some direct information about job performance. Disadvantages are that this method does not give a fully integrated picture of the job and that the incidents are not easily scaled and compared.

Diary Method

When the **diary method** is used, the job incumbents self-record their job activities in a logbook or diary. Usually, this is an unstructured, open-ended approach that requires considerable time and energy from job incumbents to complete well. Advantages of the diary method are that it gathers much information on the job as the activities happen. Disadvantages include the time it requires from job incumbents, the amount of irrelevant information collected, and the amount of time it takes to organize and analyze the information.

Group Interview Method

When job analysts use the **group interview method,** a number of job incumbents are interviewed simultaneously. The interviewer guides job incumbents in the recall and discussion of job behaviors. The advantages that combine to make this a popular method include the following: It gives a very complete picture of the job behaviors, the job incumbents do not have to write the report, and it saves time because of the use of groups to collect the information. Disadvantages are that it is difficult to analyze and not all key job behaviors may be recalled.

Individual Interview Method

When using the **individual interview method,** the job analyst conducts extensive personal interviews of representative incumbents. These interviews are usually conducted off the job, and the results from several such interviews with different job incumbents are combined to form the final job analysis. The advantages of individual interviews are that they give a rich, complex picture of the job, the employee does not have to write the report, and it is a good method to start with. Disadvantages include that this method is cumbersome and costly in terms of interview time and analysis time and that the interview depends on the accurate memory of the job incumbents. Some may not recall all parts of their job; others may try to make their job sound too good.

Observation Interview Method

The **observation interview method** is similar to the individual interview method, but takes place on the job. An analyst using this technique will watch the worker perform the job while questioning or interviewing the person about the job activities. The method is similar to individual interviews in that workers are asked about the job they are performing. The major difference is that the interview takes place on the job, where the workers' behaviors *can be observed* while they are describing them. Advantages include the following: It provides a rich, complex picture of the job, the employee does not have to write the description, and it gives first-hand information. Disadvantages include the following: It is cumbersome, requiring a lot of training and coordination to do well; it is costly in terms of the time it takes for the interview and the analysis; and when not done well, observation interviews may interfere with the work, even to the point of changing some aspects and biasing the results.

Questionnaire Method

When job analysts use the **questionnaire method,** they begin with observations of an exemplary job. The behaviors that they observe are summarized in descriptive questions. These are organized in a survey about the job that is given to a large sample of job incumbents to fill out. A major advantage of questionnaires is that they can be mailed out to get wide coverage. They are effective for job incumbents who read well and who feel comfortable with answering questions or writing descriptions of what they do. It is also possible to create effective standardized questionnaires that do not require the job analyst to have much previous knowledge about the job. Some disadvantages are that questionnaires are not good for workers who have difficulties reading or who have poor verbal skills (this can also include workers for whom English is a second language) and that the data can be time consuming to analyze.

Technical Conference Method

The **technical conference method** uses job experts (also referred to as subject matter experts, or SMEs) to describe the job. Often, the individuals who are chosen as SMEs are supervisors. These individuals meet in a technical conference to describe the job. This is a group discussion among the SMEs during which they discuss the various activities required by a job and how important each is. Advantages are that technical conferences are fast and added insights are often developed as a result of the discussion. Disadvantages include the following: The SMEs may not know the job as intimately as does the job analyst, and there is a tendency for supervisors acting as SMEs to describe what the worker "should do" rather than what is actually done.

Work Participation Method

Although the **work participation method** has never been particularly popular, it has been effective for simple jobs about which detailed knowledge is desired. With this method the job analyst learns and performs the job. Once the analyst's job performance is judged to be effective by someone who is knowledgeable about the job under study, the analyst develops the job analysis. An advantage is that the information on job behaviors is first-hand. Because the analyst personally performs the job, he or she gets a detailed feeling for what is done. Work participation has mainly been used for jobs that an analyst can learn easily and quickly. Its disadvantages are that it is time consuming and costly, particularly for complex jobs that require much training and experience to do well.

We have examined nine methods for collecting job analysis information: the checklist, the critical incident, the diary, the group interview, the individual interview, the observation interview, the questionnaire, the technical conference, and the work participation method. Each has its own advantages and disadvantages, proponents and critics. Yet surprisingly little research has been done to compare these methods objectively. One of the few such studies is summarized in Scientific Perspective 4.1.

Specific Examples of Job Analysis Instruments

Now that we have described the major methods used to collect job analysis data, we can examine in more detail several of the techniques available to the job analyst. We have chosen seven to describe briefly.

Functional Job Analysis

Originally developed by Sidney Fine in 1951–1952 as a basis for the classification system of

the third edition of the *Dictionary of Occupational Titles* of the U.S. Employment Service (1965), **functional job analysis** (FJA) is a highly structured, task-oriented approach to job analysis. Through the years, Fine has expanded the original version of FJA and now considers it "an integral part of a systems approach to human resource management" (Fine, 1989, p. vi). He is also careful to note that "Functional Job Analysis describes only the functional skills a person applies to specific job content. It does not cover . . . adaptive skills, . . . competencies concerned with managing oneself with relation to conformity and change" (Fine, 1989, p. vi). Fine (1992) described FJA as identifying:

- what people need to do to get the job done,
- the standards to which work needs to be done,

SCIENTIFIC PERSPECTIVE 4.1

Exploratory Comparative Study of Four Job Analysis Methods

Edward L. Levine, University of South Florida, Tampa; Nell Bennett, Salt River Project, Phoenix, AZ; and Ronald A. Ash, University of South Florida, Tampa.

First prize paper, 1978 National Psychological Consultants to Management Consulting Psychology Research Award competition, presented at the American Psychological Association Convention, Toronto, 1978.

Although methods of job analysis vary considerably, different methods do not necessarily lead to different end results. One aspect of science that is both fascinating and challenging is the fact that very different approaches can yield the same or highly similar results. When this happens, there is no clear-cut, best solution to choose. Such results can be highly thought stimulating.

Levine, Bennett, and Ash designed a study to evaluate the differences among four job analysis methods. They evaluated the final job descriptions on the basis of usefulness (as rated by participants), on the content and quality of the selection testing programs developed for selecting new people to the jobs, and on the costs of conducting the analyses and administering the selection battery. Four jobs were analyzed (Accountant I, Accountant II, Mental Health Worker, and Mental Health Technician). Four different job analysis methods were used (Job Evaluation, Task Analysis, Critical Incidents, and Position Analysis Questionnaire).

The big surprise was that no significant differences were observed in the exam plan content, quality ratings, or costs among the job analysis methods. The study did find that the expert raters were more knowledgeable about and comfortable with the Job Elements and Task Analysis methods. These raters also saw Job Elements most favorably, followed by Critical Incidents, Task Analysis, and, finally, the PAQ. While no significant differences were found in the selection plans based on the four different methods of analysis, there were more job constructs produced by the Critical Incident reports and more personal history constructs produced by the PAQ reports.

Source: "Exploratory Comparative Study of Four Job Analysis Methods," by E. L. Levine, N. Bennett, and R. A. Ash, 1978, Milwaukee: National Psychological Consultants to Management. Reprinted with permission.

- the training needed to achieve success,
- the amount of discretion the worker has to get the job done,
- optional paths for worker self-direction, and
- the different kinds of skills involved in getting the job done.

In analyzing jobs by studying tasks, Fine discovered that what passed for task descriptions was a hodgepodge of phrases or bits of information referring to knowledge, skills, abilities, activities, and behaviors. He spent five years sorting through data to make sense of it. Fine had 250,000 classification components derived from classifying 4,000 jobs on eight behavioral dimensions. He used the English sentence as a frame of reference; sentence structure provided his model for task statements. FJA task statements include six components. These are the subject; the action verb describing the activity; the object of the action; the observable results of the action; the tools, equipment, and other work aids used; and the degree of discretion given to the worker. Figure 4.4 illustrates a typical **FJA model sentence** worksheet.

Fine provided additional structure by examining the verbs used in the descriptions. He found that they reflected workers' mental, physical, and interpersonal capacities. The verbs could be ordered from simple to complex in terms of the contexts within which the behavior took place. This resulted in a scheme by which the selection of one verb from each ordinal hierarchy (describing a thing, a datum, and a people verb) also simultaneously described the task. Fine's summary chart of these three worker function scales is presented in Figure 4.5 on page 114 (Fine, 1989, p. 6).

FJA is applied to one job at a time. The focus is on worker behaviors. It asks what workers do to get the work done. All worker behaviors are considered in terms of their relation to "Things," "Data," and "People" functions or objects. The behaviors are described in terms of a limited number of worker functions arranged hierarchically. Actions by the worker initiate tasks; the actions are modified by knowledge, skills, and abilities to produce results that contribute to organizational outcomes. The tasks are the fundamental units of work-doing systems. All tasks involve all aspects of a worker's actions—the

Who?	Performs What Action?	To Whom or What?	Upon What Instructions? (Source of Information)	Using What Tools, Equipment, Work Aids?	To Produce/ Achieve What? (Expected Output?)
Subject	Action Verbs	Object of Verb	Phrase	Phrase	In Order to
The worker	Operates	Grader	Following work order for haul road Drawing on experience Knowledge of equipment	Grader	Maintenance of haul road

Task Statement

FIGURE 4.4   A model sentence worksheet used in functional job analysis.

Source: From S. A. Fine (1989). *Functional job analysis scales* (Rev. Ed., p. 1). Milwaukee, WI: Sidney A. Fine Associates. Copyright 1989, by Sidney A. Fine. Reprinted with permission.

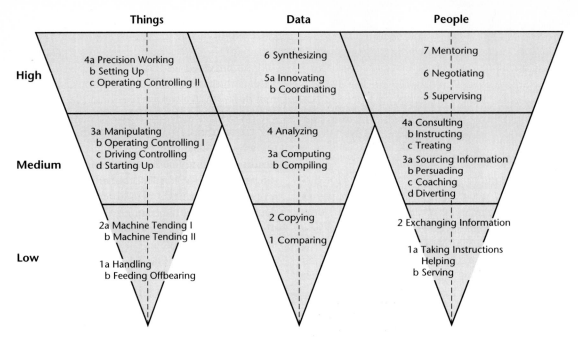

	Things	Data	People
High	4a Precision Working b Setting Up c Operating Controlling II	6 Synthesizing 5a Innovating b Coordinating	7 Mentoring 6 Negotiating 5 Supervising
Medium	3a Manipulating b Operating Controlling I c Driving Controlling d Starting Up	4 Analyzing 3a Computing b Compiling	4a Consulting b Instructing c Treating 3a Sourcing Information b Persuading c Coaching d Diverting
Low	2a Machine Tending I b Machine Tending II 1a Handling b Feeding Offbearing	2 Copying 1 Comparing	2 Exchanging Information 1a Taking Instructions Helping b Serving

1. Each hierarchy is independent of the other. It would be incorrect to read the functions across the three hierarchies as related because they appear to be on the same level. The definitive relationship among functions is within each hierarchy, not across hierarchies. Some broad exceptions are made in the next note.

2. Data is central since a worker can be assigned even higher data functions although Things and People functions remain at the lowest level of their respective scales. This is not so for Things and People functions. When a Things function is at the third level, e.g., Precision Working, the Data function is likely to be at least Compiling or Computing. When a People function is at the fourth level, e.g., Consulting, the Data function is likely to be at least Analyzing and possibly innovating or Coordinating. Similarly for Supervising and Negotiating, Mentoring in some instances can call for Synthesizing.

3. Each function in its hierarchy is defined to include the lower numbered functions. This is more or less the way it was found to occur in reality. It was most clear-cut for Things and Data and only a rough approximation in the case of People.

4. The lettered functions are separate functions on the same level, separately defined. The empirical evidence did not support a hierarchial distinction.

5. The hyphenated functions. Taking Instructions, Helping, Operating, Controlling, etc., are single functions.

6. The Things hierarchy consists of two intertwined scales: Handling, Manipulating. Precision working is a scale for tasks involving hands and hand tools. The remainder of the functions apply to tasks involving machines, equipment, vehicles.

FIGURE 4.5   Sample worker function scales from functional job analysis.

Source: From S. A. Fine (1989). *Functional job analysis scales* (Rev. Ed., p. 4). Milwaukee, WI: Sidney A. Fine Associates. Copyright 1989, by Sidney A. Fine. Reprinted with permission.

physical, the mental, and the interpersonal. Fine recognizes that performance also involves a person's quality, reflected by the worker's adaptive skills. However, these are not assessed in FJA.

A common procedure is to conduct focus group discussions using five or six people who hold the same job. These job incumbents are considered subject matter experts and are enlisted to understand the true nature of their work. They are asked to discuss five key questions:

What do you get paid for?

What do you need to know to do the work for which you are paid?

What skills and abilities do you need to do the work well?

What do you actually do?

What standards do you work toward: your own and those of others in your organization?

Answers to these questions are recorded exactly. After the session the comments made by job incumbents are grouped and refined until a clear classification/description is possible. The classification/description can be cross-validated by repeating the process with a second sample of job incumbents. The final result is a detailed narrative that explicitly describes the main elements important to the job.

Position Analysis Questionnaire

Originally developed by McCormick, Jeanneret, and Mecham (1972, pp. 346–347), the Position Analysis Questionnaire (PAQ) is a structured questionnaire that uses 187 job elements to analyze jobs. The PAQ is considered a worker-oriented approach because the elements are descriptions of general human behaviors that are used on the job, rather than the technologies used. The PAQ uses a relatively small number of job elements to describe all jobs in all situations. The job elements are organized into six major groups. As described by Ernest McCormick (1979, p. 144), the major groups and examples of each are as follows:

1. Information input. (Where and how does the worker get the information he uses in performing his job?)
   Examples: Use of written materials, near-visual differentiation.
2. Mental Processes. (What reasoning, decision-making, planning, and information-processing activities are involved in performing the job?)
   Examples: Level of reasoning in problem solving, coding/decoding.
3. Work output. (What physical activities does the worker perform and what tools does he use?)
   Examples: Use of keyboard devices, assembling/disassembling.
4. Relationships with other persons. (What relationships with other people are required in performing the job?)

   Examples: Instructing, contacts with public, customers.
5. Job Context. (In what physical or social contexts is the work performed?)
   Examples: High temperature, interpersonal conflict situations.
6. Other job characteristics. (What activities, conditions, or characteristics, other than those described above, are relevant to the job?)
   Examples: Specified work pace, amount of job structure.

To rate a job using the PAQ, the job analyst scores the job in terms of the 187 job elements. There are six standard scales with a specific rating scale used for each job element. The six scales are as follows:

Identification	Type of Rating Scale
U	Extent of use
I	Importance to the job
T	Amount of time
P	Possibility of occurrence
A	Applicability
S	Special code

An advantage of using the PAQ is the availability of **attribute profiles.** These profiles consist of six-point scale ratings of the relevance of 76 different human attributes (verbal comprehension, intelligence, dealing with people, time pressure, working alone, etc.) to the 187 job elements. Another advantage is that reliability can be derived by comparing two different analyses of the same job. In a similar fashion, it is possible to examine inter-rater reliability when multiple raters are used.

Occupation Analysis Inventory

Developed by William J. Cunningham at the Center for Occupational Education (North Carolina State University), the Occupation Analysis Inventory (OAI) is similar to the PAQ in that it uses 622 work elements. These are grouped into five major categories (information received,

FIGURE 4.6
Paradigm for the
Occupation Analysis
Inventory (OAI).

Source: From Cunningham,
J. W., Tuttle, T. C., Floyd, J. R.,
& Bates, J. A. (1971). The development of the occupation
analysis inventory: An "ergometric" approach to an educational problem. (Ergometric
R & D Report no. 3 under
grant no. OEG-2-7-070348-
2698 from the U.S. Office of
Education.) Raleigh: Center
for Occupational Education,
North Carolina State University. Reprinted with permission.

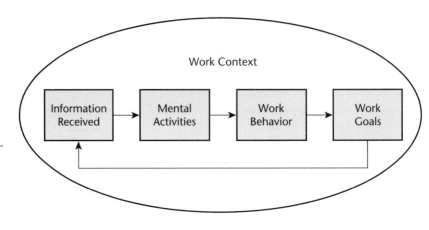

mental activities, work behavior, work goals, and
work context) as illustrated in Figure 4.6. Four of
the categories of work elements define the four
steps in the information processing cycle. The entire cycle, as well as the four steps independently,
are considered relative to the work context
within which they occur. The major frame of reference for the OAI is information processing.

To complete a job analysis using the OAI, the
job analyst rates all 622 work elements on significance to the job (0–6), extent of occurrence
(0–6), and applicability (does apply, does not
apply). Some elements have special scales. Although similar in many ways to the PAQ, the
OAI adds job-oriented (technological) work elements and goal-oriented work elements. Like
the PAQ, the OAI is based on a large amount of
data describing the relationships between ratings of human attributes and the work elements
of specific jobs. The data are organized in the
Attribute Requirement Inventory (ARI), which
provides meaningful guidance about the educational requirements of jobs. Six groups of attributes that are important for occupational education are identified. These are general vocational
capabilities, cognitive abilities, psychomotor abilities, sensory capacities, interests, and needs.
Cunningham's goal was to be able to complete
meaningful occupational clustering based on
similar educational requirements. This goal was

a primary motive behind the development of the
OAI. (Cunningham et al., 1971; cited by Mc-
Cormick, 1979).

Task Inventory

A **task inventory** typically consists of two components: a list of the tasks for the occupation being
evaluated and a response scale for rating each
task. While there are many examples of task inventories in use, the most extensive development
of this process has been done under the direction
of Raymond E. Christal (1974) at the Air Force
Human Resources Laboratory in Texas. Developing a task inventory is a complex, time-consuming
process that is typically justified only when the inventory will be used with a large number of people. The process as summarized by McCormick
(1979, pp. 123–129) includes the following steps:

1. Define scope of performance situation.
2. Locate written sources of activity statements.
3. Develop preliminary inventory (more than
   one may be needed).
4. Review the preliminary inventory or inventories.
5. Prepare revised draft of inventory.
6. Select scales to be used.
7. Administer a pilot test of the inventory.
8. Print the inventory.
9. Administer the inventory.

Automotive Mechanics Task Inventory	Page __19__ of __23__ Pages	
	CHECK	TIME SPENT
LISTED BELOW ARE A DUTY AND THE TASKS WHICH IT INCLUDES. CHECK ALL TASKS WHICH YOU PERFORM. ADD ANY TASKS YOU DO WHICH ARE NOT LISTED, THEN RATE THE TASKS YOU HAVE CHECKED.		1 Very Much Below Average 2 Below Average 3 Slightly Below Average
M. MAINTAINING AND REPAIRING BRAKING SYSTEMS	✓ If Done	4 Above Average 5 Slightly Above Average 6 Above Average 7 Very Much Above Average
1. Repair master cylinder		
2. Repair wheel cylinder	✓	4
3. Replace brake hoses and lines	✓	1
4. Replace brake shoes	✓	6
5. Resurface brake drums		
6. Adjust brakes	✓	7

FIGURE 4.7
Example of a task inventory.

Source: William H. Melching and Sidney D. Borcher (1973). *Procedures for Constructing and Using Task Inventories* (p. 35). Columbus, OH: Center on Education and Training for Employment, (formerly CVTE), The Ohio State University. Copyright 1973, by The Ohio State University. Used with permission.

Because of the difficulty in developing task inventories, it is common practice to find one that has already been developed and modify it to fit the current need. Since job incumbents can easily complete task inventories, these can generate large collections of task-specific job data. Such data can be useful for identifying job types, examining the structure of occupational groups, and planning appropriate training.

Task inventories most often are completed by job incumbents, although in some cases they are completed by supervisors or job analysts. The worker is given the task inventory with instructions such as: "Check all the tasks you perform. Add tasks you perform, but which are not listed, and rate the tasks you checked in terms of the time spent doing each" (Melching and Borcher, 1973; cited by McCormick, 1979, p. 119). A task inventory that asks auto mechanics to rate the time they spend on certain

key tasks is illustrated in Figure 4.7. One type of scale that is used with task inventories describes the job incumbent's involvement in the task. In rating involvement, Air Force research has found that using a relative-time-spent scale is better than using an absolute-time-spent scale. A second type of scale describes the incumbent's judgment or attitude relating to the task. Among the many different scales used are complexity, criticality, difficulty of learning, difficulty of performing, supervision, and satisfaction.

The reliability of task inventories can be examined in two ways. First, we can compare two administrations of the same inventory with the same job incumbents for a specific task. Following this procedure, McCormick (1979) reported studies with reliabilities varying from .35 to .87. Another way is to consider the reliability of the pool of task items that make up a given inventory. Using this approach,

McCormick found adjusted reliabilities varying from .92 to .97.

Harvey (1991) notes that task inventories that use an absolute frequency scale (instead of the more common within-job-relative frequency scale) make it possible to do meaningful cross-job, level-sensitive item and profile comparisons. In using the **absolute frequency scale,** or cross-job approach, job analysts are instructed to rate all items on a common scale, one that is the same across positions. Analysts are trained to use the scales in such a way that the numbers mean the same thing in terms of frequency of occurrence or amount of the characteristic observed, regardless of the job rated or the person doing the rating. In contrast, the **within-job-relative frequency scale** has raters evaluate the components relative to other elements of the specific job being rated. The PAQ is a good example of within-job rating. The importance-rating-scale used to rate relative importance of a dimension for the job being evaluated is: 5 = extreme, 4 = high, 3 = average, 2 = low, and 1 = very minor. Two different positions might legitimately receive high importance ratings on a behavior, but the level of sophistication required might be different. Using absolute frequency scales eliminates this confusion.

Even when using absolute frequencies, the job analyst must be careful because the task inventory method can fail to detect some of the abstract similarities and differences between jobs masked by technological influences. This can be a critical difference if one is using the job analysis for structuring a technical training program in which relatively small differentials in the course work may be critical in determining the final effectiveness of the individuals trained. Harvey is also critical of the common practice of using within-job-relative frequency scales because doing so severely limits the ability to make comparisons between jobs. By changing the rating scale used to a common metric type (cross-jobs-relative), job analysts could widely increase the cross-job comparisons that could legitimately be completed. The data would be collected under instructions to compare the dimensions across jobs, and the ratings would be collected on standard scales.

Threshold Traits Analysis

Developed by Lopez, Kesselman, and Lopez (1981), **threshold traits analysis** combines the job functions approach with analysis of the human attributes required to perform the job. Lopez, Kesselman, and Lopez defined a process requiring the job analyst to complete two ratings of each of thirty-three traits that are used to describe job performance. The first rating describes the complexity of the job function by using a four-point (0–3) scale. Parallel to that rating is a human attribute (trait) scale. It, too, is a four-point (0–3) scale, but it describes the complexity of the responses required from the workers. The list of twenty-one job functions and the thirty-three traits rated on the threshold traits analysis can be seen in the example in Figure 4.8.

Cognitive Job Analysis

Murphy and Cleveland (1991) indicate that although traditional job analysis methods provide objective information about the dimensions of the job, they may not provide the whole solution. They note that Borman's (1983, 1987) studies show that raters use dimensions that reflect their implicit theories about the job in question in order to organize their thinking. Cognitive research has shown that such implicit theories are often accurate. However, they do not necessarily yield the same results as those derived through job analysis. As summarized by Murphy and Cleveland, Borman (1987, p. 95) found that the dimensions that defined the supervisor's conceptions of job performance included the following:

- Initiative and hard work
- Maturity and responsibility
- Organization
- Technical proficiency
- Assertive leadership
- Supportive leadership

It is important to note that several of these dimensions are global traits rather than specific

Area		Job Functions	Trait	Description—**Can:**
Threshold Traits Analysis	*Physical*	Physical exertion ⟶	1. Strength	Lift, pull, or push physical objects
			2. Stamina	Expend physical energy for long periods
		Bodily activity ⟶	3. Agility	React quickly: has dexterity, coordination
		Sensory inputs ⟶	4. Vision	See details and color of objects
			5. Hearing	Recognize sound, tone, and pitch
	Mental	Vigilance and attention ⟶	6. Perception	Observe and differentiate details
			7. Concentration	Attend to details amid distractions
			8. Memory	Retain and recall ideas
		Information processing ⟶	9. Comprehension	Understand spoken and written ideas
			10. Problem-solving	Reason and analyze abstract information
			11. Creativity	Produce new ideas and products
	Learned	Quantitative computation ⟶	12. Numerical computation	Solve arithmetic and numerical problems
		Communications ⟶	13. Oral expression	Speak clearly and effectively
			14. Written expression	Write clearly and effectively
		Action selection and projection ⟶	15. Planning	Project a course of action
			16. Decision-making	Choose a course of action
		Application of information and skill ⟶	17. Craft knowledge	Apply specialized information
			18. Craft skill	Perform a complex set of activities
	Motivational	Unprogrammed ⟶	19. Adaptability–change	Adjust to interruptions and changes
		Cycled ⟶	20. Adaptability–repetition	Adjust to repetitive activities
		Stressful—Working ⟶	21. Adaptability–pressure	Adjust to critical and demanding work
		Secluded—Conditions ⟶	22. Adaptability–isolation	Work alone or with little personal contact
		Unpleasant ⟶	23. Adaptability–discomfort	Work in hot, cold, noisy work places
		Dangerous ⟶	24. Adaptability–hazards	Work in dangerous situations
		Absence of direct supervision	25. Control–dependability	Work with minimum of supervision
		Presence of difficulties ⟶	26. Control–perseverance	Stick to a task until completed
		Unstructured conditions ⟶	27. Control–initiative	Act on own, take charge when needed
		Access to valuables ⟶	28. Control–integrity	Observe regular ethical and moral codes
		Limited mobility ⟶	29. Control–aspirations	Limit desire for promotion
	Social	Interpersonal contact ⟶	30. Personal appearance	Meet appropriate standards of dress
			31. Tolerance	Deal with people in tense situations
			32. Influence	Get people to cooperate
			33. Cooperation	Work as a member of a team

FIGURE 4.8   Area, job function, trait, and activity description matrix illustrating the trait-oriented job analysis technique of Threshold Traits Analysis.

Source: From " An Empirical Test of a Trait-Oriented Job Analysis Technique," by F. Lopez, G. Kesselman, and F. Lopez, 1981, *Personnel Psychology, 34,* p. 484. Copyright 1981 by Personnel Psychology, Inc. Reprinted with permission.

abilities. Because traits are less job-specific than behaviors, using them in job analysis is less accepted. However, Borman's results suggest that supervisors use global traits rather than specific behaviors when evaluating job performance. **Cognitive job analysis** recognizes that the rating behavior of supervisors is hard to change and suggests the following (Murphy & Cleveland, 1991, p. 95):

1. Supervisors hold implicit theories of the job that define, for them, the meaning of job performance.
2. The dimensions emphasized by supervisors will not always be the same as those derived through formal job analysis.
3. It is the implicit theory, not the job analysis, that guides the supervisor's observation, interpretation, and recollection of subordinates' job performance.

Professional and Managerial Position Description Questionnaire

Mitchell and McCormick (1979) extended the process used by the PAQ to develop a similar structured job analysis questionnaire designed for use in the analysis of professional, managerial, and related positions or jobs (e.g., executives, managers, staff personnel, technicians, teachers, and instructors).

Analyzing jobs with the PAQ is quite easy. The researcher selects raters who are knowledgeable about the job. These can be job analysts, personnel managers, supervisors, and even job incumbents. Each analyst is given a copy of the Professional and Managerial Position Description Questionnaire (PMPQ) along with detailed instructions on how to complete it. The analyst then uses the questionnaire to describe the job in question. Once the form has been completed, it is combined with the forms of other analysts and sent to PAQ Services, Inc., for scoring and profiling. The service sends back a detailed printout that summarizes the analysts' ratings of the job in question and compares those ratings to the database collected from other analysts rating similar jobs in other companies using the PAQ. This documentation can be a vital part of demonstrating the validity of the job analysis process as well as the validity of any selection process that is used.

The PMPQ consists of ninety-eight different behavioral items. Each is rated in terms of its relevance to the position using one of four scales. The scales are the P scale (part of the job), C scale (complexity), I scale (impact), and R scale (responsibility). There are three major sections to the questionnaire. Section I describes job functions, Section II describes personal requirements, and Section III covers other information.

The Common Metric Questionnaire

Harvey (1990) developed the Common Metric Questionnaire (CMQ) to be applicable to all jobs. Written at an eighth grade (or lower) reading level, the CMQ uses several rating scales for each item. Items are presented in a matrix format that produces a much larger number of data points than is typically seen in worker-oriented questionnaires. Behavioral specificity is obtained by using an absolute frequency scale to indicate how many times the activity is performed hourly, daily, and so on. Items are highly specific to ensure that the behavior being rated is the same regardless of the job being rated. For example, to describe interactions with other people, the matrix describes thirteen types of people contacted (e.g., customers, regulatory officers, contractors, executives of other organizations) as rows. Each kind of person contacted is described by using dichotomous ratings describing the actions performed with them (take information from them, coordinate/schedule their activities, sell to them, persuade them, train/educate them, etc.). Instead of only thirteen rating points (one for each type of person contacted), the CMQ rates each contact on twenty scales, producing 260 rating points. The grid format makes it possible for the CMQ to avoid the problems inherent in methods that assign only a single number to describe each personal contact.

Job analysis is one of the activities that most people in business admit should be done, but

> ## PRACTICE PERSPECTIVE 4.1
>
> ### Job Descriptions That Really Work
>
> Originally, job descriptions described what are known as "input" characteristics. These are such things as when the employee is to report to work and the physical requirements of the job. The results, or "output" characteristics, are important to include because they give managers a way to measure results. Even small businesses can benefit from output job descriptions.
>
> Two young men went into the lawn care business. They quickly realized that as owner-managers they would also be performing as employees. Despite the fact there were only two people in the organization, they wrote job descriptions to define what they would do when they functioned as mowers of lawns, bookkeepers, sellers of their service, and buyers of fertilizer and equipment. Later, when they hired other workers, they wrote job descriptions of how they would perform as middle managers. Ultimately they even attached a different rate of pay to each job.
>
> Many times managers complain that some employees are not working. The belief that employees should be busy all the time does not consider the fact that some people work faster, better, or smarter than others. What is important is not that they are standing around but rather whether or not they have completed the work. If workers seem to have extra time, their job description may be too narrow. For example:
>
> A seafood distributor in the south reduced the size of the work force after adding automated
>
> truck-loading equipment. Even then, the remaining workers had some spare time. . . . (H)e called them into a meeting and suggested that they might want to spend that extra time in a training program designed to help them grow within the company. To initiate this notion, we led them through a job-description writing exercise that yielded many new activities in which they could engage during the time saved by the automated equipment. Today, three of those people have been transferred to the sales department, a direct result of a job description that indicated a need for further growth and the achievement of a higher position in the company.
>
> Some of the obvious, immediate benefits of "output" job descriptions are that they create a better understanding of what every employee is supposed to do, they define how performance will be measured, and they assist in salary administration. Job descriptions will not solve all the problems of managing a business but they can contribute to making the business more professional and easy to run. Armed with this new perspective, one of our manager friends put this sign on his desk, "You can't expect people to perform until you have told them what is expected."
>
> *Source:* From B. Robert Anderson (1976). Job descriptions that really work. *The Kiwanis Magazine* (July–August), pp. 39–54. Copyright 1976 Kiwanis International. Reprinted with permission.

they do not enjoy doing it. One reason is that we are not used to examining what we do in the kind of detail required by even the most straightforward job analysis technique. Nonetheless, the process has been proven to be extremely valuable to even the smallest of companies. As illustrated by Practice Perspective 4.1, even a company with only two employees can profit from developing clear job descriptions using job analysis.

SUMMARY

Job analysis in current industrial/organizational practice describes work behaviors, work products, and job context. Its focus is on collecting data describing observable or otherwise verifiable job behaviors performed by workers and verifiable characteristics of the job environment. Good job analysis describes observables, describes the work itself, and is verifiable and replicable. The job description that results from a job analysis will typically specify KSs (job knowledge and skills) and AOs (abilities and other characteristics). KSs are behavioral and directly observable, while AOs are often inferred.

The result of a job analysis is a job description that accurately describes the behaviors one could observe a skilled worker doing while successfully completing a job. In job analysis the smallest division of work activity is known as an element and consists of very specific motions. The next larger element is a task, which is any discrete unit of work accomplished. Tasks combine into duties, which define a given person's key work outcomes. A position collects duties and adds contextual factors to define the most elemental unit of work in an organization. Finally, related positions are combined into jobs, and related jobs into job families, which are then grouped into occupations.

A number of job analysis strategies have been developed over the years. These can be analyzed in terms of behavioral detail and the meaningfulness of cross-job comparisons. Some of the more popular methods include the checklist method, which uses prepared lists of job tasks that are checked off by raters; the diary method, which uses a logbook or diary to record job tasks when they are completed; group interviews, which question a group of job incumbents to develop job data; observation interviews, which combine on-the-job observations with interviews of job incumbents to describe on-the-job behaviors; questionnaires, which use surveys to ask large samples of employees about the job; technical conferences, in which job experts meet to discuss and describe a job; and work participation, in which the job analyst learns and performs the job being studied.

The strategies have been combined and modified to form several major methods used for most job analyses. The methods include the following.

Functional job analysis, a highly structured, task-oriented approach, develops task statements consisting of a subject, an action verb, the object of the activity, the observable results, the tools or work aids used, and the degree of worker discretion.

In the Position Analysis Questionnaire (PAQ), which uses 167 job elements in a structured questionnaire, analysts use scales to rate each item in terms of extent of use, importance to the job, amount of time used, possibility of occurrence, or applicability.

The critical-incident method combines a description of the setting, a description of the job behavior, and a description of the positive or negative consequences of the job behavior into narrative descriptions of unusually effective or ineffective job performance.

In the Occupational Analysis Inventory, which is much like the PAQ, 622 work elements are rated. All are rated on three scales: significance, occurrence, and applicability.

Task inventories use a list of tasks completed for an occupation and a rating of that task. This is a difficult and time-consuming process that has been used mainly in organizations in which there are large numbers of individuals in the jobs analyzed.

Threshold traits analysis describes a job using two scales: the complexity of the work function scale and the human attribute scale.

Cognitive job analysis is an emerging technique. A key finding to date is that supervisors have implicit theories defining jobs. These are meaningful and important because they guide the way in which supervisors observe, interpret, and remember a worker's job performance.

Finally, the Professional and Managerial Position Description Questionnaire provides a PAQ-style structured job analysis for managerial jobs.

A major resource in job analysis is the *Dictionary of Occupational Titles*. The U.S. Employment Service publishes this reference work, which contains job definitions, cross-references to similar jobs, and a description of each job in terms of the people, data, and things involved.

Job analysis is useful for many purposes. Some of the more common uses include job classification defining jobs and job families, employee selection, performance appraisal, compensation, reducing adverse impact, and test validation.

KEY TERMS AND CONCEPTS

absolute frequency scale
AO
attribute profiles
behavioral specificity axis
checklist method
cognitive job analysis
comparability of rating scales axis
criterion contamination
criterion deficiency
critical incident methods
critical incident technique
diary method
duty
element
employee selection

FJA model sentence
functional job analysis
group interview method
holistic methods
individual interview method
job analysis
job classification
job description
job family
jobs
job specifications
KS
KSAOs
observation interview method
occupation

outplacement
position
position incumbent
questionnaire method
task
task inventory
task-oriented methods
technical conference method
threshold traits analysis
trait-oriented methods
weighted checklists
within-job-relative frequency
  scale
work participation method

RECOMMENDED READINGS

American Educational Research Association, American Psychological Association, & National Council on Measurement in Education (1985). *Standards for educational and psychological testing.* Washington, DC: American Psychological Association.

Fine, S. A., and Getkate, M. (1995). *Benchmark tasks for job analysis: A guide for functional job analysis (FJA) scales.* Mahwah, NJ: Lawrence Erlbaum Associates.

Harvey, R. J. (1991). Job analysis. In Dunnette, M. D., & Hough, L. M. (Eds.), *Handbook of industrial and organizational psychology* (2nd Ed., Vol. 2). Palo Alto, CA: Consulting Psychologists Press.

McCormick, E. J. (1979). *Job analysis: Methods and applications.* New York, NY: AMACOM.

Society for Industrial and Organizational Psychology, Inc. (1987). *Principles for the validation and use of personnel selection procedures* (3rd ed.). College Park, MD: Author.

Uniform guidelines on employee selection procedures (1978). *Federal Register,* 43, 38290–38315.

U.S. Department of Labor. (1977). *Dictionary of occupational titles* (4th ed.). Washington, DC: U.S. Government Printing Office.

INTERNET RESOURCES

Job Analysis

This Virginia Tech site focuses on job analysis and classification. Most of the research in job analysis performed at Virginia Tech addresses task-inventory methods and the Common-Metric Questionnaire. This site provides a summary of new job analysis postings, an e-mail discussion list, research reports, data files, and software. A closely related site is the Personnel Systems and Technologies Corporation page (http://www.pstc.

com/) devoted to the Common-Metric Questionnaire.
http://harvey.psyc.vt.edu/JA.html

The Institute for Job and Occupational Analysis

This site provides detailed information about the Institute for Job and Occupational Analysis (IJOA). This nonprofit corporation encourages the study of the world of work in terms of the tasks, jobs, and occupations humans perform and seeks to model the human requirements quantitatively. The

site provides membership information; the latest news about job analysis, occupational research, and integrated human resource management systems; a collection of professional papers; and the institute's newsletters.
http://metricanet.com/IJOA/
BOLA (Business Open Learning Archive):
The Analysis of Jobs
This site provides notes and checklists to aid in the examination of your own job from a self-development point of view. Included are tips on how to get started, the value of different job analysis techniques, choices and constraints on job demands, a job analysis toolbox, and a discussion of traditional work study techniques.
http://sol.brunel.ac.uk/~jarvis/bola/jobs/
JOB DESCRIPTION Software
Work Science has created a computerized encyclopedia of work in a database format. The 27 MB database includes information from *The Dictionary of Occupational Titles, The Revised Handbook for Analyzing Jobs, The Guide for Occupational Exploration, The General Aptitude Test Battery, and the Standard Occupational Classification Manual.* JOB DESCRIPTION is listed in many software directories and has received several national product reviews.
http://www.workscience.com/job30.html
ERGOWEB: Job/Task Review and Analysis Tools
Ergoweb describes itself as, "the place for ergonomics on the World Wide Web." A subscription site, it offers access to a variety of ergonomic software for performing job evaluations, analyses, and job designs. Case studies and other instructional materials are also available through the site.
http://www.ergoweb.com/
The Many Uses of Job Analysis
This URL leads to an article by employee relations consultant Ethan Winning. In it he defines and describes job analysis and job description. A partial job analysis questionnaire is listed as well as a sample job description.
http://www.all-biz.com/articles/jd.htm
The Small Office Home Office (SOHO) Guidebook: Doing Job Analysis
SOHO is a large internet site that provides guidance for small businesses. The Guidebook is from SOHO's set of business tools. It provides a basic exercise that will help small business owners gather their thoughts and may be just enough analysis to get them started on searching for the right candidate to fill a particular job opening.
http://www.toolkit.cch.com/guidebook/text/P05_0210.htm
Job Analysis—Physical Demand Archives
This site provides searchable access to the Archives of the Academy of Management's Human Resources Management Division (HRNET) Internet E-Mail Discussion List on Job Analysis and focuses on physical demands. It helps answer questions such as, "If certain strength and endurance levels are required, how can I make sure the selection tools used will stand up in court?"
http://ursus.jun.alaska.edu/archives/hrnet/msg06303.html

Listservers

JOBANALYSIS: Job Analysis discussion list
listserv@listserv.vt.edu
subscribe jobanalysis firstname lastname
Job-tech: Job technologies list
listserv@uicvm.uic.edu
subscribe job-tech firstname lastname
IOOB-L: Industrial psychology discussion group
listserv@uga.cc.uga.edu
subscribe ioob-l firstname lastname

EXERCISES

Exercise 4.1

Writing Task Statements and Job Duty Descriptions

Step 1: Develop task statements.
A task is usually considered to be a discrete unit of work performed by an individual. It is a logical and necessary step in the performance of a job duty and typically has an identifiable beginning and ending.
Use the following criteria for identifying tasks:
A task is a group of related manual activities directed toward a goal.
A task usually has a definite beginning and end.

A task involves people's interactions with equipment, other people, and/or media.

When performed, a task results in a meaningful product. (Such products are not always tangible. For example, a "correct decision" is a meaningful product.)

A task includes a mixture of decision, perception, and/or physical (motor) activities.

A task may be of any size or degree of complexity. But it must be directed toward a specific purpose or separate portion of the total job duty.

Think of your current role as a student as if it were a job. On a sheet of paper, prepare a list of task statements. Aim to write at least thirty task statements. As you work, think about the job of being a student in general terms as well as specific terms. Using a broader perspective can help you think of things you might overlook if you focused only on fine grain details.

Write your task statements in the following form:

1. Use an implied subject for the task sentence (e.g., students). The implied subject is plural.
2. Use a verb that tells what function you, the job incumbent, performed.
3. Use as the object of the verb data, people, or things (machines, equipment, work aids, or tools).
4. End with a "to" or "in order to" phrase stating the purpose of your task activity.

Example: For computer operators: produce/control/monitor distributions of computer output to deliver to the proper people in response to specific project timelines.

Step 2: Prepare a composite list of task statements.

Form groups or pairs. Acting as a group of subject matter experts, have one person be the leader. Now use a modified brainstorming approach to prepare a composite list of task statements. To accomplish this, the leader will go around the table, asking each subject matter expert, in turn, to read one unique task statement. This statement is then written on a flipchart or blackboard. Anyone who has an identical statement deletes it from his or her list of task statements. Anyone who has a slight addition or modification volunteers this information, which is noted on the flipchart or blackboard. The leader continues this process until all task statements from all job experts have been transferred to the posted listing or have been deleted as duplicates.

Step 3: Sort task statements into functional groups.

Select a new group leader. This leader guides the group in a review of the completed list of task statements. The task in this step is to identify duty or functional groupings. Identify each such group with a brief name; below the name, list all of the task statements that can be categorized as being part of that group. If any participants think of additional task statements during this process, these can be added to the list. After all task statements have been assigned to a group, one person transfers the list in legible writing to a Task Rating and Evaluation Form.

Step 4: Interview workers and supervisors.

Because interviewing is an integral part of most job analysis methods, individuals who serve as analysts need to develop interviewing skills that will enable them to get the most out of each interview. In job analysis, semistructured interviews are usually the most appropriate. This is particularly true if the interviewer uses a job schedule that provides for obtaining information on each of the different aspects of the job in question.

There are three basic stages in preparing for the interview:

1. Set the objectives. (Yours is to extend your list of task statements describing the target job of student.)
2. Organize your approach. (You will use a guided interview format with a set of standard questions. You are fortunate that you do not have to worry about scheduling your interviews, since all your job experts are readily available.)
3. Plan the methods to be used. (You will manually record answers on the interview form.)

Interviewing a job incumbent (one of your fellow students): Begin with a brief statement describing the purpose of your interview. Ask the person to think about the most recent complete work day (school day) and to describe what she or he did from the start of the day to the end of it. Ask for more information any time a task is unclear. When the description is complete, ask for other tasks that are normally done but were not part of the most recent day's work. Finally, ask the questions at the end of the interview form.

Interviewing a supervisor: Ask the supervisor (your instructor) to describe a typical working day for a student under his or her direct supervision. Have your instructor describe the tasks that might come up at other times. Ask the questions at the end of the interview form to complete the task description.

Step 5: Defining the job duties.

Finally, have your group review the task statements and functional groupings of task statements to develop names and definitions for job duties. Work to ensure that your statements summarize the key job tasks and outcomes that were identified for each job duty.

Job Analysis Interview Format

Job title:
Location:
Reports to what job:
Summary descriptive statement:
Daily routine tasks:
Special tasks:
Number and type of jobs supervised directly:
How frequent is contact with:
    Superiors:
    Other departments:
    Outsiders:
Associated with what other jobs:
What are some similarities with other jobs:
Main duties and responsibilities:
Less frequent duties:
In what ways is this job unique:
What is the most difficult task in this job:
To what extent is this job structured:
What is the scope of authority in:
Other comments:

Defining Job Duties

Duty:
Description:

Duty:
Description:

Exercise 4.2

Understanding the Whole Job

At the beginning of this chapter we defined the different categories that are used in job analysis. To make this real, pick a job with which you are familiar (for example, one that you or a family member has held). Using your knowledge, fill in as many of the categories as you can. Then go to the reference section of a library and read the descriptions of the job in the *Dictionary of Occupational Titles* and the *Occupational Outlook Handbook*. Use this information to extend your worksheet.

Next, use the subject catalogue to search for books about the job. Check these for additional information. Once you have completed this background work, seek out someone who holds the job you selected and interview that person. Add the information he or she provides.

Once your analysis is complete, meet with other students and discuss the job you analyzed and how the different levels of analysis provide different perspectives on the job and its nature. Which perspective is the most meaningful? Why? Which one is the least useful? Why?

Job Analysis Worksheet

Date of analysis:
Job analyst:
Organization:
Occupation:
Job:
Position analyzed:
Related positions:
Duties:
Tasks:
Elements:
Elemental motions:

REFERENCES

Albemarle Paper Co. v. Moody (1975). 422 U.S. 405.

American Educational Research Association, American Psychological Association, & National Council on Measurement in Education (1985). *Standards for educational and psychological testing.* Washington, DC: American Psychological Association.

Ash, R. A., & Edgell, S. L. (1975). A note on the readability of the Position Analysis Questionnaire (PAQ). *Journal of Applied Psychology, 60,* 765–766.

Borman, W. C. (1983). Implications of personality theory and research for the rating of work performance in organizations. In F. Landy, S. Zedeck, & J. Cleveland (Eds.), *Performance measurement and theory.* Hillsdale, NJ: Erlbaum.

Borman, W. C. (1987). Personal constructs, performance schemata, and "folk theories" of subordinate effectiveness: Exploration in an army officer sample. *Organizational Behavior and Human Decision Processes, 40,* 307–322.

Christal, R. E. (1974). The United States Air Force occupational research project (AFHRL-TR-73-75). Lackland AFB, TX: Air Force Human Resources Laboratory, Occupational Research Division.

Cornelius, E. T., Carron, T. J., & Collins, M. N. (1979). Job analysis models and job classification. *Personnel Psychology, 32,* 693–708.

Cunningham, J. W., Boese, R. R., Neeb, R. W., & Pass, J. J. (1983). Systematically derived work dimensions: Factor analyses of the Occupational Analysis Inventory. *Journal of Applied Psychology, 68,* 232–252.

Cunningham, J. W., Tuttle, T. C., Floyd, J. R., & Bates, S. A. (1971). *The development of the Occupational Analysis Inventory: An "ergometric" approach to an educational problem.* Center for Occupational Education, Center Research Monograph No. 6. Raleigh, NC: North Carolina State U.

Fine, S. A. (1989). *Functional job analysis scales: A desk aid.* Milwaukee, WI: Sidney A. Fine.

Fine, S. A. (1992). *Seminar on Functional Job Analysis (FJA).* Presented as a professional development program under the auspices of the Wisconsin Psychological Association, Division Two, Milwaukee, WI.

Fine, S. A., & Getkate, M. (1995). *Benchmark tasks for job analysis: A guide for functional job analysis (FJA) scales.* Mahwah, NJ: Lawrence Erlbaum Associates.

Flanagan, J. C. (1954). The critical incident technique. *Psychological Bulletin, 51,* 327–338.

Griggs v. *Duke Power Co.* (1971). 402 US 424.

Harvey, R. J. (1988, April). Does the choice of worker-verses task-oriented job analysis data influence job classification results? In R. J. Harvey (Chair), *Troublesome questions in job analysis.* Symposium presented at the annual conference of the Society for Industrial and Organizational Psychology, Dallas.

Harvey, R. J. (1990). *The common-metric questionnaire for the analysis and evaluation of jobs* (field test version 1.12). San Antonio, TX: The Psychological Corporation.

Harvey, R. J. (1991). Job analysis. In Dunnette, M. D., & Hough, L. M. (Eds.), *Handbook of industrial and organizational psychology* (2nd Ed., Vol. 2). Palo Alto, CA: Consulting Psychologists Press.

Ilgen, D. R. & Hollenbeck, J. R. (1991). The structure of work: Job design and roles. In Dunnette, M. D., & Hough, L. M. (Eds.), *Handbook of Industrial and Organizational Psychology* (2nd Ed., Vol. 2). Palo Alto, CA: Consulting Psychologists Press.

Lopez, F. M., Kesselman, G. A., & Lopez, F. E. (1981). An empirical test of a trait-oriented job analysis technique. *Personnel Psychology, 34,* 479–502.

McCormick, E. J. (1979). *Job analysis: Methods and applications.* New York, NY: AMACOM.

McCormick, E. J., Jeanneret, P. R., & Mecham, R. C. (1969). *Position analysis questionnaire.* West Lafayette, IN: Occupational Research Center, Purdue University.

McCormick, E. J., Jeanneret, P. R., & Mecham, R. C. (1972). A study of job characteristics and job dimensions as based on the Position Analysis Questionnaire (PAQ). *Journal of Applied Psychology, 56,* 347–367.

Melching, W. H., & Borcher, S. D. (1973). *Procedures for constructing and using task inventories.* Center for Vocational and Technical Education, Research and Development Series No. 91. Columbus, OH: Ohio State University.

Mitchell, J. L., & McCormick, E. J. (1979). *Development of the PMPQ: A structured job analysis questionnaire for the study of professional and managerial positions* (Report No. 1). West Lafayette, IN: Occupational Research Center, Department of Psychological Studies, Purdue University.

Murphy, K. R., & Cleveland, J. N. (1991). *Performance appraisal: An organizational perspective.* Boston, MA: Allyn and Bacon.

Schmidt, F. L., & Hunter, J. E. (1981). Employment testing: Old theories and new research findings. *American Psychologist, 66,* 166–185.

Society for Industrial and Organizational Psychology, Inc. (1987). *Principles for the validation and use of personnel selection procedures* (3rd ed.). College Park, MD: Author.

Uniform guidelines on employee selection procedures (1978). *Federal Register, 43,* 38290–38315.

U.S. Department of Labor, Manpower Administration. (1972). *Handbook for analyzing jobs.* Washington, DC: U.S. Government Printing Office.

U.S. Department of Labor. (1977). *Dictionary of occupational titles* (4th ed.). Washington, DC: U.S. Government Printing Office.

U.S. Employment Service. (1939). *Dictionary of occupational titles* (Vols. I and II). Washington, DC: U.S. Government Printing Office.

U.S. Employment Service. (1947). *Dictionary of occupational titles* (2nd ed.). Washington, DC: U.S. Government Printing Office.

U.S. Employment Service. (1965). *Dictionary of occupational titles* (3rd ed.). Washington, DC: U.S. Government Printing Office.

Criteria

A journeyman is teaching an apprentice how to run a milling machine. She uses a knowledge test provided by the machine's manufacturer and an on-the-job operational evaluation. The exam covers basic knowledge of the machine and its capabilities as presented in the operator's manual, basic operation controls learned from hands-on experience, and special emergency procedures. As she compiles the test, the criterion she uses is mastery of milling machine setup and operation learned by apprentices. As the journeyman chooses test questions and operations, she has a picture in her mind of what she means by "mastery." When apprentices are successful—according to the instructor's vision of mastery, as communicated in the exam content—the assumption is that they have learned the material well and have mastered the operation of the milling machine. The problem arises when we ask how we know that the exam provides an accurate indication of the apprentice's mastery of milling machine operation. This is further complicated when we include multiple journeymen acting as instructors.

Let us say that two apprentices are learning milling machine operations, working simultaneously, each with a different journeyman instructor. Although the instructors are using the same operator's manual and machines to teach the apprentices, their on-the-job operation exams could be quite different. One journeyman's criteria for successfully learning the material might include the ability to understand various programs, to run standard parts easily and with little scrap, and to be able to describe emergency procedures. This journeyman requires that the apprentice demonstrate effective basic milling machine operation. The other journeyman's criteria might include reading the operator's manual carefully, being able to answer technical questions about the milling machine and its many capabilities, and accurately performing complicated machining functions. This instructor requires that the apprentice demonstrate sophisticated control of the milling machine. Each journeyman believes that his or her exam "best" measures an apprentice's learning. This example illustrates why industrial/organizational psychologists call issues concerning criteria, or measures of how well people perform on the job, the **criterion problem.**

In Chapter 4 we saw that a primary function of job analysis is to establish relevant measures of job performance. Job performance and success are indicators against which we can measure successful work behavior. These indicators of performance are developed during job analysis and provide the essential data that are needed to design selection techniques, training programs, job evaluation, and performance appraisals. In this chapter we will discuss the criterion construct, how it is developed, requirements for criteria, types of criteria, and how criteria are used to predict successful performance in the workplace.

DEFINING THE CRITERION CONSTRUCT

Although there is no single definition of **criterion,** it is best understood as an evaluative standard. The plural of criterion is "criteria." "Job-relevant criteria are the measures of how well people 'do,' identified and chosen by understanding the organization's needs and the duties and responsibilities of the job" (Guion, 1991, p. 333). Therefore, criteria are tools that organizations use to establish levels of individual performance in comparison to other members of the same group. Austin and Villanova (1992, p. 838) offered a practical definition of a criterion: "A criterion is a sample of performance (including behavior and outcomes), measured directly or indirectly, perceived to be of value to organizational constituencies for facilitating decisions about predictors or programs."

A criterion for a sales job at an automobile dealership might be the number of cars sold per month, the amount of money each salesperson earns for the dealership by selling cars, or the commission earned by each salesperson. Deciding which criterion to use for an assessment of effective sales will depend on the organization's needs and obligations and the specific purpose of the assessment. For example, let us suppose that the owners of an automobile dealership have made it clear to the car lot supervisor that high car sales result in increased profit. Because increased profit is the desired effect, the owners want the supervisor to hire and retain productive salespeople who will sell many cars. To apply this example to Austin and Villanova's definition, the **sample of performance** is the actual number of cars sold. The behavior is the communication skills that the salesperson applies during the sale. The outcome is the money brought to the business from the sale of automobiles. The sale of the car is of value to the organizational goals. The predictors could be the methods the business will use to hire high-performance salespeople, and the programs could be an incentive program to retain desirable performers. Establishing criteria is at the heart of making sound decisions about what is "good" and what is merely "satisfactory"—and how to gauge the difference.

Immediate, Proximal, and Distal Criteria

Now that we have established several definitions of criterion, we will address time and its impact on criteria. Tests that are used to predict performance are constricted by time factors (Blum & Naylor, 1968). Performance that a particular organization views as desirable today may not be desirable two or ten years later, due to the fluid nature of today's industries. The terms *immediate criteria, proximal criteria*, and *distal criteria* were introduced to address these concerns.

Measurements of criteria that are recorded concurrently with the predictive test are called **immediate criteria.** An example of an immediate criterion is administering a criterion-referenced test to an organization's workers. The criterion-referenced test measures an individual's specific skills or knowledge about a particular area. Measures of the employees' current performance that are assessed at the time of testing can then be immediately correlated with test scores. Measures of performance obtained near the time (but not at the *same* time) when the predictive test is given are called **proximal criteria.** Proximal criteria usually are obtained up to one year after the test date. Finally, **distal criteria** are measures of performance that will occur at some time in the distant future (over one year from the date of the prediction). Criteria can be dynamic and ever-changing. What the organization finds valuable today may become trivial or irrelevant later. Ghiselli's (1956) landmark article described the "dimensional problems of criteria" (p. 1). Ghiselli posits that performance measures should be reviewed after a considerable amount of time has passed, because a criterion is a dynamically evolving phenomenon. For example, as workers in the organization gain experience, they can become more proficient, stronger performers. This poses a problem for those psychologists who have seen criteria as being fixed, definable targets for performance.

Hofmann, Jacobs, and Baratta (1993) supported the argument that criteria are dynamic and that some individuals increase output (and therefore display improved performance) over time. They also theorized that raters, too, may change over time, making the issue even more complex. These elements of criterion will be addressed in more depth in the sections on composite criteria and multiple criteria.

Actual and Ultimate Criteria

As was previously noted, the definition of individual success always relies on individuals' conceptions. A criterion is an attempt to define the underlying characteristics of successful performance that can be established through observations of behavior. Each of us has a mental image of what it means to be a "successful worker" or a "good student." These subjective conceptions are theoretical definitions of success; they are ideal abstractions of what ultimately constitutes success for a particular job. Thus, an **ultimate criterion** is "in theory, a true measure of the degree of job success or 'satisfactoriness' of an employee at any situation at any moment in time" (Blum & Naylor, 1968, p. 176).

This ultimate criterion incorporates the various ideal notions existing in the mind of the psychologist, employer, or teacher. For example, the underlying characteristics of what constitute the concept of a "good student" are: involvement in school activities, good reputation among teachers and faculty, perfect attendance, and working knowledge of the material. All of these are components of a theoretical abstraction and subjective definition of success as a student.

The ultimate criterion is an ideal notion, thus we need to develop quantifiable measures that we can actually use to assess these ideals. These are the **actual criterion** measures. The actual criteria to assess the performance of a student might be: ratings by teachers and faculty to measure involvement in school activities, number of classes missed, tests for acquisition of knowledge, and grades. The actual criteria need to represent some of the ideal notions of the ultimate criteria. The purpose of using the actual criteria "is to obtain an approximate estimate of this ultimate criterion by selecting one or more actual criteria which we think is appropriate" (Blum & Naylor, 1968, p. 176). While the actual criteria may account for a large part of the performance defined by the ultimate criterion, they will never account for 100% of it (see Figure 5.1). This occurs in part because of errors in measurement and in part because we can never be 100% sure we have included every factor that may influence the ultimate criterion.

As the actual criterion overlaps the ultimate criterion, their intersection becomes *criterion relevance*. The more the actual (measurable) criterion represents the ultimate (construct) criterion, the larger the area of criterion relevance. Rele-

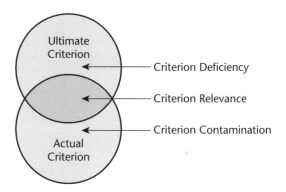

FIGURE 5.1   Criterion construct including deficiency, relevance, and contamination.

Source: From M. L. Blum and J. C. Naylor (1968). *Industrial Psychology: Its Theoretical and Social Foundations,* Revised Edition (p. 177). New York: Harper & Row. Copyright © 1968 by M. L. Blum and J. C. Naylor. Reprinted by permission of HarperCollins Publishers, Inc.

vance refers to the degree to which the measurable criterion accurately represents the construct of successful performance.

Examples of the relationship between the actual criterion and the ultimate criterion can be developed in many ways. Ultimate criteria for a highly productive, and therefore desirable, factory worker might include such characteristics as the following:

1. high level of effort
2. safety
3. commitment to work

Actual criteria for a highly productive factory worker that represent each of the conceptual, or ultimate, criteria might be the following:

1. number of products above the norm set by management
2. no documented accidents
3. zero absenteeism

Although each of the actual criteria seems to be a good representation of the ultimate criteria, a perfect match is practically impossible. This is because we cannot directly define constructs such as "high level of effort." On the other hand, we can attempt to define such abstractions by identifying their ingredients. Take, for instance, the construct of safety. A low incidence of accidents seems to be a good indication of a "safe worker" but cannot account for all of the variables that contribute to being a safe worker. Variables such as attitudes, skills, and experience all contribute to a worker being safe on the job. The part of the ultimate criterion that is not accounted for by the actual criterion is referred to as *criterion deficiency*. A criterion measure that is included in our list of actual criteria, but does not measure performance that is part of the ultimate criteria, is termed a *contaminant*. Its influence on our measure of the ultimate criterion is called *criterion contamination*. For example, attendance at work could relate to the number of accidents; a worker who was often absent could have a lower accident rate. It would be a mistake, however, to include a measure of attendance in our measures of safety because we are interested in on-the-job performance.

In the well-known article "Criteria for What?" Wallace (1965) explained that criteria should be developed to increase understanding of the reasons individuals perform at the levels they do. In other words, criteria should be based not solely on data or other information the company has on hand, but on true estimates of performance. Although it may be easier, quicker, and seemingly adequate to use existing data, such information may be incomplete or not relevant. The question we must ask ourselves is: Are the data relevant estimates or inferences of performance?

Criterion Deficiency, Relevance, and Contamination

Criterion deficiency is the area in the ultimate criterion that is not accounted for by the actual criterion (see Figure 5.1). It is impossible to eliminate criterion deficiency; there is always some part of the ultimate criterion that cannot be directly represented. As was mentioned previously,

this is partly because we cannot truly define constructs. If it were possible to quantify the ultimate criterion, criterion deficiency could perhaps be eliminated. Because this is impossible, we are restrained to improving existing strategies. Returning to our example of the safe factory worker, we must ask ourselves how much of the ultimate criterion of "works safely" was accounted for by the number of reported accidents. Surely, there is more to being a safe worker than merely avoiding reporting an accident. Issues such as what constitutes a reportable injury must be addressed if we want to truly represent the construct of safety. As was stated earlier, other hard-to-measure variables come into play that alter our measurements and contribute to criterion deficiency.

Criterion relevance is the fit, or overlap, between ultimate criterion and actual criterion (see Figure 5.1). In our example of the factory worker, the overlap between a high level of effort invested (ultimate criterion) and "produces above the norm" (actual criterion) is the degree of criterion relevance. Relevance is the degree of validity of the actual criterion. A constraint such as the condition and age of the tools or facilities may inhibit the number of products made by the employee, which would contribute to criterion deficiency.

As Figure 5.1 shows, **criterion contamination** involves aspects of the actual criterion that are not representative of the ultimate criterion but are used as attributes of the construct. Criterion contamination is caused by two factors: error and bias. **Error** occurs when the actual criterion is not correlated to any part of the ultimate criterion. Error is a random contamination. **Bias** is the systematic measurement of something other than the ultimate criterion. Both criterion deficiency and contamination are undesirable outcomes. Error lowers the correlation between the ultimate and actual criterion; bias falsely shows a fit while actually measuring something completely different. Criterion contamination differs from criterion deficiency in that contamination refers to data collected that are not representative of the construct, while criterion deficiency is the variance of ultimate criterion not accounted for by actual criterion. Criterion relevance, on the other hand, is desirable and is an important standard in industrial/organizational psychology. Criterion measures should cover as many elements as possible that are *relevant* to an individual's job (Borman, 1991).

....
CRITERIA DEVELOPMENT

The next step in developing a criterion construct is to identify relevant criteria. Nagle (1953) offered a four-step process for criterion development:

1. *Define the problem.* Defining the problem involves deciding which behavior(s) we want to assess. Each particular behavior must be distinguished through a job analysis to identify the elements that contribute to successful job performance. An example of defining a problem in a metal machine shop might be to decide that the activities of drilling and tapping steel parts are valuable to the organization.

2. *Conduct an activity analysis.* Activity analysis describes the specific behaviors that workers engage in on the job. This process can be divided into several parts. For example, the first part describes the purpose of the activity: to establish the reasons and goals of individual behavior. The machinist's behaviors on the job take place to produce drilled and tapped products. The second part makes up a description of these behaviors. This is achieved by a job analyst who describes what the person does to complete the job tasks. The third part, definition of success, is accomplished by identifying the job behaviors that indicate successful performance. This allows the organization to set levels concerning what the company views as success. The fourth part of the activity analysis, subcriteria, assigns levels of importance to each of the job activities. In other words, of all the behaviors the workers exhibit during their shift, setting subcriteria delineates which ones are the most crucial for completing the task at hand. If you are thinking that an activity analysis sounds much like a job analysis, you are correct. The implementation of a well-designed job analysis would be an acceptable way to conduct an activity analysis (Nagle, 1953).

3. *Create a definition of success.* This stage is similar to the third part of the activity analysis in that the I/O psychologist must propose a list of the behaviors that are most related to being successful on the job. At this step we can compare the different behaviors exhibited by workers that result in some workers being successful and others being unsuccessful. Once successful behaviors are defined, the next step is to assign a weight to each behavior in terms of its importance to overall task completion. This will be discussed more completely in the section on multiple and composite criteria.

4. *Develop subcriteria to measure each element of success.* Subcriteria are the individual measures of performance that we will use to define success. Examples of subcriteria for a successful assembly worker might be the quantity of production (measured by number of units produced), commitment (measured by days not absent from work), and safety (measured by the number of accidents reported). If our organizational definition of success is "produces a large number of products," each subcriterion can be carefully weighted to determine how it is related to overall successful performance. This process can provide the job analyst with an understanding of the meaning of successful performance as defined by a particular organization.

Criterion development is often completed in conjunction with a job analysis. This is because a job analysis provides the data for establishing the criteria. As was discussed in Chapter 4, job

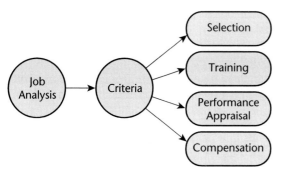

FIGURE 5.2   Criteria development and its future functions.

analysis is conducted by a job analyst to gain an understanding of the skills and traits an individual should possess to be successful on the job. As depicted in Figure 5.2, different criteria are selected for different purposes. Perhaps the most common purpose is selection. Criteria are often defined to specify elements the organization should include in their training programs. A third important use for criteria is to set areas and standards for performance appraisal. Closely related to this are questions about the worth of a particular job to the organization and issues of compensation. All issues of performance and criteria are interconnected. If an inadequate job analysis is conducted, it is unlikely we will obtain relevant criteria. Similarly, if irrelevant criteria are developed, their negative effect will be seen in subsequent programs and policy. The methods, procedures, policies, and implications of job analysis were discussed in Chapter 4.

TYPES OF CRITERIA

There are basically two types of performance criteria: objective criteria and subjective criteria. Objective criteria consist of empirical data collected by an organization. In other words, the data consist of information that is quantifiable. Data such as number of goods produced, amount of sales generated, or number of years on

the job are examples of objective criteria. Subjective criteria are data based on subjective assessment of an employee's performance. An example of a subjective criterion is supervisors' ratings of their employees' performance. In the following section we discuss objective and subjective criteria in more detail.

Measures of Objective Criteria

Objective criteria are measures of job performance that can be observed relatively free of subjective bias. Guion (1965, 1991) divided objective criteria into two major categories: production data and personnel data. Production data include measures such as amount of sales and amount of production. Personnel data include objective criteria such as turnover, absenteeism, and number of accidents.

Production

A common method of assessing performance criteria is to review records of employee production rates. These data provide the employer with information about how many units each worker produces on a daily basis. By itself this information is useless. However, if we compare individual production rates among similar employees, the figure becomes meaningful. Deadrick and Madigan (1990) used production data, or output, as a measure of performance in their research on performance stability in the garment industry. Because garment makers are compensated according to a piece rate (they are paid for each product completed), a measurement such as number of garments produced by an individual is valuable. If the daily average for dress makers in the organization is twenty dresses per day, we could conclude that an individual who produces twenty-five dresses per day is a high-performer. That is, provided that the products are free from defect.

Although production rates are a popular way to gauge performance, they are not free of bias. Vinchur, Schippmann, Smalley, and Rothe (1991) used estimates of productivity to assess the relationship between levels of performance and an incentive system. The employees who were included in this study performed tasks that were considered "heavy and non-repetitive and involved the use of such tools as air driven grinders, hammers, and chisels to clean large castings" (p. 134). This type of work differs from assembly-line work such as that at an automotive plant. Each individual working on the assembly line can produce up to the number of products allowed by the rate of the assembly line. Assembly-line work provides an example of how output measures can be contaminated. Guion (1991) indicated that output measures could be influenced by the quality of tools and material; accidents and fatigue could determine consistency of output; and other aspects of behavior (e.g., helping others) could affect production measures.

Sink and Tuttle (1989) broadened the concept of productivity to include more than simply output. In their conceptualization, it is the *combination* of inputs and outputs that yields productivity (input/output = productivity). Inputs are described as efficiency, meaning the highly capable use of energy, time, money, and other inputs. Effectiveness involves the actual production (output) of results fulfilling an intention. Combining effectiveness with efficiency gives productivity. In contrast to many measures of productivity, Sink and Tuttle's definition extends the domain to include suppliers and customers as well as production workers.

Other issues that can inhibit production rates as an indication of performance are: type of products made, the company's location, years on the job, and age of the company's facilities. For instance, if one company produces multiple products, problems would surely develop if we attempted to assess them in a unitary manner. A plastic-molding company might make yo-yos and airplane interiors simultaneously. The employees producing the yo-yos will produce a higher number of products than will the employees making large components of air-

plane interiors. In this case a **norm-based evaluation** system should be used. Norm-based assessment allows the airplane interior producers (who may produce twenty complete interiors per day) to be compared only to other airline interior producers within the organization. Another variable is the location and age of the company's production plant. A facility that was built fifty years ago will probably be filled with older machines that have slower rate capacities than those in a modern, updated facility. In this example, if the production rates of two employees from two different facilities were compared, an error could be made if the production potential of one of the workers was limited by inferior equipment. The amount of time an employee has been on the job can also result in misleading production rates. Employees with more seniority often get the better machines (and jobs). This, in turn, leads to the appearance of better production. In conclusion, even seemingly objective measures of job performance are not entirely free of bias. The human factor and the time factor constantly change the dynamic structure of criteria.

Quality

A popular formula that includes quality in the assessment of production is: Quantity of goods produced – Quantity of goods returned to the department due to defects = Number of acceptable goods per worker. Dr. Joseph Juran, a total quality management guru, defines and teaches how to create customer-oriented organizational systems. He points out that quality is an important factor because it is the customer's ultimate concern. Juran recognizes that it is the user who is really the focus in total quality management, not some abstract ideal of quality. Quality as an objective criterion can be understood by thinking of manufacturing or service delivery as a flow process. Much as small streams combine to feed water to a river, suppliers and vendors provide various information and/or materials. These move into and through the production process and are transformed into finished services or products. Further downstream in the manufacturing process, the finished goods are delivered to clients or customers, who use them. There are five specific points at which quality can be objectively checked or measured (Sashkin & Kiser, 1993, p. 59):

> First and most important, quality can be identified by whether and how well a product or service meets customers' needs and desires when in actual use. This is the first quality checkpoint. Far more common, quality is checked by final inspection of the product or service on completion. Final inspection prior to customer delivery or use is the second quality checkpoint. The third checkpoint involves the actual production or service delivery process. Statistical process control [was] designed to assess quality in the process of production and service delivery.
>
> The quality of the raw materials that are transformed into a product or service can be examined and assessed when the materials are delivered by suppliers and vendors. This is quality checkpoint four. Finally, one can go to suppliers and examine how they produce the materials they provide, to assess the quality control they exercise. This is quality checkpoint five.

Job Level

Another form of objective criteria is the job level an individual has achieved. The premise is that an individual who has progressed through the organization and achieved promotions and increased job responsibilities is a successful employee. This could be a valid way to plot achievement and success in an organization that has many levels and positions. On the other hand, organizations that lack such complex inner structures could not provide such data. Another problem with using information about job level is that there is no way to measure whether individuals who were promoted truly deserved it. This is also true of individuals who were passed over for promotion. Subjective input in the or-

ganization's promotional and career advancement process may be involved. This might occur, for example, in a retail business.

Let us use the example of a shoe store. The manager has a position opening up for "senior floor salesperson," which must be filled within the week. Two salespeople in the department are candidates for the promotion. Candidate A is John, a 45-year-old man who has been employed by the shoe company for five years. John has a reputation at the store as a good worker and a family man. Candidate B is Sandy, a 23-year-old woman who, although she has been with the store only a year, has increased sales by 40%. Faced with making a fast decision, the manager decides to give John the promotion, based on his tenure with the organization and knowledge of the job. Although Sandy is performing at a higher production level than John, she is passed over for promotion because of other factors. As this example demonstrates, job level as a form of objective criterion should be used with caution.

Sales

Sales volume is another criterion for gauging performance. Sales figures are easy to access because most organizations keep track of such statistics. Sales figures can be very useful if the employee being assessed is from the same area and is selling the same product. Using the shoe store example, if the branch manager reviewed sales records of all employees to assess their success on the job, Sandy would be the highest performer and the best candidate for promotion. As with measures of production and job level, data on sales should also be interpreted with caution. The sales records of individual employees should be compared only with the records of other sales personnel in the same area or region. Imagine, for example, two snowmobile dealerships, one in northern Wisconsin and the other in southern Illinois. Although all the salespeople are selling the same product, the salespeople in northern Wisconsin are likely to sell more snowmobiles because there is usually more snowfall in Wisconsin. Another restriction that should be placed on sales information is that only salespeople who sell the same product should be compared. For example, a sporting goods company may sell equipment at many different price levels. The salespeople in the part of the store selling golf clubs and related equipment will achieve higher sales figures than will the salespeople in the skateboard and roller-blade department. This is because golf-related products are usually considerably more expensive than skating equipment. Using sales figures as a performance measure is a popular way to define sales as an objective criterion, but overgeneralization and misuse should be taken into account.

Salary

Salary, or pay level, is another objective measure. Although salary may be a useful way to pinpoint high achievers within a group, it cannot be generalized across groups. In other words, because each group of employees has a different pay rate, it would be invalid to compare across groups. An example of this could occur at the shoe store. Sandy, the highly successful salesperson, seems to work very hard on the job, as indicated by her sales figures. Herb, her supervisor and store manager, does not seem to work as hard on his job, but he makes more money than Sandy. Herb's job as the manager is not as physically demanding as Sandy's job, but it is viewed as more important to the company's goals. If the organization is interested in successful performance based on pay rates, pay levels must be separated by job types before the organization can reach any conclusions. If the company compares Sandy's pay rate (including commissions earned from sales) with that of other sales people, a different picture will appear. Specifically, Sandy would probably be considered a top performer. We could also compare Herb's salary with other store managers' salaries within the organization. While Sandy may be at the top of her pay rate, Herb might be making only average pay when compared to his organizational peers.

Some psychologists argue that salary should not be used as a criterion measure. They point out that in most situations the use of salary is contaminated because criteria are used for performance appraisals, which, in turn, are used to determine salaries. Because of this circularity, salary is being used less often as a criterion. We believe that salary should not be used as a criterion in most situations. If it is used, all relevant factors should be taken into consideration, such as group- or norm-referenced criteria (i.e., managers compared only with managers, salespeople compared only with salespeople).

The previous types of objective criteria—production, job level, sales, and salary—are all forms of production data. As was noted earlier, personnel data such as turnover, absenteeism, and accidents are also objective measures of performance criteria. As with production data, personnel data provide numerical information about employees that can be obtained by organizations in an efficient and cost-effective manner.

Turnover

One type of objective criterion that many organizations use is turnover. **Turnover** describes the voluntary or involuntary action of an employee who is leaving the company. Turnover is actually a measure of nonperformance, because when an employee is leaving the organization for any reason, he or she is no longer performing in the organization. Tenure is the opposite of turnover, involving the individual who stays with, or is retained by, the organization. Research on turnover and tenure has been an important part of industrial/organizational psychology over the past thirty years (Campion, 1991).

Having low turnover figures is an important goal for organizations. This is primarily because companies invest significant amounts of time and money in employee selection and training. When employees leave the organization, this investment is lost. Turnover becomes especially expensive for companies that have highly sophisticated training programs. Research shows that there is no single reason for turnover; it is usually the result of multiple factors. Lee and Mitchell (1994, p. 84) provide an interesting and comprehensive list in which turnover is defined as "a complex process whereby individuals assess their feelings, personal situation, and work environment and, over time, make decisions about staying or leaving an organization." This list of reasons for turnover includes the following suggestions (Lee & Mitchell, 1994, pp. 84–85):

1. The existing models of employee turnover are too simple; leaving an organization can take place in many different ways.
2. One of the major precipitating events for employee turnover is shock to the system—an event that prompts an individual to evaluate his or her current job and perhaps compare it to other jobs.
3. Shocks are not just negative job-related factors; positive and neutral events that are both job and nonjob-related can prompt mental deliberations about leaving.
4. In some cases, employees simply leave because the shock results in scripted behavior (i.e., behavior where no extensive cognition deliberations that evaluate the current or alternative jobs take place).
5. Some employees leave organizations without considering alternatives; their central choice is to stay or leave their present company—not to quit for another organization.
6. In most cases employees make decisions about staying or leaving an organization based on fit or compatibility criterion, rather than on maximizing their subjective expected utilities.
7. Employee turnover occurs over time; only by developing methods that assess how the process evolves will researchers and managers understand why individuals chose to leave.

The conclusion is that there are multiple reasons for employee turnover. Some researchers have adopted statistical procedures to further understand the nature of turnover. Kemery,

Dunlap, and Bedejan (1989) use the product-moment correlation (see the Chapter 2 Appendix) to study the prediction–criterion relationship when plotting tenure as the criterion of interest. Finding the relationship between prediction tools (such as selection tests) and turnover might enable organizations to hire the individuals who are most likely to stay with the company. Turnover is an important element for any organization to address. After all, a company with 99% retention and 1% turnover reflects a high level of job security for tenured employees. Finding a good fit between the individual and the company can benefit the person as well.

Absenteeism

Another objective measure of performance is the rate of absenteeism. **Absenteeism** occurs when employees fail to come to work. Absenteeism is harmful to the company primarily because the employee is not at the job site performing his or her duties. Another consequence of absenteeism is that it may lead to employees leaving the company, because of their own actions or actions taken against them by the company. Mitra, Jenkins, and Gupta (1992) found a positive relationship between absenteeism and turnover ($r = .29$ to $r = .36$) in their meta-analysis study. Various reasons were found to account for these behaviors, including family illness. Fichman (1989) researched work attendance rates of coal miners, and classified absences into three categories (p. 327):

1. Voluntary absences: absences categorized as discretionary or contract days, discretionary holidays, graduated vacation days, and miscellaneous paid absences. All of these absences were paid. These were not paid sick days, because the category below provided for sick days.
2. Semivoluntary absences: absences categorized as excused unpaid and unexcused unpaid. All were unpaid. Although these may reflect some volition, they clearly cost

the individual more, making them less desirable.

3. Involuntary absences: absences categorized as on-the-job injuries, illnesses, wildcat strikes, and off-the-job injury. These absences were compensated in varying degrees. Unlike semivoluntary absences, they are not voluntary.

Employees give various reasons for not being able to come to work. Many cite family obligations or illness. Reasons for making it to work are also diverse. Hackett, Bycio, and Guion (1989) conducted a study on absenteeism among a sample of nurses working at two metropolitan hospitals. They administered questionnaires concerning the nurses' work-related attitudes, values, and personal stressors. The data in Table 5.1 show the reasons given by the nurses for both missing and attending work.

The large amount of research conducted on absenteeism indicates that understanding why people miss work is an important issue for industrial psychologists and personnel administrators alike. Organizations strive to predict which employees will have a high rate of absenteeism and which employees will never miss work without an excused leave of absence. This prediction is important enough for Harrison and Hulin (1989, p. 314) to suggest that "traditional regression and correlational analyses can generate moderately successful predictions, especially if last year's absence total is included as a predictor."

Other Objective Personnel Criteria

Four other types of objective criteria that can be obtained from personnel records are safety (accident) records, employee theft records, employee suggestions (innovation), and customer satisfaction. While keeping the numbers of reported accidents low is an important goal for an organization, getting realistic data is not an easy task. Smith (1976) noted that although accident figures are important to companies for humani-

tarian and economic reasons, they may not accurately measure the true number of accidents. An example of this is a safety incentive program initiated by a mining company to reduce the high costs of employees collecting workmen's compensation because of accidents.

The program worked like this: The work year was divided into four quarters. Employees who had no reported injuries in a given quarter were given a gift that had an estimated value of fifty dollars. Employees who were eligible to participate in the program were sorted into groups by job class. For example, truck drivers were grouped together, as were machine operators, laborers, and so on. The key to the incentive program was that to be eligible for the safety award, every member in a group must not have reported any injuries while on the job. If one member of the group reported an injury, the entire group was ineligible for the award. The result could be biased safety records. Injured employees might feel guilty about messing it up for everyone and decide not to file an injury report, especially if the injury was slight. Employees might also pressure each other not to report injuries. Although such a safety program might decrease reported injuries, thus lowering the cost of paying for injured workers, the program could also adversely affect the organization's humanitarian efforts and measurements of performance.

Another objective representation of personnel data is employee theft records. Like safety records, these are difficult, probably impossible, to validate. Although an employee may get caught stealing large sums of money or products, businesses suffer significant losses each year due to small-scale stealing. Employee theft is the most unstable measure of objective criteria.

Some investigators (Harris, 1987; Wigdor & Green, 1986) have used hands-on work samples as objective criteria. While such measures have been commonly used as predictors, their use as criteria is rare but has some important advantages. Hands-on samples reduce contamination due to factors such as production demands,

TABLE 5.1   Frequency of Nurses' Stated Reasons for Absence and Attendance*

Reasons for Absence	General Hospital	Children's Hospital	Reasons for Attendance	General Hospital	Children's Hospital
Minor illness (self)	24 (25)	28 (20)	Responsibility to co-workers	26 (28)	40 (38)
Mental health day	23 (22)	27 (19)	Guilt	12 (13)	9 (8)
Illness in the family	13 (13)	12 (9)	Loss of pay	8 (9)	9 (8)
Family social function	9 (8)	17 (12)	Avoid confrontation	8 (9)	5 (5)
Work to do at home	5 (5)	5 (3)	Responsibility to patients	6 (7)	3 (3)
Emotional problems	4 (4)	5 (3)	Unethical–dishonest	5 (6)	2 (2)
School work to do	3 (3)	3 (2)	Work left undone	3 (3)	5 (5)
Bereavement	3 (3)	8 (6)	Recently absent a lot	3 (3)	1 (1)
Physical fatigue	3 (3)		Peer pressure	3 (3)	2 (2)
Professional appointments	2 (3)	1 (1)	Not sick enough	2 (2)	
Obnoxious patients	1 (1)	1 (1)	Feel better at work	2 (2)	1 (1)
Hangover–partying late	1 (1)	8 (6)	Family pressure	2 (2)	
Frustrated with work	1 (1)	4 (3)	Save for legitimate reason	2 (2)	6 (6)
Snow storm–weather	1 (1)	2 (1)	Avoid calling in sick	2 (2)	
Misread time sheet	1 (1)		No one to do my job	2 (2)	1 (1)
Bought a house–moving	1 (1)	1 (1)	Given an enjoyable task	2 (2)	2 (2)
Nice day	1 (1)		Avoid health unit	2 (2)	
Too little time off	1 (1)	3 (2)	Avoid bad record		6 (6)
Hard to concentrate	1 (1)		Committed to work		6 (6)
No permanent ward	1 (1)		No sick time left		3 (3)
Shift change–tired	1 (1)		Save for good weather		1 (1)
Worked overtime		2 (1)	Enjoy co-workers		1 (1)
Missed bus–car problem	1 (1)	2 (1)	Need M.D. certificate		1 (1)
Extend holiday		1 (1)	Can learn new things		1 (1)
Compassionate leave		2 (1)			
Ward is overstaffed		1 (1)			
House was robbed		1 (1)			
Pregnancy		1 (1)			
Religious holiday		1 (1)			
Mad at the supervisor		1 (1)			
Peace rally		1 (1)			
Missionary work		1 (1)			

*The percentages of all events reported within hospitals appear in parentheses.

Source: R. D. Hackett, P. Bycio, and R. M. Guion (1989). Absenteeism among hospital nurses: An idiographic-longitudinal analysis. *Academy of Management Journal, 32*(2), 431. Copyright 1989 by the Academy of Management Journal. Reprinted with permission.

Hands-On Criteria

In the mid-1980s, the U.S. Department of Defense conducted a large-scale validation of the Armed Services Vocational Aptitude Battery (ASVAB). The ASVAB is a standardized test battery used by the U.S. armed forces to select new recruits for specific job-skill training. The criteria used were hands-on work samples. These work samples were carefully developed, specifically defined pieces of the job content that were selected and refined to represent a critical part of the job. These were administered in carefully controlled situations using standardized equipment and environmental parameters.

The Army, for example, developed a hands-on battery to be administered to tank crew members. This required the crew member to complete several tasks, one at a time. The crew member was observed and scored on a checklist that summarized the operations that are necessary to successfully complete the action. Some examples of these actions are the following: Position the tank cannon for firing; disassemble and reassemble an automatic hand-held weapon; operate the tactical

radio system for communicating with other friendly ground forces; and operate the tank's internal communication system. Crew member scores on these hands-on tasks were the criterion measures that were correlated with the ASVAB paper-and-pencil test scores in the Army's criterion-related validity study.

The Army found that the hands-on measures produced reliable scores with good validity. As direct samples of the tasks from the job analysis, they also reduced the contaminating influences of equipment differences, performance demands, and day-to-day environmental variation.

Hands-on performance measures also made possible the observation of behaviors such as response to enemy fire that occur infrequently or could not be easily observed on the job.

Source: Adapted from D. A. Harris (1987). Joint-service job performance measures enlisted standards project. *The Industrial/Organizational Psychologist, 24,* 36–42; and Wigdor, A., & Green, B. F. (1986). *Assessing the performance of enlisted personnel: Evaluation of joint service project.* Washington, DC: National Academy Press.

equipment differences, and day-to-day fluctuations in the environment. Prepared carefully, hands-on criteria can also create situations in which infrequent but critical on-the-job behaviors can be observed. The Defense Department's use of hands-on work samples as objective criteria in validating vocational aptitude tests is described in Historical Perspective 5.1.

An objective criterion that is being used more often is innovation. The total quality movement has placed a premium on creativity applied to work. This is tracked by using data on the number and kinds of innovations or recommendations submitted by employees. The degree of creativity present may be impossible to determine, but it is easy to track the number of sug-

gestions submitted by employees and the number of work changes that occur as a result of such suggestions.

The final objective criterion that we will describe is customer satisfaction. This criterion has proved to be important because it is emphasized in quality improvement programs and systems theory. Two types of customers are considered: External customers are the people who purchase and use the product or service. In so doing, they support the organization financially. Internal customers are other employees to whom work is assigned. Each worker is a link in a chain; each is the customer of the worker who precedes her or him in the manufacturing process and a supplier to the workers who follow them. Objectively assessing customer satisfaction is accomplished by asking two questions:

1. Are we doing the right things? (Are our customers getting exactly the products and services they need, precisely when and how they want them?)
2. Are we doing things right? (How efficient are the processes we are using to design, manufacture, deliver, and provide maintenance for our products?)

Measures of Subjective Criteria

Truly subjective criteria can be characterized by employee performance ratings. These ratings can be performed by the workers' supervisor, their coworkers, or even themselves. Performance ratings often take the form of scales that include various types of performance measures for each employee. Because subjective criteria are the product of human decision-making processes, numerous research efforts have attempted to improve the stability and reliability of such practices. Lance, Teachout, and Donnelly (1992) conducted research that compared four methods of assessment: self-ratings, supervisor ratings, peer ratings, and work samples. The data collected from 261 Air Force mechanics used scales that were intended to measure interpersonal proficiency, general maintenance, electronic systems maintenance, and pickup service and delivery. They found that the different methods of rating correlated with various aspects of performance. In other words, they found a difference in performance levels among the four methods.

Ratings can become clouded when raters receive feedback about ratees before conducting the assessment. This can occur when supervisors must provide an evaluation for employees with whom they have worked for a long time. They have a global outlook, or "feeling," about each worker that is a result of their previous experiences with that employee and can cause errors in judgment. Sharpe and Adair (1993, p. 243) refer to these errors as "the hindsight

bias phenomenon" and offer three implications for future research:

1. Some portions of the bias can be controlled by training raters to recognize the problem.
2. Cognitive and motivational explanations contribute to hindsight bias.
3. There is a need for more research that focuses on identifying processes that can reduce bias instead of merely commenting on its strength.

As we approach the twenty-first century, more and more women are entering the work force. How do the gender of the rater and that of the ratee affect the evaluation? How does race affect the rater–ratee relationship? Pulakos, White, Oppler, and Borman (1989) conducted research on 8,642 first-term enlisted Army personnel to discover whether any differences existed when Caucasian, African-American, female, and male raters were used. The raters were required to evaluate soldiers on four dimensions of job performance: technical skill, job effort, personal discipline, and military bearing. The results showed that any differences reported by the different raters (either male, female, African-American, or Caucasian) were very small. Although these data appear to be optimistic, additional research is needed.

Customer satisfaction is another subjective criterion (as well as an objective criterion). Total quality management has led many companies to look at their organization in a different, systems-oriented fashion. In the area of customer satisfaction this means examining the user of the company's outputs, whether that user is inside or outside the organization. Internal customers are fellow employees who use or receive the products. External customers are traditional customers, outside the organization, who buy and use the products. Using customers as a way of measuring effectiveness derives from opinions of people such as Armand Feigenbaum (1991), who observed that "Quality is what the customer says it is" (p. 16). An example of using external customer satisfaction as a criterion is Harvey

Mackay's Minneapolis envelope-manufacturing firm. It uses a sixty-six-item questionnaire to learn as much as possible about each customer. The questionnaire is not sent to customers; it is completed by company employees using information they obtain each time they contact a customer. By learning about their customers, involving all employees in the effort, and making this an ongoing process, Mackay Envelope Company has become very successful and is known as being highly responsive to customer needs.

Subjective criteria have also been used to describe personal measurements of job success. This occurs when an employee rates himself or herself on a performance scale. Subjective criteria, such as being satisfied with one's job, are more powerful estimates of perceived career success than are objective criteria measurements. This type of information is useful in gaining an understanding of self-assessment performance scales. Subjective criteria are also used to rate employee performance.

Debate still exists as to the best method to assess performance criteria and the best criterion to use for personnel decisions. These issues have been hotly debated by I/O psychologists, human resource managers, management, and labor. In the following section we discuss the nature of the arguments both for and against composite and multiple criteria.

Composite Criterion Versus Multiple Criteria

Earlier research suggests that all information gathered about an individual should be combined to give a single measurement of performance. The combination of data into one score is called a composite criterion (note the use of the singular, *criterion*). Other I/O psychologists posited that it was not reasonable to group all the data into one score. They maintained that measures of behavior are independent indicators of performance criteria that must be assessed individually. This insistence on keeping criteria separate is known as multiple criteria (note the

use of the plural, *criteria*). In this section we identify some of the main proponents of composite and multiple criteria, state their arguments, and examine their strengths and weaknesses.

Composite Criterion

Personnel decisions are often made by compiling an overall estimate of employee performance. This can be especially true for companies that have a large number of employees. The personnel administrator, human resource management professional, or I/O psychologist is typically faced with the challenge of combining a variety of known data (or criteria) on an employee into one composite criterion score (see Figure 5.3). Each criterion is composed of objective and subjective data. The task is to find a way to combine the separate dimensions of criteria in a fair and valid manner to find one criterion score that effectively reflects individual performance.

The next step in establishing a composite criterion is to decide how to combine the criteria. Nagle (1953) suggested weighting each criterion score to empirically combine the data. A popular way to weight the data is to use expert judges. These judges could be senior-level officers within each department, personnel and human resource administrators, and I/O psychologists. To weight the criterion scores, the expert judges must give an individual weight to each category. The weight gives more precedence to data that are more important in the decision-making process and less precedence to less important criteria. As illustrated in Figure 5.3, if the experts assign a weight to each of four criteria, we can use the following formula to combine the four criteria:

$$\text{Composite criterion} = \text{Weight (C1)} + \text{Weight (C2)} + \text{Weight (C3)} + \text{Weight (C4)}$$

Organizations that use a composite criterion technique must decide how to weight each criteria score. Brogden and Taylor (1950) suggested placing a dollars-and-cents value on employees according to estimates of their overall worth to the company. They proposed a method of "converting production units, errors, time of other

**Criteria
Data**

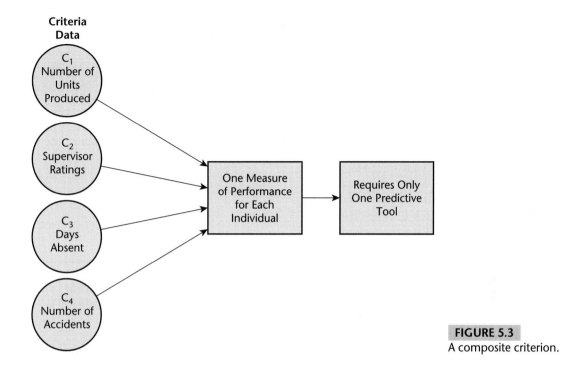

A composite criterion.

personnel, etc., into dollar units" (p. 133). The main purpose of this approach was to attach a monetary worth to each worker based on combined multiple criteria, and including the following (p. 146):

1. Average value of production or service units
2. Quality of objects produced or services accomplished
3. Overhead—including rent, light, heat, cost depreciated or rental of machines and equipment
4. Errors, accidents, spoilage, waste, damage to machines or equipment through unusual wear and tear . . .
5. Factors [such] as appearance, friendliness, poise, and general social effectiveness . . .
6. The cost of other personnel consumed. This would include not only the time of supervisory personnel, but also that of other workers

Although this list seems to be a well-rounded estimate of a worker's productivity, subjective issues such as how to measure poise and friend-liness in an objective and fair manner must be addressed. How, then, do we combine both qualitative and quantitative criteria to get a fair and realistic composite score? Siegel and Lane (1982) list three main categories for addressing the weighting dilemma: The weighting of criteria data must be either judgmental, statistical, or economic. **Judgmental weighting** is closely related to the expert opinions of judges weighting criteria. Organizational leaders usually have an idea about what behaviors are most closely linked to exemplary performance within their organizations. These judgments can be made by single individuals or by a group of individuals. The second type of weighting is **statistical weighting.** Statistical forms of weighting are based on empirical information compiled from criteria data. For example, Vance, MacCallum, Coovert, and Hedge (1988) used statistical devices to assess performance ratings of Air Force personnel. One of the benefits of using statistical weighting is that it is based on empirical data and statistical analyses that increase the levels of confidence in the outcomes.

The third type of weighting is **economic weighting,** which is supported by Brogden and Taylor's (1950) research on the dollar-value estimate of the criterion. Economic-based weighting is useful when knowledge of an employee's overall worth in terms of dollars and cents is desirable.

One additional type of weighting is **uniform,** or equal, **weighting.** This type of weighting occurs when all criteria data are given equal weights, thereby eliminating the problem of assigning different values to each criterion (Blum & Naylor, 1968). Arguments for a composite criterion are well suited for an organization seeking a single measurement of successful behaviors. However, some researchers insist that there cannot be one single estimate of performance and that a multiple-criteria approach must be adopted. In the following section we address this approach.

Multiple Criteria

In response to theorists who supported the concept of a composite criterion, many researchers claim that criteria scores cannot be grouped together into one single value of performance. Ghiselli (1956, p. 2) was one of the first to state that the composite criterion is an insufficient measure of human performance: "There is no way to combine the independent scores of an individual into a single value that will describe him [or her] uniquely." Ghiselli theorized that a criterion has many dimensions: static, dynamic, and individual. These dimensions describe criteria measures as being much too complex for any of the simple methods proposed to combine them. Guion (1961) is also a proponent of multiple criteria in decision making. He devised an order of events that should be adopted in using a composite methodology (Guion, 1961, p. 142):

1. The psychologist has a hunch (or insight) that a problem exists and that she can help solve it.
2. He [she] reads a vague, ambiguous job description.
3. From these faint stimuli, he [she] formulates a fuzzy concept of an ultimate criterion.

4. Being a practical psychologist, he [she] may then formulate a combination of several variables which will give him [her]—as nearly as she can guess—a single, composite measure of "satisfactory performance."
5. He [she] judges the relevance of this measure: (the extent to which it is neither deficient nor contaminated).
6. He [she] may judge the relative importance of each of the elements in the composite and assign a varying amount of weight to each element.
7. He [she] then finds that the data required for the composite are not available in the company files, nor is there any immediate prospect of having such records.
8. He [she] will then select "the best available criterion." Typically, this will be a rating, and the criterion problem, if not solved, can at least be overlooked for the rest of the research.

Although Guion's list is rich in satire and irony, the material in question is far from unimportant. Many organizations need to design performance assessment systems to fairly evaluate their employees. Researchers such as Ghiselli and Guion believe that criteria measures are estimates of separate behaviors that cannot be validly combined. They have found that combining the behaviors oversimplifies the criterion. Dunnette (1963, p. 252) stated, "Junk the criterion! Let us cease searching for single or composite measures of job success and proceed to undertake research which accepts the world of success dimensionality as it really exists." Instead of a combination of possibly unrelated criteria, the proponents of multiple criteria maintain that different criteria must be viewed as separate and matched with independent predictive measures.

Figure 5.4 shows various short-term records and test scores associated with different long-term performance criteria. For example, the number of customers attended to daily by a car dealer for the first few weeks of employment (P_1 = daily production records) is found to be associated with the number of cars sold per year (C_1 = number of units produced). According to the

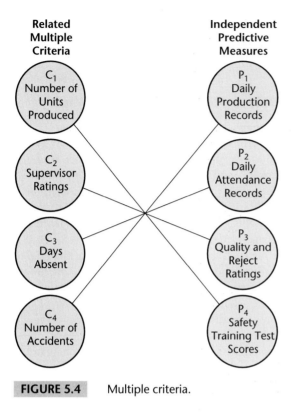

Related Multiple Criteria

- C_1 Number of Units Produced
- C_2 Supervisor Ratings
- C_3 Days Absent
- C_4 Number of Accidents

Independent Predictive Measures

- P_1 Daily Production Records
- P_2 Daily Attendance Records
- P_3 Quality and Reject Ratings
- P_4 Safety Training Test Scores

FIGURE 5.4   Multiple criteria.

figure, we can use this short-term measure (P_1) to predict two long-term criteria: long-term production records (C_1) and the number of accidents (C_4) per year.

Although it is easier and probably more cost efficient for an organization to adopt a composite criterion score for each employee, proponents of multiple criteria have shown that such procedures may jeopardize factors such as construct validity. What can we do to clear up this issue? Is there any right or wrong methodology? These issues are addressed in the following section.

Choosing a Method

Selecting a "best" method, either a composite criterion or multiple criteria, is far from easy. However, a variety of suggestions have been set forth based on the needs of individual organizations. Borman (1991) stated that both approaches—composite and multiple—are good

techniques to gauge performance behavior but that they must match the organization's needs. Borman finds value in the composite criterion approach when an organization needs an overall estimate of performance. "Qualities such as overall success, worth as an employee, and contribution to the organization must be determined in order to select persons with the highest predicted overall performance" (Borman, 1991, p. 274). In other words, a composite criterion may be a good representation of employee performance when the organization's goal is a general estimate of successful performance.

However, estimates of multiple criteria are necessary if the organization is seeking different kinds of information, such as ways to improve training or selection techniques. For specific performance criteria the organization should develop a multiple-criteria technique. Borman (1991, p. 274) further stated, "Combining such criteria in a composite masks relationships between individual predictors and the criteria, relationships that could increase understanding of predictors, criteria, and the relationships between them." Multiple criteria are especially helpful when an organization needs employees with very specific skills. For example, one performance criterion for an auto mechanic is knowledge of automotive brake systems. If the company used a composite criterion to assess the mechanic's performance, other criteria might obscure the performance rating. For instance, criteria such as a high supervisory rating on friendliness and sociability might skew the data. Suppose the mechanic failed a pencil-and-paper test about automotive brake systems, but the rest of the data from the composite criterion rating compensate for the poor brake test scores. The result will be an overall satisfactory assessment. In this situation, multiple criteria should have been used to pinpoint individual deficiencies, thereby enabling the organization to implement possible changes in training and other policies.

The choice of whether to use multiple criteria or a composite criterion is usually left to the company. Controlling costs, in addition to establishing criteria for successful performance, is very important to most companies. Carefully assessing and weighting criteria measurements are crucial in pinpointing successful performance. Campbell, McHenry, and Wise (1990, p. 315) stated that

> it seems quite reasonable for the organization to scale the importance of each major performance factor relative to a particular personnel decision that must be made, and to combine the weighted factor scores into a composite that represents the total contribution or utility of an individual's performance within the context of that decision.

In conclusion, the decision to use a composite criterion or multiple criteria should rest on the type of information requested and its intended use. If the company is looking for a general estimate of performance for use in establishing a pay rate, a composite criterion should suffice. If the organization is interested in specific performance behaviors in order to improve methods of selection or training, a multiple-criteria technique should be utilized.

REQUIREMENTS FOR CRITERIA

Building from a basic understanding of criteria, the next step is to understand the requirements for good criteria. Bellows' (1954) requirements, as modified by Blum and Naylor (1968, p. 182) stated that sound criteria should be as follows:

1. Reliable
2. Realistic
3. Representative
4. Related to other criteria
5. Acceptable to job analyst
6. Acceptable to management
7. Consistent from one situation to another
8. Predictable
9. Inexpensive
10. Understandable
11. Measurable
12. Relevant
13. Uncontaminated
14. Discriminating

Although all of these requirements are important, certain characteristics are essential and deserve further explanation.

Relevance and Construct Validity

Perhaps the most important requirement for criteria is relevance. Borman (1991, p. 272) defines relevance as "the correspondence between criteria and the actual performance demands of the target job." As we will discuss in Chapter 8 ("Personnel Decisions"), the definition of a construct is "an idea of an attribute or characteristic inferred from research" (Guion, 1965, p. 128); construct validity is "a judgement of the degree to which its [a measure's] variance can be attributed to the concept it is supposed to measure" (Guion, 1965, p. 119). In terms of our previous discussion, if the concept of relevance refers to the data provided by the interaction between the actual criterion and the ultimate criterion, then the development of the measure relevance is also part of assessing its construct validity (Guion, 1965, 1991). Guion (1991) differentiates between job relevance and construct relevance. In job relevance the purpose is the prediction of performance; construct relevance refers to understanding the meaning of the criterion scores and the inferences that could be made about the concept or construct being measured. Thus a criterion could have both types of relevance: (a) valid prediction of job behavior (job relevance—for example, number of promotions) and (b) an understanding of the attribute being measured (construct relevance—for example, the math achievement test given to accountants measures the comprehension of accounting principles).

The process of developing and establishing relevant criteria that are essential to job performance is also associated with the criterion problem. Binning and Barret (1989) suggested that the criterion problem results from researchers and practitioners abridging and cutting off the network of inferences that can be made from criterion scores. They proposed two reasons for the criterion problem. The first is that criterion measures are likely to be less psychometrically developed than other variables of the decision-making process, such as predictors. This means that criterion measurements are not as empirically sophisticated as predictors are. The second reason is that performance criteria are less rooted in the network of theoretical relationships than the predictors are (i.e., there is less research on construct validity). Binning and Barret recommended that criterion measures be researched and validated as rigorously as predictors in terms of all validation strategies.

Reliability

Another important quality that criteria must possess is reliability. **Reliable criteria** are criteria that have similar results in repeated measurements. If the performance criteria are composed mainly of production rates and absenteeism rates, evaluations should agree when carried out at different times.

In his article "Criteria for Criteria," Weitz (1961) outlined three major dimensions of criteria: time, type, and level. Time refers to the decision about when to collect the measurement data. Type of criteria refers to the particular kinds of criteria the organization chooses for a job. Level of criteria refers to the cutoff score above which performance is considered effective. However, other researchers (e.g., Austin, Humphreys, & Hulin, 1989; Ghiselli, 1956; Ghiselli & Haire, 1960) believe that criteria are dynamic entities, which change over time. They have called for establishing reliability in criteria measurements by collecting data at different times. Ghiselli and Haire stated,

> The practice of using performance data obtained during an initial period and letting it stand for ultimate or total performance completely ignores the dynamic character of the criterion and important changes that are taking place in the worker's performance.

Once again, the need for more research on criteria is stressed.

Acceptability to Management

Criteria should not only be representative of the behavior in question; they should also be regarded as practical by the organization. Criteria should be established in a timely, inexpensive manner without compromising their validity. We have reiterated the importance of more research on criteria, and there is no better place to conduct this research than in real, operating organizations. Guion (1965) states that the personnel professionals should explain to the company's top managers the benefits of a well-researched, carefully developed set of criteria. An explanation of the possibilities of saving the company money because of improved selection and training techniques almost certainly will show the worth and importance of establishing relevant criteria.

Avoiding Discriminatory Practices

As we approach the twenty-first century, a more diverse work force is evolving. Many individuals are working longer than ever before, women are entering occupations that were previously dominated by men, and a variety of ethnic groups are becoming an integral force in the work environment. Now, more than ever, criteria for successful working behavior must be very carefully composed. Varca and Pattison (1993, p. 256) suggested that we "are wary of informal promotion and selection procedures, particularly in large organizations where it is suggested that numbers of decisions can result in a basis for disparate impact." Disparate impact occurs when a company's policies or procedures on issues such as selection or promotion systematically choose only individuals from one race, gender, or other category. Criteria development is directly involved in establishing selection and promotion techniques, as seen in Figure 5.2. Some jobs may require certain levels of physical strength or mental capacity that some applicants might not possess, but if criteria are not carefully selected, disparate impact can occur. One way to increase diversity within the organization is to create larger applicant pools for new hires or promotions.

How do government regulatory agencies discover whether an organization is discriminating against minorities? Wymer and Sudbury (1992) found that employers may be faced with testers. Testers are individuals of a minority class or gender who present themselves to various companies as candidates for employment. These testers are on the lookout for discriminatory practices in the companies' hiring processes. Wymer and Sudbury state that these efforts are supported by the Equal Employment Opportunity Commission and are currently under way throughout the country. They believe that this will push companies to carefully reevaluate their selection techniques. "This will require employers to place greater emphasis and attention on their hiring processes in much the same way they have already with regard to their discharge procedures" (Wymer & Sudbury, 1992, p. 257). As we have noted, a major method to improve selection techniques is to improve criteria development and evaluation.

These requirements of criteria are important areas of concern for both the I/O psychologist and the organization. Issues such as criterion relevance, contamination, validation strategies, and all other criteria procedures contributing to personnel decisions are covered by the Uniform Guidelines (see Chapter 4) and require intense and longitudinal studies. As the government and other parts of society call for better selection techniques to improve diversity in the workplace, perhaps this result can be achieved.

RESULTS OF ESTABLISHED CRITERIA

The establishment of relevant criteria can enable an organization to improve on existing strategies, policies, and procedures. Earlier in the chapter, Figure 5.2 presented the relationship between job analysis (criteria development), criteria, and the uses for criteria. In this section we discuss the impact of criteria on issues of selection, training, job evaluation and compensation, and promotion. Practice Perspective 5.1 shows

one method that a company can use to help make criteria real and meaningful to employees.

Selection

Criteria play a most important role in employee selection. Just as people need jobs, organizations need qualified personnel who have the abilities to perform various jobs. Criteria are established through a job analysis carried out during the criteria development stage. Job analyses are conducted to specify the behaviors individuals should exhibit to be successful at their tasks. Once an organization has an idea of which behaviors constitute successful performance, it can select individuals who show promise of being effective on the job. Guion (1976, pp. 783–784) proposed an informal set of guidelines in the development of selection strategies. These tenets include the following:

1. The purpose is to predict future job performance.
2. Predictors and criteria should be selected on the basis of a job analysis.
3. Measuring instruments must be standardized.
4. Tests should be empirically evaluated.
5. Validation should be situation-specific.
6. More than one test should be used.
7. Only one criterion should be used.
8. Tests are preferred over "non-test" predictors.
9. Individual differences should be recognized in evaluating tests.
10. Tests should be considered supplements to existing employment procedures.

From this list we can see how important criteria development is in the process of selecting employees. Selection procedures are influenced not only by the standards and ethics that guide I/O psychologists, but by federal laws as well. When hearing cases concerning selection procedures, many courts inquire about the organizational job analysis procedure (Guion & Gibson, 1988) and the relationship between criteria and selection techniques. Sevy (1988) used job analysis data to compare test scores on the Correctional Officers'

PRACTICE PERSPECTIVE 5.1

How Companies Use Games to Focus Employees on Criteria

Say your company has a problem. Maybe inventory accuracy is very low. Maybe warranty costs or overhead are too high. Many companies are using games to shake things up. Whatever the criterion the company wants to focus on, it sets up a game to change the situation. For example, if a company has an easily measurable goal, such as 95% accuracy by the end of the year, it establishes a game with clear rules that everyone understands and provides some kind of payoff for a win.

Here are a few examples from a recent *Inc.* magazine article illustrating how companies have focused employee attentions on selected criteria using a gaming strategy:

Heating system manufacturer Heatway, Inc., sponsors "Guess-the-Gross" contests. "We circulate a form like a racing form at the start of every month," explains Dan Chiles, one of the two brothers who run the company. "At the bottom is a tip sheet—last month's gross, this month's gross last year, our forecasts, what on the projections we give the bank." The winner gets $25, but the real purpose is focusing people's attention on the bottom line.

Consumer products distributor Manco, Inc., is running a game called Formula 10. On its face it's no more than an elaborate employee suggestion system: Propose a way of saving sales or administrative costs and get a little plaque. But the name reflects a critical goal, which is to get Manco's selling, general, and administrative expenses down under 10% of sales. The Achilles' heel of competitors, ex-

plains company president Tom Corbo, is their high overhead levels. Manco's is low, and Formula 10 is their "secret weapon" to lower it still further.

Missouri Home Care attacks its huge workers' compensation liability with not one game but a series of games. Game 1, a while ago, consisted of prize drawings for workers who stayed injury free. In game 2, which is ongoing, managers go into the homes of randomly selected clients with a safety checklist, and workers get a $50 bonus for achieving a 100% score on all safety procedures. Game 3, which is still on the drawing board, involves some sort of bingo, with safety issues on every square.

Bill Palmer, CEO of a cabinetry company called Commercial Casework, describes the effect of one seemingly trivial managerial move. In the past the company budgeted a certain number of labor hours for each step of a job but never told employees what the budget was. A few months ago, Palmer began posting those labor budget numbers on the bulletin board. "Rather than someone telling them, 'Hey, we want you to build this table as fast as you can,' we were saying, 'We have 40 hours in the estimate.' " Before the change, Commercial Casework's jobs averaged 6% over budget. Afterward, they averaged 2% under budget, an 8% difference.

Source: Adapted from "Games Companies Play," by John Case, *Inc.* magazine, (October 1994) by Goldhirsh Group, Inc., 38 Commercial Wharf, Boston, MA 02110. Reprinted with permission.

Interest Blank (COIB) to discover whether the test was a valid predictor of performance for corrections officers, juvenile counselors, and probation officers. Sevy found that the tool moderately predicted performance ($r = .27$). In a study conducted by Nathan and Alexander (1988), validity coefficients were established for clerical abilities using five criteria: supervisor ratings, supervisor rankings, work samples, production quan-

tity, and production quality. Nathan and Alexander reported high test validity for ratings, rankings, work samples, and production quantity.

Tannenbaum and Wesley (1993) found that job analysis results established by an advisory committee are so closely related to data provided by field surveys that the latter may not be necessary. This might allow for an increased focus on other aspects of criteria. Tannenbaum and Wesley's study (1993, p. 978) emphasized another important ingredient in the criteria development process:

> Emphasis needs to be placed on the careful selection of advisory committee members. The membership should consist of well-recognized content experts and should, to the extent possible, have representation by professional perspective as well as sex, race and ethnicity, and geographic region.

To compare individuals equitably for group assessment, geographic region as well as product type must be taken into consideration in developing criteria.

Such research shows how important criterion development is in using selection techniques. In other words, criteria are inseparable from desired performance behavior.

Performance Appraisal and Promotion

As will be discussed in Chapter 6, performance appraisals are conducted to identify whether employees are exhibiting unsatisfactory, satisfactory, or above-average levels of performance. Performance appraisals consist of data collected about individual employees. Murphy (1991) found that performance appraisals can usually be classified into one of two groups: specific behaviors or classification and judgments. Estimates of specific behaviors are usually conducted when specific data, such as rate of production, are requested. Classifications and judgments are often quality-based estimates. Issues such as how well an employee relates to coworkers would fall into this category. Murphy stresses that the techniques that are used depend on the organization's needs at the time of appraisal.

Performance appraisal criteria may take the form of self-appraisals or supervisor ratings. Promotional decisions may be the result of a classification or judgment about an employee by advisors, peers, or the employee under review. In a self-appraisal, each individual rates himself or herself on such variables as intelligence, abilities,

and work skills. Peer appraisals are performance ratings about individuals that are provided by coworkers. Supervisory ratings are ratings that are made by the worker's supervisor. Hoffman, Nathan, and Holden (1991) found that when compared to production data, self-evaluations tend to overestimate ability. On the other hand, performance ratings that are made by supervisors are found to be closely related to estimated productivity. However, performance appraisals based on criteria for successful performance must be scrutinized for mistakes in measurement. If an appraisal system is heavily based on ratings conducted by other people, such as supervisors, care must be taken with performance evaluation formats. For example, Hartel (1993) found differences in ratings performed by raters when the format of the rating tool was changed. Many of these issues are discussed in Chapter 6 ("Performance Appraisal").

Performance appraisals are valuable to both organizations and the individual employees. Feedback on how each worker is performing—as seen by the organization—can be a valuable tool for increasing desired behaviors, which in turn allows individuals to better perform their jobs. Kleinmann (1993) found that when employees understand the dimensions on which they are being rated, they are able to improve their behaviors within each dimension. For more information about this study, see Scientific Perspective 5.1.

Carefully developed criteria are used to rate employees according to their individual contribution to the company. Ideally, the individuals who score the highest on performance criteria will be eligible for promotion. This allows the company to get the most out of their employees' potential and rewards successful employees with better wages and increased responsibility.

Job Evaluation and Compensation

Establishing criteria for job success also significantly contributes to job evaluation and com-

SCIENTIFIC PERSPECTIVE 5.1

**Accurate Recognition of Rating Dimensions
Improves Assessment Center Scores**

The concern many researchers had about the lack of construct validity in assessment centers led Kleinmann (1993) to explore the extent to which participants who recognized the rating dimensions in an assessment center performed better than those who did not. Participants completed a one-day assessment center with five exercises. An additional measure collected was the participants' assumptions about which dimensions would be rated and recorded. Sixty college students (twenty-three women and thirty-seven men) participated.

Participants were found to vary considerably in their ability to develop assumptions about the dimensions assessed. No participant correctly recognized all the dimensions. Three participants correctly recognized 13–16 dimensions, twelve recognized 9–12 dimensions, thirty-five recognized 5–8 dimensions, and six recognized 0–4 dimensions.

Three measures of performance on the assessment center were defined: (a) the sum of an individual's ratings on all the dimensions, (b) the estimation of the individual's management poten-

tial from the assessment center evaluation, and (c) the decision as to whether the participant would be given a job. All three of these measures correlated with the number of correctly recognized dimensions (rating a, $r = .30$, $p < .05$; rating b, $r = .44$, $p < .01$; rating c, $r = .25$, $p < .05$). In addition, participants performed better on dimensions they had recognized (mean = 3.5) than on dimensions they had failed to recognize (mean = 6.6, $p < .01$).

Kleinmann was surprised by how well his participants recognized the dimensions being evaluated by the assessment center. However, he did believe that this finding provides an explanation for the high levels of common variance found among dimensions in assessment center validity studies and negatively influences the criterion validity of assessment centers.

Source: Based on M. Kleinmann (1993). Are rating dimensions in assessment centers transparent for participants? Consequences for criterion and construct validity. *Journal of Applied Psychology, 78*(6), 988–993.

pensation. Job evaluation is a measurement devised by the organization to establish each job's worth to the company. Company leaders evaluate the various duties that individuals carry out in performing their jobs. As discussed in Chapter 12 ("Total Compensation"), questions in typical job evaluation often include the following:

Does the job require great or specialized skill?

Does the job require extensive training?

Is the job physically demanding?

Is the job psychologically demanding?

These questions are answered by the organization by reviewing the criteria data collected for each job type. The purpose of job evalua-

tions is to establish compensation or pay rates for each member of the organization. For example, the general rule is that jobs that require great skill and extensive training should involve higher levels of pay than jobs that do not have these prerequisites.

Training

Another area in which criteria play a major role is training. Job analysis enables the analyst to identify behaviors that are critical to performing assigned tasks. When the company has determined what behaviors are desirable, it must train employees, teaching them methods and techniques for accomplishing task goals. Companies spend millions of dollars annually on training programs, so it is crucial to establish valid, reliable criteria to determine whether the training employees are receiving will translate to successful job performance. Establishing relevant criteria directly affects training programs in two ways. First, criteria are estimates of job success that define the desired behaviors. For example, an effective occupational therapist is one who successfully helps patients to heal and cope with their injuries. Having criteria for achieving this, including a knowledge of the latest therapy techniques, enables the hospital staff to establish training programs that teach therapists concrete ways to help their patients.

The second way in which criteria affect training is that measures of successful performance enable organizations to monitor the effect that the training program has on employee performance. As indicated in Chapter 9, a simplified process for monitoring the success of a training program is to assess the performance of employees currently on the job, engage them in the training program, and measure their performance after completion of training. Using established criteria of successful performance, we can measure the behavioral changes the trainees exhibit after the training program. A successful training program will result in trainees' exhibiting more desirable behaviors on the job after training. Training programs are usually the direct result of criteria development, and companies use them to improve workers' skills, productivity, and safety. Training programs also provide an in-house method of measuring the effects of such programs. By monitoring and improving existing training programs, employers can fully utilize individual employees. Chapter 9 ("Training and Development") provides further explanation of training issues.

....

SUMMARY

An understanding of criteria is crucial in industrial/organizational psychology. Much research has been conducted over the past forty years to better explain criteria and their functions.

The criterion problem arises because a 100% or true criterion will never be available. Criteria are composed of complex variables that differ with each situation and each individual. The quality and success of an organization's criteria development can be only as good as the organization's ability to recognize the elements that are important to achieving success at a particular job. Discovering relevant criteria during the job analysis allows the organization to establish a good fit between workers and tasks. Identifying what it takes to be successful on the job enables the company to efficiently select people who will successfully perform these jobs. Criteria also allow for increased efficiency in terms of training. Since companies spend large amounts of time and money on training, it is desirable for them to get the best results for their investment.

Establishment of relevant criteria also provides workers with important information. An employee who has a good understanding of what is expected of him or her will be better equipped to perform the desired behaviors. If the criteria model is working correctly, employee performance is monitored through the processes of evaluation and compensation, with promotion occurring accordingly. Employees who believe that their efforts at work are noticed and rewarded generally continue to be successful employees.

The key to further understanding the complex nature of criteria lies in conducting additional research. Researchers are trying to answer the elusive questions that arise out of past research and experience.

Although criteria are abstract constructs that can never be uniformly identified through exact definitions, research efforts continue to provide more and more clues about the ultimate criterion. Increased understanding will help organizations to develop increasingly relevant criteria, thus closing the gap between criteria deficiency and criteria contamination.

KEY TERMS AND CONCEPTS

absenteeism
actual criterion
bias
criterion
criterion contamination
criterion deficiency
criterion problem

criterion relevance
distal criteria
economic weighting
error
immediate criteria
judgmental weighting
norm-based evaluation

proximal criteria
reliable criteria
sample of performance
statistical weighting
turnover
ultimate criterion
uniform weighting

RECOMMENDED READINGS

Arvey, R. D. (1979). *Fairness in selecting employees* (pp. 111–119). Reading, MA: Addison-Wesley.

Borman, W. C., & Motowidlo, S. J. (1993). Expanding the criterion domain to include elements of contextual performance. In N. Schmitt, W. C. Borman, & Associates, *Personnel selection in organizations* (pp. 71–98). San Francisco: Jossey-Bass.

Landy, F. J., & Shankster, L. J. (1994). Personnel selection and placement. *Annual Review of Psychology, 45,* 280–284.

Mcmanus, M. A., & Brown, S. H. (1995). Adjusting sales results measures for use as criteria. *Personnel Psychology, 48*(2), 391–400.

Schmidt, F. L., & Kaplan, L. B. (1971). Composite vs. multiple criteria: A review and resolution of the controversy. *Personnel Psychology, 24,* 419–434.

INTERNET RESOURCES

Selection Criteria

This site lists selection criteria for a support programmer (Unix & networks). It includes both essential and desirable criteria.
http://www.cs.utas.edu.au/Adverts/Jobs/SupProgUN/SelectionCriteria.html

Cognitive Stumbling Blocks

This abstract summarizes a study that identified cognitive stumbling blocks for telephone operators working on a large computer system. This led to a comprehensive job analysis.
http://www.ergoweb.com/Pub/Info/Ref/AppErgo/Abstract/a92105.html

EXERCISE

Exercise 5.1

Defining Criteria for Jobs

Form a group with two other students in class. Develop and agree on a job description of a student's job and the registrar's job at your university. On the basis of these job descriptions, each member in your group should independently decide on the following:

1. Job-relevant criteria for each job.
2. The different types of criteria that are important in defining effectiveness in these jobs.

3. The procedures by which one would establish the basic requirements for these criteria.
4. The goals of the university in defining these criteria and in using them for performance appraisals of faculty and for grades assignments to students.

Get together with your group to compare and discuss your criteria. Come to a consensus on the final definitions, taking into account all aspects mentioned above.

REFERENCES

Austin, J. T., Humphreys, L. G., & Hulin, C. L. (1989). Another view of dynamic criteria: A critical reanalysis of Barret, Caldwell, and Alexander. *Personnel Psychology, 42, 583–596.*

Austin, J. T., & Villanova, P. (1992). The criterion problem: 1917–1992. *Journal of Applied Psychology, 77*(6), 836–874.

Bellows, R. M. (1954). *Psychology of personnel in business and industry* (2nd ed.). Englewood Cliffs, NJ: Prentice-Hall.

Binning, J., & Barret, G. V. (1989). Validity of personnel decisions: A conceptual analysis of the inferential and evidential bases. *Journal of Applied Psychology, 74*(3), 478–494.

Blum, M. L., & Naylor, J. C. (1968). *Industrial psychology: Its theoretical and social foundations.* New York: Harper & Row.

Borman, W. C. (1991). Job behavior, performance and effectiveness. In M. D. Dunnette & L. M. Hough (Eds.), *Handbook of industrial and organizational psychology* (2nd ed., Vol. 2, pp. 271–326). Palo Alto: Consulting Psychologists Press.

Brogden, H. E., & Taylor, E. K. (1950). The dollar criterion: Applying the cost accounting concept to criterion construction. *Personnel Psychology, 3,* 133–154.

Campbell, J. P., McHenry, J. J., & Wise, L. L. (1990). Modeling job performance in a population of jobs. *Personnel Psychology, 43,* 313–333.

Campion, M. A. (1991). Meaning and measurement of turnover: Comparison of alternative measures and recommendations for research. *Journal of Applied Psychology, 76*(2), 199–212.

Deadrick, D. L., & Madigan, R. M. (1990). Dynamic criteria revisited: A longitudinal study of performance stability and predictive validity. *Personnel Psychology, 43,* 717–744.

Dunnette, M. D. (1963). A note on the criterion. *Journal of Applied Psychology, 47*(4), 251–254.

Feigenbaum, A. V. (1991, April 1). *Boardroom Reports,* 16.

Fichman, M. (1989). Attendance makes the heart grow fonder: A hazard rate approach to modeling attendance. *Journal of Applied Psychology, 74*(2), 325–335.

Ghiselli, E. E. (1956). Dimensional problems of criteria. *Journal of Applied Psychology, 40*(1), 1–4.

Ghiselli, E. E., & Haire, M. (1960). The validation of selection tests in the light of the dynamic character of criteria. *Personnel Psychology, 13,* 225–231.

Guion, R. M. (1961). Criterion measurement and personnel judgments. *Personnel Psychology, 14,* 141–149.

Guion, R. M. (1965). *Personnel testing.* New York: McGraw-Hill.

Guion, R. M. (1976). Recruiting, selection, and job placement. In M. D. Dunnette (Ed.), *Handbook of industrial and organizational psychology* (pp. 777–828). Chicago: Rand McNally.

Guion, R. M. (1991). Personnel assessment, selection, and placement. In M. D. Dunnette & L. M. Hough (Eds.), *Handbook of industrial and organizational psychology* (2nd ed., Vol. 2, pp. 328–397). Palo Alto, CA: Consulting Psychologists Press.

Guion, R. M., & Gibson, W. M. (1988). Personnel selection and placement. *Annual Review of Psychology, 39,* 349–374.

Hackett, R. D., Bycio, P., & Guion, R. M. (1989). Absenteeism among hospital nurses: An idiographic longitudinal analysis. *Academy of Management Journal, 32,* 424–453.

Harris, D. A. (1987). Joint-service job performance measures enlisted standards project. *The Industrial/Organizational Psychologist, 24,* 36–42.

Harrison, D. A., & Hulin, C. L. (1989). Investigation of absenteeism: Using event history models to study the absence-taking process. *Journal of Applied Psychology, 74*(2), 300–316.

Hartel, C. E. (1993). Rating format research revisited: Format effectiveness and acceptability depend on rater characteristics. *Journal of Applied Psychology, 78*(2), 212–217.

Hoffman, C. C., Nathan, B. R., & Holden, L. M. (1991). A comparison of validation criteria: Objective versus subjective performance measures and self versus supervisor ratings. *Personnel Psychology, 44,* 601–618.

Hofmann, D. A., Jacobs, R., & Baratta, J. E. (1993). Dynamic criteria and the measurement of change. *Journal of Applied Psychology, 78*(2), 194–204.

Kemery, E., Dunlap, J., & Bedejan, A. G. (1989). The employee separation process: Criterion-related issues associated with tenure and turnover. *Journal of Management, 15*(3), 417–424.

Kleinmann, M. (1993). Are rating dimensions in assessment centers transparent for participants? Consequences for criterion and construct validity. *Journal of Applied Psychology, 78*(6), 988–993.

Lance, C. E., Teachout, M. S., & Donnelly, T. M. (1992). Specification of the criterion construct space: An application of hierarchical confirmatory factor analysis. *Journal of Applied Psychology, 77*(4), 437–452.

Lee, T. W., & Mitchell, T. R. (1994). An alternative approach: The unfolding model of voluntary employee turnover. *Academy of Management Review, 19*(1), 51–89.

Mitra, A., Jenkins, G. D., Jr., & Gupta N. (1992). A meta-analytic review of the relationship between absence and turnover. *Journal of Applied Psychology, 77*(6), 879–889.

Murphy, K. R. (1991). Criterion issues in performance appraisal research: Behavioral accuracy versus classification accuracy. *Organizational Behavior and Human Decision Processes, 50,* 45–50.

Nagle, B. F. (1953). Criterion development. *Personnel Psychology, 6,* 271–289.

Nathan, B. R., & Alexander, R. A. (1988). A comparison of criteria for test validation: A meta-analytic investigation. *Personnel Psychology, 41,* 517–535.

Ostroff, C. (1991). Training effectiveness measures and scoring schemes: A comparison. *Personnel Psychology, 44,* 353–374.

Pulakos, E. D., White, L. A., Oppler, S. H., & Borman, W. C. (1989). Examination of race and sex effects on performance ratings. *Journal of Applied Psychology, 74,* 770–780.

Sashkin, M., & Kiser, K. J. (1993). *Putting total quality management to work: What TQM means, how to use it, & how to sustain it over the long run.* San Francisco, CA: Berrett-Koehler.

Sevy, B. A. (1988). The concurrent validity of the correctional officers' interest blank. *Public Personnel Management, 17*(2), 135–144.

Sharpe, D., & Adair, J. G. (1993). Reversibility of the hindsight bias: Manipulation of experimental demands. *Organizational Behavior and Human Decision Processes, 56,* 233–245.

Siegel, L., & Lane, I. M. (1982). *Personnel and Organizational Psychology.* Homewood, IL: Richard D. Irwin.

Sink, D. S., & Tuttle, T. T. (1989). *Planning and measurement in your organization of the future.* Norcross, GA: Industrial Engineering and Management Press.

Smith, P. C. (1976). Behavior, results, and organizational effectiveness: The problem of criteria. In M. D. Dunnette (Ed.), *Handbook of industrial and organizational psychology* (pp. 745–775). Chicago: Rand McNally.

Tannenbaum, R. J., & Wesley, S. (1993). Agreement between committee-based and field-based job analyses: A study in the context of licensure testing. *Journal of Applied Psychology, 78*(6), 975–980.

Vance, R. J., MacCallum, R. C., Coovert, M. D., & Hedge, J. W. (1988). Construct validity of multiple job performance measures using confirmatory factor analysis. *Journal of Applied Psychology, 73*(1), 74–80.

Varca, P. E., & Pattison, P. (1993). Evidentiary standards in employment discrimination: A view toward the future. *Personnel Psychology, 46,* 239–258.

Vinchur, A. J., Schippmann, J. S., Smalley, M. D., & Rothe, H. F. (1991). Productivity consistency of foundry chippers and grinders: A 6-year field study. *Journal of Applied Psychology, 76*(1), 134–136.

Wallace, S. R. (1965). Criteria for what? *The American Psychologist, 20,* 411–417.

Weitz, J. (1961). Criteria for criteria. *The American Psychologist, 16,* 228–232.

Wigdor, A., & Green, B. F. (1986). *Assessing the performance of enlisted personnel: Evaluation of joint service project.* Washington, DC: National Academy Press.

Wymer, J. P., III, & Sudbury, D. A. (1992). Employment discrimination "testers": Will your hiring practices "pass"? *Employee Relations Law Journal, 17*(4), 623–633.

Performance Appraisal

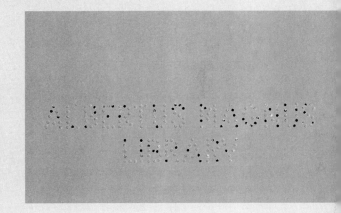

Chapter Outline

(continued)

I nternational Foods, Inc., is a large manufacturer of food ingredients. In 1986 the company instituted an extensive quality improvement initiative that included strong adherence to W. Edwards Deming's fourteen points. These describe what a business must do to survive and compete. One of these points directs management to "eliminate work standards (quotas) on the factory floor. Substitute leadership. Eliminate management by objectives. Eliminate management by numbers, numerical goals. Substitute leadership" (Deming, 1986, p. 24). Within International Foods this was interpreted as meaning that performance appraisals should be eliminated. While much money and time had been spent on teaching the quality management process, nothing had been done to change the old, existing performance appraisal process. Not only was the existing process out of sync with the new corporate quality philosophy, it was also poorly administered. Managers did not devote much time or attention to performance appraisal. The annual Employee Attitude Survey elicited many complaints about the old performance appraisal process. Not only did employees not feel fairly treated, but job actions were threatened. In one plant, a brief "informational" picketing campaign sought to "End Performance Appraisals—Substitute Leadership!" There were many problems; two of which were that managers did not take the time to objectively review performance and that employees had no opportunity for input but could only agree or disagree with their appraisals. Several of the survey

feedback meetings (small round-table discussions of survey results with employees) also exposed strong feelings about the performance appraisal process. As a result, International Foods hired an I/O psychologist to help develop a new performance feedback system that would be consistent with Deming's values and more focused on career development.

The resulting process combines performance feedback with mutual goal setting and career development. Ongoing documentation through self-report compared with management assessment and review provides regular communication between managers and direct reports. Both the manager and the employee can enter information about performance during these meetings. Every six months, a major review meeting is held to discuss key performance during the last six-month period and to discuss and set objectives for the next period. Once a year, the review includes a discussion of the employee's career goals plus active planning of actions needed for advancement. There were some initial complaints about the time demands on managers and that some of the sessions seemed awkward and uncomfortable, but managers and employees have come to believe that the effort is worthwhile.

Three years after implementation of the new process, International Foods, Inc., has received many compliments on the new system. Employee satisfaction is at an all time high on the biennial Employee Attitude Survey. Furthermore, a higher percentage of new supervisors and managers are from internal promotions.

Mississippi Farm Extension Service Performance Appraisal Case

The Mississippi Farm Extension Service was subjected to a class action suit in 1974. The service's African-American extension agents and other professional employees filed suit, claiming that the performance appraisal system was biased in favor of white employees. Initially, the courts agreed. The extension service was directed to use four factors to determine pay and performance: job category, education level, technical knowledge, and tenure. This was an interim solution. The extension service was also assigned the long-term goal of developing and implementing an objective, valid, and nondiscriminatory appraisal process.

This developmental process began with the service hiring consultants, who performed job analyses for each position. Although the consultants were not able to identify quantitative measures that were valid indices for judging an agent's job performance, they did identify forty-two elements representing critical job requirements. The court reviewed this system and found that it was nondiscriminatory in form and use. Even though the form did not use a strict numerical rating system, it was still objective because the extension service developed (and published) explicit definitions and procedures. This publication provided managers with clear criteria regarding job performance and helped to ensure that they evaluated agents and other professional employees consistently and nonsubjectively.

Source: From *Wade* v. *Mississippi Cooperative Extension Service,* 615 F. Supp. 1574 (N.D. Miss.) Modern Business Reports, D3-UP-1R, 1993.

As illustrated in this story, a performance appraisal interview can be an emotionally charged event. No one enjoys criticism, no matter how constructively it is presented:

> In survey after survey, managers overwhelmingly report dissatisfaction with their companies' performance appraisal systems. Typical complaints charge that performance appraisals are a waste of time at best, and destructive to the boss-employee relationship at worst" (Momeyer, 1986, p. 95)

The purpose of this chapter is to discuss ways to create a less emotionally loaded appraisal environment, resulting in a cooperative climate that can benefit employees, managers, and the organization. We will discuss performance appraisal system design, talking with employees, and the legal ramifications of performance appraisal. We will conclude with suggestions on how to apply research findings for improving any existing appraisal process or for developing a new one.

PERFORMANCE APPRAISAL SYSTEM DESIGN

Systems theory is an important theoretical framework from which to begin, because all organizations contain many systems and subsystems, such as reward systems, work systems, communication systems, and performance appraisal systems. These systems continuously interact; if there are problems within one system, they will most likely affect other systems and ultimately the organization as a whole. Therefore it is important that performance appraisal objectives be compatible with the needs of the entire organization. To accomplish this, a performance appraisal system should do the following (Carroll & Schneier, 1982):

1. recognize the need for user acceptance and commitment;
2. be in compliance with organizational policy and legal requirements;
3. determine a cost/benefit ratio in terms of the resources expended for system design and implementation;
4. produce psychometrically sound ratings;
5. provide useful input to other areas of the organization; and
6. maintain, motivate, improve, and manage job performance and job satisfaction.

A wheel diagram (DeVries, Morrison, Shullman, & Gerlach (1986; see Figure 6.1) can be used to illustrate how the performance appraisal system interacts with other systems in the organization.

A **systems approach** to performance appraisal dictates a continual cycle of input, output, and feedback. A central idea is the focus on how well an employee serves his or her internal and external customers. When used directly, this means having those customers complete ratings of performance, which become part of the employee's performance appraisal. This process, called 360-degree feedback, is discussed in detail later in this chapter. The systems approach also recognizes that organizations are fluid rather than static and allows for system modifications that can adapt to both environmental and organizational growth. Let us more closely examine the interactions that take place in a systems approach to performance appraisal (see Figure 6.2).

The process of designing an effective performance appraisal system starts with the identification of organizational goals. From this information, administrators can develop companywide standards, which include performance dimen-

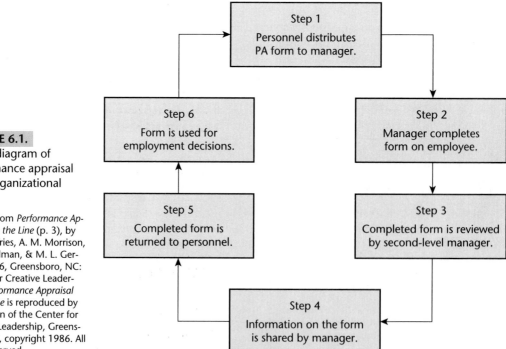

FIGURE 6.1.
Wheel diagram of performance appraisal as an organizational event.

Source: From *Performance Appraisal on the Line* (p. 3), by D. L. DeVries, A. M. Morrison, S. L. Shullman, & M. L. Gerlach, 1986, Greensboro, NC: Center for Creative Leadership. *Performance Appraisal on the Line* is reproduced by permission of the Center for Creative Leadership, Greensboro, NC, copyright 1986. All rights reserved.

Step 1
Personnel distributes PA form to manager.

Step 2
Manager completes form on employee.

Step 3
Completed form is reviewed by second-level manager.

Step 4
Information on the form is shared by manager.

Step 5
Completed form is returned to personnel.

Step 6
Form is used for employment decisions.

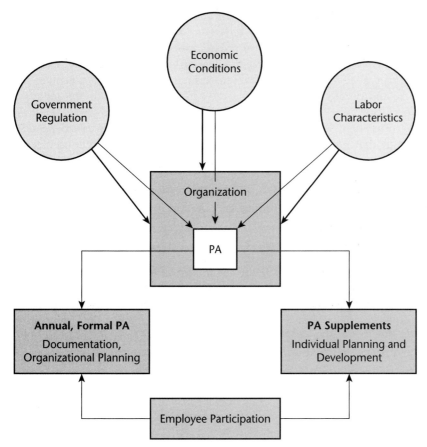

FIGURE 6.2.
Diagram of the systems approach for the design of performance appraisal processes.

Source: From *Performance Appraisal on the Line* (p. 127), by D. L. DeVries, A. M. Morrison, S. L. Shullman, & M. L. Gerlach, 1986, Greensboro, NC: Center for Creative Leadership. *Performance Appraisal on the Line* is reproduced by permission of the Center for Creative Leadership, Greensboro, NC, copyright 1986. All rights reserved.

sions such as quality and quantity of output. With these parameters identified, departmental supervisors can create performance dimensions and standards for specific jobs. These in turn become the objective criteria against which job performance can be assessed. In addition, the organization can determine the appraisal methods that will best measure performance, and then develop and carry out an appraiser training program to accomplish that end.

Once the appraisal system is in place, the supervisor can monitor employee performance to determine whether work-related behavior meets performance standards. The supervisor and the employee can then develop ways to direct the employee toward the achievement of job goals. Fi-

nally, the organization can determine the general effectiveness of the performance appraisal system by analyzing data collected from performance reviews. Consequently, the organizational goals, performance standards, appraiser training program, or even the appraisal methods themselves may be changed to improve the appraisal system.

MEASUREMENT OF JOB PERFORMANCE

Performance Criteria

A major characteristic of performance criteria is that they must be able to differentiate among individuals (Blum & Naylor, 1968). The development of criteria (discussed in detail in Chapter 5) is the process of determining performance dimensions—whether they are behavior-based or trait-based—that will permit accurate description of job performance, and differentiate the poor from the effective performer.

As discussed in Chapter 5, proponents of the multiple criteria approach argue that unrelated elements cannot be combined into any one measure of success on the job. For instance, a given employee may be an extremely high producer but is often tardy or absent. How would this person be rated? In the multiple criteria approach, the person's job performance would be viewed as a behavioral construct consisting of several dimensions that would include both the strengths (high production) and the weaknesses (late, absent) of the individual. Our worker would receive one score (a high one) for high production and a separate (low) score for attendance. Both scores would be reported in the appraisal. In contrast, if only a single score were reported, it would be impossible to give meaningful feedback to the worker on the attendance problem. A composite performance score might rate the worker's performance as "average" and give the impression that everything was all right. An example of a well-designed system using multiple criteria is described in Practice Perspective 6.1.

As suggested in Chapter 5, the opposing view suggests that job performance criteria can be meaningfully combined to form a composite measure of success. It has been argued that a composite criterion makes it easier to compare individuals and make decisions about who is most valuable to the organization. Proponents of this approach are less concerned with behavioral processes and place the major emphasis on the individual's overall worth to the organization. In this scenario the employee mentioned above would be rated by factoring high productivity along with undesirable tardiness and absenteeism. The supervisor would consider all the variables to produce an *overall* rating of the employee and his or her worth to the organization. Very different results might be obtained in different organizations. If the worker's job required the employee to work independently, tardiness and absenteeism might have a low weight in calculating the performance score. In this situation the overall rating would be high. However, if the employee worked as a part of an interdependent work team in which tardiness and absenteeism had a significant effect on overall productivity, then this aspect of their performance would have a heavier weight, and the overall rating of job performance would be low.

Performance Dimensions

Performance measurement consists of comparing actual outcomes with planned outcomes or production standards. To effectively measure job performance, it is vital that the organization precisely define the job by identifying the performance dimensions on which the employee will be assessed.

Several types of data (see Chapter 5) describe successful performance. **Objective data** are quantitative descriptions of employee outcomes, such as counts of units produced (Guion, 1961). Quantity of output, quality of output (e.g., number of errors), and speed of performance are examples of objective data. **Personnel data** consist of quantitative information about the individual's personal actions, such as absences, tardiness, rate of advancement, or accidents. Objective and personnel data are discrete and observable; they do not require appraiser opinion, judgment, or subjective interpretation. **Judgmental data,** by contrast, represent the opinions of one individual about another individual's job performance. These judgments (appraisals) can be made by comparing, ranging, rating, or evaluating the employee. Comparing involves matching two or more employees to show their performance relative to one another. Ranging ranks the employees from high to low in performance, using a common scale. Rating simply describes the performance level of an employee by using a

PRACTICE PERSPECTIVE 6.1

Westinghouse Electric Corporation

The implementation of a new compensation program for nonexempt employees forced Westinghouse to develop a complementary performance appraisal system (Cowfer & Sujansky, 1987). The company's human resource department acknowledged that it would be a mistake to create such a system without giving appraisers and appraisees the opportunity to contribute to its development. This idea is the essence of the participative approach to management. Westinghouse formed a performance appraisal task force made up of nonexempt employees and managers. With the help of an outside consultant the task force played a major role in the creation of the new appraisal system. With input and support from other nonexempt employees and managers, the task force reviewed job descriptions and wrote specific job standards. The task force members evaluated existing appraisal practices and identified them as either successful or unsuccessful. Of particular concern was the opportunity for halo effect, recency error, and central tendency error in the existing system. These efforts resulted in a new system that successfully combined proven techniques with newly created elements.

The new system called for one formal appraisal per calendar year, to take place in March, April, or May for all nonexempt employees. A new appraisal form was designed that contained job descriptions and performance standards for each position. In response to the need for documentation to support employee appraisals, the formal review was supplemented by at least three annual coaching and counseling sessions. A reference form was created to guide managers through these sessions and to serve as documentation for the formal review.

The task force also acknowledged the issue of employee development. After exploring several options, they determined that nonexempt employee developmental plans that created improvement plans for employees who received substandard ratings had a place in the formal appraisal process. The manager outlined the plan and reviewed it with the employee. The new system also required that a developmental plan be established for each employee during the formal review session.

The task force recommended that *all* management employees, even those without direct supervisory responsibilities, receive training in the new system. In fact, it was suggested that all nonexempt employees also receive training. Managers received training in how to be more effective in coaching and counseling, maintaining appropriate records, and conducting the formal appraisal session. In an attempt to communicate to employees their responsibilities within the new system, such as providing feedback and communicating with the manager, nonexempt employees' training sessions included instructions for receiving coaching and counseling. They were also encouraged to maintain their own forms of documentation regarding their performance and anything else that could affect the appraisal process.

In keeping with a participative approach to management, Westinghouse monitored the new appraisal system using feedback from both appraisers and appraisees. Specific areas of interest included the practicality of the appraisal form, the value of the coaching sessions, and the quality of performance standards. This information helped Westinghouse to determine the validity of its new appraisal program and identified areas that required further development.

Westinghouse followed all the steps that are crucial to the systems approach to performance appraisal. First, the company identified its needs and goals. Next, it determined the methods that would be most useful in meeting their needs. The creation of the new system involved employees at all levels, which increased employee commitment to, and acceptance of, the appraisal program. Finally, Westinghouse adequately trained all employees and instituted a system of monitoring the effectiveness of the new program. Not only did Westinghouse create a more successful appraisal program, it also succeeded in creating a more participative environment that had positive effects on all areas of the organization.

Source: Adapted from "Appraisal Development at Westinghouse," by D. B. Cowfer and J. Sujansky, 1987. *Training and Development Journal, 41*(7), 40–43. Reprinted with permission.

value on a standard scale. Evaluating assigns a numerical value representing the judgment of the quality of the performance. Whatever the appraisal method, the measurement of performance must be made according to some type of standard. These standards can be behavior-based or trait-based.

Behavior-based performance dimensions focus on the behaviors that are necessary for successful performance. These behaviors are derived either from the job analysis or from behaviors that have been observed and measured on the job. The critical incidents rating method and the behaviorally anchored rating scale (BARS) are two examples of behavior-based measurement techniques. These methods are discussed in detail in a later section.

Recent research has investigated the factors that can influence job analysis and performance ratings. Yammarino and Waldman (1993) had supervisors and employees rate job performance on skill dimensions and the importance attributed to those skills. In matched skill areas these ratings were positively correlated when job incumbents completed both sets of ratings and when supervisors completed both. Incumbents and supervisors agreed moderately on which skill areas were important for various managerial positions, but inter-rater agreement was much lower for performance ratings. Incumbents' ratings of job skill importance were somewhat biased by their corresponding perceptions of skill performance. They also found that supervisory ratings were less biased. The correlations between performance and importance ratings of supervisors were lower than those for incumbents. Yammarino and Avolio interpreted this finding as an indication that supervisors may have less ego involvement when providing skill importance ratings and thus may be more objective. After combining their findings with those of Waldman, Yammarino, and Avolio (1990), Yammarino and Waldman concluded that supervisory ratings may be superior to employee ratings for the purposes of job analy-

sis. It appears that incumbents and supervisors can more easily reach agreement on skill importance than on skill performance. The implication is that multiple sources of skill performance assessment are necessary in evaluating skill performance levels of individuals.

Trait-based performance dimensions focus on the personal qualities that influence performance, such as motivation, initiative, and attitude. One way to measure these factors is the **adjective checklist method.** A list of adjectives describing desired and undesired job behaviors or characteristics is given to the rater, who then checks off the adjectives that reflect the behavior of the person being rated. The difficulty with this approach is that it is open to interpretation. Different perceptions of the words on the list and the behavior or characteristics they describe can influence the ratings and affect the validity of the appraisal. Often, this method includes some personality characteristics as well. High ratings in personality characteristics do not necessarily affirm good performance. However, the validity of a trait-based system can be improved by describing relevant employee characteristics in terms of specific, job-related behaviors. In other words, the trait rating must be backed up by job facts. Finally, the appraiser and appraisee agree about the meaning of the trait as it applies to the workplace to reduce the opportunity for interpretative differences.

METHODS OF APPRAISAL

Once the dimensions for describing job criteria and behavior have been developed, the organization must decide how it will appraise performance. A variety of methods are available, each with its own combination of strengths and weaknesses. No one technique, however, can satisfy all of the expectations an organization places on a performance appraisal system (Oberg, 1972). What works well for one company may be a dismal failure for another. When choosing an appraisal method, each business must consider the many variables that are unique to its own situation, such as the type of goods or services; production and delivery methods; the ability to specify quality and quantity of output; the physical locations of work sites; employee needs, perceptions, demands, personal histories, and backgrounds; business history and background; legal requirements; and the organizational hierarchy (Henderson, 1984).

Additionally, there must be a strong understanding of organizational performance standards so that the rating method(s) selected can accurately assess employee performance in light of those standards. Carroll and Schneier (1982) and Henderson (1984) suggested a variety of rating methods. Following are a few of the most common options.

Rating Scales

The most widely used and easiest to administer measure of performance is the rating scale. In a study to identify nonmanagerial performance appraisal practices in large U.S. cities, England and Parle (1987) found that 30% (37) of the cities surveyed used the rating scale alone to assess job performance of city personnel.

Rating scales identify individual employees' strengths and weaknesses in different aspects of job performance. A **graphic rating scale** uses predetermined scales to indicate the degree of performance exhibited by the employee and observed by the appraiser. It usually consists of a list of job-related traits and descriptions of each trait and identifies the degree to which the employee demonstrates each trait. Careful attention must be given to the construction of this list. Too many intervals can result in repetition of labeling descriptors; too few intervals may omit relevant distinctions among levels of performance. Furthermore, when an uneven number of anchor points is used, appraisers are inclined to use the average (central tendency) value to avoid making a judgment. An even number of anchor points, on the other hand, has no absolute median and forces the appraiser to choose either the high or low end of a middle value.

In this technique, points are assigned to each rating to determine a value for overall performance and to compare employees against job performance standards and other employees. In some cases, weights are assigned to give added value to the more important traits. Some rating scales list job-related traits in descending order of importance, enabling both the appraiser and the appraisee to identify the most important job aspects at a glance.

Graphic scales can be presented in a variety of ways. Table 6.1 on page 168 illustrates scales that were designed to appraise employee cooperation. The six examples shown range from a single design with minimal cues to a more complex design with descriptive cues. Visual proportioning indicates a bar scale with several intervals and a high–low anchor point (Example 1). A more precise scale can quantify the response by assigning values to each interval (Example 2). Descriptors can be assigned to each interval to more clearly define the ratings (Examples 3 and 4). Numerical and verbal standards can be combined to provide precise identification of performance levels and to help eliminate response ambiguity (Example 5). Adding definitions to the rating scale further enhances the precision of the appraisal instrument (Examples 5 and 6).

In 1980, Landy and Farr extensively reviewed the research on rating scales. They concluded that performance appraisal ratings were not affected by changes in the scale format, and they called for a moratorium on further research in this area. However, in her article published in 1993, Charmine Härtel found differences attributable to the field independence or dependence of the raters. Field dependence refers to cognitive dependence on the external organization of information. A rater who is field dependent will perform better on tasks in which clear structure (a rating scale) is provided. Field independence refers to the ability to impose organization on

| **TABLE 6.1** | Examples of numerically and adjective-anchored rating scales |

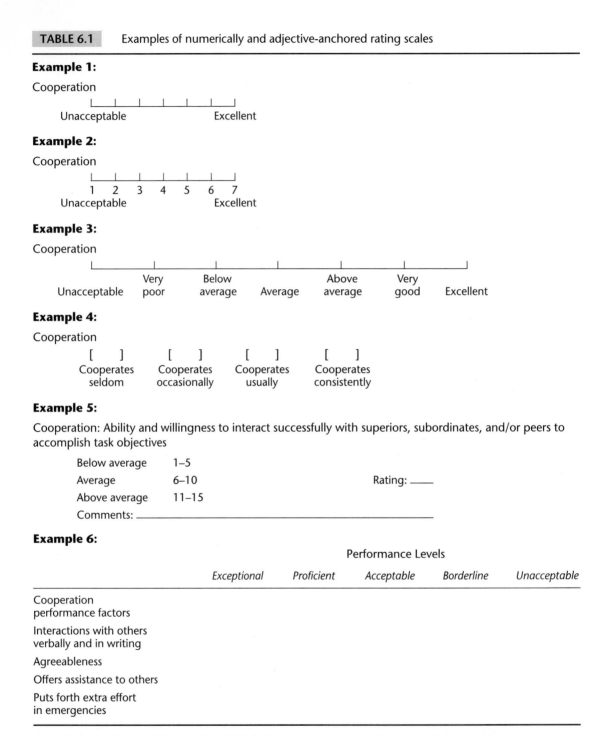

Example 1:

Cooperation

Unacceptable   Excellent

Example 2:

Cooperation

1 2 3 4 5 6 7
Unacceptable   Excellent

Example 3:

Cooperation

| | Very | Below | | Above | Very | |
| Unacceptable | poor | average | Average | average | good | Excellent |

Example 4:

Cooperation

[   ]   [   ]   [   ]   [   ]
Cooperates   Cooperates   Cooperates   Cooperates
seldom   occasionally usually   consistently

Example 5:

Cooperation: Ability and willingness to interact successfully with superiors, subordinates, and/or peers to accomplish task objectives

Below average   1–5
Average   6–10   Rating: ____
Above average   11–15
Comments: _____

Example 6:

	Performance Levels				
	Exceptional	*Proficient*	*Acceptable*	*Borderline*	*Unacceptable*
Cooperation performance factors					
Interactions with others verbally and in writing					
Agreeableness					
Offers assistance to others					
Puts forth extra effort in emergencies					

Source: From Carroll, S. J., & Schneier, C. E. (1982). *Performance appraisal and review systems: The identification, measurement and development of performance in organizations* (p. 104), by S. J. Carroll and C. E. Schneier, 1982, Glenview, IL: Scott, Foresman. Copyright 1982 by Scott, Foresman. Reprinted with permission.

information independent of the form in which it is perceived. A rater who is field independent will perform well regardless of whether the task structure (the rating scale) is clear or ambiguous. Härtel found that field-independent raters, who organized information independently of the form in which it was received, were more accurate than field-dependent raters who were cognitively dependent on the external organization of information. Field independent raters were also more confident in their ratings and less frustrated or confused by rating tasks. Härtel also found that the ratings by field-dependent raters were significantly influenced by the level of structure in the scale format. Härtel's findings indicate that rater field dependence may be an important factor to consider in designing graphic rating scales for performance appraisals.

Checklists

A **checklist** consists of a set of objective statements or adjectives that describe desired and undesired job behaviors. The appraisers do not evaluate their employees; they objectively report employee actions. If the appraisers believe that the employees have exhibited a listed trait, they check the corresponding item; if not, that item is left blank. Several items can be representative of an employee's behavior on any given job dimension. Table 6.2 provides an example of an adjective checklist.

Checklist statements can be assigned values and weights that are determined by using the mean value assigned to each statement. When the appraiser completes the checklist rating, the items are averaged to determine the overall score.

The **forced-choice checklist,** an expansion of the checklist technique, was developed to help eliminate errors from a generalized overall rating (halo errors) and errors from being too generous or critical (leniency/harshness errors). Instead of indicating the degree to which a trait is present, the appraiser merely assesses whether a particular trait is demonstrated by the employee. The forced-choice format is based on the

TABLE 6.2   Example of an adjective checklist used for performance appraisal

Position: Store Manager

_____ Considerate

_____ Works quickly

_____ Attentive to detail

_____ Knowledgeable

_____ Initiating

_____ Decisive

_____ Good leader

_____ Neat appearance

_____ Attentive to safety

_____ Cooperative

_____ Articulate

_____ Good writer

_____ Punctual

_____ Eager to learn

Source: From Carroll, S. J., & Schneier, C. E. (1982). *Performance appraisal and review systems: The identification, measurement and development of performance in organizations* (p. 120), by S. J. Carroll and C. E. Schneier, 1982, Glenview, IL: Scott, Foresman. Copyright 1982 by Scott, Foresman. Reprinted with permission.

idea that a variety of behaviors exist on any job, some effective and some ineffective. Some of the effective behaviors are highly relevant and critical for job performance; other effective behaviors are "nice" but not all that important for job performance. In contrast, some of the ineffective behaviors are also highly relevant and critical in job performance, while others are "bad" but do not really affect job performance much. A forced-choice checklist presents the appraiser with a group of statements that have been previously judged for their desirability as well as for their ability to discriminate good performance from poor performance.

For example, the appraiser may be asked to choose two of four statements that most accurately describe the employee. All choices within the group of statements appear equally favorable, so the appraiser is likely to select the statement that most accurately describes the employee. What the appraiser does not know is that one of these behaviors has been shown to be critical for job performance. An employee who demonstrates that behavior receives a higher score than does one who demonstrates the other behavior. For an example, see Table 6.3. Unfortunately, in its attempt to avoid rater bias, the

---

TABLE 6.3   Example of Forced-Choice Performance Rating Scales

---

In each group place a checkmark in front of the statement that you believe best characterizes the employee under consideration. Be sure to put only one checkmark in each group of statements.

_____   Is very patient

_____   Arrives at conclusions logically

_____   Assumes responsibility for his own mistakes

_____   Delegates work very wisely

_____   Is exceptionally fair

_____   Inspires his associates

In each group place a checkmark in front of the statement that you believe best characterizes the employee under consideration and another checkmark in front of the statement that you believe least characterizes him. Be sure to put two and only two checkmarks in each group of statements.

_____   Has a well-rounded personality

_____   Lacks force and drive

_____   Tends to be overbearing

_____   Shows foresight

_____   Displays disloyalty

_____   Is almost indispensable

_____   Makes many mistakes

_____   Has a very promising future

Source: From *Industrial and Organizational Psychology* (p. 315), by A. K. Korman, © 1971. Englewood Cliffs, NJ: Prentice-Hall, Inc. Reprinted by permission of Prentice-Hall, Upper Saddle River, NJ.

forced-choice checklist does not provide much basis for employee feedback, since the appraiser is not made aware of the values assigned to each statement. Forced-choice ratings have two serious problems: They are very difficult to construct, and raters do not like them. This is because raters feel that they are not trusted to give a meaningful rating. They also often report that forced-choice ratings have a "when did you stop beating your spouse?" sense to them.

Recent research by Reilly, Henry, and Smither (1990) demonstrated that behavioral checklists can reduce cognitive demands on the rater. This is because the scale focuses the rater's attention on specific dimension-relevant behaviors. Additionally, the rater's focus on a standard list of relevant behaviors should result in less contrast effect. That is, the rater should be less inclined to make judgments by contrasting the ratee's performance with the way the rater perceives himself or herself performing. Maurer, Palmer, and Ashe (1993) tested the impact of behavioral checklists on contrast effects. They found that although behavioral checklists were susceptible to contrast effects, they did not increase contrast. The contrast effects that they found were consistent with those previously reported. Specifically, shifts in the observed ratings were upward in the poor performance context and downward in the good performance context.

Critical Incidents

The **critical incidents method** (Flanagan, 1949) focuses on actual job behavior. The appraiser maintains a log of observed behaviors that are considered either successful or unsuccessful. This method requires close, systematic observation and is subject to the recency of events error, where the appraisal is based on recent, easily remembered behavior. If documentation of behaviors is not prompt, accurate recall is diminished and the integrity of the performance measurement instrument is threatened. Additionally, if rater guidelines are not developed, the appraiser's observations can be affected by personal bias. The appraiser's writing skills also have a significant impact on the description of critical incidents and can either enhance or detract from the employee's overall appraisal.

The critical incidents method was developed in an attempt to overcome subjectivity. However, unless the appraiser is consistent in observing and describing all critical behaviors, rater bias is not diminished. Employees may become anxious and feel less free to respond to new situations if their behavior is constantly monitored and documented. Despite these drawbacks, the critical incidents method has value because of its focus on actual job behaviors and its ability to provide appraisal ratings that are easy to defend.

Behaviorally Anchored Rating Scales

Developing **behaviorally anchored rating scales (BARS)** is a complex process that has its origins in the checklist and critical incidents methods. Each step of the procedure requires a separate group of job experts. Landy and Farr (1983) compiled a table that clearly identifies the steps in this procedure (see Table 6.4).

A BARS rating form usually consists of six to ten key performance dimensions. Each dimension is anchored with positive and negative critical incidents arranged in order of value on the rating scale. Performance expectations are clearly defined, and employees are rated on each dimension.

TABLE 6.4   Outline of procedure for developing behaviorally anchored rating scales (BARS)

Stage	Process
Identification and definition of performance dimensions	Group A of job experts identifies all important dimensions of performance for job in question. They also define conceptually each performance dimension and define high, average, and low performance on each dimension.
Generation of behavior examples	Group B of job experts gives examples of good, average, and poor job behaviors for each performance dimension. (Examples are edited by personnel researchers to reduce redundancy and to place each example in the expectation format.)
Retranslation and allocation	Group C of job experts is presented with a randomized list of behavioral examples and a list of the performance dimensions. They each independently allocate or classify each behavioral example to the performance dimension that it best represents. (A behavioral example is eliminated by the personnel researcher unless a large majority (e.g., 70%) of the group assigns it to the same performance dimension.)
Scaling	Group D of job experts evaluates the behavioral examples meeting the allocation criterion in the previous step in terms of effectiveness of the performance described.
Scale anchor selection	Personnel researcher computes the mean and standard deviation of the ratings given to each behavioral example in the scaling step. Examples are selected as anchors for each performance dimension such that items have mean values that provide anchors for the entire performance scale (from low to high) and that items have relatively small standard deviations.

Source: From *The Measurement of Work Performance* (p. 61), by F. J. Landy and J. L. Farr, 1983, New York, NY: Academic Press. Copyright 1983 by Academic Press. Reprinted with permission.

Feedback is based on information derived from behavioral anchors. However, despite its success, Borman and Dunnette (1975) found that this method was prone to halo, harshness, and leniency rating errors.

Behavioral Observation Scales

Behavioral observation scales (BOS) are similar to the BARS method, except that the appraiser indicates the frequency of occurrences of job-related behaviors. Using a Likert-type scale, in which each alternative answer has a preassigned scoring weight, the appraiser judges the employee by how often a behavior is exhibited. Table 6.5 presents an example of a scale in which each statement can be assigned the weight of 1 (almost always) to 5 (almost never). BOS can cover several aspects of job performance, overall performance being calculated by averaging individual scores on each dimension. This procedure is similar to the checklist scale because employees can be compared on each dimension as well as on overall performance. One criticism of BOS is that

---

TABLE 6.5   Example of a behavioral observation scale (BOS)

Punch Press Operator

1. Checks press for loose dies or other parts.
   Almost never   5   4   3   2   1   Almost always

2. Cleans all machine parts with proper solvents.
   Almost never   5   4   3   2   1   Almost always

3. Leaves machine running when not using it.
   Almost never   5   4   3   2   1   Almost always

4. Wears all safety equipment and clothing.
   Almost never   5   4   3   2   1   Almost always

5. Feeds machine so as to prevent jamming or other malfunctioning.
   Almost never   5   4   3   2   1   Almost always

Source: From Carroll, S. J., & Schneier, C. E. (1982). *Performance appraisal and review systems: The identification, measurement and development of performance in organizations* (p. 104), by S. J. Carroll and C. E. Schneier, 1982, Glenview, IL: Scott, Foresman. Copyright 1982 by Scott, Foresman. Reprinted with permission.

---

appraiser accuracy diminishes over time. Unless the appraiser documents every occurrence of a specific behavior, it is unlikely that he or she will be able to correctly identify the number of occurrences over a period of six to twelve months (the normal time between performance appraisals).

A strength of this method, however, lies in its effectiveness as a goal-setting instrument. A study by Tziner and Kopelman (1988) found the BOS method to be superior to the graphic rating scale with regard to goal clarity. While the graphic rating scale was unclear regarding goal actions and assumed that all employees could formulate behaviors appropriate for achieving stated goals, the BOS method aided employees in achieving goals by providing direction and examples of specific behaviors. As a result, the information included on the BOS rating form facilitates a more effective appraisal interview and feedback session.

Essay Evaluations

The appraiser, using the **essay evaluation** method, describes in essay format the employee's behavior, progress, and performance, using predetermined guidelines. Essay evaluation requires good communication and writing skills on the part of the assessor and is subject to many of the same biases as the critical incidents method. This method can be used singularly to appraise performance but is most effectively implemented in conjunction with some other, more structured form of appraisal, such as the graphic rating scale.

Management by Objectives

The **management by objectives (MBO)** approach stands apart from other methods in that it is more a management philosophy than an evaluation program. Increasingly popular since Peter F. Drucker first formalized the concept in 1954, MBO recognizes the importance of goals for directing and motivating human behavior. With this method, managers and employees work together to plan, organize, control, communicate, and evaluate objectives. Since the MBO method is a process of performance management, it re-

PRACTICE PERSPECTIVE 6.2

Key Bank of Utah

Deregulation and fierce competition from numerous sectors encouraged Key Bank of Utah to address the issue of productivity. Key Bank's concerns included ritualistic annual goal-setting meetings, ineffective performance evaluation systems, and other unproductive activities.

After hours of research, management discussions, and consultation with outside specialists, the Key Bank implemented what it termed the "Performance Management System" (Addams & Embley, 1988). Senior human resources managers combined the concepts of strategic planning, performance appraisal, and increased productivity into one integrated performance management system consisting of four steps:

1. Corporate strategies
2. Department strategies
3. Individual position descriptions
4. Individual performance planning and review

The first step addressed overall organizational goals. This time-consuming and intensive process developed the overall corporate mission statement, objectives, and strategies. The second step, developing department strategies, was designed to ensure that departmental mission statements were consistent with corporate objectives. Managers and employees from each department worked together to develop their mission statements and objectives.

Once departmental strategies were identified, individual position descriptions were analyzed and rewritten, if necessary, to meet departmental and corporate objectives. Key Bank believes that the result was a true team effort in which each employee understands how they affect corporate performance.

The final step, individual performance planning and review, measured the individual's performance in relation to his or her achievement of established accountabilities. A Performance Planning and Review (PP&R) record was developed to integrate established accountabilities with employee performance. Each accountability had six descriptors: weight, measure, standard, goal, actual performance, and personal development plan. The supervisor and employee determined the weight, measure, standard, and goal before the employee began working toward achieving results. This performance appraisal system was employee-driven. The supervisor served as the coach and worked with the employee to decide on a personal development plan.

The PP&R evaluation system became a tool for individual and organizational growth and achievement. As a result of implementing this performance management system, Key Bank realized a number of improvements: Managers had greater control over work activities, decision making moved down the chain of command, employees and supervisors felt that performance evaluations were equitable, communication among managers and between managers and employees increased, and the program helped to develop strong managers.

Source: Adapted from "Performance Management Systems: From Strategic Planning to Employee Productivity," by H. L. Addams and K. Embley, 1988, *Personnel, 66,* 55–60. Reprinted by permission of American Management Association, New York.

quires frequent feedback and assessment. Performance discussions focus on job behaviors only as they pertain to results. During the formal performance evaluation, the manager and the employee analyze objectives that have and have not been achieved and target a course of action for the next performance period.

Using a balanced sample of larger companies (with more than 500 employees) and smaller companies (with fewer than 500 employees), a recent study by Smith, Hornsby, and Shirmeyer (1996) reported that 31.8% of these companies applied the MBO approach to their performance appraisal programs. One example of an MBO approach is the Performance Planning and Review (PP&R) procedure developed by the Key Bank of Utah as described in Practice Perspective 6.2. Various objectives are set in these programs, from routine duties explicit in the language of the job to more complex goals.

However, use of this method has resulted in questions regarding the validity of MBO as an appraisal instrument.

While almost all employees would like to participate in organizational decision making, unless they are involved in determining specifically how and when they will do their work and the resources they will use, the setting of performance goals has little or no meaning. The MBO method often focuses on analyzing the ends but not the means. In many cases, if performance standards are met, the behaviors applied are considered to be acceptable and little attention is given to procuring new resources or considering other behaviors. Only when performance standards are not met is action taken to implement new behaviors.

Several other arguments have been made for the imminent failure of MBO as an appraisal system (Kane & Freeman, 1986). For example, it may undermine the very nature of a job by continually redefining the job function. Another contention is that the MBO approach to measuring job performance does not allow for comparison among employees. Supervisory discretion is at its peak with this approach. Manager bias can affect the interpretation of organizational goals, the determination of desirable objectives, and the equitable distribution of goals among employees. Likewise, the employee's ability to understand, accept, and attain job goals can be affected by subjectivity. Organizational goals may not be stated in a way that has value or meaning for the employee, and the fear of future goals being set too high may predispose the employee to avoid performance that exceeds objectives. Kane and Freeman (1986) suggested that, while MBO can be an effective planning tool, its role as an appraisal instrument should be limited.

WHO SHOULD EVALUATE PERFORMANCE?

Because to *appraise* is to give an expert judgment of value or merit, it is important to identify the person who is qualified to make accurate and effective performance appraisals. However, all appraisers bring a variety of characteristics to the evaluation. Demographic variables, psychological variables (such as personality and intellect), cognitive processes, and job-related variables (such as supervisory expertise, leadership style, and ability) all affect the way an appraiser rates an employee.

An effective appraiser is familiar with specific job responsibilities, aware of employee strengths and weaknesses, and able to assess performance according to organizational and unit goals. The appraiser records observed behaviors that affect job performance in order to recall them at the time of the formal appraisal. Finally, the appraiser creates a safe, open atmosphere in which to interact with the employee. An effective interaction should include communicating goals, praise, criticism, reward, and penalties. In addition, it should include suggestions of alternative behaviors that could make the employee more productive and lead to greater rewards and job satisfaction.

Latham and Wexley (1977) suggested that an ideal performance appraisal system should combine information from multiple sources to provide an integrated assessment. This type of integration would maximize the strengths of individual appraisers and minimize their weaknesses. Farth, Werbel, and Bedeian (1988) conducted a study that examined how information provided by different appraisers could be combined to measure an employee's performance. In the following section we will take a closer look at this study, which focuses primarily on incorporating self-appraisal performance evaluations into traditional supervisor-conducted evaluations.

Supervisor Appraisal

Most companies assign the task of employee appraisal to the immediate supervisor because that individual has the most contact with the employee. However, in a study to determine the effect of appraiser–appraisee acquaintance on performance ratings, Landy and Guion (1970) suggested that the type of contact between the appraiser and the appraisee might be a more critical factor in the reliability of ratings than the frequency of contact. The supervisor, then, would still be the best choice as an appraiser, not because of the number of contacts he or she has with the employee, but because the contact is job-relevant.

However, questions have been raised about the supervisor's ability to maintain meaningful contact with the employee, primarily because of the appraiser's dual role as judge and counselor. It has also been suggested that supervisors may hesitate to assume the role of judge, since negative evaluations of employees could have negative consequences (Carroll & Schneier, 1982). A possible solution to this dilemma lies in how the evaluation interview is handled. We will discuss this in a later section.

Supervisors often avoid conducting formal performance appraisals. This avoidance can be politically motivated (Schmitt & Klimoski, 1990). Research in this area indicates that supervisors are often more concerned with how their ratings will serve their interests as managers than with how accurate are the ratings. A supervisor may be concerned about losing a good employee if that employee's appraisal is too good. Or the concern may be that an employee in a hard-to-fill job may be lost if rated too low. These concerns can cause supervisors to increase or decrease ratings inappropriately. In some situations, supervisors may avoid completing the performance ratings. This last strategy is often preferred when the performance appraisal system allows it. Fried, Tiegs, and Bellamy (1992) examined supervisors' decisions about conducting formal evaluations during two consecutive performance appraisal periods. The main variables that affected these decisions, in decreasing order, were the length of time the employee had been under the supervisor's jurisdiction, the employee's job experience, the level of trust between the employee and supervisor,

the amount of structure the supervisor provided for the employee, and the amount of confidence the employee had in the performance appraisal system.

Another shortcoming of supervisor appraisal is that it is very difficult, perhaps impossible, for one supervisor to observe and measure the job performances of a number of employees. Supervisors are not omnipresent; they cannot possibly be aware of the range of behaviors exhibited by employees and the overall impact of those behaviors on others (Henderson, 1984). One way to counter this problem is to implement a system of self-appraisal or peer appraisal, which can then be integrated with the supervisor's evaluation.

On the other hand, supervisory ratings can be more performance related, and less susceptible to racial bias, than peer ratings (Oppler, Campbell, Pulakos, & Borman, 1992).

Self-Appraisal

Since individuals are usually very knowledgeable about their own behavior, **self-appraisal** can be a logical choice. Self-appraisal has received increased attention as more companies implement goal-setting approaches to performance appraisal. It is particularly useful for purposes of self-development programs such as identifying individual training needs. Self-appraisal not only permits the employee to assess his or her own potential and progress, it provides a forum for the employee to articulate future goals, such as personal development, job growth, and promotional opportunities. A recent book by David Peterson and Mary Dee Hicks (1996a), *Development First: Strategies for Self-Development*, provides practical guidelines for self-development in the workplace of the 1990s.

A major drawback to self-appraisal is that most individuals believe that they are average or above-average employees. Research indicates that self-appraisal ratings tend to be inflated (Farth, Werbel, & Bedeian, 1988). Lenient self-appraisals may occur if employees believe that they will lead to personal gain, such as a salary increase or promotion, and if no separate measure of performance is available. However, additional research into the validity of self-appraisals has shown that they are at least as predictive as other evaluation methods and that employees are capable of realistic self-appraisals when evaluation is restricted to observable dimensions.

In spite of ongoing arguments about the validity of self-appraisal, the people who are being appraised are the closest to the information about their own job knowledge and performance. Self-appraisals can result in greater job satisfaction, less frustration with the appraisal process, and a more meaningful performance appraisal interview. Self-appraisal also increases employee participation and provides employees with a greater sense of control over the performance review. Given these considerations, it would make sense to integrate self-appraisals into a traditional evaluation process. Farth, Werbel, and Bedeian (1988) suggested using self-appraisal as a basis for the performance appraisal interview to increase communication between appraiser and appraisee. There are some criteria that must be met for successful integration of self-appraisal techniques.

Because a self-appraisal-based evaluation system solicits employee involvement in the appraisal process, it works best in an organization that has a participative management style. Self-appraisal can be effective when employees work independently with minimal supervision. In these situations, self-appraisal can add valuable information about unique, often unobserved dimensions of the job. However, it is unlikely that any two employees will place equal importance on the same aspects of performance. Consequently, an organization that uses this technique must clearly define performance criteria to help employees prepare reliable and valid self-reports. Self-appraisals are rarely used as the sole basis for determining salary increases or promotions.

Peer Appraisal

Peers and coworkers can often offer valid insights into job behaviors. There are three peer appraisal techniques: peer rating, peer ranking, and peer nomination. **Peer rating** and **peer ranking** are handled in the same manner as supervisor rating and ranking. **Peer nomination** consists of having each member of the work unit indicate the member(s) he or she perceives as best or most competent on some specified performance dimension or characteristic. Self-nominations usually are not allowed.

There are definite drawbacks to peer appraisal. If not properly handled, peer evaluations can damage social interactions between coworkers. In addition, Henderson (1984) suggested that individuals may have difficulty assessing peer job behavior because they frequently do not have enough information about coworker job requirements and actual performance. In addition, peer perspectives and supervisory perspectives might differ with regard to specific employee jobs and accomplishments. Finally, when reward systems are competitive, peer appraisals may be prejudicial.

To minimize the influence of friendships on peer ratings, peer appraisal can be used strictly as a developmental tool to assist the employee in becoming a more effective part of the organization. Similar to self-appraisal, peer-appraisal accuracy increases when it is used to aid in personnel development, rather than to make decisions about compensation or promotion. Employing a professional counselor, either in-house or external, to review peer appraisals and to discuss them with each employee, may make possible the effective use of this technique in a nonthreatening manner that eliminates personal bias. The supervisor, then, would engage only in identifying the employee behaviors that indicate improved performance and deserve reward.

Group Ratings

Lanza (1985) recommended group appraisal as a supplement to individual appraisals. The goal of group appraisal is to build a spirit of teamwork that can result in improved productivity and morale. In the group appraisal, everyone is rated, including the supervisor. This process provides the supervisor with information about the group's interpersonal dynamics. The supervisor then interviews each employee to discuss his or her rating. Lanza warns that for group appraisal to be effective, there has to be a trusting relationship between the supervisor and the employees and confidentiality must be stressed. While this type of appraisal is best used in conjunction with other methods, it does have some significant advantages: It removes the supervisor from the role of sole rater, ratings are not tied to the reward system, ratings may be more objective, and the process could foster increased participation among the work group.

Martell and Borg (1993) examined the accuracy of group performance appraisal ratings. They found that when the ratings were delayed (five days) rather than being immediate, groups remembered the behaviors on a checklist more accurately than did individuals, although they also adopted more liberal decision criteria. No differences were found in the immediate ratings. Martell and Borg concluded that group ratings can help but do not fully solve problems of rating accuracy.

360-Degree Feedback Systems

A current method of performance appraisal that is growing in popularity is **360-degree feedback**. This appraisal method obtains ratings from all the people who surround the person being rated. The full-circle, 360-degree view, is more comprehensive than other methods of appraisal because of the variety of perspectives included. Typically, ratings are obtained from the ratee, the ratee's immediate superior, the ratee's peers, and those who directly report to him or her (all of them, or a representative sample of them). In addition, some 360-degree appraisals are completed by others who know or work with the ratee, such as customers and sales contacts, project team members, occasional work contacts inside and outside of the company, family members, and friends. In fact, almost anyone who knows or has been associated with the ratee can be a potential rater of performance. This method

has also been called multirater feedback, multi-perspective ratings, upward feedback, and full-circle feedback.

One of the reasons for the popularity of 360-degree feedback is that it provides direct, behavioral feedback to the manager about his or her impact on others. Performance appraisal systems are supposed to do this, but few succeed. The 360-degree feedback addresses a key weakness that exists in the more traditional performance appraisals for managers: they do not include feedback from subordinates or peers.

A typical 360-degree survey process develops a survey instrument or uses a published instrument that focuses on behaviors of interest. For example, the Clark Wilson Multi-Level Management Survey is designed to provide behavioral feedback on seven management tasks through which a manager moves in the day-to-day performance of his or her job. Clark Wilson (1985) theorizes a task cycle repeated time after time that can be observed and rated by others who work with the manager being assessed. This task cycle is:

1. Goal setting and clarification
2. Planning and problem solving
3. Work facilitation
4. Obtaining and giving feedback
5. Making control adjustments
6. Recognizing and reinforcing task performance

Once the survey has been developed or selected, the organization is ready to implement the process itself. The following eight steps describe a full implementation:

1. Train the trainers who will instruct others on how to conduct the surveys, how to interpret the results, how to coach others in survey-guided development, how to strengthen participative management using survey results, and how to tie existing training to survey results or develop new training as needed.

2. Administer the surveys. This can be complicated because a number of surveys will be completed for each person describing his or her behaviors. The preferred method is to use all of the person's direct reports, a sample of peers, a self-report, and a report from the person's immediate superior. Many variations are possible, depending on the feedback desired. Surveys carry an ID number for the person being rated and only a category ID for the rater. Surveys have been administered on-line, in pencil-and-paper formats, in disk formats, and by personal interview.

3. Aggregate the survey results by categories such as work groups, manager, department, or plant to assess group needs. When surveys are administered for several (or all) managers or people in a group, you can combine the results to calculate overall group ratings. These can serve as in-house norms and can be used to develop teamwork and solve group problems.

4. Coach and counsel individuals using survey feedback. The 360-degree feedback for managers is unvarnished truth that many find disturbing. Most ratees presume that they are doing a better job than what is reported on their evaluations. A trainer or I/O psychologist using 360-degree measures needs to provide support to managers or they are likely to reject all of the information in their report as meaningless. Good coaching helps managers to identify their strengths and build on those to address weak spots. Only a few areas should be targeted for development at any one time. Feedback has been given in sessions conducted internally and externally, as well as in individual and group settings.

5. Use group feedback to solve problems and build better teams. A popular approach is to develop aggregate profiles and then present them to the team. The team then discusses them and develops plans for addressing concerns.

6. Plan and coordinate training so that it addresses the behaviors profiled in the 360-degree survey. Group training can be provided for areas of high need within the organization.

7. Follow-up training and action plans to ensure that participants complete the actions they commit to.

8. Reassess participants on a regular basis to reinforce their progress and to provide a basis for evaluating the effectiveness of the program and demonstrating its validity.

Bracken (1994, p. 3) offered the following definition of a successful multirater system:

- It is reliable, providing consistent ratings.
- It is valid, because it provides feedback and is job related.
- It is easy to use, understandable, and relevant.
- It creates positive change at both the individual level and the organizational level.

The 360-degree surveys can be for individual, team, or organizational use. Many can be applied in all three applications. Common uses include development, selection, promotion, succession planning, and career planning. In most cases the most important result is the behavioral change that the managers and other participants demonstrate in response to the feedback they receive. Research at the Center for Creative Leadership (Campbell, Curphy, & Tuggle, 1995) has identified the following "best practices." These characterize people who changed the most as a result of their 360-degree feedback:

- The plan was written.
- The plan included both strengths and development needs.
- The plan capitalized on on-the-job experiences.
- The plan was drafted within two weeks of 360-degree feedback.
- The boss reviewed the draft plan.
- The boss provided periodic feedback.
- The boss was held accountable for development.
- The plan is adjustable to reflect the realities of situation.

Some organizations have adopted 360-degree feedback because it is the current fad or because the concept "feels right." However, an organization should exercise caution before committing to this process. While I/O psychology can draw from a wealth of experience in assessment, our understanding of 360-degree systems is restricted. In addition, the wide variety of methods that have been used makes comparisons difficult. Careful design and disciplined control of this form of performance assessment is needed to ensure that the results are meaningful and valid.

In conclusion, different appraisers have different views of performance, and the performance appraisal is clearly influenced by these individual perspectives. When determining who will appraise performance, the organization must be aware of the factors that influence employee ratings and must monitor the appraisal program to identify when and where these influences could occur.

....

FREQUENCY OF PERFORMANCE APPRAISALS

Although it is often recommended that performance be assessed at least annually, there is no perfect schedule for appraising employees. However, it is good personnel practice to emphasize that the performance appraisal is not simply a periodic process. Rather, it is the continuous, day-to-day responsibility of the supervisor or manager. Research has suggested that feedback on performance should be frequent. The closer in time the feedback is to the action, the more effective it will be (Henderson, 1984).

In a study to identify nonmanagerial performance appraisal practices in large U.S. cities, approximately 81% of the respondents indicated that performance appraisals of nonmanagerial employees were conducted on an annual basis (England & Parle, 1987). Only 58.9% of managerial city employees were appraised annually (Ammons & Rodriguez, 1986). Ammons and Rodriguez indicated that 24.3% of the cities appraised performance semiannually, 7.5% quarterly, and 3.7% monthly.

A performance appraisal system that relies only on the annual review to document employee progress often fails to acknowledge behavior that occurs during the first half of the year, especially if there is no ongoing formal documentation procedure. Some organizations, believing that a year is too long to wait to praise or correct performance problems, conduct informal quarterly reviews. This practice facilitates the annual review by allowing averaging of the informal quarterly reviews for each employee. It also reduces employee anxiety by deemphasizing the importance of the annual performance appraisal. Quarterly reviews can provide a forum for ongoing feedback; the manager and employee can review progress in relation to goals and can redefine goals or redirect work activities. However, informal reviews should not be held around the time of the formal appraisal, because the purpose of the informal review is not to appraise but to solve problems, facilitate accomplishments, revise the work plan if necessary, and obtain a broad range of information about performance.

Most organizations conduct their formal performance appraisals on the anniversary of the date the employee was hired. Some organizations conduct all performance appraisals during the same period of time or near a single calendar date. This gives the supervisor or manager the opportunity to review all employees' performances at the same time and to coordinate all the paperwork. Although using the same time period or single calendar date may be convenient, it is not a constructive idea. It requires the appraiser to spend a significant amount of time conducting evaluation interviews and completing forms, which can lead to a desire to "get it over with" (Henderson, 1984, p. 36). This practice makes it difficult for the supervisor or manager to evaluate performance effectively and encourages halo effect rating errors (see p. 180).

Some organizations conduct performance appraisals upon completion of a task or job cycle. Using an MBO technique, the manager and employee agree on a task or job cycle and, on completion, conduct a performance appraisal. The completion date can be either flexible or previously agreed upon by the manager and employee. An organization may also postpone conducting a performance appraisal because of extenuating circumstances, such as the employee who is performing at an unacceptable level owing to family or health problems. Since the employee is expected to improve and perform at an acceptable level in the near future, it is better to postpone the performance appraisal for a reasonable period of time than to disregard it or wait for the next formal appraisal.

INTER-RATER BIAS

Though the format may vary, most appraisal methods rely on employee ratings. Unfortunately, these ratings are almost inevitably inaccurate (Borman, 1979). Even a well-designed performance appraisal system can produce faulty results if the appraisers are not cooperative or well-trained. As will become apparent as we explore each type of bias, rating errors can be reduced by training appraisers to avoid them and by including appraisers in the process of designing the performance appraisal system.

Central Tendency Error

Central tendency error occurs when the appraiser is reluctant to use extreme ratings, either high or low. A rater making this error tends to give all employees a rating around the midpoint for all qualities. A supervisor making this error fails to discriminate among employees. This error is easily recognized when virtually all employees receive the same performance ratings.

One method that has been used to eliminate or reduce this error is the forced-distribution rating. For example, if the company were using a normal distribution, the supervisor would be required to distribute his or her ratings to ensure that 68% of the employees supervised were within one stan-

dard deviation of the mean rating for all employees, 95% were within two standard deviations, and 99% were within three standard deviations. The supervisor would check his or her ratings to confirm that the distribution of the performance scores approximated a normal curve. This method is easy to apply but it has not worked well in practice. The approach forces the supervisor to rate some employees in the outstanding and unsatisfactory categories, even when the supervisor may not believe that those employees have earned or deserve those ratings. Also, when a forced-distribution rating is used, the quality of the specific work group can have a significant effect on the ratings. An employee who is the best employee in a poor work group may get an unduly high rating. This results in less comparability of performance ratings across work groups.

Another approach that can be applied to minimize central tendency errors and to reduce ambiguity is to provide a precise definition of dimensions and anchors. Using carefully defined dimensions that have meaningful behavioral anchors creates an objective system that generates ratings that are comparable across work groups. Such ratings are more descriptive and objective because they are closely linked to the observed behaviors.

Finally, alerting appraisers to central tendency error during appraiser training can help to reduce its occurrence. When supervisors have been trained to examine their ratings of employee performance, and look for central tendency errors, they do a better job of using the full scale in their ratings. Often, such training is supported with statistical feedback to supervisors that profiles how they have rated their employees. Central tendency errors are fairly obvious when all of the ratings completed by one particular supervisor are examined and compared to the ratings of other supervisors or to other benchmarks.

Halo Effect

Halo effect is probably the most common appraiser error. It occurs when the appraiser assigns a generalized overall rating, either positive or negative, to the employee. It is not uncommon for a rater to assign approximately the same value for all traits or performance areas listed on a scale. For example, if an employee secures an excellent rating on one key task, the appraiser may rate the employee high on all tasks. The halo effect is present when (a) different raters disagree in their evaluations of the same individual in the same situation and (b) an individual's rating on a series of unrelated tasks or characteristics are highly correlated. When raters are compared, a low standard deviation for evaluation scores assigned to multiple employees can indicate an assessor who is being consistently too lenient or too strict.

Murphy and Anhalt (1992) recently suggested that halo error is not a stable characteristic of either the rater or the ratee. Instead, they found halo to be dependent on the unique rating situation. In other words, a rater may not consistently fall prey to this error; it may result from specific situational factors such as the amount of contact the rater has had with the employee or the occurrence of some significant performance problem.

Halo effect is difficult to eliminate or reduce, but there are ways to combat its occurrence. One way to reduce this effect is to rate all employees on one dimension before proceeding to the next dimension. Another approach is to use precise definitions of dimensions and anchors to discourage raters from basing their ratings on an overall (positive or negative) impression. A final approach is to ensure that appraisers are adequately trained in the use of the performance appraisal technique. However, Murphy and Anhalt (1992) found that although there was substantial variability in the levels of halo errors exhibited across rating conditions and rating sessions, there were no consistent differences among raters in their tendency to have high or low halo errors. This was true even when the exact same behaviors or characteristics were evaluated at two different times. These findings challenge the assumption that halo errors are solely due to the rater and can be controlled by rater training. Instead, halo errors appear to be a characteristic of the unique rating situation and can be reduced by rater training, coupled with situational and environmental controls.

Halo error might not be as much of a problem as some have suggested. Balzer and Sulsky (1992) proposed that, instead of using halo error as a measure of rating outcomes, it may be more appropriately used to measure the cognitive processing of the raters. For example, when performance is based on general abilities that have an effect on several job dimensions, the presence of what appears to be halo error may not indicate inaccurate ratings (Ilgen, Barnes-Farrell, & McKellin, 1993). Furthermore, it is possible for employees to perform consistently across all job dimensions. When this occurs and is reflected in consistent ratings across dimensions it should not be attributed to rater error.

Murphy, Jako, and Anhalt (1993, p. 223), in their review of the research on halo, arrived at three conclusions: "Halo is not ubiquitous, the presence of halo does not necessarily detract from the psychometric quality of ratings, and it is impossible to separate true from *illusory* halo in most field settings." They suggested that current halo indices are too ambiguous to be considered meaningful and should be discontinued.

Leniency/Harshness Error

Leniency/harshness error, another common appraisal problem, can also result in ratings that do not accurately reflect performance. The lenient appraiser tends to give higher-than-average ratings, while the harsh appraiser tends to give lower-than-average ratings. This occurs when appraisers apply their personal frame of reference to the rating scales, and is a direct sign that managers are not giving their employees ratings that truly reflect performance. Leniency errors can be recognized on annual performance appraisals when the distribution of a supervisor's employee ratings falls above the midpoint for employees. Harshness errors can be recognized when the distribution of a supervisor's ratings falls below the midpoint for employees in general. The techniques that are best suited to eliminate or reduce leniency and harshness errors are the same as those that are used to eliminate central tendency error.

Personal Bias Error

Personal bias error occurs when the appraiser's personal biases influence employee appraisals. Some appraisers are not capable of making objective judgments that are independent of their values, prejudices, and stereotypes. Other personal factors that can contaminate the appraisal process are friendship, first impressions, and irrelevant or poorly understood performance standards.

Personal bias error is also known as **perceived similarity/dissimilarity error.** Employees who are perceived as being similar in attitudes and background to the supervisor are appraised more favorably than are employees who are perceived as dissimilar. However, a study by Turban and Jones (1988) supports an alternative explanation for this phenomenon. They suggest that a perceived similarity may lead to more confidence and trust between the supervisor and the employee. This could lead to a more positive working relationship and an improved understanding of job expectations, which, in turn, would lead to deeper insights (rather than bias). Such insights could contribute to more accurate and sometimes more favorable performance appraisals.

Oppler, Campbell, Pulakos, and Borman (1992) examined the degree to which ratings associated with different race/rater/ratee combinations had the same psychological meaning. Their studies tested the Dipboye (1985) stereotype-fit model, which suggests that how raters perceive information about a particular ratee depends on the stereotypes they have about the individual. In a similar research effort, Kraiger and Ford (1985) conducted a meta-analysis that suggested that appraisers assign higher ratings to employees of the same race: African-Ameri-

can appraisers rated African-American ratees higher, and Caucasian appraisers rated Caucasian ratees higher. However, a study by Sackett and DuBois (1991) challenged this finding. This study found that African-American ratees consistently received lower ratings from both Caucasian and African-American raters. Caucasian and African-American raters differed very little in their ratings of Caucasian ratees. Similarly, Oppler et al. (1992), did not find evidence to support the stereotype-fit model in supervisory ratings. They did, however, find partial support for the model in peer ratings. Overall, they concluded that there was higher agreement between African-American and Caucasian supervisors than between African-American and Caucasian peers, regardless of the race of the ratee. In addition, they found that non-performance factors (e.g., personality, interests, intelligence) were included to some degree in determining performance ratings.

Personal bias error can be reduced through the use of detailed performance appraisal scales (or forms) and clearly defined dimensions and descriptors. Another way to eliminate or reduce this type of error is to train appraisers in the areas of effective rating, appraiser tendencies, accuracy issues, and feedback. In addition, the need to involve employees in the performance appraisal process should be emphasized.

Recency of Events Error

Most performance appraisals cover the preceding six to twelve months and should represent average performance for this period. However, there is a tendency to base ratings on the most recent behavior, which might not be representative of the total performance period. Appraisers tend to forget past behavior, especially if it has not been frequently and clearly documented.

Documentation of employee behavior throughout the entire performance period and conducting frequent appraisals are common approaches to reducing **recency of events errors.** Another approach includes using specific rating methods, such as critical incidents, Behaviorally Anchored Rating Scales (BARS), or management by objectives (MBO). These popular rating methods were discussed earlier in this chapter.

Recent cognitive research by Woehr and Feldman (1993) examined memory as a factor in appraising performance. They found that the relationship between memory (for specific information) and judgment is far more flexible than was previously assumed. Both processes are sensitive to contextual cues, both before and after observation. The information processing that occurs as part of the judgment process appears outcome-oriented. In other words, information is incorporated in the most advantageous manner to achieve the targeted outcome. They also found that the rating format can influence the way in which people process performance information.

Standards of Evaluation Error

Standards of evaluation errors occur when there is no common understanding of the meaning of the words that are used to appraise employees. Terms such as *good, fair, satisfactory,* and *excellent* may mean different things to different appraisers. This error can be reduced by precisely defining the dimensions and the descriptors on the rating form itself. Another approach to eliminating standards biases is to train appraisers to apply ratings consistently.

Conclusion

Although studying and controlling rating bias have long been popular ways to improve performance appraisals, critics of the rater bias approach disagree with the underlying assumption that the presence of rating errors signifies a lack of appraisal accuracy and that a decrease in errors implies increased accuracy. The fallacy of this assumption became apparent when bias-free appraisals were not found to be consistently accurate (Hulin, 1982; Murphy & Balzer, 1989). While it is preferable to have little to no rater

error, current research is focusing more on cognitive processing and rater characteristics in an attempt to understand disparate levels of performance appraisal accuracy.

....
COGNITION AND PERFORMANCE APPRAISAL

According to Landy and Farr (1980, p. 96):

> The major theme in the research that has been conducted in the area of performance rating has been that variables of major importance can be found in the rating scales themselves . . . rather than first level direct influences, such as cognitive operations or feelings toward the stimulus object.

All of the biases that we discussed earlier were **cognitive processes.** Why do we remember some things and not others? How do we encode information? How does cognition affect performance appraisal? Current research on performance appraisals is focused on cognitive processes.

Cognition is the acquisition, storage, retrieval, and use of knowledge. It includes such complex processes as memory, perception, learning, language, problem solving, reasoning, and decision making. Accordingly, it is an important factor in determining how an appraiser rates an employee. In part because rater biases are specific examples of cognitive effects, current I/O research is interested in cognitive processes and their impact on performance appraisal.

Feldman (1981) suggested that raters construct cognitive prototypes and schemata that affect how they perceive and organize information. *Prototypes* are abstract images that summarize distinctive properties, or best examples, of a category. They serve as internal reference points. *Schemata* (singular: schema) represent the generic ideas that we store in memory. A rater with insufficient information—about either the employee's job description or the employee's actual performance—may rely on internal prototypes or schemata when conducting an appraisal. Or appraisers may selectively attend to

---

SCIENTIFIC PERSPECTIVE 6.1

Model for Employee Assessment

As an alternative to the standard methods of performance evaluation, Girard (1988) introduced the idea that the best appraisal method may be no performance appraisal at all. Girard suggested that the best approach was to classify all employees as average and to distinguish only those who either did not meet the standards or far exceeded the standards. This approach would eliminate performance appraisals for approximately 80% of employees.

In this system, supervisors are required to maintain a file of critical incidents that document outstanding or poor performance. This information is communicated to the employee at the time the incident is recorded to keep the employee abreast of the situation. The formal appraisal is the review of this personnel file documentation. This approach requires intense observation, demands attention to proper record keeping, and is applicable to 20% or fewer of all employees. Using this system, a manager who supervised ten people would be required to maintain files for only two of the ten. Employees who did not have critical incidents in their files would be considered average performers.

Individual performance goals are established and reviewed periodically throughout the year. This approach stresses that the annual review is too infrequent for either recognition of good performance or intervention and correction of problem performance. One advantage of this system is that it eliminates recency error because it forces managers to acknowledge outstanding or poor

performance when it occurs. Additionally, separately identifying each behavior helps to eliminate halo error because each critical incident is evaluated independently of the others.

Girard also suggests that goal achievement not be directly tied to salary. Since most employees focus on compensation, the potential salary increase often overshadows the performance appraisal. Unfortunately, it is not unusual for budget constraints to prohibit appropriate increases for all employees who have achieved their goals; this can result in decreasing motivation. Separating goal fulfillment from compensatory reward gives the manager and the employee more freedom to develop and attain goals. Under a system of "no performance" appraisal, a common salary review date provides the opportunity to discuss compensation increases. The average employee receives the average increase based on companywide formulations of wage determination. Only employees with documentation of outstanding or poor performance would receive more or less than the average raise.

The focus of the no performance appraisal approach is to use a goal-setting program that emphasizes future achievement rather than past performance and to eliminate the need for the performance appraisal form in the assessment process. This model is an extension of McGregor's (1987) concept that a more effective evaluation system focuses on analysis rather than appraisal and places the accent on performance actions relative to goals, rather than on the personality of the employee.

---

some behaviors and ignore others. Specifically, an appraiser may attend to behaviors that match his or her own schema and disregard behaviors that do not (e.g., personal bias, or similarity/dissimilarity errors).

By contrast, Foti and Lord (1987) suggested that behaviors that were similar to the prototype were less accurately recalled than behaviors that were dissimilar to the prototype, indicating that

behaviors that stand out are more easily remembered. This suggests that employees who consistently perform as expected might receive less attention than employees who exhibit unexpected behaviors. This perspective has been refined into a method of appraisal that considers all employees average unless they demonstrate critical incidents of notably good or bad performance. This method is described in Scientific Perspective 6.1.

In their book *Performance Appraisal: An Organizational Perspective,* Kevin Murphy and Jeanette Cleveland (1991) provide a straightforward, cognitive model based on their review of state-of-the-art methods in performance appraisal. As we will demonstrate, this model provides a theoretical perspective that is quite different from the measurement-focused approach that was common throughout the 1970s.

THE FOUR-COMPONENT MODEL OF PERFORMANCE APPRAISAL

Murphy-Cleveland's **four-component model** is a social-psychological model that contrasts with the more classical psychometric approach. It emphasizes issues the authors believe have not received enough attention in other models of appraisal and deemphasizes issues that have been the subject of considerable research. Specifically, it defines *context* as the most important issue in appraising performance.

Performance appraisal, therefore, is seen as a goal-directed communications process that occurs within a defined organizational context. As depicted in Figure 6.3 the Murphy-Cleveland model is simplified to focus attention on the four critical elements: the rating context, the perfor-

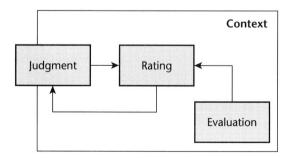

FIGURE 6.3.   The Murphy-Cleveland four-component model of performance appraisal in context.

Source: From *Performance Appraisal: An Organizational Perspective* (p. 14), by K. R. Murphy & J. N. Cleveland, © 1991. Boston, MA: Allyn & Bacon. Reprinted by permission of Prentice-Hall, Upper Saddle River, NJ.

mance judgment, the performance rating, and the evaluation of the appraisal system.

Rating Context

Emphasis on organizational context is the cornerstone of the Murphy-Cleveland model. In a 1983 review of the research on performance appraisal, Ilgen and Feldman also concluded that organizational context had not been given much attention. In 1986, Cleveland, Morrison, and Bjerke identified two broad sets of contextual issues. The first is made up of factors that relate directly to the organization's culture. The second consists of the associated internal exchanges, pressures, changes, and organizational issues that grow out of the organization's interface with its environment.

In their explanation of contextual factors Cleveland et al. adopted Brunswick's (1952) labels of **proximal variables** (those that directly influence the rater) and **distal variables** (those that indirectly influence the rater). Proximal variables include supervisor–employee interaction, the nature of the job or task, the consequences associated with the performance ratings, and time constraints that influence the rater. Distal variables include organizational climate, the value system of the organization, and the organizational structure.

In a 1989 investigation, Cleveland, Murphy, and Williams found that 70% of the more than 100 organizations surveyed reported that performance appraisal had a moderate to strong effect on two or more organizational goals. The greatest impact was on salary administration, performance feedback, and the identification of employee strengths and weaknesses. They also found that performance appraisal was typically used for a variety of purposes rather than for a single purpose. In fact, many organizations require raters to provide ratings that will be used for potentially incompatible purposes. An example would be expecting a rater to provide data that could be used for promotions or salary increases and also for providing developmental feedback. Because of this latter finding, Cleveland et al. suggested that rater perceptions and intentions were important areas to consider in performance appraisal research.

An earlier study by McCall and DeVries (1977) had pointed out the importance of context on performance appraisal. They identified five contextual factors that can *adversely* affect performance appraisals. These were as follows:

1. The typical manager is often involved in many short-term, ad hoc activities that focus on nonroutine information. Performance appraisal, on the other hand, requires preparation, formal meetings, a review of past behavior, and action based on appraisal results.

2. Organizations have limited resources and are hierarchical in structure with subjective decision making. In contrast, performance appraisal systems require administrative and developmental programs, mutual structure, and objective decision making.

3. Most assessments assume that performance varies, that a person's performance is independent of the performance of others, that what constitutes good or bad performance is clear, and that the individual can improve performance through motivation and/or development. The organizational reality may be quite different. Performance may be consistently good (or bad), it is often dependent on the performance of others, the definitions are not clear, and the performance itself may be difficult or impossible to change.

4. External demands often clash with effective performance appraisals. For example, unions favor seniority, while the performance appraisal process may seek to reward individual performance.

5. Much of the variance in ratings that is seen as rater error may be adaptive behavior as supervisors react to multiple, competing, and sometimes conflicting organizational directives.

Performance Judging

Much of the cognitive research on performance appraisal deals with the judgment process, that is, the private evaluation the appraiser makes about an employee. Two areas are central to this process: how information about performance is acquired and how information is processed to form judgments.

Factors that can influence the judgment process include observing behavior (Smith, 1976), previous impressions (Murphy, Balzar, Lockhart, & Eisenman, 1985), and the rater's feelings toward the ratee. This last factor is relatively new; it includes the degree to which the supervisor likes the subordinate (Cardy & Dobbins, 1986) and the rater's mood and temperament (Clark & Isen, 1982; Isen & Daubman, 1984; Tsui & Barry, 1986). In summary, the cognitive processing that is used to form judgments about performance is concerned primarily with the encoding and retrieval of information. Most of the research on this area focuses on inter-rater bias and error (Higgins & King, 1981; Ilgen & Feldman, 1983; Jeffrey & Mischel, 1979; Murphy et al., 1985; Williams et al., 1986).

Performance Rating

Ratings are public statements about the ratee's performance. However, they do not always represent the rater's actual judgment. For example, giving a worker a high rating on a dimension such as "quality of work" does not necessarily mean that the rater truly believes that the employee is a better performer on this dimension. It may mean that the rater has a hidden agenda and wants to convey something to the audience that will receive the performance appraisal form.

The cognitive model suggests that discrepancies between judgment and ratings cannot be explained solely in terms of the rater's desire to escape the consequence of giving low ratings. Instead, performance appraisal may emerge as a way for the rater to achieve well-defined goals, such as maximizing the likelihood that an employee will be promoted or substantiating that a promotion was justified (Cleveland et al., 1986).

The cognitive model (Murphy & Cleveland, 1991) finds that ratings are most likely to correspond with judgment in the following situations:

1. Organizational norms support distinctions between employees on the basis of their performance (Mohrman & Lawler, 1983).

2. Raters perceive a strong link between the ratings they give and specific outcomes (Landy & Farr, 1983; Thompson, 1967).

3. Raters believe that those outcomes should be based on present performance.

4. The valence (the extent to which it is attractive to a person) of those outcomes is substantially larger than the valence of the negative outcomes that are associated with giving low ratings (Vroom, 1964).

Evaluation

As we have seen, the past focus in many performance appraisal investigations has been on the appraisal's resistance to psychometric biases and errors (Landy & Farr, 1980) and on the accuracy of performance appraisal ratings.

The cognitive model does not view rater error as appraiser mishaps. Rather, rater errors may reflect desirable outcomes (Saal, Downey, & Lahey, 1980). For example, a high level of halo effect does not necessarily mean that the manager is incapable of evaluating differences in performance; it means only that the manager did not produce ratings that reflected such discrimination. Murphy and Cleveland (1991, p. 23) indicated that their "analyses suggest that many rater errors are consciously made and that failure to discriminate among persons or dimensions is often a highly adaptive behavior." For example, since organizations work hard to improve workers' performance, we could expect that some will be successful. In those instances, all employees would validly receive high ratings (reflecting the fact that the organization was getting high performance from its employees).

The word *objective* is often used in describing an effective performance appraisal. This term can be misleading, however, because it suggests the strict, quantitative, data-based approach that is commonly used in scientific endeavors. Although many studies have focused on these kinds of objectives and they are often a sound choice, there is a growing recognition that we cannot always go simply by the numbers. Nonquantitative qualities such as imagination and judgment are intrinsic to successful performance in many jobs but are very difficult to measure. As was mentioned earlier, a growing body of evidence suggests that appraisers are heavily influenced by the context within which the ratings are conducted.

While we must avoid biased, subjective judgments based on race, sex, or any other discriminatory standard, there is a growing trend toward less number-oriented, or rating-scale-based, judgments. However, personal judgment should be supported by citing specific behavioral examples and should be based on equitable, carefully established, nondiscriminatory standards of performance.

THE IMPORTANCE OF APPRAISER TRAINING

There is one universal technique that can counteract the effects of rating errors: the development of a complete training program for all appraisal system participants. Landy and Farr (1983) identified the ultimate, and most obvious, appraiser characteristic as the extent to which the appraiser has been trained to rate others. They acknowledged that this is an organizational process that later becomes the property of the rater. An organization should not assume that its appraisers possess this characteristic and should develop an appraisal system that acknowledges appraiser deficiencies and implements training to ensure that all appraisers are equally qualified. Ivancevich and Glueck (1986) stated that the major problem with performance appraisal systems is not the techniques themselves, but how they are used. Untrained appraisers or those who have little ability or motivation to evaluate can hamper even the most effective appraisal technique. The rater, then, is more critical than the method in developing an effective appraisal system.

Many employees believe that a performance appraisal is something that is done to them, a feeling that can have an adverse impact on the success of the appraisal system. Employee involvement is one way to help eliminate the sense of threat in performance appraisal. All users, both appraisers and appraisees, should have an overview of the appraisal system, its uses, objectives, and procedures. This helps employees to understand why the performance appraisal is beneficial to them as well as to the company.

The employee may need training in communication skills to provide feedback to the appraiser and to be more effective in his or her role as appraisee. The employee must also have access to the resources that will enable him or her to act in a manner that will benefit the individual and the organization. This training can be handled via employee orientation sessions, companywide update sessions, company manuals, or individual workshops. The result should be that employees have the skills and information that will enable them to use their knowledge and abilities in the best way possible.

The skills required by the appraiser are more varied because their task is more comprehensive and therefore more difficult. The appraiser's responsibility is to conduct fair, unbiased evaluations that will help to enhance individual growth and attain corporate goals. A good performance appraisal system includes five basic processes, each requiring a different skill (Wehrenberg, 1988):

1. Establish performance standards and goals
2. Observe and record performance
3. Integrate observations into a statement of overall average performance

4. Evaluate performance
5. Provide feedback to the employee

Skilled communication underlies the effectiveness of almost every step. A company with minimal resources can most wisely invest what it has in improving communication skills companywide. In addition to strong communication skills, each of the five steps requires special skills; the first four steps call for technical skills. Even though these skills may be complex, they are relatively easy to teach. Providing examples of appropriate job behaviors and opportunities to practice and refine these behaviors is an effective way to train supervisors. Many good training programs rely on techniques such as observing, modeling, role playing, and decision making. Teaching a manager to observe and record behavior can have long-term results, especially if it is a skill that will be appraised during the manager's performance review.

Training the manager to integrate observations into the performance evaluation helps to ensure rater consistency and discourages rater bias. Providing feedback requires interpersonal skills, which are not as easily taught through example and practice. Care must be taken to develop specific examples of appropriate behaviors, to model those behaviors, and to allow for practice in a variety of situations. Because the work environment is not static or predictable, not every interaction can be scripted and practiced. The approach to a given situation depends on the atmosphere of the workplace at a particular moment and the issue at hand.

As was previously mentioned, the supervisor's dual role is a critical issue in the effectiveness of any performance appraisal system. In systems that are aimed toward employee development, the supervisor serves as a coach as well as a judge. The supervisor's success in these two roles depends on communication skills. As a coach, the supervisor provides meaningful feedback about performance, sets goals that encourage growth, motivates employees to put forth their best effort, and is aware of the employees' need for self-development. As a judge, the supervisor must objectively review and accurately identify levels of performance, conduct bias-free appraisals, and effectively punish poor performance or reward satisfactory performance in line with legal requirements. Blending these two roles can be difficult.

Although training programs can be developed internally, a popular trend in industry is to purchase training programs from independent consulting firms. This not only reduces the time, effort, and money required to develop an effective training program, it also allows the organization to judge the success of the program before implementing it. Purchasing a training program is less work in a developmental sense, but great care should be taken to thoroughly investigate any new training plan. An organization should review the content of the program, ensure its legal compliance, request statistics on program validity, and have access to other firms that can provide feedback on the program's success.

•••
COMMUNICATING WITH EMPLOYEES

Goal Setting

Critics of traditional appraisal techniques (e.g., Reily & Noland, 1987) have argued that most performance appraisals focus on past behaviors and fail to address future performance. One response to this criticism is the practice of **goal setting.** While goal setting is usually linked with the MBO method of performance appraisal, it has useful applications in any appraisal system.

Goal-setting theory emphasizes cognitive processes and intentional behavior. Landy and Farr (1983) suggested that levels of performance are closely related to the goals individuals have either set for themselves or accepted from someone else. Goals differ significantly in specificity and difficulty. Locke, Shaw, Saari, and Latham (1981) discerned that performance tends to be

higher when goals are specifically stated rather than generalized. Carroll and Schneier (1982) identified several different types of goals. **Routine objectives** deal with the basic, unchanging responsibilities of the job. **Problem-solving objectives** are designed in response to specific difficulties in the work unit. **Special-purpose objectives** are designed to increase efficiency. **Self-improvement objectives** deal with overcoming personal deficiencies. The key to a successful goal-setting program is to give the employee control over the means of reaching the goal, to offer frequent feedback, and to reward goal achievement.

Feedback

Effective performance appraisal serves a dual purpose: It is a control mechanism to monitor performance and goal attainment and a feedback mechanism to foster individual growth and development (Stroul, 1987). **Feedback** is a critical part of the performance improvement and review process. It is usually given to the employee at the time of the formal appraisal, at the completion of a task or job cycle, or at informal review sessions. As was stated earlier, the closer the feedback is to the action, the more effective it is. To effectively influence performance, feedback should be an ongoing process; ideally, feedback should be given on a daily basis.

When an employee's performance is excellent, it should be rewarded; when it is unsatisfactory, it should be corrected. **Positive feedback** provides employees with recognition and appreciation of accomplishments. However, managers often concentrate on employee failures rather than on employee accomplishments. This is known as **negative feedback.** Smith (1987) suggests two alternatives for the terms *positive feedback* and *negative feedback*. **Maintenance feedback** recognizes satisfactory work, general competence, or exemplary performance. **Improvement feedback** calls attention to poor work, areas that need improvement, or problem behavior. Feedback is a useful tool with which an effective manager can engender feelings of success on the job. Employees who feel successful work harder, tackle more difficult assignments, take personal risks, and are more innovative and aware of the consequences of their actions (Weitzel, 1987). Following are guidelines for providing effective feedback based on Smith's (1987) recommendations:

1. Feedback should focus on activities that are under the employee's control.
2. Feedback should describe the situation and behavior in specific terms.
3. Feedback should allow for two-way communication between manager and employee.
4. Feedback should allow for negotiation.
5. Feedback should be constructive, not manipulative.
6. Feedback should be used to motivate the employee.
7. When giving feedback, managers should recognize that what works for one employee may not work for another.
8. Feedback should be appropriate to the employee's needs and desires.
9. The manager should not use loaded terms that encourage emotional reactions from the employee.
10. Feedback should be timely.

Brett and Fredian (1981) found that employees receive feedback in 97% of organizations that have a formal performance appraisal system, usually at the time of the evaluation interview. The feedback interview should be designed to recognize and encourage superior performance, sustain acceptable behavior, or change unacceptable behavior (Henderson, 1984). The next section identifies how these goals can be accomplished.

The Performance Appraisal Interview

The performance appraisal interview should be an ongoing communication tool rather than an annual, anxiety-producing event. Malinauskas and Clement (1987) suggest that an effective performance review should consist of a three-stage process: the preview stage, the interview stage, and the review stage.

The **preview stage** gives the supervisor the opportunity to communicate the organization's philosophy about the appraisal process; to give the employee a good understanding of performance criteria; and to set the time, place, and agenda for the actual review. Experts (e.g., Grant, 1987; Malinauskas & Clement, 1987) agree that investing time in preliminaries can help to develop a sensitive frame of mind for both the employee and the manager, helping the employee to better understand the value of the appraisal system. In addition, prereview discussion and preparation reduce the stress associated with appraisal and should ensure that there are no surprises during the assessment.

The **interview stage** is the formal meeting between supervisor and employee. During the interview, the supervisor should provide a climate in which the employee feels free to be himself or herself, an atmosphere that allows for exploration of weakness in an unthreatening way so that the employee and the supervisor can formulate plans for development and growth. **Rogerian client-centered theory** is especially applicable to the performance appraisal interview process. This theory recognizes the individual as being oriented toward positive growth and as tending to work toward self-actualization and fulfillment for self and others.

The **review stage** consists of informal meetings in which the supervisor and employee review performance objectives. It is also a period of ongoing feedback and coaching that assists the employee in improving his or her performance or working toward desired objectives. These meetings can be initiated by the manager, but placing the responsibility on the employee can help to intensify the employee's commitment and increases the likelihood that performance and satisfaction will improve.

A more specific, less global approach is provided by the microskills approach to performance appraisal. The **microskills approach** is primarily a communications strategy that focuses on developing a more intentional and well-rounded ability to interact with another individual. Ivey (1982) identified several basic attending skills that can be applied in the performance appraisal interview. A supervisor who exhibits good attending behavior recognizes the importance of eye contact, vocal qualities, and body language in any interpersonal exchange. Leaning forward and maintaining eye contact encourages employee participation and conveys the idea that the supervisor is paying attention and is interested in the employee. Sincerity and understanding can be conveyed by tone of voice and word inflection.

Another skill is the ability to ask open-ended questions beginning with *how, what,* or *why.* Effective questioning helps the supervisor to gather information and clarify issues. This technique is especially helpful in drawing the employee into the review process by giving the employee an opportunity to explain, support, or defend his or her performance. The supervisor must also be aware of, and use, other verbal methods to improve communication, such as choice of language (positive versus negative words), choice of statements (supportive versus defensive), and paraphrasing.

The successful performance review should be a dialogue in which both the manager and the employee learn something about the employee's past performance and expectations for future performance. Weitzel (1987) suggested the following eight-step procedure:

1. The warm-up. Build rapport and put the employee at ease to facilitate an honest exchange of information.
2. State the objectives. Define the structure of the interview to prepare the employee for the exchange.
3. Begin with the positive aspects of job performance to allow the individual to express pride in his or her accomplishments.
4. Stress that every behavior can be improved on to help the employee find ways to capitalize on his or her strong points.
5. Ask the employee about performance difficulties. Assess problem areas to enable the employee to generate ideas to improve future performance.
6. Discuss ways to overcome areas that need improvement. Highlight the employee's strengths as a positive way to approach weaknesses.
7. Summarize the performance review. Conclude the interview with an over-view of key points to make clear to the employee what is expected of him or her in the future.
8. Follow up. Check on the employee's progress to reinforce the performance appraisal and increase the employee's incentive to follow the performance plan.

As was mentioned previously, a problem in the relationship between supervisor and employee (as appraiser and appraisee) is the supervisor's dual role as judge and counselor. There are several approaches to resolving this conflict. One recurring theme is to keep the review of job performance and the discussion of rewards separate (Girard, 1988; Henderson, 1984; Weitzel, 1987). When rewards and performance improvement strategies are discussed at the same time, employees may not acknowledge ways in which they could improve; they may be more concerned with appearing as favorable as possible to ensure the greatest possible reward.

Coaching entails using on-the-job learning opportunities to develop an employee's skills, knowledge, and abilities. The formal performance review provides an opportunity for coaching, but it may also be done in separate sessions throughout the year. Coaching requires the same interpersonal skills as the formal review sessions and can follow much the same format in terms of identifying areas that need improvement and formulating plans to achieve desired changes. Recently, attention has also been given to providing better training to managers on coaching. A set of research-based, practical guidelines for assisting managers in gaining the knowledge and skills to coach employees can be found in Peterson and Hicks's book *The Manager as Coach: Strategies for Coaching and Developing Others* (1996b).

In conclusion, the performance appraisal interview provides the opportunity for the manager and the employee to share information. The intended results of this communication are to motivate and improve performance, enhance the relationship between the employee and the supervisor, and promote the achievement of organizational and individual goals. When two individuals work together to resolve work-related problems, their relationship can be strengthened. When both individuals understand the issues and recognize the interdependency that exists, supportive action increases. This can lead to improved job performance.

PERFORMANCE APPRAISAL AND THE LAW

The Equal Opportunity Employment Commission (EEOC) administers and enforces the Civil Rights Act of 1964, as amended in 1972, 1978, and 1991. The following characteristics and the EEOC guidelines, when combined, provide a framework for an effective performance appraisal system:

1. The appraisal system should be based on a thorough job analysis.

2. The appraisal system should be valid and job related.

3. The appraisal system should be formalized, standardized, and objective.

4. Employees should participate in establishing performance standards.

5. The appraisal system should not discriminate against individuals because of their race, color, sex, religion, or nationality.

6. Appraisers should have sufficient knowledge of the employee and the job.

7. Appraisers should have daily contact with the employee.

8. Appraisers should be sufficiently trained in the use of performance appraisal techniques.

9. Performance standards should be communicated to employees.

10. Performance appraisals should be conducted independently by more than one appraiser.

11. A formal performance appraisal should be conducted at least annually and should be summarized in writing.

12. The results must yield information that is useful in making personnel decisions.

13. Appraisers should document reasons for all employment decisions.

14. Performance appraisal records should be confidential.

15. A mechanism for appeal should be provided to employees.

16. Performance appraisal systems must be periodically evaluated and refined.

Performance appraisals have been used for a variety of purposes: as an employee development tool, as a criterion instrument in a validation study, and as a source of information on which to base employment decisions such as promotions, terminations, and salary decisions. When used as a basis for personnel actions, performance appraisals clearly fall within the purview of Title VII of the 1964 Civil Rights Act and subsequent government guidelines on employee selection (Kleiman & Durham, 1981). As a result, employers are increasingly concerned about the legality of their performance appraisals. The most legally defensible approach is to develop a properly validated system based on a job analysis to ensure that the criteria are job related. The EEOC's 1978 Uniform Guidelines state that all personnel decisions, including performance appraisal, that affect an employee's status be defined as tests, and as such are subject to the conditions of validity and reliability required of other tests examined by the courts (Fletcher & Wertheim, 1985).

Federal Laws

As we will see in Chapter 8, a number of federal laws have had an impact on personnel actions, including performance appraisal. (Henderson, 1984; Ivancevich & Glueck, 1986; Rausch, 1985). Some of the more important laws include the following:

The Age Discrimination in Employment Act of 1967 as amended in 1978

The Civil Service Reform Act of 1978 (CSRA)

The Equal Pay Act of 1963

The Privacy Act of 1974

The Rehabilitation Act of 1973 as amended in 1974 and 1978

Title VII of the Civil Rights Act of 1964, as amended in 1972 and 1978

The Vietnam Era Veterans' Readjustment Act of 1974 as amended in 1976 and 1978

Every organization needs to review the full provisions of these laws as a part of preparation to implement a new performance appraisal process. Many existing processes should also be revised to ensure that they are in compliance with the provisions of the federal laws.

Court Rulings

In addition to the laws themselves, many court rulings may affect the design of an appraisal system. Martin, Bartol, and Levine (1986) identified four types of personnel actions that figure prominently in litigation involving employment discrimination: promotion, discharge, layoffs, and merit pay. A number of rulings have identified and defined management responsibilities with regard to developing and implementing a performance appraisal system. It is important that organizations pay attention to these rulings and consider them in designing appraisal systems.

MONITORING THE PERFORMANCE APPRAISAL SYSTEM

A performance appraisal system is a complex structure with many substructures. A successful appraisal system will be implemented uniformly across the organization. Ensuring such consistency requires that some part of the organization, usually the personnel or human resources management department, maintains a longitudinal history of employee performance ratings and supervisory rating distributions. To gauge effectiveness, this information should be linked to some type of measure of production, either measured job performance or the production of specific work units.

A **performance appraisal review program (PARP)** should be developed alongside the appraisal system itself to ensure honest, accurate, and consistent application of the appraisal system. A well-designed PARP recognizes the right of each employee to review and appeal appraisals. It monitors the supervisors' use of the performance appraisal system, audits the system's effectiveness, and reports the results to the level of management that is responsible for making policy and identifying corporate goals.

Certain signals can indicate a problem within a performance appraisal system. Phillips (1987) identified the following "red flags" which can alert an organization if part or all of its system is operating ineffectively:

1. Lack of performance standards or identical standards for all employees
2. Virtually the same end-of-year rating for all employees

3. Identical written reviews for an employee from year to year
4. Disagreement between manager and employee on the date of the last appraisal
5. A manager's inability to discharge an ineffective employee because of lack of proper documentation
6. Promotions made on the basis of supervisory recommendation that prove to be unsatisfactory in practice

Another obvious indicator of an ineffective appraisal system is disgruntled employees who are not motivated by the existing appraisal and reward program.

Computer-based information systems (CBIS), also referred to as computer-aided performance appraisal (CAPA) and computerized performance monitoring (CPM), can enhance the monitoring of individual performance and the entire appraisal system. CBIS and CAPA are especially helpful to large organizations with many appraisers and appraisees. The ability of CBIS and CAPA to perform various data operations makes it possible to record and compare multiple dimensions of performance over extended periods of time as well as to compare individual performance on similar or dissimilar jobs. The rating behaviors of supervisors can also be assessed, and potential areas of discrimination, bias, or inappropriate assessment can be identified before they became a major threat to the integrity of the performance appraisal system. Computerized assistance allows for closer contact with performance appraisal data and assists in development and implementation of training programs. CBIS and CAPA permit everyone in the organization, including the employee, to be more involved in the appraisal system.

CPM has been widely used in a variety of professions, including insurance, communications, transportation, and banking. In these industries, CPM systems continuously monitor and record employee performance and are usually associated with computer-driven activities. A program keeps track of the employee's activities, their duration, and, in some cases, their success. Kulik and Ambrose (1993) studied CPM in contrast to observational data for developing performance appraisal data on secretaries. They found that the supervisors in their study were influenced more by the observational data than by the CPM. However, they also found that the supervisors did use the CPM data when making their appraisals.

Briefly, CBIS and CAPA allow performance data to be entered, stored, and retrieved by any authorized end-user. Data may include an employee's demographic information, pay status, performance ratings, and job history. Performance appraisal data can be packaged to meet the individual decision maker's specific requirements, eliminating the need to wade through useless information while at the same time protecting the confidentiality of critical or sensitive information.

In conclusion, a CBIS or CAPA program allows management and staff to determine whether rules and procedures are being followed, whether programs should be modified, eliminated or enforced; and whether employees are receiving fair, accurate, and timely appraisals (Henderson, 1984).

APPLYING THE RESEARCH

This chapter has described a range of techniques that are available to assess performance. The combinations of these methods are virtually limitless and have generated a great deal of research. Some investigators in the performance appraisal arena have expressed doubts about the generalizability, even the applicability, of the psychological research on performance appraisal. However, as Murphy and Cleveland (1991, p. 279) noted, "the generalizability of different types of research is an empirical issue; analyses such as those presented by Locke (1986) suggest that generalizability is more often the rule than the exception."

Performance appraisal will remain an important issue and will continue to be the subject of attention. Employees at all organizational levels want a louder voice in the decisions that affect their lives. They want to be treated with fairness and respect. They want useful feedback; most people want to perform well, and appropriate feedback can strongly influence performance. When people believe that they have not been fairly judged, they become increasingly willing to challenge the companies and processes that created those feelings of inequity.

The research described in this chapter is valuable background but does not ensure that a company's performance appraisal system will be successful. Clampitt (1991, p. 153) provided the following four questions as a guide to use in constructing an effective performance appraisal system:

1. Do employees know their job responsibilities?
2. Do employees know the standards of evaluation?
3. Is the informal feedback system effective?
4. Is the formal feedback system effective?

With these straightforward questions as our guide, it is possible to develop an effective approach that is consistent with many research findings. Effective performance appraisal is a formidable task. It requires skill, dedication, time, effort, and a commitment to continuous change and improvement. In the process of appraising employees, fairness and a code of ethics (both personal and legal) require the appraiser to put forth his or her best effort. The appraiser can thus create performance appraisals that are worthwhile experiences for both appraiser and employee.

SUMMARY

Performance appraisals are often stressful events in which emotions may threaten the accuracy and effectiveness of the entire appraisal system. Consequently, I/O psychologists have researched ways to make performance appraisal less emotional and more effective. One way to achieve this end is to employ a systems approach to performance appraisal. In this approach, performance appraisal is viewed as one (of many) interactive subsystem within the entire organization. This focus on interdependence encourages employees and supervisors to view job performance within an organizational context and creates a continual cycle of input, output, and feedback.

Another performance appraisal consideration is the measurement of job performance. Organizations can measure employee performance by using performance dimensions that compare actual results against planned results and rely on objective data to provide a quantitative description of performance. Appraisal data can also be provided in the form of personnel information, such as accidents or tardiness. Judgmental data are subjective evaluations of an individual's job performance by another individual.

Any decision regarding the degree of performance considered successful is based on the concepts of criterion and criteria. The multiple-criteria approach is based on the belief that job performance is multidimensional and that distinct performance dimensions should be separated in assessing overall performance. Conversely, the composite criterion approach argues that dimensions of job performance can be combined to obtain an overall measure of success on the job. Proponents of this approach also suggest that the major emphasis should be on the individual's overall worth to the organization.

A third consideration, inter-rater bias, addresses the many errors that can occur during the evaluation process. Central tendency error happens when appraisers fail to give extreme ratings and apply a midpoint rating to all employees. The halo effect occurs when appraisers apply an overall positive or negative rating to employees; this error is extremely hard to reduce or eliminate. When committing the leniency/harshness error, appraisers assign either higher than average ratings or lower than average ratings to all employees. Personal bias error occurs when raters allow their personal views to influence the appraisal process. Recency of events error occurs when appraisers base an entire appraisal on the most recent behavior. Evaluation errors are apparent when perceptual differences in the meaning of job-related definitions create ratings that do not accurately reflect job performance.

A fourth consideration is the interaction between cognition and performance appraisal. Cognition can be defined as the acquisition, storage, retrieval, and implementation of knowledge. Appraisers perceive information according to their own subjective prototypes and schemata, which can perpetuate performance appraisal error.

The Murphy-Cleveland model offers a four-component appraisal system that emphasizes context. Included in this sociopsychological model is the concept of performance judgment, which relates to how information is acquired and used to make judgments. The evaluation process is viewed as the manager's competence to employ sound performance judgment that results in valid ratings.

Once the performance appraisal system has been designed, organizations need to select a method of appraisal. The rating scale, the most widely used method, identifies the strengths and weaknesses in a person's job behaviors. The checklist method allows the appraiser to check the adjectives that describe desired or undesired job behaviors. In the critical incidents method, the rater logs all observable behaviors and uses this information to assess overall job performance. Behaviorally anchored rating scales (BARS) use critical incidents and require job experts for each rated task. Behavioral observation scales (BOS) require that the appraiser record the frequency of job-related behaviors. The essay strategy is based on skilled communication by appraisers as they write about the employee's behavior, performance, and progress. Finally, the management by objectives (MBO) method is philosophical and is most effective when used as a guideline for organizing and evaluating objectives.

Once a method has been selected, the organization needs to decide who will conduct performance appraisals. The most commonly chosen appraiser is the employee's immediate supervisor. The disadvantages of using supervisors include interview avoidance and supervisory overload. A second qualified individual is the employee. A major pitfall to this approach is that most people tend to assign themselves above average ratings. Peer appraisals can offer additional insight into a person's performance; however, social relationships can be damaged if these types of reviews are not handled properly. Group ratings provide additional assessment resources and can help to create a team environment.

The frequency of performance appraisals, appraiser training, system monitoring, and supervisor–employee communication are additional areas of concern. Companies should conduct performance appraisals more often than annually. An organization can reduce or eliminate rater error by providing the proper appraiser training. Whatever system is chosen, the organization must monitor its effectiveness, and a performance appraisal review program should be developed to aid in this process. The performance appraisal system will work only if the organization effectively communicates with its employees; many organizations are using performance appraisals as a tool for encouraging this type of communication.

KEY TERMS AND CONCEPTS

adjective checklist method

behavior-based performance dimensions

behavioral observation scales (BOS)

behaviorally anchored rating scales (BARS)

central tendency error

checklist

coaching

computer-based information systems (CBIS)

critical incidents method

distal variables

essay evaluation

forced-choice checklist

graphic rating scale

halo effect

improvement feedback

interview stage

judgmental data

leniency/harshness error

maintenance feedback

management by objectives (MBO)

microskills approach

negative feedback

objective data

peer nomination

peer ranking

peer rating

perceived similarity/ dissimilarity error

performance appraisal interview

performance appraisal review program (PARP)

personal bias error

personnel data

positive feedback

preview stage

problem-solving objectives

proximal variables

recency of events error

review stage

Rogerian client-centered theory

routine objectives

self-appraisal

self-improvement objectives

special-purpose objectives

standards of evaluation error

systems approach

360-degree feedback

trait-based performance dimensions

RECOMMENDED READINGS

Balzer, W. K., & Sulsky, L. M. (1992). Halo and performance appraisal research: A critical examination. *Journal of Applied Psychology, 77*(6), 975–985.

Borman, W. C., White, L. A., Pulakos, E. D., & Oppler, S. H. (1991). Models of supervisory job performance ratings. *Journal of Applied Psychology, 76*(6), 863–872.

Clampitt, P. G. (1991). *Communicating for managerial effectiveness.* Newbury Park, CA: Sage.

Cleveland, J. N., Murphy, K. R., & Williams, R. E. (1989). Multiple uses of performance appraisal: Prevalence and correlates. *Journal of Applied Psychology, 74*(1), 130–135.

DeVries, D. L., Morrison, A. M., Shullman, S. L., & Gerlach, M. L. (1986). *Performance appraisal on the line.* Greensboro, NC: Center for Creative Leadership.

Fisher, C. D. (1979). Transmission of positive and negative feedback to subordinates: A laboratory investigation. *Journal of Applied Psychology, 64*(5), 533–540.

King, P. (1989). *Performance planning & appraisal: A how-to book for managers.* New York, NY: McGraw-Hill.

Modern Business Reports (1986). *Performance appraisals: The latest legal nightmare.* New York, NY: Alexander Hamilton Institute.

Murphy, K. R., & Cleveland, J. N. (1991). *Performance appraisal: An organizational perspective.* Boston: Allyn & Bacon.

Peterson, D. B., & Hicks, M. D. (1996). *The manager as coach: Strategies for coaching and developing others.* Minneapolis, MN: Personnel Decisions International.

Whisler, T. L., & Harper, S. F. (Eds.). (1962). *Performance appraisal.* New York: Holt, Rinehart and Winston.

INTERNET RESOURCES

Playing God? The Performance of Appraisal
Working Papers Series 94/5 by Tim Newton and
Patricia Findlay. This site presents an abstract of
an interesting paper that criticizes past work on
performance appraisal because of methodological
limitations and argues for a broader context for
performance appraisal research.
http://spey.bus.ed.ac.uk:8080/94_5.html

Deming Electronic Network Files
This index to files in the Deming Electronic Network file area catalogues and provides access to
many interesting quality improvement papers, including a condensation of Dr. Deming's 14 Points,
with his famous edict that there should not be any
performance appraisal.
**http://deming.eng.clemson.edu/pub/den/files/
index.html**

University of Calgary Performance Appraisal
Research
This site provides references to the University of
Calgary's Department of Psychology faculty re-

search on performance appraisal by D. P. Skarlicki
and L. M. Sulsky.
**http://www.psych.ucalgary.ca/GradStudies/
IndOrgErg.html**

Goldenson Management Case Studies Index
This site is the index to the case studies in the University of Missouri–Columbia School of Journal-
ism and AEJMC Media Management Division's
Goldenson Management electronic library. The full
text of each case is provided. Many of these cases
also contain teaching notes. Several deal with performance appraisal.
http://www.missouri.edu/~jourcw/cseindex.html

HBR Classic—Douglas McGregor, AN UNEASY
LOOK AT PERFORMANCE APPRAISAL.
The full text of this classic article is available at
this URL.
**gopher://deming.eng.clemson.edu:70/00/pub/
tqmbbs/prin-pract/uneasy.txt**

EXERCISES

Exercise 6.1

Strengths and Weaknesses of Performance Appraisal Systems

Review each of the models discussed in this chapter.
Identify the strengths and weaknesses of each performance appraisal system. Some questions to consider
are the following:

1. What types of appraisal techniques are used in
   this system? What are the advantages and disadvantages of each?

2. Who is responsible for appraising performance?
   Would adding a self-appraisal enhance this system?

3. What types of rating errors could occur? Does
   this appraisal system attempt to eliminate rating
   errors? How?

4. What additional steps could be taken to ensure
   consistent performance ratings?

5. Does this appraisal system promote feedback
   and goal setting?

6. What additions could be made to this system to
   enhance communication between managers and
   employees?

7. Does this system comply with the 1978 Uniform
   Guidelines issued by the EEOC? What could be
   some of the legal ramifications of this system in
   use?

8. How does the performance appraisal system address the issue of employee training? What steps
   could be taken to improve the employee's understanding of the appraisal system?

9. Does this appraisal system provide a means for
   monitoring effectiveness? If not, how could a
   performance appraisal monitoring system be developed?

10. What other improvements could be made to this
    system?

Exercise 6.2

Developing a 360-Degree Performance Measure of Your Instructor

The purpose of this exercise is to develop a behaviorally based evaluation of your instructor's effectiveness. Using information presented in this chapter, additional library research about behaviors that exemplify effective teaching, your personal experience, and a team discussion, develop and administer a 360-degree instrument to provide performance feedback to your instructor. Use the instrument and process to evaluate your instructor. Give the results to your instructor. Review and discuss your experience.

The following are the key steps in this process.

1. Form several teams. Meet as a team to discuss your approach and make team assignments. Your team task is to research and develop a behavioral list of teacher competencies.

2. Working independently, collect information about teaching competence. Look for evidence of specific behaviors demonstrated by effective teachers and/or research evidence of effective instructional techniques.

3. Meet as a team to discuss your individual lists and definitions. Combine the lists and consolidate the result using group consensus to arrive at a list of five to ten key competencies. Define each in behavioral terms. Include specific examples when possible.

4. Pool team lists and repeat step 3 but working as a whole class. Arrive at a class consensus on the five to ten key competencies for your instructor. Define each.

5. Separate into your original teams. Now work individually or in pairs or small groups to write items that you, as students, could use to assess your teacher. Work to make these as objective as possible; that is, specify them in terms such that, if two different students observed the same behavior, they would recognize and rate it similarly.

6. Meet again in your team, selecting, combining, and refining the best items. Your goal should be to have three or four items for each key behavior and five to nine major dimensions of teaching effectiveness.

7. Working as a class, pool team items to develop a draft survey. Test the survey by giving it to several students who are not in your class. Ask them to use it to rate one of their instructors and give you feedback on how clear the items are and how easy it is to use. Revise the survey as necessary to improve it.

8. Administer the survey. Use the steps described in this chapter to collect, analyze, and feedback the results.

9. Critique your efforts. What went well for you in this exercise? If you were repeating the exercise, what would you do differently? What was the biggest challenge? How do you feel, overall, about the process? Do you believe that your 360-degree survey accurately assessed your instructor?

. . . .

REFERENCES

Ammons, D. N., & Rodriguez, A. (1986). Performance appraisal for upper level management in city governments. *Public Administration Review, 46,* 460–467.

Balzer, W. K., & Sulsky, L. M. (1992). Halo and performance appraisal research: A critical examination. *Journal of Applied Psychology, 77*(6), 975–985.

Blum, M. L., & Naylor, J. C. (1968). *Industrial psychology: Its theoretical and social foundations.* New York: Harper & Row.

Borman, W. C. (1979). Format and training effects on rating accuracy and rater errors. *Journal of Applied Psychology, 64*(2), 410–421.

Borman, W. C., & Dunnette, M. D. (1975). Behavior-based versus trait-oriented performance ratings: An empirical study. *Journal of Applied Psychology, 60*(5), 561–565.

Bracken, D. W. (1994). Straight talk about multi-rater feedback. *Training & Development,* September (Reprint).

Brett, R., & Fredian, A. J. (1981, December). Performance appraisal: The system is not the solution. *Personnel Administrator,* pp. 61–68.

Brunswick, E. E. (1952). *The conceptual framework of psychology.* Chicago: University of Chicago Press.

Campbell, D., Curphy, G., & Tuggle, T. (1995, May). *360 degree feedback: Beyond theory.* Pre-conference workshop presented at the meeting of the Society for Industrial and Organizational Psychology, Orlando, FL.

Cardy, R. L., & Dobbins, G. H. (1986). Affect and appraisal accuracy: Liking as an integral dimension in evaluating performance. *Journal of Applied Psychology, 71*(4), 672–678.

Carroll, S. J., & Schneier, C. E. (1982). *Performance appraisal and review systems: The identification, measurement and development of performance in organizations.* Glenview, IL: Scott, Foresman.

Clampitt, P. G. (1991). *Communicating for managerial effectiveness.* Newbury Park, CA: Sage.

Clark, M. S., & Isen, A. M. (1982). Toward understanding the relationship between feeling states and social behavior. In Hastorf, A., & Isen, A. M. (Eds.), *Cognitive social psychology.* New York: Elsevier.

Cleveland, J. N., Morrison, R., & Bjerke, D. (1986). *Rater intentions in appraisal ratings: Malevolent manipulation or functional fudging.* Paper presented at the First Annual Conference of the Society for Industrial and Organizational Psychology, Chicago.

Cleveland, J. N., Murphy, K. R., & Williams, R. E. (1989). Multiple uses of performance appraisal: Prevalence and correlates. *Journal of Applied Psychology, 74*(1), 130–135.

Deming, W. E. (1986). *Out of the crises.* Cambridge, MA: Massachusetts Institute of Technology, Center for Advanced Engineering Study.

DeVries, D. L., Morrison, A. M., Shullman, S. L., & Gerlach, M. L. (1986). *Performance appraisal on the line.* Greensboro, NC: Center for Creative Leadership.

Dipboye, R. L. (1985). Some neglected variables in research on discrimination in appraisals. *Academy of Management Review, 10,* 116–127.

Drucker, P. F. (1954). *The practice of management.* New York: Harper.

England, R. E., & Parle, W. M. (1987). Nonmanagerial performance appraisal practices in large American cities. *Public Administration Review, 47,* 498–504.

Farth, J. L., Werbel, J. D., & Bedeian, A. G. (1988). An empirical investigation of self-appraisal based performance evaluation. *Personnel Psychology, 41,* 141–156.

Feldman, J. M. (1981). Beyond attribution theory: Cognitive processes in performance appraisal. *Journal of Applied Psychology, 66*(2), 127–148.

Flanagan, J. C. (1949). A new approach to evaluating personnel. *Personnel, 26,* 35–42.

Fletcher, H. M., Jr., & Wertheim, E. G. (1985). Performance appraisal. In W. R. Tracey (Ed.), *Human resource management and development handbook* (pp. 238- 243). New York: American Management Association.

Fried, Y., Tiegs, R. B., & Bellamy, A. R. (1992). Personal and interpersonal predictors of supervisors' avoidance of evaluating subordinates. *Journal of Applied Psychology, 77*(4), 462–468.

Foti, R. J., & Lord, R. G. (1987). Prototypes and scripts: The effects of alternative methods of processing information on rating accuracy. *Organizational Behavior and Human Decision Processes, 39,* 318–340.

Girard, R. (1988). Is there a need for a performance appraisal? *Personnel Journal, 67,* 89–90.

Grant, P. C. (1987). A better approach to performance reviews. *Management Solutions, 32,* 11–16.

Guion, R. M. (1961). Criterion measurement and personnel judgments. *Personnel Psychology, 14,* 141–149.

Härtel, Charmine E. J. (1993). Rating format revisited: Format effectiveness and acceptability depend on rater characteristics. *Journal of Applied Psychology, 78*(2), 212–217.

Henderson, R. I. (1984). *Performance appraisal* (2nd ed.). Reston, VA: Reston.

Higgins, E. T., & King, G. (1981). Accessibility of social constructs: Information processing consequences of individual and contextual variability. In N. Cantor & J. Kihlstrom (Eds.), *Personality, cognition, and social interaction.* Hillsdale, NJ: Erlbaum.

Hulin, C. L. (1982). Some reflections on general performance dimensions. *Journal of Applied Psychology, 67*(2), 165–170.

Ilgen, D. R., Barnes-Farrell, J. L., & McKellin, D. B. (1993). Performance appraisal process research in the 1980's: What has it contributed to appraisals in use? *Organizational Behavior and Human Decision Processes, 54,* 321–368.

Ilgen, D. R., & Feldman, J. M. (1983). Performance appraisal: A process approach. In B. M. Staw (Ed.), *Research in organization behavior* (Vol. 2). Greenwich, CT: JAI Press.

Isen, A. M., & Daubman, K. A. (1984). The influence of affect on categorization. *Journal of Personality and Social Psychology, 47,* 1207–1217.

Ivancevich, J. M., & Glueck, W. F. (1986). Performance evaluation. *Foundations of personnel: Human resource management* (3rd ed., pp. 276–322). Plano, TX: Business Publications.

Ivey, A. E. (1982). *Intentional interviewing and counseling.* Monterey, CA: Brooks Cole.

Jeffrey, K. M., & Mischel, W. (1979). Effects of purpose on the organization and recall of information in person perception. *Journal of Personality, 47,* 397–419.

Kane, J. S., & Freeman, K. A. (1986). MBO and performance appraisal: A mixture that's not a solution, part 1. *Personnel, 63,* 26–36.

Kleiman, L. S., & Durham, R. L. (1981). Performance appraisal, promotion and the courts: A critical review. *Personnel, 34,* 103–121.

Kraiger, K., & Ford, J. K. (1985). A meta-analysis of ratee race effects in performance ratings. *Journal of Applied Psychology, 70*(1), 56–65.

Kulik, C. T., & Ambrose, M. L. (1993). Category-based and feature-based processes in performance appraisal: Integrating visual and computerized sources of performance data. *Journal of Applied Psychology, 78*(5), 821–830.

Landy, F. J., & Farr, J. L. (1980). Performance rating. *Psychological Bulletin, 87,* 72–107.

Landy, F. J., & Farr, J. L. (1983). *The measurement of work performance: Methods, theory, and applications.* New York: Academic Press.

Landy, F. J., & Guion, R. M. (1970). Development of scales for the measurement of work motivation. *Organizational Behavior and Human Performance, 5,* 93–103.

Lanza, P. (1985). Team appraisals. *Personnel Journal, 64,* 47–51.

Latham, G. P., & Wexley, K. N. (1977). Behavioral observation scales for appraising the performance of foremen. *Personnel Psychology, 32,* 299–311.

Locke, E. A. (1976). The nature and causes of job satisfaction. In M. D. Dunnette (Ed.), *Handbook of industrial and organizational psychology* (pp. 1297–1350). Chicago: Rand McNally.

Locke, E. A. (1986). *Generalizing from laboratory to field settings.* Lexington, MA: Lexington Books.

Locke, E. A., Shaw, K. N., Saari, L. M., & Latham, G. P. (1981). Goal setting and task performance: 1969–1980. *Psychological Bulletin, 90,* 125–152.

Malinauskas, B. K., & Clement, R. W. (1987). Performance appraisal: Interviewing for tangible results. *Training and Development Journal, 41,* 74–79.

Martell, R. F., & Borg, M. R. (1993). A comparison of the behavioral rating accuracy of groups and individuals. *Journal of Applied Psychology, 78*(1), 43–50.

Martin, C. D., Bartol, K. M., & Levine, M. J. (1986). The legal ramification of performance appraisal. *Employee Relations Law Journal, 12,* 370–396.

Maurer, T. J., Palmer, J. K., & Ashe, D. K. (1993). Diaries, checklists, evaluations, and contrast effects in measurement of behavior. *Journal of Applied Psychology, 78*(2), 226–231.

McCall, M. W., & DeVries, D. L. (1977). *Appraisal in context: Clashing with organizational realities* (Tech. Rep. No. 4). Greensboro, NC: Center for Creative Leadership.

McGregor, D. (1987). An uneasy look at performance appraisal. *Training and Development Journal, 41,* 89–94.

Mohrman, A. M., & Lawler, E. E. (1983). Motivation and performance appraisal behavior. In F. Landy, S. Zedeck, & J. Cleveland (Eds.), *Performance measurement and theory.* Hillsdale, NJ: Erlbaum.

Momeyer, A. G. (1986). Why no one likes your performance appraisal system. *Training, 23,* 95–98.

Murphy, K. R., & Anhalt, R. L. (1992). Is halo error a property of the rater, ratees, or the specific behaviors observed? *Journal of Applied Psychology, 77*(4), 494–500.

Murphy, K. R., & Balzer, W. K. (1989). Rater errors and rating accuracy. *Journal of Applied Psychology, 74*(4), 619–624.

Murphy, K. R., Balzar, W. K., Kellam, K. L., & Armstrong, J. (1984). Effect of purpose of rating on accuracy in observing teacher behavior and evaluating teaching performance. *Journal of Educational Psychology, 76,* 45–54.

Murphy, K. R., Balzar, W. K., Lockhart, M., & Eisenman, E. (1985). Effects of previous performance on evaluations of present performance. *Journal of Applied Psychology, 70*(1), 72–84.

Murphy, K. R., & Cleveland, J. N. (1991). *Performance appraisal: An organizational perspective.* Boston: Allyn & Bacon.

Murphy, K. R., Garcia, M., Kerkar, S., Martin, C., & Balzer, W. K. (1982). Relationship between observational accuracy and accuracy in evaluating performance. *Journal of Applied Psychology, 67*(3), 320–325.

Murphy, K., Jako, R., & Anhalt, R. (1993). Nature and consequences of halo error: A critical analysis. *Journal of Applied Psychology, 78*(2), 218–225.

Oberg, H. (1972). *Make performance appraisals relevant. Organizational behavior: Industrial psychology selected readings.* New York: Oxford University Press.

Oppler, S. H., Campbell, J. P., Pulakos, E. D., & Borman, W. C. (1992). Three approaches to the investigation of subgroup bias in performance measurement: Review, results, and conclusions. *Journal of Applied Psychology Monograph, 77*(2), 201–217.

Peterson, D. B., & Hicks, M. D. (1996a). *Development first: Strategies for self-development.* Minneapolis, MN: Personnel Decisions International.

Peterson, D. B., & Hicks, M. D. (1996b). *The manager as coach: Strategies for coaching and developing others.* Minneapolis, MN: Personnel Decisions International.

Phillips, K. R. (1987). Red flags in performance appraisal. *Training and Development Journal, 41,* 80–82.

Rausch, E. (1985). *Win/win performance management/appraisal.* New York: Wiley Interscience.

Reilly, R. R., Henry, S., & Smither, J. W. (1990). An examination of the effects of using behavior checklists on the construct validity of assessment center dimensions. *Personnel Psychology, 43,* 71–84.

Reily, M., & Noland, R. (1987). Beyond performance reviews. *Management Solutions, 32,* 4–15.

Saal, F. E., Downey, K. G., & Lahey, M. A. (1980). Rating the ratings: Assessing the quality of rating data. *Psychological Bulletin, 88,* 413–428.

Sackett, P. R., & DuBois, C. L. Z. (1991). Rater-ratee race effects on performance evaluation: Challenging meta-analytic conclusions. *Journal of Applied Psychology, 76*(6), 873–877.

Schmitt, N. W., & Klimoski, R. J. (1990). *Research methods in human resources management.* Cincinnati: South-Western.

Schneier, C. E., Geis, A., & Wert, J. A. (1987). Performance appraisals: No appointment needed. *Personnel Journal, 66,* 80–87.

Smith, M. (1987). Feedback as a performance management technique. *Management Solutions, 32,* 20–29.

Smith, P. C. (1976). Behaviors, results, and organizational effectiveness. In M. Dunnette (Ed.), *Handbook of industrial and organizational psychology* (pp. 745–775). Chicago: Rand-McNally.

Smith, B. N., Hornsby, J. S., & Shirmeyer, R. (1996). Current trends in performance appraisal: An examination of managerial practice. *Advanced Management Journal, 61*(3), pp. 10–15.

Stroul, N. A. (1987). Whither performance appraisal. *Training and Development Journal, 41,* 70–74.

Thompson, J. D. (1967). *Organizations in action.* New York: McGraw-Hill.

Tsui, A. S., & Barry, B. (1986). Interpersonal affect and rating errors. *Academy of Management Journal, 29,* 586–599.

Turban, D. B., & Jones, A. P. (1988). Supervisor-subordinate similarity: Type, effects, and mechanisms. *Journal of Applied Psychology, 73*(2), 228–234.

Tziner, A., & Kopelman, R. K. (1988). Effects of rating format on goal-setting dimensions: A field experiment. *Journal of Applied Psychology, 73*(2), 323–326.

Vroom, V. (1964). *Work and motivation.* New York: Wiley.

Waldman, D. A., Yammarino, F. J., & Avolio, B. J. (1990). A multiple level investigation of personnel ratings. *Personnel Psychology, 43,* 811–835.

Wehrenberg, S. B. (1988). Train supervisors to measure and evaluate performance. *Personnel Journal, 67,* 77–79.

Weitzel, W. (1987). How to improve performance through successful appraisals. *Personnel, 64,* 18–23.

Williams, K. J., DeNisi, A. S., Meglini, B. M., & Cafferty, T. P. (1986). Initial decisions and subsequent performance ratings. *Journal of Applied Psychology, 71*(2), 189–195.

Wilson, C. L. (1985). *Task cycle management: A users manual for the development of managers/supervisors, individual contributors, and organizations.* Silver Spring, MD: The Clark Wilson Group, Inc.

Woehr, D. J., & Feldman, J. (1993). Processing objective and question order effects on the causal relation between memory and judgment in performance appraisal: The tip of the iceberg. *Journal of Applied Psychology, 78*(2), 232–241.

Yammarino, F. J., & Waldman, D. A. (1993). Performance in relation to job skill importance: A consideration of rater source. *Journal of Applied Psychology, 78*(2), 242–249.

Predictors

Chapter Outline

A true story introduces us to some of the basic principles underlying the uses and abuses of predictors: A six-year-old child is sitting in front of a psychologist. The place is Israel. The time is the early period of immigration from Yemen in southern Arabia. The child, a son of new immigrants, needs to be placed in the appropriate grade in elementary school. The psychologist is testing the child. One of the items she is showing him is a picture of a man's face with only one eye and no hat. Since in Jewish religious tradition, men always wear hats and the child was raised in a religious family, he is used to seeing men wearing hats. The child looks at the picture for a long time and then says with confidence: This man is not wearing his hat!

What led to the child's answer? How accurate was this type of test for this child? How meaningful was it for the psychologist to make decisions and interpretations on the basis of the child's responses?

The answers to these questions relate to basic requirements and principles for the use of any predictors. We will discuss two main principles: reliability and validity. But first, we need to be familiar with basic terms and concepts pertaining to predictors.

BASIC TERMS AND CONCEPTS

Because issues of prediction are part of both personnel decisions and human resources management, we discuss some of the specific applications of predictors in Chapters 3 and 8. In this chapter we focus on the definitions and descriptions of predictors and current issues related to their use in industry and organizations.

In general, the process of prediction at work is based on the relationship that exists between an instrument that we use for prediction and a job behavior. A **predictor** is a variable used for forecasting job behavior; the **criterion** and job behaviors are the variables being forecasted. As Guion (1991, p. 327) specified, the prediction hypothesis "is based on an understanding of the job for which people are to be selected . . . [the] . . . specific, valued aspect of performance or other job behavior to be predicted, with one or more applicant traits hypothesized to predict it." It is the process of measuring individual differences "that is, the assignment of quantitative values to observable differences in human behavior" (Dunnette, 1966, p. 41). A **test** is any device that quantifies behavior (Kaplan & Saccuzzo, 1993). In our case it would be any predictor variable that is used in the procedure of personnel decision making, for example, psychological tests, interviews, questionnaires, references, and ratings (Campbell, 1990). A **psychological test** is a measure designed to elicit a representative sample of behavior in meeting a specific environmental demand. The behavior can be overt or covert. Overt behavior can be directly observed (e.g., the speed at which the employee moves his or her hand); covert behavior is behavior that cannot be directly observed (e.g., what the person thinks or feels) (Kaplan & Saccuzzo, 1993). Psychological tests measure psychological constructs such as intelligence, aggression, and leadership. **Objective tests** enable the decision maker to physically measure psychological behaviors. The results do not depend on the observer's judgment and are free of personal bias. **Standardized tests** use uniform procedures, material, instructions, time limits, scoring, and reporting procedures and thus reduce the subjectivity of interpretations of test scores (Anastasi, 1988).

The question of "subjectivity" in using tests, combining data accumulated about an individual, and making inferences from test scores has been an issue for years. The controversy was stimulated by Meehl's 1954 book *Clinical versus Statistical Prediction*. The question posed was: Do we take test scores, ratings, references, interview observations, and other materials about an individual and combine them subjectively (i.e., clinically) to make our decision about this individual, or do we base our decision and pre-

PRACTICE PERSPECTIVE 7.1

Clinical versus Statistical Prediction

So here is veteran Jones, whose case is under consideration at therapy staff. The equation takes such facts as his Rorschach [score], his multiphasic code, his divorce, his age, his 40 percent service-connection, and grinds out a probability of .75 of good response to therapy. . . . Here is Jones. We want to do what is best for him. We don't know for sure. . . . We act on probabilities. . . . But now the social worker tells us that Jones, age 40, said at intake that his mother sent him in. The psychology trainee describes [his scores] . . . ; the psychiatrist adds his comments, and pretty soon we are concluding that Jones has a very severe problem with mother-figure. Since our only available therapist is Frau Dr. Schleswig-Holstein, who would traumatize anybody even without a mother-problem, we

begin to vacillate. The formula gives us odds of 3 to 1 on Jones; these further facts, not in the equation. raise doubts in our minds. What shall we do? . . .

Shall we use our heads, or shall we follow the formula? Mostly we will use our heads, because there just isn't any formula, but suppose we have a formula, and a case comes along in which it disagrees with our heads? Shall we then use our heads? I would say, yes—provided the psychological situation is as clear as a broken leg; otherwise, very seldom.

Source: From P. E. Meehl (1966) "When Shall We Use Our Heads Instead of the Formula?" In E. I. Megargee (Ed.), *Research in Clinical Assessment* (pp. 651–656). New York: Harper & Row. Copyright © 1966 by Harper & Row. Reprinted by permission of HarperCollins Publishers, Inc.

diction on empirical evidence and research that provides statistical probabilities (i.e., statistical decision making)? The problem and the issue relate to the accuracy of prediction. Practice Perspective 7.1 illustrates this issue. After reviewing fifty-one different studies, Meehl (1965) found that thirty-three of them demonstrated that statistical prediction was better than clinical prediction. In seventeen studies, neither method was clearly better, and clinical prediction was better in only one study. Meehl concluded that the clinical methods for combining observation and judgment into a prediction of behavior were less accurate than were the statistical methods.

Meehl's question and conclusion describe the need for verifying the accuracy of inferences made about an individual from instruments and generalizing the inference process to all tests used in industry. These could be a psychologist's reports based on observations of the individual's drug or alcohol abuse, problems the employee has with his or her peers, or standardized tests

such as clerical or motor dexterity tests. The controversy that Meehl initiated led to other comparative studies; for example, Sines's 1970 study showed that about two thirds of the studies that used statistical prediction were more accurate than studies that used clinical prediction; and in about a third of the studies there was not much difference between the statistical and clinical methods in accuracy of prediction. Other studies (e.g., Goldberg, 1970) claimed that better prediction can be made by professional clinicians who are highly trained and experienced. An example of an effective prediction made by a professional clinician is described in Historical Perspective 7.1 on page 208.

The controversy continues, especially since the issue in industry relates to assessments made about employees on the basis of interviews, case histories, and observations. The use of personality tests in selection processes and employment settings (e.g., integrity tests) has recently reemerged. At the same time the use of computerized tests that combine information about an

An Example of Clinical Prediction

Here is an example that Meehl (1954) cites as an experienced "prediction" by a clinician:

> a patient tells a dream which begins as follows: "I was in the basement of my parents' house, back home. It seems that I was ironing, and a fellow whom I had not seen since junior high school, and whom I never went out with, and hardly knew, had brought some shirts over for me to iron for him. I felt vaguely resentful about this—oh, and by the way, he was dressed in a riding habit, of all things" (grinning). Now, this patient had said in the preceding interview that it would be too easy to get into the habit of having sexual relationships with her present

boy friend, and that since she did not really care a great deal about him, she must try to avoid this. If the phrase "riding habit" is a sexual pun, we infer that the adolescent acquaintance whom she "hardly knew" represents her present friend in the dream. The remainder of the dream and her associations to it, which I will not reproduce here, confirmed this hypothesis.

Source: From P. E. Meehl (1954). *Clinical versus statistical prediction: A theoretical analysis and a review of the evidence* (p. 71). Minneapolis, MN: University of Minnesota Press.

individual, the development of predictions, and the interpretations of scores into a fully computerized process have been growing. Doubts and debates have also been raised about computerized predictions. This is because some computer software is not suited to the particular uses to which it has been put (Hartman, 1986; Kaplan & Saccuzzo, 1993).

Industrial/organizational psychologists recognize that every process of decision making and most predictors involve subjective inferences: "Judgement is an integral part of most selection procedures. . . . The question is not whether there is subjectivity in selection decisions but whether that subjectivity is recognized, reliable, and understood" (Guion, 1991, p. 345). Judgment and subjectivity are part of performance appraisals that are used for salary increases, interviews used for decisions on promotion, and assessment centers used for decisions about development, training, or selection. If "someone is given the responsibility for considering available evidence and presumably basing a selection decision on the accumulated evidence, then judgement is part of that process" (Guion, 1991, p. 345). Proving the accuracy,

quality, and precision of any device we use in such decision making is "a must."

PSYCHOMETRIC REQUIREMENTS: RELIABILITY AND VALIDITY

The basic requirements for any instrument that is used to measure individual differences are the consistency, stability, and accuracy of scores. The empirical evidence of these characteristics of tests refers to reliability and validity (see Chapters 8 and 3). A detailed discussion of validity and the methods by which we can measure it is presented in Chapter 8, *Personnel Decisions*. In this chapter we discuss reliability and define validity so that the reader can associate these concepts with predictors and the processes that are applied in selection, human resources, and criteria.

Reliability

We frequently find discussion in the media about the dependability of mammogram tests in detecting cancerous breast cells. The allegation has been made that some of the equipment used is old, producing inaccurate results. That is, if the tests were repeated on the same patients with the same equipment by the same technicians, the results might be different and could lead to different chances of the radiologist's detecting the disease. The precision and consistency of scores "obtained by the same persons when retested with identical test or with equivalent form of the test" (Anastasi, 1988, p. 27) are called **reliability.** The term *reliability* refers to the dependability and repeatability of test scores and applies to any measure used in employment, education, and clinical situations. An example cited by Gatewood and Feild (1994) is presented in Scientific Perspective 7.1.

In theory, we might expect that scores achieved by the same individuals, taking the same test twice, would be identical. However, because

psychological characteristics and attributes cannot be defined and measured with the same precision as physical attributes, their measurement always involves errors of measurement (Gatewood & Feild, 1994). Any departure from perfect correspondence of scores is due to these errors.

Dunnette's (1966) early book on personnel selection probably has the best summary of the sources of errors in psychological measurements:

1. "Inadequate sampling of content of tests" (p. 29). Dunnette claims that tests that are assumed to measure the same attribute may sometimes sample *different* aspects of that attribute. Two forms of a mechanical aptitude test may differ in that one includes more items that measure mechanical reasoning and the other includes

---

SCIENTIFIC PERSPECTIVE 7.1

Using an Aptitude Test in Selection

A human resource manager had given an aptitude test to ten people who were applying for a computer programmer job. He took the results home to review them and make decisions. On the way home he stopped to buy some supplies; when he returned to his car, he realized that the car had been broken into and his briefcase was missing. Two days later, he successfully gathered all ten applicants again and gave them the same test. However, the same day, the police found and returned his briefcase with all the material intact. The manager now had two sets of scores achieved by the same individuals given the same test within a short interval of time.

Applicant	First test	Second test
1	35	47
2	57	69
3	39	49
4	68	50
5	74	69
6	68	65
7	54	38
8	71	78
9	41	54
10	44	59

The scores these applicants achieved on the two occasions are different, so the manager has some problems. Can he use these results to make selection decisions? Which of the two sets can he use? Should he throw away all these scores and try to base his decision on another measure?

To make his decisions, he should first apply the appropriate statistics to calculate and estimate the degree of reliability of the test, that is, the degree of dependability, consistency, and stability of the test. Only then can he make his decisions about the usability of the test and its results.

Source: Adapted from R. D. Gatewood, & H. S. Feild (1994), *Human Resource Selection,* Third Edition (pp. 154–155). Copyright © 1994. Reprinted by permission of the Dryden Press.

more items that measure the ability to manipulate objects and perceive the relationships between them. The differences in scores achieved by the same people could be due to the different sampling of items in the test.

2. "Chance response tendencies" (p. 29). Assume that you apply for a clerical job. The selection test that you are given includes multiple-choice questions about bookkeeping, about which you know nothing. Your tendency will probably be to guess the answers so that you will not turn in an empty form. Random guessing because of lack of skills or motivation leads to chance answers and scores that would probably vary if you took the test more than once.

3. "Changes in the testing environment" (p. 29). Any changes in the testing environment between repeated administrations of the same test or parallel forms of the test could affect the subjects' responses. For example, if one testing is done in an air-conditioned room and the repeat testing is done in a hot, stuffy room, the candidates' concentration may be affected, leading to different results on their tests.

4. "Changes in the person taking the test" (p. 30). Individuals may respond differently to the same tests designed to measure the same trait because of various personal reasons. Having a cold, suffering from lack of sleep, and trying to get the test over with would all affect the stability of scores achieved on the repeated testings. Dunnette indicates that care should be taken to account for the fluctuations that occur with repeated testing of some traits because of their dynamic nature. For example, the level of fatigue changes with time of day, and fatigue times are different for different individuals. If a job requires a high level of alertness, such effects should be detected in an applicant for the job. It would be important to separate the dynamic changes that occur in the level of fatigue because of the nature of the trait and to differentiate these effects from errors of measurement.

"Errors of measurement are those factors that affect obtained scores but are not related to

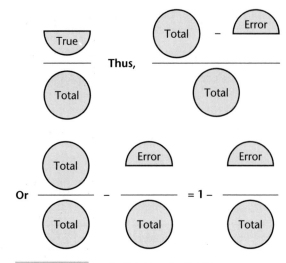

FIGURE 7.1   Definition of reliability.

Source: From M. L. Blum and J. C. Naylor (1968). *Industrial Psychology: Its Theoretical and Social Foundations,* Revised Edition (p. 40). New York: Harper & Row. Copyright © 1968 by M. L. Blum and J. C. Naylor. Reprinted by permission of HarperCollins Publishers, Inc.

the characteristic, trait, or attribute being measured" (Gatewood & Feild, 1994, p. 158). As Blum and Naylor (1968) define it, "reliability [is] a ratio of true variance to total variance" (p. 40). They represented this ratio graphically as shown in Figure 7.1.

As Figure 7.1 shows, the full circle represents the actual score a person receives on a test, that is, the **obtained score,** or the *total variance.* An example is a mechanical comprehension test score that a person obtains. That variance can be depicted as two partial circles. One portion represents the **true score,** which expresses the variance related to the behavior being measured (in our example the actual amount of mechanical comprehension the person has), and the other portion represents the *error variance,* or **measurement error.** These errors refer to the sampling, chance, and time factors discussed previously. Error variance is the part of the score that is not related to the behavior and characteristic being measured. If the person has the flu on the day he or she takes the test, performance on the mechanical comprehension test will be affected. Reliability of a measure is the ratio of the true score to the total score (shown in the top element of Figure 7.1). Another way to depict this relationship is shown in the middle part of the figure, where the true variance has been replaced by the equivalent of total variance minus error variance. The mathematical transformation (bottom formula) represents reliability: 1 minus the ratio of error variance to total variance. It is important to understand that any score a person obtains on a test is composed of the true score and the amount of measurement error influencing the obtained score. Because true scores cannot be accurately derived from obtained scores, we can only estimate the degree of reliability a test has (Gatewood & Feild, 1994).

Estimates of reliability are called **reliability coefficients.** They indicate the degree of relationship between different sets of measures of the same characteristic and can vary between .00 and 1.00. As we discuss in Appendix 2A, the higher the correlation, the higher the degree of agreement between the measures (or measurements) and the lower the amount of error variance in the obtained scores; the lower the correlation coefficient, the larger the error variance and the lower the reliability.

The estimate of the reliability coefficient is important because of the value of estimating the degree of dependency or repeatability of scores obtained by applicants and employees and because reliability affects the degree of validity. For a test to be highly valid, it has to have high reliability. However, the reverse does not hold: A test can be highly reliable but not valid for making a certain prediction. For example, "we might use the weight of individuals to predict college grades. Where weight can be measured very precisely, and thus be highly reliable, weight would be invalid as a predictor of college grades" (Nunnally, 1959, p. 95). Reliability is a necessary condition for validity, but it is not a sufficient condition for a measure to have high validity (Nunnally, 1967). There are several forms of reliability.

Test–Retest Reliability

In the **test–retest reliability** method the same test is administered to the same individuals at two different times. Because the correlation coefficient is calculated over time, it represents the **coefficient of stability.** Variations of scores achieved by the individuals across the two times indicate the influence of errors due to changes in the testing environment (e.g., noise, heat) and the person (e.g., illness, lack of sleep, stress); these variations are expressed in a correlation coefficient of less than +1.00. Dunnette (1966) claims that it is important to take into account the degree to which the memory of the first testing would affect scores achieved on the second testing and would lead to a biased correlation coefficient. To offset effects of memory, the two testings may be separated by a long interval of time.

Equivalent or Alternate Form Reliability

In the **equivalent (alternate) form reliability** method, two separate forms of the same test may be developed and administered to the subjects on two occasions. Following Dunnette's (1966) suggestion, this might be two to four weeks. The two forms are called *equivalent* or *parallel* because they have to represent the same universe of content (e.g., items representing clerical ability or typing speed), and the correlation is the coefficient of equivalence. The resulting correlation represents both the stability of scores over time and the consistency of scores across two forms of the same measure. The requirements for the forms to be parallel are that they have to contain the same number of items; item difficulty should be the same; format, instructions, and time limits should be equivalent; distribution of items from content domain should be parallel; and means and standard deviation of scores achieved by individuals on the two tests should be the same (Anastasi, 1988; Gatewood & Feild, 1994).

Internal Consistency Reliability

When only one form of the test is available, reliability can be checked either by dividing the test into two halves (**split-half reliability**) and correlating the scores achieved by the subjects on the two parts of the test administered at one point of time or by separating the scores these people achieved on the odd-numbered items and the even-numbered items (**odd-even split**) and correlating the two sets of scores. The resulting correlation expresses the degree of test precision of scores achieved at one point in time and a single test.

The assumption in internal consistency reliability measures is that all parts of the test measure the characteristic; that is, it indicates the degree of homogeneity of what the test measures across all its parts.

These methods result in a correlation that is computed on only half of the test; therefore it underestimates the reliability coefficient when it is computed on the whole test. To correct for this error and estimate the reliability coefficient of the full test, the Spearman-Brown formula can be applied:

$$r_{ttc} = \frac{nr_{12}}{1 + (n-1)r_{tt}}$$

where r_{ttc} is the corrected reliability coefficient, n is the number of times the test was increased in length, and r_{tt} is the correlation obtained on part of the test.

This estimate of reliability does not detect errors that can occur over time (e.g., changes in subjects or conditions), is appropriate only with measures that do not have time limits, and is influenced by variations in content of items and chance responses (Dunnette, 1966; Gatewood & Field, 1994).

Several other internal reliability estimates are based on a single administration of a single test.

Kuder-Richardson Reliability

The **Kuder-Richardson reliability** method takes the inter-item consistency of responses on all items; that is, the procedure averages the reliability coefficients that are calculated with "all possible ways of subdividing a measure" (Gatewood & Feild, 1994, p. 179). Thus this estimate takes into account the responses of the subjects on each of the items in the test. However, this estimate requires items to be similar and content to be homogenous. The higher the similarity of items, the higher will be the reliability estimate achieved.

Cronbach Alpha Reliability

The Kuder-Richardson method can be extended to estimate reliability from items that do not have choices of right and wrong answers. The **Cronbach alpha reliability** method can be applied to interest inventories, attitude questionnaires, and personality tests. These measures present the subject with a number of choices ranging from "strongly agree" to "strongly disagree," such as the following:

"Your supervisor listens to you when you have a suggestion"

strongly agree ____

agree ____

am not sure ____

disagree ____

strongly disagree ____

"Overall, are you satisfied with your pay?"

very satisfied ____

satisfied ____

moderately satisfied ____

dissatisfied ____

very dissatisfied ____

The alpha coefficient can estimate the internal consistency for such instruments. An alpha of .95 indicates that a test measures a particular trait well despite some heterogeneity of items (Ackerman & Humphreys, 1990). Dunnette (1966, p. 32) claims that all internal consistency estimates are based on the "pooling of correlations obtained from all possible ways of subdividing a test . . . [but] . . . that none of these methods has been shown to have any particular advantage over the odd-even method."

Validity

Because validity relates to all personnel decisions, we present an extensive discussion of the different types of validity and the methodologies for computing them in Chapter 8. When applied to predictors, **validity** refers to what an instrument measures, how well it measures it, and the supporting evidence for justifying inferences and interpretations that can be made from its scores (Society of Industrial and Organizational Psychology, 1987). In their discussion of the nature of evidence for validity, Kaplan and Saccuzzo (1993, p. 134) claim that

> obtaining data in validity studies is like gathering evidence for a court trial. Evidence for validity comes from showing the association between the test and other variables. The rules for claiming validity strictly forbid saying there is a relationship without some proof. This is similar to the legal notion of innocent until proven guilty. Proof of guilt must be persuasive. In a similar manner, we must have convincing proof that there is a relationship between two variables before we are justified in touting the connection.

TYPES OF PREDICTORS

Summarizing research on personnel selection and placement, Landy, Shankster, and Kohler (1994) considered predictors from the point of view of *what* they measure—that is, the content of the tests—and from the aspect of *how* they measure different characteristics, that is, the process by which they measure what they are supposed to measure. We will follow their guidelines in our discussion. Before we proceed with this discussion, we should note that tests can be categorized according to how they are administered and constructed.

Paper-and-Pencil Tests and Performance Tests

Paper-and-pencil tests are printed forms containing multiple-choice and/or essay questions. Often, the individual has to record the answers on a separate answer sheet. **Performance tests** involve

the manipulation of instruments. They employ three-dimensional objects and "de-emphasize language requirements" (Nunnally, 1959). Examples are some of the motor skills tests that we discuss later.

Individual and Group Tests

Individual tests are given to each subject separately. These tests call for an experienced examiner and require relatively longer time to administer. Many assessment techniques that are used for recommendation of selection and promotion of supervisors and management positions are individual tests. **Group tests** are administered to many individuals simultaneously. They can be given by a trained clerical worker, they are self-explanatory, and instructions are given to all individuals at the same time, so these tests are economical and quick. An example is the Graduate Record Examination (GRE), which is used as an entrance test for graduate schools.

Speed Tests and Power Tests

Speed tests are timed, usually with a short time such as five minutes, and the subject must stop when the allotted time is over. Speed tests often include items that have a low level of difficulty. The score is the number of items completed within the time limit. **Power tests** have no time limit or have a long enough time interval to allow the individual to complete all the test items. Items on power tests are often relatively difficult, and the score is the number of questions answered correctly.

Language and Nonlanguage Tests

Blum and Naylor (1968) added a category of tests that require the knowledge of a particular **language.** The individual has to know the language to perform and answer questions on the test, regardless of the ability being tested. **Nonlanguage tests** do not include verbal instructions or questions; they often include questions designed from shapes and forms. For example, the Army Alpha and the Army Beta were group intelligence tests constructed by a committee of psychologists during World War I to evaluate Armed Forces recruits. The Army Alpha was a verbal intelligence test constructed for recruits who knew how to read English. The Army Beta was an intelligence test for recruits who were illiterate in English.

WHAT PREDICTORS MEASURE

Cognitive Tests

Cognitive tests require "responses based on remembering information, producing ideas or solutions to problems, or perceiving, comparing, and evaluating stimuli" (Guion, 1991, p. 341). Examples are tests that can measure verbal abilities and those that measure spatial perception.

Historically, psychologists and educators have tried to differentiate the terms *ability, achievement, aptitude,* and *intelligence* from one another. Accordingly, Kaplan and Saccuzzo (1993) claim that achievement tests assess previous learning, aptitude tests measure potential for learning, and intelligence tests gauge the general potential to be able to solve problems and profit from experience. Others (e.g., Gatewood & Feild, 1994) differentiate between achievement tests, which measure the results of formalized learning experience (e.g., English grammar), and aptitude tests, which assess accumulation of nonformalized learning experiences (e.g., musical or mechanical ability). However, as these authors indicate, because any future learning requires previous experience, it is impossible to differentiate between these two behaviors. In place of the terms *achievement tests* or *aptitude tests,* they recommend that we use *ability tests* or *cognitive tests* (Guion, 1991). Ability tests can measure different content (e.g., mechanical or clerical), and they can cover different breadths of content (e.g., specific abilities and general

mental ability). We will use the term *ability tests* to include all the other concepts.

General Intelligence Tests

General intelligence (g factor, or psychometric g) has been associated with psychologists' attempts to sample and assess "a broad repertoire of skills and knowledge available to the person at a particular point in time" (Ackerman & Humphreys, 1990, p. 239). Specific ability tests measure narrower repertoires of skills and knowledge. In addition, mental ability tests have been identified as measuring cognitive abilities that indicate the level of the individual's ability to manipulate symbols, numbers, figures and words (e.g., Gatewood & Feild, 1994).

Research and development on mental ability tests have shown the following:

1. The validity studies have associated scores on these tests with scholastic success, assuming an overlap of content covered.
2. Statistical studies on the definition of intelligence (e.g., Cattell, 1971; Guilford, 1967; Spearman, 1904, 1927; Thurstone, 1938, 1947) have shown that these tests measure various abilities such as verbal, mathematical and memory.
3. Different mental ability tests can measure different combinations of these abilities. Some of these tests score each ability separately; others combine the scores into one numerical result.

Tests and testing practices have been the subjects of considerable scrutiny in recent years. There have been increasing public and professional criticism of tests, state legislative mandates for testing practices, and federal laws specifying fair uses for tests. The most frustrating of the challenges are criticisms that pertain to sex-, race-, and ethnic-based test bias. A charge of bias can be leveled against any measurement device. It is difficult to develop solid evidence to refute such charges. In addition, the term *bias* has become socially volatile. Charges of bias often evoke emotional reactions similar to those aroused by the words *discrimination* and *racism*. In response, researchers and psychometricians have focused on creating objective criteria, rigorous methods for studying bias, and controlled ways to conduct empirical investigations of test bias (Berk, 1982).

An example of the use of intelligence tests in business and industry is the popular Wonderlic Personnel Test (WPT). The test is based on the Otis Self-Administering Test of Mental Ability (1922–1929), which is one of the earliest group tests applying the spiral-omnibus format. In the **spiral-omnibus format** "the easiest items of each type are presented first, followed by the next harder of each type, and so on in a rising spiral of difficulty level" (Anastasi, 1988, p. 311). The Wonderlic is a shortened adaptation of the Otis test, including fifty items and a time limit of twelve minutes. The content includes items involving verbal, numerical, and spatial perception. It yields a single score, is available in five parallel forms, and has extensive norms tables for different occupations and various demographic, ethnic, jobs and industry groups. Test–retest and parallel forms reliability ranges between .70 and .90, the best predictability being for clerical jobs. Like the Otis, the format is with items arranged in a spiral-omnibus form. A sample item from the Wonderlic test is given in Figure 7.2.

The argument continues in industrial/organizational psychology about the utility and predictability of intelligence tests in employment decision making. Guion (1991) claims that the "recent trend in employment testing has been away from highly specific ability tests and toward more general measures . . . [with] the conclusion . . . that a general factor of intelligence is quite often a better predictor of success, in training and on a job" than specific abilities (p. 341). Schmidt, Ones, and Hunter (1992) support this argument, stating that summary of research in personnel selection favors the general mental ability theory. Landy et al. (1994) summarize their review of cognitive predictors by claiming that I/O psychologists are too busy with the argument of "how much variance in performance can be attributed to general intelligence (commonly referred to as psychometric g)" (p. 268) and how much research should concentrate on specific abilities. Their conclusions were that the relevant questions that should be emphasized are those involving interaction between motivation and abilities, personality variables, and ability levels, and that more attention should be devoted to the conditions that determine the use of specific abilities or the application of measures of g factor (e.g., the specific work conditions, the type of criteria used) (Landy et al., 1994).

Mechanical Ability Tests

Some psychologists (e.g., Anastasi, 1988) have argued that intelligence tests concentrate on the abstract use of verbal and numerical symbols but that there is a need for tests measuring more practical and concrete abilities to enhance predictability of selection in business and industry.

Sample Item, No. 5

RESENT   RESERVE—Do these words
1 have similar meanings   2 have contradictory meanings
3 mean neither the same nor opposite?

FIGURE 7.2   Sample item from the Wonderlic Personnel Test

Source: From the *Wonderlic Personnel Test,* WPT Sample Questions, © 1996 Wonderlic Personnel Test, Inc. Reprinted by permission.

Examples include tests that measure mechanical, clerical, spatial, and musical abilities.

Mechanical ability tests include subtests that measure factors associated with success in jobs involving machines and equipment. In general those are the recognition and application of mechanical principles and information, the speed and dexterity of manipulation of physical objects, and the visualization of their relationships in space. Two of the most popular tests are the Bennett Mechanical Comprehension test (Bennett, 1941) and the Minnesota Paper Form Board (Likert & Quasha, 1941–1948). Both of these tests are paper-and-pencil group tests. The Bennett test presents pictures containing objects and tools that are assumed to be familiar in Western culture. The questions related to each picture presume that subjects have had the everyday experiences that are common in an industrial society. Figure 7.3 presents an example of an item that measures mainly mechanical reasoning.

The Bennett test is a power test with no time limit. There are different forms of the test; the current two equivalent forms cover a wide range of difficulty level, with percentiles available for high school students, industrial applicants, industrial employees, and engineering schools, among others. Reported odd–even reliabilities are on the average in the .80s. Reported validity coefficients vary between .30 and .60.

The revised Minnesota Paper Form Board provides the subject with items, each containing parts of a geometrical form followed by five different assembled forms. The subject has to decide which of the five forms fit the parts when they are assembled.

There are sixty-four multiple choice questions similar to the one illustrated in Figure 7.4. The test is a paper-and-pencil test designed to measure the ability to visualize and manipulate objects in space. It has numerous norms tables for schools (e.g., grade 9, grade 10, engineering students), industrial groups, prison inmates, males, and females. Reliabilities (alternate forms and test–retest) range between .71 and .78. The reported median predictive validity with school success is .30, and .34 with job success (Likert & Quasha, 1970).

DIRECTIONS

Fill in the requested information on your ANSWER SHEET.

Look at Sample X on this page. It shows two men carrying a weighted object on a plank, and it asks, "Which man carries more weight?" Because the object is closer to man "B" than to man "A," man "B" is shouldering more weight; so blacken the circle under "B" on your answer sheet.

FIGURE 7.3

Sample test items from the Bennett Mechanical Comprehension test.

Source: From the *Bennett Mechanical Comprehension Test,* (p. 2), 1994 Printing, San Antonio, TX: The Psychological Corporation. Copyright 1942, 1967–1970, 1980 by the Psychological Corporation. Reproduced by permission. All rights reserved.

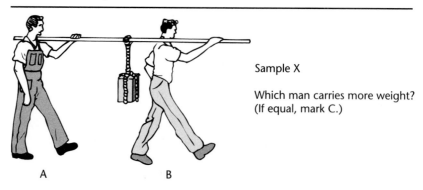

A   B

Sample X

Which man carries more weight? (If equal, mark C.)

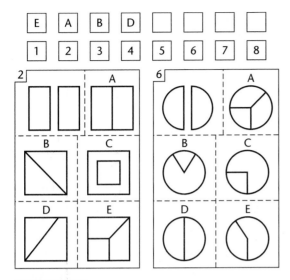

Clerical Ability Tests

Tests designed for the selection of applicants for clerical jobs have stressed perceptual speed and accuracy, mainly in processing verbal and numerical material. The Minnesota Clerical Test is a well-known and extensively used test that is intended to measure the ability "to perceive visual details quickly and accurately" (Dunnette, 1966, p. 49).

This is a paper-and-pencil test with two subtests, each including 200 items, one with the number-checking items and the other with the name-checking items. Applicants have to check identical pairs of digits or names, and the final score depends on speed and the number of errors they make. Reported reliabilities range between .70 and .90 (the test–retest range is from .70 to .80; the parallel forms average is .90). The exclusive use of these types of tests assumes that all clerical jobs are identical in terms of skills

and functions and the abilities that are required are mainly perceptual speed and accuracy. However, Pearlman, Schmidt, and Hunter (1980, p. 398) found in their study of 698 published and unpublished validity studies for five clerical job families that

> measures of verbal ability, quantitative ability, reasoning ability, memory and perceptual speed (as well as general mental ability and clerical aptitude, which are composites of some of these) are generally better predictors of clerical performance than measures of motor ability and spatial/mechanical ability.

The authors indicate that these results are similar to Bennett and Cruikshank's (1949) review, which showed that a test of general intelligence in combination with tests of accuracy and perceptual speed was the best predictor for clerical jobs. They also cite parallel results from Ghiselli's 1966 review that indicated that the best predictor for clerical occupations is the combination of intellectual abilities tests and perceptual accuracy tests.

Sensory and Physical Ability Tests

According to Guion (1991), motor, speed, and movement responses to sensory stimulations are fundamental to the performance of many tasks that are physically demanding. Although fine and gross motor coordination are important to many jobs, job analysts tend to forget them "in the jargon of [current] fashion, perception is in, but the sensory bases for perception are out" (p. 342). However, it may be essential to include the motor abilities that are required for the effective performance on the job to guard against organizations being sued for discrimination against handicapped people and women and to use in disputing claims for work injuries (Campion, 1983; Guion, 1991). Two physical manipulative tests that were constructed in the 1940s and are still in use are the Crawford Small Parts Dexterity Test (Crawford & Crawford, 1946, 1949), designed to test fine hand and finger dexterity, and the Stromberg Dexterity

Test (Stromberg, 1951), designed to measure gross motor coordination.

The Stromberg Dexterity Test requires the subject to place sixty circular blocks in holes; the blocks are then removed and turned over and have to be placed back in the holes. The Crawford requires the subject to first use tweezers to place the pins in the holes and then pick up the collars and place them over the pins (see Figure 7.5). In the second part of the test, the small screws have to be inserted in the board and then screwed into place with the help of a small screwdriver. Both tests are speed tests in which the applicants have to complete the tasks as fast as they can. Reliabilities are typically high (in the .80 to .90 range), however, the different parts of the same tests correlate much lower (around .50). This is similar to the tendency of various motor tests to have low intercorrelations. These tests are also performance tests because the individual is required to manipulate instruments, parts, and/or equipment.

Personality, Integrity, and Drug Tests

According to Azar (1995, p. 30),

> For years, industrial and organizational psychologists turned to cognitive ability as a predictor of job performance: Smarter people were considered more likely to succeed on the job. But intelligence alone is only part of the story. Creativity, leadership, integrity, attendance and cooperation also play major roles in a person's job suitability and productivity. Personality rather than intelligence, predicts these qualities.

Personality Tests

Personality traits have held psychologists' interest since the creation of psychology as a discipline. Allport and Odbert (1936) located over 17,000 words that could be used to describe personality traits. Hogan (1991, p. 875) argued that personality "refers both to a person's social reputation and to his or her inner nature: The first is public and verifiable; the second is pri-

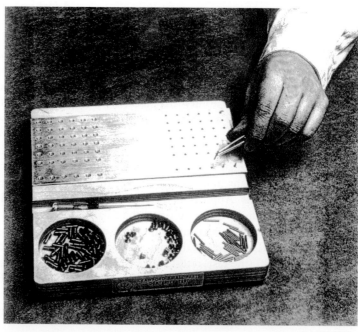

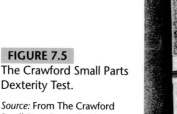

FIGURE 7.5
The Crawford Small Parts Dexterity Test.

Source: From The Crawford Small Parts Dexterity Test (p. 1), 1956, San Antonio, TX: The Psychological Corporation. Copyright 1981, 1956, 1946 by the Psychological Corporation. Reproduced by permission. All rights reserved.

vate and must be inferred." Kaplan and Sac-cuzzo (1993) claimed that personality tests measure the typical behavior of individuals, that is, traits, temperaments, and dispositions. They differentiated between structured or objective tests and projective personality tests. Objective tests of personality provide the individuals with statements to which they respond with true or false, yes or no; projective tests provide the individuals with obscure stimuli that require spontaneous responses.

Hogan's definition and Allport and Odbert's lengthy list provide insights into the difficulty of defining and measuring personality. As we mentioned previously, the ambiguity of the concept of personality has raised many criticisms of personality measures. For example, criticisms levied by Mischel (1973, 1981) against research on personality assessment include the following:

1. Poor operational definitions make it difficult to develop reliable and valid measures.
2. Individuals fail to show consistency in personality traits over time; therefore measurement is situationally specific and not generalizable.
3. At best, personality measures account for such a small proportion of variance (9%) in behavior that most of the remaining variance is accounted for by the situation.

Recently, investigators have begun to refine their definitions of personality traits. McCrae and Costa (1987) have developed refined definitions. Using factor analysis, they argued that they could describe most of human personality with the **big five personality dimensions.** McCrae and Costa argue that these five traits can be used to describe behavior in a variety of situations. More important, the value of the "big five" is that these factors have very low intercorrelations. As a result, they have greater descriptive value because they measure separate components of the human personality. See Table 7.1 for descriptions of these traits.

Relevant to industry, studies such as that of Barrick and Mount (1991) demonstrate the im-

TABLE 7.1 The Big Five Personality Dimensions

Personality Dimension	Definition
Neuroticism	A tendency to experience unpleasant emotions relatively easily
Extraversion	A tendency to seek new experiences and to enjoy the company of other people
Agreeableness	A tendency to be compassionate toward others and not antagonistic
Conscientiousness	A tendency to show self-discipline, to be dutiful, and to strive for achievement and competence
Openness to experience	A tendency to enjoy new experiences, the arts, fantasies, and anything that exposes the person to new experiences

Source: Adapted from Costa, P. T., McCrae, R. R., & Dye, D. A. (1991). Facet scales for agreeableness and conscientiousness: A revision of the NEO personality inventory. *Personality and Individual Differences, 12,* 887–898.

portance of conscientiousness in selection in the workplace. According to their study, individuals who score high on measures of conscientiousness perform above average on most jobs. An employer seeking to hire applicants who will be productive and attentive to quality may use measures of conscientiousness when selecting new employees. However, there are two camps of I/O psychologists in this matter (Azar, 1995). One (including Barrick and Mount) argues for a personality characteristic that is generic to success on most jobs. Their claim is that the construct of conscientiousness is the basic personality trait for all jobs. The other camp (including Hogan and colleagues) maintains that some jobs, such as artistic, social, and investigative jobs, require traits such as openness and not conscientiousness. The complexity of these relationships is demonstrated in Azar's (1995) jigsaw puzzle graphic (see Figure 7.6).

The value of personality tests in employment settings may be further demonstrated by review-

ing a position in which it is imperative that an individual demonstrate high levels of a particular trait. For example, in 1994, twenty-five individuals walked away from a commuter plane that crashed while approaching its final destination. Credit for the high number of survivors was given to the flight attendant who was able to prepare the passengers for impact. The passengers described the flight attendant as very calm and methodical in her preparations. According to the work of Williams (1990) and Stelmack (1990), the flight attendant may have scored high on extraversion. Both Williams and Stelmack reported that individuals who rate high in extraversion tend to be stable and not easily excitable. Therefore personality measures may provide employers with valuable information that may improve their work force, their productivity, and ultimately their profit.

It seems that these recommendations for the increased use of personality tests have also raised concerns about the influence of the specific context in which job applicants complete personality inventories. Schmidt, Ryan, Stierwalt, and Powell (1995) demonstrated that applicants answer such items (for example, items for the five-factor personality inventory) by describing how they are likely to behave at work, not in general. Schmidt et al. found that this "frame of reference" (p. 607) influences the degree of validity in predicting job performance and thus leads to implications for personnel selection. Another concern relates to determining the operational definition and the measurement of the five (or more) personality traits so that they can be used for prediction in personnel work. Disagreements about these definitions still exist, and the conclusion is that

FIGURE 7.6   *The complexity of relationships between personality traits and success on the job.*

Source: Based on John Michael Yanson's illustration in B. Azar (1995), Which traits predict job performance. *The APA Monitor, 26*(7), 30–31. Copyright 1995 by the American Psychological Association. Copyright 1995 by John Michael Yanson. Reproduced by permission.

the good news is that [the definitions of these constructs and the development of instruments to measure them] . . . will inevitably occur. The bad news is that for the next several years, the journals will be clogged with narrow methodological examinations and comparisons of alternative measuring devices (Landy et al., 1994, p. 272).

Integrity Tests

The shift in the United States from an industrial-based economy to a service/retail-based economy has resulted in changes in the selection systems that are used to hire new employees. Traditionally, aptitude and ability testing provided employers with the information to hire qualified employees. Recently, organizations have noted an increase in counterproductive behavior such as theft by employees. It was estimated in 1988 that the dollar value of theft ranged between $15 billion and $25 billion; this range increased to between $6 billion and $200 billion of loss in 1993. In addition, it has been estimated that about 45 percent of employees commit theft (Bernadin & Cooke, 1993; Hollinger, 1989; Kingston-O'Connell, 1992; Murphy, 1993). To reduce losses from theft, organizations have begun to expand their selection systems to include measures of an individual's integrity, that is, predicting the likelihood of new employees engaging in counterproductive behavior on the job.

Factors relating to theft, safety, substance abuse, and violence have been shown to be as important and relevant to selecting a job applicant (e.g., professional secretaries, Martin & Orban, 1995) as task-focused factors. A meta-analysis (Ones, Viswesvaran, & Schmidt, 1993) in organizations concluded that integrity tests are relevant to selecting applicants and are predictive of supervisors' rating of overall job performance; integrity tests predict counterproductive behaviors; and the validities of integrity tests were positive and could be generalized across situations, tests, jobs, and organizations. In fact, their conclusion was that "integrity test validities for overall job performance are second only to the validities of ability tests, work sample tests, and job knowledge tests used in personnel selection" (Ones, Viswesvaran, & Schmidt, 1995, p. 456).

A review (Sackett & Harris, 1984) of forty-two validity studies of integrity tests identified a number of factors that are commonly incorporated into measures of integrity: beliefs about the frequency and extent of theft in today's society; beliefs about how individuals who engage in counterproductive behavior should be punished; personal thoughts about theft; perceptions of how easy it is to engage in theft; the likelihood of getting caught; awareness of friends or coworkers who have engaged in theft; rationalization of theft; and personal history as it relates to counterproductive behavior.

Counterproductive behavior is usually measured by using one of two formats. The first format is referred to as *direct admissions,* and the second is a *personality-based measure.* An example of direct admission would be asking, "Have you ever stolen from your present employer?" The direct admissions format openly requests the applicant to reveal any behavior that may be considered dishonest, of low integrity, or counterproductive. These measures provide behavioral trend data that indicate the likelihood of the individual's engaging in counterproductive behavior. For example, if an applicant reveals having stolen from his or her present employer, there is a strong likelihood that the person will do so again.

The second format is a personality-based test that is much more indirect. Rather than asking applicants to discuss or record their counterproductive behaviors, this approach asks applicants to respond to items such as "I feel that it is justifiable for underpaid employees to take office supplies home for personal use." These measures look for attitudinal data that may indicate the likelihood that the individual will engage in counterproductive job behavior.

Debate has centered on the validity of integrity and honesty tests in the workplace. According to Sackett (1985), validity must be examined continually across different organizational settings to ensure that the test is functioning appropriately. More important, Sackett recommends that integrity testing be used as only one piece of information in selecting employees. Concerns were also raised about assertions that these tests measure mostly an individual's degree of conformity to particular social standards;

that individuals can lie and slant their responses in the direction of "what they should be" to look "good" for the job; and that these tests might discriminate against individuals who have a history of counterproductive behavior but may be willing or able to change their behavior (Lilienfeld, Allger, & Mitchell, 1995). The main concern was raised about what these integrity tests measure and what underlying psychological construct they assess. The questions raised were: Do these tests measure a specific trait of integrity? Is integrity part of the big five personality measures? (Camara & Schneider, 1994, 1995).

A recent argument about validity related to the legality of using polygraph tests for employment selection. It was argued that it may be inaccurate to assess integrity and honesty by physiological measures (e.g., Saxe, Dougherty, & Cross, 1985). That is, the applicant may be nervous during the process of assessment with the result that the galvanic skin responses could be inaccurate; this in turn could lead to incorrect selection decisions. With the passage of the 1988 Employee Polygraph Protection Act, polygraphs could no longer be used in employment selection by most employers. As a result, the use of paper-and-pencil honesty/integrity tests has increased in organizations for a variety of purposes, such as determining antisocial tendencies and personnel selection (Bernadin & Cooke, 1993).

[I]t is important to remember that honest behavior is a function both of the individual employee's personality and of situational pressures. Predicting employee counterproductibility in an applied setting requires assessment of a full range of organizational variables, including the existing norms of the work group, supervisor attitudes, compensation, and incentive practices, in addition to individual integrity. (Cunningham, Wong, & Barbee, 1994, p. 656)

Drug Tests

Drug testing has traditionally been used by the military and professional sports associations.

The purpose of drug testing was to ensure that relevant behaviors were not enhanced or altered by drugs in such a way that performance was affected. Recently, drug testing in the workplace has received a great deal of attention. Employers argue that drug testing improves safety in the workplace. As early as 1977, studies indicated that approximately 40% of Americans cope inadequately with problems of daily life (Knowles, 1977). The concern is that such individuals use drugs or alcohol to cope with their life problems and attempt to work while under the influence of such substances. According to Martin and DeGrange (1993), organizations lose about $100 billion per year because of drug and alcohol abuse used by 10% to 20% of their employees.

To reduce monetary losses and employment problems, organizations have increased the use of prescreening selection tests. A variety of tests exist for detecting drug and alcohol abuse, such as blood tests and brain pattern analysis (Martin & Godsey, 1992). However, urinalysis (urine analysis) and paper-and-pencil tests are the most prevalent drug testing programs in industry.

Testing of urine samples has increased in the 1980s and the 1990s, the cost per employee ranging between $30 and $70 (Gatewood & Feild, 1994; Martin et al., 1993). One of the few follow-up studies on the relationship between urinalysis results, job performance, and costs to the company is the U.S. postal study (Martin & DeGrange, 1993). More than 5000 applicants were hired regardless of their urinalysis results and followed in terms of tenure and job performance. Absenteeism and termination rates were checked after sixteen months of employment, and discipline rates for poor performance were followed for about three years. Table 7.2 shows the results.

For example, while 50% of applicants who failed the physical drug test were "frequently absent," only 34% of those who passed the test were "frequently absent." Martin and DeGrange summarized the research results, stating "that urinalysis results are related to job performance and costly counterproductive behavior" (p. 40).

TABLE 7.2   Effectiveness of Urinalysis Prescreening

Outcomes	Urinalysis Results	
	Failed	Passed
Absenteeism[a]	50%	34%
Termination[a]	15%	11%
Poor performance[b]	10%	8%

a=Sixteen months follow up; b=Three years follow up.

Source: Based on information in Martin & DeGrange, 1993, and Normand, Salyards, & Mahoney, 1990.

Criticisms against drug testing are primarily related to the right to privacy afforded by the U.S. Constitution. In addition, the validity of drug tests has often been questioned. The argument is that the test results may come back positive even when the applicant is not a substance user. Some food products, when consumed before abuse testing, produce physiological responses that are similar to those created by drugs or alcohol. For example, poppy seeds often cause positive results in tests for the use of marijuana.

Given the criticisms and concerns, how can employers continue with drug abuse testing while protecting the rights of their employees? Equally important, how can employers protect themselves from the legal concerns raised by drug testing? Angarola (1985) recommends four guidelines that employers can use to maintain a successful and fair drug testing program:

1. All employees and applicants should be given a written statement of the organization's drug-testing policy.

2. The drug-testing policy and the possibility of random drug testing should be incorporated into all employment contracts.

3. Someone should explain to all employees and applicants the medical and safety benefits

such testing policies provide. It was found that when information about the company's drug-testing program is given to applicants by someone who is highly regarded, that information affects the applicants' intentions to apply to that company (Crant & Bateman, 1990).

4. When drug testing is implemented as a routine part of employment, all employees and applicants should be aware of such policies in advance. In addition, a chief concern of a company should be to implement a program that enables careful testing and retesting of positive results (Gatewood & Feild, 1994). The purpose is to avoid labeling individuals as drug users and to reduce the risks of legal claims of defamation of character and discriminatory denials of employment (e.g., 1991 U.S. Civil Rights Act; Kingston-O'Connell, 1992).

Paper-and-pencil tests that are similar to the integrity tests are another type of drug use screening device. Like general integrity tests, some questionnaires ask direct questions such as "Do you think it is okay for workers to use 'soft' drugs at work if this does not cause poor job performance?" (Gatewood & Feild, 1994, p. 682). The tests may also ask indirect questions related to people's perceptions about others such as "How often do you think the average employee smokes marijuana on the job?" (Martin and DeGrange, 1993, p. 40).

A meta-analytic study of a psychological paper-and-pencil substance abuse test developed by Martin and Godsey (1992) showed it to be "equally effective in predicting substance abuse and theft-related criteria" (p. 23); it was least effective in predicting job performance. When comparing the costs and effectiveness of the physical and psychological drug abuse tests, Martin and Godsey concluded that although the paper-and-pencil tests would be more expensive to implement, the company can "recover most or all of this expense by reducing the number of urinalyses that are administered" (p. 41).

Recognizing the societal role that organizations must begin to fill, many organizations are taking protective steps to help employees who have substance abuse problems. **Employee Assistance Programs (EAPs)** are becoming more common in human resource departments. EAPs have been developed to provide employees with guidance and/or referral that will ultimately aid individuals to recover and/or learn new strategies for dealing with stresses and challenges.

Application Blanks

A short summary of biographical information questionnaires within the context of human resources management is presented in Chapter 3. Because application questionnaires and resumes are the most popular prescreening instruments that organizations use as predictors for job success and because biographical data questionnaires are a form of application blank, we will extend that discussion in this chapter.

Almost every applicant for any type and level of job is required to complete a series of questions that provide information about the applicant's educational background, previous work history, demographic information, and personal information. The specific information that is gathered and the form of the questionnaire that is used depend on the purpose. Some are short and include only essential information such as name, address, and Social Security number; others extend over several pages and include questions about the individual, the family, life history, and other such areas. Some forms of application blanks are questionnaires constructed by the "armchair method," in which individuals are charged with the task of constructing questions they think should be included in the questionnaire. Other forms are constructed empirically, based on statistical analysis and the relationship that has been found between each item and different aspects of job success. Two examples are weighted application blanks and biographical data (biodata).

In using the **weighted application blank** (WAB), items are first correlated with aspects of job success. Weights are then assigned to the dif-

ferent possible responses on each item on the basis of their predictability for job performance or any other effectiveness measure. The applicant's responses are scored accordingly, summarized, and used in the hiring decisions (Gatewood & Feild, 1994).

Biodata questionnaires have other labels, such as autobiographical data, background data, and biographical information blank (BIB). Some researchers (McDaniel, 1989) differentiate between background information and biodata inventories. For example, background information questionnaires and biodata questionnaires are used for various types of occupations; biodata questionnaires are always paper-and-pencil self-report questionnaires, while background information can be collected through other channels such as interviews and previous employers; biodata inventory is used mostly to predict overall job success, while background information is used to predict job behaviors such as being reliable and adjusted and having high degree of integrity. These arguments represent a major difficulty of defining items that can be characterized as "biodata." According to one definition, biodata items are those that "pertain to historical events that may have shaped the person's behavior and identity" (Mael, 1991, p. 763). Examples of such items are historical items that predict future behaviors, are verifiable, and reflect external events. Table 7.3 presents examples of various attributes and their item taxonomy.

Research on biodata questionnaires has shown that these inventories have relatively high validity coefficients. For instance, a combination of ten items predicted tenure for clerical personnel in an insurance company (Cascio, 1976). Cascio found the correlations on the validation sample to be .79 for the minority sample and .77 for the nonminority sample. Other studies have shown that in addition to their predictability, some of these inventories can be constructed so that they could be used across different organizations. For example, a meta-analytic study has shown that the biodata item validities included validity generalized across organizations,

TABLE 7.3	Examples of Biodata Items
Attributes	*Example*
Historical	How old were you when you got your first paying job?
External	Did you ever get fired from a job?
Objective	How many hours did you study for your real-estate license test?
First-hand	How punctual are you about coming to work?
Discrete	At what age did you get your driving license?
Verifiable	What was your grade point average in college?
Controllable	How many tries did it take you to pass the CPA exam?
Equal access	Were you ever class president?
Job relevant	How many units of cereal did you sell during the last calendar year?
Noninvasive	Were you on the tennis team in college?

Source: Adapted from F. A. Mael (1991). A conceptual rationale for the domain and attributes of Biodata items. *Personnel Psychology, 44*(4), p. 773. Copyright 1991 by Personnel Psychology, Inc. Reprinted with permission.

validity across various subgroups (e.g., age, gender, education), and validity over time (Rothstein, Schmidt, Erwin, Owens, & Sparks, 1990).

Criticisms of biodata questionnaires have included the possible falsification of applicants' responses to the items. Individuals applying for jobs can distort their answers in ways that might increase their chances of being selected for the job. Studies have shown that applicants for positions such as sales and nurse's assistants fake their responses according to what they consider to be socially desirable in these jobs (Kluger & Colella, 1993; Stokes, Hogan, & Snell, 1993). The extent of this distortion among applicants is unknown.

• •

HOW PREDICTORS MEASURE ATTRIBUTES

Interviews, computer testing, and assessment centers can be described from the point of view of how traits and attributes can be measured (Landy et al., 1994).

Interviews

"The interview is a selection procedure designed to predict future job performance on the basis of applicants' oral responses to oral inquiries" (McDaniel, Whetzel, Schmidt, & Maurer, 1994, p. 599). Surveys have consistently shown that the interview is the selection device that is most frequently used in industry and organizations. For example, 99% of companies surveyed in 1989 indicated that they use the interview for hiring decisions; in most of these companies, each candidate was interviewed by more than one person and the interview lasted between 36 and 60 minutes (Gatewood & Feild, 1994; Ulrich & Trumbo, 1965). The popularity of the selection interview has led to a significant amount of research and the conclusions that the interview is of limited usefulness (Landy et al., 1994) and its levels of validity and reliability are depressing (Guion, 1991). However, recent studies have led to more optimistic conclusions. For example, in contrast to the traditional belief that the employment interview has low validity, some research results indicate that it has moderate validities (Harris, 1989; McDaniel et al., 1994).

Format of the Employment Interview

The dimensions by which the formats of interviews are characterized differ among practitioners and researchers.

Group versus Individual Interview

The **group interview** format consists of more than one interviewer rating one candidate in the same interview session (also called board interview); the **individual interview** includes a single interviewer rating one individual in one session.

Structured versus Unstructured Interview

The **structured interview,** or patterned interview, provides a printed form that includes the questions, the sequence of their presentation, the method by which candidates are rated, and the method by which the rating is performed. The **unstructured interview** does not have any predetermined strategy for presenting the questions or scoring them, and the questions that are presented may vary across interviewers (Blum & Naylor, 1968; McDaniel et al., 1994). Both of these formats indicate how the information about the interviewee is collected and the degree of the interview's standardization (McDaniel et al., 1994).

Content of the Information Collected

Another way to differentiate between interviews is by the type of information that is collected during the session. McDaniel et al. (1994) distinguish between the **situational interview,** which focuses on questions about how the individual would behave in a specific situation, and the **job-related interview,** in which the questions are asked by a "hiring authority . . . [who] attempts to assess past behaviors and job related information" (p. 601). The purpose of the situational interview is to predict future job behavior in similar situations. The questions are based on activities identified as part of the job requirements. The questions in the job-related interview are not related to specific job situations.

The term *behavioral interview* is used to include questions that describe behaviors associated with maximum or typical performance on the job. McDaniel et al. (1994) believe that behavioral interviews should be categorized as situational interviews.

Validity Issues

McDaniel et al. identified the factors of structure and content of the interviews as affecting the validities of the employment interviews. Recent meta-analytic studies (see Appendix 2A and Chapter 8) have indicated that structured interviews have higher validities (e.g., .67, .63, .49, .44) than unstructured interviews (e.g., .34, .31, .33, .20) (e.g., Conway, Jako, & Goodman, 1995; Huffcutt & Woehr, 1993; McDaniel et al., 1994; Wiesner & Cronshaw, 1988). An additional parameter that was found to affect the validities of the interview was the type of criteria used as the predicted variables (McDaniel et al., 1994). The authors found that when the criterion was job performance validity coefficients ranged between .40 and .50 (Landy et al., 1994). Another important finding was that the interview validities can be generalized across varying situations (McDaniel et al., 1994).

The issues of interview validities can best be considered "in terms of four functions of the interviews" (Guion, 1991, pp. 347–349):

1. Enhancing good public relations through the interview. That can be done by the interviewee having the impression of being treated fairly, by sharing realistic information, and by motivating the interviewee to present his or her case effectively.

2. Gathering information about the applicant. This should be done by having prior information about the candidate and the job. Questions and procedures should be formalized, with emphasis on the specific behaviors relevant to the job.

3. Assessing characteristics that cannot be measured by other instruments, such as the first impression the candidate makes and friendliness. Questions still exist as to how these dimensions can be measured and how accurately they can be assessed.

4. Making hiring decisions. Interviewers are the individuals who are responsible for predicting the candidate's future work behavior. In addition, they can be involved in different phases of the organization's decision to hire, reject, or put on hold a candidate. Sometimes, they act as the final decision makers; sometimes, they make only a recommendation. These various responsibilities for decision making affect the validities of the interviews.

In summary, "about the only firm statement we can make is that well-planned, clearly structured, behaviorally focused, job-related interviews have better chances of resulting in good predictions than those that just happen" (Guion, 1991, p. 349).

Psychological Assessments

The use of psychological assessments in business settings began in the 1920s and 1930s. During this time, most psychologists were in private clinical practice or taught and conducted research in universities. In the 1930s a few psychologists began to work seriously with businesses. During World War II, many psychologists were employed full time by the military to assess the fit between new recruits and many military positions. The primary tools that they used to assess fit were paper-and-pencil tests and face-to-face interviews. After the war, some psychologists took positions with large companies. They initiated the use of assessment for business in a manner similar to that used by the military. A few psychologists formed the first psychological consulting firms that worked primarily with businesses. These psychologists adapted their clinical approach to fit the business world. A key adaptation was that assessment reports were written in business terms and focused on the characteristics that predicted success in business settings.

Today, many psychologists work as consultants to business. Some focus on individual psychological assessments. Others specialize in areas such as stress management, management development, assessment centers, selection test development, and test validation.

Research investigating the application of psychological assessment in business has not been as extensive as in other areas of applied psychology. However, the results from most of the studies that have been conducted have been supportive.

Handyside and Duncan (1954) studied first-line supervisors, using multiple assessment techniques in the hiring decision. Performance ratings were given four years after an employee was hired. Handyside and Duncan found that the most effective predictions of performance were psychological tests, personal interviews, a panel review, and letters of recommendation.

Hilton, Bolin, Parker, Taylor, and Walker (1955) evaluated the accuracy of psychological assessments. As part of the assessment, the psychologists rated each employee on five scales: sociability, organizational ability, drive, general performance, and potential for advancement. The employees were rated on job performance after six months and again after two years on the same five scales. The findings indicated that the psychologists' predictions of employee performance were accurate.

Laurent (1968) conducted a study on middle- and upper-level managers in Standard Oil of New Jersey. A group of 443 experienced managers completed psychological assessments. Four to six years later, performance information was collected that included ratings of managerial effectiveness, promotions, and salary progress. Predictors from the psychological assessments were able to differentiate the most successful from the least successful managers.

In a 1965 critique of personality research, Guion and Gottier concluded that most of the popular personality instruments should not be used as measures for decision making. Their critique temporarily brought research in the area to a halt. More recently, personality researchers have begun to reassess the usefulness and validity of personality assessment. Hough (1992) noted some past research lumped many personality characteristics together and erroneously concluded that personality does not have much predictive power for job performance. Hough's recent work shows that certain personality characteristics, such as achievement and dependability, are correlated with job performance. In the past decade, researchers have discovered that personality assessment, when used with ability testing, can improve the ability to predict the job performance of employees. Hogan (1991, p. 9) noted that "personality inventories, if they're well constructed, are just a systematic interview, . . . but unlike a regular interview they're not biased."

In using personality tests, the challenge is to provide support for the validity of the measures. Abilities are directly related to job performance, but the relationships between personality characteristics and job performance are often less concrete. For example, showing that a particular job requires a person to have a certain level of math skill is easier than showing that the person needs to be agreeable. Nevertheless, personality assessment has come back into favor as a result of improved statistical procedures, better research instruments, and more sophisticated techniques. It is now viewed as a valid and appropriate approach, particularly in the selection and development of senior managers.

Ryan and Sackett (1987) recently reviewed the practice of psychological assessments in business. They found that assessments are frequently conducted in manufacturing, banking and finance, retail businesses, and service businesses. In their summary of the practice of psychological assessment in business, Ryan and Sackett found that 56% of psychologists using assessments work in cities with populations of at least one million; individuals being assessed were predominantly white (89%) and male (76%); assessments were conducted mainly at the middle (34%) and top (25%) management levels. Several popular reasons were given for conducting assessments: final selection of candidates, promotion determination, employee development, career counseling, succession planning, initial applicant screening, and outplacement counseling.

A typical psychological assessment takes four to eight hours to complete. Ryan and Sackett (1987) found that three quarters of the psy-

chologists surveyed in their study used cognitive ability tests as part of their assessment procedure. The most popular test was the Watson-Glaser Critical Thinking Appraisal (38%), following in popularity were the Wesman Personnel Classification Test (19%), the Employee Aptitude Series (19%), the Wechsler Adult Intelligence Scale (18%), and proprietary cognitive ability tests designed by consulting firms (18%). Paper-and-pencil measures of personality were used by 78% of the psychologists. The most popular of these measures were the 16 Personality Factor Test (33%) and the Guilford-Zimmerman Temperament Survey (33%). Other frequently used measures were the California Personality Inventory (28%), MMPI (20%), Myers-Briggs Type Indicator (19%), the Edwards Personal Preference Profile (18%), and proprietary personality tests (9%). Projective tests were used by 34% of the psychologists surveyed. The most widely used projective tests were a sentence completion test (77%), the Thematic Apperception Test (43%), and the Rorschach Ink Blot Test (25%). Many assessments also included some type of simulation exercise, such as an in-basket test (60%), role plays (21%), writing exercises (14%), and sample business cases (12%).

The performance dimensions that were examined in most psychological assessments cover a wide range of skills. These include interpersonal skills, judgment and analytic skills, organization and planning skills, intellectual skills, supervisory skills, emotional maturity, leadership skills, management skills, energy, and drive. Information about the organization and particular positions within the organization is gathered through employee interviews (82%), informal discussions with managers (81%), reviews of written job descriptions (81%), discussions with supervisors (75%), and other company contacts (81%).

Hansen and Conrad (1991) describe the psychological assessment process in detail in their book *A Handbook of Psychological Assessment in Business.* Included in their handbook are examples from assessments and descriptions from users of how and why they apply the process in their companies. Hansen and Conrad (1991, p. 129) summarize the assessment process as

> personal and essentially clinical rather than psychometric or statistical. Yet it is objective and is as soundly based in scientific evidence as we can make it. Underlying our strategy is the belief that most managers already possess more talent, more motivation, and more skill than they will ever fully utilize. Our job as business psychologists is not so much to help them develop new capacities as to release those they already have. People who succeed in business all succeed in ways that are unique to their own experiences, opportunities, and personalities.
>
> Successful people do not all succeed in the same fashion. There is evidence, however, to indicate that many people fail for a common reason: they do not understand something about themselves. One of our key goals in assessment is to identify such areas and to help the individual manager develop healthy self-perceptions. The assessment and interaction with the psychologist accomplishes this by:
>
> > Helping the individual gain self-respect through increased insight into his or her own resources and aspirations.
> >
> > Creating and maintaining a healthy working environment that supports and rewards the efforts of people.
> >
> > Encouraging interpersonal cooperation and mutual support between all employees and managers.
>
> We seek, through the assessment process, to create an effective behavioral environment supportive of the individual and realized in conjunction with that person's work with his or her employer.

Meta-analyses by Barrick and Mount (1991) and Tett, Jackson, and Rothstein (1991) have shown evidence supporting personality as a predictor of job performance. Previous studies were limited by the use of poorly constructed personality measures, unreliable measures with overlapping predictors and criterion measures, or inappropriate correlational techniques (Blinkhorn & Johnson, 1990; Jackson & Rothstein, 1992).

There is a major problem in attempting to study personality as a predictor of performance in management-level employees. Performance data for this group are not readily available because formalized, objective evaluations are not routinely conducted on upper-level management personnel. Therefore most data collected on senior managers tend to be impressionistic and global in nature. Another barrier is that few organizations have enough management-level employees to allow adequate statistical analysis.

Gellatly, Paunonen, Meyer, Jackson, and Goffin (1991) demonstrated that managerial positions tend to be heterogeneous in terms of required duties and functions. Criterion performance measures are multidimensional, so many distinct personality predictors are needed for predictive research to be effective. Blinkhorn & Johnson (1990) state that these studies have a high risk of capitalizing on chance and, as a result, may find significant relationships where none exist. This is called a *type I error.*

The occurrence of a type I error is of particular concern when an investigator uses only univariate correlational techniques. Blinkhorn and Johnson (1990) emphasize the importance of using more appropriate statistical procedures, such as canonical correlation analysis. Like multiple regression, canonical correlation determines the relationship between the criterion measure and the best linear combination of predictors. The main difference between these techniques is that multiple regression uses a single criterion, whereas canonical correlation uses multiple criterion measures.

Jackson, Hagberg, and Jackson (1993) provide an example of canonical correlation applied to personality research. A battery of forty-seven personality measures was completed by 100 senior executives. The battery included the Personality Research Form, the Jackson Personality Inventory, the Survey of Work Styles, and an adjective checklist. Job performance was evaluated through the use of 360-degree feedback surveys. Each executive was rated by an average of eighteen coworkers, including their superiors, peers, and subordinates. The survey instrument had forty-four scales, such as dependability, negotiation skill, and technical skill.

Separate factor analyses were conducted on the personality scales and performance evaluations. The resulting factors were orthogonally rotated, a process that produced fourteen personality factors and six performance factors. When these data were analyzed by using canonical correlation, four canonical variants emerged. These variants accounted for 32% of the criterion variance. The variants were interpreted as personality-determined managerial styles, which were sensitive leadership, creative leadership, charismatic leadership, and authoritative leadership. For the forty-four criterion measures, corrected multiple regression correlation coefficients ranged from .31 to .70 with a median of .45.

Jackson, Hagberg, and Jackson's results demonstrate that executive performance and various leadership styles can be predicted from personality measures. The results also indicate that using a single dimension—of strong versus weak leadership—does not account for the criterion differences. The rotated canonical components were found to be bipolar. The result suggests that personality characteristics are positive predictors of certain leadership abilities and negative predictors of others.

In a related study, Hagberg, Jackson, and Jackson (1993) again used 360-degree feedback surveys to examine the same forty-four ratings of job performance on the same 100 executives. Inter-rater reliabilities ranged from .63 to .89, with a mean of .82. The investigators used a principal components factor analysis, which identified six first-order factors. Examples of these factors are directive leadership, innovative leadership, and persuasive leadership. A sec-

ond-order factor analysis discovered only two factors: goal-oriented leadership and person-oriented leadership.

The Jackson, Hagberg, and Jackson (1993) and Hagberg, Jackson, and Jackson (1993) studies led to several conclusions. First, the studies provided evidence for several leadership styles that contribute to success at executive levels. Although managerial leadership styles have often been theoretically described, these studies provided some of the first objective measurements and definitions of these styles. Second, they found that no style was appropriate for every situation. Finally, the aggregation of ratings from multiple judges was significantly more reliable than ratings from one or two judges.

Psychological assessment in business settings has evolved from the pioneering model created by Rohrer, Hibler and Replogle International (1991). This technique is popular because it meets many practical business needs, which include the following:

- The opportunity that assessment provides for individuals to describe their interests, values, abilities, personality, and motivations

- The opportunity for individuals to be given work assignments that will make maximum use of their strengths and support advancement to the highest level that is consistent with their potential

- The opportunity for individuals to be successful in work situations that fulfill their potential

- The opportunity for people to make significant contributions and achieve happiness and fulfillment in their work

- The opportunity for a company to identify and develop people with the necessary abilities to get a job done while finding people who will stay with the company and those who have the potential to eventually be managers and executives

The future of psychological assessment is encouraging because of the versatility, power, and practicality it provides as a management tool. For fifty years, psychological assessment has remained a popular and effective tool in the business world. In the future the assessment process will improve as it becomes more accurate and consistent. These refined psychological assessments will provide increased benefits to employees, managers, organizations, and businesses. Some organizations prefer to complete assessment by using internal managers. Assessment centers can be structured so that a company's managers can perform effectively as assessors. Others use psychologists, who face new challenges presented by today's work force.

Assessment Centers

An **assessment center** is a standardized evaluation of behavior based on multiple inputs. Several trained observers and techniques are used to make judgments about behavior from specially developed simulations. An evaluation meeting is held, during which assessment data are reported. The assessors discuss the data and reach consensus about performance on the specific dimensions and on the evaluation in general (Task Force on Assessment Center Standards, 1980).

Assessment centers were first used by German psychologists during the 1930s. The goal was to assess the total personality of the young officers, rather than specific traits or abilities. In the assessments, candidates completed a series of assignments, including situational tests and paper-and-pencil measures. This process was adopted by the British War Office Selection Boards and by the U.S. Office of Strategic Services.

In 1956, AT&T began the Management Progress Study. This was the start of assessment center work in business. The results have been reported in several publications (Bray, 1964; Bray & Grant, 1966; Bray, Campbell & Grant, 1973; Bray & Howard, 1983). These reports

provide useful information about managers and their development in U.S. business.

A typical assessment center begins with a job analysis and the identification of key job dimensions. This information is used to develop a battery of instruments that will assess performance on the key dimensions. The battery includes performance tests such as in-baskets, or simulations of the day-to-day items that managers deal with; leaderless group discussions; case analyses, which describe "what if" scenarios to applicants for analysis and decision making; and paper-and-pencil tests, measuring aptitudes and abilities. Assessors are usually company employees, often managers, who are carefully trained to observe and evaluate the exercises. The training must be thorough enough to ensure that the assessors understand the dimensions, are skilled observers, can categorize behavior observed into appropriate dimensions, can accurately judge the quality of behavior, and know how to complete and compile the ratings. Practice Perspective 7.2 on page 232 describes one candidate's experience with an assessment center that was used for a promotion decision.

In general, assessment centers have been found to have respectable predictive validity. They have also been well received by the courts. Occasionally, courts specify assessment centers as a method of addressing discrimination issues. Assessment centers are often criticized because of their high cost. Criticism is also directed at the inconsistency of ratings across exercises. Correlational analyses suggest that these ratings may not be sufficiently reliable.

Criterion-Referenced Tests

A **criterion-referenced test** is one that is deliberately constructed to yield measurements that are directly interpretable in terms of specific performance standards (Nitko, 1980). The following paragraphs describe the process of constructing a criterion-referenced test.

PRACTICE PERSPECTIVE 7.2

A Police Captain Makes Chief

When the current chief of police decided to retire, the Fire and Police Commission decided to use an assessment center for the selection of the next chief. A psychological consulting firm designed and administered the center. The process began with two working sessions during which an I/O psychologist helped the commission members to define the critical success factors for the new chief. Seven key dimensions were identified and defined. The consulting firm then developed a one-day executive assessment center to evaluate candidates on those dimensions.

Henry, a captain in the police department, was a candidate for promotion. He submitted his application for chief. After two interviews with the commission and a background investigation, Henry was informed that he was in the group of final candidates who were to complete the assessment center. He was told to report to the assessment site for one day of evaluation.

When he arrived, Henry was greeted by the assessment team and given an overview of the day ahead. He was scheduled to begin with some cognitive measures. He completed the Wechsler Adult Intelligence Scale, the Watson Glaser Critical Thinking Test, the Profiles Personality Measure, and the Guilford Zimmerman Personality Inventory. The battery took three hours to complete. Next, a member of the assessment team gave Henry instructions for a problem analysis and decision-making exercise along with information and data to study. After forty-five minutes of preparation, Henry was called into a briefing room, which was equipped with audio and visual aids and included a podium. Henry made a formal presentation of his decision, summarizing his thinking and responding to questions from assessors, who acted as members of the press. The conference was videotaped.

After a short lunch break, Henry was given instructions for an in-basket exercise. The task stated that he had just been promoted to chief but had been suddenly called out of town. He was given thirty-five items from his current in-basket with instructions to complete them in the next three hours. Henry studied the items and found them to be realistic. It did not take him long to feel that this was not just an exercise but something very close to the kind of items a chief had to deal with. Although he worked quickly, Henry felt time flying. He managed his time well, however, and had completed all critical items and a few of the less important ones before he had to quit. After the assessor collected the items, she gave Henry a form to summarize his impressions of the people he had "met" while working on the in-basket. He was also asked to complete a self-assessment.

Henry's last activity was a team interview with the assessors. During this interview, different assessors asked questions about Henry's experiences and background. He was asked to relate past examples of ways in which he had handled critical decisions and assignments. At the end of the interview he was invited to describe his goals for the department as its new chief.

Exhausted but confident, Henry left feeling that the day had been a fair test of his abilities. Two weeks later, he was informed he had been selected. Several months after he assumed the position of chief, Henry met again with the psychologists; together, they reviewed his assessment and developed a plan for addressing his weak spots and building on his strengths.

Specify the Purpose and Design

A test author begins by identifying his or her purpose and what basic form or design will be used in developing the test. Decisions include the objectives of the test, the importance of the results, the target population, and the kind of items that are most likely to measure the subject at the desired level.

Write the Test Items

Writing test items is a very systematic process. Procedurally, it begins with past research, moves to drafting items, then to field testing them, and finally to revising them into final form.

Review Existing Research.   Survey the literature to capitalize on other work in the same content area. Past research is also often a good indicator of the kinds of items that are best for assessing different domains.

Draft Items.   Many methods have been developed for writing test items. The author selects the one that is most effective for the domain of the test. Data-based methods are usually preferable to more subjective methods.

Field Test Items.   Once the items have been drafted, the test is given experimentally to subjects. The data can then be checked with the data provided by other measures. Also, interviews of testees can help the author to understand how and why items are working or not working.

Revise and Extend Items.   Once the field test is complete, items are revised and extended as necessary to improve their effectiveness.

Conduct the Item Analysis

Once test items have been generated, they are checked to ensure that the items measure the instructional or behavioral objectives they were designed to assess. They are also checked to determine their ability to differentiate between high and low performers on the job. Item analysis can be done by judgmental review, statistical analysis, a combination of the two, or a choice review analysis (breaking items into components and analyzing those).

Determine the Length of the Test

Short tests are often imprecise. They represent restricted samples of the target domain. Short tests are not used for making important decisions such as who will receive diplomas, li-

censes, or certificates. Longer tests are usually better measures but they must be carefully constructed. Test length is the number of test items measuring an objective. There is an optimal test length for each objective that is included in a test (Hambleton, 1983, 1987). Beck (1980) recommends that a test developer consider the following factors when thinking about test length: the importance and types of decisions to be made, the importance and emphasis given to the objectives, the number of objectives, and practical constraints, such as available testing time.

Set the Performance Standards

Most tests are used to distinguish between competent and incompetent performance and between masters and nonmasters of a subject. In these applications a cutoff point is essential. The validity of the final classification decisions depends as much on the cutoff point as on the test content. Shepard (1980) distinguished three uses for tests in classroom applications: pupil diagnosis, pupil certification, and program evaluation. Each has a different focus and, as a result, a different set of performance standards. In large-scale diagnostic tests to evaluate curriculum information or the group impact on students as a group, rigorous standards need to be applied.

Validate the Test Scores

Test scores are intended to describe examinees' performance, to assign examinees to mastery states, or to describe the performance of groups for program evaluation. Unless the test scores serve one of these purposes (i.e., have validity), they are of no use. For a more extensive discussion of validity, see Chapter 8.

Evaluate the Reliability of the Test Scores

Hambleton, Swaminathan, Algina, and Coulson (1978) defined three categories of reliability (see the previous discussion in this chapter): the consistency of mastery–nonmastery classification decisions, the consistency of the squared deviations of individual scores from the cutoff scores across parallel forms of the test, and the consistency of the individual test scores across parallel forms of the test. A fourth issue is inter-rater reliability, which examines the comparability of ratings completed by independent judges of the the same performance.

This process is time consuming but well worth the effort. More and more organizations are learning that appropriate care exercised in an evaluation process is well rewarded by improved results in the future. Once a test has been developed, it is possible to consider different ways of administering it. One of those choices, which is growing in popularity, is to administer the test on a computer.

Computer Testing

The development of computers, of a variety of procedures for item analysis, of procedures for structuring difficulty levels for test items, and of different methods of creating item pools has laid the foundation for today's **computerized adaptive testing (CAT)**. These procedures apply the development of different item pools for different groups of individuals to a common scale score. For example, in ability testing, the use of computers allows individuals to work at their own pace. Each person starts at a specific level of difficulty (usually a medium difficulty level), and the computer presents questions with a higher or lower level of difficulty depending on the individual's responses. Scoring is done by the computer. The individual's score is usually the number of items answered correctly. CAT is appropriate in employment testing (a) when there is a continuous flow of candidates and relatively small groups that have to be tested at one time; (b) when test security is important and each applicant can be tested with a different sample of items (Anastasi, 1988); and (c) when a large number of computers are available and the procedures lower the company's selection and placement costs.

We have reviewed a variety of procedures and types and methods of predictors used in industry and organizations as predictors of job performance. However, we have discussed *only a sample* of the predictors, techniques, and controversies that exist in the field. For further information the reader is referred to the recommended readings listed later in the chapter.

SUMMARY

The purposes of this chapter are to define some of the predictors of job behaviors and to review concepts and principles underlying the prediction process. Samples of predictors used in industry and organizations are reviewed.

A predictor is an independent variable that is used for forecasting criterion job behaviors. Predictors can be interviews, biographical data, psychological tests, references, and other such devices. Every predictor that is used involves a degree of judgment and subjectivity of decision making, especially in the inferences and interpretations made from test scores. The issues of subjectivity and ways to reduce it have existed in psychology and in the I/O area for many years. Meehl's 1954 book *Clinical versus Statistical Prediction* originally stimulated the controversy, leading to the conclusion that every procedure and device used for prediction should be proven to be accurate, precise, and fair.

The basic psychometric requirements for every predictor are reliability and validity. The term *reliability* refers to the precision and consistency of scores obtained by the same individuals retested with the same test or with equivalent forms of that test. The term *validity* refers to what the instrument measures, how well it measures it, and the supporting evidence for justifying inferences made from its scores.

Predictors can be categorized in a variety of ways. Paper-and-pencil tests use printed forms and performance tests require manipulation of objects. Individual tests are administered to one person at a time by an expert examiner; group tests are given to a number of individuals at one time. Speed tests have a short time limit; power tests enable the person to complete the test. Language tests require the knowledge of a particular language; nonlanguage tests are nonverbal measures of traits.

We reviewed and discussed examples of predictors that are used in industry and organizations: what predictors measure (content) and the process by which predictors measure attributes (how they measure what they are supposed to measure). In terms of content being measured, we discussed cognitive tests; examples are general intelligence tests, mechanical ability tests, clerical ability tests, and sensory and physical ability tests. We also discussed personality and integrity tests, including the recent discussion of the big five personality dimensions and their use in predicting job behaviors. The traits of neuroticism, extraversion, agreeableness, conscientiousness, and openness to experience initiated the argument as to whether some of these traits (e.g., conscientiousness) are predictive of success across most jobs or whether a particular trait (e.g., openness) is predictive of effectiveness in specific types of jobs (e.g., artistic jobs). These traits can be measured in a variety of ways, for example, by using structured, objective and projective tests.

Integrity testing is intended to predict the likelihood of counterproductive behavior on the job. In general, studies indicated that these tests have better validities in predicting a criterion that combines different aspects of counterproductive behavior (e.g., absenteeism, violence, and substance abuse) than in predicting only one aspect of that behavior (e.g., theft).

Drug and alcohol abuse testing was shown to be cost-effective for organizations. However, to achieve its purpose, it has to incorporate a well-planned program of information that can be related to applicants and employees.

The weighted application blank (WAB) and the biodata questionnaire were presented as examples of the use of application blanks. Extensive validity and meta-analytic research have shown that biodata items have high predictability for a variety of jobs and that they generalize across organizations, subgroups, and time (e.g., Rothstein et al., 1990).

For the process category of predictors we discussed interviews, psychological assessment, computer testing, and assessment centers.

Interviews are the most frequently used predictors of job behavior in industry and organizations. Recent validity and predictability studies have shown that the interview is a better predictor of job performance than was previously assumed. However, the level of validity coefficients was contingent on parameters such as the format of the interview.

Assessment centers have proven to have good predictive validity. Computer adaptive testing (CAT) uses current developments in item analysis methodology and computer technology to identify how predictors measure traits such as motor, cognitive, perceptual abilities, and achievement tests.

KEY TERMS AND CONCEPTS

assessment center
big five personality dimensions
biodata
coefficient of stability
cognitive tests
computerized adaptive testing
(CAT)

criterion
criterion-referenced tests
Cronbach coefficient alpha
Employee Assistance Programs
(EAP)
equivalent (alternate) form
reliability

group interview
group tests
individual interview
individual tests
job-related interview
Kuder-Richardson
reliability

language tests	power tests	standardized test
measurement error	predictor	structured interview
mechanical ability	psychological test	test
nonlanguage tests	reliability	test–retest reliability
objective tests	reliability coefficients	true score
obtained score	situational interview	unstructured interview
odd-even split	speed tests	validity
paper-and-pencil tests	spiral-omnibus format	weighted application
personality tests	split-half reliability	blank

RECOMMENDED READINGS

Ackerman, P. L., & Humphreys, L. G. (1990). Individual differences in industrial and organizational psychology. In M. D. Dunnette & L. M. Hough (Eds.), *Handbook of industrial and organizational psychology* (Chapter 5, pp. 223–282). Palo Alto: Consulting Psychologists Press. (We suggest concentrating mainly on pp. 224–232, 239–282.)

Arvey, R. D., & Landon, T. E. (1992). Development of physical ability tests for police officers: A construct validation approach. *Journal of Applied Psychology, 77*(6), 996–1009.

Buros, O. K. (1995). *Mental measurement yearbook* (12th ed.). Highland Park, NJ: Grython. (Read the chapters related to predictors of interest.)

Dawis, R. V. (1991). Vocational interests, values and preferences. In M. D. Dunnette & L. M. Hough (Eds.) *Handbook of industrial and organizational*

psychology (Chapter 12, pp. 833–872). Palo Alto: Consulting Psychologists Press.

Gough, H. (1976). Personality and personality assessment. In M. D. Dunnette (Ed.), *Handbook of industrial and organizational psychology,* (Chapter 13, pp. 571–607). Chicago: Rand McNally College Publishing.

Hansen, C. P., & Conrad, K. A. (1991). *A handbook of psychological assessment in business.* New York: Quorum Books.

Johns, G. (1994). How often were you absent? A review of self-reported absence data. *Journal of Applied Psychology, 79*(4), 574–591.

Joyce, L. W., Thayer, P. W., & Pond, S. B., III (1994). Managerial functions: An alternative to traditional assessment center dimensions? *Personnel Psychology, 47*(1), 109–121.

INTERNET RESOURCES

Outcome Assessment: Assessment Tools in Academe and Public Accounting

This site describes examples of the assessment tools colleges and universities are using for gathering student and alumni information. It also lists articles describing how assessment provides systematic support for making educational decisions.
http://www.rutgers.edu/Accounting/anet/ education/baker-report/baker.section4.html

The Experimental Knowledge Systems Library (EKSL) Research: Causal Modeling

This site describes how causal relationships between measured variables are tested experimentally and their use. The site has a small section where many other computer and other "autonomous agents" are described.
http://eksl-www.cs.umass.edu/research/ causal-modeling.html

Pitfalls of Data Analysis (or How to Avoid Lies and Damned Lies)

The text at this site is a summary of a workshop that addressed things that people overlook in their data analysis and the ways in which people sometimes bend the rules of statistics to show support for their own views. The site also includes suggestions for presenting statistics in ways that are clear and understandable.
http://maddog.fammed.wisc.edu/pitfalls/

The New York Times SCIENCE Tuesday, May 8, 1990: Huge Study of Diet Indicts Fat and Meat

This article reports early findings from a study in China, the most comprehensive large study ever undertaken of the relationship between diet and health. It provides an excellent example of how useful statistics can be in making sense of piles of data. http://www.fatfree.com/FAQ/china-study

Pre-employment Screening Considerations and the ADA

The paper that can be downloaded from this site describes some of the implications of the ADA in recruiting, such as whether the ADA will change the way new employees are recruited. http://janweb.icdi.wvu.edu/kinder/518scree

EXERCISE

Exercise 7.1

Developing a Selection System

The Widget Company is a manufacturer of computer parts. Because of personnel problems such as high turnover, management, with the help of an I/O psychologist, is developing a new selection system and strategy for the organization. The predictors that the company has used to date are a simple short application blank, an unstructured interview, and reference checks. The I/O psychologist is considering the addition of a variety of cognitive tests and changes in the formats of some of the previous devices used.

Get together with four other students in class. Your first task is to review the selection process as outlined in the chapter on human resources management (Chapter 3).

Following the steps outlined in Chapter 3:

1. Start with the preliminary task of accumulating the information necessary for putting together your selection strategy. For example, do the following:

   - Decide on a specific job within this company (e.g., production line or clerical) for which you are going to select the predictors.

   - Review the literature of job analysis for that job (including chapter 4, "Job Analysis") and decide on the description of the job.

   - Review the literature dealing with validity studies for similar jobs.

   - Review validity information for the predictors the company wants to use for the particular job (e.g., the Buros Mental Measurement Book, journal articles).

2. On the basis of all the information you have collected, discuss and decide the following:

   - Which of the of the previous predictors you would continue to use

   - What you would change and in what way, in terms of the specific formats and structures of each of these predictors

   - The particular cognitive predictors you want to add

   - The pros and cons of using the new set of predictors (e.g., costs and benefits to Widget of better organizational outcomes such as tenure, risks of lawsuits, satisfied employees, and so on).

REFERENCES

Ackerman, P. L., & Humphreys, L. G. (1990). Individual differences in industrial and organizational psychology. In M. D. Dunnette & L. M. Hough (Eds.), *Handbook of industrial and organizational psychology* (Chapter 5, pp. 223–282). Palo Alto, CA: Consulting Psychologists Press.

Allport, G. W., & Odbert, H. S. (1936). Trait names: A psycholexical study. *Psychological Monographs, 47* (Whole No. 211).

Anastasi, A. (1988). *Psychological testing.* New York: Macmillan Publishing.

Angarola, R. T. (1985). Drug testing in the workplace: Is it legal? *Personnel Administrator, 30*(9), 79–89.

Azar, B. (1995, July). Which traits predict job performance? *The APA Monitor, 26*(7), 30–31.

Barrick, M. R., & Mount, M. K. (1991). The big five personality dimensions and job performance: A meta-analysis. *Personnel Psychology, 44,* 1–26.

Beck, R. A. (Ed.). (1980). *A guide to criterion-referenced test construction*. Baltimore, MD: The Johns Hopkins University Press.

Berk, R. A. (Ed.). (1982). *Handbook of methods for detecting test bias*. Baltimore, MD: The Johns Hopkins University Press.

Bennett, G. K. (1941). *Test of Mechanical Comprehension*. New York: Psychological Corporation.

Bennett, G. K., & Cruikshank, R. M. (1949). *A summary of clerical tests*. New York: The Psychological Corporation.

Bernadin, H. J., & Cooke, D. K. (1993). Validity of an honesty test in predicting theft among convenience store employees. *Academy of Management Journal, 36*(5), 1097–1108.

Blinkhorn, S., & Johnson, C. (1990). The insignificance of personality testing. *Nature, 348,* 671–672.

Blum, M. L., & Naylor, J. C. (1968). *Industrial psychology: Its theoretical and social foundations*. New York: Harper & Row.

Bray, D. W. (1964). The management progress study. *American Psychologist, 19,* 419–420.

Bray, D. W., & Grant, D. L. (1966). The assessment center in the measurement of potential for business management. *Psychological Monographs,* 1980 (17, Whole No. 625).

Bray, D. W., Campbell, R. J., & Grant, D. L. (1973). *The management recruit: Formative years in business*. New York: Wiley-Interscience.

Bray, D. W., & Howard, A. (1983). The AT&T longitudinal studies of managers. In K. W. Schaie (Ed.), *Longitudinal studies of adult psychological development* (pp. 112–146). New York: Guilford.

Camara, W. J., & Schneider, D. L. (1994). Integrity tests: Facts and unresolved issues. *American Psychologist, 49,* 112–119.

Camara, W. J., & Schneider, D. L. (1995). Questions of construct breadth and openness of research in integrity testing. *American Psychologist, 50*(6), 459–460.

Campbell, J. P. (1990). Modeling the performance prediction problem in industrial and organizational psychology. In M. D. Dunnette & L. M. Hough (Eds.), *Handbook of industrial and organizational psychology,* (Vol. 1, pp. 687–732). Palo Alto, CA: Consulting Psychologists Press.

Campion, M. A. (1983). Personnel selection for physically demanding jobs: Review and recommendations. *Personnel Psychology, 36,* 527–550.

Cascio, W. F. (1976). Turnover, biographical data, and fair employment practices. *Journal of Applied Psychology, 61*(5), 576–580.

Cattell, R. B. (1971). *Abilities: their structure, growth, and action*. Boston: Houghton Mifflin.

Conway, J. M., Jako, R. A., & Goodman, D. F. (1995). A meta-analysis of interrater and internal consistency reliability of selection interview. *Journal of Applied Psychology, 80*(5), 565–579.

Crant, M. J., & Bateman, T. S. (1990). An experimental test of the impact of drug-testing programs of potential job applicants' attitudes and intentions. *Journal of Applied Psychology, 75*(2), 127–131.

Crawford, J. E., & Crawford, D. M. (1946, 1949). *Small parts dexterity test: Manual*. New York: Psychological Corporation.

Cunningham, M. R., Wong, D. T., & Barbee, A. P. (1994). Self-presentation dynamics on overt integrity tests: Experimental studies of the Reid report. *Journal of Applied Psychology, 79*(5), 643–658.

Dunnette, M. D. (1966). *Personnel selection and placement*. Belmont, CA: Wadsworth Publishing Company.

Gatewood, R. D., & Feild, H. S. (1994). Human resources selection. Fort Worth, TX: Harcourt Brace.

Gellatly, I. R., Paunonen, S. V., Meyer, J. P., Jackson, D. N., & Goffin, R. D. (1991). Personality, vocational interest, and cognitive predictors of managerial job performance and satisfaction. *Personality and Individual Differences, 12,* 221–231.

Ghiselli, E. E. (1966). *The validity of occupational aptitude tests*. New York: Wiley.

Goldberg, L. R. (1970). Man versus model of man: A rationale, plus some evidence, for a method of improving on clinical inferences. *Psychological Bulletin, 73,* 422–432.

Guilford, J. P. (1954). *Psychometric methods*. New York, NY: McGraw-Hill.

Guilford, J. P. (1967). *The nature of human intelligence*. New York: McGraw-Hill.

Guion, R. M. (1991). Personnel assessment, selection, and placement. In M. D. Dunnette & L. M. Hough (Eds.), *Handbook of industrial and organizational psychology* (Vol. 2, pp. 327–397). Palo Alto, CA: Consulting Psychologists Press.

Guion, R. M., & Gottier, R. F. (1965). Validity of personality measures in personnel selection. *Personnel Psychology, 18,* 135–164.

Hagberg, R. A., Jackson, D. N., & Jackson, D. N., III (1993, May). *Personality and performance in senior executives.* Paper presented at the eighth annual conference of the Society for Industrial and Organizational Psychology, Inc., San Francisco, CA.

Hambleton, R. K. (1987). Determining optimal test lengths with a fixed testing time. *Educational and Psychological Measurement, 47*(2), 339–347.

Hambleton, R. K. (1983) Determining the lengths for criterion-referenced tests. *Journal of Educational Measurement, 20*(1), 27–38.

Hambleton, R. K., Swaminathan, H., Algina, J., & Coulson, D. B. (1978). Criterion-referenced testing and measurement: A review of technical issues and developments. *Review of Educational Research, 48*, 1–47.

Handyside, J., & Duncan, D. C. (1954). Four years later: A follow-up of an experiment in selecting supervisors. *Occupational Psychology, 28*, 9–23.

Hansen, C. P., & Conrad, K. A. (1991). *A handbook of psychological assessment in business.* New York: Quorum Books.

Harris, M. M. (1989). Reconsidering the employment interview: A review of recent literature and suggestions for future research. *Personnel Psychology, 42*, 691–726.

Hartman, D. E. (1986). On the use of clinical psychology software: Practical, legal and ethical concerns. *Professional Psychology: Research and Practice, 17*, 473–475.

Hilton, A. C., Bolin, S. F., Parker, J. W., Jr., Taylor, E. K., & Walker, W. B. (1955). The validity of personnel assessments by professional psychologists. *Journal of Applied Psychology, 39*, 287–293.

Hogan, R. T. (1991). Personality and personality measurement. In M. D. Dunnette & L. M. Hough (Eds.), *Handbook of industrial and organizational psychology* (Vol. 2, pp. 873–919). Palo Alto, CA: Consulting Psychologists Press.

Hollinger, R. C. (1989). *Dishonesty in the workplace: A manager's guide to preventing employee theft.* Park Ridge, IL: London House Press.

Hough, L. M. (1992). The "Big Five" personality variables—construct confusion: Description versus prediction. *Human Performance, 5*, 139–155.

Huffcutt, A. I., & Woehr, D. J. (1993). *A conceptual analysis of interview structure and the effects of structure on the interview process.* Paper presented at the Seventh Annual Conference of the Society for Industrial and Organizational Psychology, Montreal.

Jackson, D. N., Hagberg, R. A., & Jackson, D. N., III (1993, May). *Dimensions of executive performance.* Paper presented at the Eighth Annual Conference of the Society for Industrial and Organizational Psychology, San Francisco, CA.

Jackson, D. N., & Rothstein, M. (1992). Evaluative personality testing in personnel selection. *The Psychologist, 6*, 8–11.

Kaplan, M. R., & Saccuzzo, D. P. (1993). *Psychological testing: Principles, applications, and issues* (3rd ed.). Pacific Grove, CA: Brooks/Cole.

Kingston-O'Connell, F. G. (December, 1992). Paper-pencil integrity tests and the issues surrounding them. Unpublished student paper, University of Wisconsin–Parkside, Psychology Dept.

Kluger, A. N., & Colella, A. (1993). Beyond the mean bias: The effect of warning against faking on biodata item variances. *Personnel Psychology, 46*(4), 763–779.

Knowles, M. (1977). The adult learner becomes less neglected. *Training, 14*(9), 16–18.

Landy, F. J., Shankster, L. J., & Kohler, S. S. (1994). Personnel selection and placement. *Annual Review of Psychology, 45*, 261–296.

Laurent, H. (1968). Research on the identification of management potential. In H. Laurent, H. D. Kolb, V. J. Benz, & D. W. Bray (Eds.), *Predicting managerial success* (pp. 1–34). Ann Arbor, MI: Foundation for Research on Human Behavior.

Likert, R., & Quasha, W. H. (1941–1948). *Revised Minnesota Paper Form Board Test.* New York: Psychological Corporation.

Likert, R., & Quasha, W. H. (1970). *Revised Minnesota Paper Form Board Test: Manual, 1970 edition.* New York: The Psychological Corporation.

Lilienfeld, S. O., Alliger, G., & Mitchell, K. (1995). Why integrity testing remains controversial. *American Psychologist, 50*(6), 457–458.

Mael, F. A. (1991). A conceptual rationale for the domain and attributes of biodata items. *Personnel Psychology, 44*(4), 763–792.

Martin, S. L., & DeGrange, D. J. (1993). How effective are physical and psychological drug tests? *Security Technology & Design, 3*(3), 38–41.

Martin, S. L., & Godsey, C. (1992, May). Validating a theoretically-based predictor of substance abuse. In

S. L. Martin (Chair), *Examining physical and psychological predictors of substance abuse.* Symposium conducted at the Seventh Annual Conference of the Society for Industrial and Organizational Psychology, Montreal.

Martin, S. L., & Orban, J. A. (1995). Are fundamental job requirements neglected in selection systems? *Journal of Business and Psychology, 9*(4), 345–353.

McCrae, R. R., & Costa, P. T. (1987). Validation of the five-factor model of personality across instruments and observers. *Journal of Personality and Social Psychology, 52,* 81–90.

McDaniel, M. A. (1989). Biographical constructs for predicting employee suitability. *Journal of Applied Psychology, 74*(6), 964–970.

McDaniel, M. A., Whetzel, D. L., Schmidt, F. L., & Maurer, S. D. (1994). The validity of employment interview: A comprehensive review and meta-analysis. *Journal of Applied Psychology, 79*(4), 599–616.

Meehl, P. E. (1954). *Clinical versus statistical prediction: A theoretical analysis and a review of the evidence.* Minneapolis, MN: University of Minnesota Press.

Meehl, P. E. (1965). Seer over sign: The first good example. *Journal of Experimental Research in Personality, 1,* 27–32.

Mischel, W. (1973). Toward a cognitive social learning reconceptualization of personality. *Psychological Review, 80,* 252–283.

Mischel, W. (1981). Current issues and challenges in personality. In L. T. Benjamin (Ed.), *The G. Stanley Hall Lecture Series,* (Vol. 1, pp. 81–99). Washington, DC: American Psychological Association.

Murphy, K. R. (1993). *Honesty in the workplace.* Belmont, CA: Brooks/Cole.

Nitko, A. J. (1980). Defining "criterion-referenced test." In R. A. Beck (Ed.), *A guide to criterion-referenced test construction* (pp. 8–28). Baltimore, MD: The Johns Hopkins University Press.

Nunnally, J. C., Jr. (1959). *Tests and measurement: Assessment and prediction.* New York: McGraw-Hill.

Nunnally, J. C., Jr. (1967). *Psychometric theory.* New York: McGraw-Hill.

Ones, D. S., Viswesvaran, C., & Schmidt, F. L. (1993). Comprehensive meta-analysis of integrity test validities: Findings and implications for personnel selection and theories of job performance. *Journal of Applied Psychology Monograph, 78,* 679–703.

Ones, D. S., Viswesvaran, C., & Schmidt, F. L. (1995). Integrity tests: Overlooked facts, resolved issues, and remaining questions. *American Psychologist, 50*(6), 456–457.

Pearlman, K., Schmidt, F. L., & Hunter, J. E. (1980). Validity generalization results for tests used to predict job proficiency and training success in clerical occupations. *Journal of Applied Psychology, 65*(4), 373–406.

Rohrer, Hibler and Replogle International (1991). Psychological assessment in international business. In C. P. Hansen & K. A. Conrad (Eds.), *A handbook of psychological assessment in business* (pp. 206–224). New York: Quorum Books.

Rothstein, H. R., Schmidt, F. L., Erwin, F. W., Owens, W. A., & Sparks, C. P. (1990). Biographical data in employment selection: Can validities be made generalizable? *Journal of Applied Psychology, 75*(2), 175–184.

Ryan, A. M., & Sackett, P. R. (1987). A survey of individual assessment practices by I/O psychologists. *Personnel Psychology, 40,* 455–488.

Sackett, P. R. (1985). Honesty testing for personnel selection. *Personnel Administrator, 30*(9), 67–76.

Sackett, P. R., & Harris, M. M. (1984). Honesty testing for personnel selection: A review and critique. *Personnel Psychology, 37,* 221–245.

Saxe, L., Dougherty, D., & Cross, T. (1985). The validity of polygraph testing. *American Psychologist, 40,* 355–366.

Schmidt, F. L., Ones, D. S., & Hunter, J. E. (1992). Personnel selection. *Annual Review of Psychology, 43,* 627–670.

Schmidt, M. J., Ryan, A. M., Stierwalt, S. L., & Powell, A. B. (1995). Frame of reference effects of personality scale scores and criterion-related validity. *Journal of Applied Psychology, 80*(5), 607–620.

Shepard, L. A. (1980). Setting performance standards. In R. A. Beck (Ed.), *A guide to criterion-referenced test construction* (pp. 169–198). Baltimore, MD: The Johns Hopkins University Press.

Sines, J. O. (1970). Actuarial versus clinical prediction in psychopathology. *British Journal of Psychiatry, 116,* 129–144.

Society for Industrial and Organizational Psychology (1987). *Principles for the validation and use of personnel selection procedures* (3rd ed.). College Park, MD: Author.

Spearman, C. (1904). General intelligence, objectively determined and measured. *American Journal of Psychology, 15,* 201–293.

Spearman, C. (1927). *The abilities of man.* New York: Macmillan.

Stelmack, R. M. (1990). Biological bases of extraversion: Psychophysiological evidence. *Journal of Personality, 58,* 293–311.

Stokes, G., Hogan, J. B., & Snell, A. F. (1993). Comparability of incumbent and applicant samples for the development of biodata keys: The influence of social desirability. *Personnel Psychology, 46*(4), 739–762.

Stromberg, E. L. (1951). *Stromberg dexterity test: preliminary manual.* New York: Psychological Corporation.

Task Force on Assessment Center Standards (1980). Standards and ethical considerations for assessment center operations. *The Personnel Administrator, 25,* 35–38.

Tett, R. P., Jackson, D. N., & Rothstein, M. (1991). Personality measures as predictors of job performance: A meta-analytic review. *Personnel Psychology, 44,* 703–742.

Thurstone, L. L. (1938). Primary mental abilities. *Psychometric Monographs* (Monograph No. 1).

Thurstone, L. L. (1947). *Multiple factor analysis.* Chicago: University of Chicago Press.

Ulrich, L., & Trumbo, D. (1965). The selection interview since 1949. *Personnel Bulletin, 63,* 100–116.

Wiesner, W. H., & Cronshaw, S. F. (1988). The moderating impact of interview format and degree of structure on the validity of the employment interview. *Journal of Occupational Psychology, 61,* 275–290.

Williams, D. G. (1990). Effects of psychoticism, extraversion, and neuroticism in current mood: A statistical review of six studies. *Personality and Individual Differences, 11,* 615–630.

Personnel Decisions

Chapter Outline

(continued)

UTILITY ANALYSIS

VALIDITY GENERALIZATION

LEGAL CONSIDERATIONS
  The Civil Rights Act of 1964
  Equal Employment Opportunity Commission
    (EEOC)
  Adverse Impact
  Affirmative Action

Summary
Key Terms and Concepts
Recommended Readings
Internet Resources
Exercise
References

. . . .

Recently, the Widget Corporation, a producer of computer parts, has been experiencing an increase in employee turnover. In addition, an employee satisfaction survey provided evidence that employees are increasingly becoming dissatisfied with their jobs. Exit interviews with employees terminating their employment with Widget supported the survey results. Further analysis showed that employees' feelings of job dissatisfaction were associated with the new computerized production lines the company had installed. Specifically, employees felt that they were not qualified to successfully operate the new lines.

In an effort to improve employee work satisfaction and reduce turnover, the top management at Widget decided to use two methods of intervention. The first created a training program, which was designed to help current employees understand and work with the computerized production lines. The second was the development and implementation of a new system for recruiting and selecting employees to replace those who left.

The steps in the old employee selection process at Widget were: reviewing applications and resumes, interviewing applicants, and contacting references provided by the applicants. Because this selection process was found to be inefficient, Widget decided to create a new selection system.

The new system is designed to increase organizational effectiveness and individual satisfaction. For example, the company wants to select new employees who have the knowledge, skills and abilities to perform the jobs on the computerized product

lines. The new selection system retains the application/resume, interview, and employment reference components of the old system, but weights them differently in making hiring decisions. New instruments were developed for use in predicting successful performance on the job, and two new assessment tools were added to the process. One of these tools measures general cognitive abilities, specifically math and verbal skills, and the second assesses knowledge of computer systems. A follow-up study was conducted to examine the outcomes associated with the new selection system. The results showed a substantial reduction in turnover, increased job satisfaction for existing and new employees, and greater profits for the company. A beneficial by-product of the new system was that it could also be used to fill other positions in the corporation.

When setting up and developing a validated selection system, I/O psychologists follow a series of steps like those presented in Figure 8.1. Note that the steps in this outline are essentially the same as the ones presented originally in the chapter on human resource management (see Figure 3.1). However, the discussion in this chapter extends that description to include the details of how criteria and predictors are chosen and applied during implementation of a selection system.

Several of the terms and concepts used in this chapter may be unfamiliar. Therefore some basic definitions are provided in Table 8.1 on page 246.

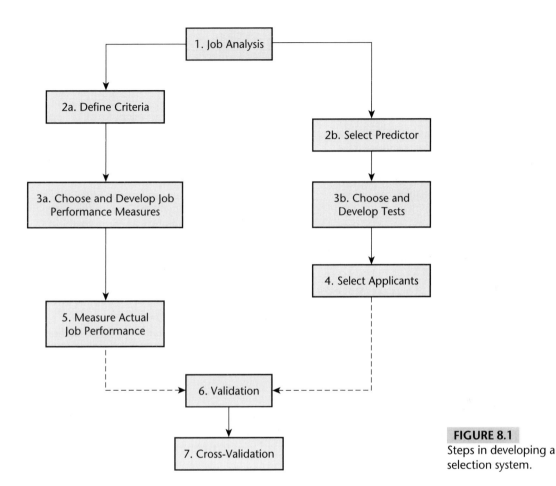

FIGURE 8.1
Steps in developing a selection system.

····································

DEVELOPING A SELECTION SYSTEM

The selection process takes place in every facet of life. For example, children preparing to play a game of kickball must select team members. This selection process is used to create the best kickball team, the one that can win the game. Children learn about other children's abilities in a variety of ways. This information may be based on personal experience, recommendations from other team members, or each child's self-reported kickball abilities and successes. The final decision about who the team members will be is based on predictions about which children have the ability to be successful ball players. The re-

sult is a group of individuals whose collective abilities are likely to make a winning team.

Human resource departments also attempt to create a winning team. They want a productive, committed, and satisfied work force, which leads to profitable outcomes for the organization. Before this team can be created, the jobs that must be filled need to be identified. For each job, the required knowledge, skills, and abilities must be specified. Using this information, management can search through the applicant pool to find individuals who best match the needs of the organization.

In our example the Widget Corporation wanted to create a selection system to match candidates with jobs on the computerized produc-

TABLE 8.1   Terms and definitions relevant to personnel selection

Terms	Definitions	Terms	Definitions
Selection	Process of choosing one or more individuals from a large pool of applicants	Test bias	Occurs when a selection instrument's prediction of success is not equivalent for all groups
Job analysis	A definition of the knowledge, skills, and abilities needed to perform the job	Adverse impact	Occurs when a selection procedure results in the hiring of, or favors, members of one group over another
Predictor	A measure of the knowledge, skills, and abilities needed to perform the job	Affirmative action	Steps to provide equal employment opportunities and thereby overcome past and present inequities
Criterion	A measure of success on the job		
Validity	The degree of support of the inference that a score on a predictor is related to a criterion score	Validity generalization	A research approach demonstrating the ability to use a predictor for similar jobs across multiple organizations or within an organization
Reliability	The degree of measurement error		
Cutoff score	A score used to delineate successful or unsuccessful completion on a test	Utility analysis	A research approach demonstrating the increase in dollar payoff from using a selection procedure instead of randomly selecting employees
Selection ratio	The number of applicants divided by the number of job openings		
Base rate	The number of successful employees divided by the total number of employees		

tion line. The number of factors that are examined during such a matching process may vary. At a minimum level, the focus is on whether an individual has the necessary knowledge, skills, and abilities for a particular job. The maximum approach considers personal and organizational variables such as motivation, interests, compensation, and physical conditions.

··

RECRUITMENT, SELECTION, AND PLACEMENT: CONCEPTS AND DEFINITIONS

Recruitment

The first step in developing a pool of applicants is recruiting. This process is bidirectional, which means that individuals can search for organiza-tions or an organization can seek out and attract the individuals. Organizations may recruit individuals through either an external or an internal process or both. The recruitment process is external when individuals outside the organization are being sought. Recruitment is internal when employees from within the organization are recruited to fill a position.

Many variables and conditions can influence the process of recruitment. Some of these are: constraints of governmental laws and regulations, unions and labor market conditions, and characteristics of the recruiters (such as gender, race, and position). It is beyond the scope of this text to cover all of them; the interested reader is referred to the list of recommended readings.

An important factor in recruiting is the "tightness of the labor market" (Guion, 1976, p. 779). If the labor market is extremely tight, there are many job openings but few individuals available to fill them. In this case the process of selection focuses on finding the best applicant from those who are available. When the job market is loose, there are many more potential applicants than job openings (such as in a time of high unemployment). The human resource manager could reject a high number of individuals and return to the labor market for applicants who are more likely to succeed in the job and the organization (Dunnette, 1966; Guion, 1976). When there is the opportunity to choose from a number of candidates the question becomes how to select the best potential employee.

Selection

Selection is the process of choosing one or more individuals from a large pool of applicants (see Table 8.1). According to Gatewood and Feild (1994, p. 3),

> Selection is the process of collecting and evaluating information about an individual in order to extend an offer of employment. Such employment could be either a first position for a new employee or a different position for an existing employee. The selection process is performed under legal and environmental constraints to protect the future interests of the organization and the individual.

According to Gatewood and Feild, this definition takes into account not only initial recruitment and employment, but also the internal moves of employees such as transfers and promotion.

Whatever the specific definition, the selection process has two components. The first is a focus on individual differences, which is essential to selecting the individuals who are most likely to succeed on the job (Cascio & Awad, 1981). The second component involves matching individuals, jobs, and organizations. Current efforts to match people with organizations extend selection decisions beyond knowledge, skills, and abilities. These investigations suggest that selecting employees only on the basis of their abil-

ities is more useful to the gatekeepers than to the applicants. Gatekeepers have the responsibility of selecting individuals for particular places or jobs (Tyler, 1995). To accomplish this goal, they take into account only the abilities of applicants. However, this process is not useful to the individuals who are seeking the jobs and organizations. The literature on person–organization fit recognizes the importance of matching an applicant's values, beliefs, and personality traits with the characteristics of an organization (Adkins, Russell, & Werbel, 1994; Dawis, 1991). The selection process and the search for a fit are conducted by *both* the individual and the organization. Porter, Lawler, and Hackman (1975, p. 131) propose that "Individuals seek a work or organization where they can fulfill their goals, and organizations try to hire people who can help them reach their objectives."

The selection process involves a multitude of factors. These include measures of motivation, abilities, skills, and needs; individuals' reactions to various leadership styles; individuals' ability to adapt to the physical and cultural climate of the organization; and employees' ability to transfer to other departments, commit, and adjust. All of these factors are important in today's world of downsizing, merging, and establishing divisions overseas (Kristof, 1996; Porter et al., 1975). On the basis of these factors, researchers have defined person–organization fit as the suitability and compatibility between organizations and the individuals they hire and employ (Dawis, 1991; Kristof, 1996). Dawis and Lofquist (1984) originally defined this process as the correspondence that exists between an individual and the environment, implying that there is a harmonious, reciprocal, and complementary relationship.

The search for fit takes place on different levels and depends on the goals of the organization and the individual (Kristof, 1996). For example, the person–group fit refers to the level of compatibility between an employee and the employee's work group. Another level of compatibility is the person–job fit. The person–job fit is the fit between the characteristics, abilities, needs, and desires of an individual and the demands, supplies, and attributes of the job (Dawis, 1991; Kristof, 1996).

An effective selection process begins with the organization's determining which level of search for fit is necessary to benefit the organization and the selected applicant. Lower turnover, lower absenteeism, improved quality and quantity of production, and increased profits are examples of beneficial outcomes. A discussion of the different levels, types, and moderators of the process of fit is beyond the scope of this text. Additional information about this area can be found in the recommended reading list.

Selection and Placement

As Figure 8.1 illustrates, developing a selection system that leads to appropriate and accurate matching is a multistep process. The success of each step is contingent on the success of the previous steps. Success at each step is determined by the quality of the information collected. The quality of each step ultimately affects the quality of the entire selection system.

The process of selection is associated with, but not synonymous with, the processes of placement. Guion (1976, p. 780) noted that "selection is a special case of placement." **Placement** involves finding the optimal job for an applicant on the basis of the particular strengths and weaknesses of that applicant (Guion, 1965, 1991; Lawler, 1980). It is also person-oriented, which means that a job is selected for an individual and that applicants are considered simultaneously for different job openings. **Selection** refers to filling a job vacancy. It is job-oriented, and only the prerequisites for a given job are considered when making hiring decisions. "In selection, the person hired is predicted to be a better performer than the person rejected. In placement, a person is predicted to be a better performer on one job than on any other" (Cascio & Awad, 1981, p. 263).

For example, Widget has five positions open for data entry technicians and fifty applicants for these positions. The goal is to select the five

individuals who are most likely to succeed in data entry. This pool of applicants will not be considered for any other job opening in the organization. Dunnette (1966, p. 2) suggests that "the need to fill a single specified job illustrates selection in its purest form . . . no thought will be given to utilizing the skills of the rejected applicants in other ways or on other jobs."

Now consider the case in which a human resource manager needs to fill three job openings. One job is for data entry, the second is for a secretary, and the third is for a receptionist. The human resource manager assesses all fifty applicants to obtain a thorough profile of their characteristics. The manager decides which three candidates will be hired by considering requirements of each of the jobs in relation to the information gathered about the applicants. This information will also be used to determine which of the applicants will be placed in each of the positions. Blum and Naylor (1968) state that placement refers to hiring the number of individuals needed to fill the same number of positions and then determining who should be offered which job.

Classification and Placement

Placement is associated with classification, but the two processes have different goals. The goal in classification is to assign each individual to a job. This type of assignment is practical for the armed forces, in which all of the people recruited have to be placed. However, classification may not be useful in the industrial world, in which a variety of problems can exist. The numbers of job openings may be different from the number of applicants, or there may be only a specific number of openings for a particular type of job. The question soon becomes one of which individuals will be hired and which job openings the individuals will fill (Guion, 1965).

The answer to this question is best summarized by Dunnette (1966). Dunnette claims that the process of "pure placement" or "vocational guidance" aims to maximize the individual's attainment of his or her goals. It ignores the fact that the organization has a limited number of jobs available and that it needs employees who are qualified for these specific jobs. When applied in their pure form, the strategies of vocational guidance are wasteful to the organization. The process of pure selection is directed toward achieving the organization's goals. It assumes that there is a limitless supply of applicants and leaves many individuals unemployed. Dunnette's suggestion is a compromise approach. For example, taking into account the resources of applicants available and the job openings, the process would be to select the best applicant for job 1. The next step is to select the best or the next-best applicant for job number 2 out of the remaining pool of applicants. At each step the aspirations and goals of the individual are also considered. The process continues until all job vacancies are filled.

To collect all the information needed to implement this process of selection and placement, we follow the steps outlined in Figure 8.1, beginning with job analysis.

Job Analysis

When a carpenter sets out to build a shelf, the first step is to identify all of the materials and tools that are necessary to complete the job. Like a carpenter, an I/O psychologist must gain information about the materials and tools that are needed to perform a particular job. The psychologist also needs information about the knowledge, skills, abilities, and working conditions associated with that job. The vehicle used to collect this information is job analysis.

As described in Chapter 4, job analysis is a method of gathering information to dissect a job into its component parts. As is stated in the 1987 Principles of the Society for Industrial and Organization Psychology (SIOP), one purpose "of job analysis is to assemble the information needed to understand the work performed on the job and the setting in which the work is accomplished" (p. 5). It is important to gather information that allows researchers to make appro-

priate decisions regarding the selection of predictors and criteria.

Cascio (1995) noted that traditional job analysis defines jobs in terms of clusters of tasks, which are task-based, but the current shift is toward a "process-based definition of work" (p. 962). Cascio defines *process* as an accumulation of activities that cut across organizations and functions, such as marketing and production. From this point of view, the development of a selection system is more complicated than shown in Figure 8.1. Most jobs are interdependent and overlap in terms of employees' functions and efforts. Because jobs are constantly evolving, the challenge exists "to move beyond valid, job-based predictors" (Cascio, p. 932) to a solution process. This process would need to address issues such as the selection of individuals to work effectively as a team, optimal use of individuals with different levels of cognitive ability, and the effective application of various personality measures.

In 1990 the Americans with Disabilities Act (ADA) was enacted. It is a good example of how job analysis can assist in developing nondiscriminatory selection procedures. The ADA prohibits employers from discriminating against any individual with a disability who, with reasonable accommodation, can perform the "essential functions of the . . . position held or designed" (Gatewood & Feild, 1994, p. 32). A detailed and accurate job analysis defines job requirements as they currently exist or as they may exist with accommodations for disabled individuals.

Criterion and Predictor Variables

According to the model of selection demonstrated in Figure 8.1, information that is gathered during the job analysis is used in the development of job-related criteria (Figure 8.1, step 2a) and the selection of predictors (Figure 8.1, step 2b). To incorporate the material discussed in Chapters 5, 6, and 7 ("Criteria," "Performance Appraisal," and "Predictors") into our present discussion, let us remind ourselves of several important points.

As Figure 8.1 shows, criterion variables are defined before the predictors are selected. These criteria will determine the standards by which job performance is evaluated (Cascio & Awad, 1981; Schmitt & Robertson, 1990). The criterion is a reliable and valid measure of effective job performance that must also be relevant, sensitive, and practical. Once we know the characteristics we seek to predict, the next step is to select the appropriate measures to assess these characteristics. The following Widget example demonstrates the process.

THE WIDGET EXAMPLE

The management personnel at the Widget Corporation used the results of their job analysis to define criterion measures. Some of the measures included the number of computer parts produced, the amount of down-time due to computer problems, absenteeism rates, and level of job satisfaction. Other indices were job commitment and job turnover.

The next step was the development of predictors to improve outcomes in areas such as productivity and turnover. Before Widget computerized its production lines, the interview process was the main predictor used. However, because the Widget Corporation is a culturally diverse company in which employees are considered members of the corporate family, it was important to select applicants who fit into the corporate culture. The study that Widget's I/O psychologist carried out suggested that the battery of predictors in the Widget study should include applications; questionnaires; resumes; personal interviews; knowledge, skills, and abilities tests (including cognitive ability); and personality tests. The job analysis determined that an individual applying to work on the computerized production lines had to have good math and verbal skills. Therefore, tests of these skills were added to the battery.

The I/O psychologist integrated personality tests into the battery. These were included to assess whether an individual is likely to be conscientious and cooperative and would get along with peers and supervisors (Barrick & Mount, 1991; Day & Silverman, 1989; Jones, 1991). Personality measures were also given to determine an applicant's disposition toward illegal and counterproductive behavior such as violence, drug use, and theft. Practice Perspective 8.1 gives

---

PRACTICE PERSPECTIVE 8.1

The Spit Test

An example of a predictor variable developed for applicants to a variety of jobs was the spit test. Dr. James M. Dabbs, Jr. discussed the link between testosterone levels and acts of violence in an interview in the *Wall Street Journal*. The correlation between testosterone and behavior has shown that the higher the testosterone, the more violent the behavior. Dr. Dabbs developed a "Spit Test," in which he tested the level of testosterone in the saliva of different people. The sample, which consisted of 2,500 subjects, was made up of men and women from a variety of socioeconomic classes and included murderers, ministers, lawyers, and farmers. Dr. Dabbs found higher levels of testosterone in the saliva of attorneys, prisoners, and the unemployed. He reported lower levels of testosterone in the saliva of ministers, farmers, and white-collar managers. However, "the idea of spit tests . . . might be as hard for employers to stomach as it is for job applicants to swallow."

Source: Sharpe, A. (November 29, 1993). Spit testing may be hard to swallow in the workplace. *The Wall Street Journal,* p. A1.

an example of a predictor designed to identify individuals with violent dispositions.

Other predictor variables that were included in the Widget battery measured physical ability and computer knowledge. The I/O psychologist had to examine each of these predictors to ensure that they met legal guidelines and that they were reliable, valid, and practical.

Our previous discussions have already defined the process of selection (step 4 in Figure 8.1). Step 5 in Figure 8.1 was discussed in Chapter 6 ("Performance Appraisal"). We now move to the discussion of validation.

Validity and Selection System Validation

The next step in the development of a selection and placement system is validation. This involves determining what the selection tests are measuring and whether they predict successful job performance (Dunnette, 1966). SIOP (1987) defines validation as an effort by which a psychologist estimates how much meaning can be attributed to interpretations made from test scores. For example, Widget wants to determine whether its experimental selection battery can predict successful performance on the computerized production lines.

Dunnette (1966, p. 113) suggests that this process is "never ending," because each additional study adds information to the interpretations of test scores. For instance, continued research at the Widget Corporation could find that test scores are related to more than just job performance. Scores may also be related to tenure, the employee's fit into the company's culture, and compatibility with peers and supervisors.

Conceptually, validity is the "degree to which inferences from scores are justified or supported by evidence" (SIOP, 1987, p. 41). At the operational level, validity is the extent to which a test measures what it is supposed to measure. In general, the validation procedures provide support for the inferences drawn from test scores.

Validation Strategies

The goals of the organization and the researcher determine which validation strategies will be used. The strategies that SIOP (1987) recognizes are construct, content, predictive, and concurrent validity. Psychologists consider content and construct validation strategies to be test-oriented (also known as descriptive validity and logical validity). Predictive and concurrent strategies are categorized as criterion-oriented (also known as criterion-related validity and empirical validity). The questions considered by these strategies are twofold:

Content and construct strategies

What can be inferred about the test itself?

What is the intrinsic nature of the test?

(Does the test measure what it claims to measure?)

Predictive and concurrent strategies

What can be inferred about criterion behaviors?

How well are predictor scores related to criterion performance?

Content Validity

Content validity establishes the extent to which items on a test represent a defined area of skill. Content validity focuses on the subject matter of the test items. This type of validity is based on the selection of appropriate test items that cover the construct area. Performance on these items is therefore "a representative sample of job performance or job-required knowledge" (SIOP, 1987, p. 37). Widget management wants to hire individuals who have an extensive level of computer knowledge. Therefore, items on the computer knowledge test must represent the range of computer knowledge skills from the most basic to the most complex.

To meet Widget's requirements, a test will need to give applicants the opportunity to demonstrate their skill level. If the test measures only one level of skill, rather than a range of possible skill levels, many applicants may receive similar scores. When this occurs, the test has failed to differentiate among applicants for hiring decisions.

Another example is an instrument designed to assess basic math skills. The items on this instrument should measure addition, subtraction, multiplication, and division. If the test includes items that require knowledge of geometry, trigonometry, and calculus, then the test no longer focuses on basic mathematics. The test is not representative of the knowledge area it purports to measure. It is important to remember that content validity can be affected when a test underrepresents or overrepresents a skill or knowledge area.

Content validity can be empirically tested in several ways. One way is to develop two independent tests of the same content area, administer both tests to the same subjects, and then compare the results. Another method is to measure whether all test items are homogeneous in the content area being sampled. A third way is to compare dimensions of the job analysis with the content area sampled in the test and then assess the degree of agreement between them.

Construct Validity

A construct is a theoretically defined trait based on empirical evidence (SIOP, 1987) with the purpose of explaining observed consistencies in behavior. Some examples of constructs are integrity, dominance, and intelligence. Examples of constructs in the work environment are leadership, clerical ability, and being a team member.

Construct validity is "an attempt to demonstrate a relationship between [the] underlying traits or hypothetical constructs and job related behavior" (SIOP, 1987, p. 37). It determines the extent to which a test measures the characteristics of a particular construct. Suppose you have applicants complete a test of leadership ability, which has been shown to measure the trait of leadership. High-scoring applicants should exhibit various behaviors related to leadership, such as guiding other employees, directing new hires, and mentoring novices. Another example is the trait of assertiveness described in Scientific Perspective 8.1.

SCIENTIFIC PERSPECTIVE 8.1

Measuring Assertiveness

Suppose you were contacted by a company to develop an instrument to measure the construct of assertiveness. These are the steps you would take:

1. Define assertiveness on the basis of its behavioral correlates. For example, the literature suggests that assertive people usually take charge of group discussions, are generally more talkative than others, and are more likely to be identified as leaders by group members.
2. Identify measures for each of the above behavioral correlates, such as personality tests, success in assertiveness training programs, and leader behavior questionnaires.

3. Validate the tests of assertiveness. Apply all forms of validation to provide evidence of the construct validity of your assertiveness tests. For example, determine whether any significant differences exist between groups of people who are more talkative and those who are less talkative, correlate assertiveness training scores with the newly developed test scores, and correlate scores on leader behavior questionnaires with the new test scores.
4. Continue to validate the test with other relevant behavioral dimensions to improve description and to be able to use the new assertiveness test across a variety of situations.

The essential steps in determining construct validity (Cronbach & Meehl, 1955), are as follows:

1. Make hypotheses about the relationship between the construct or trait and its observable behaviors (e.g., responses on the job). The construct is defined by its behavioral correlates.
2. Develop a measure of the construct or trait.
3. Identify other measures of the same construct or trait that have evidence supporting their validity.
4. Conduct correlational and experimental studies to examine the hypothesized relationships (step 1) between the test that was developed to measure the particular trait (step 2) and other measures (step 3).

Construct validity is an ongoing process. The goal is to determine the meaning associated with a test score. Validation is used to build a "total network" of interpretations and predictions associated with scores individuals receive on a test (Dunnette, 1966, p. 113). As the amount of evidence supporting a test increases, the degree of construct validity also increases, and so does the level of confidence with which the test can be used.

The purpose of content and construct validity is to provide evidence that the test assesses the domain or the construct it claims to measure. To demonstrate the difference between content validity and construct validity, suppose you are asked to create a test that measures an individual's level of integrity. When attempting to establish content validity, you want to ensure that the test items represent the range of behaviors associated with integrity. Some examples may include telling the truth, not stealing, and not cheating. Content validity demonstrates how well the test items directly reflect the job knowledge, skills, and/or behaviors measured. When demonstrating construct validity, you would first define the theoretical trait underlying integrity and then identify items that best measure that trait.

Criterion-Related Validity

In our Widget Corporation example, the company is interested in the relationship between an applicant's computer knowledge test score and the likelihood of success on the job. To investigate this relationship, criterion-related validity should be applied. This type of validity provides empirical evidence of the relationship between the predictor and the criterion. To confirm that criterion validity exists, test scores are compared with performance on the job. Suppose you conduct a criterion-related validity study of the integrity test. The results provide the correlation between scores on this test and the number of times the employee had stolen computer parts on the job. These results do not allow us to draw a conclusion about whether the test measures the underlying construct called integrity. We can only make predictions about the likelihood that the applicant will steal on the job.

Concurrent Validity. As illustrated in Figure 8.2a on page 254, **concurrent validity** is established by collecting test scores and criterion information concurrently (simultaneously) from current employees.

The relationship between the test (predictor) and the criterion is evaluated by correlating predictor scores with criterion scores. Suppose the Widget Corporation took this approach. Employees would take the computer knowledge test (predictor), and at the same time their supervisors would rate them on productivity (the criterion) without any knowledge of the corresponding predictor scores. After the data were collected, the employee test scores would be correlated with their productivity ratings. The resulting correlation coefficient, or validity coefficient, would indicate the strength of the relationship between the predictor and the criterion for current employees.

Predictive Validity. Figure 8.2b shows how **predictive validity** is established in two steps. First, the researcher collects predictor information from all applicants. Subsequently, criterion data

a. Concurrent

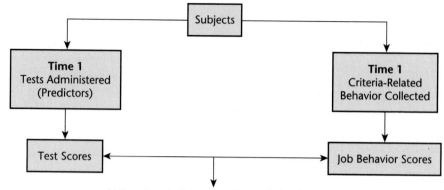

At time 1, calculate concurrent relationships.

b. Predictive

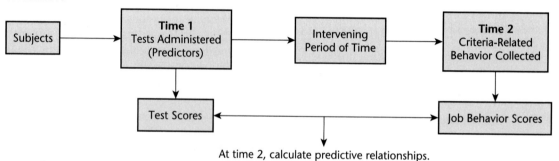

At time 2, calculate predictive relationships.

FIGURE 8.2 Criterion-related validation strategies.

Source: From *Personnel Selection and Placement* (pp. 115–116), by M. D. Dunnette (1966). Belmont, CA: Wadsworth. Original copyright 1966 by Wadsworth. Current copyright held by M. D. Dunnette. Used by permission of M. D. Dunnette.

are collected, perhaps as much as six months to a year later. As in the concurrent validity model, the relationship between the predictor and the criterion is determined by correlating predictor scores with criterion ratings.

Concurrent Validity versus Predictive Validity

Both concurrent validity and predictive validity have advantages and disadvantages in terms of issues such as motivation, time, subjects, characteristics measured, frequency of use, range restrictions, and sample size. As discussed in the following sections, comparisons between con-

current and predictive validity demonstrate that what is considered a strength for predictive validity is sometimes a weakness for concurrent validity, and vice versa.

Motivation

The motivation to do well on a predictive measure may be different for applicants than it is for employees. Concurrent validity studies use current employees who have experience in performing particular duties in a particular environment. Their test scores may be biased because there is no benefit in doing well on the test. These employees are already employed and, therefore, have less at stake than do the applicants. The

TABLE 8.2	A comparison of concurrent and predictive validation strategies	
	Validation Strategy Approach	
Variable	*Concurrent*	*Predictive*
Time	Immediate	6 months to 1 year
Subjects	Incumbents	Applicants
Characteristic measured	Actual + experience	Actual
Frequency of use	High	Less often
Range restriction	Smaller	Larger
Sample size	Larger	Smaller

predictive validity approach uses applicant data. The applicants are motivated to give their best performance on the predictor to increase their chance of securing employment.

Other factors that demonstrate the strengths and weaknesses associated with each of these strategies are summarized in Table 8.2.

Time

As indicated in Table 8.2, the time factor is the delay between administrations of the predictor and criterion measures. Each approach differs in the time required to complete data collection. The concurrent approach collects data simultaneously on the predictor and criterion measures because the sample consists of existing employees. The predictive approach is at a disadvantage because administration of the criterion measure may be delayed up to one year.

Subjects

As Table 8.2 shows, concurrent validity uses present employees and predictive validity strategy uses applicants. The main issue regarding participants is the problem of attrition, or the loss of participants before all of the data can be collected. When the predictive validity model is applied, attrition can occur at two points in the data collection process: at the time of hire or after hire but before criterion collection can occur.

This approach is often criticized because, theoretically, all of the applicants should be selected for employment. Most organizations are not likely to hire all applicants, so a loss of participants occurs at the beginning of data collection. In conducting predictive validity studies, the criterion measure is collected after the newly hired applicants have been working in a particular position for an amount of time. If an applicant's employment is terminated before the criterion data are collected, validity is affected by the reduction in sample size.

The concurrent approach is not as susceptible to attrition as is the predictive approach. The concurrent approach has the advantage of a large sample whose performance on the criterion measure is known at the time of test administration. One criticism of this approach is that there may be an erroneous increase in the validity coefficient. This can be the result of current employees' experience on the job, which allows them to master or improve the abilities measured by the predictor. The researcher is responsible for selecting the appropriate approach and being able to defend that choice.

Characteristics Measured

Another question to consider is: What does each strategy measure? A researcher who uses the concurrent validity approach must acknowledge that the predictor is measuring abilities or skills *plus* experience (see Table 8.2). Data are collected from present employees, whose test responses may be biased because of experience on the job, in the organization, and working with their peers. On the other hand, the predictive validity approach uses data from job applicants who are assumed to have no on-the-job experience. The researcher postulates that the only characteristics being measured are those the predictor purports to measure.

Frequency of Use

The concurrent model is employed more often than the predictive model, because of convenience, cost, and time considerations. Anastasi (1988) suggests that concurrent validation is often a substitute for predictive validation because it is less time consuming. From an economic perspective, organizations do not typically have the luxury of time required by the predictive validity model.

Range Restriction

As previously explained, the normal distribution represents the total possible range of scores for a particular measure. The correlation coefficient is based on the bivariate distribution of two variables, demonstrated by the shape of the scattergram. For the Widget Corporation this range of data represents the distribution of scores achieved on the computer knowledge test (predictor) and the supervisors' ratings (criterion measure). As the scattergram becomes more restricted and the distribution of scores deviates from the normal shape, the accuracy of the correlation coefficient is directly affected. As Table 8.2 demonstrates, these effects have more of an impact on the results of concurrent validity. To clarify these effects, let us examine Figures 8.3a and 8.3b. These figures show how the restriction of scores for the predictor and criterion affect the shape of the scattergram and the size of the correlation coefficient.

As Guion (1965, p. 141) describes it, the correlation coefficient assumes a linear relationship that "takes on an elliptical shape. . . . If either end of the ellipse is removed, then it obviously becomes wider relative to its length; likewise the correlation coefficient of remaining cases is

smaller." For example, the Widget Corporation's goal is to obtain a validity coefficient that is as accurate as possible. This coefficient becomes less accurate when the data from the computer knowledge test and productivity ratings do not represent the entire range of possible scores (Barrett, Phillips, & Alexander, 1981).

Figure 8.3a presents an example of range restriction for the concurrent validity strategy. The restriction occurs at the lower part of the distribution because employees who were unqualified and those who transferred, quit, or were terminated during the study are not included. The loss of these employees creates range restriction because the remaining sample consists only of successful employees. These are the employees who have high scores on the criterion. In Figure 8.3a the arrow indicates a job behavior level above which employees are considered successful. The area of the scattergram below the arrow includes employees who are considered unsuccessful. This area indicates performance data lost to the validity study. In this example, the validity study was carried out only on the forty employees remaining in the computer department (the upper part of the ellipse). The remaining part of the ellipse is rounder, and the resulting correlation amounts to only $r = .35$. Had all the original employees been included, the correlation would have been higher, because the employees who were dropped had low predictor scores and low performance.

Figure 8.3b shows the predictive model. Range restriction occurs here because of the number and types of positions available. This form of restriction happens when an organization hires only the applicants who receive scores above a cutoff point on the predictor (to the right side of the arrow on the scattergram). Because only applicants who have these final predictor scores are hired, the resulting range of scores used in the study is limited (i.e., restricted). The validity coefficient calculated on the selected forty applicants in this example is a low correlation, $r = .20$. The correlation coefficient would have been higher if all applicants could have been included. Because range restric-

a. Concurrent Validation

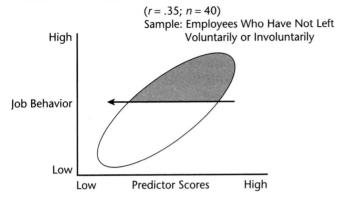

b. Predictive Validation

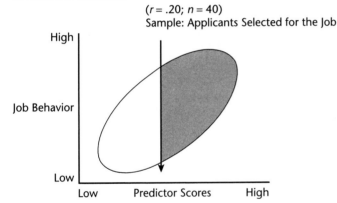

FIGURE 8.3
Range restriction
in criterion-related
validation strategies.

tion biases validity studies, some companies will try to hire all the applicants tested, at least occasionally. When this is done, the range restriction is eliminated, and a "pure" predictive validity study can be completed.

Sample Size

The issue of sample size relates to the need for statistical power. As the sample size increases, so does the researcher's ability to make appropriate conclusions based on the results of a given statistic. The goal is to have a sample that is large enough to provide a significant level of confidence in the conclusions drawn from the study's results.

For the Widget Corporation, the sample that is used for the computer knowledge test must represent the population of either current employees or job applicants and be large enough to ensure the accuracy of predictions. According to Guion (1991), estimates of sample sizes differ among researchers, but they should consist of more than the thirty to fifty participants traditionally used.

In summary, it is important to remember that studies using the concurrent validity model usually have access to larger samples because the participants are current employees. Predictive validity models include only applicants who are hired, and involve a smaller group. These small samples often fail to reflect the characteristics of the normal distribution, a result that reduces the likelihood of obtaining a stable or accurate estimate of validity.

Guion and Cranny (1982) argue that even when a researcher must work with the concurrent model, it is not an adequate substitute for predictive validity. Guion (1965) points out that the samples that are used with each approach represent different populations; the predictive approach tests applicants, while the concurrent approach tests employees.

Whichever approach is the most practical for an organization, the goal is to take advantage of individual differences in selecting employees. This allows management to choose the individuals who are most likely to succeed on the job.

Cross-Validation

The analysis of data requires an additional step to ensure the stability of the validity coefficient. Step 7, illustrated in Figure 8.1, is the process of cross-validation. For the Widget Corporation the results of the criterion-related validity study produced a regression equation and correlation coefficient that describe the relationship between performance on the computer knowledge test and productivity. To determine whether the results are due to the characteristics of the original sample, Widget must assess the stability of this relationship using another sample. The second sample is drawn randomly from either the population of applicants or the population of employees. The regression equation developed on the original sample is applied to reassess the relationship between the predictor and the criterion. An example of this process carried out by Widget Corporation for the computer knowledge and math tests is demonstrated in Practice Perspective 8.2.

The validity coefficient may be inflated, or appear larger, than it actually is. Cross-validation provides the opportunity to reassess the relationship between the predictor and the criterion, using a second sample that is similar to the first. The results of cross-validation establish a more realistic picture of test predictability.

Moderator Variables

A **moderator variable** affects the relationship between the predictor and the criterion. An ex-

---

PRACTICE PERSPECTIVE 8.2

Example of a Concurrent Validation Study

In an original concurrent validation study of sixty-five secretaries, the Widget Corporation gave each secretary the computer knowledge test and a simple math test and then collected criterion performance scores. A multiple regression analysis was performed between the two tests and the number of requisition forms completed, resulting in a multiple correlation coefficient of .79.

A second sample of sixty secretaries was drawn from the current employee population. Widget's managers determined the predicted criterion scores of the second sample by applying the original multiple regression equation. They then recalculated the multiple correlation coefficient by correlating the predicted criterion scores and the actual criterion scores achieved by the second sample, resulting in a coefficient of .75.

The managers compared the two multiple correlations (.79 and .75) and concluded that the difference between the two multiple correlations was small enough to indicate a successful cross-validation. The relationship between the two tests and the measure of productivity was stable, indicating that using the two tests to predict future performance was feasible and valid.

a. Total Sample

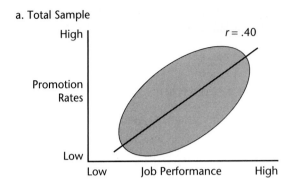

b. Males

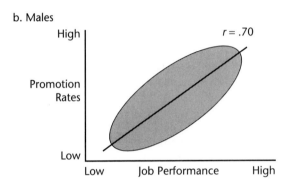

c. Females

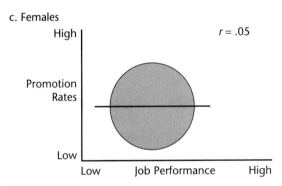

FIGURE 8.4   The moderating effects of gender.

ample of a moderator variable is gender. Suppose Widget is interested in the relationship between job performance and promotion rates and that a low positive relationship is found to exist between them. As Figure 8.4a shows, as job performance improves, so does the number

of promotions. Therefore, Widget decides that job performance should be the basis for promoting employees.

However, when gender is considered, the relationship between job performance and promotion is stronger for males (see Figure 8.4b) than for females (see Figure 8.4c). These results indicate that not all employees in Widget are measured with the same precision (Dunnette, 1966). The predictability of job performance for promotion rates is different for the two subgroups. The conclusion is that Widget must review its promotion policies to prevent discriminating against women for higher-level positions. If this promotion practice continues, a larger proportion of men will have higher-level positions than women, and women may bring discrimination charges against the company to correct this unfair practice.

In this situation, gender was not correlated with either the predictor or the criterion. However, gender did moderate, or affect, the degree of the relationship between performance and promotion. Examples of moderators that include individual differences or demographic variables are age, weight, and socioeconomic status. Statistical analyses have identified other moderator variables, which include organizational climate, management philosophy, leadership style, and job tasks over time (e.g., Schmidt, Hunter, & Pearlman, 1981). Other studies (e.g., Schmidt & Hunter, 1978) claimed that evidence of the presence of existing moderators depends on different variables, such as sample size.

Suppressor Variables

A **suppressor variable** is correlated with the predictor, rather than the criterion, and influences the accurate prediction of criterion scores. The more a predictor accounts for the variance in a criterion variable, the stronger is the relationship between those variables. A suppressor variable affects this relationship by reducing the variance in predictor scores that is irrelevant to the criterion.

An Example of Suppressor Variables

Dunnette (1966) presents the following example of suppressor variables:

$$r_{sp} = +.40$$
$$r_{vp} = .00$$
$$r_{sv} = +.70$$
$$R_{(sv)p} = +.56$$

s = spatial reasoning test (predictor)

v = verbal reasoning test (suppressor)

p = job proficiency rating (criterion)

The first correlation shows the relationship between the spatial reasoning test and job proficiency (.40). The second correlation shows that there is no relationship between the verbal reasoning test and job proficiency ratings (.00). The third correlation demonstrates that spatial reasoning and verbal reasoning are highly correlated (.70). According to Dunnette, it would seem that verbal reasoning is not a useful variable. However, when verbal reasoning is included in the correlation between spatial reasoning and job proficiency ratings, the overall multiple correlation increases to .56.

The increase in the correlation between the spatial reasoning test and job proficiency scores occurs because the verbal reasoning test accounts for variance in the spatial reasoning test that is unrelated to job proficiency ratings. The result is a reduction in the amount of variance unaccounted for in the spatial reasoning test scores. After removal of the portion of variance in the spatial reasoning test that is unrelated to job proficiency ratings, the remaining variance in the spatial reasoning test (shared with the job proficiency ratings) is proportionally larger and therefore increases the size of the relationship between the variables: $R_{(sv)p} = .56$.

Source: Dunnette, M. D. (1966). *Personnel selection and placement* (pp. 140–141). Belmont, CA: Wadsworth.

Historical Perspective 8.1 illustrates the effects of suppressor variables. Dunnette (1966) demonstrates how a suppressor variable, when incorporated into a multiple regression equation, increases the formula's predictive value.

Although the suppressor variable increases the ability to predict a criterion score, it rarely is identified. The search for a suppressor variable is costly because it is difficult to isolate variables that are not correlated to the criterion.

Moderator and suppressor variables influence the validity, or the relationship between two variables. Validity generalization (discussed later in the chapter) is often used to quantify, remove, and demonstrate the effects of moderator variables on validity.

MAKING SELECTION DECISIONS

Once a valid relationship has been shown to exist between predictors and criterion, the decision of how to select employees must be made. In making these decisions, the organization considers its own needs, the number of positions available, the labor market, economic issues, and other related factors. Additionally and supplementary to predictors' validity, the company has to take into account the factors of selection ratio and the base rate discussed in this section. All this information will help Widget's management to determine how many jobs to fill and the quality of successful applicants.

Selection Ratio

The **selection ratio** (*SR*) is the ratio of the number of job openings (*n*) to the number of applicants to that job (*N*) (*SR* = *n/N*). For example, when the number of job applicants is equal to the number of positions available, the *SR* is 1.00 (see Figure 8.5a), and all applicants are hired. The *SR* is important because it affects the quality of applicants selected and contributes to the utility, or economic value, of a predictor.

If Widget had eight job openings and ten job applicants, the *SR* would equal 8/10, or .80 (see Figure 8.5b). If there were only two job openings and ten applicants, the *SR* would equal 0.20 (see Figure 8.5c) and only two applicants would be hired. If Widget had eight job openings and four applicants, the *SR* would equal 8/4, or 2.0. In the first and second examples there are more applicants than job openings; in the last example there are more job openings than applicants. When Widget Corporation has more applicants than jobs, Widget can rank-order the applicants on the basis of their predictor scores and select the top applicants. When there are more positions than applicants (*SR* > 1.00), Widget Corporation can hire all of the applicants who are willing to take positions. However, some of the new employees may not be as productive or successful as others.

The size of the selection ratio is affected by labor market conditions, money budgeted for recruitment, and compensation available for each position. For example, in a tight labor market in which there are few applicants, the selection ratio would be large (e.g., *SR* = 8 vacancies/2 applicants = 4.00). In a loose labor market, as in periods of high unemployment, the selection ratio would be small (e.g., *SR* = 2 vacancies/8 applicants = .25). The stricter a company is in selecting and hiring job applicants, the higher is the probability of securing higher-quality employees.

Base Rate

The **base rate** compares the number of current employees who are considered successful to the

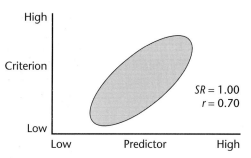

a. Scatter plot showing relationships (*r* = 0.70) between predictor and criterion. *SR* = 1.00, i.e., all applicants are being hired.

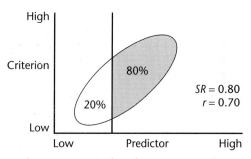

b. Same scatter plot when *SR* = 0.80. There are eight job openings for every ten applicants. Thus the lower 20 percent on the predictor can be rejected.

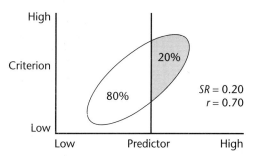

c. Same scatter plot when *SR* = 0.20. There are only two job openings for every ten applicants. Thus the lower 80 percent on the predictor can be rejected.

FIGURE 8.5   The effect of selection ratio (*SR*) on the average quality of those being hired.

Source: From M. L. Blum and J. C. Naylor (1968). *Industrial Psychology: Its Theoretical and Social Foundations,* Revised Edition (p. 47). New York: Harper & Row. Copyright © 1968 by M. L. Blum and J. C. Naylor. Reprinted by permission of HarperCollins Publishers, Inc.

total number of employees in the organization. Employees are considered successful if their score on the criterion measure equals or exceeds the organization's minimally acceptable level of performance.

The base rate serves two purposes. First, it is an indicator of the number of successful employees in the organization. This information, used with the selection ratio, can identify the applicants who will enhance the quality of the current staff. Second, the base rate provides insight into the effectiveness of a newly developed selection system. It can determine whether the new system improves the ratio of successful employees within an organization.

An example of a low base rate may be 10 successful employees/100 total employees = .10. A low base rate indicates that most of the current employees are performing poorly and that implementing a new selection system may improve the quality of the future work force. When most of the employees are performing successfully and the base rate approaches 1.0, it is not necessary to create a new selection system. The new system will not increase the number of successful employees.

Base rates can be discussed in relative or absolute terms. For example, a new selection system may improve a base rate from 5% to 10%. In absolute terms this is only a 5% improvement. In relative terms it is a 100% improvement (original 5% base rate/5% improvement).

Therefore in relative terms, lower base rates increase the likelihood that a new predictor will increase successful job performance.

The base rate is only one aspect of information that researchers use in determining whether a selection system is effective. Recent research compares the benefits of a new selection system (e.g., qualified employees, a work force with more tenure) with associated costs for the development, implementation, and administration of the system. We will discuss more of these issues later in the chapter (in the section on utility analysis).

Cutoff Scores

When validity evidence exists, **cutoff scores,** on both the predictor and the criterion, represent the minimal level of performance an organization considers acceptable (on the predictor and the job). The purpose of a cutoff score is to identify the applicants who have the highest probability of being successful on the job. Figure 8.6 is an example of a cutoff score on the criterion. Employees who perform above this criterion score are considered successful; those who perform below it are categorized by management as poor performers.

For example, suppose there are 100 questions on the computer knowledge test and productivity is measured on a scale of 1 to 5 (1 = low, 5 = superior). Widget may select a score of 3 as a minimal acceptable criterion score. This

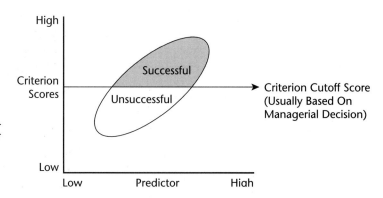

FIGURE 8.6
Cutoff score based on acceptable criterion performance.

Source: From M. L. Blum and J. C. Naylor (1968). *Industrial Psychology: Its Theoretical and Social Foundations,* Revised Edition (p. 49). New York: Harper & Row. Copyright © 1968 by M. L. Blum and J. C. Naylor. Reprinted by permission of HarperCollins Publishers, Inc.

criterion score can be used to determine the minimal acceptable score on the predictor (the computer knowledge test). If Widget finds that a significant number of individuals who receive a criterion rating of 3 also obtain a predictor score of 80, then Widget may decide that 80 is an appropriate predictor cutoff score for selection purposes.

To summarize, the criterion cutoff is set by management and influences the predictor cutoff on the basis of the validity coefficient. The minimum criterion performance is considered the point below which performance on the job is considered unacceptable. In setting the predictor cutoff score, the minimum acceptable criterion is considered because the goal is to identify the people who will perform best on the job. Regardless of the approach, the cutoff scores must be set at a point at which errors are minimized and the probability of successful performance is maximized. We discuss more of these issues in the section on selection outcomes.

Establishing a cutoff score requires more than empirical or statistical support that incorporates predictor validity, the selection ratio, and the base rate (Taylor & Russell, 1939). It also requires the test developer to make a value judgment (Cronbach, 1990; Nunnally, 1993; Thorndike, 1982). Additionally, social, economic, practical, and personal factors must be considered.

Social factors and legal requirements mandate that members of minorities and other protected groups have equal opportunity for employment. Using predictor cutoff scores that are biased against members of such a group results in applicants being unfairly deprived of employment. This process can cause personal problems for the applicants such as reduced self-esteem due to failure or stereotyping associated with group membership. Economic considerations involve the cost of selecting and training someone who is not qualified for the job. Practical considerations are the selection ratio and organizational need. Personal factors include the researcher's judgment when setting the cutoff score, and the importance of social, economic, and prac-

tical considerations in light of organizational objectives.

Expectancy Tables

After validation, selection ratio, base rate, and cutoff scores are established, and the test is approved for use in the selection process, the organization must determine how effective the test is in identifying quality applicants. According to Guion (1965), organizations need to be able to predict that the probability of selecting satisfactory employees is greater than chance. The purpose of developing selection instruments is to reduce chance errors in the prediction and selection processes.

Expectancy tables are created to establish the probability that a selected employee will turn out to be a good performer once he or she is placed on the job. The purpose is to increase the overall proportion of future satisfactory employees (Lawshe, Bolda, Brune, & Auclair, 1958). Table 8.3 is an example of an individual expectancy table that shows the probability of success on the job for each range of test scores—that is, the likelihood that an applicant with a predictor score in a specific range will attain a given level of job success. Table 8.3 shows that an applicant who scores between 5 and 10 on the aptitude test will have a lower probability of achieving an acceptable performance level (e.g., 15%) than will an individual who scores between 16 and 20 (e.g., 30%).

TABLE 8.3   Individual Expectancy Table

| Test Score | Chances of Different Level of Success | | |
	Low	Average	Superior
5–10	85%	15%	0%
11–15	60%	25%	15%
16–20	25%	30%	45%
21–25	5%	40%	55%

TABLE 8.4	Institutional Expectancy Table		
	Criterion Scores		
Selection Ratio	Low	Average	Superior
Best 15%	0	10	90
Best 40%	10	20	70
Best 75%	20	25	55

Table 8.4 is an example of an institutional expectancy table. Any organization that uses the selection ratio, discussed earlier, can use this type of chart to predict the percentage of successful applicants given a particular selection ratio. In addition, institutional expectancy charts provide the organization with information that can be used to determine a cutoff score for the selection instrument, that is, the minimum scores applicants must achieve to be hired. As Table 8.4 shows, the smaller the selection ratio (e.g., the best 15%), the higher is the proportion of selected applicants that will achieve high criterion scores in the future (90%). Therefore, when the number of jobs available is limited, the cutoff scores associated with smaller selection ratios could be used to increase the probability of selecting qualified applicants. Taking into account the various factors contributing to an effective selection process (e.g., validity, selection ratio, and utility, discussed later in the chapter) expectancy charts are effective because they "can be developed directly from empirical data, so that one's statement of what he/[she] expects in the future is precisely what he/[she] found in the past" (Guion, 1965, p. 158).

Selection Outcomes

Four possible outcomes are associated with a selection decision and the consideration of predictor and criterion cutoff scores. These four outcomes, as illustrated by Figure 8.7, are correct acceptances, erroneous acceptances, correct rejections, and erroneous rejections. Figure 8.7 shows the effects of combining predictor and criterion cutoffs on the selection outcomes.

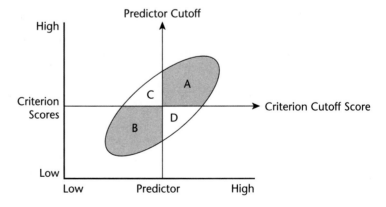

FIGURE 8.7
Selection outcomes.

Source: From M. L. Blum and J. C. Naylor (1968). *Industrial Psychology: Its Theoretical and Social Foundations,* Revised Edition (p. 49). New York: Harper & Row. Copyright © 1968 by M. L. Blum and J. C. Naylor. Reprinted by permission of HarperCollins Publishers, Inc.

Note: A = true positives
B = true negatives
C = false negatives
D = false positives

Correct acceptances, or **true positives,** represent applicants selected on the basis of predictor scores who are found to be successful at the time of performance appraisals (Figure 8.7, Quadrant A). **Correct rejections,** or **true negatives,** represent applicants who were rejected on the basis of predictor scores who would have been unsuccessful on the job if hired (Figure 8.7, Quadrant B). **Erroneous acceptances,** or **false positives,** represent applicants selected on the basis of predictor scores whose performance appraisals later determine that they are unsuccessful on the job (Figure 8.7, Quadrant D). **Erroneous rejections,** or **false negatives,** represent applicants who were predicted to be unsatisfactory employees but who would have performed well on the job if hired (Figure 8.7, Quadrant C).

The decision maker's goal is to maximize correct acceptances and rejections, while minimizing erroneous acceptances and rejections. As Blum and Naylor (1968) indicate, the purpose is to maximize the percentage of applicants employed whose performance is satisfactory (Quadrant A).

Cascio, Alexander, and Barrett (1988) discussed three scenarios involving cutoff scores in employment situations. First, some private organizations may continuously test new applicants to create a pool of potentially successful applicants. In this situation, a pool is created on the basis of the applicants' scores on the predictor. Applicants who meet or exceed the predictor cutoff score form the pool from which future employees will be selected. Applicants who do not reach the cutoff scores are not eligible for employment. The applicants remaining in the pool are then rank-ordered, from high to low, on the basis of their predictor score. When a job becomes available, the applicants with the greatest probabilities of success on the job are contacted.

The second scenario involves public organizations, in which the number of applicants far exceeds the number of available positions. In these organizations, such as the U.S. Postal Service, which is the nation's largest employer, it is not necessary to create a pool of potentially successful applicants. The organization rank-orders all applicants according to their predictor score. Because of the large number of applicants, there is less concern with the criterion cutoff score. The number of applicants allows the selection of only those applicants who are top performers on the predictor.

The third situation involves both public and private organizations, in which tests are frequently used as screening devices. Cutoff scores are often used to identify applicants who will be allowed to proceed to successive stages of the selection process. For example, important prerequisites for firefighters may include general cognitive ability, physical ability, and analytic skills. For the position of firefighter, physical ability may be considered the most important attribute, followed by general cognitive ability and analytic skills. It may be financially prudent for the fire department to allow only the applicants who meet the physical requirements to proceed through the selection process.

STRATEGIES IN SELECTION DECISION MAKING

Cascio et al. (1988) state that explicit formulas or rules dictate selection decisions. These include multiple regression, multiple cutoff, and multiple hurdles.

Multiple Regression

Multiple regression is based on three assumptions: that a linear relationship exists between the predictors and the criterion, that this relationship is additive, and that the predictors are compensatory. Because multiple regression involves the sum of two or more weighted predictor scores, this method is compensatory. That means that a low score on Test A is compensated for by a high score on Test B. Therefore an applicant may receive a low score on one predictor, but if the other scores are high enough to compensate for that low score, the applicant may still be judged acceptable. This method depends on the sum of predictor scores, so applicants whose predictor scores differ may have identical predicted criterion scores.

The following example shows the multiple regression equations for applicants A and B:

The multiple regression equation is:

$$y = a + b_1(x_1) + b_2(x_2)$$

where

y = criterion score

a = constant

b = weights given to predictors

x_1 = first predictor score

x_2 = second predictor score

Applicant A: $50 = 5 + 3(5) + 2.5(12)$

Applicant B: $50 = 5 + 3(10) + 2.5(6)$

Applicant A has a lower score on measure x_1 than on x_2. The score on x_2 is high enough to compensate for the lower score on x_1, so the applicant is considered acceptable for hire. The reverse is true of Applicant B, who received a higher score on predictor x_1. Both applicants received a predicted criterion score of 50, which will qualify them for being selected.

One disadvantage of multiple regression is that the procedures involved in the computation of multiple regression analysis are complex, which can make it difficult to explain and defend. Another disadvantage is that applicants may be approved for hire even though they have not performed satisfactorily on each component of the battery (Anastasi, 1988).

An alternative strategy is the multiple-cutoff approach, which disallows the compensatory characteristics of multiple regression. The multiple-cutoff approach considers each predictor independently of the other.

Multiple Cutoff

Compared to multiple regression, the **multiple-cutoff** selection strategy considers individual predictor scores for each attribute. Minimum cutoff scores are set for each predictor, following the assumption that a minimal level of proficiency on all predictors is required. An applicant who meets or exceeds the minimum cutoffs on all predictors is qualified to be accepted. An applicant who scores below the minimum cutoff on any of the predictors is rejected. This strategy is noncompensatory, a feature that addresses the criticism of multiple regression, so individual predictors do not compensate for each other.

For example, Widget Corporation has decided to hire computer programmers to develop programs for its mathematics software line. Management decides to give a computer knowledge test and a mathematics test to each applicant. One applicant scores above the minimum cutoff on the computer knowledge test but below the minimum cutoff on the mathematics test. Despite the applicant's high degree of computer knowledge, success as a computer programmer is unlikely because of the applicant's low level of mathematical understanding. The high computer knowledge score cannot compensate for the poor mathematics score. This approach is appropriate when minimal levels of proficiency in certain skill areas are required for successful job performance.

The main advantage of the multiple-cutoff technique is that it is easy to use and understand. No complicated mathematical formulas are required, so communicating the results to an organization's staff members is relatively easy. The multiple-cutoff technique also has disadvantages. A major one involves determining the cutoff scores for each of the predictors without discriminating against any of the applicants.

Therefore the validity of the cutoff scores must be established before using any of the tests.

Multiple Hurdles

A third selection strategy is the **multiple-hurdles** approach. This procedure involves gathering and evaluating information on predictors sequentially and over a period of time. This is a process that is analogous to the sport of hurdling. On a track, a hurdler must successively clear each hurdle to reach the finish line. Similarly, applicants must clear successive hurdles during the selection process. If an applicant does not clear any hurdle, progress to the next hurdle is not permitted, and the applicant is rejected. This strategy is like the multiple-cutoff method because it is noncompensatory.

This strategy can be advantageous to both the organization and the applicant. Unqualified applicants are identified early in the selection process. This saves an applicant the time and inconvenience of completing the entire process. The organization is spared the time and cost of further testing.

Muchinsky (1986) suggests that the accuracy of predicting job performance increases with longer observation times and successive evaluations. The cost of reaching a final decision may serve as a disadvantage to the organization. At the same time, the applicant pool decreases after each hurdle, so the cost of further testing may be reduced. Another disadvantage to the multiple-hurdle approach is the range restriction that occurs on the predictor scores. This happens because at each successive hurdle, fewer applicants continue with the next step of evaluation. The applicants who reach the "finish line" represent only the high range of the normal distribution, or the top performers.

There is no one best way to make final decisions about applicants. The strategy that is selected must best serve the organization's desired outcome when it is compared to other strategies of selection.

UTILITY ANALYSIS

Utility analysis was developed to forecast the financial benefits of a selection system (Latham & Whyte, 1994). Utility is "the degree to which a selection measure improves the quality of individuals selected over what would have happened if the measure had not been used" (Gatewood & Feild, 1964, p. 243). **Utility analysis** consists of determining the payoff of a selection procedure to the organization. It is expressed in the amount of money an organization saves because of a new selection system. The utility of a selection strategy is its usefulness and benefits to the organization as a whole.

As a quantitative approach, utility analysis ultimately becomes a balance sheet. The costs and benefits are compared to determine whether the new selection system results in financial gain. Some of the factors that are considered in determining utility are: validity of the tests, average test scores of selected applicants, and how effective selected applicants are on the job (Guion, 1991). A number of utility models exist, each differing slightly from the other with regard to overall costs and benefits.

Schmidt, Hunter, Outerbridge, and Trattner (1986) provide an example of the utility of an alternative selection system for white-collar jobs in the federal government. Results of the study suggest that increases in performance were found when selection was based on valid measures of cognitive ability, rather than evaluating education and experience. The amount of money that was saved was up to $600 million for every year the new employees continued their employment. Federal employees remain with the government an average of about thirteen years. During that time, the federal government would save almost $8 billion.

Another model of utility analysis is based on decision theory. As we mentioned before, decision theory focuses on the outcomes of selection decisions, taking into account the selection ratio, base rate, cutoff scores and percent improvement in the quality of employed applicants. Accordingly, a selection strategy is effective (has utility) to the extent to which the proportion of successful employees selected by the new strategy or new predictors is greater than the proportion of successful employees among those currently employed (i.e., those selected by "whatever selection methods used prior to the introduction of the new predictor [or strategy]" (Blum & Naylor, 1968, p. 50). With use of the quadrant reasoning in Figure 8.7 and its application to *present* employees who were selected by the *old* predictor or strategy, the percent of present employees considered successful is

$$(A + C / A + B + C + D)$$

where $A + C$ refers to the number of present employees who perform above the criterion cutoff and $A + B + C + D$ relate to all current employees in the organization previously hired by the *old* system of selection. By again using the categorization presented in Figure 8.7, but applying it to employees who were selected and hired by the *new* system (or predictor), the ratio of successful employees is

$$A/(A + D)$$

where A is the number of employees hired by the *new* system who are considered successful and $A + D$ is the number of all applicants hired by the new system.

By comparison of the two rates of success, utility is defined as the percent of improvement in the performance and quality of employees hired using the *new* selection system. This can be expressed as

$$[A/(A + D)] - [(A + C)/(A + B + C + D)]$$

A positive result will show there is utility in using the new system of selection (Blum & Naylor, 1968, p. 50).

Researchers and practitioners in I/O psychology and human resources have argued that, despite the impressive improvement utility analysis has made in the effectiveness of personnel selection decisions, two issues should be noted: the influence utility analysis has on management personnel decisions and the fact that estimating the dollar value of utility analysis outcomes is complex. For example, performance sometimes changes over time, some performance variables cannot be measured financially, and the utility benefits to the individual could be different than those to the organization.

Latham and Whyte (1994) showed that managers were not affected by possible gains and benefits of a utility analysis. Furthermore, the estimation of the results of the utility analysis reduced management support for implementing the new selection strategy. The researchers presented a group of 143 managers with a utility analysis of a selection system that would lead to improved employee performance and financial gains to the corporation. The findings indicated that these managers "did not base their decisions on the quantifiable costs and benefits of the utility analysis" (p. 41). Latham and Whyte recommended including managers in conducting utility analysis.

Boudreau (1991) claimed that attaching a dollar value to utility analysis involves a liaison between I/O personnel decision models and human resource functions such as accounting, marketing and finance. As a result, utility analysis models should address not only consequences related to productivity, but also economic and financial outcomes such as discounts, sales revenue, and taxes.

VALIDITY GENERALIZATION

The concept of **validity generalization,** as established by Schmidt and Hunter (1977), refers to the "evidence that the results of validity studies obtained in one or more studies may be appropriately applied to other situations involving the same or similar jobs" (SIOP, 1987, p. 41). The goal of validity generalization is to establish predictor validity that is generalizable across similar jobs and situations. For example, consider the case of a corporate psychologist who needs to use a test of knowledge of a computer system for applicants for a computer programmer job. An appropriate method is to examine the validity study results that Widget had achieved for its computer knowledge test in hiring its computer employees. If the test were found to be valid for Widget and if the psychologist can find evidence of other studies supporting these results, then he or she can consider adopting the test for use in that company.

Historically, Ghiselli (1966, 1973) combined the results of various validity studies that had predicted performance and training criteria for similar or identical jobs. Ghiselli found extensive variability among the reported validity coefficients, a result that led to the development of the situational specificity hypothesis. The specificity hypothesis suggests that validity studies are specific to each job and to each job situation. As a result, individual validity studies are necessary for different jobs, organizations, groups of employees and applicants, and for any test used in personnel selection. This hypothesis was accepted as a doctrine of I/O psychology until the 1970s, when Schmidt and Hunter developed the concept validity generalization and the procedures of meta-analysis (see Chapter 2, Appendix A).

In I/O psychology, the application of validity generalization focuses on the validity of employment tests. Two questions are typically investigated by researchers. One asks whether the variation in findings across studies is due to situational specificity or errors inherent in the original studies. The other asks whether, when the differences among studies are due to error, the error effects can be removed to uncover the true relationship between the predictor and the criterion.

Results of validity generalization research suggest that most variance is the result of statistical artifacts rather than of situational specificity (Hunter, Schmidt, & Jackson, 1982; Pearlman, Schmidt, & Hunter, 1980; Schmidt, Gast-Rosenberg, & Hunter, 1980; Schmidt & Hunter, 1977; Schmidt, Hunter, Pearlman, & Shane, 1979). Seven such artifacts are the following:

1. Differences among studies in criterion reliability.

2. Differences among studies in test reliability.

3. Differences among studies in range restriction.

4. Sampling error.

5. Differences among studies in amount and kind of criterion contamination and deficiency (e.g., ratings made by people who know that a subject's test scores may be biased or contaminated).

6. Computational and typographical errors.

7. Slight differences in factor structure among tests of a given type (e.g., a test measuring a similar set of abilities, but not an identical set, in which the number of abilities vary and the correlations between them vary).

Validity generalization studies (Schmidt & Hunter, 1977; Schmidt, Hunter, McKenzie, & Muldrow, 1979; Schmidt, Hunter, Pearlman, & Shane, 1979) were conducted on clerical workers and first-line supervisors. They found that statistical artifacts accounted for an average of 63% of the variance in validity coefficients, with a range of 43% to 87%. Other distributions of validity coefficients have been examined. For 152 test-job combinations an average of 72% of the variance that existed among the correlations was accounted for by the first four artifacts. (Lilienthal & Pearlman, 1983; Pearlman et al., 1980; Schmidt et al., 1980; Schmidt & Hunter, 1977; Schmidt, Hunter, & Caplan, 1981; Schmidt et al., 1979)

The 75% rule was proposed on the basis of this research. The **75% rule** states that if the first four artifacts account for 75% of the variance, then all seven artifacts could account for 100% of the variance. Therefore Schmidt and Hunter (1977) and Hunter and Schmidt (1982; 1990) rejected the hypothesis of situational specificity, assuming that error variance accounts for at least 75% of the observed variance (i.e., variance existing among validity correlations accumulated for the meta-analysis). In fact, they claimed strong evidence exists that measures of verbal, quantitative, and spatial abilities are valid predictors for job performance and job training across all jobs "in the occupational spectrum" (Schmidt, Hunter, Pearlman, & Hirsh, 1985, p. 712).

Although empirical evidence supports validity generalization, some psychologists differ as to existent issues, such as relevant moderators (Landy, Shankster, & Kohler, 1994). Others imply an overestimation derived from the cumulative research. As Burke (1984) summarized: despite the fact that validity generalization provides "an impetus toward developing procedures which permit us to derive general principles of behavior . . . to over-value the relative importance of these general conclusions based on current procedures, would be to undermine the many exceptions which also exist" (p. 113).

Validity generalization has had a significant impact on personnel selection. Specific validation studies are not needed for jobs for which validity data already exist, when a similar job has existing validity data, or when validity generalization has been shown. Validity generalization is accepted when (a) valid studies by other employers or organizations meet standards set by the Federal Executive Agency (FEA); (b) studies pertain to jobs that are comparable (as shown by a job analysis); or (c) there are no major differences in contextual variance and no differences exist in the sample composition that are likely to affect validity (SIOP, 1987).

Validity generalization demonstrates the cross-situational uses of different predictors in selection decisions. Assessment cost-effectiveness is improved, because a predictor can be used in multiple situations, for similar jobs. Validity gen-

eralization has been a fruitful area of research and continues to receive substantial attention by I/O psychologists.

....

LEGAL CONSIDERATIONS

In an attempt to demonstrate that a selection system is legally defensible and serves to advance the quality of work life for individuals, there are important components to consider. These include the issues of legally defensible job analyses, fair criterion and predictor measures, and the importance of validity and ways to demonstrate validity.

The major legal consideration in personnel selection is equal employment opportunity. Discrimination in selection can lead to serious consequences for both organizations and individuals. Discrimination leads to individuals being denied opportunities for employment, education, and the rights for residency in various areas. Organizations that are accused of carrying out unfair selection practices can lose money in lawsuits. These lawsuits may damage the organization's reputation as an equal opportunity employer. Therefore, personnel selection strategies must comply with the law.

The Civil Rights Act of 1964

The Civil Rights Act of 1964, especially the Title VII section of this act, is the main body of legislation in the area of fair employment. This act was updated in 1991. Title VII prohibits discrimination in selection or any personnel matter because of race, color, religion, sex, or national origin. The interpretation of Title VII regarding sexual orientation is currently under debate. For example, an article in the *Wall Street Journal* (Farney, 1994) states that laws protecting gay rights have been repealed in Austin, Texas, and Cincinnati, Ohio. In Austin, homosexual couples were denied health insurance because they could not be defined as married domestic partners. Early in 1997, several California-based national companies extended health insurance coverage to such domestic partners.

The Civil Rights Act prevents any conditions from being put on employment unless they are a business necessity. Conditions of business necessity are called bona fide occupational qualifications (BFOQ). BFOQs allow an employer to incorporate variables such as race, gender, and religion into their selection process if they are related to performance on the job. For example, a Catholic diocese that is seeking a Director of the Catholic Family Support Group Services could stipulate that the applicant must be Catholic. Because of the nature of the position, such a prerequisite would be considered business necessity or a BFOQ. On the other hand, the same Catholic diocese could not stipulate that the applicant be of a particular race because there is no justification for making race a BFOQ.

The Equal Employment Opportunity Commission (EEOC) was created as a regulatory agency to ensure compliance with Title VII of the Civil Rights Act. In 1978 the committee adopted the Uniform Guidelines on Employee Selection Procedures. Its purpose is to guide employers in complying with Title VII. Federal and state judicial systems also use it as standards for determining if organizations comply with Title VII.

The Principles for the Validation and Use of Personnel Selection Procedures (SIOP, 1987) is another primary set of guidelines regarding the legal aspects of personnel selection. It serves as the official statement of SIOP on the procedures for conducting validation research and personnel selection.

The 1991 version of the Civil Rights Act strengthens and reaffirms the 1964 Act. In 1989 the Supreme Court's decision in *Ward's Cove Packing Company* v. *Antonio* switched the burden of proof from the employer to the employee. Congress perceived this decision as a reduction in the effectiveness of the 1964 act and enacted the 1991 act to clarify that the responsibility of proof lies with the employer. Another part of the 1991 version of the act prohibits the adjustment of cutoff scores or the use of different cutoff scores on selection tests for different minorities and national groups. The act led to debates about "quotas in hiring in order to avoid litigation . . . [to placing] . . . greater burden on both the courts and employers to identify new ways of reducing adverse impact" (Landy, Shankster, & Kohler, 1994, p. 264).

The Equal Employment Opportunity Commission (EEOC)

As was stated before, the EEOC is a federal agency that regulates and enforces Title VII of the Civil Rights Act of 1964. Practice Perspective 8.3 presents a recent example of such enforcement. The commission consists of five members who are appointed by the President and confirmed by the Senate. Each commissioner

---

PRACTICE PERSPECTIVE 8.3

Discrimination Because of Pregnancy:
EEOC v. Ackerman, Hood, & McQueen (1992)

An organization named Ackerman, Hood, & McQueen denied a female employee a modified work schedule because she was pregnant. The organization argued that pregnancy is not a medical condition because it does not exist across gender groups. The court ruled that the designation of a medical condition is not contingent on whether it exists across gender groups. The court also ruled that it is appropriate to designate a medical condition on the basis of within-gender-group comparisons.

Source: EEOC v. Ackerman, Hood, and McQueen, 956 F.2d 944, 58 FEP 114 (10th Cir.)(1992).

serves for a term of five years. The EEOC is responsible for making policy and determining reasonable causes for unlawful discrimination. Courts do not give legal weight to EEOC rulings on reasonable cause; each court case is a new proceeding.

The EEOC has regional and district offices throughout the country. Complaints must be filed within 180 days of the believed date of violation. Complaints may be made by individuals, groups, or EEOC commissioners. The Equal Employment Opportunity Act of 1972 gave the EEOC power to sue on its own behalf or for a claimant, when it believes unlawful discrimination has occurred.

Complaints filed with the EEOC are first given to a state or local commission. The EEOC can begin its own investigation after sixty days and will seek to achieve voluntary compliance from the organization under review. A solution to the alleged discrimination is sought that is acceptable to the government, the respondent organization, and the aggrieved party. If this fails, court action can be taken. In cases that involve private employers the appropriate federal district court is addressed. Cases involving public employers are referred to the U.S. Department of Justice.

Beyond investigating charges of unlawful discrimination, the EEOC functions as an information gatherer. Organizations that have 100 or more employees must file an annual form with the EEOC, which indicates the number of women and members of minority groups that are employed in different job categories. Minority groups include African-Americans; Americans of Cuban, Spanish, Puerto Rican, or Mexican origin; Asian-Pacific Islanders; and American Indians.

Equal employment opportunity (EEO) gives women and minority populations the same access to positions that the nonminority population has. An organization's demographics should reflect the demographics of the larger social milieu and the labor market in which the organization exists. An organization must take all actions necessary in posting positions, recruiting, selecting, and integrating women and minorities into the work force. Together with affirmative action, EEO promotes diversity. We discuss this further later in the chapter.

Adverse Impact

The term **adverse impact** refers to the extent to which a selection procedure negatively affects members of a protected minority group. The **four-fifths rule,** or 80% rule, may be used to determine whether adverse impact occurs. Accordingly, adverse impact takes place when the proportion of minorities being hired is less than four fifths, or 80%, of the majority group being hired.

It is the plaintiff's (the complainant) responsibility to prove that unfair treatment has occurred. A plaintiff can present an argument as a class member, not as an individual. A pattern of discrimination must be shown before a finding of adverse impact is held up by the court. If a plaintiff is successful in demonstrating adverse impact, the employer must demonstrate the validity of the selection procedure. The employer may also have to demonstrate that no other, equally valid selection procedure would lead to a less adverse impact. Examples of court cases involving adverse impact are presented in Table 8.5.

Kleiman and Faley (1985) reviewed twelve court cases published since 1978 that dealt with adverse impact. They found that courts placed heavy emphasis on proper test development procedures. *Griggs* v. *Duke Power Company* (1971) was a landmark case in adverse impact. A selection test was shown to have adverse impact on black employees. Thirteen black employees accused Duke Power Company of practicing discriminatory employment practices. The plaintiffs charged that the selection requirements were arbitrary and screened out a much higher proportion of blacks than whites. The requirements included a high school diploma, passage of a mechanical aptitude test, and a general intelligence test. The organization did not attempt to show

TABLE 8.5   Testing and Legislation on Adverse Impact

Court Case	Year	Issue	Decisions
Griggs v. *Duke Power Company*	1971	Adverse impact	Tests must demonstrate job relatedness; the test must measure the person for the job.
Albermarle Paper Company v. *Moody*	1975	Adverse impact	An organization must identify the knowledge, skills, abilities, and criterion via job analyses.
Washington v. *Davis*	1976	Adverse impact	A test that predicts training performance demonstrates sufficient job relatedness.
Connecticut v. *Teal*	1982	Adverse impact	A multistage selection system must demonstrate that adverse impact does not occur at any stage in the selection process.

that these requirements were job-related. A district court did not find discriminatory intent by the company. An appellate court agreed with the district court's decision. Yet, the Supreme Court reversed the two previous decisions. The Supreme Court ruled that lack of discriminatory intent was not a sufficient defense against the use of employment selection devices that exclude applicants on the basis of race.

Most laws and legal policies existing today originated in efforts to overcome discrimination and unfair employment policies. According to Cascio and Awad (1981, p. 582), discrimination "involves giving a disadvantage (or advantage) to the members of one or more groups in comparison to the members of other groups. The disadvantage constitutes a non-related limitation." An example of non-related limitations is the high school diploma. One of the federal actions that is intended to regulate effects of past or present discriminatory actions or policies is affirmative action.

Affirmative Action

Affirmative action is a results-oriented policy that a contractor, by virtue of its contracts with the government, must take to ensure equal employment opportunity. The term was first used in the 1960s, when Presidents Johnson and Nixon signed executive orders requiring businesses with federal contracts to establish goals and timetables for hiring *qualified* women and minorities.

Today, the term refers broadly to policies that are focused on race, ethnicity, and gender. Companies are encouraged to institute programs that promote specific plans to recruit and hire qualified women and minorities in proportion to their existing numbers in labor pools. Affirmative action takes a proactive role in fighting employment discrimination; it attempts to overcome the effects of unfair past discriminatory practices and policies.

Although affirmative action is not a law and companies are not obligated or encouraged to hire a less qualified applicant over a more qualified one, various commentaries have associated affirmative action with different ideologies regarding racial and ethnic preferences/goals or "quotas."

Reflecting on affirmative action goals, Amirkhan, Betancourt, Graham, Lopez, and Weiner (1995, p. 140), claim that today we have a social agenda with "incompatible goals." One goal

of the civil rights movement of the 1950s and
1960s was that individual merit should be rewarded, regardless of race and gender. On the
other hand, the 1980s affirmative action policies define individual merit in terms of ethnicity
and gender. These two issues are associated with
different ideologies of affirmative action. Amirkhan et al. (1995) discuss affirmative action as
it applies to academia. However, two of the
goals pertaining to these ideologies and to the
general population are compensating for past
injustice and correcting present inequities. The
compensation for past injustice is imperative
"because ethnic minorities have been victimized
by a protracted history of prejudice and racial
discrimination[.] Affirmative action procedures
are necessary to balance the moral scales"
(Amirkhan et al., p. 141). Correcting present inequities is required because discrimination allowed members of some groups to receive
"greater shares of scarce, prized and competitive rewards than other groups" (Amirkhan et
al., p. 142). Affirmative action tries to correct
this inequity by recommending that members of
minorities be represented in the work force in
roughly the same proportion as in the general
population. It is essential to support these goals
with more research and better definitions of
what affirmative action tries to accomplish.

SUMMARY

This chapter provides an overview of the
process of selection system development and the
associated legal and ethical considerations. Employee selection has a direct impact on the organization's effectiveness and on the quality of
individual employees' work life.

Recruiting is the first step in building a pool
of applicants. When the job market is tight, organizations focus on finding the "best" applicant from those available. When the labor market is loose, organizations can be more selective
and hire only the best applicant from the larger
numbers available.

The next step is selection, the process of
choosing one or more individuals from a pool of
available applicants. Selection begins by examining individual differences in abilities and
skills, motivation, and personality characteristics. The selection process considers the person–
organization fit, which involves the person–
group fit and the person–job fit.

Placement extends the process of selection
and attempts to find the optimal job for the person on the basis of his or her unique strengths
and weaknesses. It also seeks to maximize the
individual's opportunity to attain personal goals.
Ultimately, there is a compromise, balancing the
desires and needs of the individual with those of
the organization.

Job analysis provides a detailed description
of the work performed and its setting. This information allows the organization to determine
the appropriate predictors and criteria. Criteria
variables are defined first, establishing the standards for performance evaluation. Next are predictors, which measure and assess characteristics relevant to the job.

The following step, validation, determines
the interpretations that can be adduced from
test scores. There are four strategies to validation. Content validity establishes the extent to
which items on a test represent a defined skill
or area of skill. Construct validity attempts to
demonstrate a relationship between underlying
traits and related behaviors. Concurrent validity, involving present employees, correlates their
scores on the predictor measure(s) with those on
the criterion measure(s). Predictive validity requires two steps: testing applicants at the time
of hiring and later comparing job performance
with predictor scores. Many factors affect concurrent and predictive validity. Principal among
these are motivation, time delay between measures, the subject pool, and restriction of range.

Additional steps require cross-validating the
results across the original study and a new sample. Other variables that affect the relationship
between predictors and criteria are the moderators and suppressors.

Selection decisions are based on proving that a valid relationship exists between the predictors and the criteria. Selection ratio, base rates, and cutoff scores are used in making these decisions. Expectancy tables that utilize these factors show the probability that a selected employee will be effective. In addition, they indicate the overall impact the selection decisions are likely to have on the organization.

Four possible outcomes are associated with selection decision making, using a combination of cutoff scores on the predictor and criterion measures. True positives are applicants predicted to be successful on the job who turn out to be successful. True negatives are applicants rejected on the basis of predictor scores who actually would have been unsuccessful had they been hired. False positives are accepted applicants predicted to be successful who later are found to be unsatisfactory. False negatives are applicants who were rejected because of their negative test predictions but who, if hired, would have proved successful on the job.

Next, the chapter explored three major strategies in selection decision making. The multiple regression strategy assumes a linear additive relationship among predictor variables with compensatory prediction. The multiple cutoff strategy considers individual predictor scores for each attribute measured, assuming that a minimal level of proficiency is required on each test. Failure on any of the predictors leads to rejection. The multiple hurdles strategy sequentially gathers and evaluates information on the predictors. It permits early identification and elimination of unqualified applicants. Both the multiple-cutoff

and multiple-hurdles strategies are noncompensatory. The strategy that would be best in a given situation is the one that best serves the organizational goals.

Utility analysis determines the financial benefits of a selection system to the organization. It is the degree to which a new selection process would be superior to the existing system in payoff results. Utility analysis should take into account not only the monetary consequences to the organization, but also the benefits to the individual employees.

Validity generalization refers to evidence that predictor validity could be generalized across similar jobs and situations. The results of validity generalization research suggest that most of the variance of validity coefficients found across studies are caused by statistical artifacts. Data can be examined and corrected by meta-analysis, thereby discerning whether the results can be generalized across similar jobs and situations. This process increases the cost-effectiveness of assessment because it enables validated predictors to be used in comparative situations.

The organization's goals are to improve employees' productivity and quality through fair personnel practices while avoiding discrimination. In implementing any selection system, companies need to be mindful of, and abide by, applicable laws at all levels as well as current standards of professional practice.

Giving care and concern to the multistage process will better enable an organization to achieve its goals of employee development and satisfaction and organizational productivity and profit.

KEY TERMS AND CONCEPTS

adverse impact	correct acceptances	false positives
affirmative action	correct rejections	four-fifths rule
base rate	cutoff score	meta-analysis
concurrent validity	erroneous acceptances	moderator variable
construct validity	erroneous rejections	multiple cutoff
content validity	false negatives	multiple hurdle

multiple regression	selection ratio	true positives
placement	75% rule	utility analysis
predictive validity	suppressor variable	validity generalization
selection	true negatives	

....

RECOMMENDED READINGS

Bernadin, H. J., & Cook, D. K. (1993). Validity of honesty test in predicting theft among convenience store employees. *Academy of Management, 36*(5), 1097–1108.

Dunnette, M. D. (1966). *Personnel selection and placement.* Belmont, CA: Wadsworth.

Hunter, J. E., & Schmidt, F. L. (1990). Methods of meta-analysis: Correcting error and bias in research findings. Newbury Park, CA: Sage.

Levy-Leboyer, C. (1994). Selection and assessment in Europe. In M. D. Dunnette & L. M. Hough (Eds.), *Handbook of industrial and organizational psychology* (Vol. 4). Palo Alto, CA: Consulting Psychologists Press.

Ones, D. S., Mount, M. K., Barrick, M. R., & Hunter, J. E. (1994). Personality and job performance: A critique of the Tett, Jackson, and Rothstein (1991) meta-analysis. *Personnel Psychology, 47*(1), 147–156.

Tett, R. P., Jackson, D. N., & Rothstein, M. (1991). Personality measures as predictors of job performance: A meta-analysis review. *Personnel Psychology, 44,* 703–742.

....

INTERNET RESOURCES

University of Houston Interviewing Institute
   This site provides outlines of the University of Houston Personnel Psychology Services Center's Interviewing Institute seminars on productive, risk-free interviewing.
   http://fisher.psych.uh.edu/ppsc/

Department of Business Studies, University of Edinburgh
   This is the home page for the Department of Business Studies. One section, The Worldwide Web Business Information Resource, includes links to a number of interesting human resource management articles. There is also a good section on international business.
   http://spey.bus.ed.ac.uk:8080/93_15.html

FedWorld Information Network
   FedWorld provides an integrated site from which you can search all U.S. government information services. It also hosts the servers for a number of governmental agencies providing a comprehensive central access point for locating and acquiring government information. More than 15,000 files are included and indexed at this location.
   http://www.fedworld.gov/

U.S. Government Gopher Collection at University of California, Irvine
   This listing links to a number of U.S. government, federal agency, and State of California sites and documents. On it you can find the original text of many important laws and rulings (for example, the text of the Americans with Disabilities Act).
   gopher://peg.cwis.uci.edu:7000/11/gopher. welcome/peg/GOPHERS/gov

U.S. Federal Register
   This subscription site provides the latest regulatory information and important notices from all U.S. government agencies.
   gopher://gopher.counterpoint.com:2002/

Government and Law [Wiretap] (gopher)
   This site collects government publications and notices from other sites on the web and collects them for easy reference. Some are unusual. References

are not always provided, and no claim is made for completeness or accuracy.
gopher://wiretap.spies.com/11/Gov/
The U.S. House of Representatives Internet Law Library
This site is provided by the Office of the Law Revision Counsel of the U.S. House of Representa-tives. It provides public access to the basic documents of U.S. law, including a full text-searchable copy of the U.S. Code and links to thousands of other law resources on the internet.
http://law.house.gov/1.htm

....

EXERCISE

Exercise 8.1

Establishing a New Selection Process

In July 1995 the University of California system decided to discontinue affirmative action programs for disadvantaged groups in the selection and employment of students and staff. That is, no preferential treatment in recruitment, selection, and employment were to be based on being a member of any of these groups (e.g., being female or African American). Nor would the work force at the university have to reflect the distribution of gender and minority populations in the community.

Assume that you work for an electronics company that is adopting the same social philosophy and strategy as the University of California. You are a personnel director, and you were asked to recruit, select, and place employees for sixty clerical positions (with identical job description), without considering an affirmative action program. You recruited 300 candidates. Together with the human resources director and the clerical pool supervisor, plan on the following:

1. How would you set up your selection program differently without an affirmative action program?
2. What would be your goals in setting up your selection process for these positions?
3. What would be the first three steps you would take in planning your strategy?

Your next steps would be to decide on the decision strategy (or strategies) you should apply, the validation studies you would carry out, and how you would implement all these steps to accomplish the organizational goals.

....

REFERENCES

Adkins, C. L., Russell, C. J., & Werbel, J. D. (1994). Judgments of fit in the selection process: The role of work value congruence. *Personnel Psychology, 47*, 605–623.

Amirkahn, J., Betancourt, H., Graham, S., Lopez, S. R., & Weiner, B. (1995). Reflections on affirmative action goals in psychology admissions. *Psychological Science, 6*(3), 140–148.

Anastasi, A. (1988). *Psychological testing* (6th ed.). New York: Macmillan.

Barrett, G. V., Phillips, J. S., & Alexander, R. A. (1981). Concurrent and predictive validity designs: A critical reanalysis. *Journal of Applied Psychology, 66*, 1–6.

Barrick, M. R., & Mount, M. K. (1991). The big five personality dimensions and job performance: A meta-analysis. *Personnel Psychology, 44* (1), 1–26.

Blum, M. L., & Naylor, J. C. (1968). *Industrial psychology: Its theoretical and social foundations.* New York: Harper & Row.

Boudreau, J. W. (1991). Utility analysis for decisions in human resource management. In M. D. Dunnette & L. Hough (Eds.) *Handbook of industrial and organizational psychology* (Vol. 2, pp. 621–745). Palo Alto, CA: Consulting Psychologists Press.

Burke, M. J. (1984). Validity generalization: A review and critique of the correlational model. *Personnel Psychology, 37,* 93–115.

Cascio, W. F. (1995). Whither industrial and organizational psychology in a changing world of work. *American Psychology, 50*(11), 920–939.

Cascio, W. F., Alexander, R. A., & Barrett, G. V. (1988). Setting cutoff scores: Legal, psychometric, and professional issues and guidelines. *Personnel Psychology, 41*(1), 1–24.

Cascio, W. F., & Awad, E. M. (1981). *Human resources management: An information systems approach.* Reston, VA: Reston.

Cronbach, L. J. (1990). *Essentials of psychological testing* (2nd ed.). New York: HarperCollins.

Cronbach, L. J., & Meehl, P. E. (1955). Construct validity in psychological tests. *Psychological Bulletin, 52,* 281–302.

Dawis, R. V. (1991). Vocational interests, values, and preferences. In M. D. Dunnette & L. Hough (Eds.) *Handbook of industrial and organizational psychology* (Vol. 2, pp. 833–871). Palo Alto, CA: Consulting Psychologists Press.

Dawis, R. V., & Lofquist, L. H. (1984). *A psychological theory of work adjustment.* Minneapolis: University of Minnesota Press.

Day, D. V., & Silverman, S. B. (1989). Personality and job performance: Evidence of incremental validity. *Personnel Psychology, 42*(1), 25–36.

Dunnette, M. D. (1966). *Personnel selection and placement.* Belmont, CA: Wadsworth.

Equal Employment Opportunity Commission (EEOC) (1978). Uniform guidelines on employee selection procedures. *Federal Register, 43,* 38, 290–38, 309.

Farney, D. (1994, October 7). Gay rights confront determined resistance from some moderates. *The Wall Street Journal,* pp. A1, A4.

Gatewood, R. D., & Feild, H. S. (1994). *Human resource selection.* Fort Worth, TX: Harcourt Brace College Publications.

Ghiselli, E. E. (1966). *The validity of occupational aptitude tests.* New York: John Wiley & Sons.

Ghiselli, E. E. (1973). The validity of aptitude tests in personnel selection. *Personnel Psychology, 26,* 461–477.

Griggs v. Duke Power Company, 401, U.S. 424 (1971).

Guion, R. M. (1965). *Personnel testing.* New York: McGraw-Hill.

Guion, R. M. (1976). Recruiting, selection, and job placement. In M. D. Dunnette (Ed.), *Handbook of industrial and organizational psychology* (pp. 777–828). Chicago: Rand McNally.

Guion, R. M. (1991). Personnel assessment, selection, and placement. In M. D. Dunnette & L. M. Hough (Eds.), *Handbook of industrial and organizational psychology* (Vol. 2, pp. 327–397). Palo Alto, CA: Consulting Psychologists Press.

Guion, R. M., & Cranny, C. J. (1982). A note on concurrent and predictive validity designs: A critical reanalysis. *Journal of Applied Psychology, 67,* 239–244.

Hunter, J. E., & Schmidt, F. L. (1990). *Methods of meta-analysis: Correcting error and bias in research findings.* Newbury Park, CA: Sage.

Hunter, J. E., Schmidt, F. L., & Jackson, G. B. (1982). *Meta-analysis: Cumulating research findings across studies.* Beverly Hills: Sage.

Jones, J. W. (1991). Assessing privacy invasiveness of psychological test items: Job relevant versus clinical measures of integrity. *Journal of Business Psychology, 5*(4), 531–535.

Kleiman, L. S., & Faley, R. H. (1985). The implications of professional and legal guidelines for court decisions involving criterion-related validity: A review and analysis. *Personnel Psychology, 38,* 803–833.

Kristof, A. L. (1996). Person-organization fit: An integrative review of its conceptualization, measurement and implication. *Personnel Psychology 49*(1), 1–49.

Landy, F. J., Shankster, L. J., & Kohler, S. S. (1994). Personnel selection and placement. *Annual Review of Psychology, 45,* 261–296.

Latham, G. P., & Whyte, G. (1994). The futility of utility analysis, *Personnel Psychology, 47*(1), 31–46.

Lawler, E. E. (1980). The individualized organization: Problems and promises. In A. D. Szilagyi, Jr., & M. J. Wallace (Eds.), *Readings in organizational behavior and performance* (pp. 85–95). Santa Monica, CA: Goodyear.

Lawshe, C. H., Bolda, R. A., Brune, R. L., & Auclair, G. (1958). Expectancy charts: If, then theoretical developments. *Personnel Psychology, 11,* 545–559.

Lilienthal, R. A., & Pearlman, K. (1983). *The validity of federal selection tests for aid/technicians in the health, science, and engineering fields.* Washington, DC: U.S. Office of Personnel Management.

Muchinsky, P. M. (1986). Personnel selection methods. In C. L. Cooper & I. T. Robertson (Eds.), *International review of industrial and organizational psychology 1986* (pp. 37–70). New York: John Wiley & Sons.

Nunnally, J. C. (1993). *Psychometric theory.* McGraw-Hill: New York.

Pearlman, K., Schmidt, F. L., & Hunter, J. E. (1980). Validity generalization results of tests used to predict training success and job proficiency for clerical occupations. *Journal of Applied Psychology, 65,* 373–406.

Porter, L. W., Lawler, E. E., & Hackman, J. R. (1975). *Behavior in organizations.* New York: McGraw-Hill.

Schmidt, F. L., Gast-Rosenberg, I., & Hunter, J. E. (1980). Validity generalization results for computer programmers. *Journal of Applied Psychology, 65,* 643–661.

Schmidt, F. L., & Hunter, J. E. (1977). Development of a general solution to the problem of validity generalization. *Journal of Applied Psychology, 62,* 529–540.

Schmidt, F. L., & Hunter, J. E. (1978). Moderator research and the law of small numbers. *Personnel Psychology, 31,* 215–232.

Schmidt, F. L., Hunter, J. E., & Caplan, J. R. (1981). Validity generalization results for two job groups in the petroleum industry. *Journal of Applied Psychology, 66,* 261–273.

Schmidt, F. L., Hunter, J. E., McKenzie, R. L., & Muldrow, T. W. (1979). Impact of valid selection procedures on work-force productivity. *Journal of Applied Psychology, 64,* 609–626.

Schmidt, F. L., Hunter, J. E., Outerbridge, A. N., & Trattner, M. H. (1986). The economic impact of job selection methods on size, productivity, and payroll costs of the federal work force: An empirically based demonstration. *Personnel Psychology, 39,* 1–29.

Schmidt, F. L., Hunter, J. E., & Pearlman, K. (1981). Task differences as moderators of aptitude test validity in selection: A red herring. *Journal of Applied Psychology, 68,* 166–185.

Schmidt, F. L., Hunter, J. E., Pearlman, K., & Hirsh, H. R. (1985). Forty questions about validity generalization and meta-analysis. *Personnel Psychology, 38,* 697–798.

Schmidt, F. L., Hunter, J. E., Pearlman, K., & Shane, G. S. (1979). Further tests of the Schmidt-Hunter Bayesian validity generalization procedure. *Personnel Psychology, 32,* 257–281.

Schmitt, N., & Robertson, I. (1990). Personnel selection. *Annual Review of Psychology, 41,* 289–319.

Society for Industrial and Organizational Psychology (SIOP), Inc. (1987). *Principles of the validation and use of personnel selection procedures* (3rd ed.). College Park, MD: Author.

Taylor, H. C., & Russell, J. T. (1939). The relationship of validity coefficients to the practical effectiveness of tests in selection. *Journal of Applied Psychology, 23,* 565–578.

Thorndike, R. L. (1982). *Applied Psychometrics.* Houghton Mifflin: Boston.

Tyler, L. E. (1995). The challenge of diversity. In D. Lubinski & R. V. Dawis (Eds.), *Assessing individual differences in human behavior.* Palto Alto, CA: Davies-Black.

CHAPTER

9

Training and Development

Oceans is a century-old firm that provides harbor, ship assist, tanker escort, and ocean transportation services. It has a long tradition of excellent customer service and is famous for its "We're Ready" motto. Recently, Oceans decided to upgrade its sales training activities. The company wanted to establish a consistent, fundamental program that would provide a forum for the Oceans salespeople to discuss the company's diverse product lines and to build the sales team. The company hired a consulting I/O psychologist to assist it.

The consultant evaluated the current state of sales force readiness using two standardized surveys: the Sales Relationship Survey (SRS) and the Sales Organization Survey (SOS). The SRS yielded scores for five key sales skills (relating, discovering, advocating, supporting, and customer service). The SOS ranked basic sales skills according to the need for development. Oceans' needs in priority order were closing, negotiation, self-management, call planning, market planning, account development, management support, product knowledge, discovering, follow through, presentations, and relating. On the basis of the survey results, the consultant recommended three courses: one to develop basic sales skills, one to develop sales negotiation skills, and one to help salespeople better understand their customers on an interpersonal basis.

One year after implementation, Oceans believes that the programs have been very successful. Its customer satisfaction survey showed significant improvement. This has been further confirmed by positive customer feedback. There are several cross-product teams working on developing cross-sale opportunities and strategies. Finally, a reassessment of the salespeople using the SRS and SOS showed improvement in most of the skills measured. A second series of training is now planned to continue to build call-planning and market-planning skills, the two areas that did not improve as a result of the previous training.

As the Oceans example illustrates, training is "the systematic acquisition of attitudes, con- cepts, knowledge, rules, or skills that result in improved performance at work" (Goldstein, 1991, p. 508). A successful training program includes developing and improving motor, cognitive, and/or interpersonal skills with the intention of attaining individual and organizational goals. This definition emphasizes training as a sequential, preplanned process that improves existing skills and develops new skills. That is, training strives to develop the skills of new employees and to improve the deficient skills of current employees to enhance performance. Personnel training demonstrates three primary characteristics:

1. It is a psychological process that leads to a relatively permanent change in a behavioral tendency resulting from experience and practice (Howell, 1976). In other words, it is a learning experience. On completion of training, the individual knows how to do something he or she did not know how to do previously. Training does not aim toward temporary changes in behavior, such as those resulting from different levels of motivation, nor does it include behavioral changes resulting from injury or physiological adjustments. For example, limping as the result of an accident or having to wear glasses to be able to read the small print of this chapter are changes in behavior that would not be attributable to training.

2. Well-designed training includes a formal purpose for achieving specific organizational objectives; an informal learning process that occurs among employees; and the skills, knowledge, and attitudes that the individual brings to the job.

3. Finally, training prepares employees for the attainment of individual as well as organizational goals. While a company's training program should be designed to meet organizational objectives, a successful program will meet individual objectives as well (e.g., increase in salary, attainment of promotion, and the development of skills needed to advance within the organization).

Some of the important issues that must be addressed in developing a training program (Tannenbaum & Yukl, 1992; Towne, 1985) are the following:

1. The purpose(s) or intention(s) of the training program must be determined and must be clearly stated to trainees.

2. The personnel involved must be considered, including both the trainer(s) and the trainee(s). For example, highly skilled trainers require different kinds of preparation than employees who were recently promoted to a training position; an organization that is training blue-collar workers on technical skills will use different training methods than will an organization that is training white-collar workers on interpersonal skills.

3. Trainees should be viewed as active, adult participants during all the stages of training.

4. Training materials (audiovisual equipment, textbooks, or computers) and procedures must consider the objectives of the training program, the pretraining and posttraining environments, the trainees' existing skills and characteristics, and the criteria used to gauge the effectiveness of the training program.

5. Finally, the program design must include a way to evaluate the effectiveness of the training system.

The goal of this chapter is to provide an overview of the basic principles of learning and training that have emerged from psychological research. From this research we summarize guidelines that can promote learning in applied settings. The chapter also describes a systematic approach to training. Such an approach begins with the assessment of training needs, which is explored from the perspectives of the organization, the task, and the person. Next we examine the training itself. Because training methods vary in type, applicability, and effectiveness, the section on techniques reviews both on-site and off-site methods and discusses some cur-

rent training technologies. In this section we also discuss leadership development and career counseling for managers. Although they are not "techniques," these two areas are unique and often are characterized by specially designed approaches. The final focus in our systematic approach to training is the evaluation of training programs, including issues of criterion relevance, and experimental design. Our description of a systematic approach to training ends with an examination of the goals of training with attention to the major forms of training validity.

....

PRINCIPLES OF LEARNING AND TRAINING

Training programs must enable employees to learn the skills they need to perform satisfactorily on the job. An understanding of several learning theories can help to provide the foundation for any training effort.

A number of learning theories are in existence today. This chapter focuses on the two theories most relevant to personnel training: the *connectionist theory* and the *social/cognitive learning theory* (Cascio & Awad, 1981).

The Connectionist Approach to Learning

The connectionist approach to learning consists of two processes: classical conditioning and operant conditioning.

Classical Conditioning

Bass and Vaughan (1966) defined **classical conditioning** as the formation of an association between a conditioned stimulus and a response. This association is developed through the repeated presentation, within a controlled relationship, of the conditioned stimulus with the unconditioned stimulus that originally elicited the response.

Training in organizations rarely uses the classical approach because the objectives of training programs are to impart more than a simple automatic response to a specific, conditioned stimulus.

Operant Conditioning

Operant conditioning is different from classical conditioning primarily in that the subject is active rather than passive in making responses to produce desired consequences. Consequences are either pleasant by their very nature or rewarding through the avoidance of aversive or punishing situations. Examples of positive consequences are promotions or salary increases. (For an interesting compendium of reward alternatives, see Bob Nelson's 1994 book *1001 Ways to Reward Employees*.) These positive reinforcements increase the likelihood of sustaining the behavior that precedes them. An example is the piecework system, in which the employee is rewarded directly for each unit of production. Productive behavior will increase as long as the reward is associated with the production.

In operant conditioning terms, negative reinforcement presents an adverse stimulus until the desired behavior occurs. Because the target behavior eliminates the aversive stimulus, the subject learns to avoid the negative consequences. Examples of negative reinforcements at work are pay withheld and being fired.

Training programs that use operant conditioning principles in business are called **organizational behavior management** (OBM). Three elements are necessary to control operant behavior: the behavior itself, the antecedents of the behavior, and the consequences of the behavior. In organizational behavior management, many aspects of the work environment (e.g., the presence of coworkers, the presence of supervisors, written instructions, and physical settings), individually or in combination, take on antecedent control.

Komaki, Barwick, and Scott (1978) reported an application of OBM that was used to reduce lost time due to accidents in a bakery. The problems were defined not as accidents, but as the assessment and control of safe behavior (e.g., walking around conveyers, cleaning up spills). An observational coding system was developed. Trained observers recorded safety behaviors for fifty-five minutes, four times a week. (Capturing the actual behavior on the job is important to OBM.) The workers were shown slides of safe and unsafe practices, followed by a discussion. The consequences in this study were two: Feedback was given on levels of safety, and supervisors verbally recognized safe practices whenever they saw them. The intervention increased the frequency of recorded safe behaviors 37% over the baseline in one department and 28% in the second department.

Other successful OBM interventions have been reported in the areas of safety, absenteeism, lateness, sales performance, and production.

Social and Cognitive Learning Theory

Bandura (1974) suggested that, at least for humans, learning does not occur automatically. He stated that conditioning is mediated by mental operations that are more complex than the simple pairing of repetitive events. The critical factor in distinguishing human learning from animal learning is that "people learn to predict [events] and to summon up appropriate anticipatory reactions" (p. 859). **Social learning theory** stresses the social and cognitive aspect of learning. We do not operate in isolation; rather, we observe the performance of others and the consequences of their actions. These consequences are perceived as rewards or punishments, depending on whom we use as referents. We then evaluate the observed consequences and rehearse the actions mentally until we are presented with the opportunity to perform them ourselves. Outcomes lead us to modify our behavior and make the necessary corrections, using memorized information and observations of modeled behavior as a guide. In contrast to the connectionist view, which links a stimulus to a response, social learning theory does not require a stimulus or a response. Instead, Bandura (1974, 1977, 1986) included in his theory of learning concepts such as memory, reasoning, judgment, motivation, emotion, and self-esteem.

Research has shown that social and cognitive learning theory can be successfully applied to many training situations (e.g., Burnaska, 1976; Latham & Saari, 1979; Moses & Ritchie, 1976). In industrial applications this theory can provide insight into how new employees learn tasks involving complex mental processes (Tannenbaum & Yukl, 1992). One such process is metacognition, a construct that can distinguish proficient from nonproficient learners. Howell and Cook (1989) defined metacognition as the self-monitoring mental ability of learners to differentiate mentally between what they know and what they need to learn. Processes such as decision making, interpretation of feedback, learning from experience, and motivational variables, such as perception of one's own ability to achieve a goal (e.g., Kanfer & Ackerman, 1989), are now part of the cognitive and social models of training.

Latham (1989) observed that social and cognitive learning theory was adopted by I/O psychologists for the following reasons:

1. It takes individual differences into account by identifying cognitive dimensions such as **self-efficacy,** the "belief that one can execute a given behavior in a given setting" (Latham, 1989, p. 265), and outcome expectancies, the "belief that the given outcome will occur if one engages in the behavior" (Latham, 1989, p. 265). For example, Frayne and Latham (1987) found that the higher a trainee's judgment of his or her capacity to perform the job (self-efficacy), the higher was his or her attendance record.

2. It provides a basis for explaining behavior. The theory enables I/O psychologists to use operant principles by adding the concept of cognition, including the interaction between environment, mental processes, and behavior, to the explanation of performance at work.

GUIDELINES TO PROMOTE LEARNING

Research has suggested guidelines that can be used to promote more effective and efficient learning (e.g., Bower & Hilgard, 1981; Hall, 1982) in training and development programs. Following are some of the suggested guidelines.

Overview and Importance

The first step in conducting an effective training program is to make learners aware of training program objectives and the reasons for learning the new material.

Reinforcement

Any reward that increases the probability of the occurrence of an immediately preceding specific behavior is, by definition, a **reinforcer** (e.g., recognition, pay increase, social acceptance). The effectiveness of various reinforcers changes when training different individuals and different subgroups such as gender, age, ethnic background, skills, and personality. For example, London and Bassman (1989) found that individuals are most concerned about their jobs and careers during the "midlife crisis" (p. 338). Providing reinforcement for tasks well done can help an individual to overcome this crisis.

Another example of the use of reinforcements is provided by Emery Air Freight (Feeney, 1973) experience. Emery established a project in which employees who performed well were verbally recognized by their supervisors immediately after the performance. The project resulted in a sizable increase in effective employee performance and associated savings of about $3 million to the company.

Shaping

Conditioning can be expedited by reinforcing closer and closer approximations of desired behaviors. This procedure is referred to as **shaping** behavior. Wexley and Latham (1981) describe the shaping procedure that was applied to train employees for punctuality. A trainee who consistently is fifteen minutes late to work is first praised if he is only fourteen minutes late. Successively, as the demand for punctuality increases, praise is given only when the employee gets closer and closer to being on time. Finally, praise is given only when the employee arrives to work exactly on time.

Conditions of Practice

Milkovich and Glueck (1985) showed that practice is essential for learners to master the task at hand and should continue beyond the point at which the task can be successfully repeated. Because unit size can affect the rate of learning, units should be kept small. However, the way a task is divided and the subsequent benefits to the learning process vary among different types and difficulties of tasks and individuals.

Another factor that can affect practice is the timing, or spacing, of practice trials. The two most common approaches are massed trials and distributed trials. In **massed trials,** everything that is to be learned is presented at one time and is steadily practiced until it is mastered. This approach is most appropriate for short, less com-

plex material. In contrast, **distributed trials** are spread out over time and are most beneficial in learning lengthy or difficult material.

Feedback

Feedback is information given to the learner about the effectiveness of his or her responses. Having trainees practice skills without feedback results in little or no improvement in behavior because the trainees do not know whether their responses are correct. Feedback is probably the single most important reinforcement and incentive tool for human learning. Feedback provides trainees with the knowledge of how they are doing, reinforces appropriate behaviors, and prevents inadequate behavior patterns from recurring. The brief experiment described in Scientific Perspective 9.1 illustrates the power of feedback.

Transfer

Transfer of training refers to the extent to which the knowledge, skills, or attitudes acquired during training will transfer to the job site (Tannenbaum & Yukl, 1992). Transfer of training is evaluated by the extent to which behavioral changes are apparent in actual job performance. To maximize transfer of training, we match the

---

SCIENTIFIC PERSPECTIVE 9.1

Feedback Experiment

To practice the effects of immediate feedback on learning, try the following simple experiment with your peers:

Have one person stand about ten feet from an encircled area marked by chalk. Give the subject twenty pennies and have him or her throw the pennies into the marked circle under three conditions:

1. Eyes covered, no feedback.
2. Eyes covered with detailed feedback indicating where the coins landed. Provide direction

   on the way the individual has to correct his or her movements for the coins to land in the circle.
3. Eyes not covered and freedom to see and direct movements when throwing the coins.

   In principle, performance should get respectively better moving through conditions 1 to 3, as each condition provides additional feedback.

training elements as closely as possible to the elements of the job. This is done by conducting a careful assessment of the tasks to be learned and using that information in the design of the training program. In addition, reward systems must be similar in the training situation and the job situation. For more complex jobs, such as management duties, it is essential that trainees understand the principles by which problems are solved, both in training and on the job.

It is difficult to ensure transfer in complex, higher-level jobs. For example, a bank teller will not find much deviation between training and job environments, while an individual who is trained for leadership development may find little direct application of training to the job. This is because the duties performed by a manager are so complex that it is difficult to obtain an accurate task assessment and to design a program that encompasses the variety of tasks involved in successful managerial performance.

Other factors also can affect training transfer. Ford, Quinones, Sego, and Sorra (1992) examined transfer from training to job performance for Air Force Aerospace Ground Equipment graduates. They found that transfer from the training program to the job depended on the different opportunities trainees had to perform the tasks they had learned in the program. Among other factors, these opportunities were related to the supervisor's perception of the capability of the trainee. Trainees who were perceived by their supervisors as highly competent were asked to perform more complex tasks on the job and therefore were given more opportunities to transfer their skills to the job site.

Another example of the effects of the trainer's perception and interpretation of material is seen in the train-the trainer method. **Train-the-trainer** begins with one master trainer, who then trains the individuals who in turn deliver the programs. In very large applications there may be several levels of train-the-trainer. The master trainer trains a group of senior trainers, who in turn train groups of plant trainers, who in turn train employees.

Deming (1986) expressed serious concerns about this process. He claimed that something is lost in each translation. He conceptualized the train-the-trainer process as being like dropping a ball bearing down a funnel. Even though the ball bearing is directed by the funnel, when it drops out at the bottom, it may bounce in different directions. In the same way the master trainer's first students do not all learn the material exactly the same way as the master trainer did. When they teach their classes, they start at different places than did the master trainer. In this way, diffusion of the content may occur at each successive step. This can result in training being substantively different from the original intent. For example, training dealing with sexual harassment and bias may actually foster instead of reducing them.

Gagné (1962) proposed an alternative set of learning principles relevant to training and development. These principles differ from those in traditional learning approaches in that they deemphasize the initial learning of responses. Gagné believed that humans already have the necessary responses in their response repertoire before training and that all that is needed to accomplish a task is to learn the proper sequencing of responses.

According to Gagné, every task or job involves a set of distinct component activities. He suggests that these task components are mediators of the final task performance. That is, their presence ensures positive transfer to a final performance, and their absence reduces such transfer to near zero.

Consequently, Gagné suggested that the basic principles of training design should consist of (a) identifying the component tasks of a final performance, (b) ensuring that each component task is fully achieved, (c) arranging the total learning situation sequentially to ensure optimal mediational effects from one component to another, and (d) organizing the sequence to start with the simplest components of behaviors and proceed to the more complex components.

Every organization should use many, if not all, of the learning strategies described above.

Although research has shown that learning principles "have limited utility for designing training to develop the complex skills required in most organization jobs" (Tannenbaum & Yukl, 1992, p. 404), their use would enhance the effectiveness of any training program.

Adult Learning

It is estimated that in 1994, training expenditures exceeded $50 billion and an estimated $13.4 billion were spent on training of adults in management positions (U.S. Department of Education, 1994). In industry the term *adult* includes such roles as "worker, spouse, parent, and retiree" (Alkin, Linden, Noel, & Ray, 1992a, p. 30; 1992b). However, the emphasis is on the worker role at all organizational levels and across all positions.

With changes in technology, international business, the demographics of the work force, and the globalization of industry, the concepts and principles of adult education and adult learning have become part of the formal training programs supported by employers. In all of these programs, adults are being recognized as a unique group of individuals, and adult education is regarded as a lifelong process of learning. Essential to this process of learning are the components of self-teaching and self-direction, with special emphasis on the active role of the learner.

The designation of adult learners as a "unique subgroup in need of specialized study, theory and educational practices" (Zemke & Zemke, 1995, p. 31), led to the use of the term **andragogy** in theories of adult education. The term is derived from the Greek words "anere," meaning adult, and "agogus," which refers to the process of helping others to learn (Knowles, 1990). Using the term *andragogy,* Knowles (1978, 1980, 1984) created a theory applied specifically to adult learning and training. Knowles (1978) claimed that the andragogial model of adult learning is a process model that is concerned with providing procedures and resources for involving the learner in this process. The ele-

ments necessary for such a process are as follows (Knowles, 1978, pp. 108–109):

1. establishing a climate conducive to learning
2. creating a mechanism for mutual planning
3. diagnosing the needs for learning
4. formulating program objectives . . . that will satisfy these needs
5. designing a pattern of learning experiences
6. conducting these learning experiences with suitable techniques and materials
7. evaluating the learning outcomes and rediagnosing learning needs.

Knowles (1990) makes the following assumptions, which are basic to adult learning:

1. The need to know. Adults' learning is effective when they understand what they have to learn and how it would benefit them.

2. The need to be self-directing. Adults learn better and retain longer what they have learned when they feel responsible and in charge of their undertakings. The facilitator and trainers must make the learners aware that they are perceived as being able to take responsibility for decision making. The learners may feel confused and anxious when asked to take charge of planning and learning their projects, but will be energized after starting to work on them.

3. Greater volume and quality of experience. Adults accumulate more experience as they become older. Because these experiences are unique to each individual, the emphasis should be on providing a variety of procedures and resources that will fit the learner's background and experiences. Knowles claims that the best approaches to provide such individualized instruction would be experiential methods such as group discussions, simulation exercises, and field training.

4. Readiness to learn. Adults learn better when they are prepared to learn things perceived to result in satisfaction and success. Zemke and Zemke (1995) indicate that providing opportunities to learn at times when the trainee is receptive to learn is an important factor enhancing both motivation and the retention of material and skills. They labeled this timing the "window of opportunity" (Zemke & Zemke, 1995, p. 32). For example, providing training to promoted managers and supervisors immediately after promotion and giving them the opportunities and equipment to practice (e.g., computers and software) would have greater impact than delaying the training until a more convenient time. Zemke and Zemke (1995, p. 32) concluded that "the longer such training is delayed, the less impact it appears to have on job performance."

London (1989) claimed that the principles of adult learning determine the design of training programs. Self-pacing training programs and the use of advanced new technologies and tools during training will provide the trainee with a sense of control over learning, opportunities for practice and feedback, and timely rewards. Zemke and Zemke (1995) suggested that three factors should be taken into account in designing a training program:

1. Be knowledgeable about adult motivation. Adults cannot be forced to learn. Find out about their desire to learn and their needs to acquire new experience. Motivation can also be enhanced by helping trainees to have a sense of increasing their self-esteem and a perception of personal growth (e.g., the expectation of line employees who are involved in team and participative group work that they will be liberated from management authority).

2. Be knowledgeable about curriculum design that enhances opportunities for self-directing learning. Focus on a single concept or critical issue; provide activities with some challenge and realism that involve active participation; have clear, planned feedback, recognition, goals, and expectations; carefully plan for intervention when a company changes strategies (e.g., in marketing or production); and plan overlap and transfer from training to the job.

3. Be knowledgeable about adults in the classroom. Increase benefits of learning by providing a comfortable environment (e.g., light, heat); engaging trainees in establishing goals;

combining methods of discussions, debates, and presentations; providing opportunities for exercising and practicing the new skills.

The best summary of the andragogial model is Knowles's (1990, p. 612) own example:

> During this past year I have been trying to learn to use a microcomputer to write letters, articles, and books, and I have been having a difficult time. The instructional manuals and software programs are written by engineers who do not understand that adults are task-oriented learners, so they instruct me to memorize information about how the machine works and the commands that will make it work. I spent hours memorizing information I had no idea how to use, and I proceeded to forget most of it. Then I started teaching myself how to use the computer to write letters, articles, and books, and although the manuals were not very helpful, I eventually was able to get the microcomputer to do the work I needed. I would have learned much faster and more easily if the manuals and software programs had been organized around life tasks (i.e., how to write a letter, how to write a report, how to personalize form letters, etc.).

It should be clear from this discussion that an effective training program will combine learning theory, a social and cognitive theoretical framework, and principles of adult learning. For example, Gist (1989) found that a training method composed of cognitive modeling, practice, and reinforcement led to significantly higher self-efficacy than did a method involving practice and lecture alone.

SYSTEMS APPROACH TO TRAINING

The **systems approach** to training involves systems engineering applied to the design of an instructional program (Silvern, 1972). This approach, which has been used for the past thirty years, identifies training as a subsystem within the organizational system. "One must be concerned with objectives of the total system rather than objectives of any component within the system" (Blum & Naylor, 1968, p. 252) and with the interaction among components. For example, the selection and hiring of employees with higher job-relevant skills and abilities will lead to a higher level of training; the reverse is true of hiring people with lower ability levels (Goldstein, 1991). Training that results in an increase in production in one department (e.g., the spinning department) will be ineffective unless the next department (e.g., the weaving department) can process the increased input and the final products can be sold at a profit.

Following Katz and Kahn's (1978) conceptualization of organizations as open systems, Figure 9.1 depicts training as a system. A continuous sequence of steps, from inputs through adaptation, is facilitated by a constant cycle of evaluation, feedback, and improvement.

The **input phase** of the systems approach refers to the trainees' existing aptitudes and skills as well as the projected organizational goals and objectives. Existing skills and aptitudes

are determined either during the selection of new employees or through the course of performance appraisals for incumbents. Organizational goals and objectives are defined after a needs assessment (see next section).

The **transformation phase** consists of the training itself and addresses both its contents and its methods. Training content includes the new skills, knowledge, and other characteristics that trainees are expected to learn and develop. Training methods are the means by which the content is taught. The first component of methods is the procedure used. Task analysis and performance evaluations are two such methods that are used to collect data to determine the specific skills and knowledge required for successful performance. Task analysis is discussed later in this chapter, and performance appraisal is reviewed extensively in Chapter 6. The second component of methods is the process followed. For example, a curriculum design maps all the learning activities of a particular training course. This includes how a concept will be pre-

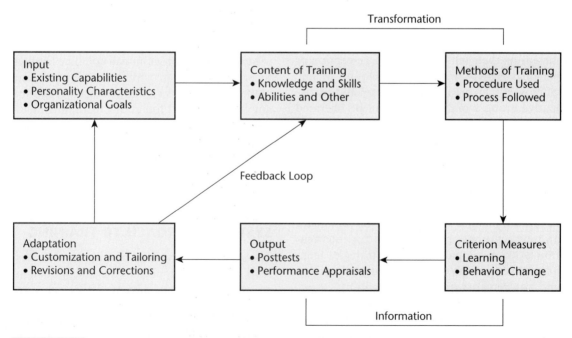

FIGURE 9.1 Diagram of the systems approach to training.

sented, how it will be related to what the trainee already knows, how it will be practiced, and how on-the-job application will be facilitated and reinforced.

The next step in Katz and Kahn's systems approach is the **information phase.** This phase ensures that trainees have effectively learned what the training was designed to teach and that they apply it when they are back on the job. Criterion measures evaluate both knowledge (the information learned) and behavior change (the ability to act differently). The output facet in information emphasizes the importance of follow-up after employees have been on the job for a period of time. It is vital to ensure that the trainees both retain the knowledge acquired and use it to increase their proficiency on the job. These are evaluated through posttests and performance appraisals. The information phase also provides data for the next step in the systems approach.

The **adaptation phase** is the last phase in the systems approach. Its purpose is to assess the entire training program on the basis of the information received from the posttests and performance evaluations. This information is used to modify the training process used, as well as to determine whether it is meeting the organization's goals and objectives. Adaptation of the program involves tailoring and customizing training to improve the fit to the organization, individuals, and situations. For example, a program may need to be adapted to suit changes in organizational goals, existing skills of new employees, and the fact that training will be carried out abroad. Furthermore, adaptation can provide information that can be used as input in the content development of a new planning cycle of training. The last component, the **feedback loop,** makes the systems approach to training a continuous, self-correcting process.

The systems approach has been included in the research on training for many years. Goldstein (1991) developed an instructional technology model for training that incorporated the idea of the feedback loop and the systems per-

spective. His model emphasizes the steps of needs assessment, learning experiences designed to achieve instructional objectives, and performance criteria. It takes into account the pretraining and posttraining organizational environment and the socialization process of employees within the organization. This process continually evaluates training outcomes and assesses areas that need modification throughout the feedback loop. Figure 9.2 on page 292 illustrates Goldstein's model.

The main components of this model are needs assessment, training and development techniques, evaluation designs, and validity of training goals.

Needs Assessment

The first step in the training process is to determine what employees need to learn to successfully perform on the job. This is done by performing a needs analysis through which the training objectives are formulated. Traditionally, this process has consisted of analysis of the organization, the task, and the person (McGehee & Thayer, 1961; Morey & Esch, 1992). Goldstein and Buxton (1982) argued that it is important that all three analyses be included to ensure the success of a training program. In fact, it would seem illogical, if not impossible, for a training department to develop a successful program without analyzing the organization and its objectives, the job tasks, and the people who will perform the work under review. Unfortunately, this is a frequent occurrence. According to Tannenbaum and Yukl (1992), only 27% of the companies they surveyed had any procedures in place for assessing training needs for their managers. Yet organizations are spending more than $40 billion a year on a variety of training programs (Goldstein, 1991).

Organizational Analysis

In conducting an **organizational analysis,** the assessors' main goal is to investigate the organization as a whole. One reason is that examina-

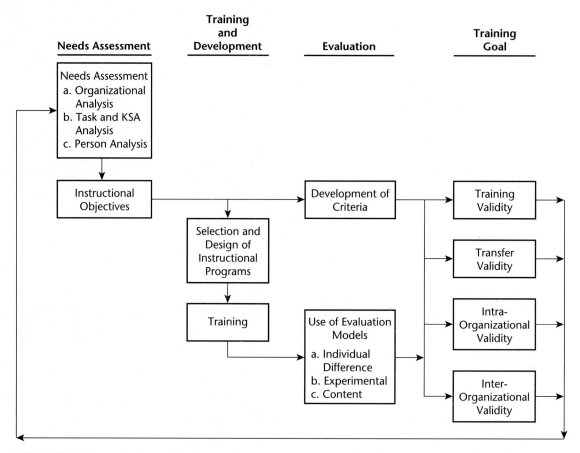

tion of systemwide components can determine whether training will lead to behavioral changes that will permanently transfer back to the job (Goldstein, 1991). Wexley and Latham (1981) found that this process involved examining the organization's interface with the external environment in which it operates, the attainment of its objectives, its human resources, and its internal climate. Organization analysis attempts to operationally define the extent to which (a) training objectives are linked to organizational objectives, (b) training objectives change alongside changes in organizational man-

agement, and (c) progress in training is linked to progress in the achievement of organizational objectives (Latham, 1989; Morey & Esch, 1992). One such objective is accommodating the cultural diversity of organizations. This has been of considerable interest to companies in the United States. An example of training that supports objectives defined by organizational analysis is the police training program in Los Angeles described in Practice Perspective 9.1. Organizational analysis can serve as a basis for developing the broader content areas of the training program.

PRACTICE PERSPECTIVE 9.1

Community Policing Approach

The American Psychological Association suggests in a report on children and violence that police departments and citizens should form a working partnership, known as community policing, to control crime in their neighborhoods. In its report entitled "Violence & Youth: Psychology's Response," APA's Commission on Violence and Youth calls on law enforcement agencies to start or expand community policing efforts. The programs should include cultural sensitivity training and encourage increased participation by community leaders.

Implementing community policing requires changes in the way police departments select, train, supervise, and evaluate officers, creating a new role for police psychologists, said Ellen Scrivner, Ph.D., a consultant to the Commission on Violence and Youth:

It represents a dramatic change from repressive styles of policing and the 'we-they' element of the police culture that has dominated law enforcement for so many years. . . . Psychologists can help develop new screening procedures to select appropriate recruits for the community police role. They can also develop training procedures to help older 'by-the-book' officers adapt to the changing requirements. . . .Because community police operate more independently and interact more closely with the public, they need help developing skills in com-

munications, problem-solving, decision-making, conflict resolution, negotiation tactics and time management.

Victoria Havassy, a Ph.D. police psychologist who participated in the venture, commented that in Los Angeles County, where about 85 languages are spoken, the sheriff's department recently developed a cultural diversity training program. In the program, trainees learn about the dominant cultures in their area, and appropriate ways of addressing those residents. The program developers found that many officers believed they had to be aloof and suspicious with members of certain minority groups in order to protect themselves. Part of the training involves showing the officers that they can't treat every Hispanic or African-American person they encounter as a criminal.

The program also challenged the officers to learn about their own biases. In a test, recruits were given photographs of individuals and were directed to identify which ones they believed were drug dealers, murderers, or members of other deviant or distinct groups. But after making the selections, the participants learned that the photos were all of senior-ranking law enforcement officers.

Source: Excerpts from "Community Policing Approach Suggested," by Scott Sleek, 1993, *APA Monitor*, December, 1993, p. 33. Copyright 1993 by the American Psychological Association. Reprinted with permission.

The environment in which an organization operates determines the type of training that should be conducted. For example, whether an organization functions internationally or locally will affect training. An organization with international divisions would consider cross-cultural training, such as teaching employees to adjust to different cultures, learn appropriate languages, and become aware of specific customs. An example of this type of training is the assimilation training a German company used to prepare its

staff for cross-cultural management (Thomas, 1990). The training concerned Chinese perceptions, cognition, and actions. It consisted of forty-one hypothetical interactions involving different Chinese behavioral norms in business and was intended to teach managers the behaviors appropriate to these situations.

A company that functions solely within its own country might concentrate on internal climate constraints, such as the hierarchical order of the company and relationships with management. Components of the environment that are taken into account during organizational analysis include:

1. The organization must financially support training. Even though training is thought of as an investment in the overall profitability of the organization, the amount of financial support can affect training options. A small, family-owned business probably would not be able to invest substantial amounts of capital into an elaborate, computerized training program, while a larger corporation would be financially able to make this large investment. Often, training is viewed as an unnecessary expense when it does not achieve desired results and is considered to be an important investment when it is successful. Stability of financial support occurs when training is integrated into the organization's strategic, human resource, succession, and employee/management selection plans. (For a discussion of the planning process, see Chapter 3.)

2. Training must consider whether the organizational environment is dynamic or relatively stable. Organizations that operate in rapidly changing environments must be able to readily adapt their training programs to keep current with new technologies. This can be accomplished by paying close attention to the adaptation phase of the systems approach, which allows for reevaluation and modification of the training program. On the other hand, organizations that operate in relatively stable environments may develop highly effective programs and maintain them over time with little change.

An organization's objectives are driven by its strategic plan (see Chapter 3) and can be stated in long- and short-term goals, as well as corporate and departmental goals. According to Bass and Vaughan (1975), long-term objectives need to be established in broad areas for the entire company; next, specific goals and strategies should be stated for the various components of the company as a means of achieving these broad objectives. This, in turn, allows the asses-

sor to formulate specific training objectives for each department, as well as broad training areas for the entire organization. Since both stable and dynamic organizations change over time, the objectives—whether long-term, short-term, departmental, or systemwide—must be continually reviewed and revised.

3. A third aspect of organizational analysis is estimating how many people need immediate training and how many will require future training (Wexley & Latham, 1981). This is usually part of the organization's personnel plan (see Chapter 3). Each organization should perform some type of employment forecasting and planning, whether formal or informal. Informal methods are usually intuitive in nature; formal techniques employ a variety of sophisticated statistical methods. Formal planning is necessary for large organizations with high growth rates, high employee turnover, and rapid changes in technology and product lines.

4. The final aspect of an organizational analysis is the climate in which an employee will perform. Bass and Vaughan (1975) described climate as a reflection of the attitudes of organizational members toward various aspects of work, supervision, company procedures, goals and objectives, and membership in the organization. As early as 1953, Fleishman stated that the effects of training will transfer only when reinforced by the departmental climate. Research (e.g., Rouillier & Goldstein, 1990) on the effects of organizational climate over the years has confirmed its impact on the transfer process. This is an important consideration. If the organizational climate does not allow for a certain behavior, then training for that specific behavior would be a waste of time unless it is the training department's intention to change the climate. It is possible to change an organization's climate, but only with the support of all the components of the organization. For example, if supervisors were trained to include employees in decision making (i.e., participative management), the company should ensure that the supervisors will be reinforced by their managers for this behav-

ior and that this will be the philosophy of the company through all levels of management.

Transfer of training is a part of the posttraining environment. Situational cues that enhance transfer, as summarized by Tannenbaum and Yukl (1992), include (a) "goal cues that serve to remind trainees to use their training" (p. 421), (b) supervisor and peer behavior that supply the situational cues for the application of the learned behavior, and (c) training tasks and equipment designed to be similar to the job situation. The opportunity to use what has been learned in training is an additional situational cue that can provide a positive posttraining environment. For instance, "existing managers [can] let new managers know they are doing a good job when they use their training" on the job (Goldstein, 1991, p. 526).

Task Analysis

The second type of needs assessment analysis is task analysis, which consists of assessing the actual duties and responsibilities that are required to complete a specific job. According to Goldstein and Gilliam (1990, p. 135), task analysis is the "determination of which tasks are required on the job and which skills and abilities are critical in learning to perform these tasks." It is important to determine the knowledge, skills, abilities, and other characteristics (KSAOs) that are necessary for successful performance to define specific training objectives for each individual job title (see Figure 9.2). As Goldstein (1991, p. 527) commented, task analysis is not a "description of the worker, but rather a description of the job."

In most organizations, task analysis is part of a job analysis that is completed in designing the selection procedures for the position. Job analysis is the first and most important step in preparing to train for skill development (Piskurich, 1991). It is at this stage that particular attention is focused on the performance standards required of employees, the tasks in which they will be engaged, the methods they will use on the job,

and, most important, the way they will learn these methods (McGehee & Thayer, 1961).

In developing training programs for new employees and current employees who have been promoted, the main goals are to determine what can be accomplished via training and what must be learned through experience on the job. This distinction is important, not only because it is difficult to teach something that can be best learned by experience, but also because using ineffective methods is a waste of time and money. For example, certain chefs might find it impossible to teach others how to judge whether a sauce has the right taste or consistency. Following the recipe does not guarantee that the sauce will have the desired taste. The ingredients can be measured precisely, but their quality and strength may vary. These elements in the recipe are difficult to quantify. Skilled chefs, however, have learned to use their sense of taste to make the adjustments that make the sauce taste the way they want it. This type of knowledge can be obtained only through trial and error or on-the-job experience.

A variety of methods can be used in a task analysis. Methods for collecting data include observing a current job incumbent, interviewing and surveying both the incumbent and supervisors, examining the requests made to trainers from supervisors, comparing successful and unsuccessful job incumbents, and reviewing performance appraisals, personnel files, and production records. Other methods include collecting incidents on the job that lead to effective and ineffective performance and using validated questionnaires for job analysis (e.g., the Position Analysis Questionnaire; Tannenbaum & Yukl, 1992).

Person Analysis

The final type of analysis in needs assessment is the person analysis. In a person analysis the assessor considers who will receive training and the type of training they will receive. Three main groups of people receive training: new employees, current employees who have been promoted, and current employees who have performance deficiencies. The training can take place individually or in groups.

Unless the selection procedure ensures that current employees already have the qualifications for successful job performance, the training department should not assume that new employees have those skills. For example, if an organization finds that using a photocopy machine is an important skill for office personnel, it should include training in how to use the photocopy machine unless the skill for using this type of machine is included in the selection procedure. In developing training objectives for new hires, all aspects of the job should be included. Then, if trainers find that an individual has a certain skill, they can tailor the training program for that individual to avoid redundancy. In the photocopy example, if this skill is not part of the selection process but the trainer finds that all trainees are well-versed in photocopy machine operations, this section of training can be eliminated. At the group level, exposure to knowledge that a few employees have already learned must be tolerated so that all employees ultimately have the knowledge they need for successful performance.

Frequent and effective employee evaluations allow for the detection of substandard performance, which can be remedied through training. The tool that is often used for identifying performance problems is the performance appraisal. Substandard performance due to factors such as poor motivation or the use of antiquated machinery cannot be improved through training. However, substandard performance due to the lack of specific skills or knowledge *can* be remedied through training. Training current employees is usually done individually unless a specific deficiency is found in many employees or an effort is being made to upgrade the skills of employees in a specific targeted area. In these situations, group training is usually more cost-effective.

Person analysis incorporates the idea of individual differences. For example, the person's age and phase in his or her career can affect the type of training (or retraining) needed. Addi-

tional factors that are often considered include differences in training time required by people in different age groups, the motivation of older trainees, individual self-determination, self-paced learning processes, and feelings of employment security (London & Bassman, 1989; Sterns & Doverspike, 1989). Sterns and Doverspike (1989, p. 326) believe that the most important issues are "to sensitize managers to workers' potential and to be aware that managers may be discriminating against middle-aged and older workers by not providing adequate and well-designed training and retraining programs."

We have seen how a complete needs assessment must include analyses of organizational objectives, specific job duties and responsibilities, and the people who will be trained. This is a difficult task but a necessary one if we are to maximize the effectiveness of training programs. Mitchell (1981, pp. 49–50) suggested the following steps for conducting a sound needs analysis:

1. Monitor the standard sources of information in order to proactively identify needs before they become obvious.
2. Identify the types of problems in each area and determine those that are training related.
3. Gather data to establish present levels of performance.
4. Examine the feasibility of training as a solution to the problems.
5. Determine the size and scope of the program.
6. Justify the cost of the program.
7. Search for and identify the particular training needs of different employee subgroups (such as women, older workers, and minorities) and plan training and costs accordingly.

Effective needs assessment is a dynamic, ongoing process that must respond to the changing nature of organizations. Objectives, job duties, and the employees all change over time. The successful organization is constantly aware of its fluid nature and will conduct frequent needs assessments to ensure continued employee satisfaction and productivity.

Training and Development Techniques

After training needs and goals have been established by conducting a needs assessment, the needs are translated into specific objectives, and a training program is designed to achieve those objectives. In deciding on training techniques, it is imperative to take into account the various advantages and disadvantages, as well as the costs, of each technique. The technique that is best suited to a particular organization will meet organizational objectives while staying within budget. Despite the claim that the distinction between on-the-job and off-the job training is becoming blurred (Tannenbaum & Yukl, 1992), we believe that the traditional categorization of training methods is still pertinent. This section focuses on a variety of techniques that are used to train employees in today's workplace.

On-Site Techniques

On-site training occurs on the same job site as the one in which the worker will be expected to perform. Typically, on-site training is used when an employee has to learn a multifaceted task or an entire job. The major approaches for on-site training are on-the-job training, job rotation, and mentoring. On-site training is usually less expensive than off-site training. Because training takes place on the job, the transfer of the skills is better, and close relationships to the trainer usually result in better tailoring, feedback, and learning. Several weaknesses of on-site techniques are that the employees who are selected to provide the training, though technically skilled, may lack the interpersonal and training abilities needed to effectively teach others, job rotation can take long periods of time, and mentoring can be biased toward the personal beliefs or agenda of the mentoring manager.

On-the-Job Training. Tracey (1984) described on-the-job training as the most common, most widely accepted, and most necessary method of training employees in the skills that are essential for acceptable job performance. Seventy-five percent of all training in organizations has been done on the job (Mitchell, 1981). In-on-the job training, new trainees are placed with experienced workers to learn job tasks through observation and imitation. This technique was used, for example, by a large textile factory in Israel. New employees were placed in front of machinery on the floor. These machines were fitted with thirty or more spindles for the purpose of making yarn from fibers and spinning more than one thread at a time. Each trainee was placed on one machine, and an experienced employee who was responsible for several machines showed the trainee how to work with the spindles. The experienced employee provided feedback, direction, and correction *while the trainee was performing the job.* When the trainee was judged able to cope with a single machine (subjectively as well as by tracking errors), the number of machines for which he or she was responsible was increased.

Because trainees learn while producing, the on-the-job method is relatively inexpensive. In addition, it typically does not require special training space or equipment. Trainees receive immediate feedback about the correctness of their behavior, which often speeds learning. Finally, on-the-job training dramatically increases the likelihood of positive transfer, the appropriate use of the new learning in the work environment.

On-the-job training does have limitations. For example, the employees who serve as trainers are usually chosen because they are "skilled" workers and may lack the interpersonal skills necessary to train another. Also, experienced employees may perceive the trainee as a threat to their own job security. They may feel burdened by additional training duties and/or hurried because the time allowed for the training is often far too brief and added to other ongoing duties. In selecting trainers, special attention should be given to their social skills, their desire to teach, and their technical competence. To maximize the learning process and its effectiveness, trainers should be well versed in the proper methods of instruction, in principles of learning, and in the standardization of techniques for teaching new employees and evaluating their progress (Mitchell, 1981; Nilson, 1991).

Job Rotation.   **Job rotation** provides trainees with a series of job assignments in various parts of the organization (Wexley & Latham, 1981). Trainees may spend several days, months, or even years in different departments throughout the organization. The main objective of this approach is to expose trainees to a variety of positions and departments within the organization to give them a systemwide perspective of the organization, an understanding of the relationships among its various parts, and an opportunity to establish a working rapport with other employees throughout the company.

An illustration of this method is the experience of a student who received her undergraduate degree in psychology with a concentration in I/O psychology. She was selected as a personnel representative at a large national electrical manufacturing company. Her initial responsibilities included the design and execution of a performance appraisal program for lower- and middle-level managers. The company tailored a training program to fit her specific needs. The initial training involved learning organizational goals, the communities served by the company, and corporate policies. The next step included a review of existing job analyses of related positions, performance evaluation systems, and procedures for promotion. The last phase of her training was a job rotation program lasting about one year. While working in each of the assigned departments, she learned the functions of various managers and departments, the relationships among them, the climates (both formal and informal) in each department, and departmental goals; she met personnel and established rapport. By the time she completed her job rotation training, this new representative had solid knowledge of the entire organization.

When job rotation is used for blue-collar workers, it frequently is limited to the immediate department or work station. Many produc-

tion teams and cells rotate workers through all work stations. This helps a worker to understand the full nature of his or her work and makes it possible for the team to easily move people to different stations as needed. In training white-collar managers, job rotation is more extensive, involving more departments or areas of the company, and takes longer. This is because the role of a manager is more complex, usually requiring a wider variety of skills and a broader knowledge and understanding of the company.

For job rotation to be effective, these principles should be followed:

1. Job rotation must be tailored to the needs and capabilities of individual trainees (Bass & Vaughan, 1966).
2. The specific period of time trainees spend in each department should depend on the rate at which they learn new material.
3. Trainees' performance should be monitored by trained and experienced personnel who offer guidance, reinforcement, and feedback.

Mentoring.   The concept of sponsoring, or mentoring, is similar to the apprenticeships that are typical of craft trades (Wilbur, 1987). **Mentoring** occurs when a senior, experienced, influential person provides guidance and support in a protege's career development or takes a personal interest in another individual's development (Mahler, 1991). In management training that uses mentoring, a subordinate is assigned to a person who is several levels above the trainee in the management hierarchy and whose task is to help or champion the trainee. Mentoring can include the formation of relationships on two levels: informal relationships, which are spontaneous rather than managed or structured by the organization (Chao, Walz, & Gardner, 1992), and formal programs, which are organized and managed by the organization. In both cases, training is provided through the mentor's career-related and psychosocial roles. The career-related role includes functions such as coaching, protection, and assigning challenging activities to the protege. An example of this type of role is helping the trainee meet new colleagues (Chao et al., 1992). The psychosocial role includes the functions of friendship, counseling, and other activities that help the protege's self-image, such as sharing a career history with the protege and expressing empathy for his or her feelings (Chao et al., 1992).

Mentoring is a powerful learning model because it provides the trainee with direct, constant, and focused contact with the trainer and the trainer can tailor instruction to the trainee's progress. Because of this direct relationship and the mutual immediate feedback, mentors can ascertain whether trainees are actually learning the material and can shape the trainees' behavior accordingly, using reinforcement and feedback. A disadvantage to mentoring (Lawrie, 1987) is that mentors may subtly program trainees to think in a particular way about corporate or departmental philosophies.

Skills may be taught through mentoring, but most often what is learned from the mentor is a set of values or attitudes toward organizational priorities. Some instances in which mentoring makes sense are when the trainee's position requires impeccable customer relations, when large amounts of capital investment are at risk, or when a department manager nears retirement.

Successful mentors are apt to exhibit mentoring characteristics in activities outside the workplace, such as teaching in an educational setting or leading a community group. Once mentors have been selected, they should be instructed as to the importance of the learning and reinforcement strategies that are crucial to a successful mentoring program, review the particular trainee and job situation to develop a specific mentoring plan, and earn the trainee's respect by showing empathetic understanding, listening with interest and comprehension, and explaining and communicating effectively.

Off-Site Techniques

Traditionally, off-site techniques have been geared toward the attainment of specific skills rather than toward learning a multifaceted task or an entire job (as in on-the-job training). A major weakness in off-site techniques is that learning might not transfer easily from the training environment to the job site. A recent trend in training combines on-the-job and off-the-job training by providing clues and feedback through sophisticated equipment, monitoring operations, and troubleshooting diagnostic techniques (Tannenbaum & Yukl, 1992).

Classroom Lecture. The lecture method is defined as a semiformal discourse in which the instructor presents a series of events, facts, concepts, or principles (Tracey, 1984). A primary advantage of this method is the opportunity to relay information simultaneously to a large group of trainees.

However, using the lecture method alone allows for little interaction between the instructor and the trainee because a lecture is usually one-way communication. The trainee passively listens to the lecturer, and there is little or no provision for the exchange of ideas. Consequently, the instructor must be aware of trainees' misconceptions, inattention, and other difficulties and must take measures to remedy them immediately. To maximize its effectiveness and increase feedback, the lecture method can be combined with other methods. For example, trainers can combine the lecture with a discussion approach, the trainer serving as both a lecturer and a facilitator (Griffin & Cashin, 1989). An illustration of this combination is the way in which a general psychology course is being taught at a Midwestern university. Lecture classes include sixty to ninety students and cover basic principles, definitions, and theories. Three or four times a semester, the lecturer divides the class randomly into groups of five students. Class time is allocated for the groups to meet to divide the material covered in class to date and decide on the method by which discussions will be conducted. Students can prepare the review material to be presented to their groups in the form of multiple-choice questions and summary and discussion questions. After the group discussions the instructor circulates among the groups answering questions and stimulating additional discussion. At the end of the hour, students rate each other on preparation and participation. Feedback from students has confirmed that these discussion sessions help them to clarify and comprehend the lecture material. Methods such as this can help trainers to modify lecture-based approaches to meet the needs of a particular group of trainees.

Conference.   The conference method facilitates understanding through two-way communication. This technique has proved to be "particularly suitable for acquiring and understanding conceptual data" (Bass & Vaughan, 1966, p. 98) and for facilitating changes in behaviors and attitudes. Tracey (1984) suggested that learning takes place in direct proportion to the amount of individual participation in the learning process. The demand for participants to be active in the process promotes increased comprehension and can result in more permanent learning. This method follows some of the principles of operant learning—specifically, feedback and motivation. Students learn more when they ask questions in class, get answers from the instructor, and are encouraged to participate in the learning process by engaging in a discussion of the material under review.

On a negative note, a relatively large amount of time must be devoted to the conference method and its preparation to ensure success. Tracey stated that the thoroughness of the preparation before the meeting determines the quality of the discussion and the outcome of the conference.

For the conference method to be a valuable learning experience, as well as a method for enhancing individual participation, the group should be limited to a maximum of fifteen people. The amount of time needed for the discussion of a subject is directly proportional to the number of trainees in the group. Group members should possess similar backgrounds. For example, if half of a group of skilled machinists

have at least five years of experience and the other half of the group are beginners with no experience, the desired degree of discussion will be difficult to obtain. The leader has to be trained in leading a discussion and in administering reinforcement and feedback. Group members have to be willing to participate.

Audiovisual.   The use of **audiovisual aids** began during World War II, when large numbers of personnel needed training and very few instructors were available to provide it. Audiovisual aids ensured the military of training uniformity and provided the capability to train vast numbers of people simultaneously.

Audiovisual aids include such devices as slides, audio recordings, films, and videotapes. They should not be used in isolation, however; audiovisual aids are most effective when used in conjunction with other methods, such as a lecture or a discussion. As with the lecture method, audiovisual presentations can create passive audiences. However, if instructors use a discussion together with audiovisual aids, feedback is possible, the audience becomes participative, and the session becomes interactive rather than one-way or passive. For example, student group presentations in an organizational psychology class were videotaped. The class later observed the tapes, and students commented on the content of material covered by each group and the manner in which it was presented. Students incorporated these comments into their term papers. The comments were also used to revise presentations in future classes.

Schneier and Beatty (1978) stated that audiovisual devices can "capture" experts in a particular area, ensuring the quality and correctness of the material presented. Films and videotapes seem to be effective because, as Howell (1976) noted, they permit a dramatic illustration of certain kinds of information that could not readily be conveyed in any other way. For example, videotapes of actual and simulated bank robberies are used to teach bank tellers what procedures to follow during a robbery.

Simulation and Games Methods

One of the main principles of training is the transfer of training, that is, practicing behaviors similar to those used on the job to enhance the transfer of skills from the training site to the job situation (Schneier & Beatty, 1978). This principle is central to the **simulation method** of training. In "simulations, some essential features of an activity are duplicated without portraying reality itself" (Thornton & Cleveland, 1990, p. 190); "a game involves one or more players who are given . . . [information] . . . rules to follow, and roles to play" (p. 190).

Simulations present trainees with real-world problems and/or situations and allow them to experience the consequences of their decisions. A primary benefit of this method is that poor decision making does not result in the actual loss of a job, pay, or profits. Rather, using simulations provides employees with the opportunity to learn how to avoid future negative consequences but to do so within a safe, nonpunitive environment. The space program used simulators to train astronauts on what conditions to expect when they reached space. The success of the program was due in part to the accuracy of these simulations and the degree to which they prepared astronauts for the demands of space travel.

Supervisory development sometimes uses simulation by assigning the roles of supervisor and subordinate to two supervisory trainees. In one such application the "supervisor" trainee questions the "subordinate" trainee about unexcused absences. In such situations, new supervisors can practice appropriate ways of giving corrective feedback to employees. When playing the role of subordinate, they develop a perspective on the effectiveness of the approach they are learning. Originally, simulations were developed for the training of technical and motor skills. Now they have become highly useful for investigating and teaching almost the entire gamut of organizational behavior (Bass & Vaughan, 1966; Thornton & Cleveland, 1990).

In general, simulations vary in group size (e.g., from one to twenty participants; (Thornton &

Cleveland, 1990) and in task or project complexity (e.g., from an accounting exercise in which a trainee must calculate and make decisions regarding the transfer of monies from one department to another, to a simulation game including an entire hypothetical international organization). According to Thornton and Cleveland (1990), the parameters that influence the success of simulation training include the time spent on training, group size, type of feedback, tutoring aids, and others.

Critics of simulations have raised some concerns. They question the type of learning processes involved, the effects of simulation on immediate and long-term performance and the need for careful and detailed preparation for feedback, reinforcement, and practice (Tannenbaum & Yukl, 1992). These issues and others related to the major forms of simulation training are discussed in more detail in the following sections.

Role Playing. **Role playing** involves the unrehearsed acting out of a situation by two or more individuals under the direction of a trainer (Tracey, 1984). Each participant is presented with a situation in which he or she assumes a role and acts it out as he or she thinks the role *should* be played. Role playing has been used to simulate real-life situations and dilemmas that participants may encounter on the job.

Some major advantages of role playing are that participants explore various approaches to a solution while not encountering penalizing consequences as a result of their actions. They also develop diagnostic skills with regard to potential problem areas, learn how others view certain situations, and develop communication and interpersonal relations skills.

An example of role playing is the shop steward being placed in the role of his or her department manager, and the manager being placed in the role of the shop steward. The task is to decide on punitive actions toward a routinely tardy employee. Assuming these reversed roles and acting out solutions on the basis of these roles can help participants to better understand the other person's perspective, search for compromise, and open the channels of communication.

One of the disadvantages of this technique is that a large amount of time needs to be allotted for trainee briefings, performances, and follow-up discussions. Additional problems may arise if some participants are too timid to engage in role-playing sessions or if they become resentful when receiving corrective feedback on their role play performance. Whatever problems arise, a capable instructor is the key to successful role playing, as direction and guidance are essential elements of this technique.

Business Games.   **Business games** are carefully controlled simulations that focus on general management principles and/or specific problems. Most business games are created to stimulate decision-making strategies and are designed to include carefully arranged, competitive elements. Because clear-cut solutions to problems are not readily apparent, participants are encouraged to develop their own solutions. Exercise 9.2 is a business game that is used to develop insights into team building. These games are used to develop leadership skills, to improve decision-making abilities, and to improve technical performance, cooperation, and teamwork.

Business games are also used internationally. For example, they have been used to teach collective bargaining in the Soviet Union (Davidov, Neverkovich, & Samoukina, 1990); as an intervention mechanism to prepare women for nontraditional careers in the United States (Hammer-Higgins & Atwood, 1989); and as a developmental device in the Israel Defense Forces (Lipshitz & Popper, 1990). They can vary from simple games such as the in-basket game (involving hypothetical memos and letters to be handled by the subject) to an extensive, computerized, large-scale simulation of an international company (involving many subjects, sophisticated equipment, and a variety of international divisions and functions).

A famous large-scale simulation is the Center for Creative Leadership's organizational simulation, Looking Glass, Inc. This is a simulation of a glass-manufacturing corporation. It includes twenty positions ranging across three divisions and four levels (plant manager, director, vice-president, and president). The divisions face different environments, ranging from volatile to stable. The simulation attempts to replicate reality as managers and leaders perceive it and to demonstrate what leadership is like in complex settings. Participants are assessed and coached according to their performance (McCall & Lombardo, 1978).

One advantage of simulations is that long periods of time can be condensed into one- or two-week sessions, which can provide participants with valuable experience that might take months or years to gain on the job. In addition, business games can be fun, motivating the participants to become highly involved in the subject matter while undergoing stresses similar to those associated with real-life situations.

A major disadvantage of simulations is that they are more expensive than other approaches, and when computers are involved, costs rise even further because of programming expenses, time spent on the equipment, and the additional personnel required for computer operations.

Vestibule Training.   **Vestibule training** is a technique in which employees are trained off the job but on actual equipment or equipment that closely simulates what they will use on the job (Dessler, 1984). This method is often used in training assembly-line workers when it is too costly or hazardous to train them on the job. Vestibule training is also used extensively to teach complex skills, such as driver training or pilot training, when training on the job could be disastrous.

As in on-the-job training, vestibule training often minimizes transfer problems. It permits the instructor to organize and control learning conditions such as immediate reinforcement, accurate feedback, opportunities for practice and repetition, and a progressively difficult learning sequence. However, this technique can be quite expensive for the organization because of the cost of the equipment, the amount of time the trainee needs to be away from the actual job, and the additional space needed to implement the training.

Sensitivity Training. **Sensitivity training** (or T group training) is a discussion method whereby members are encouraged to express their reactions to, and interpretations of, others' behavior. A trainer is present but does not lead the discussion. Sensitivity training has no specific agenda, no specific goals, and little structure. The subject matter is "the actual behavior of the individuals in the group, or the 'here and now' "(Campbell, Dunnette, Lawler, & Weick, 1970, p. 237). Participants provide evidence of peer behaviors, such as hostility, insecurity, defensive reactions, and dishonesty. Sensitivity training does not aim toward developing participants' decision-making skills; rather, it serves to increase their awareness of how they perceive and react to others.

The goal of this technique is to enhance interpersonal skills and to sensitize individuals to interrelationships with others by taking trainees out of the structure of relationships defined by the organizational hierarchy and placing them in a situation with no authority figure or defined role-specific behaviors. The need to create new ways for participants to react to each other can teach them to better understand the needs, attitudes, and emotions of others. Ronen (1989) claimed that this method could be an effective training device for employees in international organizations; it could enhance their awareness of, and sensitivity to, cross-cultural differences in norms, values, and behavior patterns in various countries and thus increase their communication skills in these settings.

Sensitivity training sessions are long, and may last from a few days to several weeks. They usually involve an average of ten to twelve participants and one trainer and are held away from the workplace to minimize interruptions. Participants are recommended by an immediate

supervisor and/or manager who believes that they require training in human relations.

Sensitivity training is a controversial method. Although it originated in clinical psychology as a form of psychotherapy, it lacks professional clinical procedures and supervision. In addition, it can be a traumatic experience for those who participate because the discussions that evolve during a session often become personal, heated, and involved. For these reasons, sensitivity training has received mixed reviews. Opponents argue that it is unethical when participation is mandatory and can even be dangerous, since the effects may be irreversible. Advocates of sensitivity training argue that participants increase their understanding of themselves as well as those around them and that organizational profits improve as a result of increased sensitivity among employees.

Time spent away from the organization, professional fees, and travel expenses combine to make the cost of sensitivity training high. Sensitivity training can also backfire, especially when tough, hard-nosed decisions are required. For these reasons and the reasons stated above, sensitivity training is a tool that must be used with caution.

Behavior Modeling. **Behavior modeling,** which is based on social learning theory (Bandura, 1977), proposes that new behaviors can be learned by systematically exposing a trainee to a target behavior. The trainee rehearses the target behavior, receives positive reinforcement for successful performance, and repeats the sequence until learning is successful. Modeling occurs when the person who is imitated is seen as being competent, powerful, friendly, and of high status within the organization (Wexley & Latham, 1981). For example, Morey and Esch (1992) described the training of sorters in a large national delivery company. The supervisor-trainer acted as the model who initially performed the tasks, while the trainees observed and listened to descriptions and explanations. Next, the trainees performed side by side with the modeler, who provided immediate feedback and correction of

PRACTICE PERSPECTIVE 9.2

Description of Interaction Modeling

Interaction modeling is the generic name for a new type of supervisory training program. It gives supervisors the critical skills they need to handle employee performance problems and the confidence to use those skills on the job.

Research has shown that after undergoing the program, supervisors can more effectively deal with problems involving employee performance, employee work habits, tardiness and absenteeism, disciplinary action, employee complaints, goal setting and review, discrimination complaints, and resistance to change.

Program participants practice skills by role playing real situations that they are facing or have faced. Possible on-the-job application of each skill is discussed. Targets for on-the-job application are set. Higher-level managers are trained to encourage application.

The skill areas that are taught, such as orienting the new employee or handling employee

complaints, are chosen on the basis of organization needs. Programs are varied from plant to plant within the same organization depending on need. The content of each program is based on the results of an organization survey that identifies the actual problems confronting the supervisors being trained.

A film or videotape showing a supervisor dealing effectively with a specific employee situation gives the participants a vivid example of how to deal with the situations. Over 80% of classroom time is spent in skill practice sessions in which supervisors build their skills in dealing with employee situations. Specific review sessions and management support sessions reinforce the supervisors' use of the interaction skills in dealing with on-the-job problems.

Source: Excerpts from *Interaction Management,* a registered trademark and copyright of Development Dimensions International, Inc., Pittsburgh, PA. Adapted with permission.

errors. This method was augmented by additional feedback in the form of repeated paper-and-pencil quizzes. Another popular application of modeling is the commercial training program on interaction modeling developed by Development Dimensions International. This program is described in more detail in Practice Perspective 9.2.

Behavior modeling can be used as a specific off-site technique or as a subtle component of other methods, such as mentoring. Whether it is used in isolation or as part of a composite training program, the effectiveness of modeling depends on whether the model's behaviors are reinforced, the behaviors are presented in a clear and concise manner, allowing for accurate imitation by trainees, and the behaviors are sequentially presented from simple to complex.

Research supports the use of behavior modeling in training situations. Burke and Day (1986, p. 242) found that behavior modeling is a "sound method for improving learning across situations

as measured by subjective criteria." Many practitioners believe that behavior modeling can be directly responsible for behavioral changes, in contrast to other training methods that attempt to change behavior indirectly through attitudinal or value changes (Mayer & Russell, 1987). A well-designed, well-implemented program can lead to behavioral changes in the learners, which can increase positive performance throughout the organization (Robinson, 1988).

Even though there is a significant amount of support for this technique, some researchers question its overall effectiveness. Mayer and Russell (1987) found no evidence that behavior modeling was more cost-effective than other methods. Additionally, this type of training is difficult to use in some situations. For example, it would probably be ineffective to try to teach decision-making skills with behavior modeling, because this technique is best used in training overt behaviors rather than internal processes. Some recent suggestions (e.g., Gist, 1989) speculate that it may be possible to be successful with other abilities, such as idea generation or interpersonal relationship skills, by varying the modeling process.

Technology-Based Techniques

Training technology has entered into a new and exciting era through the expanded use of computer-based learning techniques. These techniques improve the quality, increase the productivity, and extend the availability of training, education, and development because their design can be closely matched to what we know about adults as learners (Reynolds, 1983). Properly designed computer-based learning can respond to individual differences in rates of learning, previous knowledge, different learning styles, and individual preferences. For example, since computer-based learning is a self-paced method of instruction, each trainee can advance according to his or her own learning rate and can begin training at his or her personal level of expertise. A meta-analysis of more than seventy-five studies found that computer-based learning produced significant gains in positive attitudes and achievement (Kulik, Kulik, & Cohen, 1980). In addition, learning time was reduced by 25–50% over other methods.

There are several computer-based training methods. The following are descriptions of some of the more popular ones.

Programmed Instruction. The **programmed instruction** technique emerged in the late 1950s in educational settings. However, it was not applied to personnel training until the 1960s. Programmed instruction (PI) is a specific method based on the application of operant principles. An example is our previously cited training program at Emery Air Freight. However, most research in the application of PI has been conducted in educational settings rather than in industry (Latham, 1989). An example from a programmed textbook is illustrated in Historical Perspective 9.1 on pages 306–307.

The material to be learned in PI is presented in a series of units that progress from simple to complex. The learner responds to each step and receives immediate feedback. If the response is correct, the trainee proceeds to the next step. If the response is incorrect, the material is presented again until a correct response is elicited. Linear approaches to PI are designed to ensure success on each step before the learner advances to the next step. Branching approaches allow the learner to skip steps or to accelerate the process on the basis of past success. In linear programs, each learner receives the same material in the same sequence; branching programs provide individual learners with unique sequences selected on the basis of their answers to questions presented by the program. The equipment for presenting the material to the learner can be a booklet containing the stimuli on one page and the correct responses on the following page, a teaching machine controlled by the learner, or a computer. Historical Perspective 9.1 presents an example of the linear approach to programmed instruction.

Feedback, reinforcement contingent on correct responses, successive approximation, and the application of specific schedules of reinforcement are the learning principles underlying PI programs (Latham, 1989). Thus, trainees are active participants in the learning process, are exposed to chunks of material, progress at their own pace, and receive immediate feedback. On a practical level, PI is an efficient method for presenting structured material that can decrease the amount of training time by approximately one-third (Nash, Muczyk, & Vettori, 1971).

Programmed instruction has several negative aspects:

1. It does not seem to improve the acquisition of knowledge or its retention over time compared to other conventional lecture methods.
2. It is appropriate to a somewhat limited range of training objectives (Hinrichs, 1976). For example, because of its low social involvement, PI is of limited use for training that deals with social interaction skills.

Programmed Instruction

This example is an excerpt taken from a PI program that was originally used to teach students at a large Midwestern university and eventually published in book form. The operant principles of behavior are based on a book by Holland and Skinner (1961). Readers proceed through the book on a frame basis, turning the page after each frame to see the correct answer and the next frame. Two pages are exhibited to illustrate how this works.

Set 1	PART 1 Reflex Behavior **Simple Reflexes** Estimated time: 23 minutes **Turn to next page and begin** ▶
stimulus (tap on the knee) 1-7	Technically speaking, a reflex involves an eliciting stimulus in a process called elicitation. A stimulus_____ a response. 1-8
threshold 1-15	The fraction of a second which elapses between "brushing the eye" and "blink" is the ___ of the reflex. 1-16
threshold 1-23	The greater the concentration of onion juice (stimulus), the ____ the *magnitude* of the response. 1-24
elicit 1-31	In the pupillary reflex, a very bright flash of light elicits a response of greater_____than a weak flash of light. 1-31
latency 1-39	A solution of lemon juice will not elicit salivation if the stimulus is _____ the threshold. 1-40
(1) magnitude (2) latency 1-47	Presentation of a stimulus is the "cause" of a response. The two form a(n) _____. 1-48

▷	A doctor taps your knee (patellar tendon) with a rubber hammer to test your _____. 1-1
elicits 1-8	To avoid unwanted nuances of meaning in popular words, we do not say that a stimulus "triggers," "stimulates," or "causes" a response, but that it _____ a response. 1-9
latency 1-16	In the patellar-tendon reflex, a forceful tap elicits a strong kick; a tap barely above the threshold elicits a weak kick. Magnitude of response thus depends on the intensity of the _____. 1-17
greater (higher, larger) 1-24	Onion juice elicits the secretion of tears by the lachrymal gland. This causal sequence of events is a(n) _____. 1-25
magnitude (intensity) 1-32	A response and its eliciting stimulus comprise a (n) _____. 1-33
below (less than, sub-) 1-40	The latency of a reflex is the (1) _____ between onset of (2) _____ and _____. 1-41
reflex 1-48	The layman frequently explains behavior as the operation of "mind" or "free will." He seldom does this for reflex behavior, however, because the _____ is an adequate explanation of the response. 1-49

Source: From *The Analysis of Behavior* (pp. 1–2), by J. G. Holland and B. F. Skinner, 1961. New York: McGraw-Hill. Copyright 1961 by McGraw-Hill Book Company, Inc. Reprinted with permission.

3. It requires trainees who are sufficiently well motivated to work more or less independently (Tracey, 1984).
4. Trainees must possess a certain reading level, so illiterate people are excluded.
5. Developing an effective system is time consuming and costly, requiring a developer who is skilled in all facets of PI system development.

Latham (1989) indicated that any self-directed training program should be designed to match individual learning styles and existing knowledge. Goldstein (1993) added that PI techniques are more effective and satisfying when they are combined with other modes of learning, such as conferences or discussions.

Computer-Assisted Instruction. In its earlier stages, PI was available in either specially designed booklets or texts (for example see Historical Perspective 9.1). After the dawn of the computer age, training departments integrated programmed instruction with computer science technology. The principles underlying PI evolved into **computer-assisted instruction** (CAI): self-based instruction structured in steps or units with immediate feedback, presented via computers. CAI is a sophisticated version of PI in which the learner interacts with the computer to gain access to stored information (Howell, 1976).

The storage and memory capabilities of the computer allow the trainer to continuously assess the trainee's progress, keep accurate performance records, adapt the method and the material to fit the trainee's needs, and train a number of employees simultaneously. Research also indicates that, as with PI, the CAI method decreases learning time (Goldstein, 1993). However, since CAI is an application of PI, they share not only advantages, but also disadvantages.

Goldstein (1993) indicated that CAI has three specific limitations:

1. It is costly to design, set up, and maintain an effective CAI program, including writing and validating a program as well as purchasing expensive computer equipment.
2. Research regarding the effectiveness of CAI is limited.
3. The influence of CAI on the satisfaction, motivation, and development of trainees is still unknown.

Fauley (1981) indicated five factors that can help an organization to determine whether to implement a CAI training program:

1. Stability. CAI can adapt to minor changes, but the time and expenses associated with developing longitudinal training programs have to be estimated to determine the benefit to the organization.

2. Audience. CAI may be a viable method of training if the target audience is relatively large and is expected to remain so in the future.

3. Trainee location. Organizations that have many scattered locations can benefit from CAI by lowering the cost of transporting trainees to and from training centers.

4. Interaction. Using CAI for simulations, case studies, and branching sequencing takes full advantage of this technology.

5. Cost-effectiveness. The dollars that are saved over time in terms of greater productivity could offset the higher initial cost of installing a CAI system. Therefore before an organization invests in such a system, a cost–benefit analysis must indicate that it would eventually pay for itself.

Interactive Videodisc Instruction. Interactive video is the combination of videodiscs and microprocessor technologies. Like CAI, **interactive videodisc instruction** combines the effects of video and film with the interactive capabilities of the computer.

Jenkins, DeBlois, and Matsumoto-Grah (1985) suggested that interactive instruction was designed to provide learners with hundreds of preplanned options. These options are based on prior knowledge of the learners' unique interests, abilities, feedback preferences, primary language ability, and learning styles. An interactive videodisc lesson allows learners to create their own learning experience because it lets learners intervene and make frequent decisions about the lesson content and delivery. This distinguishes the interactive format from the presequenced format of most traditional instructional materials, such as texts, workbooks, films, and slide or tape presentations, which treat all learners alike. A description of one such program is presented in Practice Perspective 9.3 on page 310.

The process that makes videodisc interactivity possible is referred to as **branching.** The branching technique allows for alternative tracks to be taken, depending on the speed of the learner. For example, learners can access detailed information, see only the materials they need or want to see, repeat material or perform remedial work when needed, and pose a question without being limited to only one correct answer.

Other benefits of audiovisual techniques, as cited by Goldstein (1993), also hold true for the videodisc: It can be used by a variety of learners; it allows for controlled training in situations in which instructors cannot travel; it can present time-sequenced material (e.g., circumstances leading to collisions in driving lessons); it can deliver material that cannot be presented via other training methods; and it allows for replays if necessary.

Some disadvantages of the interactive videodisc technique, as cited by Tracey (1984), include the cost of the equipment and the requirements for highly competent learning specialists and computer programmers to prepare the materials. Interactive videodisc instruction is best used in conjunction with other methods to enhance the learning environment and to help prevent learner boredom.

Closed-Circuit Television. **Closed-circuit television** is a method in which the trainees' performance of a specific task is videotaped and then replayed and reviewed by the trainee. It permits trainees to view themselves shortly after performing various activities, provides immediate feedback, and allows trainees to see how they actually perform from the trainer's point of view. This feedback may be valuable in a variety of training situations, from learning a golf swing to learning to be sensitive to one's pattern of responses in social situations. Trainees are able to gain beneficial knowledge regarding the correctness of their actions or their behavioral shortcomings when viewing their videotape. In short, the videotape provides a sense of how others may perceive them.

However, closed-circuit television cannot stand alone as a training technique; it must either precede or follow another method. For example, trainers in a customer service organization would provide trainees with prior information, perhaps in lecture form followed by a videotaped role play. If the trainees do not have this prior knowledge, it would be senseless to tape their actions, unless their actions prior to instruction were to serve as a baseline for before- and after-comparisons.

Another drawback to the closed-circuit television method is the cost. At a minimum, a camera, a recorder, and a monitor are needed. Recent decreases in costs have made the basic equipment much more economical. This method is useful only in situations in which the skills taught can be actually seen. Using the closed-circuit technique in training computer skills would offer little benefit; nevertheless, in training interpersonal skills it would be beneficial.

Satellite-Delivered Instruction. **Satellite-delivered instruction** provides live, interactive training and has the ability to receive, as well as transmit, information. As a result of satellite-delivered instruction, employees have easy access to timely and important business, management, and technical information. The variety of satellite-delivered programs has grown to include management and communication seminars, computer literacy classes, and graduate degree courses, to mention a few. Along with increased accessibility, satellite-delivered instruction enables employees to attend training sessions

PRACTICE PERSPECTIVE 9.3

A Description of Interactive Videodisc Technology Used to Teach Selling Skills

Goldstein (1993) cited the training of interpersonal skills as an example of the effective use of interactive videodisc (IVD) technology. Training in effective interpersonal skills, such as selling, remains one of the biggest challenges in training today. In many of the top insurance companies, for example, at least 75% of the new sales personnel leave after three years, largely because they are unable to develop sufficient sales skills to make an adequate income from their commissions.

A combination of automated audiovideo feedback and interactive videodisc or computer-based training is now being used to teach sales skills or to aid in early recognition that an employee is not suited to sales. One IVD system uses a laserdisc player, a touchscreen monitor and a PC coupled with a videotape recorder, camera, and microphone. The IVD presents full-motion video and audio demonstrations of skills such as presenting credentials, then provides review exercises with proper and improper examples of those skills. Trainees can interrupt the presentation of a skill when a mistake is made and offer a critique of the action. Feedback is given on the appropriateness of their critique.

The camera or audio recorder is then used to allow the students to demonstrate proper behavior. Trainees face a new customer (provided on the IVD) and practice the skill that they just saw modeled. (Although the "customer" on the IVD cannot respond in all of the unexpected ways a real person might, this will change with advances in artificial intelligence.) Their performance is recorded on videotape along with the customer's conversation. Students can practice in privacy and then review their performance based on a set of criteria (from the IVD) and evaluate their own behavior. They can erase and repeat, practicing as many times as they wish. When they believe that they have successfully transferred the training to their performance, trainees can show the tape to the supervisor, who provides advanced coaching.

In a pilot evaluation program, insurance agents using this training program had a 16% increase in calls, a 24% increase in kept appointments, and a 43% increase in approach interviews with clients. In addition, new hire training time was reduced 30% over traditional classroom methods, and the subsequent on-the-job training curve decreased. For example, one agency that had been using the IVD system for over a year compared ten agents who used the system with seventeen trained by traditional methods. The ten who used the IVD program were at a level eighteen months ahead of the control group after the completion of training. Although it is difficult to separate the impact of the IVD training from other changes in the company, revenues have gone up since introduction of the system, and the agent retention rate has increased.

IBM has also experimented with an IVD system coupled with a videocamera for teaching sales skills. In a comparison with their traditional person-to-person role-playing training, they found that trainees using the IVD system did much better in structuring their sales calls and developing sales skills.

A second, similar program uses CD-ROMs combined with audio feedback. Full-motion video is available on CD-ROMs. For some training situations, such as telephone sales, audio feedback is actually closer to the real job situation, and full-motion video is not needed. CD-ROMs also cost approximately $2000 less per training station than IVD, have larger storage capacity, and can be used more easily for nontraining applications.

Sources: From Beverly Geber, "Goodbye Classrooms (Redux)," *Training,* Vol. 27, No. 1, January, 1990 Copyright 1990. Lakewood Publications, Minneapolis, MN. Reprinted with permission. All rights reserved.

without leaving their work locations, eliminating the time and travel expenses that constitute the majority of costs associated with training. As Arnall (1987) noted, training by satellite allows a company to give an entire work force access either to its best trainer or to a particular expert and offers immediate dissemination of information that cannot be matched by any other medium.

There are two basic types of satellite-delivered instruction: horizontal programming and vertical programming. **Horizontal programming** allows an organization to purchase preproduced and/or live video programs packaged by subject. This method offers an extremely cost-effective means of addressing standardized information, allowing the training staff to focus on training needs unique to the organization.

Vertical programming is the transmission of specialized material, rather than preproduced programs. Because the demonstrations are live, the course can be structured interactively through the use of call-in question-and-answer periods. This added advantage is usually not possible with horizontal programming because most such productions are prerecorded, rather than live, presentations. However, vertical programming is also much more costly because of the additional equipment needed to transmit the material, as well as the costs associated with the development and production of the programs. Here again, recent advances in technology are making this easier and less costly. Picture-Tel, a commercial system, provides all the necessary equipment in an integrated package that can be used to set up a two-way videoconference room in any organization. Many Kinkos print shop locations across the United States have videoconferencing facilities that are available on a per-use basis for very nominal rental. A number of organizations have begun using this technology for team meetings, conferences, and training which involves people in remote locations.

Satellite-delivered instruction has a variety of uses outside the realm of training. It can be used for introducing new product lines, for teleconferencing, and for communicating with customers, suppliers, and other corporations. It is particularly advantageous for communication on international levels. The additional uses for satellites help to justify the costs of implementing this system.

Management and Leadership Training

Nadler (1984) and Hersey and Blanchard (1988) have suggested that the development of executives, managers, and supervisors has taken on new meaning. This is due in part to heightened international competition, the world economy, and the acceleration of technological, social, and other elements. These developments lead corporations, government organizations, and other businesses to design training programs with worldwide perspective. Dessler (1984) stated that, although management development is important for several reasons, the main reason is that promotion from within is a major source of management talent. Dessler further suggested that because most individuals who are promoted to management positions require some additional training, management development courses are essential for providing organizational continuity by preparing employees and current managers to smoothly assume higher-level positions.

Unfortunately, most management training is designed around untested concepts or the "fad of the day." One way to avoid this faddism is to examine the competencies needed for management. In a major study of managers, Boyatzis (1982) determined which characteristics of managers were related to effective performance in a variety of jobs in a variety of organizations. His model, presented in full in his book *The Competent Manager: A Model for Effective Performance*, used twenty-one characteristics that were evaluated in 2,000 people drawn from twelve organizations and forty-one different management jobs.

The method was job competence assessment. The steps in this process were as follows:

- Choosing an appropriate measure of job performance
- Collecting data on the managers

- Generating a list of characteristics that are judged to lead to effective performance
- Obtaining item ratings by the managers
- Computing a weighted list of characteristics
- Analyzing and clustering characteristics
- Conducting interviews to collect behavioral examples of significant managerial activities
- Coding interviews for characteristics or developing the code and evaluating the interviews
- Relating the coding to job performance data
- Choosing tests and measures to assess the competencies identified
- Administering tests and measures and scoring them
- Relating scores to job performance data
- Integrating the results
- Statistically and theoretically determining and documenting the causal relationships among the competencies and between the competencies and job performance

The result of the Boyatzis study was the identification of six clusters of competencies:

The goal and action management cluster included the following competencies: concern with impact, diagnostic use of concepts, efficiency orientation, and proactivity.

The leadership cluster contained competencies of conceptualization skill, self-confidence, and use of oral presentations.

Two competencies made up the human resource management cluster: managing group processes and use of socialized power.

Skills needed for the directing subordinates cluster were developing others, spontaneity, and the use of unilateral power.

The focus on others cluster contained the competencies of perceptual objectivity, self-control, and stamina and adaptability.

The last cluster, specialized knowledge, reflected the specialized knowledge needed by managers and their specific social roles.

The kind of information provided by the Boyatzis study and model is useful in selecting and designing special training programs for managers. Managerial training needs to involve

more than teaching participants about the functions of management. Evidence that these and other generic characteristics can be developed through specific training and education has been provided by Boyatzis (1976), McClelland (1978), McClelland and Burnham (1976), McClelland and Winter (1979), Miron and McClelland (1979), and Winter, McClelland, and Stewart (1983).

The process of developing a training program for managers is no different from the processes that are used to develop programs for any other group in an organization. However, the techniques vary considerably because of the complexity of a manager's role within the organization. For example, problem solving, decision making, career counseling, motivating, and directing employees are just a few of the areas in which a manager must display competence. Training the abstract skills needed by managers is difficult; the techniques that are used rely on both off-site and on-site methods. This combination of methods will vary for each organization, position, and individual. Off-site techniques include business games, conferences, role playing, satellite-delivered instruction, behavior modeling, and interactive video. On-site techniques include on-the-job training, job rotation, and mentoring.

Dessler suggested that on-the-job experience is the most popular form of management development. However, preferred techniques differ by organizational level; in-house programs are preferred for first-line supervisors and external conferences and seminars are widely used for top executives.

Career Development

Milkovich and Glueck (1985) defined **career development** as a formal, structured activity that an organization offers its members for increasing the awareness, knowledge, or capabilities that affect career direction and progression. The organization's role includes assisting with the development of insight into abilities and career needs, the formulation of possible career plans, and training and development to meet the requirements for career advancement. Organizations are realizing the benefits of career development, which has been shown to reduce labor turnover and increase the number of candidates with potential for promotion.

Wexley and Latham (1981) suggested that the primary goal of career development is to enhance employees' awareness about themselves and their career goals by using an information-based (i.e., cognitive) strategy. Career development sessions are usually conducted either by supervisors or by members of the training team at an on-site location; however, they may be held off-site as well. The person who conducts career planning is often highly trained in the administration of diagnostic tests. Career counseling requires that the counselor be able to interpret test results correctly and counsel employees effectively. Career planning personnel need to be aware of job availability and the prerequisites for successful job performance. With this knowledge they can develop career paths that fit individual and organizational needs.

Wexley and Latham (1981) believe that a career specialist could help an individual set realistic career objectives, plan a sequence of steps for obtaining those objectives, and brainstorm ways of overcoming individual problems that threaten to block goal attainment. Gilley (1988) suggested that career development must focus on long-term results and account for individual diversity. To accomplish these goals, resources and methods other than the traditional classroom approach are needed, such as involvement in professional organizations and experience-based training. An additional ingredient is involvement of both the individual and the organization. As Noe and Schmitt (1986) suggested, employee involvement (in the job or career) was found to be an important precondition to success in training and in the workplace.

Comparing Techniques

It is essential to give careful consideration to the selection of training methods to achieve effective employee training. As Table 9.1 on page 314 indicates, each method can be applied in various combinations to achieve particular training objectives. For example, researchers have found no difference between the effectiveness of the lecture and conference methods for acquiring knowledge (Hill, 1960; Watson, 1975). Programmed instruction, on the other hand, is superior to both the lecture and conference methods in the acquisition and retaining of knowledge (Nash et al., 1971). Several studies have shown that the conference, role playing, and sensitivity training methods are superior to the lecture method for changing attitudes (Festinger & Carlsmith, 1959; Lewin, 1968; Underwood, 1965). Lawrie (1987) added that mentoring is also an effective device for producing changes in attitude. Role playing proved to be superior for teaching problem-solving skills, and Tracey (1984) found that the business game and computer-based methods were effective for training problem-solving skills. The computer-based methods produce effective results in knowledge acquisition and retention (e.g., Tracey, 1984). For retraining, research suggests that the PI, lecture, and conference methods are equally effective (e.g., Nash et al., 1971).

Evaluation of Training Programs

The purpose of the evaluation phase in a training program is to determine overall impact as well as the effectiveness of each component. Tracey (1984) stated that the primary objective of an evaluation program is to collect data that will serve as a valid basis for improving the training system and maintaining quality control over its components. This objective is similar to the systems approach to training. As Goldstein (1993, p. 19) summarized, "in this framework a research approach is necessary to determine which programs are meeting their objectives." Examples of such considerations are presented in Table 9.2 on page 315.

According to Goldstein, the evaluation process includes two important features: establishing "measures of success (criteria)" (p. 26) and

| TABLE 9.1 | Effectiveness of different training methods for various training outcomes |

Method	Acquiring Knowledge	Changing Attitudes	Problem Solving	Knowledge Retention
On-the-job training	✓	✓	✓	✓
Job rotation	✓		✓	
Mentoring	✓	✓	✓	
Lecture	✓			✓
Conference	✓	✓		✓
Audio visual/ closed circuit TV	✓			✓
Role playing		✓	✓	
Business games		✓	✓	
Vestibule	✓			✓
Sensitivity		✓		
Behavior modeling	✓	✓		✓
Programmed instruction	✓			✓
Computer-based training (computer-assisted instruction, interactive videodisc)	✓		✓	✓
Satellite	✓		✓	✓

Source: Adapted from *Training in Industry: The Management of Learning* (p. 94) by B. Bass and J. Vaughn, 1966. Belmont, CA: Wadsworth. Copyright 1966 by Wadsworth Publishing. Reprinted with permission.

determining which evaluation models will best examine the level of effectiveness. Accordingly, the evaluation program should be regarded as a continual process that collects and reviews data as a basis for training program revisions (Goldstein, 1991).

Criteria

Training program evaluation should begin with a consideration of criteria measures. Kirkpatrick (1987) suggested four criteria for training evaluation: reaction criteria, learning criteria, behavioral criteria, and results criteria:

1. Reaction criteria measure trainees' reactions and feelings about the training program. They question both content and process to determine what trainees learned and whether they found the learning experience valuable.

2. Learning criteria measure the extent to which "principles, facts, and techniques were

understood and absorbed by the conferees" (Kirkpatrick, 1987, p. 8). Training objectives define the measures (pencil-and-paper exams, classroom demonstrations, presentations, etc.) used to evaluate learning in the training program, *not* on the job.

3. Behavioral criteria measure the transfer of training behaviors to behaviors on the job. For example, how applicable is what you have learned as a student in a business communication class to your effectiveness in writing memos and reports in your job as a personnel director?

4. Results criteria measure the payoff of the training program in terms of the organizational goals and objectives for which it was designed. For example, reductions in turnover and grievances and increases in morale, quantity, and quality of production would be considered by applying these criteria.

TABLE 9.2   Advantages and disadvantages of a sample of training techniques.

Method	Advantages	Disadvantages
On-the-job training	Inexpensive Positive transfer Immediate feedback	Inadequate training for the trainee
Job rotation	Gaining overall perspective of organization Understanding interrelationships between departments	Must be tailored to each trainee Expensive
Mentoring	Direct, constant, and focused contact with trainer Constant supervision Immediate feedback and reinforcement Probability of tailoring training to the individual	Costly Trainee is programmed in thinking and behavior

Because criteria should be selected on the basis of the needs assessment, they should be in accordance with the objectives of the particular training program. Additionally, this selection should reflect both training performance and job effectiveness (Goldstein, 1993). For example, reaction and learning criteria are internal criteria that measure how successful trainees are in the training program; they do not assess the impact of the training on job behaviors or on the achievement of organizational goals. Therefore data on all four criteria are essential.

Additional categories of criteria, as suggested by Goldstein (1991, 1993) include criterion- and norm-referenced criteria. Criterion-referenced measures compare individual achievement to a predetermined behavioral objective based on the needs analysis. For example, word-processing eighty words per minute without any spelling errors would establish the degree of competence attained by the trainee. Norm-referenced criteria compare trainees' achievements to those of other trainees. For example, if grades were determined on the basis of the distribution of scores of students in class, a grade of A would mean that the student is better than

90% of the other students in class. In an analysis similar to the types of criteria discussed in the chapter on performance appraisal, Goldstein (1991, 1993) categorized criteria as objective (such as ratings on numerical scales) and subjective (such as the aesthetic appeal of fabric woven).

Evaluation Designs

Once the criteria used to measure training effectiveness have been determined, attention must be given to proper evaluation design. Howell (1976) stated that it is not sufficient merely to evaluate the amount of change accomplished by the training program, even if the change can be verified through proper experimentation. Rather, the critical issue is whether the change transfers positively to the actual job situation. Because training is a continuous and self-correcting process, managers should monitor it constantly and answer the following questions (Goldstein, 1991):

1. Did any changes occur?
2. Did the training program lead to these changes?
3. Can these changes be generalized to new trainees?

TABLE 9.3	A summary of evaluation designs			

Designs	Pretest	Training	Posttest	Compare
Preexperimental				
Posttest				
Experimental group	—	Yes	X	Only descriptive
Pre/post				
Experimental group	X_1	Yes	X_2	Before and after scores
Experimental				
Control group				
Experimental group	X_1	Yes	X_2	The changes for the two groups
Control group	X_3	No	X_4	in pretest and posttest scores
Solomon design				
Experimental group	X_1	Yes	X_2	The experimental group's test
Control group 1	X_3	No	X_4	scores, $X_1 - X_2$, to $X_3 - X_4$, to
Control group 2	—	Yes	X_5	$X_1 - X_6$, $X_3 - X_6$, etc.
Control group 3	—	No	X_6	
Quasi-Experimental				
Time-series designs				
Experimental group	X_1			The effects of training $X_3 - X_4$ to
	X_2			$X_1 - X_2$, $X_2 - X_3$, $X_4 - X_5$, $X_5 - X_6$
	X_3	Yes	X_4	
			X_5	
			X_6	
Nonequivalent control				
Experimental group	X_1	Yes	X_2	See the control group.
Control group	X_3	No	X_4	Groups not randomly assigned

Source: Cook, T. D., Campbell, D. T., & Peracchio, L. (1990). Quasi experimentation. In M. D. Dunnette & L. M. Hough (Eds.), *Handbook of industrial and organizational psychology* (Vol. I, pp. 491–576). Palo Alto: Consulting Psychologists Press. The data in the table are from "Quasi Experimentation," by T. D. Cook, D. T. Campbell, and L. Peracchio, 1990, in M. D. Dunnette & L. M. Hough (Eds.), *Handbook of industrial and organizational psychology* (Vol. I, pp. 491–576). Palo Alto: Consulting Psychologists Press; I. L. Goldstein, 1991, "Training in work organizations," in M. D. Dunnette & L. M. Hough (Eds.), *Handbook of industrial and organizational psychology* (Vol. II, pp. 508–619). Palo Alto: Consulting Psychologists Press; and I. L. Goldstein, I. L., 1993, *Training in organizations.* Pacific Grove, CA: Brooks/Cole.

To answer these questions and be able to control for various threats to the validity of the training program, Cook, Campbell, and Peracchio (1990) and Goldstein (1991, 1993) identified three categories of evaluation design: the preexperimental design, the experimental design, and the quasi-experimental design (see Table 9.3).

Pre-Experimental Designs. In the **posttest design method**, trainees are given an examination on completion of training. This design is the least expensive. Because the trainees are measured only after receiving training, it is very difficult to ascertain whether changes resulted from training or were due to extraneous variables, such as prior experience or knowledge or increased motivation. It would be impossible for an organization to justify the costs associated with training based on this method alone.

In the **pretest/posttest design method,** trainees are assessed before and immediately after training. Howell (1976) suggested that this design reduces the possibility that the final performance is a function of preexisting capabilities. Because this method does not include a control group, it is difficult to determine cause-and-effect relationships between training and changes in behavior (Goldstein, 1993). Any differences in the performance of trainees between the pretest and posttest might be associated with effects such as testing conditions, differences in test formats, or other intervening variables. However, both the posttest and pretest/posttest designs can help to determine whether any change has occurred (Goldstein, 1993).

Experimental Design.   To determine absolutely that behavioral changes resulted from training, a complete experimental design must be used.

The experimental design compares pretest and posttest changes in trainees (the experimental group) with pretest and posttest changes for a comparable control group. Both groups are given the pretest and posttests, but only the experimental group is given training. The control group may engage in some other activity that is unrelated to the training program. Any differences in performance between the two groups would then be due to the effectiveness of the training program. Because subjects are selected randomly from the population and assigned randomly to experimental and control groups, variables that might affect the internal validity (such as pretesting effects) are controlled.

Goldstein (1993) noted that additional controls on effects might influence the validity of the training program. The **Solomon four-group design** includes an experimental group and three control groups. The experimental group is exposed to a pretest, training, and a posttest; one control group takes pretests and posttests but is not trained; the second control group is

given training and a posttest; and the third control group is given only a posttest (see Table 9.3). This design permits the trainer to determine different effects, such as the effects of pretesting or the effects of events that occurred during training that were unrelated to the content of the program.

This type of experimental design is costly, is time consuming, and requires many trainees. Small organizations often lack the resources to conduct a complete experimental design of evaluation. For this reason they may use less scientific methods. The result is that many organizations fail to properly evaluate their training programs. Unfortunately, this may be far more costly to the organization in the long run than conducting a careful evaluation. This is particularly true if the training involves teaching skills that are preexisting or unrelated to satisfactory job performance. It is imperative that the results obtained in the evaluation phase be compared to the original training objectives. In this way the organization can plan continuing modification of the program, making revisions to close any gaps between training results and organizational goals and objectives.

Quasi-Experimental Designs.   There are many natural social and work situations in which it is impossible to exert the full control required in experimental designs. The quasi-experiments involve only partial control over stimuli such as assigning subjects to control and experimental groups. **Quasi-experimental designs** are a compromise between the necessity of conducting evaluation investigations and the availability of organizational resources (Campbell & Stanley, 1963; Goldstein, 1993). Goldstein (1993, p. 197) summarized it best when he stated that these designs are "useful in many social settings where investigators lack the opportunity to exert full control over the environment."

A **time-series design** conducts a series of pretraining and posttraining testing with one group. As shown in Table 9.3, several pretests are given to a group of future trainees with about equal time intervals between tests. After training, an initial posttest measures any changes in behavior, followed by two additional posttests (again with more or less the same time intervals). To be considered training effects, changes between pretest 3 and posttest 4 ($X_3 - X_4$) should be considerably larger than any other changes in criterion scores, that is, between pretests ($X_1 - X_2$, $X_2 - X_3$) and between posttests ($X_4 - X_5$, $X_5 - X_6$).

Other changes in criteria scores could result from threats to internal validity, such as testing effects. However, this design does not control for threats to external validity (Goldstein, 1993). For example, since only one group is used, the results of the training program might be particular to this group of trainees and therefore could not be generalized or used with other groups.

The **nonequivalent control-group design** is similar to the control group design; the difference is that in this design, employees are not assigned randomly to groups. Thus the differences in gain scores between the experimental group and the control group could result from history effects, pretesting effects, or other internal validity factors. These threats are similar to the threats found in the control group design. However, Goldstein (1993) claimed that the fact that the participants were entire groups of workers in normal settings may reduce some threats to external validity. For example, the Hawthorne effect and interaction with the experimental setting are eliminated. Although participants in the experimental and control groups are not randomly assigned, this design is easier for the organization to conduct. It also enables the evaluator to train and evaluate large groups of employees and thus increases the validity of generalization.

We have seen that training program design should include a practical, well-planned, operational evaluation program. Sussman and Robertson (1986), in a comparative analysis of various validation designs, concluded that different designs yield different statistical and operational advantages. They recommend conducting more than one research design to validate each training program.

Validity of Training Goals

Goldstein (1978, 1991, 1993) suggested that the validity of any training program can be assessed along four dimensions. Each of these strategies poses a different question (Goldstein, 1991, p. 590):

1. Training validity. How did the trainees perform on the criteria established for the training program?
2. Transfer or performance validity. Did the trainees' performance match the level of criteria established for success back on the job?
3. Intraorganizational validity. Is the training program equally effective with different groups of trainees within the same company? When approaching a new group of trainees, trainers should take into account the kinds of people to be trained, task similarity, any changes in the organization, whether the current training program is the same as the previous program, and the evaluative results of the original training program.
4. Interorganizational validity. Is the training program equally effective in companies other than the one in which it was developed? Using a program developed in another organization, without first ensuring that the needs assessment factors are the same, and that the program was validated "is asking for trouble."

An effective training program should include the following in its preplanning stage: (a) an evaluation process that integrates relevant criteria and (b) validity designs that are appropriate for evaluating success in achieving the overall purpose. The four validity designs can be arranged in hierarchial order; training validity is the easiest to achieve, and interorganizational validity is the most difficult. Each level not only includes its own particular shortcomings, but also poses a threat to the levels below (Goldstein, 1978). For example, some of the deficiencies associated with training validity include a lack of established objectives, a lack of random assignment of trainees to experimental and control groups, and the failure to collect a sufficient amount of accurate data. The lack of specific organizational goals, an inadequate task analysis, and an organizational conflict are possible threats to performance validity. An inadequate training evaluation, an irregular training effect, or unintended changes in the training program over a period of time are some of the factors that compromise intraorganizational validity. Finally, a major threat to interorganizational validity is any dissimilarity found between organizations in terms of tasks, needs, climates, jobs, or products.

These unwanted effects can influence what training scientists call internal validity and external validity (e.g., Cook et al., 1990; Goldstein, 1991, 1993). The term **internal validity** refers to the ability to conclude that it is the training program itself that led to changes in the criteria used to establish training and transfer validity (see Goldstein's questions 1 and 2 on page 315). It is necessary to control biasing effects such as the history effect, the testing effect, and the differential effect in striving for internal validity. The **history effect** can occur when events other than the training occur at the same time as training and influence the resulting measurements. For example, the resignation of a favorite instructor in the middle of training would probably influence the final test scores of the trainees without having affected the instructional material covered. The **testing effect** is the influence of pretests on posttest results. For example, by taking a pretest, trainees are sensitized to the importance of some areas of the material. When they come to that portion of the training, they are more attentive than trainees who did not have the pretest. The result is that the pretested trainees have higher scores on the posttest in part because they guessed what would be measured. The **differential effect** focuses on the selection of the trainee groups for comparison. An example of this effect would be to select an experimental group of trainees with previous job-related experience and a control group of workers with no previous experience. Differential effects can jeopardize internal validity if they are not controlled by the experimental design of

the training program. Other variables that pose a threat are discussed in more detail by Cook et al. (1990) and Goldstein (1993, pp. 191–196).

External validity attempts to substantiate intraorganizational validity and interorganizational validity. It is also concerned with questions such as whether the training program can transfer to other groups of trainees, new situations, and a variety of settings (Goldstein, 1991). Sussman and Robertson (1986) characterized external validity as a concern about generalization. For example, if an original training effort was conducted with a group of skilled machinists, the training could not be generalized (or applied) to unskilled personnel in the same or a different organization.

Internal validity is a precondition to external validity and, together with other controls, enables generalization to "all types of persons in all settings at all times and with all operational representations of the cause and effect. Threats to external validity are therefore factors that limit such generalization" (Cook et al., 1990, p. 509). These threats include the interaction of the characteristics of the trainees with the particular training. For example, would the level of mechanical skill trainees have prior to training determine the results of their posttraining tests for maintenance of machine tools?

Another threat is what Goldstein (1991, p. 576) calls the "reactive effects of experimental settings." Simply selecting a group of students to participate in an experiment would influence their behavior regardless of the training itself. This is known as the Hawthorne effect. Described in more detail in Chapters 1 and 13, the Hawthorne effect results when trainees feel special because they were selected to participate in the experiment. This feeling leads to increased motivation and productivity. It can also improve the learning in response to training. Additional threats can influence external validity, and trainers should take care to control for external validity when designing an evaluation study. See Goldstein (1993) for a full discussion of these effects.

SUMMARY

A successful training program will develop and improve motor, cognitive, and/or interpersonal skills with the intent of meeting both individual and organizational goals. Effective personnel training is based on principles of learning derived from psychological research and theories. The two learning theories that are relevant to training and development are the connectionist theory and the social learning theory. The connectionist approach includes two main processes: classical conditioning and operant conditioning. Social learning theory stresses the social and cognitive aspects of learning. Adult learning principles modify techniques to accommodate the special learning needs of adults.

Learning theory provides many guidelines for designing effective training. The following are some important guides in designing a training program: Present an overview and explain the importance of the training material; reinforce appropriate behaviors; allow for shaping, guiding, and imitating key model behaviors; provide practice conditions; relay feedback; and ensure the transfer of new learned behaviors back to the job.

The systems approach views training as a subsystem within the organizational context that consists of cyclical phases. The systems approach is the preferred approach for designing, implementing, and evaluating training programs. It includes four phases: input, transformation, information, and adaptation. The continuous and self-correcting process of this cycle is often referred to as feedback loop learning.

Another major concern for I/O psychologists is the assessment of training needs. This is accomplished by conducting an organizational analysis, a task analysis, and a person analysis. By assessing these three areas, I/O psychologists create a starting point for the implementation of training.

With large-scale training programs, organizations often use a method called train-the-trainer.

A master trainer trains the individuals who will deliver the programs. Some knowledge and experience are lost in this process, so it needs to be used carefully and monitored.

Training techniques can be categorized as on-site, off-site, and technology-based. On-site techniques allow the learner to experience the job while actually performing or observing it. On-site techniques include on-the-job training, job rotation, and mentoring. Off-site techniques teach trainees off the actual job site. The most popular off-site approaches are classroom lecture, conferences, and audiovisual. The simulation and games approach includes business games, vestibule training, sensitivity training, and behavior modeling.

Technology-based learning occurs in both on-site and off-site applications. As a separate category it is characterized by various applications of technology to enhance the training. Representative of technology-based approaches are programmed instruction (PI); computer-assisted instruction, a sophisticated version of programmed instruction; interactive videodisc instruction; closed-circuit television; and satellite-delivered instruction and videoconferencing, which permit training that includes interaction with locations that can be anywhere around the world.

Leadership training and career development are special areas of interest that have assumed importance with the increasing competitiveness of the global economy. More organizations promote from within, a strategy that requires potential managers to obtain leadership training. Career development offers employees the chance to develop and plan their career objectives while providing the organization with reduced turnover and an increased number of candidates for promotion.

The final activity in a training effort involves training program evaluation. Three important features define this process: criteria, validity, and evaluation design. Criteria, or measures of success, include reaction criteria, learning criteria, behavioral criteria, and results criteria. Training program validity can be determined along four dimensions: training validity, transfer of performance validity, intraorganizational validity, and interorganizational validity. Evaluation programs can be conducted along three separate designs: preexperimental, experimental, or quasi-experimental.

KEY TERMS AND CONCEPTS

adaptation phase
andragogy
behavior modeling
behavioral criteria
branching
business games
career development
classical conditioning
closed-circuit television
computer-assisted instruction
differential effect
distributed trials
external validity
feedback
feedback loop
history effect
horizontal programming
information phase
input phase

interactive videodisc instruction
internal validity
job rotation
learning criteria
massed trials
mentoring
needs analysis
nonequivalent control-group
 design
operant conditioning
organizational behavior
 management
person analysis
posttest design method
pretest/posttest design method
programmed instruction
quasi-experimental design
reaction criteria
reinforcer

results criteria
role playing
satellite-delivered instruction
self-efficacy
sensitivity training
shaping
simulation method
social learning theory
Solomon four-group design
systems approach
task analysis
testing effect
time-series design
train-the-trainer
transfer of training
transformation phase
vertical programming
vestibule training

RECOMMENDED READINGS

Bass, B. M., & Vaughan, J. A. (1966). *Training in industry: The management of learning.* Belmont, CA: Brooks/Cole.

Chawla, S., & Renesch, J. (Eds.) (1995). *Learning organizations: Developing cultures for tomorrow's workplace.* Portland, OR: Productivity Press.

Craig, R. L. (1996). *Training and development handbook.* New York: McGraw-Hill.

Goldstein, I. L. (1991). Training in work organizations. In M. D. Dunnette & L. M. Hough (Eds.), *Handbook of industrial and organizational psychology* (Vol. II, pp. 508–619). Palo Alto: Consulting Psychologists Press.

Goldstein, I. L. (1993). *Training in organizations.* Pacific Grove, CA: Brooks/Cole.

Merry, U., & Allerhand, M. E. (1977). *Developing teams and organizations: A practical handbook for managers and consultants.* Reading, MA: Addison-Wesley.

Peters, T. J. (1994). *The pursuit of WOW!: Every person's guide to topsy-turvy times.* New York: Vintage Books.

Piskurich, G. M. (Ed.) (1993). *The ASTD handbook of instructional technology.* New York: McGraw-Hill.

Senge, P. M. (1990). *The fifth discipline: The art and practice of the learning organization.* New York: Doubleday-Currency.

INTERNET RESOURCES

Training and Management Development via the Internet

> This site is devoted to exploring corporate training and management development via the Internet. It includes articles describing e-mail conferencing, electronic bulletin boards, Web sites, and MOOs. There are links to other training and management development resources as well. It was developed by Dr. Ralph F. Wilson.
>
> **http://cac.psu.edu/~cxl18/trdev/**

CBT Systems. Computer Based Training: Demos

> A site demonstrating computer-delivered solutions for corporate and industrial training.
>
> **http://www.cbtsys.com/CBT/demos/ demchoice.htm**

Pennsylvania State University Education Technology Services

> This site provides guidance for using educational technology to enhance teaching and learning, to learn more about teaching and learning using technology, to integrate digital media into courses and research, and to access resources that support learning.
>
> **http://ets.cac.psu.edu/**

American Society for Training and Development

> This site provides detailed information on the American Society for Training and Development and easy access to its services and resources. The Training and Performance Links section provides the most comprehensive list of human resource development and performance improvement links on the Internet.
>
> **http://www.astd.org/**

The University of Houston—Clear Lake Trillium Model

> This site describes a telecommunications product support capability model named Trillium. It pro-

vides a good real-world example of human resource development and management development design.

http://ricis.cl.uh.edu/trillium/t3modc42.html

Advanced Training Systems for the Next Decade and Beyond

> This site, developed by the American Institute of Aeronautics and Astronautics, Inc., describes intelligent computer-aided training based on artifical intelligence technology to support aerospace mission training.
>
> **http://www.jsc.nasa.gov/cssb/icat/docs/ NextDecade.html**

U.S. Department of Energy Office of Training and Human Resource Development—Training Information Clearinghouse

> This central site has current information about Department of Energy resources, courses, newsletters, and standards. Its Learning Resources/Materials section is a valuable source of technical reports on instructional processes. Its section on nuclear facility personnel selection, qualification, and training details technical training for demanding nuclear safety regulations.
>
> **http://cted.inel.gov/cted/**

www.pikeperry.co.uk

> This site specializes in links to resources for company training departments. A landmark site on the Internet, it provides high-quality information and links on all aspects of management development for the United Kingdom. Some areas that are addressed include professional training, training providers, training products, personality tests, outplacement and career consultants, publications, and a directory of scholarly electronic conferences on human resources and industrial psychology.
>
> **http://www.pikeperry.co.uk/ppp/md/md.htm**

EXERCISES

Exercise 9.1

Training Program Design

The Webster Corporation is a fourteen-year-old company that manufactures plastic furniture for children. Its current selection procedure for hiring factory personnel is inadequate and unvalidated. Because the corporation is not aware of the skills that are needed for satisfactory performance, it cannot correctly identify the skills and aptitudes of new personnel or correctly assess current employees in conducting performance appraisals.

The training program consists of a brief orientation in lecture format, followed by placement with an incumbent for on-the-job training. The new employee remains with the trainer until the incumbent decides that the new employee is performing at an acceptable level, at which time the new employee is placed in a permanent position. Six months after training, the trainee's performance is reviewed.

Use the information provided about the Webster Corporation to do the following:

1. Explain how the systems approach could be used to analyze the company's current training program.
2. Explain how each phase of the systems approach would benefit training at the Webster Corporation.
3. Use the systems approach to redesign the Webster Corporation's training program.

Exercise 9.2

Origami Flapping Bird Toy Company

Purpose
To design and develop team processes that will optimize manufacturing performance and quality of the child's toy Flapping Bird.

Materials
Seventy-five to one hundred sheets of 8½ by 11 inch colored paper. The preferred variety is colored on one side and white on the other.

Parts list
Four pairs of scissors, two rulers, one pencil, one roll of cellophane tape, and 100 5 × 8 inch index cards.

1 set of folding instructions

1 stand

1 Flapping Bird

Process
The goal is to build as many high-quality Flapping Birds as you can in fifteen minutes. To do so, you must work cooperatively with your team. The team that succeeds will be awarded a prize.

Flow
Divide the class into a minimum of two teams (three to five participants per team).

Give each team a supply of materials. They can examine the materials, but they cannot practice folding the Flapping Bird.

The challenge
As teams, you have fifteen minutes to plan how you will work to construct as many high-quality Flapping Bird toys and stands as you can. Once manufacturing begins, you will have fifteen minutes to build the toys.

Each toy will be inspected for quality. Sloppy construction is cause for the toy to be scrapped.

The best-performing team is the one that builds the most high-quality Flapping Birds in the fifteen minutes.

Any questions?

Steps

1. The groups are given fifteen minutes to plan. They cannot practice folding Flapping Birds or precut their materials.
2. After fifteen minutes, the groups are given fifteen minutes to manufacture as many toys as they can. Completed toys are submitted to the instructor for quality control. Acceptable toys will be correctly folded, with no extraneous folds or unneeded creases. Each bird will sit on a storage platform 12 inches above the table. Unacceptable toys and/or platforms are discarded. (Have a large wastebasket ready to receive them.)
3. When the teams are ready, say, "Go." Call out time every five minutes. Count down the last five minutes.
4. At the end of time, say, "Stop." Count acceptable Flapping Birds manufactured by each team and award the prize to the winner.

Debrief the exercise

How did each team plan its manufacturing process?

How was this similar to other manufacturing processes?

What went well for the teams?

What would they do differently if repeating the task?

What team characteristics contributed to completing the task?

What team characteristics got in the way of completing the task?

How did the teams plan to complete the task?

Did one person or several manage and direct the team?

How did the teams share responsibility?

What are some general observations?

Flapping Bird Toy Folding Instructions

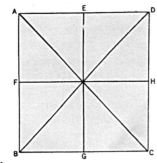

1.
Fold on line F—H. Unfold. Fold on line G—E. Unfold. Now fold diagonals A—C and D—B.

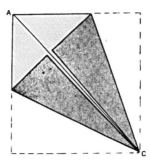

2.
Fold step 4 of Basic Shape No. 1 so narrowest point is at C. Unfold. Repeat fold with narrowest point at A. Unfold.

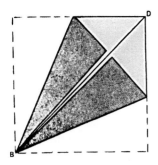

3.
Repeat folds for corners B and D.

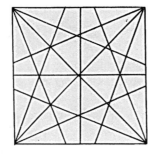

4.
Open your folded paper. This is how the creases look. Do all your folding on these lines.

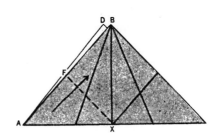

5.
Fold B up to meet D. Push A—X in between D and B and crease along F—X. (See figure 6.)

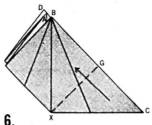

6.
Fold X—C in between D and B and crease along G—X. (See figure 7.)

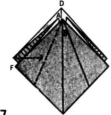

7.
Open A and B and push fold F—I in between A and B. Crease along I—B.

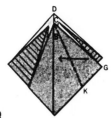

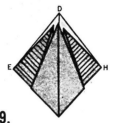

8.
Open B and C and push G—K in between B and C. Crease along K—B.

9.
The shape now looks like this. Turn shape around and repeat; push in folds with points E and H.

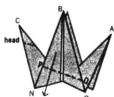

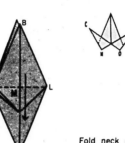

10.
Fold D down on line L—J.

11.
This is how the shape looks. Turn it around with flap M facing you (see figure 12).

12.
Fold B down on line J—L. Turn shape over so B is at top, and C and A are nearest you.

neck   tail

13.
Fold neck up on dotted line G—N. Unfold. Now fold tail up on dotted line F—O. Unfold. Push neck up, in L and K. Reverse crease on G—N. Push tail up, in between I and J. Reverse crease on F—O.

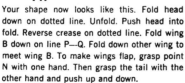

14.
Your shape now looks like this. Fold head down on dotted line. Unfold. Push head into fold. Reverse crease on dotted line. Fold wing B down on line P—Q. Fold down other wing to meet wing B. To make wings flap, grasp point N with one hand. Then grasp the tail with the other hand and push up and down.

Finished Flapping Bird

Source: From "Fun With Origami, 17 Easy-to-do Projects and 24 Sheets of Origami Paper," pp. 15–16. Instruction book by Harry C. Helfman, Copyright 1991 by Dover Publications, Inc. Reprinted with permission.

REFERENCES

Alkin, M. C., Linden, M., Noel, J., & Ray, K. (1992a). Adult education. *Encyclopedia of education research* (6th ed., Vol.1, pp. 30–35, 238–244).

Alkin, M. C., Linden, M., Noel, J., & Ray, K. (1992b). Management training and development. *Encyclopedia of education research* (6th ed., Vol. 3, pp. 763–769).

Arnall, G. C. (1987). Satellite-delivered learning. *Training and Development Journal, 41,* 90–94.

Bandura, A. (1969). *Principles of behavior modification.* New York: Holt, Rinehart & Winston.

Bandura, A. (1974). Behavioral theory and the models of man. *American Psychologist, 29*(12), 859–869.

Bandura, A. (1977). *Social learning theory.* Englewood Cliffs, NJ: Prentice-Hall.

Bandura, A. (1986). *Social foundation of thought and action: A social cognitive theory.* Englewood Cliffs, NJ: Prentice-Hall.

Bass, B. M., & Vaughan, J. A. (1966). *Training in industry: The management of learning.* Belmont, CA: Brooks/Cole.

Bass, B. M., & Vaughan, J. A. (1975). Assessing training needs. In C. E. Schneier & R. W. Beatty (Eds.), *Personnel administration today: Readings and commentary* (pp. 308–314). Reading, MA: Addison-Wesley.

Blum, M. L., & Naylor, J. C. (1968). *Industrial psychology: Its theoretical and social foundations.* New York: Harper & Row.

Bower, G. H., & Hilgard, E. R. (1981). *Theories of learning.* Englewood Cliffs, NJ: Prentice-Hall.

Boyatzis, R. E. (1976). Power motivation training: A new treatment modality. In F. Seixas & S. Eggleston (Eds.), Work in progress on alcoholism. *Annals of the New York Academy of Sciences, 273,* 525–532.

Boyatzis, R. E. (1982). *The competent manager: A model for effective performance.* New York: Wiley Interscience.

Burke, M. J., & Day, R. R. (1986). A cumulative study of the effectiveness of managerial training. *Journal of Applied Psychology, 71*(2), 232–245.

Burnaska, R. F. (1976). The effects of behavior modeling upon managers' behaviors and employees' perceptions. *Personnel Psychology, 29,* 329–335.

Campbell, D. T., & Stanley, J. C. (1963). *Experimental and quasi-experimental designs for research.* Chicago: Rand McNally.

Campbell, J. P., Dunnette, M. D., Lawler, E. E. III, & Weick, R. E. (1970). *Managerial behavior, performance and effectiveness.* New York: McGraw-Hill.

Cascio, W. F., & Awad, E. M. (1981). *Human resources management: An information systems approach.* Reston, VA: Reston Publishing.

Chao, G. T., Walz, P. M., & Gardner, P. D. (1992). Formal and informal mentorships: A comparison on mentoring functions and contrast with nonmentored counterparts. *Personnel Psychology, 45*(3), 619–636.

Cook, T. D., Campbell, D. T., & Peracchio, L. (1990). Quasi experimentation. In M. D. Dunnette & L. M. Hough (Eds.), *Handbook of industrial and organizational psychology* (Vol. I, pp. 491–576). Palo Alto: Consulting Psychologists Press.

Davidov, V. V., Neverkovich, S. D., & Samoukina, N. V. (1990). On functions of reflection in game education of managers. *Voprosy-Psikhologii,* May–June, 3, 76–84. (From PsycLIT Database, 1991, Abstract No. 28–73827).

Deming, W. E. (1986). *Out of the crises.* Cambridge, MA: Center for Advanced Engineering Study, Massachusetts Institute of Technology.

Dessler, G. (1984). *Personnel management* (3rd ed.). Reston, VA: Reston Publishing.

Fauley, F. E. (1981). When to use CAI in training. In R. Zemke, L. Standke, & P. Jones (Eds.), *Designing and delivering cost-effective training and measuring the results* (p. 170). Minneapolis: Lakewood.

Feeney, E. J. (1973). *Behavioral engineering systems training.* Hamden, CT: E. J. Feeney Associates.

Festinger, L., & Carlsmith, J. M. (1959). Cognitive consequences of forced compliance. *Journal of Abnormal and Social Psychology, 58,* 203–210.

Fleishman, E. A. (1953). Leadership climate, human relations training, and supervisory behavior. *Personnel Psychology, 6,* 205–222.

Ford, K. J., Quinones, M. A., Sego, D. J., & Sorra, J. S. (1992). Factors affecting the opportunity to perform trained tasks on the job. *Personnel Psychology, 45*(3), 511–527.

Frayne, C. A., & Latham, G. P. (1987). Application of social learning theory to employee self-management of attendance. *Journal of Applied Psychology, 72*(3), 387–392.

Fredricksen, L. W. (1982). *Handbook of organizational behavior management.* New York: Wiley.

Gagné, R. M. (1962). Military training and principles of learning. *American Psychologist, 17,* 83–91.

Gilley, J. W. (1988). Career development as a partnership. *Personnel Administrator, 33,* 62–68.

Gist, M. E. (1989). The influence of training method on self-efficacy and idea generation among managers. *Personnel Psychology, 42*(4), 787–806.

Goldstein, I. L. (1978). The pursuit of validity in the evaluation of training programs. *Human Factors, 20,* 131–144.

Goldstein, I. L. (1991). Training in work organizations. In M. D. Dunnette & L. M. Hough (Eds.), *Handbook of industrial and organizational psychology* (Vol. II, pp. 508–619). Palo Alto, CA: Consulting Psychologists Press.

Goldstein, I. L. (1993). *Training in organizations.* Pacific Grove, CA: Brooks/Cole.

Goldstein, I. L., & Buxton, V. M. (1982). Training and human performance. In M. D. Dunnette & E. A. Fleishman (Eds.), *Human performance and productivity: Human capability assessment* (pp. 135–177). Hillsdale, NJ: Lawrence Erlbaum Associates.

Goldstein, I. L., & Gilliam, P. (1990). Training issues in the year 2000. *American Psychologist, 45*(2), 134–143.

Griffin, R. W., & Cashin, W. E. (1989). The lecture and discussion method for management education: Pros and cons. *Journal of Management Development, 8*(2), 25–32.

Hall, J. F. (1982). *An invitation to learning and memory.* Boston: Allyn & Bacon.

Hammer-Higgins, P., & Atwood, V. A. (1989). The management game: An educational intervention for counseling women with nontraditional career goals. *Career Development Quarterly, 38*(1), 6–23.

Hersey, P., & Blanchard, K. H. (1988). *Management of organizational behavior: Utilizing human resources* (5th ed.). Englewood Cliffs, NJ: Prentice-Hall.

Hill, R. J. (1960). *A comparative study of lecture and discussion methods.* White Plains, NY: Fund for Adult Education.

Hinrichs, J. R. (1976). Personnel training. In M. D. Dunnette (Ed.), *Handbook of industrial and organizational psychology.* Skokie, IL: Rand McNally.

Holland, J. G., & Skinner, B. F. (1961). *The analysis of behavior.* New York: McGraw-Hill.

Howell, W. C. (1976). *Essentials of industrial and organizational psychology.* Homewood, IL: Dorsey Press.

Howell, W. C., & Cook, N. J. (1989). Training the human information processor: A review of cognitive models. In I. L. Goldstein (Ed.), *Training and development in organizations.* San Francisco: Jossey-Bass.

Jenkins, M. J., DeBloois, M. L., & Matsumoto-Grah, K. Y. (1985). Future firefighting—by the book or by screen. *Training and Development Journal, 39,* 36–39.

Kanfer, R., & Ackerman, P. L. (1989). Motivation and cognitive abilities: An integrative/aptitude-treatment interaction approach to skill acquisition. *Journal of Applied Psychology, 74,* 657–690.

Katz, D., & Kahn, R. L. (1978). *The social psychology of organizations* (2nd ed.). New York: Wiley & Sons.

Kirkpatrick, D. L. (1987). Techniques for evaluating training programs. In D. L. Kirkpatrick (Ed.), *More evaluating training programs* (pp. 4–16). Alexandria, VA: American Society for Training and Development.

Knowles, M. S. (1978). *The adult learner: A neglected species* (2nd ed.). Houston: Gulf Publishing.

Knowles, M. S. (1980). *The modern practice of adult education: From pedagogy to andragogy.* Chicago: Association Press.

Knowles, M. S. (1984). *Andragogy in action.* San Francisco: Jossey-Bass Publishers.

Knowles, M. S. (1990). Adult learning: theory and practice. In L. Nadler and Z. Nadler (Eds.), *The handbook of human resource development* (pp. 6.1–6.23). New York: John Wiley & Sons.

Komaki, J. L., Barwick, K. D., & Scott, L. R. (1978). A behavioral approach to occupational safety: Pinpointing and reinforcing safety performance in a food manufacturing plant. *Journal of Applied Psychology, 63,* 434–445.

Kulik, J., Kulik, C., & Cohen, P. (1980). Effectiveness of computer-based college teaching: A meta-analysis of findings. *Review of Educational Research, 50,* 525–544.

Latham, G. P. (1989). Behavioral approaches to the training and learning process. In I. L. Goldstein, *Training and development in organizations: Frontiers of industrial and organizational psychology.* San Francisco: Jossey-Bass.

Latham, G. P., & Saari, L. M. (1979). Applications of social learning theory to training supervisors through behavior modeling. *Journal of Applied Psychology, 64,* 239–246.

Lawrie, J. (1987). How to establish a mentoring program. *Training and Development Journal, 41,* 25–27.

Lewin, K. (1968). Group decision and social change. In D. E. Maccoley, T. M. Newcombe, & E. L. Hartley (Eds.), *Readings in social psychology* (pp. 197–211). New York: Holt.

Lipshitz, R., & Popper, M. (1990). Gaining power and viability in management development programs. *Leadership and Organization Development Journal, 11*(4), 23–27.

London, M. (1989). *Managing the training enterprise.* San Francisco: Jossey-Bass.

London, M., & Bassman, E. (1989). Retraining mid-career workers for the future workplace. In I. L. Goldstein, *Training and development in organizations.* San Francisco: Jossey-Bass.

Mahler, M. J. (1991). *The gift of mentoring.* Unpublished manuscript, International Association of Personnel Women.

Mayer, S. J., & Russell, J. S. (1987). Behavior modeling training in organizations: Concerns and conclusions. *Journal of Management, 13,* 21–40.

McCall, M. W., & Lombardo, M. M. (1978). *Looking Glass, Inc: An organizational simulation,* Operational Manual, Vol. I (Center for Creative Leadership Technical Report Number 12, October, 1978). Greensboro, NC: Center for Creative Leadership.

McClelland, D. C. (1978). Managing motivation to expand human freedom. *American Psychologist, 33*(3), 201–210.

McClelland, D. C., & Burnham, D. H. (1976). Power is the great motivator. *Harvard Business Review, 54*(2), 100–111.

McClelland, D. C., & Winter, D. G. (1979). *Motivating economic achievement.* New York, NY: Free Press.

McGehee, W., & Thayer, P. (1961). *Training in business and industry.* New York: John Wiley & Sons.

Milkovich, G. T., & Glueck, W. F. (1985). *Personnel—human resource management* (4th ed.). Plano, TX: Business Publications.

Miron, D., & McClelland, D. C. (1979). The impact of achievement motivation training on small business. *California Management Review, 21*(4), 13–28.

Mitchell, F. G. (1981). Developing an international marketing training approach. *Training and Development Journal, 35*(11), 48–51.

Morey, N., & Esch, J. (1992). *An analysis of the training program for United Parcel Service package sorters.* Unpublished paper.

Moses, J. L., & Ritchie, R. J. (1976). Supervisory relationships training: A behavioral evaluation of the behavioral modeling program. *Personnel Psychology, 29,* 337–343.

Nadler, L. (1984). *The handbook of human resource development.* New York: John Wiley & Sons.

Nash, A. N., Muczyk, J. P., & Vettori, F. L. (1971). The relative practical effectiveness of programmed instruction. *Personnel Psychology, 24,* 397–418.

Nelson, B. (1994). *1001 ways to reward employees.* New York: Workman Publishing.

Nilson, C. (1991, May). How to train employees one-on-one. *Supervisory Management,* p. 3.

Noe, R. A., & Schmitt, N. (1986). The influence of trainee attitudes on training effectiveness: Test of a model. *Personnel Psychology, 39*(3), 497–524.

Piskurich, G. M. (1991). Quality through self-directed learning. *Training &Development, 45,* 45–48.

Reynolds, A. (1983). An introduction to computer-based learning. *Training and Development Journal, 37,* 34–38.

Robinson, J. (1988). Beam me up, Scotty. *Training and Development Journal, 42,* 46–48.

Ronen, S. (1989). Training the international assignee. In I. L. Goldstein, *Training and development in organizations.* San Francisco: Jossey-Bass.

Rouillier, J. Z., & Goldstein, I. L. (1990). *The determination of positive transfer of training climate through organizational analysis.* Unpublished manuscript. College Park, MD: University of Maryland.

Schneier, C. E., & Beatty, R. W. (1978). *Personnel administration today; Readings and commentary.* Reading, MA: Addison-Wesley.

Silvern, L. (1972). *Systems engineering applied to training.* Houston: Gulf Publishing.

Sterns, H. L., & Doverspike, D. (1989). Aging and the training and learning process. In I. Goldstein (Ed.), *Training and development in work organizations: Frontiers of industrial and organizational psychology.* San Francisco: Jossey-Bass.

Sussman, M., & Robertson, D. U. (1986). The validity of validity: An analysis of validation study designs. *Journal of Applied Psychology, 71*(3), 461–468.

Tannenbaum, S. I., & Yukl, G. (1992). Training and development in work organization. *Annual Review of Psychology, 43,* 399–441.

Thomas, A. (1990). Interkulturelles handlungstraining als personalentwicklungsmassnahme. *Zeitschrift-fur-Arbeits-und-Organisationspsychologie, 34*(3), 149–154.

Thornton, G. C., & Cleveland, J. N. (1990). Developing managerial talent through simulation. *American Psychologist, 45*(2), 190–199.

Towne, D. C. (1985). Training systems: An overview. In W. R. Tracey (Ed.), *Human resources management and development handbook* (pp. 1317–1326). New York: AMACOM.

Tracey, W. R. (1984). *Designing training and development systems* (rev. ed.). New York: AMACOM.

Underwood, W. J. (1965). Evaluation of laboratory methods of training. *Training Director's Journal, 19,* 34–40.

U.S. Department of Education. (1994). Expenditures on education and training—USA (1995 estimates). *Training* (October).

Watson, C. E. (1975). The effectiveness of the case study method. *College Student Journal, 2,* 109–116.

Wexley, K. N., & Latham, G. P. (1981). *Developing and training human resources in organizations.* Glenview, IL: Scott, Foresman & Company.

Wilbur, J. (1987). Does mentoring breed success? *Training and Development Journal, 41,* 38–41.

Winter, D. G., McClelland, D. C., & Stewart, A. J. (1983). *Competence in college: Evaluating the liberal university.* San Francisco, CA: Jossey-Bass.

Zemke, R. & Zemke, S. (1995). Adult learning: What do we know for sure? *Training, 32*(6), 31–37.

Motivation: Theories and Applications

O n October 19, 1992, in the *University of Wisconsin–Parkside Communique,* J. Henneman reported the results of a satisfaction survey conducted by the University Office of Public Relations and directed by Professor J. Thomas. (Henneman, 1992). The sixty-five-question survey, devised by the American College Testing Corporation, was mailed to 7000 graduates to survey their opinions about the education they had received at UW–Parkside. There were 2564 respondents. The results stated that, in general, alumni were satisfied with the education they received at UW–Parkside. For example, two thirds of respondents felt that their education prepared them for their current job. African American graduates indicated more satisfaction than the general alumni population. Ten percent of the respondents expressed satisfaction with the university's social and cultural atmosphere and campus activities. Because the number of students enrolling at the university is essential to its survival, it is helpful if satisfied alumni spread the word in the community to motivate existing students and encourage prospective students to enroll.

The concepts, research, and applications of motivation and job satisfaction are closely interrelated. Although they are often treated individually in research, they are frequently combined in application and practice. We therefore believe it is important to deal with these two topics in an integrated way. Our discussion uses a single framework across Chapters 10 and 11. The amount of material covered is extensive because both of these areas have been popular in research and practice. For the convenience of the reader and to be consistent with many traditional presentations of motivation and satisfaction, we have divided our narrative into two chapters.

Chapter 10 begins with our framework integrating motivation and job satisfaction in a way that is consistent with how these concepts are used in applied practice. Chapter 10 also emphasizes motivation because of its strong experimental research base and the fact that moti-

vation theory is the basis for much job satisfaction work.

Chapter 11 examines how motivation theory is used to create job satisfaction. Satisfaction is a popular area in applied practice. Most of its concepts, however, are firmly rooted in motivation research.

Job satisfaction and motivation are of central interest to I/O psychologists in part because of their applicability to such areas as performance, productivity, turnover, and absenteeism. As a result, most organizations that have the financial means to do so conduct some type of satisfaction survey and try to find ways to motivate their employees. Results of such a survey are described in Practice Perspective 10.1.

In 1990, Katzell and Thompson stated that the subject of motivation had received more attention in recent journals and textbooks than any other area in organizational behavior. In an American Psychological Association literature review, Locke (1976) summarized the total number of references to job satisfaction to be at least 3,350. Despite the significance of these two subjects and the accompanying literature, few references deal with the relationship between motivation and job satisfaction.

Conceptually, job satisfaction and job motivation are interrelated. Motivation refers to how behavior is initiated and directed and to the conditions responsible for it (Campbell, Dunnette, Lawler, & Weick, 1970); job satisfaction reflects a feeling of contentment resulting from the fulfillment of important job values. Both theories attempt to explain why people work and what they work for. Knowing what motivates employees and providing the stimuli necessary to fulfill those job expectations furnish a basis of specific factors on which managers should focus.

To better understand each of these constructs, we will first review some existing definitions and discuss the relationships between them. We will then summarize the theoretical and empirical research for each concept.

PRACTICE PERSPECTIVE 10.1

Making a Job Worth the Hassle

In an article in the *Milwaukee Journal,* Patricia Braus (1992, p. 3) posed the question many Americans ask: "Is my job worth the hassle?" The claim was that U.S. workers in 1992

> want time for work, family, friends, and themselves. They also want interesting jobs, financial security and a chance to get ahead. . . . Not long ago happy employees accepted the terms employers offered; unhappy employees were free to leave. . . . But now, highly motivated workers are frustrated by slow-growing companies that cannot reward their initiative.

According to the results cited in the article, only 27% of workers are satisfied with their company's health insurance and benefits; 41% with their job,

35% with job security, and 31% with the opportunity the company gives them for learning new skills. However, different kinds of workers have different sets of needs, and companies should respond accordingly so as to invest their benefit money in the ways that are most useful. For example, General Electric's Capital Financial Services Company increased productivity and reduced turnover by eliminating a layer of managers and by giving more responsibility to lower-level employees.

Source: Based on Braus, P. (1992, December 13). More and more [American workers] are asking: Is their job worth the hassle? *The Milwaukee Journal, News Plus, J2,* pp. 1, 3.

JOB SATISFACTION

Job satisfaction is a set of favorable or unfavorable attitudes that employees hold about their work. Early definitions (e.g., Blum & Naylor, 1968) emphasized job satisfaction as a general attitude resulting from specific attitudes in three areas: job factors, individual characteristics, and group relationships outside work. Attitudes are considered to be beliefs, feelings, and action tendencies that constitute a valuative judgment of one's environment. Thus job satisfaction is an affective evaluation of the job environment (Mitchell, 1979). Later definitions emphasized the affective, or subjective, nature of these feelings. For example, Locke (1976) defined job satisfaction as a pleasurable emotional state resulting from the appraisal one makes of his or her job or job experiences. Dawis and Lofquist (1984) defined job satisfaction as a feeling based on the worker's estimate of the extent to which the work environment fulfills one's needs. Though job satisfaction has been defined in various ways,

the notion of subjective feelings such as "liking and disliking" (Hoppock, 1935) and "affective responses" (Smith, Kendall, & Hulin, 1969) and the existence of needs that have to be fulfilled (e.g., Dawis, 1991; Locke, 1976) run through most of these definitions. Feelings identify satisfaction, and needs explain the process. For example, *Webster's New World Dictionary of American English* (1994, p. 1193) defines the term "to satisfy" as the process by which we fulfill someone's needs, expectations, wishes, or desires.

Needs, then, underlie satisfaction and are assumed to exist before satisfaction. It is necessary for us to have needs to "feel" whether we are satisfied or dissatisfied, whether we "like" what we receive and achieve or "dislike" it. According to Dawis (1991) and Dawis and Lofquist (1984), the definition of needs takes into account the individual's requirement for particular reinforcers and the level of significance the individual assigns to each reinforcer. A need is a necessity; it is a lack of something that is useful, required, or desired (*Webster's New World Dic-*

tionary of American English, 1994). These needs, inclinations, or tendencies lead to motivation, because they are intrinsic to the different actions we take to secure specific outcomes.

These outcomes are important because they affect the organization's productivity, turnover, and absenteeism. Individual consequences, such as stress and mental health difficulties, affect not only individual employees but also the organization as a whole. We will discuss this in more detail in Chapter 11. First, let us move to a definition of motivation and to a discussion of the conceptual overlap between motivation and satisfaction.

MOTIVATION

As early as 1943, Hull defined motivation as a set of variables that energize behavior. Motivation regulates and directs behavior toward need satisfaction and goal achievement. Over the years, this underlying theme has remained the same. Blum and Naylor (1968) indicated that motivation could refer to individual activation resulting either from internal conditions (those existing within the individual) or from factors that exist in the individual's environment. These two conditions are interdependent and continuously interactive. For example, we look for food when we feel hunger; in our society, we know that when we are hungry and the external environment allows it, we have to earn money to get the food to satisfy the hunger.

In a comprehensive summary of motivational theories and definitions, Katzell and Thompson (1990) surmised that there are two categories of theories: **endogenous theories,** which deal with internal variables such as feelings of fairness, beliefs, values, and expectations, and **exogenous theories,** which emphasize variables that are introduced and can be changed via "external agents." Examples of external agents include praise from others, feedback, and money. Katzell and Thompson (1990) believe that endogenous variables are amenable to indirect change. It is

easy to see how these categories are interactive. For example, a worker's attitude toward a supervisor could change if an expected bonus were not granted at a time when the worker needed more money to feed his or her children.

To simplify, we will limit our definition of motivation to include only need-satisfying processes in work situations. Accordingly, motivation is defined as the willingness to exert different levels of effort toward achieving organizational goals and satisfying existing needs. Unsatisfied needs, which create tension within the individual, guide (or motivate) him or her to seek the goals that will satisfy needs and reduce tension. Dawis and Lofquist (1984) indicated that achievement of these particular goals can lead to feelings of satisfaction because it leads to a sense of harmony with both internal and external environments.

Motivation and satisfaction are not directly observable; they can only be inferred from observing behavior. We know that a person is motivated or satisfied only because he or she told us so or behaved in an indicative manner (e.g., studied longer hours to achieve a grade of A in class and then completed a questionnaire indicating a high level of satisfaction with the class). Therefore, most current definitions of motivation refer to processes (Kanfer, 1990; Katzell & Thompson, 1990) that are inferred from behaviors. These processes involve individual personality, beliefs, knowledge, abilities, and skills. Because all of these vary with different individuals, theories of motivation must take into account the "intra- and inter-individual variability in behavior" (Kanfer, 1990, p. 78). The result is a variety of theories and definitions, each emphasizing different aspects of these conditions and processes.

PRINCIPLES AND DEFINITIONS

Katzell and Thompson (1990) summarized the principles and definitions of fourteen different motivational theories. Some common terms were used across theories that we need to define to better understand the interrelationship between job satisfaction and motivation. Significant terms include needs, motives, incentives, reinforcers, rewards, goals, and goal attainment.

Needs or Motives

The concept of **needs** refers to the "conditions which are required to sustain the life and well-being of a living organism" (Locke, 1976, p. 1303). According to Blum and Naylor (1968), needs can stem from a physiological imbalance such as hunger, thirst, or lack of sleep and/or a sense of disequilibrium created by the social pressures to which the individual is exposed. Examples of social pressures include the pressure to conform to the way other students dress or to production norms of work peers. These needs are learned or acquired. Cherrington (1991) separated acquired needs into psychological needs such as the need for prestige, and sociological needs such as the need for social interaction. Whenever disequilibrium occurs, the individual is motivated to reduce the imbalance and return to a normal, balanced state. For example, we will try to get enough sleep to be able to function physically; we will make friends to satisfy the need for social involvement; we will work hard to achieve promotion and prestige.

Incentives

Blum and Naylor (1968) defined an **incentive** as an activating, inciting force that bolsters the individual's activity in the direction of particular goals. Katzell and Thompson (1990) extended the concept by characterizing incentives as a feature of the situation. These situational characteristics lead the worker to associate certain behaviors with a reward; for example, high product quality is associated with supervisor praise. Of course, a supervisor's praise would be effective only if the individual had a need for this type of praise. Therefore, an incentive is a factor that determines the level of effort a worker will invest in the job. The anticipation that rewards can be achieved enhances the worker's motivation to seek such rewards (Steers & Porter, 1991).

Reinforcers

Human behavior operates on the environment to produce positive consequences and is repeated by the individual to achieve these consequences (Skinner, 1953). Examples of consequences include food, water, money, and praise. A **reinforcer** is any condition that increases the probability of the occurrence of a specific behavior.

The emphasis is on pleasurable consequences (goals) and on the fact that the individual has to perform some specific action to achieve these goals. In this way, a contingency is created between a particular behavior and corresponding consequence. For example, you have to work to be paid; this is an **if–then relationship**: Work is the behavior; pay is the positive consequence. Reinforcement as applied to behavior does not assume the existence of a drive or a need; it is included in theories of motivation because it provides a means of controlling behavior (Steers & Porter, 1991).

Rewards

Positive reinforcers can be defined as **rewards.** They are the stimuli that satisfy needs and therefore encourage the behaviors that produce them (Katzell & Thompson, 1990). This definition assumes the existence of a prior condition, such as a need, that requires satisfaction.

How can we differentiate between incentives and rewards?

1. The basic difference is that while reward theories do not assume the existence of needs, incentive theories hypothesize the existence of drives and needs as well as the necessity to satisfy them to survive both physically and psychologically.

2. Rewards and incentives together are assumed to fulfill the functions of motivation (arouse, direct, and maintain effort of work behavior). We will use the stimulus–response dia-

I. Reinforcer (= S^R)

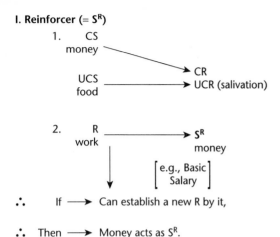

1.   CS
      money

      UCS ──────────→ UCR (salivation)
      food

2.   R ──────────→ S^R
      work   money

                    [e.g., Basic]
                    [Salary   ]

∴   If ──→   Can establish a new R by it,

∴   Then ──→   Money acts as S^R.

II. Incentive

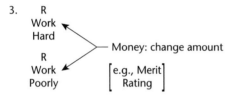

3.   R
      Work
      Hard

                    ─── Money: change amount
      R
      Work
      Poorly   [e.g., Merit]
                      [Rating   ]

∴   If ──→   With *changes* in *amount* of money,
               the person will work harder-or-
               poorly, then money also has
               motivational = incentive value.

CS: Conditioned Stimulus
CR: Conditioned Response
UCS: Unconditioned Stimulus
UCR: Unconditioned Response
R: Response
S^R: Secondary Reinforcing Stimulus

FIGURE 10.1   Stimulus–response diagrams illustrating primary and secondary reinforcers and incentives.

gram in Figure 10.1 to explain these two functions (Kimble, 1961; Opsahl & Dunnette, 1966).

We can establish and learn a new response (behavior) using a reward as a reinforcer; once the response has been learned, we can also use this reward as an incentive to change the level of effort put forth in performing the established behavior. For example, pairing money with a primary reinforcer (such as food) will establish the

value of money as a secondary reinforcer (see step 1 in Figure 10.1). Step 2 in the figure shows that once money has acquired the properties of a reinforcer, the probability is that individuals will work to achieve money (pay). The attainment of pay is contingent on the operant response of working; therefore, the probability of the occurrence of the behavior of working will increase if money is a valued reward. Step 3 in Figure 10.1 shows that once the contingency between working and pay is established, we can then use the reward of money as an incentive. When variations in the level and amount of reinforcement produce variations in the effort expended toward achieving the reward, this reward has acquired the motivating properties of an incentive. Steers and Porter (1991, p. 12) noted that "as the size of the reward varies, so too would the motivation to seek such a reward." Step 3 in Figure 10.1 shows that as changes are made in the amounts of money paid, these are associated with higher or lower levels of production.

Goals and Goal Attainment

A **goal** is an objective that must be obtained to reduce the imbalance created by needs and motives (Blum & Naylor, 1968). The attainment of a defined, needed goal is both motivating and reinforcing.

THE INTERRELATIONSHIP BETWEEN MOTIVATION AND JOB SATISFACTION

Although psychological theorists use motivation and job satisfaction in different ways, often separating them for ease of description and discussion, we believe that the two concepts are so interrelated that it is helpful to integrate them into a single framework. An incentive refers to the motivating properties of a goal. However, the goal will serve as an incentive only in response to a need (innate or acquired). For example, when an organism is hungry, food would be an incentive; the organism's goal is to satisfy its need for

PRACTICE PERSPECTIVE 10.2

Basic Motivational Concepts

We all know that "you can lead a horse to water, but you can't make him drink." The horse will search for water only when thirsty. Thirst is the need; the anticipation of finding water is the motivating force underlying the behavior, or the incentive. Finding the water is the reward. In other words, drinking would be a satisfier. Since this behavior culminates in pleasurable consequences, the water would also serve as a reinforcer; that is, the horse will repeat this pattern of behavior when thirsty.

In the work environment, motivation becomes more complex. Needs are seldom simple physiological ones, but include motives such as having an interesting or challenging job, being able to take the initiative to do things without needing approval, and being able to influence or direct others. The underlying motivating force attached to these is still referred to as an incentive, but such incentives are complex. When a job or situation directly provides elements that an individual sees as satisfying a need, that job or situation acts as a reward or satisfier. When this is a highly desired outcome, the job or situation can be a reinforcer as well.

Quite often the notion of reward is equated with pay. This is based on the assumption that money is the driving force behind motivation. This notion is hard to defend now that employees are better informed about their jobs and looking for opportunities to solve problems, participate in decisions, share in ownership, and have reasonably secure employment. Although money will remain important as a motivator, as people move away from subsistence-level living, more complex reward systems become necessary.

food. When the motivating goal (e.g., food) is achieved and fulfills an accompanying need (e.g., hunger), the goal acquires the property of a satisfier. The example in Practice Perspective 10.2 describes basic motivation in more detail.

Motivation and satisfaction are different concepts, but they are interrelated. As a result, there are some operational principles we should keep in mind:

1. The idea of motivating employees has to be linked with satisfying employees.

2. When installing a motivation program, one has to make sure that the incentives used (e.g., seniority, profit sharing, health insurance) are associated with employee needs. That is, employees will consider the programs to be incentives if employees feel that they need the programs and if the programs satisfy the employees. It is important to remember that needs interact. They are dynamic, changing within and between individuals as well as in response to a changing environment.

Certain aspects and consequences of motivation can be identified within the organizational environment. Kanfer (1990) claimed that a definition of motivation has to include three factors: (a) the antecedents, or independent factors that affect behavior (e.g., the group norms); (b) the variables that intervene and influence the relationships between the independent factors that affect motivation and their consequences (e.g., the individual's expectancies); and (c) the dependent variables, that is, the motivational consequences. Most definitions of motivation concentrate on these consequences, that is, what a person does, how hard the employee works, and how long he or she works. Thus Kanfer's motivational consequences take into account the *direction* of the worker's behavior, for example, absenteeism; the *intensity* or magnitude of this behavior, for example, effort used in performance levels; and the *maintenance* or *persistence* of behavior, for example, productivity measured over long periods of employment. These general variables are included in the definition of motivation in the workplace: It is an arousal of a set of energetic forces that originate both within and beyond an individual's being to initiate work-related effort and to determine its direction, intensity, and duration (Katzell & Thompson, 1990; Pinder, 1984). In short, work motivation is usually described as a process that moves people either intrinsically or extrinsically toward a goal.

At the turn of the century, managers were concerned with simplifying tasks to increase production. Employees worked on assembly lines, performing the same tasks over and over throughout the workday. They were not given the opportunity to turn in finished pieces of work because they were involved only in a few steps of the production effort. Although this method was cost-effective for the employer, em-

ployees were often bored and unsatisfied. Fortunately, this view has changed over the years. Managers now recognize that employees are more satisfied and motivated when they are assigned more complex duties.

Managers now use a variety of methods to motivate employees based on certain assumptions or conclusions they make about their employees and about what is necessary to get the job done. Many managers might agree with Latham (1988), who stated that the employee is an energy storage system capable of a wide variety of responses. Changing various conditions, such as the nature of the job, and providing more cues for secondary drives, such as curiosity and exploration, might lead to highly effective behavior. Latham identified two basic contradictory

TABLE 10.1   Motivational theories, definitions, and examples

Theories	Definitions	Examples
Needs theories	Innate or acquired dispositions that arouse and direct behavior.	Needs hierarchy; ERG; need achievement; two-factor theory
Reinforcement theories	Behavior is elicited by being rewarded appropriately and having positive consequences.	*Examples:* Operant conditioning (behaviorism)
Instrumentality-expectancy theories	Behavior is motivated by the expectation that effort and performance will lead to obtaining desired results.	Valence-instrumentality-expectancy (VIE); Porter and Lawler model
Equity theories	Behavior is determined by individuals' need for justice or fairness in organizational procedures. Through social interaction at work, individuals evaluate whether there is a balance (justice) between the inputs (e.g., their effort, seniority) and the outcomes (e.g., money) of their work. These ratios of outcomes to inputs are compared to those of co-workers, the profession, and other referents. Equity will result if there is a judgment of equality between these ratios (Katzell et al., 1990; Kanfer, 1990; Steers et al., 1991).	Adams' equity theory; two-component model of justice

themes concerning employee motivation. The first theme is that one cannot motivate others; one can only create the conditions that will allow people to motivate themselves. The second theme is that by focusing on the individual, that is, on the person's behavior, needs, drives, and goals, one can indeed motivate that individual. Both of these viewpoints are discussed in the following section on motivational theories.

. . . .
SOME THEORIES OF MOTIVATION

To better organize and understand theories of motivation, we have listed and defined some major theories in Table 10.1. The theories in the table are discussed in the following sections.

Needs Theories

Maslow's Needs Hierarchy

Maslow's hierarchy of needs suggests that there are various progressive levels of needs. Maslow (1954, 1970) postulated five categories of needs: physiological, safety, social, esteem, and self-actualization (see Figure 10.2 on page 340). These are arranged from lower- to higher-level needs. According to Maslow, this process is dynamic. Individuals are motivated by the lowest, most basic needs in this hierarchy that remain unsatisfied; once a level of needs is satisfied, it no longer motivates behavior; the next higher level in the hierarchy becomes the dominant motivator.

In work settings, higher-level needs are rarely reached, in contrast to lower-order needs for

Theories	Definitions	Examples
Goal-setting theories	Intentions, how people think about themselves and the environment, and their determination to act influence motivation. When employees have defined, specific, and attractive goals and when they participate in setting these goals, performance will be affected. For example, money is an effective motivator when obtaining it is contingent on achieving particular goals.	Locke's theory
Intrinsic-motivation theories	Motivation could be enhanced by providing employees with conditions that will create feelings of contentment and pleasure. Intrinsic motivation concentrates on higher needs such as challenge at work or a sense of having control over work conditions.	Cognitive evaluation theory

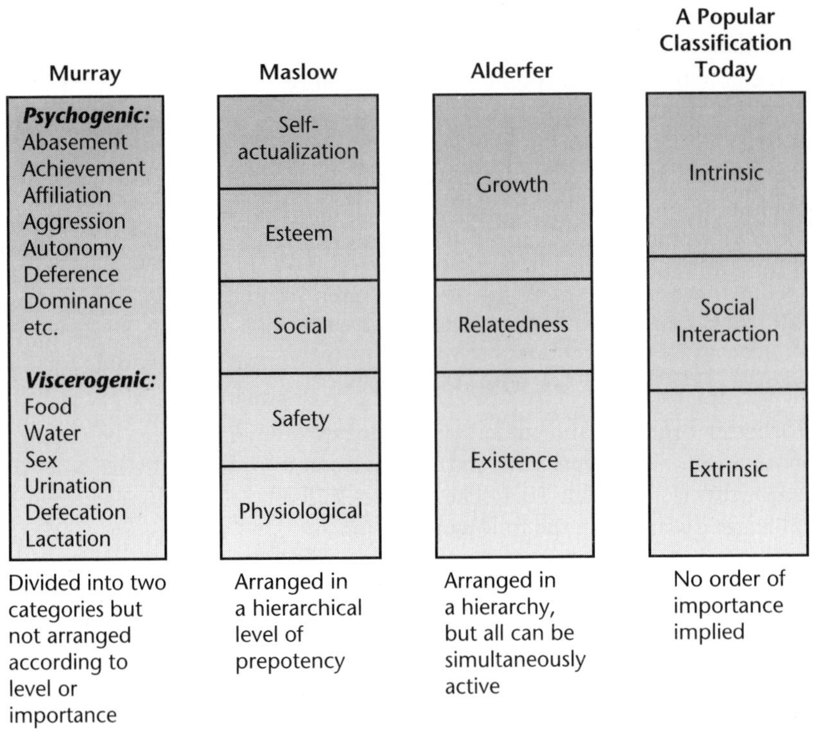

Murray	Maslow	Alderfer	A Popular Classification Today
Psychogenic: Abasement Achievement Affiliation Aggression Autonomy Deference Dominance etc.	Self-actualization	Growth	Intrinsic
	Esteem		
	Social	Relatedness	Social Interaction
Viscerogenic: Food Water Sex Urination Defecation Lactation	Safety		
	Physiological	Existence	Extrinsic
Divided into two categories but not arranged according to level or importance	Arranged in a hierarchical level of prepotency	Arranged in a hierarchy, but all can be simultaneously active	No order of importance implied

FIGURE 10.2

Comparisons of needs hierarchies.

Source: From *Personnel Management* by D. J. Cherrington, © 1991. Reprinted by permission of Prentice-Hall, Upper Saddle River, NJ.

which some level of satisfaction is a physiological necessity. Employees are less motivated to work toward achieving self-actualization, because self-actualization seems less attainable in the work environment than the lower-order needs such as food and safety. This is especially true for lower-level workers, because their jobs do not provide as many opportunities to reach higher-level need satisfaction.

Two important questions in current research are: Does the hierarchy exist? Is there a progression of gratification moving from lower to higher level needs? In his summary of the research, Cherrington (1991) concluded that there is no clear evidence to support Maslow's categorization of needs. In large measure, this is because it has been difficult to develop reliable scales to measure Maslow's needs (Staw, 1984). To date, empirical studies have shown only partial support for the existence of the hierarchy and its proposition that there are changes in the strength of different levels of needs (Kan-

fer, 1990; Wahba & Bridwell, 1976). However, some evidence has been found for the existence of an independent need category of self-actualization.

Lawler and Rhode (1976) claimed that research supports only part of Maslow's theory: that needs become less important to the individual once they are satisfied. The exception to this is the need for growth. Research indicates that this need becomes more important the more it is satisfied and appears to be insatiable. They also stated that there is little evidence that the hierarchy exists beyond the security level of needs. This assertion suggests that there is only a two-level hierarchy; once the needs for existence and security (one level) are satisfied, a number of other needs can come into play simultaneously, for example, social and autonomy needs (second level). Cherrington (1991) generalized this conclusion, claiming that higher-level needs can activate the individual while lower-level needs are only partially satisfied. For instance, artistic and cultural activities may satisfy the higher-level needs of people whose needs for food and shelter are not fully satisfied. Alderfer (1972) claimed that needs at different levels can be active simultaneously.

Although Maslow's theory lacks empirical support, it is still a popular theory of motivation (Cherrington, 1991). This may be because it was designed as a model to describe individual behavior, rather than a model to predict future behavior. In addition, it has a simplicity of form that appeals to people and makes it easy to remember. This simplicity has made it popular in management training programs, in which "Maslow's pyramid" is often the theory of motivation that students learn and remember. Additional research that takes into account age, gender, occupation, and other dimensions of individual differences is needed to prove whether Maslow's model predicts employee behavior in an organizational environment (Kanfer, 1990).

Alderfer's ERG Theory

Alderfer's ERG theory (1969) consolidated Maslow's five levels to only three: existence needs (E), relatedness needs (R), and growth needs (G) (see Figure 10.2). **Existence needs** include the survival needs, that is, Maslow's physiological and safety needs. **Relatedness needs** deal with social interaction, recognition, and status from others. **Growth needs** focus on the employee's desire to achieve and develop individual potential; they include Maslow's self-esteem and self-actualization needs. Alderfer's theory differs from Maslow's in that, although the levels are continual, they may overlap at times. This overlap means that one could proceed from level to level without fully satisfying the needs of previous levels.

Kanfer (1990) noted that while both Maslow's and Alderfer's theories were popular during the 1960s, they currently receive very little attention. This might be the result of studies that show mixed results regarding the models' basic assumptions. Lawler (1971) concluded that there is evidence that needs exist on at least two levels, but there is no empirical evidence that they exist

on more than two levels. Overall, there is very little support for the assumption that needs are organized into a specific number of levels, or for the assumption that there is a fixed hierarchy of needs that controls behavior (Locke, 1976). Additionally, studies relating need theories to organizational settings have concluded that research does not show that needs change as individuals rise in organizations (Campbell & Pritchard, 1976), and longitudinal studies are needed to discover differences in need satisfaction related to different organizational levels.

Examining Alderfer's and Maslow's theories further, Rauschenberger, Schmitt, and Hunter (1980) claimed that in both theories the concept of need hierarchy was *disconfirmed;* some of their data contradicted Maslow's concept of the person being dominated by one need at a time. It seems that there is little evidence supporting the conclusion that these models enable managers to predict individual employees' specific behaviors in order to satisfy particular needs (Locke, 1976). In spite of the attacks on these theories and the failure to validate their assumptions, they still play a strong indirect role in current theories such as expectancy theory (Staw, 1984), which is discussed later in the chapter.

McClelland's Socially Acquired Needs Theory

Another motivation theory based on needs is **McClelland's socially acquired needs theory** (e.g., Atkinson & Raynor, 1974; McClelland, 1961, 1985). This theory is based on the learned, cultural needs that motivate individuals to pursue satisfying goals. According to McClelland, previous experiences involving either success or failure can be used to predict future behaviors that result in the most positive outcomes. McClelland assumes that there are three needs: the need to achieve, the need for affiliation, and the need for power.

1. The **need for achievement** (nAch) is defined as the need to compete, achieve, and excel relative to a set of standards. High-need achievers have the desire for personal achievement, assuming the responsibility to perform tasks better than they have been done before. They seek immediate feedback and choose to work alone with tasks of moderate difficulty. These individuals will not select tasks with a high or low probability of success because the first would be too easy and the second would be too risky. McClelland believes that nAch is important to entrepreneurial success; nAch individuals would be successful at running their own business or divisions of an organization. This characteristic could be important for managers, because high nAch employees accomplish their assigned tasks.

2. The **need for power** (nPow) is the need to control others and to have impact on one's environment. When an individual learns that influencing others' behavior and controlling one's environment are associated with satisfaction, he or she learns the power motive (McClelland, 1985). Bowditch and Buono (1985) indicated that if we follow McClelland's reasoning, motivation is changeable through experience, even in adulthood. Accordingly, these motives become dependent variables rather than independent variables. McClelland (1970) further stated that there are two types of nPow: the personal power need, when the individual strives toward complete control, such as a sergeant over his or her soldiers, and the social power need, when the individual strives to achieve organizational goals through his or her group. Managers who have a high level of social nPow are those with the potential to be extremely effective and successful.

3. The **need for affiliation** (nAff) is the need for close and friendly interpersonal relationships. High nAff individuals value the feelings of others, seek approval, and try to conform to the standards of others (Cherrington, 1991). They work well in an environment of mutual understanding and support.

McClelland also assumed the existence of a leadership motive. In a longitudinal study of 237 nontechnical managers at American Telephone and Telegraph, McClelland and Boyatzis (1982) found that a pattern of moderate to high nPow, low nAff, and a high score in the way a person feels about using power coercively, that is, activity inhibition (House & Singh, 1987), was associated with managerial success as measured by promotion patterns. The need for achievement was associated with success only at the lower technical job level. Questions still exist about cause-and-effect relationships between leadership patterns and success and the need to identify other personality characteristics associated with success (McClelland & Boyatzis, 1982).

Reinforcement Theories

Reinforcement theory is based on a behavioral philosophy of rewarding correct responses. In other words, employees will repeat behaviors that have been positively reinforced and will refrain from behaviors that have not been positively reinforced. Both need and reinforcement theories are based on Thorndike's "law of effect," which posits that responses followed by satisfaction are likely to recur in similar situations, whereas those followed by dissatisfaction are less likely to recur in similar situations (Thorndike, 1911). While need theories assume the existence of an internal state, such as a drive or need, reinforcement theories emphasize consequences (Steers & Porter, 1991). The individual's behavior operates on the environment to produce consequences; pleasant results increase the frequency of the occurrence of the accompanying behaviors, and a conditional (contingent) relationship is formed. Effective behavior should be followed by reward so that it will be repeated; ineffective behavior should *not* be reinforced (or should be punished) to reduce its reoccurrence. This is the operant behavior principle that we discussed in Chapter 9 ("Training and Development").

According to Steers and Porter (1991, p. 12), strict reinforcement theory is not a theory of motivation because "it ignores the inner state of the individual . . . [that is] . . . it does not concern itself with what energizes or initiates behavior." However, they claimed that because reinforcement theory does emphasize principles of direction and maintenance of behavior (see the definition of motivation), it can provide a means to analyze "what controls behavior" (Steers & Porter, 1991, p. 12); that is, it can be viewed as a motivational mechanism (Katzell & Thompson, 1990). Some important characteristics of this theory include: (a) an emphasis on consequences of performance (such as pay, praise, or profit sharing); (b) the design of reinforcement schedules (such as continuous, intermittent, immediate, or delayed) (see the discussion in Chapter 9); and (c) the significance of performance assessment techniques (Katzell & Thompson, 1990; Komaki, Coombs, & Schepman, 1991). For a more detailed discussion of performance assessment techniques, see Chapter 6 ("Performance Appraisal").

Managers who understand reinforcement theory can apply reinforcement schedules to reward, and therefore motivate, their employees. Continuous reinforcement schedules provide rewards each time the desired behavior occurs. Intermittent reinforcement schedules do not reward employees for each desired behavior; rather, employees receive rewards at unspecified intervals. Delayed reinforcement schedules reward employees on a regular but delayed schedule (such as the first of the month) or for a specific volume of production (for example, the number of cars sold).

Employees often base their behavior on how they believe their managers will compensate them. Following Lawler's (1971) model of pay and organizational effectiveness, Milbourn (1980, p. 43) summarized how to tap pay as a motivational force:

> a reward system is effective only when the rewards used are valued by the recipients; the reward is tied directly to performance. Pay should not be used as a motivator when: (a) the level of trust between workers and managers is low, (b) when job performance is difficult to measure, and (c) when large pay cannot be used to reward the best employees.

Hamner (1977) suggested the following managerial guidelines:

1. Managers should clearly identify exactly which behaviors are desired. In other words, they should set explicit performance criteria.

2. Managers should provide a variety of rewards as potential reinforcers.

3. Managers should be conscious of individual differences when implementing reward systems; certain rewards may reinforce some employees but not others.

4. Managers should help employees to set goals, and timely feedback must be provided about the employee's progress toward achieving those goals.

5. Managers should administer rewards immediately after the desired behavior is exhibited. In addition, they must reward *only* desired behaviors.

Komaki et al. (1991) provides an example of a four-step application of positive reinforcement in a wholesale bakery, where injury rates had increased. Her study, described in Scientific Perspective 10.1 on page 344, illustrates the significant impact positive reinforcement can have in the workplace when managers take the time and trouble to apply these principles.

Operant Conditioning and Behavior Modification

Organizational behavior modification appears to be a continuation of reinforcement theory: Behavior is modified by making rewards contingent on desired behaviors, which is the definition of operant conditioning (Hamner, 1991). Many of the basic assumptions of operant conditioning that are used in the workplace began with Skinner's (1953, 1969) work in operant conditioning. Skinner assumed that human behavior could be determined and maintained through interaction with the environment. This concept is important to managers because of the relationship between job satisfaction and motivation and its partial dependence on the work environment. Bowditch and Buono (1985, p. 53)

SCIENTIFIC PERSPECTIVE 10.1

A Four-Step Program of Positive Reinforcement Reduces Accident Rate

Komaki et al. (1991) provided an example of a four-step application of positive reinforcement in a wholesale bakery, where injury rates had increased. To introduce and maintain a safety program, the following program was designed:

1. Specific behaviors were determined and defined, for example, "Walk around conveyer belt." All definitions had an interrater reliability of 90% or better.
2. Desired performance was assessed by the observation of trained observers, who recorded safe and unsafe behaviors.
3. Feedback was provided on positive behaviors by publicly posting a graph showing safety scores of groups of employees.

4. Follow-ups of five and one-half weeks in one department and thirteen and one-half weeks in another department showed improvements from 70% to 96% and from 78% to 99%, respectively. (Percentages indicate overall safe performance.)

Follow-up after one year indicated significant drops in accident rates. Komaki et al. suggest that a simple four-step positive reinforcement program can sustain employee motivation.

Source: Based on "Motivational Implications of Reinforcement Theory," by J. L. Komaki, T. Coombs, and S. Schepman, 1991. In R. M. Steers and L. W. Porter (Eds.), *Motivation and work* (pp. 87–107). New York: McGraw-Hill.

examined current ideas relating to this relationship and concluded:

> The concept of operant conditioning is useful to explain the relationship between satisfaction and performance. Originally, it was thought that high satisfaction in the work place led to high job performance. Today, however, it is generally agreed that it works in reverse, that is, high performance that is sufficiently rewarded (reinforced) leads to high satisfaction, which in turn sustains high performance.

Setting up appropriate reinforcement schedules and linking them to desired performance will lead to, and maintain, higher levels of motivation. Concurrently, introducing punishment (e.g., reprimand) to reduce the frequency of undesired behaviors may be effective, but this method is controversial. It can produce side effects such as a damaged self-image and a decrease in quality and/or quantity of performance of the employee's work group if group members identify with the punished member (Hamner, 1991). A work environment that is based on

punishment rather than reward produces anxiety in employees. This type of environment can negatively affect not only productivity, but also overall employee satisfaction, which may then lead to hostile or defensive behavior (Dubrin, 1984). Practice Perspective 10.3 gives an example of a situation in which a company's plan to cut down the number of jobs has been suspected of inducing sabotage.

Reward and punishment are two of the most powerful concepts available to managers in controlling employees. As we mentioned at the beginning of the chapter, these controls can be divided into two categories: intrinsic and extrinsic factors. **Intrinsic factors** are nonmaterial in nature and include feelings of achievement, satisfaction, growth, esteem, and knowledge. **Extrinsic factors** include material rewards such as pay, fringe benefits, and desirable working conditions. These factors are sometimes called internal and external factors. They are discussed in more detail later in this chapter and in Chapter 11.

The effects of reinforcement on motivation have been studied for a variety of employees

PRACTICE PERSPECTIVE 10.3

Job Cuts Lead to Sabotage

DETROIT – General Motors Corp. said its campaign to trim thousands of jobs appears to have provoked an incident of sabotage in an Oshawa, Ontario, plant.

GM sent home a shift of workers at Oshawa plant No. 1 Wednesday after it discovered that somebody had put salt on 40 freshly painted car bodies. The company said workers there are angered by the activities of a group of GM productivity experts from Detroit, which has spent the past few weeks in Oshawa proposing changes that would eliminate jobs.

A Canadian Auto Workers union official rejected that notion, however, saying it wasn't clear if hourly workers were responsible for the action. "All they've got is a bunch of allegations that shouldn't even be in the press," said Jim Nimigon, vice president of Local 222, adding that the union condemns any act of sabotage.

The car bodies, which will be scrapped, were sabotaged during the night shift by an hourly worker in a restricted area, said Tayce Wakefield, director of public relations for General Motors of Canada. She said the company had been inter-

viewing workers since the incident in an effort to determine who was responsible.

More than 1,000 workers on the day shift reported to work at 7 a.m. Wednesday but they were sent home at 9 a.m. because of the ruined cars. Sending the workers home was the only prudent thing to do until GM could determine the cause of the sabotage, Ms. Wakefield said.

The union, however, is upset that the workers were sent home without pay. "I think it's a very convenient way to get around paying these workers." said Mr. Nimigon. The day shift wasn't there when GM says the cars were sabotaged, he said.

Ms. Wakefield countered: "It's all the same group of employees."

GM's efforts to trim its size rapidly and cut costs have provoked two strikes by the United Auto Workers union in the U.S. since August. The company said it's unaware of any plant besides Oshawa where vehicles were intentionally damaged.

Source: From "GM Says a Worker Sabotaged New Autos at a Plant in Canada," (p. A7), *The Wall Street Journal,* Dec. 21, 1992. Reprinted by permission of The Wall Street Journal, © 1992 Dow Jones & Company, Inc. All rights reserved.

(e.g., bus drivers, real estate agents, baseball players); in different types of organizations (e.g., hospitals, the Marine Corps); and in different countries (e.g., the United States, Scandinavia). Komaki et al. (1991) summarized fifty-one studies and observed that in forty-seven of these studies, positive reinforcement resulted in "substantial improvements in performance" (p. 92). The effective application of rewards in organizational settings combines both extrinsic and intrinsic factors, or, following Katzell, Thompson, and Guzzo (1992), consists of an interaction of exogenous causes and endogenous processes. That is, organizations should design jobs that are internally rewarding (e.g., encourage a sense of contribution) and that provide rewards for good performance (e.g., pay).

Instrumentality-Expectancy Theory

People often make decisions on the basis of the value of receiving some type of reward in return for their effort and then act accordingly. This process includes the expectation that work (action, effort) will result in performance that is instrumental to receiving a valued reward. It is the basis of **valence-instrumentality-expectancy (VIE) theories.** VIE theories include Katzell and Thompson's (1990) endogenous process, or, in simpler terms, the cognitive process of decision making. These theories are also classified as **cognitive-choice theories** (Kanfer, 1990).

Vroom's (1964) book on work motivation served as the basis for many VIE theories. His assumption was that individual behavior at work is voluntary and that people make choices be-

HISTORICAL PERSPECTIVE 10.1

Instrumentality-Expectancy Evaluation of Enlisting in the Navy

Following is a classic example of instrumentality-expectancy theory in practice (Blum & Naylor, 1968). An individual considers joining the Navy. Although he believes joining will mean postponing college, it would increase his chances of securing a better (Navy) job. Postponing education is a certainty (instrumentality = 1.00) and has a negative valence (e.g., –.50). Getting a better job in the Navy is believed to have a high likelihood (instrumentality = .80) and has a positive valence (e.g., +.90). The valence of volunteering (the outcome) is a function of the sum of the valences of all anticipated outcomes multiplied by their instrumentalities:

$$V = f[(-.50 \times 1.00) + (+.90 \times .80)] = .22$$

The results indicate that this person will have a moderately positive feeling toward joining the Navy now.

Source: From *Industrial psychology: Its theoretical and social foundations* (p. 337) by M. L. Blum and J. C. Naylor, 1968, New York: Harper and Row.

tween voluntary responses. The individual must be motivated to make a certain response. The three subjective factors that initiate and direct this behavior are:

1. Valence relates to the attractiveness or desirability of a given reward or outcome. The person's desire or aversion for particular outcomes is based on "the anticipated satisfaction or dissatisfaction" (Vroom, 1964, p. 15) associated with them. For example, promotion or an increase in pay may have positive valence for the individual; being transferred, being forced to retire, or losing a job may have negative valence. The emphasis is on the belief and the expectation the individual has about achieving satisfaction from specific outcomes.

2. Instrumentality relates to the individual's belief that a particular outcome will lead to (be instrumental in attaining) additional (second-level) outcomes that are valent to individual rewards. For example, students believe studying to be instrumental to passing exams, which in turn is believed to be instrumental to receiving a diploma, which is expected to lead to a desired job (Pinder, 1991). This is an example of an outcome–outcome relationship.

Historical Perspective 10.1 gives an illustration of how instrumentality and expectancy are combined in a mathematical formula to calculate the valence of an outcome. Historical Perspective 10.1 illustrates the overall effect on the attraction (valence) of volunteering to join the Navy that is created by: (a) considering further education, (b) the belief that such education would lead to a better job, and (c) the belief that a better job is immediately available in the Navy.

These propositions express the way a person feels about specific outcomes, not the actual action taken or the choices made. Because of this, Vroom added the concepts of expectancy and force to improve the prediction of outcomes.

3. Expectancy relates to the "belief concerning the likelihood that a particular act will be followed by a particular outcome" (Vroom, 1964, p. 17). The relationship here is between action and outcomes (e.g., performing at a high level and achieving security).

4. Force is the intensity, or "motivational force" (Pinder, 1991, p. 148), with which the individual has to act to create satisfying outcomes (e.g., to make money) and avoid dissatisfying outcomes (e.g., a lack of security).

As Vroom (1964, p. 19) stated, "an outcome with high positive or negative valence will have no effect on the generation of a force unless there is some expectancy that the outcome will be attained by some act." Force, then, is a func-

SCIENTIFIC PERSPECTIVE 10.2

Using VIE to Examine the Value of Money in Attaining Security

To understand how valence, instrumentality, and expectancy are associated with behavior, let us examine Opsahl and Dunnette's (1966) example of how money is instrumental for achieving security. If money is believed to be a means (instrumental) to obtain security, which has positive valence, then

money itself will acquire positive valence. The probability, then, of his [her] making money-seeking responses depends on the degree so his/[her] desire for security multiplied by his/[her] expectancy that certain designated job behaviors lead to attaining money." (p. 97).

Thus

$$V \text{ of money} = f(V_{ds} \times I_{as})$$

$$\text{Force}_{\substack{\text{of making money} \\ \text{seeking job behaviors}}} = f[\,\text{Sum}(E_{as} \times V_{ds})],$$

where

V = valence

f = function of

ds = desirability of security

I = instrumentality

as = likelihood of attaining security

E = strength of expecting to attain security through the specific job behaviors

Source: "The role of financial compensation in industrial motivation," by R. L. Opsahl and M. M. Dunnette, 1966, *Psychological Bulletin, 66,* pp. 94–118.

tion of all the valences of all the outcomes multiplied by the strength of the individual's expectancy of achieving these outcomes through performing the act (Opsahl & Dunnette, 1966). We can see how this works in Scientific Perspective 10.2, which examines how money is instrumental for achieving security.

When applying these concepts to levels of performance in the workplace, the individual will consider all the valences, instrumentalities, and expectancies that are believed to be associated with the different performance levels that could result in desired outcomes. People base their choices about levels of effort applied to the job on the greatest payoff that they perceive to be associated with different alternatives (Mitchell, 1979). Vroom assumed that levels of motivation result from the individual's choice to perform at that level.

The VIE theory has resulted in a number of expanded studies. Discussing all of these theories is beyond the scope of this chapter; Porter and Lawler's (1968) model will be discussed in Chapter 11. In general, in spite of variations in concept definitions, the basic concepts of Vroom's model have been retained. Subsequent studies (Mitchell, 1979) investigated issues such as the causes of individual expectancies. An example is Kopelman's (1976) study, which showed that employees' perceptions and expectancies were related to the company's responsiveness to variations in individual work behavior. Other studies looked at personality variables, showing that locus of control, religious beliefs, self-esteem, and other factors are related to expectancies of the relationship between action and outcome (e.g., Lied & Pritchard, 1976); and at organizational climate (e.g., leadership style, job importance), showing a relationship to employee expectancies (James, Hartman, Stebbins, & Jones, 1977).

The empirical evidence for the VIE model varies (Campbell & Pritchard, 1976). The theory does not represent a "very powerful [explanation] of behavior . . . [but] the heuristic value of the expectancy framework will remain as a powerful force in organizational psychology" (Campbell & Pritchard, 1976, p. 92). As the result of efforts to validate the model, recent summaries have focused on methodological problems (e.g., Campbell & Pritchard, 1976; Kanfer, 1990; Mitchell, 1979; Steers & Porter, 1991). Some of the most important issues raised by this research, as reported by Pinder (1991), are as follows:

1. The between/within issue. Although the theory intends to predict individual behavioral choices (*within* individuals), most of the research concentrates on the between-individuals approach. This approach involved correlating VIE scores collected across individuals with measures of actual behavior on the job. The between-individuals approach ignored differences between people in perception, abilities, and levels of rewards. Testing for the validity of the expectancy theory by comparing the predicted choices of goals and the actual goals achieved, Tubbs, Boehne, and Dahl (1993) stated that conclusions drawn from studies conducted with the two methodologies (between and within) often are contradictory. Thus, comparing study results from the two methods is like comparing apples and oranges (Tubbs et al., 1993, p. 372).

2. Low validity and reliability were found for the factors of valence, instrumentality, and expectancy.

3. Incorrect mathematical procedures were used to test relationships among factors, such as effort and ability.

4. Performance ratings were used as criteria, rather than measuring effort as the predicted (dependent) variable.

5. The researchers neglected to take into account that people are not always as rational as the theory assumes. They may not have all of the necessary information about all possible outcomes or about the relationship between action and outcomes (Mitchell, 1979). Rather, people often make choices and act on the basis of subjective perceptions and beliefs.

Some of the implications of expectancy theory for management (Bowditch & Buono, 1985; Pinder, 1991; Steers & Porter, 1991) include:

1. To serve as motivators, outcomes must be desired by individuals. Managers must therefore try to identify outcomes that employees believe to be rewarding.

2. Employees must perceive that their efforts (work behavior) will result in good performance and success. They must believe that there is a connection among their behavior, the circumstances surrounding the job (e.g., appropriate equipment), their training, their abilities, and success on the job.

3. Organizational reward systems must provide sufficient flexibility in reinforcing individuals, or no link will be formed between differences in performance and outcomes.

"[R]ecently there have been many appropriately-conducted studies, [which] leave us with grounds for optimism that the theory is a reasonably valid model of the causes of work behavior" (Pinder, 1991, p. 156).

Equity Theory

Equity theory is concerned primarily with the issue of justice. An individual's contribution to any situation is based on his or her perception of a fair, just, and equitable distribution of outcomes among people (in a given situation) in proportion to the input of each person. The individual expects a balance between the ratio of personal inputs to outputs for a given situation. The individual then compares the personal ratio to the ratios of the other people in that situation. Only people whom the individual considers worthy of personal comparison are included. (Kanfer, 1990; Mahoney, 1979; O'Reilly, 1991). Inputs, or costs to employees, include variables such as job qualifications, age, skills, education, and amount of effort required to perform the job. Outputs, or rewards, include pay, fringe benefits, status, and self-worth. Like expectancy theory, equity theory is an endogenous theory (Katzell & Thompson, 1990), because it deals with variables such as individual perceptions and attitudes. Because it is based on the comparisons an individual makes to others, motivation is viewed as a social comparison process (Mitchell, 1979).

A primary characteristic of equity theory is that not only do employees compare costs with rewards, they compare them to the perceived costs and rewards experienced by others. This is known as **distributive justice**, or the fair sharing of rewards. Equity, then, is a cognitive process. It is "a social exchange theory of distributive justice . . . [assuming] that individuals seek fairness" (Kanfer, 1990, p. 102) and similarity of ratios of output to input in an exchange relationship.

The most prominent equity theory is Adams's (1965) **social exchange theory.** According to this theory, equity exists when the person's ratio of outcomes to inputs equals the ratio of outcomes to inputs of comparable others:

$$(O_p/I_p) = (O_a/I_a)$$

where O is outcome, I is inputs, p stands for person, and a stands for another.

Perceived inequity is experienced when the ratios are not equal:

$$(O_p/I_p) < (O_a/I_a)$$

or

$$(O_p/I_p) > (O_a/I_a)$$

People are motivated when they believe they are treated inequitably; they will try to remove the source of discomfort and injustice and achieve a sense of equity. Their objective is to achieve equity by employing various methods, such as (a) changing the outputs (e.g., asking for a pay increase); (b) changing the inputs (e.g., increasing or decreasing effort on the job); (c) changing the referent other (e.g., from employees in his or her own department to similar employees in other departments); (d) leaving the situation; or (e) trying to alter the inputs or outputs of others.

The theory of social exchange demonstrates the relationship between motivation and satisfaction. When employees believe that the ratios between the self and the other are relatively equal, they will be satisfied. On the other hand, when employees believe that there is ratio inequality, states of tension and dissatisfaction result, motivating the individual to (cognitively or behaviorally) restore equality. For example, in academia, where salary increases are often fixed and based largely on publication credits, a faculty member who did not receive a salary increase might accuse other faculty members of falsifying their number of publications to merit salary increases. Alternatively, he or she could look for another job in an institution that has a fairer salary system.

Because of the serious ramifications of positive or negative inequity, employers must be aware of the perceived inequity of employees. Adams (1965) reviewed some of the possible consequences: Employees who believe they are overpaid have been known to increase the quantity or quality of their work; those who feel underpaid may reduce their work efforts to compensate for missing rewards. However, individual differences must also be taken into account. Each employee has a unique idea of inequity, and what is acceptable to some employees will not be acceptable to others. Predictions made from equity theory were effectively summarized by Mowday (1991), as shown in Table 10.2 on page 350.

As Table 10.2 indicates, experimental situations were manipulated with underpayment and overpayment as the two conditions of inequity, and with hourly and piece rate as the procedures of pay. The results are similar to those in Scientific Perspective 10.3 on page 351, which summarizes two studies by Greenberg (1988, 1990a). The first examined the impact of being in a "better office." The second investigated the effect on theft of being "poorly paid." Both studies supported equity theory predictions.

Overall, equity theory research shows that predictions about underpayment inequity are stronger than those for overpayment and peo-

TABLE 10.2   Equity theory predictions of employee reactions to inequitable pay

	Underpayment	*Overpayment*
Hourly payment	Subjects who are underpaid by the hour produce less or poorer-quality output than equitably paid subjects.	Subjects who are overpaid by the hour produce more or higher-quality output than equitably paid subjects.
Piece-rate payment	Subjects who are underpaid by piece rate will produce a large number of low-quality units in comparison with equitably paid subjects.	Subjects who are overpaid by piece rate will provide fewer units of higher quality than equitably paid subjects.

Source: From R. T. Mowday, "Equity Theory Predictions of Behavior" (1991). In R. M. Steer and L. W. Porter, *Motivation and work behavior* (p. 115). New York: McGraw-Hill. Copyright 1991 by McGraw-Hill. Reprinted with permission.

ple's reaction to inequity depends on their perception of how the inequity was created, such as the way decisions were made and explanations provided of the distribution of rewards (e.g., Greenberg, 1988, 1990b). Folger and Konovsky (1989) administered a survey examining 217 employees' reactions to decisions about pay raises. The survey asked, "How fair do you consider the size of your raise to be?" (p. 119). Folger and Konovsky discovered that the procedures that applied to the distribution of pay increases (e.g., feedback by the supervisors) were associated with a feeling of satisfaction with the rewards given. This is consistent with Greenberg's (1987, p. 60) observation that "considerations of how outcomes are determined as well as what they are" have to be included in theoretical formulations and in organizational application of compensation. Individual perceptions about the fairness of the procedures that are used to determine the distribution of rewards (distributive justice) have been shown to influence organizational outcomes (e.g., Greenberg, 1990b; Ryer & Stone, 1993). However, this discussion is beyond the scope of our review, and we refer interested readers to the list of recommended readings.

Goal-Setting Theories

Goal-setting theories are related to expectancy-valence theories and are characterized as meta-cognitive self-regulatory motivational theories because they engage higher-level cognitive proc-

esses (Kanfer, 1990). A basic assumption in these theories is that individuals have intentions about the amount of time and effort they are willing to spend on the performance of selected goals. The decision to allocate time and effort is a rational one (cognitive) and therefore is similar to the cognitive focus of expectancy theories (Mahoney, 1979). Nevertheless, goal-setting theories differ in their emphasis on the intentions of the individual to act and the effect these intentions have on the performance level of the individual. In fact, "the person's conscious intentions (goals) are the primary determinants of task-related motivation since goals direct our thoughts and actions" (Bowditch & Buono, 1985, p. 52).

The best-known goal-setting model in industrial/organizational psychology is Locke's (1968) model. It emphasizes the way individual goals can lead to motivation to act and assumes that for the individual to be motivated, it is necessary for him or her to be committed to the achievement of specific, desired goals. In other words, employees' choices, or actions, reflect their reward preferences. The role of management in this situation is to make the path to attaining these rewards as clear as possible to motivate employees toward good performance. However, as Latham and Locke (1991, p. 357) observed, it is difficult to motivate individuals because "motivation comes from within the individual and therefore cannot be observed directly." Incen-

SCIENTIFIC PERSPECTIVE 10.3

Two Field Experiments Using Equity Theory

In two field experiments, Greenberg (1988, 1990a) obtained results that were relatively consistent with the theoretical predictions of equity theory. In the 1988 experiment, insurance company employees were temporarily and randomly assigned to offices of coworkers who were considered to be of equal status, higher status, or lower status. Some employees remained in their own offices; this was the control group. As predicted, compared to employees who were transferred to offices with equal-status coworkers, those who were assigned to offices with higher-status coworkers raised their performance, and those who were assigned to offices with lower-status coworkers lowered their performance (as measured by number of life insurance applications).

In another experiment, Greenberg (1990a) compared theft rates among employees in manufacturing plants during a period in which pay was temporarily reduced 15%. His subjects were non-union employees working in three Midwestern plants for thirty weeks. Because two large contracts were lost (for plants 1 and 2), the host company temporarily reduced its payroll across the board for the two plants. In plant 1, Greenberg created "the adequate explanation" condition. In this condition the president met with all employees and explained the causes of the pay cut and of its duration (ten weeks). Plant 2 was used for the "inadequate expla-

nation" condition. Here, only a short meeting was held with employees. The amount of the cut was announced, but no other information or explanation was offered. No pay cuts were made in plant 3, and it was used as a control group.

Statistical data on theft and on self-report feelings of pay equity revealed that both the plants in which pay was reduced had significantly higher theft rates than the control plant did. However, the "adequate explanation" plant had a significantly lower theft rate than the "inadequate explanation" plant. Post hoc tests showed that employees in the "inadequate explanation" plant experienced the highest degree of perceived inequity. "Workers whose pay reduction was adequately explained to them did not express heightened payment inequity while their pay was reduced" (Greenberg, 1990a, p. 565).

The results of both studies followed equity theory predictions. Workers who felt underpaid raised their inputs by stealing tools and supplies and expressed feelings of inequity.

Sources: From "Equity and workplace status: A field experiment," by J. Greenberg, 1988, *Journal of Applied Psychology, 73*, pp. 606–613, and "Employee theft as a reaction to underpayment inequity: The hidden cost of pay cuts," by J. Greenberg, 1990, *Journal of Applied Psychology, 75*, pp. 561–568.

---

tives such as money or participation are tools managers can use to direct employees' motivation toward achieving organizational objectives. The most efficient method by which these and other incentives will affect motivation is through setting individual goals. Campbell and Pritchard (1976, p. 110) provided a summary list of the "basic ingredients" of Locke's model:

1. Individuals make conscious decisions about which goals to pursue. These goals (or intentions) serve as the motivational basis for the level of effort expended on the job. According

to Campbell and Pritchard (1976), goals have two properties: They direct individual behavior, and once the individual commits himself or herself to a goal, more effort will be put into accomplishing it. The first property comprises the directional aspect of motivation; the second property expresses its energizing aspect (see our discussion of the definition of motivation).

2. Changing the values of incentives on the job will affect behavior only if the goals are made more attractive. For example, increasing monetary bonuses for production would affect production only if the level of production were made challenging enough to achieve.

3. Satisfaction and dissatisfaction with performance depend on whether the individual has reached and achieved a difficult but fair performance goal. For example, raising the goal of loading trucks to the legal allowable net weight of 94% from the previously attained loading weight of 58% to 63% would be a difficult but fair goal.

Locke's theory argues that setting goals for employees should include defining specific, rather than vague, goals—for example, "[work to] increase sales by 10 percent, rather than to improve sales" (Latham and Locke, 1991, p. 366). It should also include setting challenging, attainable goals. If goals are unfair or unreachable, they could lead to dissatisfaction and low performance. Campbell and Pritchard (1976) warn that although goal setting is an effective method for motivating employees, it should be used correctly, together with good management, fair payment, a sound quality control system, and other considerations.

Much of the empirical research in organizational behavior has concentrated on two motivational theories: goal-setting theory and equity theory. Research on goal-setting theory focuses on the relationship between goals and behavior on the job. Recently, researchers have been studying issues related to the way individuals choose goals and the factors that determine commitment to these goals. Reviews of this literature (e.g., Kanfer, 1990; Locke & Latham, 1990; Locke, Latham, & Erez, 1988; O'Reilly, 1991) have indicated that:

1. Goals assigned by the supervisors have as much influence on motivation as goals determined by participative decision making between the individual and the supervisor. This remains true as long as other factors (such as the type of instruction given by the supervisor and the degree of supervisor support) are held constant.

2. Three factors influence goal commitment (Locke et al., 1988): (a) **external factors,** such

as the legitimate authority of the people making the goal assignments (e.g., supervisors), the effects of peer pressure (e.g., union-determined standards of production), the importance of group success and its congruence with individual goals, the valence and probability of the achievement of a desired incentive and reward (e.g., money), and the employee's belief that the achievement of goals will not lead to punishment (e.g., layoffs); (b) **interactive factors,** such as employee participation in setting goals (e.g., representative goal setting in which an elected representative of the group negotiates with the experimenter (Erez & Early, 1987)), cultural factors (e.g., the individualistic concept of contribution in the United States compared to the collectivist values in the Israeli kibbutz, as found by Erez and Early (1987)); and (c) **internal factors,** such as self-reinforcement (e.g., "I really like it"), and the way one judges one's own capacity to perform (e.g., "I can do it!").

Our discussion of the goal-setting theory illuminates two important points: The concepts and processes of motivation and satisfaction are repeatedly deliberated together, and there is an obvious relationship between goal-setting theory and expectancy theory. For example, a recent study by Tubbs et al. (1993) examined the effects of assigned goals on performance by using the following expectancy theory concepts: the person's judgment of the probability of achieving outcomes or rewards (expectancy), the desirability of these rewards (valence), and the force (intensity of motivation) to act.

SUMMARY

To better understand human behavior in the work environment, I/O psychologists have extensively researched the concepts of job motivation and satisfaction. Motivation is often described as how work behavior is initiated and directed and the conditions under which it occurs. It is a process by which individuals fulfill their needs within the work environment. Satisfaction is commonly defined as the feeling of contentment people achieve as the result of achieving job needs. It is also thought of as a set of attitudes the employee holds about the work tasks and environment. Motivation and satisfaction are not mutually exclusive. Rather, the two concepts are interrelated: Obtaining a better understanding of one allows for a clearer understanding of the other.

In studying motivation and satisfaction, it is important to possess an understanding of some common theoretical terms, such as needs, motives, incentives, reinforcement, and goals. Needs or motives are defined as a lack of something that is either required or desired. An incentive is a stimulus that directs individuals toward a particular goal and influences the level of effort they invest in the job. Reinforcements consist of the positive consequences a person experiences after demonstrating a certain behavior. Rewards increase the likelihood that the reinforced behavior will occur again. Rewards are positive reinforcements intended to satisfy needs, and thereby encourage repetition of the original behavior. The achievement of goals reduces the imbalance created by needs. Employees who attain their desired goals are usually motivated and satisfied employees. Despite the apparent interrelationship between motivation and satisfaction, they are associated in varying degrees with different theories.

The first set of motivation theories—needs theories—holds that people work to satisfy their needs. Maslow categorized five different levels of needs in his hierarchy. He theorized that individuals can satisfy higher-order needs only after lower-order needs have been met. In Alderfer's ERG theory, which is a variation on Maslow's needs hierarchy, the five categories of needs are reduced to three levels: existence needs, relatedness needs, and growth needs. According to Alderfer, a person can move from level to level without first satisfying previous levels. Another model, McClelland's socially acquired needs theory, addresses the ways in which people's goals are influenced by their culture. McClelland defines three needs: the need to achieve, the need for affiliation, and the need for power.

Reinforcement theories are the second type of motivational theories. These models suggest that employees will repeat behaviors that have had positive consequences in the past. Employees will modify their behavior according to the type and schedule of reinforcement offered to them.

Instrumentality-expectancy theory hypothesizes that people are motivated by the expectation that their work will be instrumental in receiving a valued outcome. The four important factors inherent in this theory are valence (attractiveness of an outcome), instrumentality (belief that outcomes will lead to other outcomes), expectancy (belief that the specific action will lead to a desired outcome), and force (the effort a person invests to achieve the desired outcome). An employee evaluates these factors and selects the behaviors perceived as most effective.

Equity theory states that individuals are concerned with a fair and just distribution of rewards. They consider their own efforts and compare them to the perceived efforts of others. People expect that a balance should exist between their work efforts and the rewards those efforts produce. They believe that the ratio of their efforts to the rewards obtained should correspond to the ratios they observe operating for their fellow workers. Equity theory predicts that a person's motivation is adversely affected when the person believes that his or her effort-to-reward ratio is unfair (i.e., when too much work is required for too little reward) and when the person assumes that other workers earn greater rewards for equal or less effort.

Goal-setting theory defines motivation as the intent of an employee to meet certain goals. Workers consider the amount of time and effort that is necessary to achieve these goals. This theory offers guidelines with regard to realistic goal-setting in order to increase the chance of achieving these goals.

KEY TERMS AND CONCEPTS

Alderfer's ERG theory
cognitive-choice theories
distributive justice
endogenous theories
equity theory
existence needs
exogenous theories
expectancy
external factors
extrinsic factors
force
goal

goal-setting theories
growth needs
if–then relationships
incentive
instrumentality
interactive factors
internal factors
intrinsic factors
Maslow's hierarchy of needs
McClelland's socially acquired
    needs theory
need for achievement

need for affiliation
need for power
needs
reinforcement theory
reinforcer
relatedness needs
reward
social exchange theory
valence
valence-instrumentality-
    expectancy (VIE) theories

RECOMMENDED READINGS

Kanfer, R. (1990). Motivation theory and industrial and organizational psychology. In M. D. Dunnette & L. M. Hough (Eds.), *Handbook of industrial and organizational psychology* (Vol. 1, pp. 75–170). Palo Alto, CA: Consulting Psychologists Press.

Locke, E. A. (1976). The nature and causes of job satisfaction. In M. D. Dunnette (Ed.), *Handbook of industrial and organizational psychology* (pp. 1297–1349). Chicago: Rand McNally.

Steers, R. M., & Porter, L. W. (Eds.). (1991). *Motivation and work behavior.* New York: McGraw-Hill.

INTERNET RESOURCES

Foundation for Enterprise Development
   This site, maintained by the nonprofit Foundation for Enterprise Development is devoted to promoting equity compensation, employee ownership and involvement, and other high-performance business strategies. There are sections on high-performance companies and leading companies that use stock compensation, as well as a resource library of over 250 articles, case studies, and research on employee motivation and empowerment.
   http://www.fed.org/index.html

The Will to Work: What People Struggle to Achieve
   This site presents a series of articles about motivation by Manfred Davidmann including "Community Leadership and Management," "What People Struggle to Achieve," "The Will to Work," "Remuneration, Job Satisfaction and Motivation," and "Struggle for Independence and Good Life."
   http://ww.demon.co.uk/solbaram/articles/willwork.html

CommWeek's 1995 Network Managers Salary Survey
   A report by John T. Mulqueen of CommWeek that describes the 1995 annual survey results showing that job freedom, career opportunities, and job responsibilities outweigh compensation in what many network managers feel matters most about their jobs.
   http://techweb.cmp.com/cw/010296/salary1.htm#chart5

Surcon International Employee Opinion Survey
   Description of Surcon's employee opinion survey including a summary of results and an explanation of those results. A good example of the ways in which companies assess their employees' motivation.
   http://www.surcon.com/Enhanced/Surveys/emplopin.html

Homework Information Center
   This site presents information and suggestions for motivating children to complete homework. It goes beyond this, however, to include sugges-

tions for time management and positive work motivation.

http://www.pace-ed.com/homequiz.html

The Achiever: Recognizing the Best

This site presents information on a commercially available personality test that professes to measure work motivation. It is a good example of the types of measures that are available and used to assess personality and work motivation as a part of the selection process.

http://www.personalitytesting.com/achiever/

Human Resource Management & Organizational Behavior (Nijenrode Research Center for Organizational Learning)

This site presents links to articles on organizational learning and sections on employee motivation and empowerment, the "60-second Issues Audit," and the Positive Employee Relations Council (PERC).

http://www.nijenrode.nl/nbr/hrm/

....

EXERCISE

Exercise 10.1

Motivation at Manhattan Manufacturing

Mr. Smith, an employee from another department at Manhattan Manufacturing, was appointed supervisor of the instrument repair section. This section was part of a large development engineering group. Technicians had to have the skills to diagnose and repair equipment. This had to be done quickly and accurately to avoid repeatedly repairing the same unit.

According to past practice, Mr. Smith, as supervisor, inspected all incoming work. He then assigned the work to specific technicians according to the nature of the job. After they had completed the repairs, Mr. Smith inspected their finished work and returned it to the proper department.

During his first few weeks on the job, Mr. Smith made no changes in the established procedures. Rather, he concentrated on getting acquainted with the employees, watching them work, and sometimes working with them. He soon realized that production

was low and that there was a large backlog. Mr. Smith found that when technicians worked together, they spotted problems more quickly than when they worked autonomously and that the present system was not allowing the technicians to work efficiently or to exert their highest efforts.

1. The technicians described are affected by a number of factors. Using the facets of motivation described throughout the chapter, list all the factors that could influence the technicians' motivation.
2. Using one or two motivational theories, explain the level or levels at which the technicians are most likely working.
3. Provide several suggestions for enriching the technicians' jobs to increase their motivation.
4. Assuming that the technicians' jobs have been enriched, describe the different intrinsic and extrinsic rewards the technicians might experience or that the corporation could make available to them.

....

REFERENCES

Adams, J. S. (1965). Inequity in social exchange. In L. Berkowitz (Ed.), *Advances in experimental social psychology* (pp. 267–300). New York: Academic Press.

Alderfer, C. P. (1969). An empirical test of a new theory of human needs. *Organizational Behavior and Human Performance, 4,* 142–175.

Alderfer, C. P. (1972). *Existence, relatedness, and growth: Human needs in organizational settings.* New York: Free Press.

Atkinson, J. W., & Raynor, J. O. (1974). *Motivation and achievement.* Washington, DC: Winston.

Blum, M. L., & Naylor, J. C. (1968). *Industrial psychology, its theoretical and social foundations.* New York: Harper & Row.

Bowditch, J. L., & Buono, A. F. (1985). *Organizational behavior.* New York: Wiley & Sons.

Campbell, J. P., Dunnette, M. M., Lawler, E. E. III, & Weick, K. E., Jr. (1970). *Managerial behavior, per-*

formance, and effectiveness. New York: McGraw-Hill.

Campbell, J. P., & Pritchard, R. D. (1976). Motivation theory in industrial and organizational psychology. In M. D. Dunnette (Ed.), *Handbook of industrial and organizational psychology* (pp. 63–130). Chicago: Rand McNally.

Cherrington, D. J. (1991). Need theories of motivation. In R. M. Steers & L. W. Porter (Eds.), *Motivation and work* (pp. 31–44). New York: McGraw-Hill.

Dawis, R. V. (1991). Vocational interests, values, and preferences. In M. D. Dunnette & L. M. Hough (Eds.), *Handbook of industrial and organizational psychology* (Vol. 2, pp. 833–871). Palo Alto, CA: Consulting Psychologists Press.

Dawis, R., & Lofquist, L. H. (1984). *A psychological theory of work adjustment: An individual differences model and its applications.* Minneapolis, MN: University of Minnesota Press.

Dubrin, A. J. (1984). *Foundations of organizational behavior: An applied perspective.* Englewood Cliffs, NJ: Prentice-Hall.

Erez, M., & Early, P. C. (1987). Comparative analysis of goal-setting strategies across cultures. *Journal of Applied Psychology, 72*(4), 658–665.

Folger, R., & Konovsky, M. A. (1989). Effects of procedural and distributive justice of reactions to pay raise decisions. *Academy of Management Journal, 32*(1), 115–130.

Greenberg, J. (1987). Reactions to procedural injustice in payment distributions: Do the means justify the ends? *Journal of Applied Psychology, 72*(1), 55–61.

Greenberg, J. (1988). Equity and workplace status: A field experiment. *Journal of Applied Psychology, 73*(4), 606–613.

Greenberg, J. (1990a). Employee theft as a reaction to underpayment inequity: The hidden cost of pay cuts. *Journal of Applied Psychology, 75*(5), 561–568.

Greenberg, J. (1990b). Organizational justice: Yesterday, today, and tomorrow. *Journal of Management, 16*(2), 399–432.

Hamner, W. C. (1977). Using reinforcement theory in organizational settings. In H. L. Tosi & W. C. Hamner (Eds.), *Organizational behavior and management: A contingency approach* (pp. 388–395). Chicago: St. Clair Press.

Hamner, W. C. (1991). Reinforcement theory and contingency management in organizational settings. In R. M. Steers & L. W. Porter (Eds.), *Motivation and work behavior* (pp. 61–87). New York: McGraw-Hill.

Henneman, J. (1992, October 19). Survey finds satisfaction. *University of Wisconsin-Parkside Communique,* pp. 1, 3.

Hoppock, R. (1935). *Job satisfaction.* New York: Harper & Row.

House, R. J., & Singh, J. V. (1987). Organizational behavior. *Annual Review of Psychology, 38,* 669–718.

Hull, C. L. (1943). *Principles of behavior.* New York: Appleton-Century-Crofts.

James, L. R., Hartman, A., Stebbins, M. W., & Jones, A. P. (1977). Relationship between psychological climate and a VIE model for work motivation. *Personnel Psychology, 30,* 229–254.

Kanfer, R. (1990). Motivation theory and industrial and organizational psychology. In M. D. Dunnette & L. M. Hough (Eds.), *Handbook of industrial and organizational psychology* (Vol. 1, pp. 75–170). Palo Alto, CA: Consulting Psychologists Press.

Katzell, R. A., & Thompson, D. E. (1990). Work motivation, theory and practice. *American Psychologist, 45*(2), 144–153.

Katzell, R. A., Thompson, D. E., & Guzzo, R. A. (1992). Job satisfaction and job performance. In C. J. Cranny, P. C. Smith, & E. F. Stone (Eds.), *Job satisfaction* (pp. 195–217). New York: Lexington Books.

Kimble, G. A. (1961). *Hilgard and Marquis' conditioning and learning.* New York: Appleton-Century-Crofts.

Komaki, J. L., Coombs, T., & Schepman, S. (1991). Motivational implications of reinforcement theory. In R. M. Steers & L. W. Porter (Eds.), *Motivation and work* (pp. 87–107). New York: McGraw-Hill.

Kopelman, R. E. (1976). Organizational control system responsiveness, expectancy theory constructs, and work motivation: Some interrelations and causal connections. *Personnel Psychology, 29,* 205–220.

Latham, G. P. (1988). Employee motivation: Yesterday, today, and tomorrow. In J. Hage (Ed.), *Futures of organizations* (pp. 205–226). Lexington, MA: Lexington Books.

Latham, G. P., & Locke, E. A. (1991). Goal setting—A motivational technique that works. In R. M. Steers & L. W. Porter (Eds.), *Motivation and work* (pp. 357–370). New York: McGraw-Hill.

Lawler, E. E., III (1971). *Pay and organizational effectiveness: A psychological view.* New York: McGraw-Hill.

Lawler, E. E., & Rhode, J. G. (1976). *Information and control in organizations.* Santa Monica, CA: Goodyear Publishing Company.

Lied, T. R., & Pritchard, R. D. (1976). Relationship between personality variables and components of the expectancy-valence model. *Journal of Applied Psychology, 61*(4), 463–467.

Locke, E. A. (1968). Toward a theory of task motivation and incentives. *Organizational Behavior and Human Performance, 3,* 157–189.

Locke, E. A. (1976). The nature and causes of job satisfaction. In M. D. Dunnette (Ed.), *Handbook of industrial and organizational psychology* (pp. 1297–1349). Chicago: Rand McNally.

Locke, E. A., & Latham, G. P. (1990). *A theory of goal setting and task performance.* Englewood Cliffs, NJ: Prentice Hall.

Locke, E. A., Latham, G. P., & Erez, M. (1988). The determination of goal commitment. *Academy of Management Review, 23*(1), 23–39.

Mahoney, T. A. (1979). Justice and equity in compensation. In T. A. Mahoney (Ed.), *Compensation and reward perspectives* (pp. 190–194). Homewood, IL: Richard D. Irwin.

Maslow, A. H. (1954). *Motivation and personality.* New York: Harper & Row.

Maslow, A. H. (1970). *Motivation and personality.* New York: Harper & Row.

McClelland, D. C. (1961). *The achieving society.* New York: Van Nostrand Reinhold.

McClelland, D. C. (1970). The two faces of power. *Journal of International Affairs, 24,* 29–47.

McClelland, D. C. (1985). *Human motivation.* Glenview, IL: Scott, Foresman.

McClelland, D. C., & Boyatzis, R. E. (1982). Leadership motive pattern and long-term success in management. *Journal of Applied Psychology, 67,* 737–743.

Milbourn, G., Jr. (1980). The relationship of money and motivation. *Compensation Review, 12*(3), 33–44.

Mitchell, T. R. (1979). Organizational behavior. *Annual Review of Psychology, 30,* 243–281.

Mowday, R. T. (1991). Equity theory predictions of behavior in organizations. In R. M. Steers & L. W. Porter (Eds.), *Motivation and work* (pp. 111–131). New York: McGraw-Hill.

Opsahl, R. L., & Dunnette, M. M. (1966). The role of financial compensation in industrial motivation. *Psychological Bulletin, 66*(2), 94–118.

O'Reilly, C. A., III (1991). Organizational behavior: Where we've been, where we're going. *Annual Review of Psychology, 42,* 427–457.

Pinder, C. C. (1984). *Work motivation theory, issues, and applications.* Glenview, IL: Scott, Foresman.

Pinder, C. C. (1991). Valence-instrumentality-expectancy theory. In R. M. Steers & L. W. Porter (Eds.), *Motivation and work* (pp. 144–164). New York: McGraw-Hill.

Porter, L. W., & Lawler, E. E. (1968). *Managerial attitudes and performance.* Homewood, IL: R. D. Irwin.

Rauschenberger, J., Schmitt, N., & Hunter, J. E. (1980). A test of the need hierarchy concept by a Markov model of change in need strength. *Administrative Science Quarterly,* 654–670.

Ryer, A. J., & Stone, E. F. (1993, June). *Effects of grade appeal outcome on faculty attitudes and perceptions of procedural justice.* Paper presented at the meeting of the American Psychological Society, Chicago, IL.

Skinner, B. F. (1953). *Science and human behavior.* New York: Macmillan.

Skinner, B. F. (1969). *Contingencies of reinforcement.* New York: Appleton-Century-Crofts.

Smith, P. C., Kendall, L. M., & Hulin, C. L. (1969). *The measurement of satisfaction in work and retirement: A strategy for the study of attitudes.* Chicago: Rand McNally.

Staw, B. M. (1984). Organizational behavior: A review and reformulation of the field's outcome variables. *Annual Review of Psychology, 35,* 627–666.

Steers, R. M., & Porter, L. W. (Eds.). (1991). *Motivation and work behavior.* New York: McGraw-Hill.

Thorndike, E. L. (1911). *Animal intelligence.* New York: Macmillan.

Tubbs, M. E., Boehne, D. M., & Dahl, J. G. (1993). Expectancy, valence, and motivational force functions in goal-setting research: An empirical test. *Journal of Applied Psychology, 78*(3), 361–373.

Vroom, V. H. (1964). *Work and motivation.* New York: John Wiley & Sons.

Wahba, M. A., & Bridwell, L. G. (1976). Maslow reconsidered: A review of research on the need hierarchy theory. *Organizational Behavior and Human Performance, 15,* 212–240.

Webster's new world dictionary of American English. (1994). New York: Prentice Hall.

CHAPTER

11

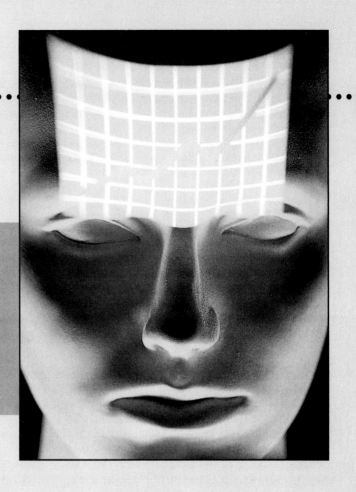

Job Satisfaction: Theories and Applications

he Midwestern Printing Company was strug-
gling for survival. In an effort to remain competitive, it had won a number of position
and wage concessions from its unions and made
many changes in management. The new management team was concerned about continuing high
production costs, excess absenteeism, and high turnover. An I/O psychologist was hired to conduct a
morale survey.

Job satisfaction was one composite scale on the
survey. Midwestern's score was well below the average for companies that had used the standardized
survey. Once the results had been compiled, the I/O
psychologist met with managers to discuss them. A
highly participative approach was selected for the
discussions. Managers met with small groups of employees to review the results and discuss them with
employees. These discussions were enlightening.
Employees held many misconceptions about management and management intent. Some of these
were clarified. Action plans were implemented using
small groups of volunteers. Plans were reviewed
by a union–management team before being implemented.

A six-month follow-up survey found job satisfaction significantly improved. Unfortunately, the effort
came too late. Eight months after the original survey, Midwestern Printing declared bankruptcy and
closed.

This chapter continues our review of motivation and job satisfaction. Chapter 10 presented
our framework integrating motivation and job
satisfaction in a way consistent with how these
concepts are used in applied practice. It also emphasized motivation because of its strong experimental research base and the fact that motivation theory is the basis for considerable work on
job satisfaction. This chapter focuses on job satisfaction, a popular area in applied practice.
Most of its concepts, however, are firmly rooted
in research on motivation.

As was mentioned at the beginning of Chap-
ter 10, **job satisfaction** is an attitude; that is, it is

a predisposition to respond to one's environment in a favorable or unfavorable manner
(Steers & Porter, 1991). We either like or dislike
something, and we can measure the extent of
this feeling on a continuum ranging from very
positive feelings to very negative feelings. However, feelings and attitudes must not be confused
with morale. While job satisfaction is an expression by individual workers of their feelings
toward the job, morale refers to a composite of
the attitudes of a group of employees toward
the job. Morale, then, is the expression of a group
based on the belief that group goals are compatible with individual goals (Locke, 1976).

Years of organizational research have resulted in the conclusion that attitudes are related to various work behaviors (Steers &
Porter, 1991). The relationship between job satisfaction and organizational outcomes (e.g., job
performance) has intrigued organizational researchers for nearly fifty years (Iaffaldano &
Muchinsky, 1985). Organizations continue to
measure employee job satisfaction because of its
assumed relationship to cost reduction through
greater productivity, reduced absences, errors,
turnover, and other such outcomes. (Cranny,
Smith, & Stone, 1992). Prevalent among these
assumed outcomes is an interest in the association between performance and job satisfaction.
For example, Iaffaldano and Muchinsky (1985)
reviewed 217 studies when conducting their
meta-analysis of this relationship. Working with
specific scales measuring job satisfaction, Fried
(1991) found nearly 200 such studies. We will
offer a more detailed discussion of these relationships later in the chapter.

According to Fisher and Locke (1992), there
has been more progress in understanding the
causes of job satisfaction than in illuminating its
effects. They believe that an innovative approach is needed to measure outcomes, using
"multi act criteria" or "aggregate" resulting
behaviors, such as job avoidance, constructive
protest, aggression, and others. Specific examples of these behaviors include tardiness (trying
to avoid work by coming late) or confronting

the supervisor with problems (in order to work them out). "We conclude that a great many acts may be taken in response to job satisfaction and dissatisfaction—far more than the tired old troika of performance, turnover, and absenteeism that have been the focus of much past research" (Fisher & Locke, 1992, pp. 186–187). However, as Fisher and Locke recognize, simply predicting "aggregate behaviors" is not enough. In an attempt to move beyond mere prediction, this section begins by reviewing principal theories of job satisfaction and then discusses the research concerning the "old troika."

JOB SATISFACTION THEORIES

Herzberg's Two-Factor Theory

The **two-factor theory,** also known as the **motivator-hygiene theory,** addresses both motivation and satisfaction and is based on Maslow's hierarchy of needs. The two-factor theory is classified as belonging to the subgroup of **content theories,** theories that attempt to identify the needs that must be met for the individual to be satisfied on the job. Locke (1976) evaluated Maslow's needs hierarchy and Herzberg's motivator-hygiene theory as the two primary content theories. The two-factor theory is also part of Katzell and Thompson's (1990) **motive/need theory,** which is included in the exogenous category of motivation theories. Herzberg's theory uses the term **motivators** to include satisfying experiences. Because of this, Herzberg's theory is an excellent example of the conceptual and definitional overlap between the processes of motivation and satisfaction.

Two-factor theory is based on a 1959 study of 203 engineers and accountants conducted by Herzberg, Mausner, and Snyderman. The authors asked the subjects to describe incidents at work that led them to feel either exceptionally satisfied or exceptionally dissatisfied with their job. Analysis of these incidents led to the con-

clusion that there are two categories of factors. The first category included experiences that led more often to satisfaction than to dissatisfaction (78% versus 22%). These involved incidents that were intrinsic to the job, such as responsibility, advancement, the work itself, achievement, and recognition. They dealt with job content and were classified as motivators. The second category covered factors that more often led to job dissatisfaction (64% versus 36%). These dissatisfiers were factors that were extrinsic to the job and included environmental factors such as company policy, supervision, salary, interpersonal relations, and working conditions. Unlike the motivators, these dissatisfiers produced short-term changes in job attitudes and had no effect on employee motivation. Herzberg (1976) labeled these dissatisfiers **hygiene factors.** Hygiene factors are different from motivators. As Herzberg stated,

> when I [punish] my dog . . . he will move. And when I want him to move again, I must [punish] him again. Similarly, I can charge a man's battery, and then recharge it, and recharge it again. But it is only when he has his own generator that we can talk about motivation. He then needs no outside stimulation. He *wants* to do it (p. 19).

To summarize, for Herzberg, satisfaction and dissatisfaction are based on two different sets of needs: motivators and hygiene needs. Motivators originate within the individual; hygiene needs stem from the environment.

The two-factor theory is based, to some extent, on Maslow's needs hierarchy. Maslow's physiological, safety, and social needs are assumed to be provided by society, which includes organizational environments. Since the general perception is that these needs *should* be provided by society, securing them would lead to a feeling of neutrality (0 in Table 11.1 on page 362); not having them would lead to a feeling of dissatisfaction. For instance, feeling hungry makes it necessary to earn money to purchase food. The desire to earn money, then, becomes a

TABLE 11.1	Maslow's needs hierarchy and Herzberg's two-factor theory	
Maslow's Needs	*Herzberg's Factors*	*Job Attitude*
Physiological	Hygiene factors	Dissatisfaction ⟶ 0
Safety		
Social		
Ego needs	Motivators	Satisfaction ⟵ 0
Self-actualization		

specific drive. We expect to obtain money to buy food; not having it would evoke a sense of frustration and dissatisfaction.

It is the higher-order needs, such as ego and self-actualization, that are difficult to achieve and that the environment is not expected to provide. Achieving these needs would provide a sense of psychological growth. Growth needs are satisfied by the tasks inherent in the job content that serve as motivators and satisfiers; not satisfying them would lead to an attitude of neutrality (0 in Table 11.1), that is, to a feeling of no job dissatisfaction. Satisfaction and dissatisfaction are not opposite processes; they involve two separate sets of factors. According to Herzberg, fulfilling hygiene needs leads only to a temporary absence of dissatisfaction, and employee demands (for salary increase or fringe benefits, for example) will recur and escalate.

Steers and Porter (1991) believe that the implications of this theory are clear: Organizations can increase employee motivation by designing jobs that provide opportunities for personal challenge, responsibility, advancement, and growth. Herzberg initiated two concepts by which these new job designs could be accomplished: **job enlargement,** in which employees are given more of the same kinds of activities within which they can apply existing skills (horizontal expansion) (Steers & Porter, 1991, p. 413). **Job enrichment** means that employees are afforded opportunities to increase their repertoire of skills and are given the chance to move vertically to other jobs within the organization (vertical expansion).

Most of the research on Herzberg's two-factor theory was conducted during the 1950s and 1960s. Since then, "[the] Herzberg dual factor model [has] simply been absent from current research" (Mitchell, 1979, p. 252). Mitchell suggested that this absence is probably due to a general shift away from needs theories. In addition, subsequent studies have failed to support Herzberg's assumption of two separate factors, one leading only to satisfaction and the other only to dissatisfaction (Locke, 1976; Steers & Porter, 1991). A detailed description of this research is beyond the scope of this chapter (see the Recommended Readings at the end of this chapter); following is a brief review of some primary criticisms:

1. Factors that are categorized as motivators (psychological) and as hygiene (physical) could lead to both satisfaction and dissatisfaction. For example, various actions by management may enhance an employee's interest in the job, in pursuing promotion, or in assuming more responsibility (Locke, 1976).

2. Herzberg did not account for individual differences in the effects of motivators and hygiene factors on satisfaction and dissatisfaction. For example, individuals may respond differently to job expansion. While some employees could view expansion as job enrichment, others may view it only as additional responsibility.

3. Vroom (1964, p. 129) argued that any research results showing differences in the effects of satisfiers and dissatisfiers may actually stem from a sense of defensiveness within the individual:

> Persons may be more likely to attribute the causes of satisfaction to their *own* achievements . . . on the job. On the other hand, they may be more likely to attribute their dissatisfaction, not to personal inadequacies or deficiencies, but to factors in the work *environment,* i.e., obstacles presented by company policies or supervision.

Herzberg's main contributions to understanding job satisfaction include his impact on the literature of motivation and satisfaction and his attention to the importance of nonfinancial factors that affect job satisfaction and motivation (e.g., supervisory style or personal growth). Finally, he initiated a tremendous number of replication studies that tried to prove or disprove his theory, and those stimulated even further research and discussion.

Lawler's Facet Satisfaction Model

In contrast to the content theories discussed above, **process theories** study and identify the processes that initiate, sustain, and terminate behavior. That is, process models of job satisfaction attempt to specify the variables that cause satisfaction (e.g., expectancies, perceptions, etc.) and result in particular outcomes. Thus Lawler's **facet satisfaction model** is a combination of a process theory, an equity theory, and a theory that accounts for individual difference in terms of subjective perception. As a process theory, the facet satisfaction model is regarded as an extension of Vroom's VIE motivation model. It includes some of its basic parameters, such as expectancy and instrumentality. As Lawler (1971, pp. 101–102) stated, "my own inclination . . . [in choosing a theoretical basis upon which to build the motivation model] . . . is toward expectancy theory." For example, the Porter and Lawler (1968; Lawler & Porter, 1975) motivation model includes the concepts of effort-per-

formance probability and reward value, or **valence** (see Figure 11.1 on page 364). Effort-performance probability relates to the employees' subjective belief that the level of effort invested in performance will result in a desired level of performance. Reward valence is based on employees' perceptions of the benefits associated with the intended level of performance. For example, employees who are given the choice of producing ten, fifteen, or twenty units of car parts per hour will behave according to (a) the level they believe they can produce and (b) the level of production that has the best (perceived) chance of leading to desired rewards (Lawler, 1991).

Lawler's (1971, 1973) satisfaction model is a derivative of Porter and Lawler's (1968) motivation theory. As Figure 11.2 shows, motivation leads to satisfaction through the person's perceived association between effort and performance, moderated by that individual's ability to perform the job and his or her expectation of attaining rewards. Rewards can be both external and internal. **External rewards** can be positive or negative and are provided by the environment—for example, praise, feedback, or pay. **Internal rewards** originate from the feelings an individual has about performing the job—for example, feelings of personal worth, pride, or accomplishment. As we will discuss later in the chapter, "satisfaction is best thought of as a result of performance rather than as a cause of it" (Lawler, 1991, p. 510), a concept that is quite different from Herzberg's theory that "a happy worker is a good worker." In addition, as indicated in Figure 11.2 on page 365, satisfaction can influence motivation, depending on the individual's beliefs about whether performance will result in the desired consequences. Lawler assumes that the relationship between motivation and satisfaction is circular.

Similar to equity theory, facet theory is a **comparison theory**, which includes both self and social comparisons to determine the level of satisfaction with the job or any of its facets (as-

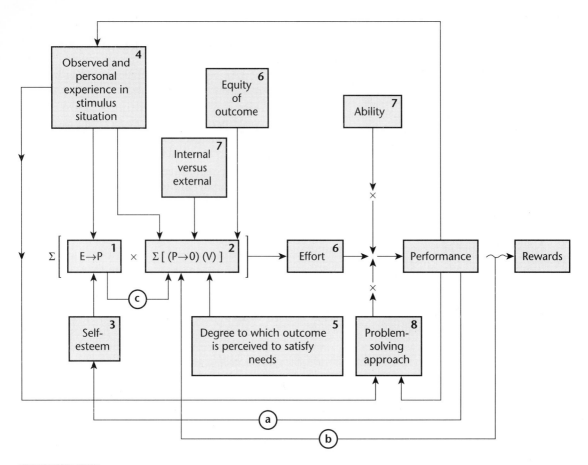

pects). This comparison process emphasizes the role of perceived inputs and outputs (Lawler, 1971; Staw, 1984). The facet satisfaction model is also a **discrepancy model:** A person's satisfaction is determined by the difference, or discrepancy, between what the person believes his or her reward (e.g., pay) actually is (see box *b* in Figure 11.3), and the perception of what it should be (see box *a*, in Figure 11.3). Overall job satisfaction is defined as the difference between "all the things a person feels he/[she] should receive from . . . [the] . . . job and all the things he/[she] actually [does] receive" (Lawler, 1973, p. 77). Lawler regards the facet satisfac-

tion model as distinct from the equity model: Equity theory emphasizes a comparison of the perceived ratio of inputs and outputs of oneself to other people; discrepancy theory addresses the difference between the individual's perception of what "is" and what "should be." Locke (1976) argued that these models involve two levels. Lawler's discrepancy theory provides the actual model, and equity theory identifies "some of the factors that determine what an individual's desired level of pay will be" (p. 1321).

Facet satisfaction theory accounts for individual differences by emphasizing personal perceptions and subjective beliefs. As shown in Fig-

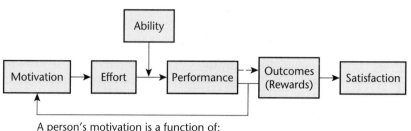

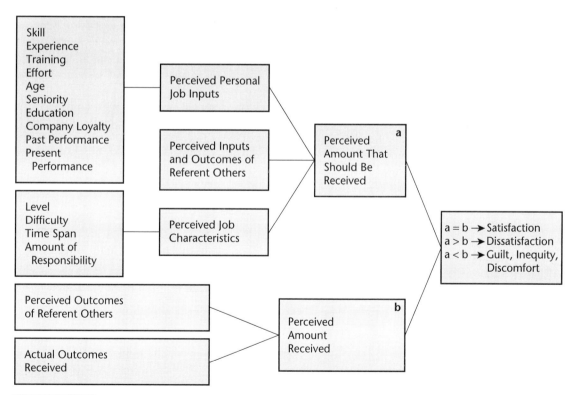

FIGURE 11.2
Lawler's model of the relationship between motivation and satisfaction.

Source: From *The Handbook of Organizational Behavior* by Jay W. Lorsch, Editor, (1987). Englewood Cliffs, NJ: Prentice-Hall, Inc. Copyright 1987 by Prentice-Hall, Inc. Reprinted with permission of J. W. Lorsch.

ure 11.3, a person's job input includes factors such as skills, age, training, and abilities. Perceived job demands influence the person's feelings about what his or her outcomes should be, compared to the referent other's inputs and outcomes. This concept is taken directly from equity theory and emphasizes the importance of the way we perceive reality, not reality itself (Lawler, 1973; Milbourn, 1980).

The best summary of the model is provided by Lawler (1973, 1991) and Lawler and Rhode (1976, p. 30): "Job satisfaction is best thought

FIGURE 11.3   Lawler's model of job satisfaction and its determinants.

Source: From *Motivation in Work Organizations* (p. 75) by E. E. Lawler, III, 1973, New York: McGraw-Hill. Copyright 1973 by McGraw-Hill. Current copyright held by E. E. Lawler. Reprinted with permission.

of as a reaction people have to what happens to them at work." Each person has his or her own mental map of behaviors to choose from and outcomes that will satisfy the person's needs. Thus, organizations should provide employees with rewards that are perceived as having value. Some implications of this model include the following:

1. People expect that input will be proportionate to output. Accordingly, people with high levels of input should receive greater rewards (such as more money) than people with lower input, or they will be dissatisfied.

2. Most people believe that the more difficult the (perceived) job demands, the higher the perceived rewards. If this relationship is not satisfactory, the employee will be dissatisfied.

Much of the literature on expectancy theory combines models such as Vroom's (1964) VIE theory, Porter and Lawler's (1968) motivation model, and Lawler's (1971) satisfaction model. We will limit our discussion to Lawler's discrepancy model and will use his original term "pay desire satisfaction" (PDS) (Lowenberg, Powaser, & Farkash, 1989, p. 209) to mean the "difference between the person's desired pay level and his[her] perception of [the] present situation."

Although a number of studies have been conducted to test the specific components of facet theory, such as the relationship between satisfaction and performance and turnover, very little research has been carried out to test models of self-comparison (intra-individual) and specifically the facet theory as a whole (Staw, 1984; Weiner, 1980). This might be because the model "is so global" (Staw, 1984, p. 635) or because the model itself and much of the related research deal with the specific reward of pay (Weiner, 1980). As we will discuss in the chapter on compensation, the policy of pay secrecy exists in many companies, resulting in issues such as the tendency to subjectively overestimate one's performance and underestimate one's pay, having the reverse perceptions about the inputs and outputs of others (Milbourn, 1980). This subjectivity has resulted in a bias that confounds

any study that is carried out in organizations with such policies.

Research on Lawler's model has studied issues such as the variables determining pay satisfaction, the importance of demographic variables in the magnitude of PDS and other modified discrepancy scores, and the relationship between PDS, pay satisfaction, and administrative factors. Following are some examples.

Dyer and Theriault (1976) modified Lawler's 1971 model to include additional variables that are assumed to affect pay satisfaction (see Figure 11.3 for Lawler's determinants). The primary additional factor was the perception of pay system administration, that is, the procedures employers use to make wage and salary decisions. Pay dissatisfaction can result even when an employee feels that his or her pay is equitable but the way pay is determined and administered is not compatible with one's expectations. Dyer and Theriault's main finding was that "between 40% and 50% of the variance in pay satisfaction was explained by . . . [the modified model]" (1976, p. 603), including pay system administrative procedures.

More recently, Weiner (1980) compared the effectiveness of Lawler's original model (1971) and Dyer and Theriault's (1976) modified model in predicting employee feelings of pay satisfaction. She administered the Minnesota Satisfaction Questionnaire (MSQ) to 186 full-time employees in a medium-size public service organization. Among questions that the study posed were how much one's salary should be in comparison to that of others in the same organization and in other companies, the fairness of pay increases, the administration of pay increases, and the performance appraisal system. These questions enabled Wiener to calculate discrepancy scores of pay satisfaction, scores for the administrative model of Dyer and Theriault, and scores for pay satisfaction. Comparison to the Lawler model concluded that Dyer and Theriault's model was better equipped to: (a) predict employee behavior resulting from pay dissatisfaction (e.g., leaving the company); and (b) explain the contribution of variables, such as policies of pay increases and perceived accuracy of performance evaluation, to employee feelings of pay satisfaction.

Lawler (1971) and Dyer and Theriault (1976) also emphasize the importance of pay criteria as one of the aspects of pay system administration that can affect satisfaction. Discrepancy scores were calculated by finding the difference between the criteria that employees believe have actually been used to determine their pay and the criteria they believe should be used. Lowenberg et al. (1989) used this concept to test the relationship between PDS scores of criteria and what employees consider to be the appropriate pay differentials (APDs) among positions with various responsibilities and at different organizational levels (Lowenberg, 1977). While the definitions of "fair and just" levels of pay and pay increases are dealt with extensively in psychology, the subjective feelings of what is considered by employees to be **fair differentials of pay** have been ignored in research.

Lowenberg (1977) devised a questionnaire measuring demographic variables of participants, APDs, PDS, and actual salary levels, which was distributed to 137 salaried employees in a medium-size Midwestern organization (Lowenberg et al., 1989). The specific results and their implications are beyond the scope of this chapter, and we refer the reader to the original articles. However, the results did indicate that the relationship between what were considered appropriate pay differentials among positions at different levels within the organization and their PDS scores was curvilinear. That is, if PDS scores can be used to measure satisfaction, then Lowenberg's results suggest that both employees who were not satisfied with the criteria used to determine their pay and those who were very satisfied thought that the pay differentials should be smaller than they were. These results held across different levels of pay and salary. In other words, they did not follow Lawler's (1981) conclusion that higher pay would be associated with a higher level of satisfaction. Rather, they

indicated that "individuals with both higher and lower pay levels [were] dissatisfied with the pay structure in their organization and, therefore, [desired] different, and what they perceive to be more appropriate, pay-differentials" (Lowenberg et al., 1989, p. 209).

Another issue in the research on discrepancy theory is the effect of individual differences on the magnitude of actual salary given various standards of comparison; for example, "What salary do I deserve? What do I feel other people receive?" (Rice, Phillips, & McFarlin, 1990). Rice et al. suggest that using four personal discrepancy measures would predict pay satisfaction, even when actual levels of pay are held constant. Their results suggest that using multiple discrepancy measures that take into account personal standards of comparisons and controlling for pay levels can predict levels of pay satisfaction. In a study of university faculty, Huber, Seybolt, and Venemon (1992) found that personal perception of determinants of pay and individual variables such as age, gender, and pay level are related to pay satisfaction. The practical implication of these studies is that "compensation professionals are likely to encounter difficulties because of employee differences in standards of comparison" (Rice et al., 1990, p. 392). Therefore, management should consider various employees' perceived standards of fair differences of pay, criteria of pay, and other factors. "At minimum, . . . it may behoove compensation professionals to measure different standards of comparison [for various employees] in their work force" (Rice et al., 1990, p. 392).

The relationship between discrepancy measures and direct measures of pay satisfaction were assumed to be primarily positive (e.g., Lee & Martin, 1991; Rice et al., 1990). Lowenberg, Kingston-O'Connell, and Conrad (1993) distributed a revised form of the Lowenberg (1977) questionnaire to faculty members in a Midwestern university. Their results suggested that, at least for that sample, the relationship between the two measures of satisfaction was nonlinear, even when salary levels were held constant. For example, overall pay satisfaction was highest for faculty members who had moderate discrepancy scores and whose salaries ranged from $30,500 to $41,499 (moderate salary).

It is surprising that, despite the practical nature of Lawler's satisfaction model and the importance of the personal, perceptual, and job factors that it includes, there is not much research applying it to organizational situations. When implementing procedures of pay distribution, organizations must take into account employees' perceptions about the fairness of these processes (Cropanzano & Folger, 1991).

Work Adjustment Theory

Dawis and Loftquist (1984) defined tenure as the amount of time an individual remains on the job. The purpose of **work adjustment theory** is to predict the probability that the individual will adjust to his or her environment and the length of time the individual will stay at the job. The primary factor affecting tenure is satisfaction; tenure is related to both the employee's satisfaction with the job (*satisfaction*) and the employer's satisfaction with the employee's quality of performance (*satisfactoriness*). The theory's assumption is that employees with substantial tenure are satisfied with their work environment and are satisfactory to the work environment. This theory was developed as the result of extensive research conducted during the Work Adjustment Project at the University of Minnesota (1969). Katzell (1994) described it as an inductive approach, built on the accumulation of research information over the years. We will detail Dawis and Lofquist's (1984) explanation of the theory, using Figure 11.4 to illustrate it.

The mutual process by which the employer and the employee react and respond to meet each other's requirements is a continual process called **work adjustment.** The degree to which these requirements are met is the *correspondence* between the individual and the employer. The far left side of Figure 11.4 illustrates the individual's **work personality,** including abilities to perform the job and the individual's needs and values. The right side of this half of the figure represents the **work environment,** including the abilities and skills required for effective performance and the reinforcers provided by the employer to fulfill the individual's needs (e.g., benefits, opportunities for creativity, achievement). Work adjustment theory states that "work adjustment can be predicted from the correspondence of the work personality and the work environment" (Dawis & Lofquist, 1984, p. 57). The correspondence between the individual's abilities and the ability requirements of the job (illustrated by the top two boxes in the left half of Figure 11.4) leads to a degree of *satisfactoriness*. The degree of satisfactoriness leads to one of four employer-determined work outcomes: The individual is retained, transferred, promoted, or fired. From the individual's perspective, the correspondence between the individual's needs and values and the reinforcer patterns provided by the job (illustrated by the lower boxes in the left half of Figure 11.4) leads to a degree of *satisfaction*. The degree of satisfaction leads to one of two employee-determined work outcomes: The person remains on the job or quits. As illustrated by the model, both satisfactoriness and satisfaction are necessary for the individual to remain on the job. Thus "tenure is the outcome of work adjustment" (Dawis & Lofquist, 1984, p. 56). Any of the other satisfactoriness or satisfaction outcomes results in a new job for the individual and a new process of work adjustment.

The theory has been used to predict employee turnover and adjustment to career and vocational counseling and has contributed to research on job satisfaction, person–environment fit, and person–organization fit (Chatman, 1989; Katzell, 1994; O'Reilly, Chatman, & Caldwell, 1991).

CORRELATES OF JOB SATISFACTION

At the beginning of the chapter we mentioned that work motivation can be described as a process that energizes and moves people, either in-

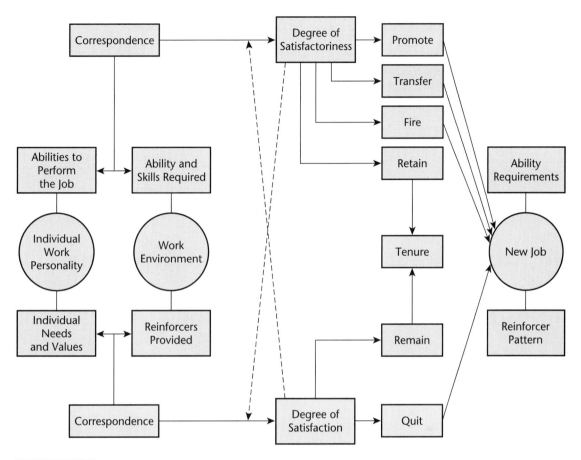

FIGURE 11.4   Work adjustment model.

Source: From *A Psychological Theory of Work Adjustment* (p. 62), by R. V. Dawis and L. H. Lofquist, 1984, Minneapolis: University of Minnesota Press. Copyright 1984 by University of Minnesota Press. Reprinted with permission.

trinsically or extrinsically, toward a goal. We also described job satisfaction as a feeling of contentment resulting from achieving these particular goals. Since job satisfaction is the process that is closer to work behavior, most research centers on correlates of job satisfaction. We should remember that these processes are interdependent, which is why the following summary relates to both concepts.

Longitudinal, nationwide studies (e.g., Davis & Newstrom, 1985) indicate that general job satisfaction has historically been relatively high and stable in the United States. Although the

proportion of dissatisfied employees to satisfied employees is modest, it should be noted that these conclusions may or may not be accurately extrapolated to a population of millions of other workers. The measurement of job satisfaction is conducted primarily because of its assumed relationship to the short-term goals of increased individual productivity, reduced absences, errors, and turnover (Smith, 1992). In her article "In Pursuit of Happiness" (1992), Pat Smith describes a feeling of satisfaction and its effects on work behavior as analogous to a major river of life satisfaction (see Figure 11.5).

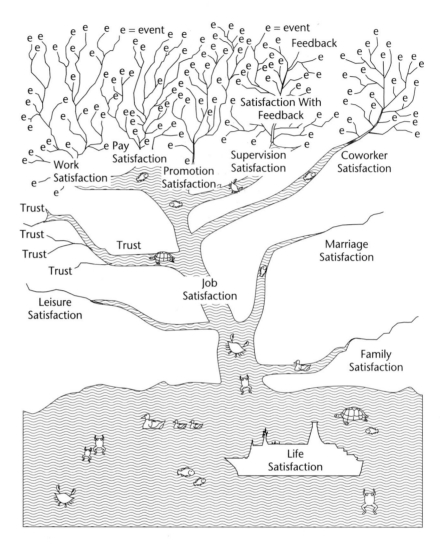

FIGURE 11.5

The river of satisfaction.

Source: From Job Satisfaction: How People Feel About Their Jobs and How It Affects Their Performance (p. 8), by C. J. Cranny, P. C. Smith, and E. F. Stone, 1992. New York: Lexington Books. Copyright 1992 by Lexington Books. Reprinted with permission.

The River of Satisfaction
The flow from events at work through facet satisfactions to general job satisfaction and life satisfaction.

The river originates in, and is influenced by, small rivulets that form creeks, which in turn combine to form small rivers, which eventually form a major river. The analogy is this: A person's overall experiences affect different facets of satisfaction (e.g., pay satisfaction), all of which affect job satisfaction and general life satisfaction. Each facet affects behavior on the job, and all of them combine and interact to result in errors, withdrawal from work, and other outcomes. These interactive relationships have been summarized by Locke (1976, p. 1335): "Satisfied people are more satisfied with their life, have better physical and mental health, and tend to be on the job more frequently and leave the organization less frequently than those who are dissatisfied."

There are many correlates of job satisfaction. We will limit our discussion of the correlates of job satisfaction to the key **input correlates** (individual characteristics and situational variables) and to the **output variables** of job performance (withdrawal, absenteeism, turnover, and theft). Later in the chapter, we will discuss other correlates such as life satisfaction and job stress.

Input Correlates

Individual Characteristics

Individual differences are the variations that exist among individuals in terms of personal characteristics. People have unique personal identities and respond in different ways to particular situations. Examples of individual differences that are relevant to this discussion include variations in personality, age, gender, or race. These differences are important because of their effects on selection, power, performance, and the ability to benefit employers.

Personality. Managers must take into consideration the fact that differences occur within people as well as between people. Individual needs and desires change over time; strategies need to be devised to meet these changing needs. These variations moderate the way in which people react to organizational strategies and try to obtain their objectives (Organ & Hamner, 1982). To help practitioners treat individual employees differently, Dubrin (1984) suggested taking into account the following list of characteristics:

1. Energy levels and resistance to fatigue.
2. The level of importance attached to intrinsic job rewards.
3. Individual reactions to various leadership styles.

4. The need to interact with others.
5. Levels of ability with regard to handling responsibility.

Managers who identify these influences can create the environmental conditions preferred by employees.

Other personality characteristics are related to job satisfaction. For example, Type A behavior has been found to be positively related to job satisfaction, and levels of impatience and irritability have been negatively related to job satisfaction (Bluen, Barling, & Burns, 1990). Lee, Ashford, and Bobko (1990) argued that when employees with higher levels of control believe that they are interacting with Type A dimensions (e.g., competitiveness, aggressiveness, high achievement), they exhibit higher levels of job satisfaction (see also Spector, 1986). Self-esteem and moods were also shown to be related to job satisfaction. For example, satisfied employees exhibit higher levels of self-esteem and lower levels of negative mood (e.g., Locke, 1976; Winefield, Tiggemann, Winefield, & Goldney, 1991).

Age. Early findings of the relationship between age and job satisfaction indicate a U-shaped, or curvilinear, relationship. That is, job satisfaction is high in younger age groups, declines later, and improves in older employees (Gruneberg, 1979). One explanation could be that career development acts as a moderator. Some time in midlife, employees realize that their career aspirations are not as likely to be fulfilled as they had once hoped. Later in their careers, employees realize new job potential, and their levels of job satisfaction tend to increase. Toward the end of their work life, when employees prepare for retirement, levels of job satisfaction tend to remain stable. Additional research has shown that job satisfaction is positively correlated with age. Weaver (1980) conducted a seven-year national survey of over 4700 employees. The results suggested significant differences in job satisfaction between age groups in each of the seven years. In addition, Weaver found that there were no significant changes in job satisfaction across the seven years.

Several researchers have attempted to explain the various relationships found between age and job satisfaction. Weaver (1980) measured global job satisfaction and concluded that while the relationship may be unresponsive to social change and thus remain stable, components of job satisfaction can improve or worsen over time. Organ and Hamner (1982) found that employees begin work with unrealistic expectations about what they will get out of their jobs. When employees discover that their jobs fall short of their original expectations, they endure the first decade of work, gradually becoming more discouraged. Eventually, employees modify their expectations to fit their current state of employment and begin to see their jobs more positively, resulting in higher levels of job satisfaction. It may be that other variables modify the relationship as well. For example, older, married, and experienced workers were found to be more satisfied than were young, unmarried, and less experienced workers (Khaleque & Rahman, 1987).

Hopkins (1983) argued that age is positively related to job satisfaction because expectations and attitudes toward the workplace change over time. The likelihood of being satisfied increases with age as the employee adjusts to the growing difficulty of finding alternative employment. Individual perspectives and expectations change as people age, and job satisfaction eventually relies not only on the completion of tasks, but also on the social roles the employee plays in the work environment. Age, therefore, has a significant influence on job satisfaction. The changes of roles and status that occur naturally as part of the aging process, along with the general climate of the work environment, can influence employee satisfaction (Hopkins, 1983).

Gender and Race. Gender and race may affect aspirations, job performance, evaluation by others, and perceived job satisfaction. Gender and race are characteristics that have set minority and female employees apart from the so-called dominant white males who in the past held the power in most organizations. In general, Caucasian men were found in higher-level jobs and had the majority of control over minority employees. (For the remainder of this section we will use the term *minorities* to include women.) It has been suggested that the low levels of job satisfaction among minorities may be due to a lack of opportunity to pursue the higher-level, powerful jobs usually held by white men. Studies of job satisfaction with regard to gender and race show varied results.

Weaver (1980) suggested that African-Americans were less satisfied with their jobs than Caucasians and that no difference existed between males and females. It seems that members of minorities (including women) who experience high levels of job satisfaction are those who occupy the same types of jobs as white males have traditionally held, such as management positions. Members of minorities in these higher-level positions are given greater autonomy and better pay than they would receive in the traditionally available, lower-level jobs. On the other hand, the occupations that members of minorities often hold involve lower-level jobs, different promotion aspects, lower pay, and fewer of the other opportunities that may satisfy higher-level needs (Gruneberg, 1979).

Fricko and Beehr (1992) explained differences in levels of job satisfaction by the level of congruence individuals had between their career aspirations, their college majors, and their jobs. Their results showed that the higher level of satisfaction for the male group could be explained by the fact that these factors were consistent. Their gender matched with jobs that had high male concentrations, and the jobs were congruent with their college majors. The least satisfied group consisted of females who held jobs in which there was a high concentration of females (i.e., traditional gender congruent). These jobs did not match their college majors.

Perceptions of job satisfaction and the assumptions made about minorities also account for differences in employee satisfaction. For example, stereotypical expectations can lead to various feelings of satisfaction. Fifteen years ago, this led to the conclusion that "Women might be expected to be more satisfied with their jobs than men because their lower expectations are consistent with the female role in the home" (Hopkins, 1983, p. 86). Members of minorities are often found to be less satisfied than nonminority individuals. Cox and Blake (1991, p. 46) stated that this could be because most organizational cultures are the "white [male] . . . culture," which is associated with stereotypes of ideal chiefs (Triandis, Kurowski, & Gelfand, 1994) and "best" employees. These stereotypes, in turn, can lead to cultural conflict and frustrations over career growth and development for both African-Americans and women. The result is lower levels of satisfaction with the job (Konar, 1981; Weaver, 1980).

Situational Variables

It is difficult to discuss the antecedents of job satisfaction without considering the various situational characteristics of satisfaction. **Situational characteristics** can be intrinsic or extrinsic factors, as well as causal. The debate regarding intrinsic and extrinsic factors goes back to Herzberg's two-factor theory (Herzberg, Mausner, & Snyderman, 1959) and relates intrinsic sources of satisfaction to the job itself (e.g., recognition, type of work) and extrinsic factors to variables such as pay, supervision, and organizational climate (Dawis, 1991; Gruneberg, 1979). The causal nature of situational characteristics stems from Locke's (1976) work. He defines **events** as the factors that directly cause satisfaction, such as the type of work (its complexity, level of responsibility, difficulty, and job status), pay and issues of equity, and promotion. **Agents** are defined as the moderators that intervene between events, conditions, and feelings of satisfaction—for example, supervisors, coworkers, subordinates, management, and the organization as a whole. Regardless of how situational characteristics are interpreted, in the final analysis

they include similar factors. The difficulty is that the amount of research on these factors is vast. Therefore we will describe only a few examples.

Job Status.   Job status is one of the attributes of work itself and is one of Locke's (1976) conditions. Job status presents the employee with challenges regarding processes such as decision making and new learning responsibilities. An example is provided by Sheppard and Herrick (1972) in their research regarding blue-collar workers. They defined the term "blue collar blues" as the feeling some manufacturing and construction laborers have about the absence of opportunity to progress to desired higher-level jobs that would provide them with opportunities for creativity, responsibility, control, and other characteristics related to job satisfaction.

Societal Values.   Societal values placed on various jobs can also moderate between job status and satisfaction. For instance, construction workers wear hardhats, act tough, and drive pickup trucks, whereas executives wear suits, have "nice" manners, and drive expensive cars. Stereotypic values such as these are often displayed in daily life and perpetuate certain standards with which employees compare themselves. People's tendency to compare themselves to these societal standards leads to varying levels of satisfaction with the position and status of their present job.

Pay.   Pay is another extensively studied factor that is considered to be both an event and a condition (Locke, 1976). Most of the research has focused on the relationship of pay to job satisfaction or on pay as an independent facet of job satisfaction, using the rewarding properties of money to investigate the relationship of pay to outcomes such as performance and turnover. Most of the initial work emphasized money as a symbol (Gellerman, 1963, 1968). Because money is effective only when it can be exchanged for other goods, such as food, shelter, security, achievement, prestige, or power (Milbourn,

1980), it serves as a secondary incentive or reinforcer (Opsahl & Dunnette, 1966).

Also, because pay is but one facet of job satisfaction, the question is the extent to which it is related to overall satisfaction. Variables such as levels and amount of pay, pay structure and administration, the importance individuals assign to pay, and individual differences (e.g., gender) can affect the relationship of pay and overall satisfaction (Huber et al., 1992; Lawler, 1971, 1973; Locke, 1976; Lowenberg et al., 1989; Rice et al., 1990; Staw, 1984). In general, as Locke (1976, p. 1328) stated: "Job satisfaction results from the attainment of values which are compatible with one's needs . . . [including] . . . rewards for performance which are just, informative, and in line with the individual's personal aspirations." Pay equity, pay fairness, and distributive justice play a major role in the effects of money on job behavior and on its relationship to overall job satisfaction. There are a variety of pay programs, such as individual plans, group plans, organizational plans, benefits programs, and bonuses, each having positive and negative effects on employee behavior (Steers & Porter, 1991) and on the relationship between pay and overall job satisfaction. We will discuss these questions further in the chapter on compensation.

Lawler and Porter (1975) demonstrated that for pay to affect employee behavior, it must create the belief that good performance will lead to high pay, demonstrate the importance of pay, minimize the negative consequences of strong performance, and create conditions such that good performance is related to positive factors other than pay alone.

The fact that different employees place varying emphasis on money indicates that individual differences must be identified with regard to the degree of importance various employees place on money. By taking into account the variety of employee needs, managers can develop a successful system for motivating and satisfying their employees. Successful pay systems can lead to desired organizational outcomes such as high job performance and low turnover.

Others. Additional determinants of job satisfaction that have been identified by Locke (1976) as agents include the type and the perceived treatment of employees by supervisors, the way an individual perceives himself or herself, the method by which communication is channeled, promotional opportunities, and working conditions. The relationship between these factors and job satisfaction may depend on the importance one assigns to the various facets of job satisfaction (e.g., Rice et al., 1990).

Output Variables

Job Performance

Most of the interest in job satisfaction is the result of its apparent relationship to job performance. A common belief among managers is that job satisfaction directly affects performance and that high satisfaction always leads to high employee performance. However, research indicates that satisfied workers may be high, average, or even low producers; to illustrate, Vroom's (1964) initial review indicated the mean correlation coefficient between job satisfaction and performance to be only +.14. One of the most cited recent review of studies dealing with the relationship between satisfaction and performance is the meta-analysis conducted by Iaffaldano and Muchinsky in 1985. A review of 217 studies led the authors to confirm the conclusion that the relationship is relatively low and that it is "disconcerting that 20 years and at least 200 satisfaction-performance correlations later, the average correlation was found here to be nearly the same (+.146)" (p. 266), with the best estimate of the true population correlation still very low (+.17).

Schwab and Cummings (1973), identified three different theoretical points of view to explain the relationship between these two variables:

1. The view that satisfaction leads to performance:

Satisfaction ⟶ Performance

Examples of this position include the early human relations movement and Herzberg's motivation theory.

2. The view that satisfaction and performance are not directly related and that there are other variables that intervene and moderate this relationship:

Satisfaction — ? — Performance

(e.g., pressure at work may relate independently to being satisfied and to high production, creating an artificial relationship between satisfaction and the amount produced). This school of thought originated in the 1950s and is still present in current research (e.g., Cherrington, Reitz, & Scott, 1971; Jacobs & Solomon, 1977).

After extensive review, for example, Locke (1976, p. 1334) concluded that "job satisfaction has no direct effect on productivity." Katzell, Thompson, and Guzzo (1992, p. 196) also introduced a model explaining the relationship between these two elements as part of a "larger model of work motivation." Katzell et al. postulated an indirect relationship between satisfaction and performance, with intervening variables such as effort, goals a person adopts, and others affecting this relationship. Their conclusion was that job satisfaction and job performance covary when the following conditions are met: The job yields intrinsic rewards; extrinsic rewards are related to performance and are perceived to be equitable; there is a high level of involvement in the job; and the individual has clear goals at work. Cherrington, Reitz, and Scott (1971) believe that reinforcement of performance creates the relationship between performance and the feelings of satisfaction. Reinforcement is responsible for the correlations found between job satisfaction and performance (see Scientific Perspective 11.1 on page 376).

3. The view that performance leads to satisfaction (Schwab & Cummings, 1973):

Performance ⟶ Satisfaction

This more current view is circular: High performance, contingent on different intervening variables, leads to high satisfaction, which in turn is dependent on various intervening factors, leading to high performance. Porter and Lawler suggest that the relationship between performance and satisfaction is more direct than the relationship between satisfaction and performance. Satisfaction is viewed primarily as the dependent variable (see Figure 11.6 on page 377).

Relevant to this discussion is the distinction that was previously made between the two types of rewards: intrinsic and extrinsic. Intrinsic rewards are governed solely by individual employees. In other words, individuals reward themselves for good performance (e.g., with feelings of accomplishment); Extrinsic rewards are those over which the organization has some control, such as pay, promotion, status, and security. Extrinsic rewards are often cited as satisfying lower-level needs (e.g., safety), in contrast to intrinsic rewards, which are said to satisfy higher-level needs (e.g., self-actualization).

Because of the way they are dispensed, intrinsic rewards are assumed to be more directly related to job performance than extrinsic rewards are. This is because the correlation between extrinsic rewards and performance can be relatively weak if the organization does not present rewards effectively. Therefore there is a need for managers and organizations to establish a strong connection between job performance and extrinsic rewards if rewards are to influence performance. Rewarding individuals when a specific level of job performance is reached leads individuals to regard rewards as being associated with performance.

Along with an effective system of reward distribution, high performance can also be achieved by implementing challenging work goals. Factors that can affect these demands include individual ability, commitment to goals, feedback, self-efficiency, and the complexity of the task itself. High performance can lead to both internal and external rewards, which can serve to fulfill

SCIENTIFIC PERSPECTIVE 11.1

Reinforcement Explanation of the Relationship between Satisfaction and Performance

Cherrington, Reitz, and Scott (1971, p. 533) hypothesized that "there are no inherent relationships between satisfaction and performance" and there is no causal relationship between these variables. However, there is a natural relationship between appropriate reinforcement and reported feelings of satisfaction. It is the contingency between performance and reinforcement that lead to the observed covariation between satisfaction and performance. For example, when performance is *appropriately* rewarded, the following situations can occur:

Situation 1

High performance is reinforced by high reward, which in turn leads to a high level of satisfaction:

Low performance is reinforced by a low level of reward, which in turn leads to a low level of satisfaction:

In both of these cases an analysis of the relationship between satisfaction and performance

would result in a positive correlation, even though there is no direct relationship between them.

When performance is *inappropriately* rewarded, the following results can occur:

Situation 2

High performance is reinforced by low reward, which in turn leads to a low level of satisfaction:

Low performance is reinforced by a high level of reward, which in turn leads to a high level of satisfaction:

Low performance ⟶ High reward

High satisfaction

In both of these cases the correlation coefficient between performance and satisfaction (satisfaction and performance) would result in an artificial negative relationship between satisfaction and performance.

Thus, according to Cherrington et al. (1971), it is the relationship between the reward and the feelings of satisfaction that produces these correlations and not the direct relationships between satisfaction and performance.

---

individual needs and lead to improved performance. This fulfillment of needs may instill within the employee a commitment to the organization and a willingness to accept future tasks. It is important to note that research in this area has also investigated the relationship between incentives and performance. For example, monetary incentives have been shown to be unrelated to

performance, but they influence it indirectly through personal goal setting and commitment to the goals set (Locke, 1968; Wright, 1989).

The importance of intervening factors in the relationship between satisfaction and performance and their function in management policies has been the focus of recent studies. For example, the rater's knowledge of the level of

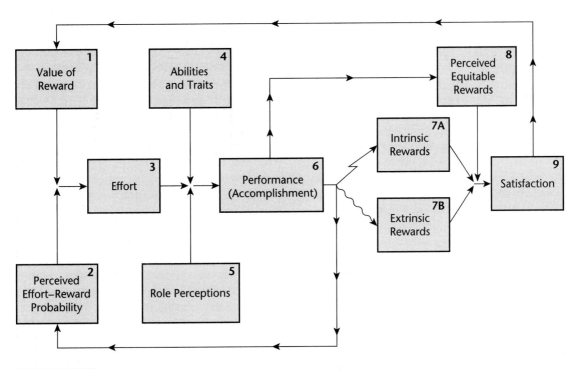

FIGURE 11.6   The revised Porter and Lawler model: performance and satisfaction.

Source: From "Valence-Instrumentality-Expectancy Theory," by C. C. Pinder. In R. M. Steers and L. W. Porter. *Motivation and Work Behavior* (p. 151), 1991. New York: McGraw-Hill. Copyright 1991 by McGraw-Hill. Reprinted with permission.

individual job satisfaction was found to bias the ratings. Smither, Collins, and Buda (1989) found that when the raters knew the task satisfaction of the ratees, their appraisals of these individuals' performances led to incorrect correlations between satisfaction and performance. Knowing that an employee is satisfied with his or her job led to more favorable evaluations than when the employee was known to be dissatisfied with his or her job.

Another recent finding is that the level of analysis that is applied to the relationship between performance and satisfaction contributes to the strength of the relationship and its application in management policies. As Ostroff (1992) emphasized, most of the research showing weak relationships was conducted on the individual level and investigated the correlation between individual feelings of job satisfaction and individual levels of job performance. However,

analyses at the organizational level, that is, the relationship between employees' feelings about their jobs and organizational performance, resulted in stronger correlations. When investigating 364 schools from 36 states, Ostroff measured individual teachers' levels of satisfaction and the organizational performance of each school. Organizational performance was assessed by measuring student achievement in reading and math, the percentage of student dropouts, teacher turnover, and other factors. Ostroff's conclusion was that "organizations with more satisfied employees tended to be more effective than organizations . . . with less satisfied employees . . . [with] . . . these relationships . . . somewhat stronger than those typically observed at the individual level" (Ostroff, 1992, p. 969).

We can conclude that the relationship between satisfaction and performance is more complex than the simple assumption that an employee's happiness is directly related to his or her productivity. More empirical evidence is needed to allow management to apply these concepts to organizational policies. Specifically, more research addressing the complex interaction between individual and organizational variables is needed to enhance both individual and organizational performance.

Withdrawal

The second output variable we will discuss is **withdrawal** from work. There appears to be a relationship between the level of job satisfaction, turnover, and/or absence from work. In a review of the research concerning these relationships, Porter and Steers (1973) found that both turnover rates and absenteeism increase as job satisfaction decreases.

It is commonly believed that dissatisfied workers are less likely to come to work than are satisfied workers. Absenteeism is costly to the organization in terms of lower productivity, the cost of temporary replacement, and overstaffing. Taking these factors into account, Steers and Rhodes (1978) estimated that the costs of absenteeism in the United States may average as high as $26.4 billion per year for large corporations.

Job turnover has also been cited as a result of job dissatisfaction. Job turnover has financial consequences that can affect the organization, both directly and indirectly. One example is the costs associated with replacing workers, such as effectively hiring and training new employees. In addition, employees who remain with the organization may suffer decreased satisfaction from the loss of valued coworkers and the disruption of established social patterns.

Porter and Steers (1973) suggested that absenteeism and turnover should not be thought of as similar responses. They regard absenteeism as a spontaneous response generated by voluntary and involuntary behaviors. Turnover, on the other hand, is a conscious process by which one evaluates present and future alternatives when deciding to stay with or leave the organi-

zation. To better understand these behaviors, we will take a more detailed look at absenteeism and turnover in the following sections.

Absenteeism

Absenteeism is pervasive and expensive. It is found in all countries and in virtually all organizations. Because it is so common and so expensive, it is an area that brings quick, opinionated responses from managers. Rhodes and Steers (1990, p. 1) reported hearing of a manager "who felt so strongly about absent workers that he once stated his company had no problem with absenteeism but it did have a significant turnover problem because every time employees were absent he fired them!" There is also informal evidence that more and more employees feel that an occasional absence from work is part of their "psychological contract"; it is justified in their minds by low wages or poor working conditions. Nevertheless, managers and organizations can do something to reduce absence at work if they are willing to address the problem systematically.

There have been several attempts to create models that explain and reduce absenteeism (for example, see Brooke & Price, 1989; Nicholson, 1977; Steers & Rhodes, 1978, 1984). A recent extension of the Rhodes and Steers (1990) model provides useful diagnostic categories and relationships for examining individual attendance behavior. As can be seen in Figure 11.7, Rhodes and Steers's **diagnostic model** includes three major attendance components. The first component is major influences on attendance motivation; these include the three elements of organizational practices; absence culture; and employee attitudes, values, and goals (see the leftmost boxes in Figure 11.7). The second component is major influences on perceived ability to attend (attendance motivation) and actual attendance (see the three boxes at the center of the figure). The third component is the role of societal context and reciprocal relationships. Those are the attendance barriers of illness and accidents, family

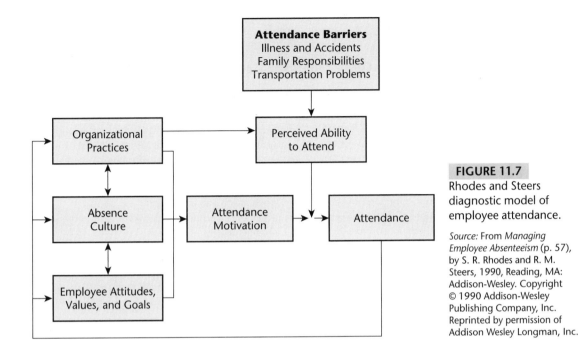

Attendance Barriers
Illness and Accidents
Family Responsibilities
Transportation Problems

Organizational
Practices

Perceived Ability
to Attend

Absence
Culture

Attendance
Motivation

Attendance

Employee Attitudes,
Values, and Goals

FIGURE 11.7
Rhodes and Steers
diagnostic model of
employee attendance.

Source: From *Managing
Employee Absenteeism* (p. 57),
by S. R. Rhodes and R. M.
Steers, 1990, Reading, MA:
Addison-Wesley. Copyright
© 1990 Addison-Wesley
Publishing Company, Inc.
Reprinted by permission of
Addison Wesley Longman, Inc.

responsibilities, and transportation problems (see the top box in the figure). We will examine each of these components.

Influences on Attendance Motivation. Rhodes and Steers (1990) describe three major interactive factors that influence attendance motivation. These are organizational practices, absence culture, and employee attitudes, values, and goals.

Organizational practices create the organizational context that encourages or discourages attendance. There are several ways in which organizations provide this context. Company absence control policies describe what management defines as acceptable and unacceptable levels and reasons for absences. A sample company philosophy statement is presented in Practice Perspective 11.1 on page 380.

Work design factors are another type of organizational practice. These include cycle time, role discretion, task identity, and job stressors. Attendance figures for nonmanagerial positions are lower in part because these positions rank lower in regard to cycle time. An employee working on an assembly line sees the completion of his or her task almost immediately, whereas a manager making a decision may not see that decision become effective for six months or more (i.e., cycle time). Companies that use a strategy focused on work design put their efforts into improving the attractiveness of the work environment.

Recruitment and selection procedures are another important organizational practice. These procedures determine who will be hired and who will be rejected. Companies can improve attendance by recruiting and selecting employees who have better previous records of attendance.

Attendance can also be improved by communicating clear job expectations to employees and applicants. These expectations should include the acceptable levels of absence. This is often done through realistic job previews, careful orientation regarding company policies, the attendance policies themselves, performance appraisals, and reward practices. Other ways companies reinforce good attendance are public recognition, monetary bonuses for perfect atten-

---

PRACTICE PERSPECTIVE 11.1

ChemCorp's Philosophy Statement

We recognized that special and patient attention would have to be given to establishing the management climate. If this were not done, the total effort would not meet our expectations. Without a favorable management climate, the competent people needed for the achievement of the objectives could not be recruited and retained. Furthermore, without a favorable management climate, the response of the people to the establishment of the objectives would be to neither accept them nor support them.

Some of the recognized important conditions in a productive management climate that would have to be cultivated are these:

1. *Mutual trust* between coworkers and among organizational groups at all levels.
2. *Freedom of the individual* to perform his duties his own way, so long as required results are obtained, and to express his own views without fear of ridicule or retribution.
3. *Openness* of everyone to questions and to suggestions about matters of mutual interest.
4. *Acceptance of accountability* for his own performance by each employee.
5. *Mutual support* for the achievement of shared goals among all employees.
6. *Acceptance of change* and involvement in the change process at all levels.
7. Concern for the *welfare of the other person* in any joint activity.
8. *Restraint of harmful assertion of superiority* ego by the individual.

Source: From *Managing Employee Absenteeism* (p. 117–118), by S. R. Rhodes and R. M. Steers, 1990, Reading, MA: Addison-Wesley. Copyright © 1990 Addison-Wesley Publishing Company, Inc. Reprinted by permission of Addison Wesley Longman, Inc.

---

dance, and allowing employees to accumulate a paid "absence bank." Time in the absence bank can be cashed in for additional pay or vacation time at year's end. Other companies use good-attendance banquets or even a good-attendance poker system (see Practice Perspective 11.2).

Schmitz and Heneman (1980) reviewed ten studies of absenteeism, all of which reported reductions following various forms of positive reinforcement. Rhodes and Steers (1990) reviewed thirteen additional positive reinforcement studies that also reported improvements in absenteeism resulting from the programs. Their general conclusion was that attendance can often be improved when a company offers positive incentives for good attendance.

Another interactive factor that influences attendance motivation is absence culture. **Absence culture** is a "set of shared understandings about absence . . . legitimacy and the established 'custom and practice' of employee absence behavior and its control" (Johns & Nicholson, 1982, p. 136). Absence culture influences attendance motivation in three ways: First, where specific norms exist, communicating an appropriate level of attendance or absence leads employees to adjust their behavior to these norms. Second, if such norms do not exist, an employee observes the behaviors of other employees and uses them as a guide. Finally, through efforts to get all employees to think alike (cultural salience) and to increase trust, the culture can moderate the relationship between individual values and attendance motivation.

Companies can incorporate absence consciousness into their approach to recruitment and selection, into the standards and expectations of behavior they establish for their employees, and by designing the work so employees feel that it is constructive and meaningful. For an example of a sociotechnical redesign of jobs, see Historical Perspective 11.1.

Employees' attitudes, values, and goals constitute the third influence on attendance mo-

PRACTICE PERSPECTIVE 11.2

Poker Lottery System for Reducing Absenteeism

In the poker system for reducing absenteeism, employees are given a playing card each day when they arrive at work (Pedalino and Gamboa, 1974; Tjersland, 1972). At the end of the week, the person who has the highest poker hand wins a cash award. In one firm, the cash award amounted to 20 dollars for the highest hand in each department (Pedalino & Gamboa, 1974). This firm posted cards and hands of each employee on the bulletin board. The unscheduled absence rate decreased from 3.01% during the thirty-two weeks before the poker hand intervention to 2.46% during the plan, a reduction of 18.27%. Moreover, over the same time period the absenteeism rate of four comparison groups increased 13.79%. (Rhodes & Steers, 1990, p. 77).

tivation. Important here are the centrality of work, personal work ethic, and employee job expectations.

Influences on Perceived Ability to Attend. The second component of the Rhodes and Steers (1990) model theorizes that attendance motivation leads to actual attendance but is constrained by the employee's perceived ability to attend. **Involuntary absenteeism** forces the individual away from work because of accident or illness. This can be influenced by attendance barriers (e.g., illness, accidents, family responsibilities, and transportation problems) or by organizational practices (e.g., company sponsored day-care, car pooling, physical fitness programs, wellness programs, company-provided transportation). The model hypothesizes that individual employees, as they assess their perceived ease in attending work, take into account both the attendance barriers and the organizational relief efforts.

HISTORICAL PERSPECTIVE 11.1

Gains Pet Foods Work Redesign Effort

Gains Pet Foods opened a new plant in Topeka, Kansas, in the early 1970s. This plant was designed to have the following key features:

1. Autonomous work groups
2. Integrated support functions
3. Challenging job assignments
4. Job mobility and rewards for learning
5. Facilitative leadership
6. Managerial decision information for operators
7. Self-government for the plant community
8. Physical and social contexts that supported each other
9. A learning and evolving culture

As a result of the new plant design, only 70 employees were needed to operate the plant instead of the 110 employees originally planned. After eighteen months of operation the fixed overhead of the new plant was only two thirds that of a matched comparison plant. Other results were 92% fewer quality rejects and a 9% lower absenteeism rate over the same period.

Source: Adapted from Walton, R. E. (1972). How to counter alienation in the plant. *Harvard Business Review, 50*(4), 50–60.

PRACTICE PERSPECTIVE 11.3

A Stress Management Program Improves Attendance

A comprehensive stress management program was implemented in a large financial institution. It began with a twenty-minute health evaluation interview (Seadmonds, 1982, 1983). This assessed the presence of work stress–related symptoms as well as the individual's coping mechanisms. When stress symptoms were identified in employees, those individuals were referred to other health manage-ment programs (blood pressure and weight con-trol programs, exercise, biofeedback, relaxation programs, psychiatric consultation, and career-planning programs) and were given educational materials about stress management.

Illness absenteeism dropped significantly as a result of the health evaluation interview and refer-ral (Rhodes & Steers, 1990).

This means that the reality of the situation is less a factor in absenteeism than how the employee perceives it. One employee may see car trouble as a valid reason to be absent. Another employee may see it simply as a challenge to be met.

Companies can enhance their employees' ability to attend work. It has been demonstrated that employees are more likely to come to work when companies can help them solve their transporta-tion problems, child-care problems, and health problems. Three increasingly popular approaches for enhancing employee health are stress man-agement programs (see Practice Perspective 11.3), physical fitness programs, and smoking cessation programs. Table 11.2 summarizes the effects of programs that are designed to improve the employee's ability to attend.

TABLE 11.2   Effects of programs that can improve employees' ability to attend work

Program	Has Effect on
Self-management training	Perceived self-efficacy
Health management programs	Illness
Stress management	
Physical fitness	
Smoking cessation	
Restricting smoking in the workplace	Illness
Employee assistance programs	Illness
Changing hours of work	Illness
Shift work	Illness
Alternate work schedules	Nonwork responsibilities
Employer-assisted child-care	Nonwork responsibilities

Source: From *Managing Employee Absenteeism* (p. 126), by S. R. Rhodes and R. M. Steers, 1990, Reading, MA: Addison-Wesley. Copyright © 1990 Addison-Wesley Publishing Company, Inc. Reprinted by permission of Addison Wesley Longman, Inc.

Role of Societal Context and Reciprocal Relationships. The third major component in the Rhodes and Steers (1990) model addresses the broader work environment provided by the societal context. Major influences here are the general societal norms concerning work, the value of work, and the economic and labor market conditions. An example of these influences is the contrast between the current societal contexts for work in Japan, where hard work, long hours, and dedication are emphasized, and in the United States, where a casual approach, shorter hours, and individual freedom are emphasized. Another example is a tight labor market, when employers will accept a wider range of behavior than they consider ideal for the job.

There has been much controversy about the role that job satisfaction plays in predicting absenteeism. Some studies do not distinguish among the different types of satisfaction and of absenteeism that are being measured. Managers need to understand that absenteeism is not necessarily the result of dissatisfaction; rather, it is often the result of outside situational factors. Understanding the different types of absenteeism allows managers to exert some control over further absences.

Turnover

In general, satisfaction is also correlated with turnover. The relationship between job satisfaction and turnover has been the subject of much research (e.g., Carsten & Spector, 1987; Davis & Newstrom, 1985).

The results of these studies indicated that although a large proportion of turnover is associated with behavior, other factors also may be included, such as age, tenure, economic opportunity, and work-related issues. For instance, young employees who have limited job tenure, a lack of commitment to the organization, and a perception of job insecurity tend to search for other jobs. Surprisingly, many young employees quit their jobs despite knowing that there are limited employment opportunities elsewhere.

Muchinsky and Morrow (1980) proposed a **turnover model** that may explain the variations in levels of satisfaction and turnover. They described three determinants of turnover: economic opportunity, individual factors, and work-related factors. Although job dissatisfaction was the primary reason for a decision to quit, economic opportunity had the greatest effect on turnover. This model proposes that during economic hardship, when levels of unemployment are high, fewer employees are likely to leave their jobs, no matter what their level of dissatisfaction.

By contrast, this model proposes that during periods of low unemployment and high opportunity, dissatisfied employees are more likely to search for different employment. This relationship produces a high correlation between satisfaction and turnover. Because the economy acts as a determinant, satisfaction may be the best predictor of turnover during periods of economic opportunity.

Mobley (1982) found that both the job itself and the working conditions affect job satisfaction. If job satisfaction is low, these factors lead to thoughts of quitting. Employees then evaluate other employment possibilities, comparing them to their present job situation. The decision to quit or to stay is based both on an overall evaluation of working conditions within the job and on the availability of other jobs.

As was explained earlier, behavioral intentions are a significant factor in the satisfaction–turnover relationship. The decision to quit is a process that usually begins with dissatisfaction and is influenced by other situational factors that may or may not cause the individual to leave the organization. The decision to quit a job is not one an individual takes lightly. This is because the decision is also tied to many other aspects of the person's life.

Theft

Employee theft has often been linked with job dissatisfaction. The concern about equity (fairness at work) has also been related to employee theft (Gruneberg, 1979). As equity theory explains, employees learn to expect that if they work hard, they will be compensated. Stress results when unfair treatment affects the employee's perceived sense of equity. When employees feel this tension, they take action to reduce the stress.

Employees often seek such outlets as working harder, using drugs or alcohol, or talking with a spouse to reduce levels of perceived stress. If these methods do not help, frustration often sets in, and employees may act out in a hostile manner against the company. Aggressive activities include sabotage (see Practice Perspective 10.4), theft, and destruction of company property.

When treated unfairly, employees may steal in an attempt to compensate themselves for perceived injustices at work; they want to receive what they believe the company owes them. Sieh's (1987) study on employee theft concluded that the levels of inequity did not determine the types of responses, but individuals who experienced high levels of unfairness usually confronted their problems. Most workers did not engage in deviant actions but instead went to the union with their problems in search of help. Employees with high levels of job satisfaction may be less likely to steal from their employers.

Employee theft within the company can be costly. Sieh (1987) suggests that managers identify possible opportunities within the organization that can provide appropriate outlets for the release of employees' frustration.

MEASUREMENT OF JOB SATISFACTION

This chapter has discussed theories of job satisfaction, consequences of job satisfaction, and individual differences. However, we have yet to discuss how job satisfaction data are collected and measured. Overall job satisfaction can be measured by devices such as the Hoppock Job Satisfaction Scale and the General Faces Scale. Certain facets of job satisfaction can be measured by the Job Description Inventory and the Minnesota Satisfaction Questionnaire. While attitude questionnaires such as these are scaling devices that provide information about job satisfaction, the approach that is used will make a considerable difference in the conclusions that are drawn.

The wide variety of measurement techniques that are currently available include objective questionnaires, interview techniques, exit interviews, action tendency scales, overt behavior ratings, and various indirect techniques.

Objective Questionnaires

Rating scales such as the Job Descriptive Index (JDI) and the Minnesota Satisfaction Questionnaire (MSQ) have been highly researched and are often described as relatively theory-free measures of job attitudes. The JDI is a carefully constructed and widely used scale that originated as part of the Cornell studies of satisfaction (Hackman & Oldham, 1975; Smith, Kendall, & Hulin, 1969). It was developed to measure five aspects of job satisfaction: satisfaction with supervision, coworkers, pay, promotional opportunities, and the work itself. A composite score of satisfaction also can be calculated from the JDI. Unlike many other scales, the JDI was carefully developed and documented. It can be completed with relative ease because it is easy to apply and understand, and it is easy to score. The fact that the JDI is such a widely used measuring device gives its users the opportunity to communicate and compare information about job satisfaction.

The MSQ was devised by Weiss, Dawis, England, and Lofquist (1967). It measures twenty aspects of satisfaction that are related to individual needs. Examples are need for achievement, need for advancement, and need for compensation. The scale includes 100 items, each of which is rated by the respondent on a five-point scale ranging from not satisfied to extremely satisfied (Dawis & Lofquist, 1984).

Although other methods of measuring job satisfaction are used, such as interviews, action tendency scales, and observations of overt behaviors, attitude scales are some of the most common devices in use today.

Group and Individual Interviews

Interviews are generally unsuccessful in predicting employee performance and are ineffective when used to predict what employees will report on rating scales (Bass & Barrett, 1981; Guion, 1991; McDaniel, Whetzel, Schmidt, & Maurer, 1994). This may be because the interview is time consuming, expensive, and, by itself, not sufficiently effective to accurately predict job satisfaction. However, when interviewing is used in conjunction with questionnaires or other methods, it can provide the information necessary to predict job satisfaction. Additionally, individual and group interviews can provide managers with information regarding the attitudes revealed by job satisfaction scales. After identifying which factors are dissatisfying, employees and managers can discuss such factors in an attempt to increase overall satisfaction. A broader discussion of the interview can be found in Chapter 7.

Exit Interviews

By the time an exit interview is conducted, it is often too late to retain the employee. The exit interview provides an opportunity to discover what factors led the employee to decide to leave the organization. Managers can determine whether the resignation was due to some fault of the corporation that could have been avoided or whether the resignation was unavoidable because it was due to personal reasons. In cases such as health problems, continued education, a better job offer, or family relocation, corporations cannot affect the employee's departure.

If the resignation is unavoidable, reasons for quitting are often stated. But, if the resignation is avoidable, employees may be reluctant to express their feelings and reasons for resigning. Therefore, it is often recommended that a neutral person conduct the exit interview. To encourage communication and to maintain confidentiality, this person should not be someone with whom the employee regularly worked, but rather someone from a different area or level in the organization (e.g., a district manager rather than the departing employee's direct supervisor). Finally, the survey method is a useful alternative for securing greater objectivity and information from exiting employees about their reasons for leaving the company.

Action Tendency Scales

Job attitudes can be described as behaviors that are observed in particular situations. **Action tendency scales** place employees in specific, simulated situations and ask them to react to the situation on the basis of their feelings. These scales provide information to the corporation about how employees will respond to certain situations when and if they occur on the job. This information may aid corporations in planning task settings and preparing for unusual circumstances. Action tendency items tend to report more dissatisfaction than other evaluative rating forms because employees are given the opportunity to state their grievances about work dilemmas.

Overt Behaviors

Overt behaviors are behaviors that are directly observable in the workplace. Managers can subjectively gauge employee attitudes by observing employees in their natural work settings. Behaviors such as high absenteeism, turnover, time wasting, and tardiness can all be directly measured and may be predictors of low satisfaction.

JOB AND LIFE SATISFACTION

Smith's (1992) **"river of satisfaction"** is an excellent summary of the relationship between job and general life satisfaction (see Figure 11.5). It is clear that, "job satisfaction is one of the components of life satisfaction. Together with satisfaction about marriage, family, leisure, and other nonwork satisfactions, it makes up the effluent into the gulf of life satisfaction" (Smith, 1992, p. 9). This interaction between satisfaction at work and satisfaction with life originates with the belief that people have difficulty separating work from other aspects of their lives. In their meta-analysis of studies dealing with the relationships between work and life satisfaction, Tait, Youtz-Padgett, and Baldwin (1989) stated that a majority of the research in this area stems from the assumption that work is a central involvement to many people and from the importance associated with work in U.S. society.

Kabanoff and O'Brien (1980) tested three models of the work–leisure relationship: (a) the generalization, or spillover, hypothesis, which assumes that a positive correlation exists between work and leisure and that satisfaction in one area influences satisfaction in the other area; (b) the compensation hypothesis, in which a negative correlation is assumed to exist between work and leisure, with dissatisfaction in one area compensated for by satisfaction in the other; and (c) Dubin's (1956) hypothesis that satisfaction in life is independent of work satisfaction, particularly in an industrial society. Kabanoff and O'Brien (1980) found only a weak relationship between work satisfaction and life satisfaction and concluded that all three models were too simplistic and did not satisfactorily explain the connection between work and leisure. They also indicated the importance of variables that may moderate these relationships, such as personality variables, cultural differences, and demographic variables.

A review of the literature conducted by Tait et al. (1989) concluded that over the years, research findings varied widely. Results ranged from doubting the existence of a relationship between life and job satisfaction to the assumption that variables such as gender act as moderators. The results of their meta-analysis showed that contrary to these individual findings, there

is a "strong positive relationship between job and life satisfaction . . . and that work should not be studied in isolation from extrawork concerns" (Tait et al., 1989, p. 504). They also supported the importance of gender as a moderator. For example, although the strength of the relationship between work and life satisfaction was stronger for men than for women in studies conducted before 1974, this difference was not apparent in studies conducted after 1974. One explanation for this change is that women have become more involved in their jobs. As a result, their life activities, identities, and overall satisfaction are now determined not only by their families, but also by their careers.

These results are indicative of current thinking in I/O psychology: that satisfaction at work and satisfaction with life, or what Smith (1992) calls "happiness," are related and that there is indeed an "overlap between work and nonwork experiences" (Tait et al., 1989, p. 502). The spillover of job stress to family life described in Practice Perspective 11.4 is another area of overlap.

Factors that influence the relationship between work and life satisfaction have been the focus of several recent studies. To illustrate, self-employed individuals were found to have a stronger relationship between job satisfaction, their life in general, and family life (Thompson, Kopelman, & Schreisheim, 1992). In an attempt to address job dissatisfaction, Judge and Locke (1993) found that individuals who are happy with their lives are more likely to be satisfied with their jobs and that job satisfaction played a role in a person's rating of his or her well-being. For example,

> if one's married and family life were exceptionally happy, one might go to work in a positive mood and interpret events in a positive light. The opposite could occur if one went to the job in a bad mood because of an unhappy family situation. (p. 486)

Cognitive processes, especially dysfunctional thought processes (e.g., extreme dependence on others, perfectionism, or overgeneralization), were found to affect happiness both on the job

Job Stress Survey

In a survey of 2399 employees in a large corporation, Youngstrom (1992) demonstrated that job stress and work environment spill over to family life. For example, a job can be an obstacle to spending time with families or can affect individuals' moods and thus relationships with spouses. An organization that supports family needs affects satisfaction with parenting and success on the job. Employees' success in balancing work and family responsibilities was found to depend mainly on the ages of the children, the demands of the job, and the supportive nature of the supervisor with regard to family demands.

Spillover of family problems to work involved factors such as degree of family support and child-care problems. Gender was found to moderate between the degree of stress on the job and reaction to members of the family. For example, women who had stressful jobs were found to be more irritable with their children. Men who were dissatisfied with their jobs devoted more time to their children.

Source: From "Juggling job, family? Sensitive employer helps," by N. Youngstrom (December 1992), *APA Monitor,* p. 33.

and in nonwork settings. The degree to which individuals believe that they must depend on others, be perfect in performing their tasks, or generalize from one event to others can affect their levels of both job and life satisfaction.

It is apparent that an interdependence exists between satisfaction with work and satisfaction with life in general. Most contemporary researchers agree that there is, in fact, a "unity of life and labor" (Thompson et al., 1992, p. 738). The challenge to I/O psychologists, then, is to investigate and attempt to explain the interrelatedness of employee happiness and life, family, leisure, health, and work.

JOB STRESS, WORK, AND HEALTH

Occupational stress has become an important focus of recent research. Ilgen (1990) suggests that "the health of the work force [is] one of the most significant issues of our time . . . [with] health issues in the work place . . . approaching crisis proportion" (p. 273).

Hinkle (1974) conducted a study that examined AT&T employees who had suffered heart attacks. The results showed that 90% of these em-

ployees worked two jobs and/or more than sixty hours a week. These work habits were believed to result in prolonged emotional strain. The control group consisted of employees with no history of heart attacks. Only 20% of these employees worked two jobs and/or more than sixty hours a week. In a related study, Orth-Gomer and Ahlbom (1980) found that psychological stress at work predicted the risk of employees developing heart disease within a five-year period. This risk was six times higher than that for the control group. House, Strecher, Metzner, and Robbins (1986) found that experiencing high job stress twice in a ten-year period produced a death rate three times higher than that produced by experiencing high job stress only once.

Ironson (1992) conducted a literature review and summarized the relationship between job stress and selected health outcomes (see Figure 11.8 on page 388). As a result, Ironson developed a model that focuses on three major components. One component concerns the sources of stress, including intervening variables affecting the job stress–health relationship. Another component addresses the physiological measure of stress. The third component addresses health outcomes.

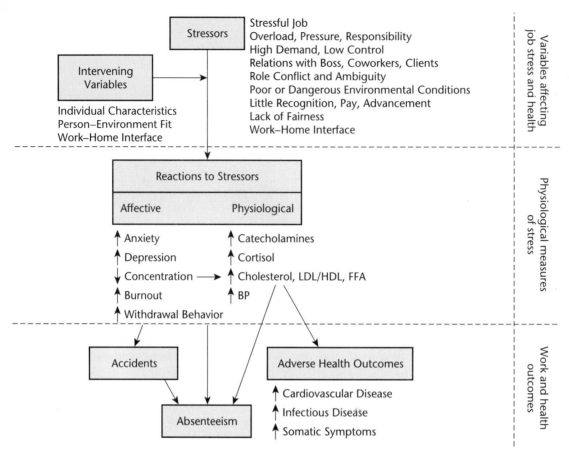

FIGURE 11.8   Ironson's model relating job stress to health outcomes, absenteeism, and accidents.

Source: From "Work, Job Stress, and Health," by G. Ironson. In *Work, Families, and Organizations,* (p. 35), S. Zedeck (Ed.), 1992, San Francisco, CA: Jossey-Bass, Inc. Copyright 1992 by Jossey-Bass Inc. Reprinted with permission.

Stressors and Intervening Variables

Investigators recognize that some jobs are more stressful than others, and the popular press periodically publishes articles listing "the most stressful jobs." In an effort to understand the validity of job-related stress, researchers have explored the dimensions and combinations of dimensions that make a job stressful. A related issue that has been examined is why a job is perceived as stressful for one individual but not for another.

The broadest level of stress analysis examines jobs as a whole. These studies consider issues ranging from differences in diseases (Cobb & Rose, 1973) to differences in suicide rates (Kaplan & Sadock, 1991). Studies conducted at this broad level do not differentiate between people who are attracted to these jobs and those who are not; nor do they identify the dimensions that make the job stressful.

The job stressor approach examines individual dimensions of stress of a job. Ironson's (1992) review identified fourteen facets of job stress (see Practice Perspective 11.5) that had been measured subjectively and objectively. The facet approach is more specific and provides more in-

PRACTICE PERSPECTIVE 11.5

Ironson's Facets of Job Stress

Ironson's 1992 review of the literature identified fourteen facets of job stress. These facets have been measured in various studies and provide a way of examining job stress that is more targeted than other whole-job approaches.

1. Work overload—having too much work to do or work tasks that are too difficult.
2. Work underload—having too little to do or work tasks that are too easy, are boring, or fail to tap the individual's capabilities.
3. Ambiguity—having unclear work objectives or no understanding of what is expected on the job or how to accomplish the objectives.
4. Role conflict—the perception of incompatible or incongruent demands, inadequate facts or resources to do the job, or conflicts between personal values and organizational values.
5. Time pressure—not having enough time to do the work.
6. Job insecurity—uncertainty about continued employment with no viable alternative jobs available.
7. Environmental conditions—working in unpleasant conditions: noise, dirt, odors, or excessive physical demands.

8. Nonparticipation—lack of say in decisions affecting one's job, lack of respect or recognition.
9. Physical risks—danger of accidents, small error leading to large damage.
10. Heavy responsibility—responsibility for people or large amounts of money, small error leading to large damage.
11. Interpersonal relations—working with friendly or unfriendly, cooperative or uncooperative supervisors, coworkers, or clients.
12. Pay—earning enough or too little money.
13. Promotion, growth, and development—advancing or not advancing in work, getting to learn new skills.
14. Perceived equity—experiencing discrimination on the job because of sex, race, ethnic background, or physical characteristics; fairness in distribution of rewards.

Source: From "Work, Job Stress, and Health," by G. Ironson, In *Work, Families and Organizations* (pp. 37–38), by S. Zedeck, (Ed.), 1992, San Francisco, CA: Jossey-Bass. Copyright 1992 by Jossey-Bass, Inc. Reprinted with permission.

formation about the stressful aspects of a job than the whole-job analyses. However, using facet analysis creates complex models of job stress that are difficult to apply.

Karasek, Theorell, Schwartz, Pieper, and Alfredsson (1982) used the facet approach to develop a model that suggests that high demand and low control are a stressful combination in a job, a result that has been supported by animal studies (Brady, Porter, Conrad, & Mason, 1958; Davis & Berry, 1963; Kaplan, Manuck, Clarkson, Lusso, & Taub, 1982; Weiss, 1971) Additional evidence suggests that positive intervening variables may buffer the impact of job stressors (Hinkle, 1974).

The person–environment fit model addresses the issue of intervening variables by explaining why a stressor for one person may not be a stressor for another. For example, some people thrive on chaos and challenge, while others prefer a routine. To understand this issue, a job stress model must take into account the needs and responses of the individual as well as the demands and circumstances of the job. Caplan, Cobb, French, Harrison, and Pinneau (1975) and French, Caplan, and Van Harrison (1982) attempted to develop this type of model. Nevertheless, attempts to develop a job stress model that takes into account individual differences led to disappointing results. For example, the person–environment fit model added only a small amount (1.5%) of predictability to the facet model.

Medical researchers exploring factors related to cardiovascular disease commonly study characteristics of individuals. But their research does not often focus on the relationship between job stress and the individual's health. The increasing number of dual-career families has prompted investigations into the work–home interface. There is evidence that home stress *and* work stress affect health, further complicated by the spillover from one area to the other (Klitzman, House, Israel, & Mero, 1990). For example, female managers do not unwind at home as quickly as do male managers. This factor may contribute to the increased negative effects of job stress on the health of female managers. Beyond this, researchers have not found differences in the rate of heart disease between women who work and those who are homemakers. The researchers found a higher rate of heart disease in working women with three or more children than in homemakers with three or more children (Haynes & Feinlieb, 1980). Some businesses are now providing day-care for children of working mothers, a practice that increased employee attendance and reduced turnover (Ward, 1991).

Responses to Stress

Responses to stress are many. Research has demonstrated a number of short-term physical and biochemical responses to stress. Physical measures of stress have the advantage of being highly objective. The two major biological systems that are involved in stress reactions are the sympatho-adreno-medullary (SAM) system and the hypothalamic-pituitary-adreno-cortical (HPAC) system. The SAM system yields the famous "fight-or-flight" pattern of response in which the person prepares to fight for survival or to flee the situation. Responses included in this pattern of behavior are increases in the heart rate, blood pressure, blood flow, norepinephrine, and epinephrine. In contrast, the HPAC pattern increases vigilance but may cause a person to freeze. There is increased ACTH from the pituitary and other hormones, such as cortisol from the adrenal cortex. A detailed summary of this research is available in Schneiderman and Tupp's book *Behavioral Medicine* (1985).

The last part of the Ironson (1992) model addresses specific health effects associated with occupational stress, including cardiovascular stress, heart disease, and hypertension. Research has shown that air traffic controllers have four times more hypertension and six times as many new cases of hypertension than do second-class airmen. One of the basic differences between the two groups is that air traffic controllers are highly experienced technicians working in high-stress jobs, whereas second-class airmen are moderately experienced Air Force servicepeople working in lower-stress jobs (Cobb & Rose, 1973). Studies have also found higher levels of stress in blue-collar workers and managers than in engineers and scientists (French & Caplan, 1973). Female clerical workers appear to be particularly at risk for coronary heart disease (Haynes & Feinlieb, 1980). Similarly, real estate agents and lawyers have higher rates of heart disease than do teachers (Kasl, 1986).

Work overload, whether measured in quantity or in level of difficulty, contributes to stress and heart disease (Theorell & Floderus-Myrhed, 1977). High demand jobs are associated with high risk for developing health problems (Karasek, Baker, Marxer, Ahlbom, & Theorell, 1981). Work situations that combine a hectic work pace with low latitude for decision making are related to increased risk of myocardial infarction (Alfredsson, Karasek, & Theorell, 1982). Overload has also been found to be associated with cigarette smoking and with drinking to escape the pressure of work (French & Caplan, 1973; Margolis, Kroes, & Quinn, 1974).

Other dimensions are related to similar health problems. These include problems with social relations at work, role conflict and ambiguity, lack of career development and opportunities for growth, monotony, job insecurity and job loss, physical conditions, shift work, and financial problems. Measures that can reflect the effects a person's job has on health include measures of absenteeism and accident rates. However, these measures may reflect more than health problems alone.

Managing job stress is a prime issue in organizations. Recent reviews of stress management programs indicate that most of these programs involve a clinical counseling approach to dealing with stress at work (Ivancevich, Matteson, Freedman, & Phillips, 1990; Sallis, Trevorrow, Johnson, Hovell, & Kaplan, 1987). This approach focuses on one of three outcomes:

1. *Altering the stressor:* This means making a change in a positive direction. For example, if an employee is frustrated by a supervisor who is very directive in style, the employee can become more assertive and respond more honestly. This can help to clear the air and reduce stress. Some people become workaholics, having a compulsion to work. They do not take vacations or take time to recharge. They allow tension to build until it becomes problematic. This situation should be approached like other addictive behaviors. The employee needs to admit that the problem exists, identify enabling behaviors or situations, and seek appropriate support.

2. *Avoiding the stressor:*

    a. Walking away can control stress. Responsible walking away means that the employee controls the schedule rather than letting it control him or her. The employee should avoid working late and know when to admit being overcommitted and need to cut back.

    b. Letting go is releasing issues that are no longer important. This includes areas in which the employee is no longer productive and abandoning lost causes. Letting go of relationships can be especially difficult because a sense of loss is experienced.

    c. Saying no is a critical control factor. If a person cannot say no when it is appropriate, then saying yes also loses its value. The employee should consider whether his or her response really means yes or is simply acquiescence.

    d. Knowing limitations is one of the most difficult tasks related to stress. It is often hard for individuals to admit that they cannot accomplish everything they would like to accomplish. It is also hard to admit that current performance may not be as effective as past performance.

    e. Learning to delegate responsibility and authority can help to break old thinking patterns. It can release an individual from the belief that the only way to have something done right is to do it themselves. Delegating responsibilities can also help to eliminate or reduce feelings of guilt because they did not do something themselves.

3. *Accepting the stressor:*

    a. Building the capacity to handle stress takes many forms. Increasing the body's physical stamina will also increase physical resistance. This can be accomplished through careful attention to diet, exercise, stress, and relaxation.

    b. Mental adjustment to stress involves changing the perception of the stressor to something less threatening. Adjustments may include providing personal time, adopting an effective time management system, and positive thinking. An effective approach to self-perception uses a symptom checklist, which uses self-examination questions to guide the discovery of possible sources of stress (see Practice Perspective 11.6 on page 392).

PRACTICE PERSPECTIVE 11.6

Stress Symptom Checklist

This is an example of a stress symptom self-help checklist given by a consulting organization as basic guidance to managers who are experiencing job stress but who do not recognize why this is happening to them.

Symptoms	*Cures*
Feeling that one can never accomplish enough.	What do I want from my job?
Experiencing consistent work overload.	What do I need now that I do not have?
Working longer hours and enjoying it less.	What should I change about my current behavior?
Finding it hard to make a decision.	Evaluate all the drugs that you take.
Noticing consistent fatigue.	Have a physical exam and a psychological evaluation.
Experiencing problems in concentration.	Isolate sources of greatest stress.
Feeling lonely.	Shake up your routine.
Having sleeping difficulties.	Challenge your body with a new physical activity.
Becoming more pessimistic.	Concentrate on revitalizing a friendship.
Feelings of incompetence.	Change habits that are personally destructive.
Experiencing headaches.	Develop a special confidant.
Having job dissatisfaction.	Find new mental tasks.

SUMMARY

Job satisfaction is an ambiguous concept, covering a broad scope of individual work experiences. It involves complicated motivational behaviors. It differs among individuals, as well as within individual employees. As a consequence, measuring job satisfaction is a subjective process. Job satisfaction scales are not always predictive of job performance, just as job performance is not always predictive of job satisfaction. This results from the various effects that different job facets have on individual employees.

Locke found thousands of studies on job satisfaction with the literature suggesting that the issue of job satisfaction is important: Employees are concerned with the content of their jobs and are interested in psychological fulfillment. They

want jobs that enhance their lives at work as well as at home.

This chapter has shown that various individual inputs, conditions, and agents may influence job satisfaction. Research on job satisfaction and job performance has identified how rewards are correlated to both dimensions and how rewards may enhance production levels, regardless of satisfaction. By noting the many facets that affect job satisfaction, managers can be made aware of individual differences and can ensure that all employees are rewarded according to their individual needs.

The challenge facing I/O psychologists lies in determining how best to measure job satisfaction. This is an important consideration, since the approach that is used can affect the conclusions. Group and individual interviews can be time consuming and costly and should not be used in isolation. The exit interview provides employees with the opportunity to voice their opinions without the threat of termination. Action tendency scales attempt to measure the employee's response to, and attitudes toward, various job situations. Another measure is to simply observe the employee's overt behaviors as an indication of job satisfaction.

Job satisfaction is an attitude, a predisposition to respond to one's environment in a positive or negative manner. Research on job satisfaction has centered on the relationship between organizational and individual outcomes. Herzberg's two-factor theory relates to both satisfaction and motivation. For example, proper emphasis on hygiene outcomes can lead to an absence of dissatisfaction, whereas proper emphasis on motivator outcomes can lead to a feeling of satisfaction. Lawler's facet satisfaction model is a process theory that regards satisfaction as the subjective perception workers have about their efforts and the corresponding rewards.

Another theory of job satisfaction is the work adjustment theory, which includes the prediction of tenure. The level of correspondence between the individual and his or her work environment enables the organization to make this prediction. The theory assumes that a person who has stayed on a job for a long time has adjusted to his or her work environment. These theories attempt to explain job satisfaction conceptually; however, there are a number of other factors that correlate with job satisfaction.

Job satisfaction is related to a variety of independent characteristics. Input correlates comprise all the aspects the worker brings to the job, including individual differences, personality, age, gender, and race. External factors that affect job satisfaction for the individual include situational characteristics and pay. Finally, output factors associated with work satisfaction include job performance, withdrawal, absenteeism, turnover, and employee theft.

An example of a specialized application of psychology to the world of work is work done in the area of occupational or job stress. Some studies explore a number of facets involved in job stress. Other studies take a broader view. One effective model examines the person–environment fit. This model helps to explain why what may be stressful for one person is not stressful for another. Different sources of job stress exist. Examples are work overload, work underload, ambiguity, role conflict, time pressure, job insecurity, environmental conditions, nonparticipation, physical risks, heavy responsibility, interpersonal relations, pay, promotion, growth, development, and perceived equity. Stress management programs use clinical counseling to help stressed individuals manage their problem. Three major approaches are used: altering the stressor by changing directions; avoiding the stressor by walking away, letting go, or saying no; and accepting the stressor by building up the capacity to handle it or changing one's perception of it.

KEY TERMS AND CONCEPTS

absence culture	facet satisfaction model	motivator-hygiene theory
action tendency scales	fair differentials of pay	motivators
agents	hygiene factors	motive/need theory
comparison theory	input correlates	output variables
content theories	internal rewards	process theories
diagnostic model	involuntary absenteeism	river of satisfaction
discrepancy model	job enlargement	situational characteristics
events	job enrichment	turnover model
external rewards	job satisfaction	two-factor theory

valence

withdrawal

work adjustment

work adjustment theory

work environment

work personality

RECOMMENDED READINGS

Cranny, C. J., Smith, S. C., & Stone, E. F. (1992). *Job satisfaction: How people feel about their jobs and how it affects their performance.* New York: Lexington Books.

Germann, R., Blumenson, D., & Arnold, P. (1984). *Working and liking it.* New York: Ballantine Books.

Gruneberg, M. M. (Ed.). (1976). *Job satisfaction: A reader.* New York: Wiley.

Hansen, C. P., & Conrad, K. A. (1991). *A handbook of psychological assessment in business.* New York, NY: Quorum Books.

Kotter, J. P., & Heskett, J. L. (1992). *Corporate culture and performance.* New York: The Free Press.

Lawler, E. E., III, (1971). *Pay and organizational effectiveness: A psychological view.* New York: McGraw-Hill.

Lawler, E. E., III, (1991). *High-involvement management.* San Francisco: Jossey-Bass.

Rhodes, S. R., & Steers, R. M. (1990). *Managing employee absenteeism.* Reading, MA: Addison-Wesley.

Smith, P. C., Kendall, L. M., & Hulin, C. L. (1969). *The measurement of satisfaction in work and retirement.* Skokie, IL: Rand McNally.

INTERNET RESOURCES

CCH Business Owner's Toolbox

Among other useful things, this site contains a fourteen-page job satisfaction survey in rich text format, consisting of fifty-seven questions addressing major morale issues such as attitudes about bosses, coworkers, the future, amount of work, and physical working conditions. It can be downloaded, modified, printed, and used at no cost to the organization.

http://www.toolkit.cch.com/default.htm

Assessing the Effects of Organizational Commitment and Job Satisfaction on Turnover: An Event History Approach, by Scott D. Camp, Ph.D., Federal Bureau of Prisons

Posted at this address is an abstract of a paper describing turnover among correctional workers. It examines the relationship between job satisfaction and organizational commitment. It confirms that higher organizational commitment leads to lower turnover. A full copy of the paper is available for download.

http://www.bop.gov/ore/camp_tpj.html

Gender Differences and Empowerment: Initial Findings, by Dafna Eylon, University of Richmond

This site summarizes a study of 135 MBA students who completed an empowerment intervention in a simulated business setting. It investigates how women's ways of working differ from those of men in the context of empowerment.

http://blue.temple.edu/~eastern/eylon.html

13th Annual White Paper Report on U.S. Industry Safety and Health Practices

This site presents the full text of the annual report of the industrial safety and hygiene professionals. A section summarizes the annual survey of job satisfaction. This is a good example of a printed report of the results of a job satisfaction survey.

http://www.safetyonline.net/wp/home.htm

The Personality, Job Satisfaction and Turnover Intentions of African-American Male and Female Accountants

This site reports the results of several studies investigating the personality characteristics, job satisfaction attitudes, and turnover intentions of a sample of male and female African-American accountants. The objective was to understand why recruiting of African-Americans into the accounting field has been lagging.

http://les.man.ac.uk/cpa96/txt/glover.txt

EXERCISES

Exercise 11.1

Investigating Job Satisfaction and Performance

Develop a brief questionnaire to measure key elements of job satisfaction. Include in your design several items to assess the individual characteristics of personality, age, gender, and race. Write items to measure the situational variables of job status, societal values, and pay. Limit your questionnaire to fifty items. Also, design a brief measure of job performance.

Identify a group of people who are currently employed. Make arrangements to administer your job satisfaction measure to this group and to collect job performance data as well. (One strategy that can be used is to have your measures designed as 360° feedback surveys. Have each person complete a survey and give copies to the employees who report directly to them and one to their manager.)

Compile your results. Examine the level of satisfaction on your satisfaction scales and the level of performance. Do the most satisfied employees perform better? Why or why not? Describe your results in terms of motivation and the job satisfaction theories discussed in this chapter. How are your findings similar to, or different from, those of other studies of job satisfaction and individual performance? Which motivation and which job satisfaction theory provide the best framework for understanding your results?

Exercise 11.2

Job Enlargement or Enrichment to Increase Satisfaction

Many investigators have found that job enlargement and job enrichment are associated with increased job satisfaction. Another common finding is that enriched jobs are viewed as more meaningful than more routine jobs.

Develop a design for an investigation of the impact of job enrichment on job satisfaction. Be sure to carefully define job satisfaction for your study. Tie your definition to the theoretical models described in this chapter. Add the behavioral indices that you will use to assess changes in job satisfaction.

In the design of the study, consider the key factors on which you want to focus. Also consider which of the many possible comparisons you want to use. A few suggestions are young versus old workers, males versus females, blue-collar versus white-collar workers, recent employees versus old timers, and higher-educated versus less-educated workers. When possible, state hypotheses that predict job satisfaction on the basis of the theories described in the chapter.

If you have the time and the opportunity, collect and analyze data for your study.

REFERENCES

Alfredsson, L., Karasek, R., & Theorell, T. (1982). Myocardial infarction risk and psychosocial work environment: An analysis of the male Swedish working force. *Social Science and Medicine, 16,* 463–467.

Bass, B. M., & Barrett, G. V. (1981). *Man, work, and organizations: An introduction to industrial and organizational psychology.* (2nd ed.). Boston: Allyn & Bacon.

Bluen, S. D., Barling, J., & Burns, W. (1990). Predicting sales performance, job satisfaction, and depression by using the achievement strivings and impatience-irritability dimensions of Type A behavior. *Journal of Applied Psychology, 75,* 212–216.

Brady, J., Porter, R., Conrad, D., & Mason, J. (1958). Avoidance behavior and the development of - gastroduodenal ulcers. *Journal of Experimental Analysis of Behavior, 1,* 69–72.

Brooke, P. P., Jr., & Price, J. L. (1989). The determinants of employee absenteeism: An empirical test of a causal model. *Journal of Occupational Psychology, 62,* 1–19.

Caplan, R. D., Cobb, S., French, J. R. P., Jr., Harrison, R. V., & Pinneau, R. R., Jr. (1975) *Job demands and worker health* [HEW Publication No. (NIOSH)75–160]. Washington, DC: U.S. Government Printing Office.

Carsten, J. M., & Spector, P. E. (1987). Unemployment, job satisfaction, and employee turnover: A meta-analytic test of the Muchinsky model. *Journal of Applied Psychology, 72,* 374–381.

Chatman, J. A. (1989). Improving interactional organizational research: A model of person-organization fit. *Academy of Management Review, 14*(3), pp. 333–346.

Cherrington, J. D., Reitz, H. J., & Scott, W. E., Jr. (1971). Effects on contingent and noncontingent reward on the relationship between satisfaction and task performance. *Journal of Applied Psychology, 55*(6), 531–536.

Cobb, S., & Rose, R. M. (1973). Hypertension, peptic ulcer, and diabetes in air traffic controllers. *Journal of the American Medical Association, 224*(4), 489–492.

Cox, T. H., & Blake, S. (1991). Managing cultural diversity: implications for organizational competitiveness. *The Executive, 5*(3), 45–56.

Cranny, C. J., Smith, P. C., & Stone, E. F. (1992). *Job satisfaction: How people feel about their jobs and how it affects their performance.* New York: Lexington Books.

Cropanzano, R., & Folger, R. (1991). Procedural justice and worker motivation. In R. M. Steers & L. W. Porter (Eds.), *Motivation and work behavior* (pp. 131–143). New York: McGraw-Hill.

Davis, R., & Berry, F. (1963). Gastrointestinal reaction during a noise avoidance task. *Psychological Reports, 12,* 135–137.

Davis, R., & Newstrom, J. (1985). *Human behavior at work: Organizational behavior.* New York: McGraw-Hill.

Dawis, R. V. (1991). Vocational interests, values, and preferences. In M. D. Dunnette & L. M. Hough (Eds.), *Handbook of industrial and organizational psychology* (Vol. 2, pp. 833–871). Palo Alto, CA: Consulting Psychologists Press.

Dawis, R., & Lofquist, L. H. (1984). *A psychological theory of work adjustment: An individual differences model and its applications.* Minneapolis, MN: University of Minnesota Press.

Dubin, R. (1956). Industrial workers' worlds: A study in the central life interests of industrial workers. *Social Problems, 4,* 3–13.

Dubrin, A. J. (1984). *Foundations of organizational behavior: An applied perspective.* Englewood Cliffs, NJ: Prentice-Hall.

Dyer, L., & Theriault, R. (1976). The determinants of pay satisfaction. *Journal of Applied Psychology, 61*(5), 596–604.

Fisher, C. D., & Locke, E. A. (1992). The new look in job satisfaction research and theory. In C. J.

Cranny, P. C. Smith, & E. F. Stone, *Job satisfaction: How people feel about their jobs and how it affects their performance.* New York: Lexington Books.

French, J. R. P., Jr. & Caplan, R. D. (1973). Organizational stress and individual strain. In A. J. Marrow (Ed.), *The failure of success* (pp. 30–66). New York: AMACOM.

French, J. R. P., Jr., Caplan, R. D., & Van Harrison, R. (1982). *The mechanisms of job stress and strain.* New York: Wiley.

Fried, Y. (1991). Meta-analytic comparison of the job diagnostic survey and job characteristics inventory as correlates of work satisfaction and performance. *Journal of Applied Psychology, 76*(5), 690–697.

Fricko, M. M., & Beehr, T. A. (1992). A longitudinal investigation of interest congruence and gender concentration as predictors of job satisfaction. *Personnel Psychology, 45*(1), 99–118.

Gellerman, S. W. (1963). *Motivation and productivity.* New York: American Management Association, Vail-Ballou Press.

Gellerman, S. W. (1968). *Management by motivation.* New York: American Management Association, Vail-Ballou Press.

Gruneberg, M. M. (1979). *Understanding job satisfaction.* London: Macmillan.

Guion, R. M. (1991). Personnel assessment, selection, and placement. In M. D. Dunnette & L. M. Hough (Eds.), *Handbook of industrial and organizational psychology* (Vol. 2, pp. 327–397). Palo Alto, CA: Consulting Psychologists Press.

Hackman, J. R., & Oldham, G. R. (1975). Development of the job diagnostic survey. *Journal of Applied Psychology, 60,* 161.

Haynes, S. G., & Feinlieb, M. (1980). Women, work and coronary heart disease: Prospective findings from the Framingham Heart Study. *American Journal of Public Health, 70*(2), 133–141.

Herzberg, F. (1976). One more time: How do you motivate employees? In M. M. Gruneberg (Ed.), *Job satisfaction: A reader.* New York: John Wiley & Sons.

Herzberg, F., Mausner, B., & Snyderman, B. (1959). *The motivation to work.* New York: Wiley Books.

Hinkle, L. E., Jr. (1974). *The effect of exposure to culture change, social change and changes in interpersonal relationships on health.* New York: Wiley.

Hopkins, A. H. (1983). *Work and job satisfaction in the public sector.* Totawa, NJ: Rowman & Allenheld.

House, J. S., Strecher, V., Metzner, H. L., & Robbins, C. A. (1986). Occupational stress and health among men and women in the Tecumseh Community Health Study. *Journal of Health and Social Behavior, 27,* 62–77.

Huber, V. L., Seybolt, P. M., & Venemon, K. (1992). The relationship between individual inputs, perceptions, and multidimensional pay satisfaction. *Journal of Applied Social Psychology, 22,* 1356–1373.

Iaffaldano, M. T., & Muchinsky, P. M. (1985). Job satisfaction and job performance: A meta-analysis. *Psychological Bulletin, 97,* 251–273.

Ilgen, D. R. (1990). Health issues at work. *American Psychologist,* 273–282.

Ironson, G. (1992). Work, job stress and health. In Zedeck, S.(Ed.), *Work, families, and organizations.* San Francisco: Jossey-Bass Publishers.

Ivancevich, J. M., Matteson, M. T., Freedman, S. M., & Phillips, J. S. (1990). Worksite stress management interventions. *American Psychologist, 45*(2), 252–261.

Jacobs, R., & Solomon, T. (1977). Strategies for enhancing the prediction of job performance from job satisfaction. *Journal of Applied Psychology, 62,* 417–421.

Johns, G., & Nicholson, N. (1982). The meaning of absence: New strategies for theory and research. In B. M. Staw and L. L. Cummings (Eds.), *Research in organizational behavior* (Vol. 4). Greenwich, CT: JAI.

Judge, T. A., & Locke, E. (1993). Effect of dysfunctional thought processes on subjective well-being and job satisfaction. *Journal of Applied Psychology, 78*(3), 475–490.

Kabanoff, B., & O'Brien, G. E. (1980). Work and leisure: A task attributes analysis. *Journal of Applied Psychology, 65*(5), 596–609.

Kaplan, H. I., & Sadock, B. J. (1991). *Synopsis of psychiatry.* Baltimore, MD: Williams & Wilkins.

Kaplan, J. R., Manuck, S. B., Clarkson, T. B., Lusso, F. M., & Taub, D. (1982). Social stress, environment, and atherosclerosis in cynomolgus monkeys. *Arteriosclerosis, 2,* 359.

Karasek, R., Baker, D., Marxer, F., Ahlbom, A., & Theorell, T. (1981). Job decision latitude, job demands, and cardiovascular disease: A prospective study of Swedish men. *American Journal of Public Health, 71*(7), 694–705.

Karasek, R. A., Theorell, T. G. T., Schwartz, J., Pieper, C., & Alfredsson, A. (1982). Job, psychological factors and coronary heart disease: Swedish prospective findings and U.S. prevalence findings using a new occupational inference method. *Advances in Cardiology, 29,* 62–67.

Kasl, S. (1986). Stress and disease in the workplace: A methodological commentary on the accumulated evidence. In M. F. Cataldo & T. J. Coates (Eds.), *Health and industry* (pp. 52–85). New York: Wiley.

Katzell, R. A. (1994). Contemporary meta-trends in industrial and organizational psychology. In M. D. Dunnette & L. M. Hough (Eds.), *Handbook of industrial and organizational psychology* (Vol. 4, pp. 2–89). Palo Alto, CA: Consulting Psychologists Press.

Katzell, R. A., & Thompson, D. E. (1990). Work motivation, theory and practice. *American Psychologist, 45*(2), 144–153.

Katzell, R. A., Thompson, D. E., & Guzzo, R. A. (1992). Job satisfaction and job performance. In C. J., Cranny, P. C., Smith, & E. F. Stone (Eds.), *Job satisfaction: How people feel about their jobs and how it affects their performance* (pp. 195–217). New York: Lexington Books.

Khaleque, A., & Rahman, M. A. (1987). Perceived importance of job facets and overall job satisfaction of industrial workers. *Human Relations, 40*(7), 401–416.

Klitzman, S., House, J. S., Israel, B. A., & Mero, R. P. (1990). Work stress, nonwork stress and health. *Journal of Behavioral Medicine, 13*(3), 221–243.

Konar, E. (1981). Explaining racial difference in job satisfaction: A re-examination of the data. *Journal of Applied Psychology, 66,* 522–524.

Lawler, E. E., III (1971). *Pay and organizational effectiveness: A psychological view.* New York: McGraw-Hill.

Lawler, E. E., III (1973). *Motivation in work organizations.* Monterey, CA: Brooks/Cole.

Lawler, E. E., III (1981). *Pay and organization development.* Reading, MA: Addison-Wesley.

Lawler, E. E., III (1991). The design of effective reward systems. In R. M. Steers & L. W. Porter (Eds.), *Motivation and work* (pp. 507–530). New York: McGraw-Hill.

Lawler, E. E., & Porter, L. W. (1975). The effects of performance on job satisfaction. In K. N. Wexley & G. A. Yukl (Eds.), *Organizational behavior and industrial psychology* (p. 32–39). New York: Oxford University Press.

Lawler, E. E., & Rhode, J. G. (1976). *Information and control in organizations.* Santa Monica, CA: Goodyear.

Lee, C., Ashford, S. J., & Bobko, P. (1990). Interactive effects of "Type A" behavior and perceived control on worker performance, job satisfaction, and somatic complaints. *Academy of Management Journal, 33,* 870–881.

Lee, R., & Martin, J. E. (1991). Internal and external referents as predictors of pay satisfaction among employees in a two-tier wage setting. *Journal of Occupational Psychology, 64*(1), 57–66.

Locke, E. A. (1968). Toward a theory of task motivation and incentives. *Organizational Behavior and Human Performance, 3,* 157–189.

Locke, E. A. (1976). The nature and causes of job satisfaction. In M. D. Dunnette (Ed.), *Handbook of industrial and organizational psychology* (pp. 1297–1349). Chicago: Rand McNally.

Lowenberg, B. H. (1977). *Employee perception of norms of pay differentials.* Unpublished manuscript.

Lowenberg, G., Powaser, P. R., & Farkash, A. (1989). Determinants of the relationship between pay desire satisfaction and appropriate pay differentials relative to income levels. In B. J. Fallon, H. P. Pfister, & J. Brebner (Eds.), *Advances in industrial/organizational psychology.* Amsterdam: Elsevier Science Publishers.

Lowenberg, G., Kingston-O'Connell, F. G., & Conrad, K. A. (1993, June). *Pay-desire satisfaction (PDS), pay-satisfaction and demographics: Nonlinear relationships in academia.* Paper presented at the annual convention of the American Psychological Society, Chicago, IL.

Margolis, B. L., Kroes, W. H., & Quinn, R. P. (1974). Job stress: An unlisted occupational hazard. *Journal of Applied Medicine, 16,* 654–661.

McDaniel, M. A., Whetzel, D. L., Schmidt, F. L., & Maurer, S. D. (1994). The validity of employment interview: A comprehensive review and meta-analysis. *Journal of Applied Psychology, 79*(4), 599–616.

Milbourn, G., Jr. (1980). The relationship of money and motivation. *Compensation Review, 12*(3), 33–44.

Mitchell, T. R. (1979). Organizational behavior. *Annual Review of Psychology, 30,* 243–281.

Mobley, W. H. (1982). *Employee turnover: Cause, consequence, and control.* Reading, MA: Addison-Wesley.

Muchinsky, P. M., & Morrow, P. C. (1980). A multidisciplinary model of voluntary employee turnover. *Journal of Vocational Behavior, 14,* 43–77.

Nicholson, N. (1977). Absence behavior and attendance motivation: A conceptual synthesis. *Journal of Management Studies, 14,* 231–252.

Opsahl, R. L., & Dunnette, M. M. (1966). The role of financial compensation in industrial motivation. *Psychological Bulletin, 66*(2), 94–118.

Organ, D. W., & Hamner, W. C. (1982). *Organizational behavior: An applied psychological approach.* Plano, TX: Business Publications.

Orth-Gomer, K., & Ahlbom, A. (1980). Impact of psychological stress on ischemic heart disease when controlling for conventional risk indicators. *Journal of Human Stress, 6*(1), 7–15.

O'Reilly, C. A., III, Chatman, J., & Caldwell, D. F. (1991). People and organizational culture: A profile comparison approach to assessing person-organization fit. *Academy of Management Journal, 34*(3), 487–516.

Ostroff, C. (1992). The relationship between satisfaction, attitudes, and performance: An organizational level analysis. *Journal of Applied Psychology, 77*(6), 963–974.

Pendalino, E., & Gamboa, V. V. (1974). Behavior modification and absenteeism: Intervention in one industrial setting. *Journal of Applied Psychology, 59,* 694–698.

Porter, L. W., & Lawler, E. E. (1968). *Managerial attitudes and performance.* Homewood, IL: R. D. Irwin.

Porter, L. W., & Steers, R. M. (1973). Organization, work, and personal factors in employee turnover and absenteeism. *Psychological Bulletin, 80,* 151–176.

Rhodes, S. R., & Steers, R. M. (1990). *Managing employee absenteeism.* Reading, MA: Addison-Wesley.

Rice, R. W., Phillips, S. M., & McFarlin, D. B. (1990). Multiple discrepancies and pay satisfaction. *Journal of Applied Psychology, 75*(4), 386–393.

Sallis, J. R., Trevorrow, T. R., Johnson, C. C., Hovell, M. F., & Kaplan, R. M. (1987). Worksite stress management: A comparison of programs. *Psychology and Health, 1,* 237–255.

Schmitz, L. M., & Heneman, H. G., III (1980). Do positive reinforcement programs reduce employee absenteeism? *Personnel Administrator, 25*(9), 87–93.

Schneiderman, N., & Tupp, J. T., (1985). *Behavioral medicine: The biopsychosocial approach.* Hillsdale, NJ: Lawrence Erlbaum.

Schwab, D. P., & Cummings, L. L. (1973). Theories of performance and satisfaction: A review. In W. E. Scott & L. L. Cummings (Eds.), *Readings in organizational behavior and human performance* (pp. 130–141). Homewood, IL: Irwin.

Seadmonds, B. C. (1982). Stress factors and their effect on absenteeism in a corporate employee group. *Journal of Occupational Medicine, 24,* 393–397.

Seadmonds, B. C. (1983). Extension of research into stress factors and their effect on illness absenteeism. *Journal of Occupational Medicine, 25,* 821–822.

Sheppard, H. L., & Herrick, N. W. (1972). *Where have all the robots gone? Worker dissatisfaction in the "70's."* New York: Free Press.

Sieh, E. W. (1987). Garment workers: Perceptions of inequity and employee theft. *British Criminology Journal, 27*(2), 174–190.

Smith, P. C. (1992). In pursuit of happiness. In C. J. Cranny, P. C. Smith, & E. F. Stone (Eds.), *Job satisfaction: How people feel about their jobs and how it affects their performance.* New York: Lexington Books.

Smith, P. C., Kendall, L., & Hulin, C. L. (1969). *The measurement of satisfaction in work and retirement: A strategy for the study of attitudes.* Chicago: Rand McNally.

Smither, J. W., Collins, H., & Buda, R. (1989). When ratee satisfaction influences performance evaluations: A case of illusory correlation. *Journal of Applied Psychology, 74*(4), 599–605.

Spector, P. E. (1986). Perceived control by employees: A meta-analysis of studies concerning autonomy and participation at work. *Human Relations, 39,* 1005–1016.

Staw, B. M. (1984). Organizational behavior: A review and reformulation of the field's outcome variables. *Annual Review of Psychology, 35,* 627–666.

Steers, R. M., & Porter, L. W. (Eds.). (1991). *Motivation and work.* New York: McGraw-Hill.

Steers, R. M., & Rhodes, S. R. (1978). Major influences on employee attendance: A process model. *Journal of Applied Psychology, 63,* 391–407.

Steers, R. M., & Rhodes, S. R. (1984). Knowledge and speculation about absenteeism. In P. S. Goodman and R. S. Atkin (Eds.), *Absenteeism: New approaches to understanding, measuring, and managing absence* (pp. 229–275). San Francisco, CA: Jossey-Bass.

Steers, R. M., & Rhodes, S. R. (1990). *Managing employee absenteeism.* Reading, MA: Addison-Wesley.

Tait, M., Youtz-Padgett, M. Y., & Baldwin, T. T. (1989). Job and life satisfaction: A reevaluation of the strength of the relationship and gender effects as a function of the date of the study. *Journal of Applied Psychology, 74*(3), 502–507.

Theorell, T., & Floderus-Myrhed, B. (1977). Workload and risk of myocardial infarction: A prospective psychosocial analysis. *International Journal of Epidemiology, 6,* 17–21.

Thompson, C. A., Kopelman, R. E., & Schriesheim, C. A. (1992). Putting all one's eggs in the same basket: A comparison of commitment and satisfaction among self-employed men. *Journal of Applied Psychology, 77*(5), 738–743.

Tjersland, T. (1972). *Changing worker behavior.* New York: American Telephone and Telegraph Company, Manpower Laboratory.

Triandis, H. C., Kurowski, L. L., & Gelfand, M. J. (1994). Work diversity. In H. C. Triandis, M. D. Dunnette, & L. M. Hough (Eds.). *Handbook of industrial and organizational psychology* (Vol. 4, (p. 769–827). Palo Alto: Consulting Psychologists Press.

Vroom, V. H. (1964). *Work and motivation.* New York: John Wiley & Sons.

Ward, B. (1991, April). Corporations and kindergartens. *Sky,* 28–39.

Weaver, C. N. (1980). Job satisfaction in the United States in the 1970's. *Journal of Applied Psychology, 65,* 364–367.

Weiner, N. (1980). Determinants and behavioral consequences of pay satisfaction: A comparison of two models. *Personnel Psychology, 33,* 741–757.

Weiss, D. J., Dawis, R. V., England, G. W., & Lofquist, L. H. (1967). *Manual for the Minnesota Satisfaction Questionnaire.* Minnesota Studies in Vocational Rehabilitation, XXII. Minneapolis: Industrial Relations Center, Work Adjustment Project, University of Minnesota.

Weiss, J. (1971). Effects of punishing the coping response (conflict) on stress pathology in rats. *Journal of Comparative and Physiological Psychology, 77,* 14–22.

Winefield, A. H., Tiggemann, M., Winefield, H. R., & Goldney, R. D. (1991). A longitudinal study of the psychological effects of unemployment and unsatisfactory employment on young adults. *Journal of Applied Psychology, 76,* 424–431.

Wright, P. M. (1989). Test of the mediating role of goals in the incentive-performance relationship. *Journal of Applied Psychology, 74*(5), 699–705.

Total Compensation

**CREATING A TOTAL COMPENSATION
    PROGRAM**
Planning
Implementation
Management

Summary
Key Terms and Concepts
Recommended Readings
Internet Resources
Exercises
References

• •

A bank hired an I/O psychologist to help put a group of branch employees on a pay-for-performance system. The branches were small and in many ways ideal locations for group performance-based pay. Unfortunately, management did not know what kind of performance it required from each branch. One group of managers viewed branches as collectors of assets; the desired performance was anything that increased deposits, bringing cash into the bank. A second group of managers viewed branches as profit generators; the desired performance was selling a variety of profitable products. The third group viewed branches as outdated and costly to maintain with no way to be profitable. The three groups of managers were unable to agree on a purpose for the branches or a strategy. As a consequence, no pay-for-performance system was established (Lawler, 1990).

Pay is a complex issue for organizations. In fact, it is more complicated than most managers realize. Most companies strive to attract, motivate, and retain employees who fulfill organizational objectives. One way to achieve this goal is to create and implement appealing compensation and benefit packages. To be effective, organizations should use all elements of pay, including **direct pay** (cash compensation, salary, and wages) and **indirect pay** (benefits) (Schuster & Zingheim, 1992, p. xi). Most individuals consider cash, or direct pay, to be the main source of income; examples of direct pay are salaries and bonuses. Benefits, or indirect payments, are symbols of security and well-being (Gerhart & Milkovich, 1992). Some examples of the types of benefits that today's employees desire are health programs, pensions, legally required pay-

ments such as Social Security, flexible benefits (e.g., elder care and child care), quality circles, and financial and retirement counseling. We discuss these benefits later in this chapter.

The total compensation package that an organization offers determines, in part, whether employees will consider employment with a company, stay with that company, and continue to produce in a way that is beneficial to both the company and themselves. Direct pay makes up the lion's share of compensation programs. On the average, 72% of a compensation program is accounted for by direct pay, and 28% is composed of benefits (Gerhart & Milkovich, 1992). However, benefit programs are the "carrots" that attract individuals to a company. "Today, the interviewees are asking the questions . . . they are comparing and contrasting benefits packages right in front of the interviewers" (Clolery, 1994, p. 26).

Total compensation is an ongoing process; it does not stop once the employee is on board. To initially attract an employee, compensation must be competitive. To retain the employee, that competitiveness must continue and often improve. Lawler (1990) believes that organizations must create pay systems that match the goals and direction of the organization, its employees, and its clientele.

The success of compensation programs and their credibility with employees depends on the partnerships that organizations form with their employees. These include involving employees in decisions about rewards and designing individual total compensation packages (Lawler, 1986a; McCaffery, 1988; Schuster & Zingheim, 1992). The *Wall Street Journal* claims that the old social contract "between employers and em-

SCIENTIFIC PERSPECTIVE 12.1

The Impact of Gainsharing Programs

T. R. Stenhouse (1995) cited a study in which the research team had surveyed a few thousand employees from a Fortune 500 company. Two groups were studied: the experimental group, in which gainsharing was implemented, and a control group, without gainsharing. As is defined elsewhere in this chapter, gainsharing is any method by which an organization shares its financial gains from productivity and cost savings with the employees who contributed to these gains.

Data were collected and analyzed at the beginning of the program and at seven, fourteen, and twenty months into the program. The last set of data was collected three months after the gainsharing program was eliminated. Results indi-

cated that the gainsharing program stimulated long-term performance and enhanced peer communication. The author's conclusion was that

> these results bode well for managers who fear making organizational changes; . . . clearly, a properly designed and implemented gainsharing program, with fair monetary outcomes for employees, can result in [better organizational conditions than before the program was implemented]. (Stenhouse, 1995, p. 78)

Source: From "The Long and Short of Gain Sharing," by T. R. Stenhouse, 1995, *The Academy of Management Executive, 9*(1), pp. 77–78. Copyright 1995 by The Academy of Management. Reprinted with permission.

ployees, in which companies promise to ensure employment . . . lifelong job security, promotions and raises . . . is dead, dead, dead." (Lancaster, 1994, p. B1). The new social contract suggested by Lancaster should involve more than just a compensation package; organizations should "make work more satisfying" and offer employees conditions that are ethical and decent (see Scientific Perspective 12.1).

A SHORT HISTORY: THE LEGAL PERSPECTIVE

The history of compensation and benefits can be illustrated in part by examining the laws that have evolved regarding these programs. The American Compensation Association and the American Society for Personnel Administration (1988) reviewed the relevant laws that have had an impact on compensation and benefits. Some examples are:

1. The Davis-Bacon Act of 1931 required construction contractors that hold federal con-

tracts to pay the wage rates and benefits that prevail in any local geographical area.

2. The Social Security Act of 1935 placed a federal tax on payrolls to provide pensions to retired and disabled employees and to secure survivors' benefits and medical benefits to the aged.

3. The Walsh-Healey Act of 1936 was similar to the Davis-Bacon Act of 1931 but required all firms that did business with the government to pay the going rate for a geographical area. It also stipulated overtime for employees who worked over forty hours a week.

4. The Fair Labor Standards Act of 1938 addressed the issues of minimum wage, overtime, child labor, and record keeping.

5. The Equal Pay Act of 1963 prohibited pay discrimination based on sex for jobs that required the same skills, effort, and responsibility.

6. Title VII, the Civil Rights Act of 1964 (amended by the Equal Opportunity Act of 1972 and updated in 1991) prohibited employment discrimination based on sex, skin color, race, religion, or national origin.

7. The Age Discrimination in Employment Act of 1967, amended in 1975, 1978, and 1986, prohibited employment discrimination against individuals between the ages of forty and seventy because of their age.

8. The Employee Retirement Income Security Act (ERISA) of 1974 regulated the funding, administration, and investment of pension funds, and required the distribution of annual reports. The purpose of this act was to provide protection against a pension program's going bankrupt.

This list is not all encompassing, but it does illustrate the significance of creating norms of fairness and equity in compensation to fulfill the social contract:

> no other area of managing relationships with employees is more likely to create problems of achieving fairness than compensation administration—setting wage and salary rates, evaluating jobs, and providing monetary and nonmonetary benefits (Wallace & Fay, 1988, p. 4).

The rest of the chapter will summarize pay satisfaction theories and provide explanations of various reward programs. Recently, some practitioners and researchers (e.g., McCaffery, 1988; Schuster & Zingheim, 1992) have claimed that the "traditional" (beginning in the 1940s) references to direct and indirect pay strategies are no longer realistic. What is needed now is a merging of direct pay with various benefit packages. These two types of compensation should be integrated according to the specific requirements of the organization and its employees. For purposes of clarity we will use the terms *financial reward systems* and *nonfinancial reward systems* and will integrate these terms into our discussions of direct and indirect payments.

The current labor market, with its changing political and economic environments (e.g., global markets, government deficits, and increasing costs of benefit programs), directly and indirectly affects compensation programs. Our discussion includes several current compensation models with a caveat to the reader that dynamic changes are taking place. The purpose of this chapter is to provide a general overview of compensation so that readers will recognize the significance of compensation in theories of I/O psychology.

THE PSYCHOLOGICAL PERSPECTIVE

One of the most important challenges facing organizations today is how to motivate employees to work more productively while simultaneously increasing their job satisfaction. As was discussed in the chapters on motivation and job satisfaction, theories of motivation and satisfaction relate pay to employees' behavior at work. "Pay is important to people as a reward, and to organizations as . . . a tool . . . to facilitate organizational effectiveness" (Schuster & Zingheim, 1992, p. 19). Studies have shown that pay expectations are not always ranked as the highest motivator. For example, Opsahl and Dunnette (1966) ranked pay sixth out of ten in terms of importance; Lawler (1971) ranked pay third in importance. The underlying assumption of all compensation programs is that these rewards are related either directly or indirectly to performance and tenure and that it is important for organizations to combine extrinsic rewards (e.g., pay and promotion) and intrinsic rewards (e.g., sense of growth and responsibility) to achieve these goals. To better understand the relationship between compensation concepts and psychological research, let us briefly review some examples of relevant theories from Chapters 10 and 11.

Expectancy Theory

Expectancy theory is based on the ideas that individuals have expectancies about the consequences of their behavior and that a person will act in order to achieve desired outcomes. The premise behind expectancy theory is that the higher are a person's expectations of receiving a reward, whether it is an increase in salary, job security, or status, the harder that person will work to attain that reward.

Goal-Setting Theory

Locke (e.g., 1976) claimed that goals serve as intervening factors between pay and performance. The goal-setting process is most likely to enhance an employee's performance when goals are specific, challenging, and accepted by the employee. Goals are most likely to be realized if an employee receives feedback and support from a supervisor and is rewarded for achieving performance goals.

Equity Theory

Equity theory (Adams, 1965) deals both with the balance an individual perceives between the outcome achieved and the input required, and with his or her perception of how equitably that balance compares with coworkers. Outcomes include variables such as promotions, salary increases, and recognition. An individual who perceives that he or she is inequitably compensated will feel dissatisfied.

Lawler's Facet Model

Pay satisfaction and perceptual equity also serve as the basis for equity theory. The original model (Porter & Lawler, 1968) stated that satisfaction occurs when actual rewards surpass or equal rewards that are perceived as equitable. Dissatisfaction occurs when rewards that are perceived as equitable exceed the actual rewards. Lawler (1971, 1973, 1991) emphasized individual perception and hypothesized that the level of pay satisfaction is associated with the degree of discrepancy between the employee's perceived present pay level and what he or she believes that pay level should be. Employees' feelings about pay levels and poli-

cies are emphasized in these theories (Gerhart & Milkovich, 1992).

Reinforcement Theory

The behaviorist school suggests that when behavior is followed by a consequence, such as a good word from the supervisor, pay, or promotion, the probability is high that this behavior will be repeated. Thus, management can influence employees' behavior by rewarding successful behavior. However, this model does not view perception, subjective feelings of fairness, or expectancies as significant variables. Only the relationship between observed behaviors and rewards establishes the patterns of employee behavior. Punishment is not considered to be as effective as rewards. Withdrawing pay or a bonus might reduce the probability of repeating noneffective behaviors, but a more effective method would be to reinforce desired behavior and not reinforce undesired behavior. As Gerhart and Milkovich (1992, p. 518) summarize,

> applied to employee compensation, this implies that the receipt of a monetary reward following high employee performance will make high performance more likely in the future. The emphasis is on the importance of *actually experiencing* [italics added] the reward.

Two-Factor or Motivator-Hygiene Theory

Herzberg's (1966) two-factor, or motivator-hygiene, theory proposes that individuals have two sets of needs. The first set consists of hygiene factors that relate to the physical environment where the work is performed. These factors are the context within which the work occurs and include variables such as company policies, supervisors, physical work conditions, coworkers, and pay appropriate to the work done or the level of responsibility assumed. The second set of factors consists of motivators that fulfill higher needs; these are content variables such as challenging tasks, recognition, and the nature of the work performed. The theory proposes that if hygiene needs are not met, the person will become dissatisfied; however, meeting hygiene needs leads only to neutral feelings toward the job, not to satisfaction. On the other hand, when motivator needs are met, the person feels satisfied. A major difference between this theory and the other theories we have described is that the two-factor theory proposes that pay is not related to job satisfaction and that feelings of being equitably compensated lead only to an impartial feeling about the job. However, being paid equitably is a necessary condition for content factors to be able to lead to feelings of satisfaction.

Central to the first four theories is the individual's perception that the organization treats him or her fairly. These subjective feelings were found to moderate between pay and behavior (Gerhart & Milkovich, 1992). Employees' judgments and satisfaction with their pay, pay increases, and disparities of pay affect organizational outcomes (Dornstein, 1988; Huber, Seybolt, & Venemon, 1992; Koch, 1982). Employees will judge any act of the organization that is related to pay and benefits to be "just" or "unjust." These acts and judgments will help to determine employee satisfaction, loyalty to the company, and quality of work (Sheppard, Lewicki, & Minton, 1992). Concepts such as salary increases being perceived as appropriate to individual performance and the distribution of pay being considered just and unbiased are at the core of the theoretical conceptualization (with different variations) of most compensation theories (Greenberg, 1987; Lowenberg, Kingston-O'Connell, & O'Connell, 1994; Pernick, 1994; Sheppard et al., 1992; Rice, Phillips, & McFarlin, 1990).

In summary, underlying any total compensation approach is the strategy's influence on employee behavior through attitudes and perceptions, contingency with desired job behaviors, and job satisfaction.

WAGE AND SALARY ADMINISTRATION

Wage and salary administration determines the amount of payment an employee receives; it specifies the "rules and procedures by which pay program[s] [are] administered" (Wallace & Fay, 1988, p. 412). These pay programs are forms of compensation that include both monetary and nonmonetary rewards to employees. Monetary compensation includes variables such as wages, salaries, premium payments, bonus payments, and benefits. Wages are paid to employees who have not secured continuous employment and are paid on an hourly scale. Salaries are usually paid to professionals and managerial employees on a monthly or biweekly basis. **Base pay** is the hourly rate or salary paid for a job performed; it does not include premium payments, bonus payments, or benefits. **Premium payments** are extra payments beyond the base rate of pay for work completed in addition to regularly scheduled work periods. Examples of premium pay are payments for holidays, Sundays, night shifts, or weekends. **Bonus payments** are direct additional payments, usually paid as a lump sum, on top of the base salary. Bonus payments might be given to individuals or groups to reward their team effort. **Benefits** consist of "rewards other than base salary. The three major types are security and health benefits, pay for time not worked, and free or reduced cost services" (Wallace & Fay, 1988, p. 396). A key part of wage and salary administration is the analysis of the jobs in the organization in terms of their content and value. This process is called *job analysis*. It includes developing job descriptions and evaluating jobs in terms of their worth.

Job Analysis

Most organizations pay on the basis of the type of job for which people are hired. The emphasis is on the job, not the person, and the process is based on job evaluation and salary surveys. Job evaluation is a formal process that provides a way of maintaining internal equity within the company by determining the value of individual jobs. It requires a careful job analysis. Equally important are **salary surveys** which provide a means of ensuring external equity by comparing such measures as base salary, bonuses, and company policy with those of comparable organizations. Job analysis was described in Chapter 4; job evaluation and salary surveys will be discussed in this chapter.

Job Description

The first step in a job evaluation is to develop job descriptions that summarize the important aspects of a job, including the duties, responsibilities, supervisory relationships, and job requirements. Job descriptions are based on a job analysis. As defined in Chapter 4, **job analysis** is a systematic study of the tasks included in a specific job; the knowledge, skills, and abilities that are required to perform a job; time factors; situational factors, such as the use of technology; and interpersonal and group interactions. Job analysis provides the information necessary to create job evaluations and job descriptions, which ultimately determine the rate of pay for a particular job.

As described in Chapter 4, **job descriptions** are used for recruitment, selection, placement, orientation, training and development, performance appraisals, promotions and transfers, career planning, labor relations, and job evaluations. Because of these numerous potential applications, it is critical that the job description reflect an accurate picture of the job under review (Smith, Benson, & Hornsby, 1990).

Job Evaluation

Job analysis also establishes the elements for **job evaluation**, which is the process of determining the relative position of one job to all other jobs within a company. Job evaluations seek to "es-

tablish fair competitive values for individual occupations" (Yoder & Staudohar, 1982, p. 350) and serve as the formal process by which pay rates and pay grades are determined for various jobs. They provide administrative procedures for establishing pay structures, rating each job within the structure, and assigning distinct pay rates to different jobs by comparing them in terms of various factors such as skills required, effort, responsibility, and working conditions. Job evaluation identifies the elements described in the job analysis and job description that are compensable, establishes internal relationships among jobs, and compares these rates to those in the external market (Schuster & Zingheim, 1992). Internal equity and fair compensation are maintained when jobs with the same values across all sections of the organization receive the same uniform base rate pay. Job evaluation is believed to influence behavior by indicating to employees what is considered important and by encouraging them to apply these behaviors to achieve a goal, such as promotion (Gerhart & Milkovich, 1992).

Organizations must also establish external equity, that is, make base rates comparable to what other organizations pay for the same jobs, to attract and retain employees. Both factors determine the "going rate" for a job by combining the demands of specific jobs, the availability of employees for these jobs in the marketplace, and the internal comparison of skills and other factors within the company.

Issues of equity and fairness have recently been associated with the concept of comparable worth. As stated by the 1963 Equal Pay Act (see the previous list of related laws), men and women should have the same pay when they perform jobs that are the same or similar in skills, effort, and responsibility.

However, as Table 12.1 on page 408 indicates, despite the Equal Pay Act and acceptance of the concept of equal pay for equal work, many women continue to be compensated at lower rates than their male counterparts. Surveys such

TABLE 12.1   Gender disparity in compensation levels. In 155 corporate law departments, compensation of women falls short of that of men.

Title	Median Male Compensation	Median Female Compensation	Percent of Gap
General counsel	$262,000	$210,750	19.6
Chief assistant	174,000	152,000	12.6
General counsel of subsidiary	169,800	156,650	7.7
Section head	155,000	134,931	13.0
Senior counsel	121,950	113,600	6.9
Expert attorney	111,687	107,800	3.5
Attorney	84,000	79,200	5.7
Junior attorney	64,675	60,000	7.2

Source: From "Gender Gap," *The Wall Street Journal,* Dec. 9, 1994, p. B6. Copyright 1994 by Dow Jones & Company. Reprinted with permission of The Wall Street Journal. All Rights Reserved Worldwide. Data from Price-Waterhouse 1994 Law Department Spending Survey.

as the one presented in Table 12.1 support the argument that jobs that are of comparable worth should receive the same level of pay. That is, jobs that are assumed to have the same value, which is comparable across different jobs (such as nursing versus parking meter maintenance) should be paid at the same rate (Wallace & Fay, 1988).

Four widely used methods of job evaluation are ranking, classification, factor comparison, and point factor. Table 12.2 provides a summary of these approaches.

Job Ranking

One method of job evaluation is **job ranking.** The most popular form of job ranking requires a committee appointed by management to rank jobs from lowest to highest according to the overall value of the job. The value of each job is determined by its worth to the organization. This type of job evaluation is the simplest and requires the least amount of administrative labor.

To get around the difficulties of having no standard of comparison, some organizations use the **paired comparison system.** In this system, evaluators compare two jobs and determine which is the more valuable. A third job is then compared to the first choice, and each job is then compared to every other job in all possible pairs. The value of each job is the number or

TABLE 12.2   Summary approaches to job evaluations.

	Whole Job	Specific Job Factors
Job versus job	Ranking method	Factor comparison method
Job versus standard	Classification method	Point method

Source: From *How to Administer Wage-Salary Programs and Perform Job Evaluations,* by R. W. Beatty, N. F. Crandall, C. H. Fay, R. Mathis, G. T. Milkovich, and M. J. Wallace, Jr., New Brunswick, NJ: Copyright © 1979 by the authors. Reprinted by permission.

preference it receives. Finally, the jobs are ranked according to these values.

Several advantages of the ranking system are its simplicity, speed, and low cost. Disadvantages include inconsistencies due to the evaluators' subjective judgments, difficulty in justifying the results because there is no record of the judgments, and the fact that while the ranking system indicates that one job is more difficult than another, it does not determine the area or level of difficulty.

Classification Method

The **classification method** has also been called the rating or grading system because each job is compared to a predetermined standard or "yardstick." The yardstick has categories for defining job difficulty and value. The salary administrator first decides how many value categories a job should have, then defines each category with factors basic to the job. For janitorial jobs, category I might involve no pretraining, only orientation training, direct supervisory control, and the ability to work night shifts. Category II might involve simple training in the use of basic tools such as a floor-waxing machine, direct supervisory control, and night shifts. The next step is to compare each job against this descriptive yardstick and place the job in the slot that most accurately describes its characteristics and level of difficulty (Wallace & Fay, 1988; Sibson, 1981). The number of categories can range from five to over fifty. This method is often used by the government to evaluate civil service jobs.

Among disadvantages of the classification method are a lack of consideration for geographical location (such as the higher cost of living in New York than in Arkansas) and the market demands for particular jobs.

The next two job evaluation systems, factor comparison and point factor, weigh individual jobs by assigning point values to different job elements. In factor comparison a job is measured against other jobs in a company; the point factor method measures a job against a previously determined scale.

Factor Comparison

As Wallace and Fay state (1988), the **factor comparison method** compares a job with other jobs on the basis of the degree to which the rated job possesses particular factors. In other words, this method compares jobs on specific aspects of the job rather than on the job as a whole. The five factors that are most commonly used in this process are mental requirements, physical requirements, skills requirements, job responsibilities, and working conditions (Wallace & Fay, 1988).

Key jobs are selected from the entire set of jobs to be evaluated; usually, ten or fifteen are sufficient. A correct selection of the key jobs is important because the whole evaluation process is based on these key jobs. Key jobs are ranked in terms of each of the factors that are found to be common to all the jobs. The market pay rate is then allocated to each key job and divided across the factors. For example, for the job of janitor, 10% of the pay would be associated with mental requirements, 55% with physical requirements, 5% with responsibilities, and 30% with working conditions. When all the key jobs have been analyzed and each element has been weighted, the averages of these weight percentages are computed. All jobs are then compared to the key jobs on each element, weights are computed, and the total point value for each job is compiled.

A disadvantage of this method is that it is complicated and difficult to explain to employees. An advantage is that when it is done correctly, it is more reliable than most methods. It also takes into account both the internal and external equities of the jobs under review (Wallace & Fay, 1988).

Point Factor System

The **point factor system** is similar to the classification method, except that the job is evaluated on a separate scale for each factor. A separate standard, or yardstick, is constructed for the different degrees of each factor, and jobs are rated against each yardstick. Burgess

(1984, p. 122) suggests four steps to develop a point factor plan:

1. Choose suitable job factors.
2. Define each factor and each degree.
3. Assign point values to each degree of each factor.
4. Evaluate each job in terms of the assigned point values.

The factors that are selected depend on the types of jobs and the kind of organization. An illustration is a set of factors such as education, experience, mental demands, and responsibility. The number of points for all factors is determined and allocated to each factor. The points are then divided and assigned to each level of each factor. The total number of points for each job is the sum of its factor points.

The disadvantages of the point factor system include the difficulty of selecting relevant compensable factors, defining degrees for each factor, and establishing appropriate point values. The number of compensable factors is also difficult to establish. Some of the most widely used compensable factors are education and/or experience required, visual and/or mental demands, supervisory responsibility, working conditions, analytical ability, and decision making. The number of compensable factors varies with each organization.

The advantages of the point factor system are that it is easily adaptable to many industries and, if properly administered, can be legally defended.

Automated Job Evaluation Plans

Advanced technology has introduced automation to the process of job evaluation. Many consulting firms offer the service of developing an **automated job evaluation plan,** which is usually a variation of the point factor method. The consulting firm works with company representatives to determine the compensable factors and the weights that should be given to each factor. A package then is put together for the company that includes all of the technology necessary to operate the program.

Considerable work is involved in installing a new automated job evaluation plan. The first step is to ensure that all employees understand the proposed plan. For example, Company K decided to install a new automated job evaluation plan. The plans that Company K had previously used involved one plan for nonexempt employees and another for exempt employees. Both plans were variations of the point factor plan. The new automated plan combined both plans, so all employees were evaluated under the point factor method. A questionnaire, including questions about the duties performed on the job and relevant employee data, was sent to all employees. Group meetings were held, the new evaluation plan was explained to all employees, and questions were addressed. The process resulted in the employees' perceptions that they had input into and control over decisions about their salary.

The most difficult part of automating a job evaluation plan is in determining the compensable factors and assigning weights to those factors. The compensable factors that Company K used were experience, knowledge and skill, analytical ability, independent judgment, consequence of error, internal and external contacts, use of confidential data, freedom of action, job demands, and work environment. The range of compensable factors included the lowest and highest jobs within Company K.

Although automation provides a timely totaling of scores and lends more credibility to the decision-making process, it does not eliminate the need for job evaluation committees.

Surveys

Surveys supplement the job evaluation process by providing a basis for external equity. Information received from surveys includes base salary data, bonus amounts, hiring rates, and company policy data. There are many surveys on the market that can assist with the process of compensation planning and job evaluation. For example, the surveys conducted by the U.S. Bureau of Labor Statistics (BLS) are relatively inexpensive and include a large number of jobs and companies. Widely used federal government surveys are the Area Wage Survey and the Professional, Technical, Administrative and Clerical survey. The usual procedure for conducting a survey is for a representative from the company conducting the survey to visit individual companies and work with the wage and salary administrator to obtain salary data for jobs that have the same duties and responsibilities as those in the survey.

Surveys are also conducted by consulting firm specialists who focus on specific professions, such as accountants, scientists, or lawyers. They can also be carried out by wage and salary departments, often in response to problems with hiring rates, high turnover, or requests to find out whether certain jobs are competitively paid. Surveys can be conducted via questionnaires, telephone, or visits and reviews by specialists.

....

DIRECT PAY

Schuster and Zingheim (1992, p. 84) claim that base pay "is used to reflect the relative importance of jobs, to compete economically for talent in the external marketplace, and to acknowledge differences in performance among people." In direct pay situations, there are two foundations for determining the base pay: paying for the individual and paying for the job (Lawler, 1990; Schuster & Zingheim, 1992).

Payments that are based on the employee and his or her job performance are either skill-based, based on piece rate, or merit-based.

Skill-Based

The **skill-based method** is also referred to as "pay for knowledge." An individual's pay is determined by the level of the skills or tasks mastered, regardless of whether the skills are actually used on a specific job. Individuals are paid for learning skills that are valuable to the organization and may lead to higher-level jobs. The belief is that skill-based pay motivates employees to acquire a wider range of skills for different jobs in the organization. The skill-based approach has been in favor in recent years because (a) it offers more flexibility and results in less turnover and absenteeism and (b) employees take more ownership of their work. In addition, it allows employees to be self-managing and innovative because they feel they can exercise some control over their pay (Lawler, 1990). Because employees earn pay increases as they acquire new skills, the skill-based method of payment appears to produce higher levels of satisfaction and motivation. Often, professional organizations (such as universities, law offices, and research and development labs) pay the person, not the job, through implementing a skill-based method of payment (Lawler, 1981). For an example of a successful skill-based pay program, see Practice Perspective 12.1 on page 412 which reports the experience of Tellabs.

In some countries (e.g., Israel), pay programs that emphasize the person take into account variables such as age, number of dependents, seniority, and years of experience (Lawler, 1990).

Many programs focus not on skills or on individual needs, but on the employee's performance. Two examples of these types of programs are piece rate and merit systems.

Piece Rate

Piece rate payments are based directly on an employee's output; payment is made for each piece, or any other unit, of work produced. For example, in a machining company, Joe Johnson produces ten couplings a day. The piece rate for couplings is $10.00 per coupling; therefore Joe makes $100.00 a day. Sue New produces six couplings a day; consequently, Sue makes only $60.00 a day. This method of payment is directly tied to employees' production rates and is based on the assumption that individuals should be given goals and be rewarded for their performance. One company that is famous for its piece rate pay system is Lincoln Electric

PRACTICE PERSPECTIVE 12.1

Tellabs Pays for Knowledge

Tellabs is a rapidly growing company of 1800 employees that designs, manufactures, and services equipment for voice and data transmission for international telephone companies.

In 1986 the company converted to an all-salaried work force and formed cells of work teams. Job titles and restrictive job descriptions were eliminated. All employees are now called *associates*. The associates are taught joint problem solving and new job skills and receive pay increases for improved performance and versatility. The total quality effort and redesign of the environment increased product quality while reducing work in progress (work that has been started but is currently on hold waiting for materials or decisions) by 95%, lot sizes by 65%,

engineering design revision time by 90 %, space requirements by 65%, labor costs by 54%, and lead time from six weeks to two days.

Tellabs uses a pay-for-knowledge plan and merit pay. The rate for each employee is keyed to the number of tasks mastered. More than 90% of employees have learned additional skills. Performance is evaluated semiannually, pay levels being in the rate range based on merit. The company also has a modified gainsharing plan. Empowerment and career enhancements are nonmonetary reward systems.

Source: Myers, M. S. (1991), *Every employee a manager* (3rd ed., pp. 36–38). Adapted as submitted. Copyright 1991 by Pfeiffer, an imprint of Jossey-Bass Inc., Publishers.

(see Practice Perspective 12.2). Schuster & Zingheim (1992) argue that the piece rate method encourages behaviors that contradict cooperation and involvement, entails high administrative costs, and creates supervisors who "function as record keepers rather than as facilitators, coaches, and trainers" (p. 170).

The Merit System

In the **merit system** of payment, the most common method, salary increases are based on performance, seniority, or any other individual equity basis (Wallace & Fay, 1988). The merit pay system is based on appraising individual per-

PRACTICE PERSPECTIVE 12.2

Lincoln Electric Piece Rate Pay Plan

Famed for productivity 250% above its industry norms, Lincoln Electric pays its employees well. (In 1991 the average wage was over $40,000 a year.) Lincoln is a manufacturer of welding equipment, electric motors, and related equipment.

Each production employee is evaluated on piecework performance and given performance ratings by his or her supervisor. Bonuses have averaged 70% of base pay for the last ten years. In

the past decade the company has been shifting its culture from the highly disciplined one of the past to a more participative one. Employees own over 40% of the stock and have a strong influence in the way the company is run.

Source: Myers, M. S. (1991), *Every employee a manager* (3rd ed., pp. 37–38). Adapted as submitted. Copyright 1991 by Pfeiffer, an imprint of Jossey-Bass Inc., Publishers.

Level of Performance Measurement

Effect on Base Compensation	Individual	Group
Added in	Merit pay	
Not added in	Merit bonus Piece rate Commission	Gain sharing Profit sharing Ownership

FIGURE 12.1 Level of performance measurement.

Source: Modified and reproduced by special permission of the Publisher, Consulting Psychologists Press, Inc., Palo Alto, CA 94303 from Employee compensation: research and practice by B. Gerhart and G. T. Milkovich (1992). In *Handbook of Industrial and Organizational Psychology* (Volume 3, p. 513) by Marvin D. Dunnette and Leaetta M. Hough. Copyright 1992 by Consulting Psychologists Press, Inc. All rights reserved. Further reproduction is prohibited without the Publisher's written consent.

formance and effort. By establishing, or attempting to establish, a clear performance–reward relationship, this method is assumed to increase motivation and retain successful employees (Lawler, 1989). The Gerhart and Milkovich grid (see Figure 12.1) is probably the best way to differentiate merit from piece rate and other related programs.

Merit pay is added into the base pay, whereas piece rate and bonuses are not. The distribution of raises is centered around a mean raise amount, and the increases are carried into future calculations of pay. These pay approaches are part of individual-based performance, in contrast to group-based performance reward strategies (Burgess, 1984; Gerhart & Milkovich, 1992). Pay increases based on individual performance follow expectancy theory, which predicts that pay will influence effort and accomplishments if the individual believes that these actions lead to rewards such as higher pay (Wallace & Fay, 1988).

A merit system is based on a formal program of pay-for-performance that is directly tied to performance appraisal. Here is a simplified example of performance indicators. For poor, fair, good, and outstanding performances, salary increase percentages might be as follows:

Performance Indicator	*Merit Increase*
Poor	0%
Fair	3%
Good	5%
Outstanding	7%

For example, Freddie Fair is an employee performing at the "fair" level. If Freddie Fair's current salary is \$5.00 an hour, then he would receive a pay increase based on 3% of \$5.00, or \$ 0.15. Freddie's new salary would be \$5.15 an hour. Most merit increase guidelines are more involved than this example, but the basic premise is the same. The most important feature of the merit method of payment is that it is based on actual job performance.

For pay to be an effective motivator, employees must perceive a relationship between performance and pay. This relationship depends on the perceived fairness, objectivity, and effectiveness of the performance appraisal system (see Chapter 6). Lawler (1990, p. 72) claims that since most organizations rely on subjective performance appraisal systems, "in the eyes of many employees merit pay is a fiction . . . [and] . . . rather than contributing to motivation and a positive culture, it can nourish a distrust of . . . the organizations." The result is a decrease in satisfaction and motivation. Also, employees who earn the larger merit raises take away from the merit raises of other employees by reducing the pool of funds available for distribution. This can create competition, which can hurt morale and productivity. According to Milkovich, Wigdor, Broderick, and Manor (1991), recent studies examining the relationships between merit pay and measures of individual job satisfaction, motivation and pay satisfaction, and performance ratings have produced mixed results.

Gainsharing

Gainsharing is similar to profit sharing in that a bonus pool of money is created when a company's productivity exceeds a forecasted target. Conversely, if productivity falls short of the target, no bonus is created. It is an "award that shares group improvements in productivity, cost savings, and quality with each employee in the group" (Schuster & Zingheim, 1992, p. 166). As Lawler (1990, p. 110) explains, "in a typical gainsharing plan, financial gains in the organization's performance are shared on a formula basis with all the employees in a single location or plant." A base period is established that is used for comparison to determine whether a gain has occurred. This gain is the basis for the gainsharing. To be fair, only costs that can be controlled are included in computing the gain. Under most gainsharing plans, employees receive half of the bonus pool, and the company retains the rest. The workers' portion of the bonus pool is generally paid out monthly or quarterly in a lump sum, all employees receiving an equal amount or an amount using the same percentage of their base pay. Another feature of most gainsharing programs is the employee suggestion program. Savings and productivity gains that come from employee suggestions get credited in some systematic way to the bonus pool. The most common forms of gainsharing plans are the Scanlon Plan (see Historical Perspective 12.1), Improshare, and the Rucker Plan. All three plans have two features: a formal approach to measuring productivity and a participative management style.

In the 1970s a number of large companies installed gainsharing. Companies such as General Electric, Motorola, TRW, Dana, 3M, Firestone, Rockwell, Amoco, and Mead implemented gainsharing in their plants. The process has also moved outside of manufacturing. Gainsharing plans have been used by Holiday Inns, Taco Bell, Xerox, and Lincoln National Life Insurance. Lawler (1990, p. 112) believes that the key reason for these increases is that "gainsharing plans are more than just incentive plans; they are an organizational development technology . . . based on a participative approach to management and often used as a way to install or reinforce other participatory management practices."

Gainsharing plans have had a number of positive results in organizations. The suggestions program improves work methods and procedures. Higher pay and greater participation make it easier to attract good employees and to retain existing ones. High motivation and involvement in work methods improve quality and the rate of output. Some disadvantages of gainsharing plans include the following: Salary and training costs increase. More support personnel are needed to administer the plan. Suggestions may create unmet expectations for the organization and may meet with resistance from support staff. Considerable time is spent in meetings, and decisions may be slow.

Bonus Payments

A **bonus** is a one-time, lump-sum payment made in addition to an individual's base salary. The purpose of a bonus is to provide an incentive to work hard; therefore, bonus plans are also referred to as incentive plans. Bonus plans can be tied to individual, group, or organizational performance. Examples of group and organization-wide bonuses include gainsharing and profit sharing, respectively. Profit-sharing bonuses are based on the profits of the organization and its ability to pay. Gainsharing is based on the costs of production and productivity of a group. Individual, merit-based bonuses are directly related to employee performance, are awarded once a year, and reflect current performance and individual success. "If someone performs poorly, it will show up immediately in [his or her] pay. Thus, a person under a bonus plan cannot coast for a year and still be highly paid, as [he or she] can be under the typical salary increase plan" (Lawler, 1994, p. 166). Evidence suggests that individual bonuses are better tied to motivation and retention than are group performance bonus programs (Gerhart & Milkovich, 1992; Lawler, 1990).

The Scanlon Plan

The Scanlon Plan is the best-known gainsharing plan. It was developed in the 1940s and 1950s by Joe Scanlon, a former steelworker and union leader who pioneered the concept of employee involvement working with Dr. Douglas McGregor at the Massachusetts Institute of Technology. The Scanlon Plan focuses on labor costs relative to productivity. Bonuses are awarded to employees on the basis of a measure of plant or company performance. Scanlon felt strongly that employee interest and contributions could best be stimulated by giving the employees a maximum amount of information about company problems and successes, then soliciting their suggestions about how to solve the problem or get the job done. In the Scanlon Plan, management and employees share common goals. Scanlon proposed that organizations use a suggestion system much like today's quality circles. Every suggestion is reviewed and responded to. Some organizations have added small incentives or bonuses for suggestions that are adopted and have significant economic impact. Lawler (1986b, pp. 158–159) notes,

> The genius of the Scanlon Plan, and of Joe Scanlon, is the recognition that a commitment to participation and joint problem solving is not enough. Effective use of participatory management requires a congruence between the pay system of the organization and its other features. Joe Scanlon was one of the first to articulate the influence of the fit between pay systems and management philosophy on an organization.

Reviews and summaries by Bullock and Lawler (1984), Lawler (1990), and Lawler and Jenkins (1992) of studies on the Scanlon Plan indicated that 70–75% of its applications were considered successful. Those reviews listed the following likely outcomes when a Scanlon Plan is successfully implemented (Bullock & Lawler, 1984, p. 160; Lawler, 1990, pp. 115–116):

1. Coordination, teamwork, and sharing of knowledge at lower levels are enhanced.
2. Social needs are recognized through participation and mutually reinforcing group behavior.
3. Attention is focused on cost savings, not just quantity of production.
4. Acceptance of change due to technology, market, and new methods is greater because higher efficiency leads to bonuses.
5. Attitudinal change occurs among workers, who demand more efficient management and better planning.
6. Workers try to reduce overtime and to work smarter, not harder or faster.
7. Workers produce ideas as well as effort.
8. More flexible administration of union–management relations occurs.
9. If present, the union is strengthened because it is responsible for a better work situation and higher pay.

The type of bonus plan that is used depends on the type of business and the company philosophy. For example, in many companies the management group often receives high, direct bonus payouts because of traditional beliefs that the managers are responsible for the increases in profitability. A few companies have taken a different approach (see Practice Perspective 12.3 on page 416). They distribute bonuses widely, under the belief that every employee plays a role in the company's successes. It is still rare, however, that large bonuses are paid to all employees. A company's philosophy is often unwritten, though it is a major factor in devising the bonus plan. The formal written part of most bonus plans includes the percent of bonus paid and timing of payment. Employees who are not in sales, middle management, or executive jobs are usually given bonuses that are linked to individual contributions. A research scientist who discovered a new use for one of the company's products would thereby contribute to his or her company's overall success. This individual is not a salesperson, manager, or executive, but his or her single contribution to the company warrants an individual bonus. A bonus also might be awarded for a suggestion about company policy that ultimately saves the organization time or money. This is usually referred to as a suggestion award.

Profit Sharing

Profit sharing plans enable employers to contribute a share of the company's profits to its employees. The introduction of profit sharing in the United States can be traced back to 1794. It is one of the more prominent group financial incentive plans in use today (McCaffery, 1988). According to Lawler (1990), at least one third of U.S. organizations have some form of profit sharing.

There are various types of profit-sharing plans. One is a cash type, in which quarterly, semian-

nual, or annual payments are made to employees. The second type is the popular deferment plan, in which employers distribute the profit-sharing bonus into a retirement fund. A third type of profit sharing involves a combination of the first two, in which there is a partial payout with a deferment.

Profit sharing differs from gainsharing in that it does not necessarily have a participative management component and it does not use formulas that measure only increases in productivity or profiles against a historical base. Though most profit-sharing plans serve as a supplement to a pension plan, others use profit sharing as a primary fund for retirement income (Crehan, 1984). The amount of the bonus distributed to each employee depends on factors such as the percentage of profit the company makes, the employee's total annual income, and, infrequently, the individual's performance. Because most profit-sharing programs are not related to individual performance, they "are much less ef-

PRACTICE PERSPECTIVE 12.4

Wells Fargo Bank's Profit-Sharing Program

The Wells Fargo Bank has made profit-sharing payments irregularly, according to management discretion. In 1989, management decided that the bank had had a good year. Each employee was given a check for $500 and a coupon for $35 to be awarded to the colleague who had been most helpful to him or her.

There is little chance that this kind of program affects motivation because there is little chance that employees can influence whether or not a bonus is paid. It is a clear case of rewards that have no impact on motivation.

Source: Lawler, E. E., III. (1990). *Strategic pay* (p. 124). San Francisco, CA: Jossey-Bass.

fective than gainsharing plans in influencing motivation and in producing the kind of social and cultural outcomes that are associated with gainsharing" (Lawler, 1990, p. 124).

Several positive outcomes can be achieved through profit sharing. These include the symbolic and communicative value of paying employees on the basis of performance, making the concept of profits concrete for employees, and the ability to adjust the organization's labor costs according to its ability to pay them. (When profits go up, labor costs go up, and vice versa.) Key issues in profit sharing are how much of an individual's pay should be at risk, how the profits should be shared, and whether the plan will have any impact on employees' motivation and behavior. For an example of a plan with little motivational value, see Practice Perspective 12.4.

INDIRECT PAYMENTS AND BENEFITS

Indirect pay includes benefits such as retirement benefits, health and welfare benefits (e.g., health insurance, life insurance, disability insurance, pension), pay for time not worked (e.g., vacation, sick leave), and legally required payments (e.g., Social Security). Benefits amount to about 28% of total compensation. The importance of benefits is that employees perceive them as representative of security and well-being, and employers use them to attract and retain employees (Gerhart & Milkovich, 1992; Schuster & Zing-

heim, 1992). In general, "satisfaction with benefits increases with improved coverage and decreases with greater costs to employees" (Gerhart & Milkovich, 1992, p. 539). The authors concluded that the current increases in payments made by employees for their benefit programs, coupled with the reductions in coverage received, will decrease satisfaction with pay. However, their evidence also indicated that benefits such as pension and health care programs are associated with reduced voluntary turnover.

Legally Required Payments

Employers are legally required to provide three types of benefits to their employees: Social Security, unemployment compensation, and workers' compensation. The purpose of these legally mandated benefits is to provide each employee with some degree of financial protection on retirement, termination, or injury.

Social Security

The Social Security Act was passed in 1935 and became effective in 1937. The primary goal of **Social Security** is to assist the elderly by guaranteeing them a minimum standard of living. It provides a major source of income for many retired employees.

Social Security is financed through matched contributions of employers and employees. Originally, employees became eligible for full benefits at age sixty-five. Because of the program's financial problems, the Social Security law was changed in 1983. Revisions include (a) delaying the time period of eligibility by two years for individuals born after 1938, (b) increasing the contributions of employers and employees, and (c) requiring that employees contribute to the plan for a specified number of quarters. To be eligible for Social Security benefits, individuals born before 1929 are required to work twenty-six quarters, or six and a half years, and individuals born after 1929 are required to work forty quarters, or ten years (DeCenzo & Holoviak, 1990).

McCaffery (1988) noted that when the Social Security program was first implemented, it was viewed mainly as a retirement income system that covered about 60% of all working people. Currently, in addition to retirement payments, Social Security provides survivor's insurance and disability insurance. **Survivor's insurance** benefits are extended to survivors of a deceased employee in the form of annuities. The amount that is paid is based on a number of factors, such as the age of the survivor and the number of dependents (DeCenzo & Holoviak, 1990).

Disability insurance offers protection to employees who become too disabled to work. This benefit is divided into two categories: short-term disability insurance and long-term disability insurance. **Short-term disability insurance** is designed to replace income lost in the event of a nonoccupational accident or sickness and is usually provided for a period of six months or less. **Long-term disability insurance** provides replacement income for an employee who still cannot return to work when the short-term coverage has ended. The program is designed as a federal insurance program. Because of the federal deficit and budget problems, "the social security system is in a state of disarray," and it is difficult to predict to what extent the program will remain solvent (Wallace & Fay, 1988, p. 276).

Unemployment Compensation

The Social Security Act of 1935 provided the foundation for unemployment compensation in-

surance. The purpose behind the development of **unemployment compensation** was to protect individuals in the event of job loss due to circumstances beyond their control, such as plant closings or layoffs. It allows individuals to receive assistance while they search for work. Though funding for unemployment compensation is obtained from a combination of federal and state tax imposed on the taxable wage base of the employer, the states retain the power to design and administer their own unemployment compensation programs (DeCenzo & Holoviak, 1990). Unemployment compensation is generally provided for up to twenty-six weeks, but it might be extended in response to unusual circumstances. An individual must meet a few requirements to be eligible for unemployment compensation, but two factors that are considered in determining the amount a worker receives are the individual's previous wage rate and length of employment.

Workers' Compensation

Workers' compensation programs are controlled at the state level and are funded by the employer. McCaffery (1988) indicated that the first workers' compensation programs were enacted in 1911 to compensate employees or their families for permanent or total occupational disability or death. Since 1948, every state has established some type of workers' compensation program. Employee benefits are based on fixed schedules and can be provided through monetary payments, the payment of medical expenses, or a combination of both (DeCenzo & Holoviak, 1990). Since employers are the sole contributors to workers' compensation programs, they can motivate companies to maintain a safe working environment.

Supplemental Income

Many companies provide workers with one or more types of **supplemental compensation**. Although employees receive these forms of financial compensation as a supplement to their regular pay, they also serve as group incentive plans designed to increase employee motivation and worker productivity (Sibson, 1981). The various forms of supplemental compensation provided by employers can be divided into two major categories: defined benefit plans and defined contribution plans. Both of these programs are variants of pension plans.

Defined Benefit Plans

Defined benefit plans are designed to "provide participants with a specified, definite benefit at retirement" (Rosenbloom & Hallman, 1991). Plans vary, but in the traditional pension plan, the employer's contribution typically is based on a number of factors, such as an employee's current age, years of service, expected life span, and expected retirement date. Benefit plans usually use a formula that takes into account length of service and earnings. Employers who use defined benefit plans claim that these programs recognize "loyalty" to the organization by enabling employees to plan for specific levels of retirement income while giving the employer the opportunity to calculate costs and funding (Schuster & Zingheim, 1992). These programs originally were designed to maintain standards of living after retirement by supplementing Social Security retirement benefits. Therefore these benefits are paid out when an employee retires or, in some cases, when an employee quits, is discharged, or dies (Sibson, 1981). In 1974 the Employee Retirement Income Security Act (ERISA) was passed to regulate pension plans. ERISA requires employers who offer pension plans to adhere to certain rules in return for favorable tax benefits (Wallace & Fay, 1988).

Defined Contribution Plans

Defined contribution plans have great appeal to both employers and employees, because they can be implemented in a variety of forms. These plans generally cost less for employers than defined benefit plans and are easier to implement and administer. Additionally, employees enjoy the flexibility defined contribution plans offer with respect to plan contributions, investment options, loan provisions, and disbursement options (McCaffery, 1989; Schuster & Zingheim, 1992). Some of the most common contribution plans are employee stock ownership plans, stock purchase plans, stock option plans, profit sharing, thrift or savings plans, and gainsharing.

Under **employee stock ownership plans,** money is borrowed from a financial institution, and company stock is used as collateral for the loan. As the loan is repaid, the security that is used for the loan is placed into an employee stock ownership trust and is distributed to the employee on retirement or separation from the company at no cost to the employee.

Stock purchase plans allow employees to buy shares of company stock, with the company contributing a specified amount for each unit of an employee's contribution. The stock might be offered at a fixed price that is usually below the market price and is paid for in full by the employee. Benefits are then distributed in terms of company stock.

Stock option plans contain contracts that restrict the period during which an employee may exercise stock options. In other words, the employee can purchase only a specified number of shares of stock, at a set price, during a specific period of time. When exercising this option, an employee can either keep the stocks or sell them for cash on the open market.

After a probationary period of (usually) one year an employee might choose to join a **thrift plan.** Under this plan the employee contributes a specified percentage of his or her pay, and that amount is then matched in some proportion by the employer. The employee and employer contributions are invested, and fund balances are paid to employees when they separate from the company.

In addition to salary and wages, employees receive compensation in the form of benefits. Generally, benefits comprise the part of an employee's compensation that is not covered under direct pay, bonuses, or long-term income. Since total compensation is the sum of direct pay and benefits, these two elements are viewed as complementary. For this reason, compensation planners often view employee benefits as an essential part of the total compensation package. In fact, both pay and benefit structures have the same goals: to attract, motivate, and retain employees. Because of the impact that benefits have on employees, it is important for an employer to offer a benefit package that employees view as competitive and fair. Though it is unlikely that one single benefit package can meet the needs of all employees, companies should try to consider overall employee preferences when designing a benefit package.

Initially, employee benefits were regarded as minor additions to wages, but by the early 1980s, benefits were perceived as a major element of total compensation (McCaffery, 1988). With the rapid expansion of benefits and the substantial increase in their value, benefits have become very popular. Wallace and Fay (1988, pp. 266–267) identified a number of reasons for their popularity:

1. During World War II, wage controls made it virtually impossible to use salaries as an instrument to attract, motivate, and retain employees.
2. It is cost-effective for a company to provide benefits because group coverage is cheaper than individual coverage.
3. Inflation reduces the value of the dollar, making benefits more desirable than wages.
4. Unions have found benefits to be an effective and profitable bargaining tool.
5. Providing benefits to employees gives the appearance that employers feel a sense of responsibility for their employees.
6. Some benefits have become governed by the federal or state government or both.

The broad range of employee benefits that are currently offered have different values to different people. Though benefit values can change depending on the events that occur in a person's lifetime, it seems that some benefits never lose their appeal. For example, McCaffery (1988) indicated that when individuals in an employee benefits course were asked to list employee benefits in order of importance, most individuals listed health or medical coverage first. Generally, health insurance is viewed as a core benefit; a total benefit package might also include dental care, vision care, or a prescription drug plan, but these are not viewed as core benefits and are usually offered separately.

The insurance benefits that are discussed in this chapter are health insurance, dental insurance, vision care, prescription drug plans, and life insurance. We will also review newly emerging flexible benefit plans.

Health Insurance

Employees generally regard medical expense benefits (for the employees and their families) as essential coverage to be provided by employers (Rosenbloom & Hallman, 1991). Studies (e.g., Dreher, Ash, & Bretz, 1988) suggest that satisfaction with benefits increases with improved coverage and decreases with higher employee costs. Recently, controversy has arisen over the issue of whether the United States should have a universal social health insurance system that would provide a basic level of medical care for all of its citizens. While this debate continues, employers still maintain the primary responsibility of providing health care protection to employees and their dependents.

The primary purpose of health insurance is to protect employees and their immediate family members from the high costs associated with a major illness. However, both the employee and employer can profit from this benefit. For example, an employee who is troubled by health problems and by the accompanying anxiety about having to pay the medical bills might not perform well on the job. Providing health insurance, then, may induce higher productivity, since the employee would be secure in the fact that health care was readily available and affordable. It might also encourage employees to take better care of themselves with corresponding reductions in costs associated with health-related problems such as sick time.

PRACTICE PERSPECTIVE 12.5

Health Insurance Premiums

Health insurance premiums rose 4.8% in 1994, the lowest increase in eight years. Despite a 40% drop in the rate of increase from 1992 to 1993, workers and companies are pinched because the rise outpaces both inflation (2.3%) and workers' earnings growth (2.5%), according to a survey of 1037 employers by KPMG Peat Marwick. Because of the debate over health care costs, and six years of profits to insurers, only single-digit premium increases are likely in coming years

Source: From "Health Insurance Premiums Rise," p. A1, Wall Street Journal Staff, 1994, *The Wall Street Journal,* Oct. 4, 1994. New York: Dow Jones & Company, Inc. Copyright 1994 by Dow Jones & Company, Inc. Reprinted with permission of The Wall Street Journal. All Rights Reserved Worldwide.

Today, most employers offer group health insurance coverage to their employees. Over the past fifty years there has been a noticeable expansion in the kinds of health insurance benefits offered to employees. Many medical benefit plans now cover expenses for alcohol and drug abuse treatment, home health care, and extended care facilities. Some employers provide incentives to employees who participate in preventive wellness programs (McCaffery, 1988; Rosenbloom & Hallman, 1991).

However, because increases in health care costs have outpaced both inflation and earnings growth (see Practice Perspective 12.5), many employers have shifted some of the costs of health insurance to employees through additional payroll deductions, higher deductible levels, and copayment requirements. Although many employees have expressed their anger regarding this matter, the trend has continued.

Efforts to reduce the costs of health benefits have also led to cuts in coverage that have caused financial devastation to families that have a seriously ill member. This sad reality is reported in Practice Perspective 12.6.

A number of health insurance programs are currently available. Three major types of coverage are traditional health insurance, health main-

---

PRACTICE PERSPECTIVE 12.6

Impact of Illness on Employment

2100 patients hospitalized for serious illnesses and their families were interviewed by Ron Winslow, a staff member of the Wall Street Journal. He reported that patients in the study (with an average age of 62 years) were diagnosed with illnesses such as severe congestive heart failure, metastatic colon cancer, and acute respiratory failure. Although 96% of the families had health insurance, 31% lost most or all of their savings, and 29% lost their major source of income. Especially affected were younger families with patients who were under 45 years old. These families did not have the Social Security and pension benefits that were more likely to continue with patients 65 years or older.

Source: From "Health Benefits for Seriously Ill Found Lacking," (p. B6, Column 5), Ron Winslow, 1994, *The Wall Street Journal,* Dec. 21, 1994. New York: Dow Jones & Company, Inc. Copyright 1994 by Dow Jones & Company, Inc. Reprinted with permission of The Wall Street Journal. All Rights Reserved Worldwide.

tenance organizations (HMOs), and preferred provider organizations (PPOs). Each of these health care insurance programs provides protection in a different way.

When employers first began offering medical benefits, the only type of medical insurance available was offered in the form of **traditional health insurance programs.** This type of insurance is usually provided through health care organizations such as Blue Cross/Blue Shield. The health provider charges commonly depend on the actual use of its services by the employees. These organizations function on a nonprofit basis and operate within specific geographic boundaries. However, as Rosenbloom and Hallman (1991, p. 83) stated, "the Blues are no more 'nonprofit' than are mutual insurance companies, which technically are owned by their policyholders."

In 1973 the Health Maintenance Organizations Act was passed. To comply with this law, a company that provided health insurance to its employees had to offer alternative health care coverage. Specifically, any company with at least twenty-five employees living in a health maintenance organization service area was required to offer membership in that organization to employees as an alternative to traditional group health coverage (McCaffery, 1988). Although there are various types of **health maintenance organization** (HMOs), they are all structured to provide high-quality health care to members at a fixed cost. These organizations provide services on a fixed, periodic, and prepaid basis; that is, charges consist of flat amounts per person or per family. The fundamental principle behind the HMO is preventive maintenance. It is believed that by having access to prepaid care, members are apt to visit their physicians more often, allowing potential problems to be discovered at an early stage, or even eliminated, before they have a chance to become a major health risk.

Preferred provider organizations (PPOs) negotiate and contract with employers or insurance companies to provide health care services

for a fixed fee. In return for accepting fixed fees, the employer or insurance company promises to encourage employees to use the PPO's services. The main incentive for providers to accept lower fees is an increase of patient volume, which ultimately results in more services being covered. The difference between these programs and HMOs is that users of PPO services are not restricted to specific health providers (McCaffery, 1988; Rosenbloom & Hallman, 1991). PPOs try to combine the best of HMOs and traditional insurance programs.

In addition to the three major types of health coverage just mentioned, many employers have recently entered into self-funding arrangements to provide good-quality health insurance at a lower cost and to receive relief from state insurance regulations. In this self-funding type of arrangement an employer provides a formal plan to employees, whereby the employer directly pays, and is responsible for, all or part of the benefits specified under the plan (DeCenzo & Holoviak, 1990).

With increasing costs of health insurance, organizations are trying to cut expenses by using the services of **managed-care firms.** Managed-care firms are what Hymowitz and Pollock (1995) call "gatekeepers." They control and monitor the type and amount of care employees receive, resulting in savings to the employer of "as much as 30% in treatment costs" (p. A1). They do not provide the care themselves but direct employees to service providers that are willing to adhere to the cost requirements. A criticism of this approach is that the result is less effective treatment with greater costs to employers if the health problems lead to absenteeism and emergencies. Practice Perspective 12.7 describes an example of such consequences.

Supplemental Health Programs

With the extension of types of health benefits offered, a variety of **supplemental health programs** are becoming more popular. Some examples are dental benefits, vision care, and prescription drug plans.

PRACTICE PERSPECTIVE 12.7

Problems with Managed Care

[An employee] drank, drove—and died—on the way home from a treatment session at an alcohol-abuse clinic. The . . . employee was 33 years old, a heavy drinker, and had been directed into treatment by his employer. Many traditional insurance plans would have covered a 28-day inpatient stay at a detox center. But two years earlier [the company] had turned over mental-health coverage to a managed-care firm that promised to cut the state's costs dramatically. For the [employee], that meant outpatient treatment at a clinic 40 minutes from

his home. And it meant he had to drive to and from his sessions. . . . It came as no surprise to people who knew him that alcohol was found in his blood after he crashed his car into a house late one night . . . and was killed.

Source: From "Psychobattle: Cost-Cutting Firms Monitor Couch Time, as Therapists Fret," (p. A1), C. Hymowitz and E. J. Pollock, 1995, *The Wall Street Journal,* July 13, 1995. New York: Dow Jones & Company, Inc. Copyright 1995 by Dow Jones Inc. Reprinted by permission of The Wall Street Journal. All Rights Reserved Worldwide.

Dental Plans. Dental care plans probably have sustained the most growth of any employee benefit plan. In 1986, about 95 million individuals in the United States were covered by various dental plans. The sources that provide and finance dental care plans are often the same as those used for medical coverage plans. An additional source is nonprofit dental service corporations sponsored by state dental associations. These programs are unique because they emphasize preventive care, they have a maximum coverage limit per year for each insured person, they have rigorous requirements for eligibility, and they control service costs by requiring dentists to submit descriptions and estimated costs of the treatment in advance (Crehan, 1984; Rosenbloom & Hallman, 1991).

Vision Care Plans. In 1976, the United Auto Workers negotiated vision care as an employee benefit. Since that time, only a few employers have provided this benefit to employees. McCaffery (1988) indicated that in 1986, only 21% of major companies had vision care plans. The sources that provide vision care are those used for core medical coverage and state optometric associations.

Prescription Drug Plans. Prescription drug expenses are covered for most employees under

their group medical plans. Employees are reimbursed under a comprehensive medical plan for their expenses for medicine, though this may be contingent on either a deductible or coinsurance provisions.

Collective bargaining, such as the United Auto Workers negotiations in 1967, is usually the force leading to the implementation of basic prescription drug plans (Rosenbloom & Hallman, 1991). McCaffery (1988) noted two cost control developments that have helped to reduce the cost of prescription drug plans: generic drugs and mail-order drug arrangements.

Life Insurance Plans

The primary purpose of life insurance is to assist a family with the loss of a deceased wage earner's income. In 1968, about 98% of all workers were covered by some form of life insurance (Nash & Carroll, 1975). Typically, it was term life insurance provided on a group basis because of the low cost of a group contract and because some occupations were insurable only under a group contract arrangement.

Various types of plans provide protection for the survivors of deceased employees. Some examples are: basic term life insurance, supplemental term life insurance, survivor income benefit insurance, paid-up life insurance, and universal life insurance. All of these programs, using different forms of contributions and levels of participation by employees and employers, are designed to provide an additional sense of security to employees. Gerhart and Milkovich (1992, p. 540) indicate that programs such as life insurance are "linked to salary levels, and thus, indirectly tied to experience. By linking these benefits to seniority, it is assumed that employees will be more reluctant to change employers."

Flexible Benefit Plans

Traditional benefit programs were designed to meet the needs of the "typical" wage earner: a married man in his mid-thirties, raising two children, who owned his own home and had two cars. However, marked changes in the composition of today's work force and in workers' attitudes toward employment and personal lifestyle have made the traditional pay and benefit approach too rigid, unable to satisfy the needs of today's diverse and nontraditional workers (Wallace & Fay, 1988). These demographic changes, along with the rising costs of benefits, have inspired employers to seek alternative benefit programs. This has led to the increasing popularity of a package of flexible benefits, sometimes referred to as *cafeteria benefits*. The appeal of **flexible benefit plans** lies in the freedom and control employees have to choose a benefit package that suits their personal needs. Under a typical flexible benefits plan, a base plan ensures minimum levels of medical, life, and disability insurance. Beyond this core coverage, employees choose from a number of options with regard to how they want their benefit dollars distributed. For example, older employees may prefer more retirement benefits, young and middle-aged married employees with children may prefer to focus on life insurance, and single individuals might choose plans that emphasize vacations and time off (Lawler, 1990).

There are five basic approaches to structuring a flexible benefits program, and most companies take into consideration their employees' needs and preferences in determining the best flexible benefits plan to offer. The five basic plans are flexible spending plans, additional allowance (add-on) plans, mix-and-match options, core-plus plans, and modular plans (Schuster & Zingheim, 1992).

Under a **flexible spending plan,** employees are allowed to set aside a specific amount of money to pay for certain medical, legal, and dependent care services with untaxed dollars.

The **additional allowance plan,** or add-on plan, provides the core benefit package but also allows employees to purchase additional benefits. This plan often is used when an employer wishes to increase benefit levels for employees while maintaining the existing benefits.

Mix-and-match options offer employees the opportunity to redesign their existing benefits by choosing different levels of coverage in certain benefit areas.

The **core-plus plan** is designed to reduce core benefits by offering a two-part plan consisting of fixed core coverage and flexible credits. These credits may be used to buy additional benefits or extend coverage or may be sold back to the employer for cash.

Modular plans consist of a number of modules (or benefit packages), each containing the same benefits but having different levels of protection. An employee selects one module (an entire package) and cannot substitute any of the coverage.

The use of flexible benefit plans has advantages for both the employee and the employer. Lawler (1981) indicated that a survey conducted in a company that had a flexible benefit program found a high level of employee satisfaction with the plan. It appears that this kind of benefit program might increase the value of the benefit package from the employee's perspective and has the potential of benefiting both the employee and the employer. It assists individuals to attain the rewards they need and value. At the same time, it guarantees the organization that the money is being spent in ways that have a positive impact on employees. DeCenzo and Holoviak (1990) noted that in some cases, providing employees with a flexible benefit plan results in improved employee morale. McCaffery (1989) indicated that employers who had already implemented flexible benefit plans believed that these programs created competitive advantages in terms of recruiting, motivating, and retaining workers.

In spite of these advantages, these types of plans have a few problems. Some major concerns include poor benefit choices made by employees; too much adverse selection, which means that low-risk employees ignore certain types of coverage and high-risk individuals seek increased coverage in a particular area; difficulty in communicating the plans to employees; and the cost and complexities of administering the plans. To combat these problems, employers can provide a minimum core of coverage of risky areas to reduce poor selection by employees; implement a variety of pricing strategies to keep adverse selection to a minimum; provide pamphlets, seminars, and continued employee assistance to introduce and effectively communicate the plans to employees; and use advanced computer programs to decrease costs and keep administrative complications to a minimum. The research (Barber, Dunham, & Formisano, 1992; Dreher et al., 1988; Gerhart & Milkovich, 1992) indicates that increased employee training concerning possible benefits, as well as communication that provides accurate information, are associated with increased levels of benefit satisfaction. Barber et al. (1992) also found some increase in overall levels of employee satisfaction.

Regardless of the advantages and disadvantages of flexible benefit plans, they are becoming increasingly popular as organizations that use these types of benefit plans report positive results. This approach communicates to employees that the organization perceives them as mature adults who can make their own decisions about their careers and personal lives, and their benefits (Lawler, 1990, p. 50).

Pay for Time Not Worked

There are a number of instances in which employees are paid for time not worked. Such payments often exist as a result of collective bargaining; however, more employers have come to recognize these nonwork payments as a hidden benefit in terms of rewarding performance. The assumption is that employees who are allowed to spend time away from the physical and mental stresses of a job will be more rested and ultimately more productive when back on the job. However, evidence about these relationships is conflicting (Schuster & Zingheim, 1992; Sibson, 1981). Schuster and Zingheim (1992, p. 258) indicate that "paid time off . . . averages 13.1 percent of payroll, which includes vacation, sick leave, holidays, personal time-off allowances, jury duty, paid rest periods, and paid lunch periods." As employees place increasing value on leisure time, these types of benefits have become more important—and relatively the most expensive. The typical forms of nonwork pay situations are vacation, holidays, and sick leave.

Vacation

Vacation plans can vary a great deal, although in most cases the number of weeks of vacation offered is related to the employee's length of service with the company. A common vacation plan is a two-week vacation after one year of service, three weeks after five years of service, and four or more weeks after ten years of service. Because many long-term employees find it difficult to schedule their earned vacation time, some employers have provided an option known as vacation banking, in which the employer pays for banked, or unused, time at a later date (DeCenzo & Holoviak, 1990).

Holidays

Almost every company offers payment for some paid holidays. McCaffery (1988) indicated that employees in the United States average about ten holidays a year. However, the actual number of holidays an employer observes is influenced by the company's geographic location and the nature of the business.

One option that some employers provide is personal days, sometimes referred to as floating holidays. Personal days are chosen by employees and are usually offered on a year-to-year basis. It is estimated that "each added holiday . . . costs a company an average of 0.25 percent of payroll" (Rosenbloom & Hallman, 1991, p. 403).

Sick Leave

Nearly all companies pay their employees for days not worked due to illness. The number of sick days offered to employees varies among organizations. Many employers have found that paid sick leave tends to be one of the most abused benefits. Because some employees view this benefit as earned time off, they may use sick leave as if it is vacation leave (Wallace & Fay, 1988). McCaffery (1988) concluded that effective communication can help to resolve this problem; however, some companies have found other solutions through plan redesign. One approach is referred to as **total time off** (TTO). This method combines vacations, holidays, and sick leave into a total time-off package. This plan is structured so that each employee is given a "bank account" of days as a substitute for the traditional time-based benefits, and the employee can make withdrawals as needed.

Employers have come to realize the likelihood of workers being absent from work due to circumstances beyond their control. Most companies now protect employees against the loss of income due to other occurrences, such as a death in the family, jury duty, and military leave. Other nonwork payments are provided to employees during working hours. The most common of these are coffee breaks, rest breaks, and lunch hours.

NONFINANCIAL REWARDS

The effectiveness of employees at work is influenced by the total working environment. Financial rewards interact with various nonfinancial rewards to affect employee effectiveness on the job. The type of compensation mix that is offered affects the attraction and retention of employees (Lawler, 1990). Various types of nonfinancial rewards have different effects on different individuals: "extensive benefits, for example, may be highly attractive to an individual with a large family and a spouse at home, while [these same] benefits may be only minimally attractive to a single employee . . . [new to] . . . the labor market" (Lawler, 1990, p. 203).

Rothman (1987) noted that some features of the work environment seem to have a psychological value because of their impact on worker attitudes and overall effectiveness. Some people care whether they have a carpet or a window in their office; others would rather have a personal secretary. However, because organizations have limited resources, they often have to determine the specific mix of pay and nonpay rewards that they can offer (e.g., promotion opportunities, physical conditions, participation in decision making and type of supervision) (Gerhart & Milkovich, 1992). Summarizing some of the literature on the effects of various job characteristics on employees' motivation, Gerhart and Milkovich proposed that research provides simultaneously supporting and nonsupporting evidence. For example, expectancy theory asserts that work outcomes, such as pay or recognition, will increase motivation only if they have value to the individual. Other studies that followed Herzberg's model found that the degree of importance associated with pay depends on the particular method used in the study. (Self-reports indicated that pay was not very important; direct observation methods indicated that pay was very important.)

Following is a short discussion of examples of nonfinancial rewards, specifically, personal work factors, physical conditions, work environment, management styles, company image, and job perquisites.

Personal Work Factors

The personal fulfillment some individuals experience from doing their jobs has more value than direct pay. Employees who have a personal interest in their jobs or are given the opportunity to utilize their skills are likely to be productive workers. Two factors that employees often regard highly are independence and degree of challenge. A meta-analysis conducted by Spector (1986) concluded that high levels of perceived control by employees were associated with high levels of job satisfaction, performance, motivation, and commitment. Sandler (1984) pointed out the significance of a meaningful and challenging job, as well as the importance of allowing employees to set work goals. Findings by Schnake and Cochran (1985) suggest that employees who have challenging work goals experience less conflict within the working environment when goals are clear and specific. A more recent study conducted by Roberson (1990) supports these findings. The type of work not only determines the level of direct pay, but also has considerable psychological value.

Physical Conditions

The physical work environment can also affect employees' productivity. Some physical factors that are commonly examined are cleanliness, lighting, decor, comfort, and safety. Studies have shown that these physical factors affect workers' performance, satisfaction, and motivation. For example, in a study conducted by Oldham and Rotchford (1983), the findings showed that various office characteristics (such as openness of interior design, work space, accessibility, and office lighting) related significantly to job satisfaction. It seems that a closed office environment offers privacy but isolates employees, whereas an open environment provides more freedom but invites interruptions. Cangelosi and Lemoine (1988) noted that a solution to this dilemma could be the use of modular furniture that would provide comfort and privacy, yet allow for an interactive atmosphere.

Companies need to keep in mind, when attempting to improve work areas, that they should not go overboard with improvements.

Improvements that employees view as ornate or plush might actually contribute to a reduction in productivity, because the employees will see the improvements as unnecessary and therefore not of value.

Another factor that pertains indirectly to the work environment and that employees perceive as valuable is the location of a company. Sibson (1981) indicated that with the high price of gasoline, easy access to shopping centers, public transportation, schools, and day care might have additional appeal for individuals seeking employment.

Management Styles

Another important factor is the company's management style, which plays a significant role in whether employees perceive that they are being treated fairly and with respect (Sibson, 1981). For years, the conventional management style was an autocratic approach, characterized by an organizational structure with multiple levels of supervision and a policy of centralized decision making. Under this management style, authority and decision making are governed by top managers, who establish policies and procedures and expect employees to adhere to the rules with little or no input.

Management styles that incorporate **employee involvement** (EI) **systems** are becoming increasingly popular. Although the United States has been slow to accept these systems, laws have been passed in many other countries requiring managers to share decision making with their subordinates. Dulworth, Landen, and Usilaner (1990) indicated that in 1987 the U.S. General Accounting Office (GAO) surveyed 962 Fortune 1000 companies and reported that the majority had implemented some form of employee involvement program. According to their findings, the primary purpose of these programs was to improve productivity, quality, employee morale, and motivation. Rohr Industries, Inc., in Hagerstown, Maryland, has had an EI program in place for several years and reports a

30–50% improvement in morale from that program (Overman, 1990). What works for one company, however, may not work for another. An organizational assessment should be conducted to determine which EI system would best fit a company's current state and future goals. The most common forms of EI systems are survey feedback, employee participation groups, quality circles, and self-managing work teams.

Survey feedback uses employee attitudes, collected via surveys, as part of a problem-solving process in which survey data are used to promote, structure, and measure the effectiveness of employee participation.

Employee participation groups consist of diverse forms of employee involvement, such as employee work councils or task teams, that are not represented in either quality circles or self-managing work teams.

Quality circles are groups of volunteers from a specific work area that meet regularly to identify and suggest solutions to work-related problems. These individuals then communicate their suggestions to management.

Self-managing work teams are responsible for an entire product or service and make decisions about task assignments, work methods, and other administrative functions.

All of these systems are designed to increase employee participation in decision making. Dulworth et al. (1990) mentioned that giving employees more control over their activities might result in increased worker productivity because employees will feel a sense of responsibility with regard to the company's success. Most companies have reported that the major reason for introducing an EI system was to improve productivity and quality. However, the employer is not the only one who can benefit from EI systems. Bassin (1988) maintained that the benefits of teams have led to increased worker stimulation, satisfaction, and motivation.

Even though EI systems are steadily gaining in popularity, some employers are still appre-

hensive. Two reasons for their reluctance are the inability to integrate such a system with an organization's present system and the complexity involved in changing an organization's structure. Because each component of the organization must be modified, this can lead to intense pressure on the organization and its employees. George (1987) noted the need to recognize the long-term effort of eliminating an organization's hierarchical structure, because the implementation of an EI system requires a strong commitment of time and resources.

In addition to these concerns, some managers perceive EI systems as a threat to the traditional roles that have provided managerial security, authority, and level of responsibility. This area might be somewhat difficult to deal with because of the importance many managers attach to these aspects of their jobs.

Company Image

Company image can also contribute to employee productivity. For example, if an organization is perceived as progressive, well known, and successful, it is likely to be viewed as a prestigious company with which to be associated. As Sibson (1976) indicated, successful companies tend to be more exciting, offer greater employment opportunities, and have higher standards than other companies. If a company promotes standards of excellence, then employees are apt to feel a sense of pride in their work. Therefore, there is some psychological value to working for a company that produces first-rate products and treats its employees and clients with respect.

In addition, a company that has a positive relationship with the community should be able to attract and retain workers. Oftentimes, companies will distribute resources to a community in a variety of ways that can lead to a favorable relationship. For example, many companies provide financial backing to help support local social and educational activities.

Perquisites of the Job

Other special benefits that companies can provide to their employees are **perquisites,** sometimes called "perks" for short. These are usually offered to employees in specific jobs or management levels in addition to the normal financial benefits. Though these benefits do not result in a direct financial reward, they are believed to have psychological value that can help to motivate or retain employees by providing a sense of prestige and status (Sibson, 1981). The primary purpose of perquisites is to enhance the employee's perception that a company's compensation is fair and competitive. In fact, many perquisites supplement basic benefit programs by supplying a service or benefit without changing the employee's pay. Perks normally add to retirement, disability, and survivor protection plans (Ellig, 1982).

Employers offer a variety of perquisites. Some are offered across the board to all employees; others are provided specifically to higher-level employees.

Perquisites Offered to All Employees

The range of perquisites a company offers depends on the company's size, location, human resource management philosophy, and type of business. Some of the most common perquisites are titles, free parking, moving expenses, employee discounts on company products, subsidized or free meals, company loans and credit unions, service awards for employees who have been with the company for many years, recreational facilities located on company premises, flexible work hours, tuition reimbursement, and employee assistance programs that help workers deal with personal or work-related problems.

Because of changes in work force demographics, two rapidly emerging benefits are child care and elder care programs. With an increased number of two-income families and single parents, the need for child care has become important. Werther (1989) indicated that approx-imately two thirds of all women with children under the age of fourteen are working today. Only a few companies currently provide child care for employees, either on site or at a nearby facility. For example, Levi Strauss, Procter & Gamble, and Hoffmann-LaRouche have received national recognition for providing child care assistance to their employees.

Another growing concern for many employees is the responsibility of providing care for aging parents. Because of improvements in standards of living and medical technology, people are living longer than ever before. In fact, the fastest-growing part of the population in the United States today are people who are eighty-six years old and older (Werther, 1989). IBM is a pioneer in offering a national network of consulting and referral agencies that assist employees in selecting a nursing home for elderly parents or aid in resolving other associated problems.

Child care and elder care programs have advantages for both employees and employers. Through these programs, employees can receive assistance in resolving stressful matters, and employers are apt to find a reduction in sick leave and tardiness, which may result in an increase in productivity. Additionally, these two benefits can complement a company's overall compensation package, giving organizations an edge in terms of recruiting, motivating, and retaining employees.

Executive Perquisites

Executives often receive the same perks as other employees, but the eligibility and terms may be more liberal. Vacations are a good example. If the vacation policy at a company is two weeks after one year of employment, three weeks after five years, and so on, the executive might be eligible for additional vacation time on the basis of age rather than years of service. For example, executives between the ages of forty and forty-nine might receive four weeks of vacation; those between ages fifty and fifty-nine might get five weeks, and those aged sixty and above might get six weeks (Ellig, 1982). The reason for this disparity is that vacation is normally based on time with a company and executives often do not remain at a company for more than five to ten years.

Other executive perquisites may include being able to work at home, sabbaticals, outplacement assistance, parking spaces, access to executive dining rooms, company automobiles, chauffeured limousines, legal services, tax assistance, and financial counseling. This list is not complete; the type and amount of perquisites vary according to the individual company.

Many companies go to the other extreme and try to downplay perquisites. Lawler (1990) describes these companies as egalitarian organizations. As such, they are in direct opposition to the hierarchial approach, which includes the awarding of the perquisites. In the egalitarian organization there is an attempt to keep lines of communication open among all management levels. For example, Federal Express expects all of its managers to perform production tasks on a regular basis. At Federal Express the office layout minimizes the role of perquisites. According to Lawler (1990, p. 171),

> Ross Perot, a former member of the GM board and founder of EDS, has suggested radical elimination of perquisites for GM corporate executives. As he has pointed out, the perquisites tend to separate executives from their consumers and their employees.

One perquisite that was not mentioned previously, because many employees as well as executives have them, is offices. The size of an office often signals the status of the employee at a glance. The fact that an office has windows may indicate that an individual is a director or a vice-president. Honda has eliminated offices entirely; all employees sit in open office areas (Lawler, 1990). Five years ago, Kemper Insurance decided to use the same approach in its human resources department. According to the vice-president of human resources at the time, this gave

employees a sense of openness and accessibility. The trend may be to downplay the existence of perquisites, but it is difficult not to extend additional benefits to executives, since benefits are used to initially lure executives to the company and to retain them in the long run.

In summary, employees have certain expectations about nonfinancial rewards, and each individual places a different value on each type of reward. To many individuals, some of the nonfinancial rewards might be considered basic requirements that a company should offer. If these basic requirements are not fulfilled, employees and potential employees might seek employment elsewhere (see Practice Perspective 12.8).

CREATING A TOTAL COMPENSATION PROGRAM

The ultimate goal of a total compensation program is to attract, motivate, and retain employees to meet organizational goals and objectives. A company's ability to attract and retain desirable individuals depends heavily on a total compensation program that contains an appropriate mix of compensation elements. These elements include wages and salaries, incentives, benefits, perquisites, and other nonspecific rewards. Since no two organizations are alike, the total compensation program needs to be designed to meet the specific needs of the organization. This involves extensive planning by the compensation committee, which is usually composed of human resource management personnel of all levels. However, in some cases a board of directors or outside consultants are involved as well (Sibson, 1981). There are three basic stages in creating a total compensation program: planning, implementation, and management.

Planning

Though each company's compensation program will differ, there are key issues that must be addressed during the initial design of a total com-

PRACTICE PERSPECTIVE 12.8

Importance of Factors beyond Compensation

Hal Lancaster claims that factors other than just financial compensation are "the glue . . . [that holds] . . . the company together." He cites examples such as Sun Microsystems, which offers counseling to its employees to discuss and test their skills for other job prospects. Texas Instruments has a policy of informing employees a year in advance about possibilities of layoffs. Other examples are courses offered by companies on leadership, corporate values and culture, and creative thinking, which allow employees to transfer skills to other jobs when nec-

essary; valid and "candid" performance evaluations; and advance notice of company decisions that would affect individual futures. In general, organizational environments in which employees know that anagement keeps lines of communication open and honest are part of the new social contract affecting employees' effectiveness on the job.

Source: From "Managing Your Career" (p. A1), by H. Lancaster, 1994, *The Wall Street Journal,* November 29, 1994. New York: Dow Jones & Company, Inc. Copyright 1994 by Dow Jones & Company, Inc. Reprinted with permission of The Wall Street Journal. All Rights Reserved Worldwide.

pensation program. Some of these issues are business objectives, work force characteristics, competition, cost, and total compensation strategy.

Business Objectives

Two factors that must be considered are the organization's human resource management philosophy and its strategic business plan. Both elements are essential to the success of a benefit program. The human resource philosophy represents a fundamental belief about employees and the employer–employee relationship, and the strategic business plan details the direction a company expects to take in the future.

Work Force Characteristics

A benefit package should be designed with the employees' interests taken into consideration. For a benefit package to be of value to employees, it must be perceived as useful. Today's compensation managers realize the importance of paying attention to employee needs, as well as recognizing the goals and objectives of organized employee groups, such as unions.

Competition

For a company to design a competitive benefit package, it must first define the market in which

it intends to compete and then compare its benefit plan to those of the principal competitors.

Cost

To keep the costs of benefit plans in perspective, a cost analysis of benefit proposals should follow the assessment of employee interests and needs. With the assistance of financial, tax, and insurance specialists, the compensation committee can then collect and analyze the cost data for a variety of approaches to fulfilling an organization's compensation objectives (McCaffery, 1989).

Total Compensation Strategy

A company should provide its employees with the best mix of pay and benefits that are valued by employees and cost-effective for the company. Once the plan is established, an employer–employee relationship of mutual respect can evolve, which should be conducive to achieving the organization's overall goals and objectives.

One final point to be made about the planning of a total compensation program is employee involvement. Although many companies allow employees to participate in the planning of compensation programs, since it is believed that this will motivate them and ultimately increase productivity, Wallace and Fay (1988) held that there is no empirical evidence to support this notion.

Implementation

The implementation of a total compensation program involves putting the program into operation and outlining the necessary policies and procedures. Once a compensation program is introduced, application is an ongoing process. Inevitably, some unforeseen problems will arise that will require revisions and adaptations to the original plan.

An important aspect of implementation is to ensure that the plan is communicated clearly to employees at all levels to avoid any misconceptions. Companies usually communicate their compensation program to employees through such means as announcements, orientation and training sessions, periodic meetings, and the distribution of employee handbooks. After providing employees with this information, compensation managers should extend open lines of communication to employees, inviting feedback on how well employees understand and value the total compensation package.

Management

Once a compensation program has been implemented, it must be continuously managed to ensure that it meets the organization's needs. Through the use of audits and budgets, compensation managers can determine just how effective the program really is (Wallace & Fay, 1988).

Since modifications to the program are inevitable, a compensation program must be flexible enough to respond to changing standards and guidelines. Yet any changes made to the compensation program must be structured so as to continue to support organizational goals. In fact, the individuals who are responsible for

compensation program management must be aware of the practices that are implemented in other areas of personnel to make sure these support the total compensation program (Sibson, 1981). Finally, to keep a compensation program current, it must be constantly reviewed and analyzed. Therefore, compensation managers must stay informed of any new options as they become available.

The best compensation program is a plan that serves the interests of both the employer and employees. It must have the ability to attract, motivate, and retain people while simultaneously supporting the organization's goals, objectives, policies, and practices.

SUMMARY

Organizations use compensation and benefits packages to attract, motivate, and retain employees. The history of compensation programs dates back to the Davis-Bacon Act of 1931. Present-day legislators and companies are still trying to define the most effective total employee compensation program.

From a psychological standpoint, pay seems to be closely related to the concepts of motivation and satisfaction. Expectancy theory holds that employees have certain expectations about the results of their behavior. Consequently, employees tend to act in a manner that they believe will lead to desired outcomes. Equity theory explains pay satisfaction as the employee's perceived balance between inputs and outcomes compared to the individual's perceptions of the inputs and outcomes of coworkers. Goal-setting theory states that a person will be satisfied with his or her pay, and will exhibit successful job performance, if specific and challenging goals are established.

Herzberg's two-factor theory suggests that employees might not be satisfied, regardless of pay, because pay is a hygiene factor. Lawler's model states that employees compare the relationship between actual rewards and rewards perceived as equitable and will be satisfied only if this relationship is perceived as equal.

Organizations provide employees with direct pay (e.g., base pay) and indirect payments (such as legally required pay and benefits). The design and administration of pay depend on a valid job evaluation. The four most common methods for job evaluation are job ranking, classification, factor comparison, and point factor systems.

All U.S. organizations are legally required to provide three major financial benefits: Social Security, unemployment compensation, and workers' compensation. Social Security is a fund created by equal employee and employer contributions to offset financial expenses after retirement. Also included in this category are survivor's insurance and disability insurance. Unemployment compensation was created to aid individuals in the event of job loss. Workers' compensation, maintained solely by the employer, offers financial assistance to employees and/or their families should the employee be permanently injured or killed on the job.

In addition to receiving a base salary, employees often receive supplemental income such as defined benefit plans or defined contribution plans. Most organizations offer employee health insurance and other plans such as dental, vision care, prescription drug, and life insurance. However, these traditional plans have not always met the needs of the work force, and flexible benefit plans have been created. These plans may be flexible spending accounts, additional allowance plans, or modular plans. In addition, employees are often allowed to take paid time off, usually in the form of vacations, holidays, or sick leave.

Many employees consider nonfinancial rewards to be as important as financial rewards. Nonfinancial rewards can include personal work factors, physical conditions, the work environment, management styles, company image, and job perquisites.

The literature recommends the following stages as guidelines in establishing a total compensation package: planning, which involves the company's business objectives, work force characteristics, the competition and perceived costs; implementation, which includes package operation and the development of policies and procedures; and management, which includes continuous budgetary and audit program assessment.

KEY TERMS AND CONCEPTS

additional allowance plan	employee stock ownership plan	mix-and-match options
automated job evaluation plans	factor comparison method	modular plan
base pay	flexible benefit plans	paired comparison system
benefits	flexible spending plan	perquisites
bonus	gainsharing	piece rate payments
bonus payments	health maintenance organization	point factor system
classification method	indirect pay	preferred provider organization
core-plus plan	job analysis	premium payments
defined benefit plan	job descriptions	profit-sharing plan
defined contribution plan	job evaluation	quality circles
direct pay	job ranking	salary surveys
disability insurance	long-term disability insurance	self-managing work teams
employee involvement systems	managed-care firms	short-term disability insurance
employee participation groups	merit system	skill-based method

Social Security	supplemental health programs	total time off
stock option plan	survey feedback	traditional health insurance
stock purchase plan	survivor's insurance	program
supplemental compensation	thrift plan	unemployment compensation

RECOMMENDED READINGS

Beatty, R. W., Crandall, N. F., Fay, C. H., Mathis, R., Milkovich, G. T., & Wallace, M. J. (1979). *How to administer wage-salary programs and perform job evaluations.* New Brunswick, NJ: Authors.

Cowherd, D. M., & Levin, D. I. (1992). Product quality and equity between lower level employees and top management: An investigation of distributive justice theory. *Administrative Science Quarterly, 37*(2), 1–14.

Gerhart, B., & Milkovich, G. T. (1992). Employee compensation: research and practice, In M. D. Dunnette & L. M. Hough (Eds.), *Handbook of industrial and organizational psychology* (pp. 482–569). Palo Alto, CA: Consulting Psychologists Press.

Kohn, A. (1993). *Punished by rewards: The trouble with gold stars, incentive plans, A's, praise, and other bribes.* Boston: Houghton Mifflin.

Lawler, E. E., III (1991). *Paying the person: A better approach to management.* [Center for Effective Organizations Publication G91-4 (189)]. Los Angeles: University of Southern California, School of Business Administration.

Lawler, E. E., III (1994). *Motivation in work organizations.* San Francisco: Jossey-Bass. (Suggested reading includes Chapter 6, pp. 143–187.)

Schwoerer, C., & Rosen, B. (1989). Effects of employment-at-will policies and compensation policies on corporate image and job pursuit intentions. *Journal of Applied Psychology, 74*(4), 653–656.

INTERNET RESOURCES

Employee Benefits Group, Inc.
This commercial site provides a description of deferred compensation and other benefit strategies that give a business a big edge in attracting and retaining key people. Deferred compensation can provide retirement benefits on a selected basis. More important, it can add big benefits over and above those provided in a regular compensation plan.
http://www.ebg.com/

Association for Services Management International Studies/Reports
This site presents the text of several valuable reports on benchmarking. These include "Impacting the Bottom Line," "Closing the Gap," "The Formula for Performance and Revenue Optimisation," and "Charting the Course Toward the New Millennium."
http://www.afsmi.org/

Partner/Shareholder Compensation Techniques
This site presents a review of the basics used by law practices in determining associate compensation. It was written by John P. Weil & Company, a group of law practice management consultants. A related document, **http://seamless.com/jpw/new/peereval.html,** provides thoughts about peer evaluation as a part of the compensation process.
http://seamless.com/jpw/new/compensa.html

Foundation for Enterprise Development
This site, which is maintained by the nonprofit Foundation for Enterprise Development, is devoted to promoting equity compensation, employee ownership and involvement and other high-performance business strategies. The site's Guide to Equity Compensation outlines an approach companies can use in evaluating and designing an effective equity compensation strategy.
http://www.fed.org/index.html

AN & H Compensation Services
This commercial site presents brief summaries of a number of different compensation services available through consultants. It is a good example of the areas of interest and work with respect to compensation.
http://www.cin.ix.net/anh/comp-ben.html

EXERCISES

Exercise 12.1

Practice Designing Benefit Packages

Using different underlying philosophies, create two benefit packages for each of the following individuals. Use the examples of benefits offered to employees that are given in the chapter. Also link your compensation package to the appropriate psychological theory or theories. For example, write a compensation plan for a single working mother of three who is employed by a company that has a participatory management style and which believes in sharing gains with employees.

A single working mother of three

A sixty-year-old widowed woman

An eighteen-year-old male attending college

A thirty-year-old woman who does not own a car

A man who has a wife and four children

A male veteran with a disability

Exercise 12.2

Designing Your Own Preferred Compensation Package

After reading this chapter, you have an appreciation for the complexity of pay reward systems in organizations. M. Scott Myers (1991) developed a simple, effective representation of this complexity. He uses a cube with the three dimensions of individual monetary factors, group monetary factors, and nonmonetary factors (see Figure 12.2). This design gives eighty-one systems from which an organization can assemble its own most workable combinations. Using more blocks

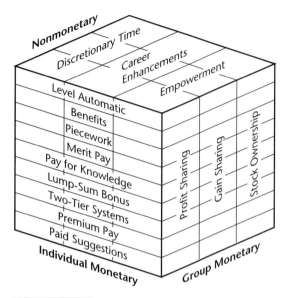

FIGURE 12.2   Myers's three-dimensional reward system model.

Source: Myers, M. S. (1991), *Every employee a manager* (3rd ed., p. 32). Adapted as submitted. Copyright 1991 by Pfeiffer, an imprint of Jossey-Bass Inc., Publishers.

is not necessarily better; what works best is a complementary combination of at least one key factor from each of the three major dimensions. Using Myers's factors and the information from this chapter, design the total compensation program that you would most like in the job you take after you complete your degree.

REFERENCES

Adams, J. S. (1965). Inequity in social exchange. In K. Berkowitz (Ed.), *Advances in experimental social psychology* (pp. 267–299). New York: Academic Press.

American Compensation Association and American Society for Personnel Administration. (1988). *Elements of sound base pay administration* (2nd ed.). Scottsdale, AZ: Author.

Barber, A. E., Dunham, R. B., & Formisano, R. A. (1992). The impact of flexible benefits on employee satisfaction: A field study. *Personnel Psychology, 45*(1), 55–75.

Bassin, M. (1988). Teamwork at General Foods: New and improved. *Personnel Journal, 67*(5), 62–70.

Bullock, R. J., & Lawler, E. E. (1984). Gainsharing: A few questions and fewer answers. *Human Resource Management, 23*, 23–40.

Burgess, L. R. (1984). *Wage and salary administration: Pay and benefits.* Columbus, OH: Charles Merrill.

Cangelosi, V. E., & Lemoine, L. F. (1988). Effects of open versus closed physical environment on employee perception and attitude. *Social Behavior and Personality, 16*(1), 71–77.

Clolery, P. (1994, October). Crafting a cost-wise benefits plan for your firm. *The Practical Accountant,* 26–32.

Crehan, H. F. (1984). Types of noncash compensation. In M. L. Rock (Ed.), *Handbook of wage and salary administration* (2nd ed., chap. 43). New York: McGraw-Hill.

DeCenzo, D. A., & Holoviak, S. J. (1990). *Employee benefits.* Englewood Cliffs, NJ: Prentice Hall.

Dornstein, M. (1988). Pay equity evaluations of occupations and their bases. *Journal of Applied Psychology, 18,* 905–924.

Dreher, G. F., Ash, R. A., & Bretz, R. R. (1988). Benefit coverage and employee cost: Critical factors in explaining compensation satisfaction. *Personnel Psychology, 41*(2), 237–254.

Dulworth, M. R., Landen, D. L., & Usilaner, B. L. (1990). Employee involvement systems in U.S. corporations: Right objectives, wrong strategies. *National Productivity Review, 9*(2), 141–155.

Ellig, B. R. (1982). *Executive compensation: A total pay perspective.* New York: McGraw-Hill.

George, P. S. (1987). Team building without tears. *Personnel Journal, 66*(11), 122–129.

Gerhart, B, & Milkovich, G. T. (1992). Employee compensation: research and practice. In M. D. Dunnette & L. M. Hough (Eds.), *Handbook of industrial and organizational psychology* (pp. 482–569). Palo Alto, CA: Consulting Psychologists Press.

Greenberg, J. (1987). Reactions to procedural injustice in payment distributions: Do the means justify the ends? *Journal of Applied Psychology, 72*(1), 55–61.

Herzberg, F. (1966). *Work and the nature of man.* Cleveland, OH: World Publishing.

Huber, V. L., Seybolt, P. M., & Venemon, K. (1992). The relationship between individual inputs, perceptions and multidimensional pay satisfaction. *Journal of Applied Social Psychology, 22*(17), 1356–1373.

Hymowitz, C., & Pollock, E. J. (1995, July 13). Psychobattle: Cost-cutting firms monitor couch time, as therapists fret. *The Wall Street Journal,* pp. A1, A4.

Koch, J. V. (1982, October). Salary equity issues in higher education: Where do we stand? *AAHE Higher Education Bulletin,* 7–14.

Lancaster, H. (1994, November 29). Managing your career. *The Wall Street Journal,* p. B1.

Lawler, E. E., III. (1971). *Pay and organizational effectiveness: A psychological view.* New York: McGraw-Hill.

Lawler, E. E., III. (1973). *Motivation in work organizations.* Pacific Grove, CA: Brooks/Cole.

Lawler, E. E., III. (1981). *Pay and organization development.* Reading, MA: Addison-Wesley.

Lawler, E. E., III. (1986a). *The new pay* (CEO publication G84–7[55]). Los Angeles, CA: University of Southern California.

Lawler, E. E., III. (1986b). *High-involvement management.* San Francisco: Jossey-Bass.

Lawler, E. E. III. (1989). Pay for performance: A strategic analysis. In L. R. Gomez-Mejia (Ed.), *Compensation and benefits* (pp. 136–181). Washington, DC: Bureau of National Affairs.

Lawler, E. E., III. (1990). *Strategic pay.* San Francisco, CA: Jossey-Bass.

Lawler, E. E., III. (1991). The design of effective reward systems. In R. M. Steers & L. W. Porter (Eds.), *Motivation and work* (pp. 507–530). New York: McGraw-Hill.

Lawler, E. E., III. (1994). *Motivation in work organizations.* San Francisco: Jossey-Bass.

Lawler, E. E., & Jenkins, G. D., Jr. (1992). Strategic reward systems. In M. D. Dunnette & L. M. Hough (Eds.), *Handbook of industrial and organizational psychology* (Vol. 3, pp. 1040–1055). Palo Alto, CA: Consulting Psychologists Press.

Locke, E. A. (1976). The nature and causes of job satisfaction. In M. D. Dunnette (Ed.), *Handbook of industrial and organizational psychology* (pp. 1297–1349). Chicago: Rand McNally.

Lowenberg, G., Kingston-O'Connell, F. G., & O'Connell, M. (1994). Predictive relationships: Pay satisfaction, and pay-differentials as moderated by income in an egalitarian organization [Summary]. *Proceedings of the 23rd International Congress of Applied Psychology, 67.*

McCaffery, R. M. (1988). *Employee benefit programs: A total compensation perspective.* Boston: PWS-Kent.

McCaffery, R. M. (1989). Employee benefits and services. In L. R. Gomez-Mejia (Ed.), *Compensation* and benefits (3rd ed., pp. 101–135). Washington, DC: Bureau of National Affairs.

Milkovich, G. T., & Wigdor, A. K. (Eds.), with Broderick, R. F., & Manor, A. S. (1991). *Pay for performance: Evaluating performance appraisal and merit pay*. Washington, DC: National Academy Press.

Myers, M. S. (1991). *Every employee a manager* (3rd ed.). San Diego, CA: University Associates.

Nash, A. N., & Carroll, S. J., Jr. (1975). *The management of compensation*. Monterey, CA: Brooks/Cole.

Oldham, G. R., & Rotchford, N. L. (1983). Relationships between office characteristics and employee reactions: A study of the physical environment. *Administrative Science Quarterly, 28*(4), 542–556.

Opsahl, R. L., & Dunnette, M. D. (1966). The role of financial compensation in industrial motivation. *Psychological Bulletin, 66*(2), 94–118.

Overman, S. (1990, May). Worker, management unite. *HR Magazine*, 38–41.

Pernick, R. (1994). Review of organizational justice: The search for fairness in the workplace. *Academy of Management Executive, VII*(1), 87–89.

Porter, L. W., & Lawler, E. E. (1968). *Managerial attitudes and performance*. Homewood, IL: Irwin Dorsey.

Rice, R. W., Phillips, S. M., & McFarlin, D. B. (1990). Multiple discrepancies and pay satisfaction. *Journal of Applied Psychology, 75*(4), 386–393.

Roberson, L. (1990). Prediction of job satisfaction from characteristics of personal work goals. *Journal of Organizational Behavior, 11*(1), 29–41.

Rosenbloom, J. S., & Hallman, G. V. (1991). *Employee benefit planning*. Englewood Cliffs, NJ: Prentice Hall.

Rothman, M. (1987). Designing work environments to influence productivity. *Journal of Business and Psychology, 1*(4), 390–395.

Sandler, L. (1984). The successful and supportive subordinate. *Personnel Journal, 63*(12), 40–45.

Schnake, M. E., & Cochran, D. S. (1985). Effect of two goal-setting dimensions on perceived intraorganizational conflict. *Group and Organization Studies, 10*(2), 168–183.

Schuster, J. R., & Zingheim, P. K. (1992). *The new pay*. New York: Lexington Books.

Sheppard, B. H., Lewicki, R. J., & Minton, J. W. (1992). *Organizational justice: The search for fairness in the workplace*. New York: Lexington Books.

Sibson, R. E. (1976). *Increasing employee productivity*. New York: AMACOM.

Sibson, R. E. (1981). *Compensation* (rev. ed.). New York: AMACOM.

Smith, B. N., Benson, P. G., & Hornsby, J. S. (1990). The effects of job description content on job evaluation judgments. *Journal of Applied Psychology, 75*(3), 301–309.

Spector, P. E. (1986). Perceived control by employees: A meta-analysis of studies concerning autonomy and participation at work. *Human-Relations, 39*(11), 1005–1016.

Wallace, M. J., Jr., & Fay, C. H. (1988). *Compensation theory and practice* (2nd ed.). Boston: PWS-Kent.

Werther, W. B., Jr. (1989). Childcare and eldercare benefits. *Personnel, 66*(9), 42–45.

Yoder, D., & Staudohar, P. D. (1982). *Personnel management and industrial relations*. Englewood Cliffs, NJ: Prentice Hall.

Communication In Organizations and Social Interactions

What happens when an organization fails to communicate effectively with its employees? A major manufacturing company had decided that they needed to lay off about one-third of their union work force in order to manage production costs and remain competitive in a global market. This company had been a family-owned business for about fifty years, but had recently been purchased by a large manufacturing conglomerate. The new management team was composed of some members who had been with the original family owners and newer members brought in by the conglomerate. The newer managers had not had a chance to get to know many of the employees who would be affected by the layoff, while the managers with more tenure had formed strong relationships with several of these same employees.

On the day the layoff was to be announced, management met with the union in the morning to discuss the situation and to let the union be involved in how this communication would be transmitted to the employees. The original plan was to make an announcement to all employees by noon, followed by a press conference to alert the surrounding community of the impending layoff. However, as the discussion among three factions (more tenured management, new management, and the union representatives) became heated, it became clear that they would not meet the noon deadline. The talks ended about 3:30 P.M., a press release was issued, and the layoff became public knowledge.

The result of this method of communicating the layoff was that first shift employees left work at 3:00 P.M. and learned of the layoff on the evening news. Receiving the information in this manner added insult to injury to many employees, who felt that management owed it to them to let them know first before informing the local media. Since the layoff was not scheduled to begin for at least six months, management was left with employees who were not only uncertain about their future, but also angry and resentful at the way they had been told that their future was in jeopardy.

Ultimately, management's inability to efficiently communicate news of the layoff resulted in much lower morale and production than if it had met with employees and shared the news in a more concerned, open manner. For example, the management team could have held a company assembly to announce the layoff, or could have informed all supervisors, who would then hold departmental meetings to tell employees the news on a more personal level. Either of these methods would have been preferable to letting employees hear of the layoff on the local news.

It seems that as more devices are created to facilitate communication, it becomes more difficult to connect with a human being. When you call your friends, you talk to their answering machines. They return your call and talk to your answering machine. Many large organizations use computerized operator systems, which ask you to make a series of choices. Pushing the appropriate numbers on your telephone allows you to listen to various types of recorded information. Letters are sent by fax, new friendships develop on the Internet, and teleconferences have become commonplace. These trends suggest that interpersonal, face-to-face communication may eventually become a thing of the past. However, today's work environment still requires daily interaction between employees and their supervisors, coworkers, and vendors.

The business world is marked by changing consumer demands, rapid new product development, corporate mergers and takeovers, and expanding international markets. This fluid environment creates a strong need for effective communication in the workplace. Janis (1989) addresses this issue through research on policy making, investigating the influence of social and psychological factors on uncorrected misperceptions and miscalculations. Starbuck and Nystrom (1981) propose that adaptability is an important concern in these changing circumstances. According to Starbuck and Nystrom, lack of adaptation will turn a company into a temporary entity. Their theory may help to explain why only 2% of all businesses created are still in existence after fifty years.

Effective communication benefits an organization by decreasing the occurrence of misperceptions and increasing its adaptability to changing conditions. Within the organization, communication affects areas such as employee selection, motivation, job performance, job satisfaction, performance appraisal, and training programs. Communication also influences the relationship between an organization and its environment. This relationship depends on the interactions between employees and clients, vendors, and shareholders.

Communication is a process through which information is transmitted from a sender to a receiver (Greenberg & Baron, 1993). To be effective, communication must include the clear transfer of information and a shared understanding of what that information means (Robbins, 1996).

Organizations are essentially information-processing systems (Gerloff, 1985). The environment sends information to the organization, where it is received and processed. Then the organization becomes the sender, transmitting information back to the environment, often as a product or service. The development of effective communication skills requires an understanding of how communication influences this information-processing system. This understanding can be gained by examining the functions of communication.

FUNCTIONS OF COMMUNICATION

Scott and Mitchell (1976) were able to identify four major functions of communication. These functions include:

1. *Information:* Managers must have access to pertinent information for use in considering alternatives, future events, and the potential outcomes of decisions. The ability to effectively transfer information is a valuable asset to the decision-making process.

2. *Motivation:* Effective communication can motivate employees and encourage employee commitment to organizational goals. To accomplish this, employers must provide clear descriptions of their expectations of employees and the employees' level of performance. It is also important to inform employees of the positive consequences of good performance.

3. *Emotion:* There is a social component inherent in all work environments. Communication allows employees to air their frustrations or satisfaction with subordinates, peers, or managers. It is a vehicle through which workers can express their feelings and needs.

4. *Control:* The communication of company policies and procedures controls employee behavior by clearly outlining acceptable and unacceptable work behaviors. This type of information helps to establish company norms that clarify specific duties, sources of authority, and the potential outcomes of noncompliance.

It is important to understand why communication is a critical component in the work environment. It is also helpful to be aware of how information travels within an organization.

DIRECTION OF COMMUNICATION

The structure and management philosophy of an organization determine its communication trends and networks. Factors such as the levels of management, supervisor–employee ratios, and the physical environment combine to determine how information is processed. Another important factor to consider is the direction, or flow, of communication within the company. The flow may be downward, horizontal, or upward (see Table 13.1 on page 442).

Downward communication originates with top management and filters down to employees on the bottom rungs of the organizational ladder. This type of transmission is usually formal and is often in written form (Harris, 1993). It is used to provide job instructions, explain procedures, and conduct performance appraisals (Katz & Kahn, 1978). An example of the flow

TABLE 13.1	Media for employment communications	

Oral	Written

I: Downward

1. Personal instructions	1. Instructions and orders
2. Lectures, conferences, committee meetings	2. Letters and memos
3. Interviews, counseling	3. House organs
4. Telephone, public address systems, movies, slides, closed-circuit television	4. Bulletin boards
5. Whistles, bells, etc.	5. Posters
6. Social affairs, including union activities	6. Handouts and information racks
7. Grapevine, gossip, rumor	7. Handbooks and manuals
	8. Annual reports
	9. Union publications

II: Upward

1. Face-to-face reports and conversations	1. Reports
2. Interviews	2. Personal letters
3. Telephone	3. Grievances
4. Meetings, conferences	4. Suggestion systems
5. Social affairs	5. Attitude and information surveys
6. Grapevine	6. Union publications
7. Union representatives and channels	

III: Horizontal

1. Lectures, conferences, and committee meetings	1. Letters, memos, reports—carbons, ditto, and mimeograph
2. Telephone, intercom systems, movies, slides, closed-circuit television	2. House organ
3. Social affairs, including union activities	3. Bulletin boards and posters
4. Grapevine, rumor	4. Handbooks and manuals
	5. Annual report
	6. Union publications

Source: From *Personnel Management and Industrial Relations* (7th ed.). (p. 320), by D. Yoder and P. D. Staudohar, 1982, Englewood Cliffs, NJ: Prentice Hall. Copyright 1982 by Prentice-Hall, Inc. Reprinted by permission of Prentice-Hall, Upper Saddle River, NJ.

of downward communication might begin with a memo from the company president to all managers. The managers then transmit the message to their employees.

Horizontal (or lateral) **communication** is characterized by exchanges between employees, between managers, or within work units and departments. Sometimes it is more efficient to communicate directly with a peer group than to send the information through the organizational hierarchy. This type of communication tends to be direct and informal and is often transmitted verbally. A departmental staff meeting is a good example of horizontal communication. Other examples include two employees discussing a project and secretaries setting up a rotating lunch schedule.

Upward communication flows from subordinates to superiors. This type of communication gives management the opportunity to learn how employees receive and understand managers' downward communications (Adler, 1991). It also allows supervisors to monitor the effectiveness of workers' activity while giving employees

PRACTICE PERSPECTIVE 13.1

360-Degree Feedback Can Change Your Life

Here's how it works. Everyone from the office screwup to your boss, including your crackerjack assistant and your rival across the hall, will fill out lengthy, anonymous questionnaires about you. You'll complete one too. Are you crisp, clear, and articulate? Abrasive? Spreading yourself too thin? Trustworthy? Off-the-cuff remarks may be gathered too. A week or two later you'll get the results, all crunched and graphed by a computer. Ideally, all this will be explained by someone from your human-resources department or the company that handled the questionnaires, a person who can break bad news gently. You get to see how your opinion of yourself differs from those of the group of subordinates who participated, your peer group, and the boss.

What's most interesting about feedback is the huge variety of unpredictable comments—and potential learning—that it delivers. Most people are surprised by what they hear. Only a fraction of managers have a good grasp of their own abilities. Those with certain kinds of blind spots are routinely judged less effective by co-workers.

The president of Raychem, a $1.5 billion electronics and electrical equipment company in California, says he didn't get any major surprises about himself but he was intrigued to learn that he wasn't fooling his subordinates either. They told Robert Saldich he wasn't good at contingency planning. His reaction: "Shucks. I haven't been hiding here."

Jo Malik, manager of a team of engineers at AT&T, got nicked for his vigorous temper. That was not a big revelation—he was already working on correcting it. But he was startled to learn that when his direct reports asked him about the company's plans for the group, he often scrunched up in his chair. His subordinates thought he was being evasive. "I was just trying to come up with the answer," he says. "If I were being evasive, I would have said I couldn't answer."

Most revealing to Malik was that his subordinates expected things of him he'd never imagined. "I found out I need to articulate the vision and mission of our little unit. I was surprised."

Many companies are using feedback for cultural change, to accelerate the shift to teamwork and employee empowerment. Jerry Wallace, an up-and-coming manager at General Motors, was surprised by his feedback too. The message that hit Wallace hardest was a common one: excess control. "The strongest message I got was that I need to delegate more," he says. "I thought I'd been doing it. But I need to do it more and sooner. My people are saying, 'Turn me loose.'"

A few conditions are crucial for feedback to make a difference. Obviously, the person has to want to change. To make the most of the process experts say you should talk over the results with everyone who participated. Ideally, your boss will have already had training from human-resources personnel on how to respond when you come for help. But with or without the boss, pick a small number of shortcomings to fix and decide on a few concrete remedies.

Says Patricia Russo, head of AT&T's business communications unit: "I think we're just beginning to see the power of this." So far, the feedback on feedback is positive.

Source: From "360° Feedback Can Change Your Life," by B. O'Reilly, *Fortune*, Vol. 120, No. 2, pp. 93–100, October 17, 1995, New York: Time, Inc. Copyright 1995 by Time, Inc. All rights reserved.

the chance to evaluate supervisors' performance. Upward communications may be formal or informal, written or verbal. An example of upward communication could be a union's demands to the company president, an employee meeting with a supervisor to report on a current project, or notes placed in an employee suggestion box (see Practice Perspective 13.1).

Multiple-source feedback, also referred to as 360-degree feedback, is an example of communication that is downward, horizontal, and upward. It is possible to standardize multiple-source feedback, which provides information about the organization at large. To provide the data, all employees complete a survey that evaluates management personnel. Multiple-source feedback can also be customized, which involves gathering information about a specific individual. For example, data may come from a self-report, subordinates' reports (upward communication), peer reports (horizontal communication), and a manager's report (downward communication). Respondents remain anonymous, a practice that allows employees to respond truthfully and without fear of negative consequences.

The type of instrument used in multiple source feedback is usually an "Agree/Disagree" scale or a "Descriptive/Nondescriptive" scale. The respondent rates the individual who is the subject of the feedback on a continuum, often from 1 to 10. For example, an item may state, "Is on time for meetings." If the individual who is being rated is always late, the score may be a 2 out of 10 possible points. These scales may have from 25 to 100 items and could take from 10 to 60 minutes to complete (Campbell, 1995).

· ·

TYPES OF COMMUNICATION

One-Way versus Two-Way Communication

Communication can be one-way or two-way in nature. **One-way communication** occurs when a sender issues a message to a receiver or a set of receivers. The sender does not know whether the message is understood, because the receiver does not provide feedback. One critical difficulty with this method is that a large number of misperceptions can occur (see Practice Perspective 13.2).

The bulls-eye model provides another example of one-way communication (Myers & Myers, 1982). This method is similar to an archer (the sender) aiming an arrow (the message) at a target (the receiver), and shooting. The arrow may or may not hit the bulls-eye. A sender must construct and present a message that can be clearly understood. Without the aid of feedback from the target, sometimes even the best "archer" can miss the mark in terms of sending an effective message.

Two-way communication is interactive, characterized by reciprocity and active listening. It enhances understanding by using feedback from receiver to sender. Myers and Myers (1982) refer to this as the ping-pong model of communication because participants take turns being sender and receiver. The sender transmits a message, and the receiver responds. The sender then answers the receiver's response, and the process continues in this manner until both parties reach a consensus on the meaning of the original message. One drawback of this model is its failure to address some complex dynamics, such as the influence of unique personal interpretations and even misinterpretation that can occur in oral exchanges. These common complexities are often due to factors such as voice volume and tone, body language, and social style. However, the two-way method is a significant improvement over one-way communication because the feedback that it adds enables both participants to ensure that their message was understood as they intended and, if not, to correct it.

Transactional communication views communication as a process that develops between two entities. It recognizes the interdependence and reciprocity between sender and receiver. This method also acknowledges individual perspective as a relevant variable in any communication effort. An example of transactional communication might be two employees of an advertising agency, Bob and Terry, who meet to create a new slogan for their client. Bob comes up with a few ideas, and Terry adds ideas of her own. They list all of their ideas and then narrow the list to

PRACTICE PERSPECTIVE 13.2

An Example of the Principle of Reciprocity

The most dramatic example of the principle of reciprocity that I ever encountered involved an executive in one of my client companies. One day he addressed a meeting of all of his field managers. His topic was his pride and joy: a major cost-reduction campaign that he had personally engineered. He went on at some length, citing economy after economy that he had found with his eagle eye and his sharp pencil. When he finished there was some polite applause. Then a grizzled old veteran stood up. He was nearing retirement, and felt he could afford to be candid. "Sir," he said, "maybe you've pushed this cost-cutting business too far. The men are starting to grumble. They say their workload is getting too big. They say they don't have enough time to do the job right any more."

The executive was tired. He'd had a bad day. He was not in his best form. So he exploded. "Damn it!" he said. "That's a bunch of crap! Anybody who says that doesn't know what they are talking about! Every one of these cuts is absolutely justified! Do you hear that? Nobody's workload is too heavy. You're just listening to a bunch of lazy guys making lame excuses. I don't want to hear any more of this nonsense! Do I make myself clear?"

He had indeed, and he got his wish. After that, none of the field managers passed on reports about the rising tide of resentment and dissatisfaction in the field force. About a year later, the executive was flabbergasted when hundreds of field employees signed a petition demanding the formation of a union. They had returned the compliment. The executive had cut himself off from feedback, which is something that no manager in his or her right mind should ever do. It's about as smart as standing on your own oxygen tube.

Source: From *The Management of Human Relations* (p. 51), by S. W. Gellerman, 1967, New York: Holt, Rinehart and Winston, Inc. Copyright 1967 by Rinehart and Winston, Inc. Reprinted with permission.

three potential slogans. Bob suggests a revision in the first slogan, and Terry agrees. Their interactions continue in this fashion, and they revise slogans until they come up with a product that is mutually acceptable. Bob and Terry depend on each other to provide reciprocal feedback and engage in a process of communicating and fine-tuning their ideas.

Communication Networks

Communication networks are formal and informal organizational channels through which information travels. **Formal communication channels** transmit information vertically through the organizational hierarchy. These communications are usually written, highly structured, professional interactions. They tend to focus on production issues, including information about the division of work in the organization (Gerloff, 1985). The goal of most formal communication is to effectively manage resources and coordinate efforts. A formal channel in the workplace could be a memo dictating a new policy or regulation, an annual performance appraisal, or an employee interview.

Formal channels may be any of several small-group networks. Figure 13.1 on page 446 shows three common networks (Robbins, 1996). The **chain network** links members through the formal chain of command. Each employee communicates with only one other employee at a time, either directly above or below the sender-employee in the organization hierarchy. The **wheel network** encourages information to flow from supervisor to employees in a formal, one-

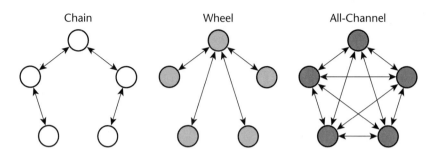

FIGURE 13.1

Three common small-group networks.

Source: From *Organizational behavior* (7th ed.) (p. 7), by S. P. Robbins, © 1996, Englewood Cliffs, NJ: Prentice-Hall. Reprinted by permission of Prentice-Hall, Upper Saddle River, NJ.

on-one manner. The **all-channel network** allows all employees to communicate with each other in multiple directions.

Some networks work better than others in different situations. Simple problem-solving tasks can be communicated through the chain or wheel network because they do not usually require multiple communications. More complex problems can be effectively addressed with an all-channel network that allows a multidirectional flow of communication (Shaw, 1964). It is important to remember that a particular network may work best in a particular situation but no single network is consistently superior to the others. Table 13.2 lists some of the characteristics of the three types of network.

Informal communications travel in all directions and encompass the social aspects inherent in any work situation. They are usually used to support the overall production effort but are

more relaxed and unstructured than formal communication. Gerloff (1985, p. 288) suggests that "individuals are sometimes able to use the informal communication system to compensate for the information-processing deficiencies of the formal system." Informal communication is usually spontaneous, face-to-face conversation that occurs between peers or employees and supervisors.

Two types of informal communication networks are the grapevine and the rumor mill. The **grapevine** is a network in which information is distributed very quickly through informal channels in the workplace (Greenberg & Baron, 1993). This is similar to playing "telephone," also known as "gossip," with a group of people: One person whispers a message into the ear of another, who then whispers the message to another, until the last person receives the message. When the last person repeats the mes-

TABLE 13.2   Small-group networks and effectiveness criteria

	Networks		
Criteria	Chain	Wheel	All-Channel
Speed	Moderate	Fast	Fast
Accuracy	High	High	Moderate
Emergence of a leader	Moderate	High	None
Member satisfaction	Moderate	Low	High

Source: From *Organizational behavior* (7th ed.) (p. 383), by S. P. Robbins, © 1996, Englewood Cliffs, NJ: Prentice-Hall. Reprinted by permission of Prentice-Hall, Upper Saddle River, NJ.

sage aloud, it is usually significantly different from the original message. The humorous result of this game is the primary problem with grapevine communication: The essence of the initial message is often garbled or inaccurate.

Suppose the president of a large corporation asks an assistant to bring a file to a board meeting. The assistant overhears the words "corporate merger" and tells the vice-president's assistant about it. The information is then shared with a secretary, who shares it with a friend in the accounting department. Within hours the news has spread throughout the organization. Employees become concerned about the ramifications of a possible takeover, which may or may not actually be in the making. The corporate officers might have been approached by another firm and decided to reject the offer. Perhaps the board was discussing the takeover of another company.

This scenario is an illustration of how rumors spread in the workplace. **Rumors** are messages that are based more on speculation than on fact. They are extreme cases of inaccurate information. "Rumors [tend to] run like wildfire through organizations because the information they present is so interesting and ambiguous. [This] ambiguity leaves it open to embellishment as it passes orally from one person to the next" (Greenberg & Baron, 1993, p. 508). One problem with rumors is their damaging effect. Suppose the employees believed the rumor that the company was going to be taken over by another corporation. This change could result in new policies and procedures or maybe even downsizing. The employees might begin to worry about their tenure at the firm. This stress could affect worker motivation, satisfaction, and production. Although the takeover might be imaginary, the stress created by rumors can be very real and can have a significant impact on the organization.

Formal communication can be one-way, not allowing feedback, while informal communication can be damaging because of grapevine transmission or rumor mills. However, both types

of communication are necessary in the work environment. Formal communication is effective in setting official guidelines and organizational policy. It also provides a forum within which employees can officially share and document their concerns. Informal communication nurtures the social and emotional factors in the workplace, often creating an environment that is "employee friendly."

These concepts have evolved from a variety of management philosophies that provide a foundation for organizational communications.

MODELS OF ORGANIZATIONAL STRUCTURE AND COMMUNICATION

The Classical School

The classical school of organizational management is an early theory of management that focuses on production. One of its primary components is the concept of **scientific management.** This model takes a mechanistic view of production, which sees employees as hired hands. Scientific management is concerned with increasing output to secure economic gains for both labor and management (Corman, Banks, Bantz, & Mayer, 1990). Therefore, it is concerned primarily with what the worker can accomplish, rather than with the worker as a human being (Harris, 1993). Industrial engineers and economists are responsible for the creation of this theory. It is still used in varying degrees in today's work environments.

F. W. Taylor was a mechanical engineer and a strong proponent of scientific management. He held an executive position in the steel industry during the early 1900s, and conducted time-and-motion studies of employees shoveling coal at the Bethlehem Steel Company. This research became his trademark contribution to the scientific management model (Taylor, 1947). Taylor believed that structure was of primary importance to an organization. He thought manage-ment and workers should share equally in labor and responsibility. However, Taylor suggested that managers are responsible for workers' out-put. He proposed that employees' performance would improve if it were directly related to pay. Taylor believed that employees were motivated by financial need and would act to secure in-come. Taylor also believed that conflict was the result of improper use of scarce resources. He advocated the need for clear job designs based on a scientific analysis of the best way to per-form any task, and supported scientific selection and training of employees.

The scientific management model stresses a downward flow of information, assuming that this is the most logical method for dispensing in-formation. However, this type of one-way com-munication does not allow for comments or feed-back from employees to management. It also ignores the informal, social, and peer communi-cations that are inherent in any organization. The assumption is that workers will understand what they are told and will comply with man-agerial directives so that they will obtain finan-cial compensation. This model does not con-sider the emotional or motivational functions of communication. According to scientific man-agement theory, financial gain is the only moti-vating factor for employees.

The classical school is also responsible for the development of the **bureaucracy.** A bureaucracy is a hierarchy that focuses on rules, professional qualifications, and impersonal relationships. It is a highly formalized organizational structure with minimum flexibility (Harris, 1993). Weber (1947), a German sociologist, stressed that bu-reaucracies impose order through regulation and suggested that people would naturally re-spond to clear authority. Weber's bureaucracy disapproved of hiring employees on the basis of family connections or any other special privi-leges. He thought organizations needed to focus on individual ability and should hire employees on the basis of their technical competence.

Corman et al. (1990, p. 14) describe bureau-cracy as a social tool that "legitimizes control of many by the few." They suggest that bureaucra-cies are excessively rigid and nonadaptive and stifle human creativity. Some key bureaucratic elements include reliance on expertise, equal treatment of workers, specific standards, exten-sive record keeping, and enforcement of rules and regulations.

Communication in a bureaucratic setting fol-lows a highly formalized communication struc-ture. It originates at the top of the organizational hierarchy, and communication among peers is almost nonexistent. The "production function of communication is strongly emphasized at the expense of its innovation and social functions. It ignores the complexity of human motivation and the richness of human resources" (Myers & Myers, 1982, p. 30).

The bureaucratic organizational structure encourages conformity to organizational norms and group think. Janis (1982) describes **group think** as the phenomenon of a group thinking alike and ignoring information that could im-pede consensus. Group think produces a "high dependency upon a cohesive group of fellow (employees) for social support" (Janis, 1989, p. 220). Conformity takes precedence over cre-ativity or group brainstorming, and new ideas that do not fit the status quo are not welcome.

The Behavioral School

The behavioral school challenged classical the-ory when researchers discovered that employees who felt good about themselves and their envi-ronment were more satisfied and productive than those who did not. The behavioral school suggested that improving the social aspects of the workplace would make employees more con-tent with their jobs and therefore, more produc-tive (Harris, 1993). The behavioral approach had an employee-oriented perspective. Employ-ees were seen as more than just hired hands. Proponents of this model recognized the importance of the emotional and social components of human behavior in the workplace.

The Human Relations Model

The **human relations model** is a product of the behavioral school. This model uses an informal organizational structure and stresses the importance of social factors in the workplace and the need for individual motivation and growth (Myers & Myers, 1982). The human relations model was based on the **Hawthorne studies** (see Historical Perspective 13.1 on page 450). As was discussed in Chapter 1, these studies were conducted between 1927 and 1932 by Elton Mayo, a professor of industrial research at Harvard University. This research was designed according to the mechanistic view but resulted in the development of a new school of thought regarding organizational management.

Communication within the human relations model is quite different from what occurs in the classical model. The human relations model encourages employee feedback as communication flows upward and laterally throughout the organizational hierarchy. In direct opposition to the classical model, informal communication among workers is a critical part of the human relations movement.

Human relations theorists believe that financial rewards alone are not enough to motivate employees (Argyris, 1957). They stress the importance of effective leadership, communication skills of management personnel, and the social function of communication in the workplace. These are seen as primary means of increasing employee motivation, satisfaction, and production. According to this model, informal communication and peer relationships are as important to employee motivation as are directives issued from top management.

The Human Resource Model

A second model that the behavioral school developed is **human resource management.** This approach was developed when managers realized

the benefits of employee involvement in the design and execution of work. Employees were found to perform best when they were internally and externally motivated (Heath, 1994).

Human resource management draws from the classical and behavioral schools in defining the optimal work environment as a "structured development combined with an awareness of human needs" (Harris, 1993, p. 52). This approach views employees as resources rather than merely hired hands or social beings.

A cornerstone of human resource theory is McGregor's (1960) Theory X and Theory Y assumptions about human behavior at work (see Historical Perspective 13.2 on page 451). Theory X follows the classical school of thought, viewing workers as lazy, lacking in ambition, and needing careful direction and supervision. Theory Y adheres to the behavioral approach, suggesting that workers need opportunities for growth, desire meaningful work, and will participate in creating meaningful work if given the chance (Harris, 1993).

McGregor's (1960) model has several implications for communication. Theory X mandates clear, one-way communication that originates at the top of the organizational hierarchy. Theory Y stresses communication that is informal, open, innovative, and multidirectional. This theory focuses on the integration of personal needs and organizational goals. It suggests that management should create a structure that simultaneously allows fulfillment of employee needs and organizational objectives.

According to McGregor's (1960) model, employees need to feel involved in what is happening in the company. This sense of connection and purpose provides a sense of power and inclusion for the employees. Production will increase as trust develops and workers feel they are an integral part of the organization's success or failure (Harris, 1993; Myers & Myers, 1982).

Another contributor to the human resource model was Likert (1961, 1967), who introduced the general concept of work teams, or familylike

HISTORICAL PERSPECTIVE 13.1

The Hawthorne Studies

1. *The illumination experiment, and the Hawthorne effect.*

   In the mid-1920s the National Research Council's illuminating Engineering Society conducted a series of studies on industrial lighting at the Hawthorne (Illinois) plant of the Western Electric Company. The council intended for the researchers to determine the relationship between lighting conditions and workers productivity. Results of these experiments were startling. As illumination went up in the room of the experimental group productivity also went up as expected. However, surprisingly, productivity went up also in the control group where lighting had remained constant. When the experimenters *decreased* the intensity of the lighting in the experimental room expecting productivity to go down, productivity still went up. As lighting further decreased productivity continued to go up. Something peculiar was obviously at work and it did not seem to have much to do with lighting conditions. It seemed that the workers' productivity was related to the special attention they were getting. As "research participants" workers felt motivated to produce more. This effect, the "Hawthorne effect" as it came to be known, refers to the tendency of people to behave in unusual ways when they know they are singled out, observed, and generally given special attention. Clearly the Hawthorne effect could not be accounted for in the terms of classical theory.

2. *The relay assembly test room experiment.*

   In the relay assembly test room a group of six women were assigned to assemble telephone relays. A variety of changes were introduced in the conditions of the job: group payment, incentive breaks, shorter working hours, and refreshments. After each of these treatments was introduced, productivity went up. Then the relay assembly test went back to its original 48-hour six-day week, with no incentives, no breaks, and no refreshments. Productivity went *up*. And it went up to the highest level yet recorded.

   At that point it became clear to the researchers that *human elements* such as workers, motivation and attitudes, social relations and supervisory attitudes and *not* the purely physical and technical conditions of the job had an effect on workers productivity.

3. *The bank wiring assembly observation room experiment.*

   In the last phase of the Hawthorne studies the bank wiring observation room experiment was set up to test some of the premises formulated at the conclusion of earlier experiments. A group of nine male workers who assembled terminal banks for telephone exchanges were involved in that phase of the study. They were a highly integrated group with their own norms and code of conduct. The researchers wanted to test the effects of a group piecework incentive pay plan. They assumed that the workers would seek their own economic interest and increase their production by having faster workers pressure the slower ones to improve their output. Yet group pressure did not quite work the way the researchers had anticipated. Once the worker group had defined what constituted the acceptable output for a day's work and, once they knew they could reach it, the workers slacked off, particularly the faster ones. Violating the group norm by being a "rate buster" and overproducing or by being a "chiseler" and underproducing was definitely unacceptable by the group's own standards. The researchers concluded that wage incentives were less effective in determining an individual worker's productivity than the sense of security and acceptance offered by the work group which not only set its own standard of production but exerted strong group pressure to achieve, maintain, and not exceed that standard.

Source: From *Managing by Communication: An Organizational Approach* (p. 37), by M. T. Myers and G. E. Myers, 1996, New York: McGraw-Hill. Copyright 1996 by McGraw-Hill. Reprinted with permission.

Douglas McGregor's Theory X and Theory Y: Basic Assumptions

Theory X

1. The average human being dislikes work and will avoid it.
2. Most people must be coerced, controlled, with punishment to get them to put forth adequate effort toward achievement of organizational objectives.
3. The average person prefers to be directed, wishes to avoid responsibility, has little ambition and seeks security above all.

Theory Y

1. Expenditure of physical and mental effort is as natural as play and rest.
2. External control and threat of punishment are not the only means to bring about effort toward organizational objectives. People will exercise self-control and self direction in the service of objectives toward which they are committed.
3. Commitment to objectives is a function of the rewards associated with their achievement.
4. The average person learns under proper conditions to seek rather than avoid responsibility.
5. The capacity to exercise a relatively high degree of imagination and creativity in the solution of organizational problems is widely distributed among the population.
6. Under the conditions of modern industrial life, the intellectual potential of the average human being is only partially utilized.

Source: From *Managing by Communication: An Organizational Approach* (p. 40), by M. T. Myers and G. E. Myers, 1996, New York: McGraw-Hill. Copyright 1996 by McGraw-Hill. Reprinted with permission.

groupings, within the organization. This model is often referred to as the **linking-pin model,** because managers belong to both the group of managers and the group that includes their subordinates. Inclusion in both groups allows managers to serve as linking pins. They encourage shared communication and decision making by consolidating upward and downward communication within the organization.

Harris (1993) provided a different view of the linking-pin model. Harris regarded managers as pins that connected the entire organization, rather than as links between two disparate groups (managers and subordinates). This version of the linking-pin model calls for a participative approach rather than an "us–them" dichotomy between managers and employees.

Likert (1967) proposed four systems of management (see Table 13.3 on page 452). These systems include (1) Exploitative-Authoritative, (2) Benevolent-Authoritative, (3) Consultative, and (4) Participative. System 1 closely resembles scientific management and McGregor's (1960)

Theory X model of management. System 4, which is the linking-pin model, parallels McGregor's Theory Y. Systems 2 and 3 represent varying degrees of Systems 1 and 4.

Differences in communication are apparent in each system of Likert's (1967) model. Communication becomes more informal, personal, multidirectional, and effective in moving from System 1 to System 4. Participative management, or System 4 management, is the clear favorite. This form of management is characterized by frequent, accurate, trusted communication that flows in all directions.

The Systems School

The **systems school** is also based on the behavioral model. It refers to the idea that the whole is greater than the sum of its parts. Every organizational system consists of subsystems, subsubsystems, and so on (Heath, 1994). Each of these subsystems joins to make up the whole, which is an organization that creates specific products or services. Communication is a continuous proc-

TABLE 13.3	Explanation of Likert's Four Systems of Management

System 1: Exploitative–Authoritative

1. Top-to-bottom chain of command—one-way communication.
2. Employees not trusted by management.
3. Fear is the major motivator for employees.
4. Mistrust permeates communication atmosphere.
5. At lower levels of the organization, an informal organization develops with different goals from leadership.

System 2: Benevolent–Authoritative

1. Majority of decisions made at the top.
2. Some decisions made at lower levels.
3. Motivation based on rewards and punishment.
4. Management gives off signals of trusting employees.
5. An informal organization develops that might work with the overall goals of the organization.

System 3: Consultative

1. Lower level management actually implements policies set by upper management.
2. Two-way communication between different levels of the organization.
3. A strong, informal organization operates that may resist or support the organization.
4. Workers have considerably more control and responsibility.
5. Management exhibits some significant trust in employees.

System 4: Participative

1. A team effort is used for decisions.
2. Trust exists throughout the organizations.
3. Extensive communication at all levels and between all levels.
4. Formal and informal structures have common goals and might be the same.
5. Motivation arises from participation by employees.

Source: From *Managing by communication: An organizational approach* (p. 7), by M. T. Myers and G. E. Myers, 1996, New York: McGraw-Hill. Copyright 1996 by McGraw-Hill. Reprinted with permission.

ess, or transaction, that occurs between and within systems and subsystems. For example, the

> marketing (system) interlocks with the manufacturing system, which joins the people (system) within the organization who create a product along with vendors (another system) who supply raw materials and persons who supply and service manufacturing equipment (yet another system) (Heath, 1994, p. 93).

Two major contributors to the systems school were Katz and Kahn (1978), who developed the **open systems model.** Katz and Kahn proposed that an organization, as a system, operates like a framework rather than a theoretical entity. The framework is used to examine organizations as goal-oriented, integrated wholes, consisting of interacting and interrelated parts (Harris, 1993). Information comes into the system environment as input, is processed, and returns to the environment as output. The output can then become input for another system. Input may consist of energy, money, personnel, or information. It can be processed by a variety of methods, techniques, or procedures. The resulting output can be either a product or a service (Harris, 1993).

Open systems differ from closed systems in that they continuously exchange energy with the environment through input and output. To survive, an open system organization must constantly receive new energy from the environment. An open system continuously strives for a productive balance between input, transformation of input, and output (Berrien, 1976). This balance is achieved by monitoring several characteristics, or processes, that safeguard against becoming a closed system. These include boundaries, dynamic homeostasis, entropy, feedback, differentiation, and equifinality.

Boundaries distinguish the organization from its environment. They recognize that the organization is dependent on, yet separate from, its environment. Boundaries are not physical barriers but flows of communication. Rogers and Argawala-Rogers (1976) point out that although communication between the organization and its environment is important, communication flows more freely within the organization than between the organization and its environment.

Dynamic homeostasis describes the fluid balance of input, transformation, and output that occurs within an open system and between the system and its environment. It is a state in which deviations in one subsystem are compensated for by changes in related subsystems (Berrien, 1976). For example, if a malfunction in machinery temporarily slows production, the sales force should be alerted to make certain that customers are given realistic delivery dates. The deviation in the production subsystem is compensated for by the sales subsystem. When a system fails to maintain dynamic homeostasis, it can fall prey to entropy, disorganization, or failure.

Entropy occurs when open systems become closed. The system fails to maintain dynamic homeostasis by discontinuing the cycle of input, transformation, and output. An example of entropy occurs when a company spends more money manufacturing a product than it receives from selling it. By not receiving input about the market value of the final product or price increase in the materials needed to make the product, the flow of communication is interrupted or blocked. One way to prevent this break in communication is to use the process of feedback.

Feedback allows the system to maintain its open state by soliciting information about its activities (Myers & Myers, 1982). It provides signals to the organization about how it is functioning in relation to the environment. Negative feedback alerts an organization that it is deviating from its planned course of action and allows management to decide which actions may be necessary to get back on track. An extended drop in sales would be a form of negative feedback, perhaps indicating a deviation in marketing or production.

Differentiation and specialization are rapidly becoming functions of open systems. Until recently, a company president was familiar with each employee's specific daily activities. However, today's organizations are complex and diverse. Corporate managers realize that they cannot master all of the organizational functions. Therefore they hire employees who have specialized training in particular areas. The successful open system recognizes the need for diversity and specialization. It creates and maintains specific subsystems to provide expertise in a variety of functions.

The principle of **equifinality** states that an objective can be met under a variety of conditions and through diverse methods (Myers & Myers, 1982). A single method is rarely effective in all situations. The workplace is a dynamic environment, and what works well one day may be a failure the next. Suppose legislation is passed that changes the acceptable level of pollutants from automobile exhaust systems. This legislation would dictate a change in automobile design and production. An auto manufacturer that clings to an old method of production would quickly become a closed system because of noncompliance with the new regulations.

The systems model suggests that communication plays an essential role in the relationships between and within organizational subsystems. Communication is regarded as a dynamic process that incorporates production and socially related exchanges. There is a strong focus on social relationships which led to the development of contingency theory.

Contingency Theory

Contingency theory assumes that the most effective organizational structure is situational, that is, developed in response to and dependent on the specific situation for which it will be used (Harris, 1993). Similar to the principle of equifinality, the contingency model recognizes that different situations require different organizational styles. "Contingency theory starts where Katz and Kahn left off and builds on the premise that situational and environmental factors must be included in any organizational analysis" (Myers & Myers, 1982, p. 51). Contingency theory promotes a situational approach to management that considers all of the environmental variables and tasks to be accomplished (Harris, 1993). Differentiation and integration are two concepts that are essential to understanding this model.

Differentiation is a concept defined by Lawrence and Lorsch (1967) of Harvard University. They examined the relationship between internal and environmental factors in organizations. The results of this study showed that organizational subsystems differ in tasks, people, and structures. For example, employees in a sales department are often autonomous, gregarious individuals who operate under deadlines but have flexible schedules. In contrast, production line personnel frequently work in isolation or in teams and adhere to a rigid schedule. Attributes

that are found within the larger system are referred to as elements of differentiation (Lawrence & Lorsch, 1967).

Integration is the process of coordinating subsystems to meet organizational goals. For example, the sales force needs to know the production capabilities of the manufacturing teams. A backlog can be created when more products are ordered than can reasonably be produced. This can result in customer dissatisfaction and may threaten the future of the organization. The production line manager must clearly communicate to the sales force information about production capabilities and the amount of required lead time. Integration is departmental collaboration that ensures that all subsystems remain autonomous and still meet the overall goals of the organization.

The contingency model suggests that managers must develop open attitudes and skills that encourage effective communication with people who are different from themselves. It suggests that integration can be achieved in a variety of ways. These range from the hierarchical integration of the classical model to compromise through communication, which is typical of the open system model. Lawrence and Lorsch (1967) suggest that ineffective organizations often fail to recognize differentiation between organizational departments and the need for integration. They assume that all departments are homogeneous and will work in harmony. Lawrence and Lorsch believe that the most effective organizations are those that are highly differentiated and integrated.

The act of communicating includes the transmission of information and a shared understanding of that information. Communication is more a process than an act. Several activities must occur for a communication effort to be successful.

Communication Process Model

The **communication process model** (Berlo, 1960) consists of several components (see Figure 13.2).

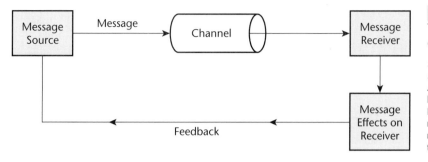

FIGURE 13.2
The process model of communication.

Source: Adapted from *The Process of Communication: An Introduction* (pp. 30–32) by D. K. Berlo, © 1960 by Holt, Rinehart and Winston, Inc. and renewed 1988 by D. K. Berlo, reproduced by permission of the publisher.

The source encodes a message, which is sent through a channel, to be decoded by the receiver. After receiving and decoding the message, the receiver experiences the effects of the message. Then the receiver sends information to the source to indicate that the message was received and understood. This model is presented here in a simplified form but provides a framework for analyzing the communication process.

The **message** is an idea that initiates the communication process. It may be physical or verbal. The message must be encoded to create shared meaning, which is critical to effective communication. **Encoding** is the process whereby a message is transformed into signals that can be carried by a communication channel. Encoding is influenced by the skills, attitudes, knowledge, values and beliefs of the source. The message is influenced by the way in which the source translates, or encodes the idea into a meaningful message.

The encoded message is then sent through a channel to the receiver. The **channel** is the medium that is used to transmit the information. It could be a newspaper, book, billboard, memorandum, letter, speech, or conversation. The type of channel that is employed depends on the intended audience and the nature and urgency of the message.

Decoding occurs when the message is received. **Decoding** is the process of filtering a message according to the receiver's personal skills, attitudes, knowledge, beliefs, and values. For exam-ple, if the receiver is illiterate, the lack of reading ability will mediate the effectiveness of a written memo. The **receiver** is the person, or intended audience, to whom the message is directed.

For communication to be effective, the source must consider his or her personal knowledge, skills, and attitudes as well as those of the receiver. The source must use a channel, words, and symbols that the receiver will easily recognize. For example, imagine that you are taking a class in which the professor talks "over your head." Professors are hired because of their expertise in a particular area. However, that expertise does not ensure that they have effective communication skills. Professors should assess the knowledge level of the students in teaching a course. Only then can lessons be prepared and presented in a manner that facilitates understanding and assimilation by the majority of students.

Communication effects are the intended results of the communication effort. Changes in the receivers' behavior can occur as a result of the transmission. For example, most professors want the communication effects of a lecture to be increased knowledge of the topic under study. Students can demonstrate this new knowledge on an exam or in practical exercises.

The final part of this model is **feedback,** which underlies the entire communication process (see Figure 13.2). Feedback is the response from the receiver to the source that indicates whether the intended message was received and understood.

Positive feedback informs the source that the message was received and understood as intended. **Negative feedback** indicates that the message was not correctly received or was misunderstood.

Students provide feedback to professors every semester through class discussions, assignments, and exams. If all students in a class performed poorly on an exam, this would constitute negative feedback. It would be clear that the audience (students) did not understand the professor's message.

The communication process model is a useful framework that emphasizes key components of effective communication. This model stresses the importance of multidirectional communication. It also highlights the critical role of feedback in the communication process. Flawed communication can result from a problem in any of the components or a breakdown somewhere in the process.

Wilson Learning Model

The Wilson Learning Corporation (1982) model of communication consists of three types of translations (see Figure 13.3). The first is the translation of the sender's thoughts into the sender's words. The second type is the translation of the sender's message into the words the receiver will understand. The third is the translation of what the receiver hears and the receiver's beliefs.

The first translation in a communication effort is internal. The sender translates the intended message internally before sending it. The second translation is external, between the sender and the receiver. It is not uncommon for a receiver to misinterpret a message during this translation. The sender's initial intent may not be clearly articulated because of a poor internal translation by the sender or misinterpretation by the receiver. The final translation is internal. It involves what the receiver believes was said and the receiver's thoughts or intentions about

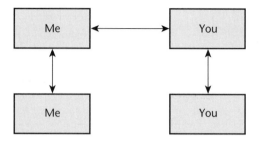

FIGURE 13.3   The three "conversations" model: the ones you have with yourself (Me–Me), the ones others have with themselves (You–You), and the ones you and others have with each other (Me–You).

Source: From *Connecting with People* (pp. 14–15), by Wilson Learning Corporation, 1982, Eden Prairie, MN: Wilson Learning Corporation. Copyright 1981 by Wilson Learning Corporation. Reprinted with permission.

the message. A receiver may have ideas about the information being transmitted. If the receiver believes that the intent of the message is different from the intent of the sender, the result may be garbled communication.

Even with simple communications, these three translations can produce errors in understanding. This problem is minimized when active listening skills are used. **Active listening** is a process by which the receiver gives feedback by paraphrasing the message to the sender. This ensures that the original intent was accurately transmitted. The receiver is encouraged to ask questions that will clarify the intended meaning. The sender and receiver continue this dialogue until the message contains a shared meaning for both parties.

PERSONAL FACTORS AFFECTING COMMUNICATION

Communication is a complex process, influenced by a variety of factors. Although the general organizational structure and management philosophy affect communication, as was discussed previously, smaller communication networks also play a role. For example, an individual's ability to process information can affect the communication process. Personal communication style can add to, or detract from, interpersonal communications. Nonverbal postures can provide clues to the underlying meaning of a message. The relationship between the sender and the receiver, the nature of the message itself, and the credibility of the source can all influence the process of communication.

Cognition and Communication

Cognition, in a general sense, denotes the thought processes that accompany an individual's actions. The variances in individual thought processes are referred to as individual differences. Individual differences are present in all dimensions, such as physical attributes, personality characteristics, interests, attitudes, and abilities. These unique differences make it difficult to develop rules that apply universally to all human behavior. People may share some characteristics, but they are not uniform across all dimensions. Individual differences are also found in terms of perception. Perception can be defined as a "process by which individuals organize and interpret their sensory impressions in order to give meaning to their environment" (Robbins, 1996, p. 132).

When several individuals are exposed to the same experience, they may react to or interpret that experience differently. A multitude of factors mediate individual perceptions of reality. How the world is perceived varies from person to person and may not be an accurate reflection of the environment. Perception is an important component of organizational communication because individual work behavior is based on a perception of reality, rather than on reality itself. Therefore, individual differences in perception play an important role in communication, especially in the processes of interpretation, understanding, and feedback.

According to the Wilson Learning model (see Figure 13.3), several translations occur when individuals communicate. People do more than merely respond to the sensory input that surrounds them. They process information cognitively and then react to the interpretations that result from this processing effort.

Failing to keep information to a reasonable level can result in **information overload.** This occurs when too much information is provided for the receiver to process. Miller (1960) discovered several common responses to information overload: omission, error, filtering, approximation, and escaping. **Omission** occurs when too much information is provided and the receiver fails to process some of it. **Error** refers to processing the information incorrectly. **Filtering** is the act of sifting out information that is perceived as less important. **Approximation** occurs when the recipient generalizes all of the information and offers a blanket response. **Escaping** occurs when the receiver does not deal with the information at all. Information overload can cause unnecessary stress in the workplace, which can result in misinterpretation and ineffective communication.

The issue of how much information needs to be shared leads to the question of how much the receiver really needs to know. What information is extraneous and threatens to confound or halt effective communication? Today, speedy collection and transmission of information are valued, sometimes to the neglect of information that is relevant and useful. Some people believe that it is best to amass and consider all of the available information. The **limited information collection principle** (Nadler and Hibino, 1990) disagrees. Nadler and Hibino propose that the only data to collect and consider are data that are essential to the bigger picture. Suppose you are in a performance appraisal conference with your supervisor. It may be distracting for the supervisor to discuss the performance of some of the individuals who work under you. The supervisor should limit the discussion to your own work behaviors, your own feelings about your performance, and developing personal or professional goals for the upcoming review period.

Selective Perception

Selective perception is a type of filter that is used to block out stimuli that will be disregarded and to select stimuli that require attention. This is an important cognitive tool because it is impossible to process all of the stimuli that are present in the environment. Selective perception allows individuals to avoid sensory overload. The decisions about which stimuli to attend to and which to disregard may be made consciously or unconsciously.

It appears that two factors play a role in the selection process. The first factor involves personal motives and attitudes. For example, suppose you had to rush to an early morning class and missed breakfast. Once in class, you found the material to be tedious and boring. Perhaps the lecture was on a chapter you had read and easily understood. You might start to think about what you want to order in the cafeteria as soon as the class is over. Your personal motive, to fill an empty stomach, would then guide your attention.

The second factor that affects the selection of stimuli is external influence. The extent to which a situation or object stands out from others around it is significant in terms of selection. This phenomenon is also known as **salience**. An example of salient stimuli might occur when a coworker who has just returned from vacation walks into a meeting with a deep tan. If the other employees were not tan, this person would stand out and would be salient. However, if everyone in the room had recently returned from tropical vacations, the salience of the coworker would be reduced.

Selective perception also provides a shortcut used in judging others. Rather than attending to every aspect of the environment, one can use selective perception to process bits and pieces of information. The way a person speaks, walks, or dresses will catch one's attention. Selective attention allows quick judgments to be made about others, but presents the risk of developing an incomplete or inaccurate picture.

The manner in which an individual perceives others is related to how that individual is likely to communicate in the work environment. It is easier to communicate with individuals who are perceived as similar to oneself. However, employees are rarely in a position to choose their coworkers and often work with people who are very different from themselves. It is important to be aware of selective perception and to make sure initial judgments do not shortchange coworkers.

Attribution Theory

A second factor that influences perception is attribution. This refers to identifying the causes of other people's behavior. **Attribution theory** examines the tendency to judge others according to the meanings we attribute to given behaviors (Kelley, 1972). Several characteristics are involved in the judgments made, including internal/external causation, distinctiveness, consensus, and consistency (Robbins, 1996). Figure 13.4 shows a model of the processes involved in attribution theory.

When making a judgment about other people, individuals typically assume that their behavior is caused by internal or external factors. **Internally caused behaviors** are believed to be under the control of the individual. **Externally caused behaviors** are thought to be the result of factors that are outside individual control. Attribution theory suggests that errors may occur in assigning attributes to others. Evidence shows that the influence of external factors is underestimated and the influence of internal factors is overestimated (Miller & Lawson, 1989; Ross, 1977). For example, suppose a coworker is late for work. According to attribution theory, initial thoughts are likely to attribute the coworker's

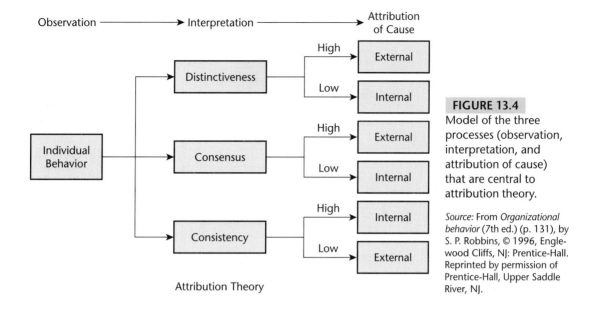

Observation ——————→ Interpretation —————————————→ Attribution
of Cause

FIGURE 13.4

Model of the three processes (observation, interpretation, and attribution of cause) that are central to attribution theory.

Source: From *Organizational behavior* (7th ed.) (p. 131), by S. P. Robbins, © 1996, Englewood Cliffs, NJ: Prentice-Hall. Reprinted by permission of Prentice-Hall, Upper Saddle River, NJ.

Attribution Theory

lateness to his or her inability to keep track of time (an internal force) instead of to the possibility of a flat tire or traffic jam (an external force).

Distinctiveness relates to whether a person behaves similarly across a variety of situations. For example, is the person who is late for work also prone to taking long lunches and missing project deadlines, or is tardiness out of character for this person? Distinctiveness influences our perception of the behavioral consistency of others. Consistent behavior is often attributed to internal causes, while inconsistent behavior will be attributed to external causes.

Consensus relates to the individual's behavior in relation to others. For example, an employee's tardiness might be judged differently if a snowstorm caused most employees to be late on the same day. The tardy behavior is not as salient as it would have been if just one person had been late and therefore stood out from the crowd. When consensus among the behaviors of a certain group is high, the cause is more likely to be attributed to external causes. However, when consensus is low (only one individual is

late), internal attributes are usually thought to cause the behavior.

Consistency relates to whether the person behaves in the same fashion over time. For example, is the employee regularly late for work or is this behavior an aberration? According to attribution theory, low-consistency behaviors are perceived as being externally caused. High-consistency behaviors are likely to be perceived as resulting from internal attributes. Individuals are assumed to have control over their actions. An incident may occur that is out of the individual control, but this should not be a frequent occurrence for someone who is judged to be consistent.

Greenberg and Baron (1993) suggest that attribution theory involves making and interpreting observations. The observations are then assigned an external or internal attribution of causality (see Figure 13.5 on page 460). **Fundamental attribution error** occurs when an incorrect causal attribution is assigned to an individual's behavior. This bias is related to the underestimation of external factors and the overestimation of internal factors.

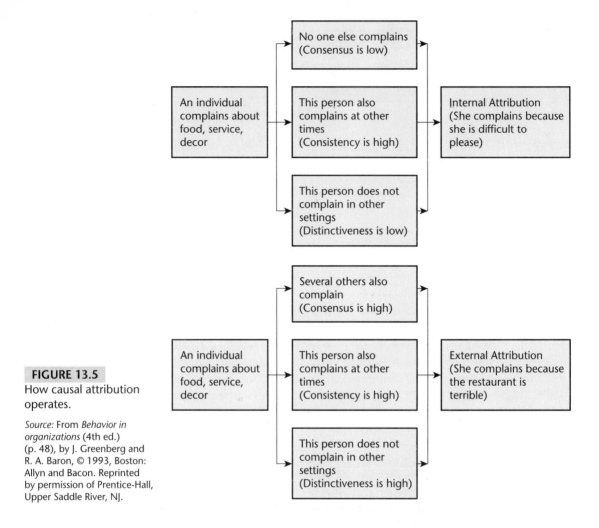

FIGURE 13.5
How causal attribution operates.

Source: From *Behavior in organizations* (4th ed.) (p. 48), by J. Greenberg and R. A. Baron, © 1993, Boston: Allyn and Bacon. Reprinted by permission of Prentice-Hall, Upper Saddle River, NJ.

Schemas

Schemas are cognitive frameworks, developed through experience, that are used to organize perceptions of the environment. **Schemas** are generalized concepts summarizing important characteristics that are common to a large number of experiences, events, and actions (Matlin, 1994). It is easier for us to understand something when we have had previous exposure to similar information. The previous exposure provides a framework (or schema) with which to link the new information. For example, an indi-

vidual's first experience with a computer is quite challenging. However, as computer literacy increases, additional computer exposure becomes less threatening and easier to assimilate. Initial computer experiences construct an internal schema with which future computer-related information is connected. Schemas are the cognitive building blocks that organize our perceptions of the world.

Once schemas have been formed, they can have a powerful effect. Suppose you had a bad experience with a professor in the history department and you received a low grade in the course.

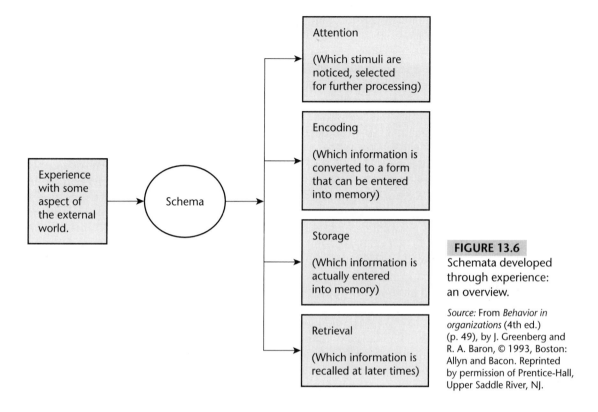

FIGURE 13.6
Schemata developed through experience: an overview.

Source: From *Behavior in organizations* (4th ed.) (p. 49), by J. Greenberg and R. A. Baron, © 1993, Boston: Allyn and Bacon. Reprinted by permission of Prentice-Hall, Upper Saddle River, NJ.

Years later, you are required to take another history course. The schema that developed from the first experience will initially influence your expectations of the second class. If you have a positive experience in the second class, you may replace the preexisting negative schema regarding history classes with a positive one.

In the work environment, schemas are developed for most situations. Information that fits neatly into a specific schema tends not to be noticed. For example, an employee might not notice that the mail is delivered every morning at the same time. Timely mail delivery fits into that employee's schematic framework. Suppose that one day the mail were not delivered or were delivered by someone in a Santa Claus outfit. These events would likely demand the employee's personal attention. They would not fit into the employee's schema and therefore would grab his or her attention.

Figure 13.6 provides an overview of schemas. Cognitive schemas influence what information is attended to, whether information is encoded and stored, and whether it will be retrieved. The concept of schemas can significantly affect our perceptions of the environment. Suppose you are asked to complete a task that is unfamiliar to you. This task may take longer to complete than a related task because you have not yet developed a schema for the new experience. The next time you complete this task, it may seem easier and take less time because you can activate a preexisting schematic framework.

Stereotypes

Stereotypes are special types of schemas that categorize people who share certain traits, roles, or characteristics into specific groups (Greenberg & Baron, 1993). Information that is consistent with the stereotype tends to be remembered, and information that is incongruent with the stereotype is often disregarded. This contributes to the difficulty in attempting to change individuals' stereotypes. Thus, supervisors may be stereotyped as being focused on production and adhering to organizational norms, rather than being concerned with employee satisfaction. Suppose Bill is assigned to Rose, a new supervisor. Bill and Rose meet to discuss Bill's personal and professional growth. Goals are set that will facilitate Bill's growth and work satisfaction while he is in Rose's department. Rose's behavior is incongruent with Bill's past experience (or schema) of supervisory behavior. Therefore, Bill's schema may influence his perception of Rose, and he is likely to stereotype her as a production-oriented supervisor. It may take several meetings with Rose for Bill to create a new schema for supervisors that includes genuine concern with employee satisfaction.

Projection

In **projection,** individuals make the assumption that other people are similar to themselves. Betsy goes to work only to receive a paycheck. She is not really satisfied with her job nor concerned about advancement. Betsy assumes that her coworkers share this outlook. She projects her characteristics onto others and may see her coworkers as more homogeneous than they really are (Robbins, 1996).

Many factors influence how people and situations are perceived in the work environment. These factors are mediated by personal styles and preferred roles, which contribute to individual perceptions and subsequent behaviors.

PERSONAL STYLE AND COMMUNICATION ROLES

People can communicate the same message in a variety of ways. Failing to recognize different styles may result in confusing or ineffective evaluations of others. The concept of individual differences relates to how we perceive the world and also involves how perceptions are communicated to others. To minimize the occurrence of incorrect judgments, it is important to become familiar with your personal communication style. It is also helpful to learn to recognize key elements of styles that are different than your own.

Loden and Rosener (1991) identified eleven elements of personal communication style. They suggest that if these characteristics are not identified, they often lead to garbled communications. Table 13.4 shows the behavioral polarities of each element. Try to determine your style as you review each continuum. For example, is your mode of interaction more initiating or listening? Do you place more weight on facts or on intuition? Recognizing your own preferences is the first step toward understanding how your style may differ from the styles of others. Understanding these differences may allow you to become more tolerant in your communication efforts.

To aid people in their interpersonal communications, Wilson Learning Corporation (1990) defined four social styles: the Analytical, the Driver, the Expressive, and the Amiable (see Figure 13.7 on page 464). Social style is determined by how coworkers view an individual employee, rather than by how an individual views himself or herself. The individual whose style is being identified is asked to distribute questionnaires to five colleagues. The survey consists of work style questions, which are designed to identify the subject's social style. The average perception of the employee by others is referred to as *social style*. This model does not assume that people always behave in a predictable way. Rather, the model identifies the behaviors with which an individual is most comfortable and therefore uses most often. These dimensions are critical for categorizing behavior. The dimension of responsiveness reflects whether an individual responds more to

TABLE 13.4	Behavioral polarities: elements of communication style

Mode of Interaction: Initiating versus Listening
The degree to which one initiates discussion or listens and responds as a primary mode of interaction.

Reference Point: Individual versus Group
The degree of emphasis placed on personal involvement and achievements versus group involvement and achievement in communications.

Authority Base: Facts versus Intuition
The degree to which one relies on factual data versus intuitive judgments as the basis for reasoning and persuading.

Degree of Self-Disclosure: Impersonal versus Personal
The emphasis placed on tasks versus sharing personal data in building new relationships and communicating with others.

Mode of Expression: Rational versus Emotional
The degree of reliance on rational descriptions and facts only versus emotional reactions and embellishment.

Method of Support: Challenge versus Agreement
The degree of challenge versus praise and agreement used to support others' ideas, views, and so on.

Method of Disagreement: Confrontation versus Compliance
The degree of confrontational versus compliant behavior exhibited in conflict situations.

Vocal Characteristics: Low versus High
The vocal pitch, accent, and volume displayed in verbal communications.

Method of Assertion: Direct versus Indirect
The degree of reliance on direct statements describing one's position or point of view versus indirect references, use of questions, and so on.

Physical Proximity: Distant versus Close
The degree of physical distance versus closeness maintained and preferred in interactions with others.

Reliance on Protocol: High versus Low
The degree of emphasis placed on formality and tradition versus spontaneous behavior in communications with others.

Source: From *Workforce America: Managing employee diversity as a vital resource* (pp. 89–90), by M. Loden and J. B. Rosener, 1991, Homewood, IL: Business One Irwin. Copyright 1991 by Business One Irwin. Reprinted with permission.

task-related stimuli or to people-related stimuli. The dimension of assertiveness profiles whether a person reacts assertively (tell-directed) or non-intrusively and inquiringly (ask-directed). An individual's preferred style of interaction is de-fined by the person's colleagues on these two dimensions.

Four styles are defined by the combination of the two dimensions. An individual with **Driver** preferences makes statements, is assertive, and

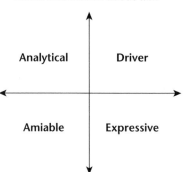

Task-Directed Responsiveness
Reserved
Actions controlled or careful
Wants facts and details
Eyes serious
Limited use of hands
Limited expression of personal
  feelings, storytelling, or small
  talk
Shares information about task

Ask-Directed Assertiveness
Seldom uses voice to emphasize
  ideas
Expressions and posture are quiet
  and nonintrusive
Deliberate, studied, or slow in speech
Asks questions more often than
  makes statements
Tends to lean backwards

Tell-Directed Assertiveness
Emphasizes ideas by tone change
Expressions are obvious
Quick, clear, or fast paced
Makes statements more often than
  asks questions
Decisive, lets one know what is
  wanted
Tends to lean forward to make a
  point

Analytical	**Driver**
Amiable	**Expressive**

People-Directed Responsiveness
Animated, uses facial expressions
Actions open or eager
Limited expression of facts
Friendly gaze
Hand gestures, palms up, open
Shares personal feelings
Tells stories, makes small talk

FIGURE 13.7   Guidelines for recognizing social styles. Recognition is most accurate when one dimension is observed at at time.

Source: From *Social Style Series* (p. 14), by Wilson Learning Corporation, 1990, Eden Prairie, MN: Wilson Learning Corporation. Copyright 1976, 1980, & 1990 by Wilson Learning Corporation. Reprinted by permission of Wilson Learning Corporation.

focuses on the task rather than on the people performing the task. Drivers want to know what needs to be accomplished. This does not mean that a Driver does not care about people or never asks questions. It suggests that Drivers are concerned with results, and with getting work done in a timely and efficient manner.

A person with an **Amiable** style tends to ask questions and be concerned with the "people" part of the task. The Amiable style differs from the Driver style in terms of preferred focus. Amiables enjoy the social component of the workplace and are usually concerned with how people feel about their work. This does not imply that Amiables disregard the task at hand. They are concerned both with getting the job done and with the feelings of the people involved. Amiables are interested in why people feel as they do or why they prefer to perform one task over another.

Social Style Summary

Categories and Names

	Amiable	Analytical	Driver	Expressive
Political Leaders				
American Presidents:	Jimmy Carter	Gerald Ford	Richard Nixon	Ronald Reagan
American Military Leaders:	Dwight Eisenhower	George Marshall	George Patton	Douglas MacArthur
International Figures:	Princess Diana	Queen Elizabeth	Margaret Thatcher	Desmond Tutu
Entertainers/Singers				
TV Celebrities:	Magnum	Bob Newhart	Barbara Walters	Carol Burnett
Talk Show Hosts:	Merv Griffin	Dick Cavett	Phil Donahue	Joan Rivers
TV/Movie Characters				
Peanuts Characters:	Charlie Brown	Schroeder	Lucy	Snoopy
MASH Characters:	Radar	Major Winchester	Colonel Potter	Klinger
Golden Girls Characters:	Rose Nylan	Sophia Petrillo	Dorothy Spornak	Blanch Devereaux
Star Trek Characters:	Uhura	Spock	Captain Kirk	Scotty
Sports				
Tennis Figures:	Chris Evert Lloyd	Bjorn Borg	Billie Jean King	John McEnroe
Sports Figures:	William Perry	Tom Landry	Vince Lombardi	John Madden

FIGURE 13.8   Examples of famous people and characters demonstrating selected social styles.

Source: From *Social Style Series* (p. 15), by Wilson Learning Corporation, 1990, Eden Prairie, MN: Wilson Learning Corporation. Copyright 1976, 1980, & 1990 by Wilson Learning Corporation. Reprinted with permission.

An **Analytical** style is characterized by individuals who ask questions but focus on the task to be completed. Analyticals are process-oriented and focus on how the work should be done, rather than on the end result. The Analytical working style is concerned with facts, data, and empirical findings. While both Drivers and Analyticals are concerned with the task, Drivers tend to issue directives rather than ask the questions that might come from an Analytical.

People who exhibit the **Expressive** style are concerned with creative ideas rather than facts or details. They make statements and are more interested in whom they work with than the process or the outcomes. Expressives thrive in environments where they can participate in creating the "big picture." They prefer to have fun at work and are quick to share their ideas.

Figure 13.8 provides examples of each of the four social styles (Wilson Learning Corporation, 1990). The styles are illustrated through the examples of well-known individuals.

Each style has a preferred mode of communication. Drivers generally prefer that the focus be on the task or desired result. They may not appreciate small talk or any activity that detracts from accomplishing the task. Expressives typically appreciate active listening and respond well to open questions. Humor, a relaxed approach, and relating on a personal level work well in communicating with an Expressive individual. Amiables pay particular attention to tone of voice and body language. Threatening or overbearing behavior will not create effective communication with an Amiable. Analyticals respond well to questions about their processes or conclusions. They prefer to deal with details and facts rather than with relational issues.

Combining the Loden and Rosener (1991) model and the Wilson Learning Corporation (1990) model may improve our understanding of style in communication. These models come from different sources and may not fit together perfectly, but they do have similarities. Try to associate the eleven elements in Table 13.4 with a corresponding Wilson social style. Which style would be more concerned with listening to a fellow employee: an Amiable or a Driver? Would an Analytical speak at a lower volume than an Expressive? Would an Amiable be overly concerned with facts or initiating production? Which style(s) would favor confrontation over compliance? The models overlap, more than one working style fitting with more than one element.

Having a working knowledge of styles can affect communication. However, the knowledge must be employed to improve communication in the workplace.

The third dimension in the Wilson Learning Corporation (1990) model is versatility. **Versatility** is "the degree to which a person is perceived as adapting his or her behavior [or style] to meet the concerns and expectations of others" (Wilson Learning Corporation, 1992, p. 41). It is the ability to temporarily modify one's style to make someone with a different style more comfortable. This results in a more effective communication.

To illustrate, an Expressive going into a meeting with a Driver would exhibit high versatility by keeping social talk to a minimum and focusing on the task at hand. The Driver focuses on the task, and the Expressive concentrates on the people involved with the task. Therefore, while the Expressive might be more comfortable informally chatting for a while and bouncing around some new ideas, the Driver will want to get down to business and move to the next item on the agenda. Analyticals display high versatility by avoiding a lengthy discussion of facts or minute details when dealing with Expressives. This is because Expressives can become bored with details, preferring to focus on future potential and ideas for new projects.

Low versatility occurs when individuals cling to a preferred style. For example, an Analytical may insist on reciting the statistical processes that are necessary to complete a project. Expressives would probably lose interest early in the discussion and stop giving the Analytical their full attention. This is not because the Expressive does not appreciate the Analytical's hard work; it is merely a matter of style, and the person's comfort zone in interactions. Low versatility limits the communication process and may be responsible for garbled, or even misinterpreted, transmissions. Suppose a Driver exhibits low versatility during a meeting with an Amiable. The Amiable wants to ask questions about the people connected with the task, and the Driver wants to focus on the fundamentals. A Driver exhibiting high versatility would temporarily move out of his or her comfort zone to accommodate the Amiable's style and discuss the people component of the task under review. Additionally, the Amiable could demonstrate high versatility by temporarily accommodating the Driver's style, for example by reviewing the numbers and setting concrete goals. Mutual flexing enhances communication by avoiding the biases built into one's preferred style and comfort zone.

Versatility is a pivotal concept in regard to social styles. Wilson Learning Corporation's (1990) social styles model is enhanced when individuals demonstrate high versatility. The need for high versatility diminishes for people who have the same style, but it is useful to have a variety of styles applied in any work unit. Each style has its own strengths and the potential to make unique contributions to any work effort.

If all members consciously engage in high-versatility behaviors, a work environment can be created that is respectful of, and able to adapt to, all working styles.

Nonverbal Communication

The words you choose, the words you do not say, your style of dress, and the manner in which you control your body and voice can significantly affect how a receiver will interpret your message. It has been said that "talk is cheap" and that nonverbal behaviors can provide clues about how people really feel. Suppose you are meeting with your doctor to discuss some recent medical tests. The doctor does not make eye contact, fidgets in the chair, and mumbles that more tests need to be conducted but there is nothing to worry about. The meeting ends abruptly as the doctor bolts from the room. Is the doctor's nonverbal behavior congruent with the words that were spoken? The doctor was uncomfortable, preoccupied, and worried. The source of the doctor's discomfort may have nothing to do with you. However, the nonverbal behaviors may lead you to question whether the doctor was withholding important information about your health.

Knapp (1972) proposed three major categories of nonverbal behavior: kinesics, paralanguage, and proxemics. Kinesics are actions such as eye contact, gestures, or physical body movement. Paralanguage refers to nonword sounds, such as "uh-huh" or "hmm," which may be encouraging or discouraging. Proxemics is the distance between communicators. Where people choose to situate themselves in relation to each other can have an impact on how their message is interpreted.

Assume that you are going to meet with a professor. You walk into the professor's office and are invited to sit down. The professor moves out from behind the desk, sits in a chair beside yours, looks directly at you when you speak, nods, and says, "Mm-hmm" occasionally. How would you feel? Would you believe you had the professor's full attention? Would you feel confident that the professor wanted to hear what you had to say? Now suppose you walk into a professor's office and remain standing because you have not been invited to sit down. The professor remains seated behind the desk and continues to look at papers lying on the top of the desk as you speak. The professor remains silent until you finish speaking, then looks up and says, "Anything else?" How would you feel about this professor's nonverbal behaviors?

Two additional nonverbal cues are an individual's style of dress and how the person uses his or her time. Malloy (1975) suggests that clothing style is an indicator of position within the firm and level of competence. For example, an individual who is dressed in a conservative business suit is assumed to have more authority than a person dressed in green coveralls.

An individual's pattern of time management also has implications for communication. Suppose you are called to your supervisor's office. You arrive, and the secretary tells you the supervisor will be with you in a moment. You sit outside the office for forty minutes before the supervisor is ready to see you. As the meeting begins, the telephone rings, and your supervisor talks for ten minutes. The secretary comes in a few minutes later with a message, and the meeting is disrupted again. What message did the supervisor communicate by making you wait and allowing frequent interruptions? The supervisor's use of time may have communicated to you, nonverbally, that other concerns were more important than meeting with you. If the meeting had started on time and telephone calls had been held, the nonverbal message conveyed to you would have been that this meeting was important.

Nonverbal communication consists of more than just body language. Nonverbal cues include body movements, tone of voice, volume, and any type of communication that either does not use words or uses words to convey a

Subsystem	Nonverbal Communication Description
Hand Movements	There are three types of hand movements: 1. Emblems are hand movements that are understood in a specific culture or occupation. An example is a thumbs-up gesture. 2. Illustrators are gestures that relate to what is being said, such as pointing or accentuating. 3. Adaptors are touching of oneself or other objects. Self-adaptors are often associated with anxiety, guilt, hostility, and suspicion.
Facial Expressions	When used, these are generally understood. Examples are smiling and frowning. Even when people suppress facial expressions, they may make very short expressions lasting only a fraction of a second that reflect their true feelings.
Eye Contact	Eye contact is a major regulator of conversation. Although there are individual differences, eye contact suggests understanding and interest.
Posture	Posture is the way people position their bodies with regard to other people. This can be a closed position with arms folded to reflect exclusion or the opposite to show inclusion. Having congruent positioning reflects agreement or acceptance.
Proxemics	How people use interpersonal space can express intimacy, social distance, and public distance. For example, standing close indicates intimacy, and sitting at the head of a table indicates status. Sitting alongside a desk indicates openness; sitting behind the desk while the other person is in front indicates a superior-subordinate relationship.
Body Rhythms	How people move in relation to others, frequency of speaking, and speaking turns provide clues to meaning being conveyed.
Speech	Choice of words can reflect involvement or distance, or enthusiasm or lack of it.

FIGURE 13.9   Nonverbal communications.

Source: From *Management Information Systems: Conceptual Foundations, Structure, and Development* (2nd ed.), by G. B. Davis and M. H. Olson, 1985, New York: McGraw-Hill. Copyright 1985 by McGraw-Hill. Reprinted with permission.

meaning beyond their strict definitions (Mc-Caskey, 1979). For example, saying, "I'll just *die* if I don't get that promotion!" instead of "It would be nice to be considered for promotion" can create a stronger sense of the same basic message.

The nonverbal components of communication are significant influences. Studies on the effects of communication (Harrison, 1970; Mehrabian, 1972) show that facial expressions account for over 50% of the effect: 30% is from voice tone and inflection, and less than 10% is from the actual content of the message. This may be because communication occurs on two levels: the level of what is actually said (content) and the level of how it is conveyed (relationship).

Figure 13.9 (Davis & Olson, 1985) offers a summary of nonverbal behaviors. Which behaviors in each subsystem would encourage or discourage effective communication in a work environment? Organizational culture, or climate, often dictates the verbal and nonverbal behaviors that are appropriate and acceptable within an organization.

Organizational Culture

Organizational culture can be defined as a system of shared meaning among members that distinguishes one organization from another (Becker, 1982; Schein, 1985). Organizational culture determines the context for the work environment by shaping the attitudes and behaviors of employees (Robbins, 1996). It defines what is meant by the statement "This is how things are done around here."

This sense of shared meaning can be further delineated by a set of seven key elements developed by a number of researchers (Betts & Halfhill, 1985; Glaser, Zamanou, & Hacker, 1987; Gordon & Cummins, 1979; Robbins, 1996):

1. *Innovation and risk taking.* The degree to which employees are encouraged to be innovative and take risks
2. *Attention to detail.* The degree to which employees are expected to exhibit precision, analysis, and attention to detail.
3. *Outcome orientation.* The degree to which management focuses on results or outcomes rather than on the techniques and processes used to achieve these outcomes.
4. *People orientation.* The degree to which management decisions take into consideration the effect of outcomes on people within the organization.
5. *Team orientation.* The degree to which work activities are organized around teams rather than individuals.
6. *Aggressiveness.* The degree to which people are aggressive and competitive rather than [cooperative or] easygoing.
7. *Stability.* The degree to which organization activities emphasize maintaining the status quo in contrast to growth. (Robbins, 1996, pp. 681–682)

These elements provide a framework for determining organizational culture. The elements combine to create cultures that are unique to each organization. Company rankings on each of these factors are fairly accurate indicators of the organization's overall culture.

An organization's culture serves several functions. It distinguishes the organization from other companies. It provides a sense of identity for employees by allowing them to identify their affiliation with the firm. It encourages employees to act out of self-interest and creates a sense of

loyalty to the organization. It also provides the "social glue that helps hold the organization together by providing appropriate standards for what employees should say and do" (Robbins, 1996, pp. 687). This last function is significant because it dictates the communication-related behaviors that are appropriate and acceptable within a particular organization.

For example, a graphic designer for Sony Music creates album covers, posters, and other promotional pieces for Sony recording artists. Typical work attire may consist of worn blue jeans, a comfortable shirt, and cowboy boots. A graphic designer wearing a banker's "power suit" to work would stick out like a sore thumb. The nature of the job (working with messy artistic materials) and the nature of the industry (entertainment) dictate that blue jeans are appropriate within the culture of Sony's art department. The casual culture of this department encourages communication with peers and supervisors that is lateral and highly informal.

However, because of Sony's status as a worldwide conglomerate, the art department is only one of many subcultures within the organization. A **subculture** within an organization consists of people who share certain cultural characteristics, such as working with art. Simultaneously, they share important characteristics of the organization as a whole, such as being employees of Sony. For example, the image portrayed by the art department may be one of a hip, young company, but Sony has a variety of business interests and locations worldwide. The subcultures that are found in the upper management levels of Sony will be significantly different from the subculture of the art department. Corporate managers, financial analysts, and legal consultants communicate nonverbally by wearing business suits to work. Their communications may be formal and hierarchical as they attempt to exert control over a multitude of national and international branch locations.

The nature of the product or service, the overall management philosophy, the size of the company, and many other factors play a role in creating organizational cultures and subcultures. Once these cultures are in place, they have a significant impact on all facets of organizational communication.

Additional Factors

Cognition, personal style, nonverbal behavior, and organizational culture all have an impact on communication in the work environment. Several additional factors can affect how information is transmitted at work.

A speaker's credibility can affect communication. An individual who is recognized as an expert in a particular field will have more credibility than a layperson. Assume that you are involved in some type of litigation. You are likely to place more weight on an attorney's advice than on advice from a friend. The degree to which the speaker is perceived as trustworthy is another significant factor. Low levels of trust lead to increased distortion. If the speaker is not perceived as trustworthy and has significant influence over the receiver's career, distortion increases even more (Read, 1962).

The power relationship between individuals can sometimes introduce bias into the communication process. For example, it may be easier to admit making a mistake to a peer than to a teacher or manager. This is related to the potential negative consequences associated with disclosing your error. The consequences are minimized with a peer because of the equal power balance in your relationship. With a teacher or manager, however, the consequences may include a lower grade or loss of your job.

Message content can distort communication. For most people it is easier to relay good news than bad news. A sender who manipulates information so that it will be more favorably received by the recipient engages in filtering the message (Robbins, 1996). The sender tries to filter the message into what the recipient most likely wants to hear. The number of links in the chain of communication also affect the accuracy of the message. The more links there are in the chain, the higher is the possibility for miscommunication, especially if the message is filtered along the way. As workloads increase, messages tend to become simplified; employees have less time to communicate when they are under stringent deadlines. Unfortunately, this type of time crunch can lead to the omission of valuable information (Aldag & Stearns, 1991).

As was mentioned previously, Janis (1982) introduced the concept of group think. This occurs when the need to conform to group norms mediates the abilities of individual group members to critically assess information. Group think dictates that reaching consensus and maintaining group membership is more important than making an informed, relevant decision. Group think can confound a message if the mentality of the group and the need to conform to that mentality override a critical analysis of the information under review.

Individual culture refers to an employee's cultural background, which has a profound effect on individual behavior. Practices that are acceptable in one country may be unacceptable or even illegal in another country. Cultural differences also exist within a country. People behave differently in Alabama than they do in New York City or Seattle. Geographical differences are combined with the diverse ethnic composition of the United States, which creates a need to be aware of a multitude of cultures in the workplace. For example, consider Maria, a Hispanic account executive. She comes from a traditional Hispanic home, where women are taught to be subservient to men. It may be difficult for Maria to behave assertively with her male manager. Maria's cultural background could detract from her performance in a workplace that values assertive behavior.

Adler (1991) suggests four rules for improving cross-cultural communication:

1. Assume that differences exist until similarity is proven. Do not assume that individuals

from other cultures interpret information as you do. As we discussed earlier, past experience is a powerful mediator in terms of how we process information and form our schemas of the world. People with different life experiences will most likely give different meanings to the same set of information.

2. Emphasize description rather than interpretation or judgment. Focus on what is said, and describe what you heard or saw. To avoid misunderstanding, first paraphrase what you heard and then check to make sure your restatement is correct.

3. Be empathetic. Put yourself in the other person's shoes. What must it be like for that person to communicate with you? What is the emotional content of his or her message?

4. Treat your initial impressions as working hypotheses. Do not jump to conclusions or make hasty judgments once you have completed the steps outlined above. Realize that because of the differences between you and the other person, you must continue to gather information; there is no way you can understand his or her perspective after a brief exchange.

Cultural diversity is one of a nation's greatest resources. Successful solutions are more likely to be found when a variety of perspectives are used to address a problem. We will examine some of these in Chapter 16. Unfortunately, cultures usually adhere to an ethnocentric approach, and the dominant culture is usually considered superior to others. This view is limiting and potentially harmful to people of all ethnic backgrounds.

New technologies in communication are providing tremendous opportunities for change in the traditional workplace. Tools such as pagers and cellular phones provide immediate access to employees. Personal computers and fax machines allow employees to work from their homes or communicate with the office when they are on vacation. E-mail, electronic scheduling, and Internet access allow communication among employees, clients, and vendors anywhere in the world.

Studies have shown that the quality of work generated through computer-mediated work groups is similar to that of face-to-face groups (Barnes & Greller, 1994; Dubrovsky, Kiesler, & Sethna, 1991; Straus & McGrath, 1994). This provides the opportunity for more individuals to work with coworkers from a variety of locations. Workers may be more productive and efficient if they can work from home when necessary.

Communication is being conducted more frequently through e-mail and scheduled meetings and less often over the telephone, with faxes, or through teleconferences (Haythornthwaite, Wellman, & Mantei, 1995). These patterns represent the development of computer technology, which allows computer-supported group decision making and encourages the use of electronic communication networks (Fulk & Boyd, 1991). The major impact of future technology will probably be in the areas of individual work support, group work support, advanced organizational automation, and enhanced global communication (Thach & Woodman, 1994).

KEY COMMUNICATION SKILLS

It is important to remember that communication occurs with people who are different from ourselves. We do not communicate in a vacuum but interact with others who most likely see the world differently than we do. Perceptions, social styles, and schemas will mediate how individuals attend to the people and situations in their lives. It might seem there are so many variables that clear communication is virtually impossible to achieve. However, some concrete methods are available to guide our interactions.

Wilson Learning Corporation (1982) suggests the following four tools for effective communication: responsive listening, questioning, restating, and empathy. Wilson Learning Corporation states that mastering these skills can facilitate sound communication by helping a person indicate a willingness to communicate with others.

1. Responsive listening is characterized by "giving signs of interest that encourage the other person to say more [and] includes both verbal and nonverbal communication" (Wilson Learning Corporation, 1982, pp. 14–15). Making eye contact, positioning your body in a friendly manner, nodding, making sounds of agreement, requesting more information, and displaying appropriate facial expressions all facilitate responsive listening.

2. Questioning can be broken into three parts: closed questions, open questions, and rhetorical questions. **Closed questions** solicit short, factual, or yes/no answers. For example, "Is your paper finished?" is a closed question because it allows for a yes/no answer: Either the paper is done or it is not. **Open questions** encourage longer, more subjective responses. For example, "How are you doing on that paper? Any problems?" is an open question. Open questions tend to solicit information about the respondent's feelings, opinions, and preferences. **Rhetorical questions** are questions to which the answer is usually known in advance. Thus, asking someone whether she or he would like to earn more money is fairly rhetorical, because most people would respond affirmatively. Asking employees whether they would be comfortable reporting to work at 8:00 A.M. may be rhetorical if the employees have no choice: Either they report to work on time or they jeopardize their employment.

3. Restatement is the act of repeating what you think the other person said. It is not advisable to mimic the other person word for word. Rather, the purpose of restatement is to repeat what you heard, in your own words, to circumvent misunderstanding. Restatement is, in effect, a form of feedback. It focuses on the facts and

clarifies the listener's understanding of the other person's intended meaning.

4. The final component of this model is **empathy**. We display empathy when we acknowledge another person's feelings without judging those feelings. We do not have to agree or disagree—we simply acknowledge the other person's emotions. We do this because most information is composed of more than just facts. Total meaning is actually a combination of facts and feelings. Acknowledging the emotional content of any message serves to make the speaker more comfortable and perhaps more willing to communicate in the future.

There are organizational techniques that can be implemented to aid in effective communication on a larger scale. Heyman (1994) offers the following suggestions:

1. Training employees continuously to create a sense of shared content and clear understanding of particular jobs and the jobs of others.

2. Making the responsibility for decision making compatible with job function to maximize the chance that decisions will be made by the individuals who are best suited (possessing the knowledge and experience) to make sound choices.

3. Creating a corporate culture that encourages both formal and informal communication that flows in all directions.

4. Establishing backup communication systems to ensure that if one system or channel fails, another is ready to disperse information. For example, if most company information is distributed via electronic mail, a secondary system should be in place in case of computer malfunction.

5. Holding employees accountable for their actions and responsible for specific aspects of organizational functioning. A clear delineation of responsibility provides a structure for effective communication by outlining who is responsible for communicating what specific information.

These suggestions for effective communication are not exhaustive, but they do outline some major issues to consider in sharing information with others. It is also important to know how to measure and monitor the effectiveness of communication.

....
HOW TO MEASURE ORGANIZATIONAL COMMUNICATION

Implementing strategies for improving or maintaining effective communication is not sufficient. You must be able to measure whether the strategies are effective. Several methods have been suggested for this process.

A **sociogram** is a common sociometric measure that sociologists originally devised to learn about group formations. A sociogram is a visual display showing which people communicate with each other within a predetermined group. The benefit of this type of illustration is that it provides a quick overview of communication patterns within a work group. Given the makeup of the group and member responsibilities, a sociogram can highlight whether the group is communicating at an expected level. Sociograms can highlight clique formations or illuminate potential leaders. They also can objectively measure employee preferences with regard to employee associations (Yoder, Heneman, Turnbull, & Stone, 1958). Figure 13.10 on page 474 illustrates a sociometric survey of office workers used to determine order of preference in terms of desired work interaction patterns, that is, who talks to whom at work. The sociogram represents each person as a circle. A line connecting two circles indicates communication between the two people. The number on each half of the line signifies the person's preference (first, second, or third) in communicating with the connected coworker. Using this plot, we can prepare a summary table ranking each person's respective choices. This information is significant to management because group soli-

darity produces less absences and a higher level of production.

A major drawback to using sociograms is that they do not provide information about the nature of the communication. Therefore, while sociograms are helpful, they provide only partial information about communication trends. They are usually used as only one part of a battery of measurement devices.

A second type of measuring tool is **activity sampling.** As the name implies, researchers take samples of communication activity at certain points in time. For example, a group of researchers might interrupt employees at the same time each day to determine their current communication format (casual conversation, telephone call, writing or reading a letter). Several samplings are conducted over time to provide a baseline measurement. Using this method, an organization can determine which types of communication are applied across a variety of job-related functions or situations. A limitation is that this method requires numerous researchers and interrupts the work flow of the people who participate in the sample group.

A third type of communication measure is called **Episodic Communication Channels in Organization (ECCO) analysis** (Davis, 1953). ECCO analysis investigates the speed at which news travels through an organization by documenting when individuals receive a piece of information. First, information is selected for review. After the information has been dispersed, employees complete a questionnaire that contains the transmitted message and may ask, "Did you know this information by yesterday at five o'clock?" Employees then record whether they knew all of the information, part of the information, or none of the information. Respondents record from whom they first heard the news and how it was delivered (verbally, in written form, via e-mail, etc.). ECCO analysis is intended to measure the speed and direction in which information travels and to identify communication patterns within an organization.

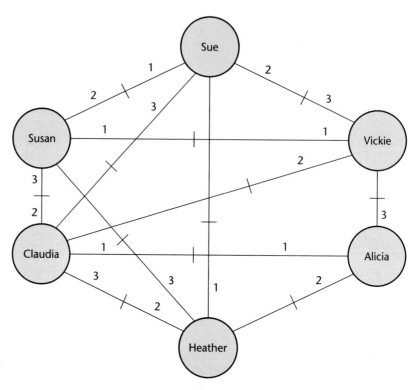

FIGURE 13.10

Examples of a sociometric survey of office workers ($N = 6$) and the associated sociogram.

Employee	1st Choice	2nd Choice	3rd Choice
Alicia	Claudia	Heather	Vickie
Claudia	Alicia	Susan	Heather
Heather	Sue	Claudia	Susan
Sue	Susan	Vickie	Claudia
Susan	Vickie	Sue	Claudia
Vickie	Susan	Claudia	Sue

The **Flesch index** (Flesch, 1948) estimates the readability of written material. It uses the number of syllables per 100 words and the average sentence length in the following formula:

Reading ease = $206.84 - 0.85W - 1.02S$

For example, suppose the number of syllables in a 100-word passage is 154 and the sentence length is 15 words. If the numbers are inserted into the formula, the result is

$206.84 - 0.85(154) - 1.02(15) = 60.64$

The level of reading ease for these 100 words is 60.64. To give this number meaning, the Flesch index places it on a scale from 0 (very difficult) to 100 (very easy). Our example is in the Flesch range of 60–70, which is the "Standard" range. It is typical for seventh and eighth graders. Flesch estimates that 83% of adults in the United States can read at this level.

This method has a number of applications in the workplace. It is useful in determining whether a piece of written correspondence is suitable for its intended audience. If the intended readers of a technical manual have a high school education, on the average, it would be challenging for them to receive a manual that was written at the graduate school level. These employees would likely become frustrated as they muddle their way through a complex manual, and valuable production time would be lost in the process. Employee safety could be threatened if they could not comprehend the material in the manual and used complicated machinery without adequate instruction.

These methods serve a variety of useful purposes in determining whether communication efforts are working well or there is a need for further development. However, each method is specific. Therefore it is advisable to incorporate a battery of measurement devices to secure a holistic view of an organization's level of communication efficacy.

SUMMARY

Organizational communication is a pivotal component to the success of any company. Communication affects several valuable functions at work, including the transfer of information, employee motivation, allowing employees to express their feelings about their work, and controlling employee behavior. A corporation's management philosophy will dictate how communication flows within the organizational hierarchy (upward, downward, or laterally); whether communication is one-way, two-way, or transactional; and whether the communication is formal or informal. Some examples of management philosophies are scientific management, which includes bureaucracy, and the behavioral school, which includes the human relations model, the systems school, and contingency theory.

Communication originates with a source. The source encodes the message before sending it through a channel to a receiver, who then decodes the message on receipt. Receivers can give feedback to the sender to ensure that the message was understood as the source intended. Feedback can be either positive or negative. Positive feedback indicates that the message was received and understood as intended; negative feedback reflects back to the source that the message was misunderstood.

People are unique; therefore individual differences play a key role in effective communication. Human cognitive abilities mediate how people perceive information. Several principles can affect communication at work, specifically selectivity, attribution, schema, stereotypes, and projection. Working styles and the ability to temporarily move out of a preferred style to make a coworker comfortable can increase communication efficacy.

Nonverbal communications include style of dress, use of time, physical movement, proximity, and paralanguage, all of which augment any verbal message. Organizational culture dictates what types of communication are acceptable within a particular company and distinguish one organization from another. The speaker's credibility, the power relationships between employees, and the content of the message all play a role in any communication effort. Individual cultural backgrounds can also affect communication at work.

Finally, researchers use several sociometric techniques to measure communication in the workplace. These methods include sociograms, activity sampling, ECCO analysis, and the Flesch index.

KEY TERMS AND CONCEPTS

active listening
activity sampling
all-channel network
Amiable
Analytical
approximation
attribution theory
boundaries
bureaucracy
chain network
channel
closed questions
communication effects
communication process model
consensus
consistency
contingency theory
decoding
differentiation
distinctiveness
downward communication
Driver
dynamic homeostasis
empathy
encoding
entropy
Episodic Communication
    Channels in Organization
    (ECCO) analysis

equifinality
error
escaping
Expressive
externally caused behavior
feedback
filtering
Flesch Index
formal communication
    channels
fundamental attribution
    error
grapevine
group think
Hawthorne studies
horizontal communication
human relations model
human resource
    management
informal communications
information overload
integration
internally caused behavior
limited information collection
    principle
linking-pin model
message
multiple-source feedback
negative feedback

omission
one-way
    communication
open questions
open systems model
organizational culture
positive feedback
projection
receiver
responsive listening
restatement
rhetorical questions
rumors
salience
schemata
scientific management
selective perception
sociogram
stereotypes
subcultures
systems school
transactional
    communication
two-way communication
upward communication
versatility
wheel network

RECOMMENDED READINGS

Chawla, S., & Renesch, J. (Eds.). (1995). *Learning organizations: Developing cultures for tomorrow's workplace.* Portland, OR: Productivity Press.

Clampitt, P. G. (1991). *Communicating for managerial effectiveness.* Newbury Park, CA: Sage.

Hall, D. T. (Ed.). (1991). *Career development in organizations.* San Francisco, Jossey-Bass.

Merrill, D. W., & Reid, R. H. (1981). *Personal styles and effective performance: Make your style work for you.* Radnor, PA: Chilton Book Company.

Pascarella, P., & Frohman, M. A. (1989). *The purpose-driven organization: Unleashing the power of direction and commitment.* San Francisco: Jossey-Bass.

Peters, T. (1994). *The pursuit of WOW!* New York: Vintage.

Robbins, S. P. (1996). *Organizational behavior* (7th ed.). Englewood Cliffs, NJ: Prentice Hall.

Rothschild, W. E. (1993). *Risktaker, caretaker, surgeon, undertaker: The four faces of strategic leadership.* New York: John Wiley & Sons.

Suzaki, K. (1993). *The new shop floor management: Empowering people for continuous improvement.* New York: The Free Press, A Division of Macmillan, Inc.

INTERNET RESOURCES

American Communication Association
Home page of the American Communication Association, this site provides easy access to many papers and resources about communications in organizations, communication law, and resources for teaching and research.
http://www.uark.edu/depts/comminfo/www/ACA.html

Bibliography of Organizational Computer-Mediated Communication
This site presents an organized bibliography of computer-mediated communication, including research studies, literature reviews, reports of new hardware and software, and theoretical papers and discussions.
http://shum.huji.ac.il/jcmc/rudybib.html

Assessing and Improving Your Organization
A basic article by David Chaudron, Ph.D., about the symptoms, diagnosis, and cures of organizational problems.

http://www.electriciti.com/~dchaudron/assess.htm

The Implication of Communication Process Approach to Genesis and Reproduction of Organizational Structure
This site presents a paper by Naoki Wakabayashi that considers the implication of the communication process approach to changing organizational structure. It examines recent sociological theories that focus on the initial or structuring phase of social change.
http://ifrm.glocom.ac.jp/ifrm/w01.003.html

A Business Researcher's Interests
This site provides access to a searchable knowledge map of contemporary business, management, and information technology issues. Over 1800 links are provided to full-text articles, papers, magazines, journals, case studies, tools, and other resources.
http://www.brint.com/interest.html

EXERCISE

Exercise 13.1

To Motivate, You Have to Communicate

Following is a list of eight areas that are often considered in evaluating job satisfaction. Rank them in the order in which you think the employees in your organization would give them priority.

Rank

____ Credit for the work they do (1)

____ Understanding and appreciation (2)

____ Comfortable physical working conditions (3)

____ Interesting work (4)

____ Counseling for personal problems (5)

____ Job security (6)

____ Fair pay with salary increases (7)

____ Promotion on merit (8)

Now compare your results with those of over 3000 employees from a company in the Midwestern United States. The ranking of the satisfaction areas from most important to least important for the 3000 employees was 1, 4, 7, 2, 8, 5, 3, 6. The managers of these employees were asked to rank the same eight areas in the order that they thought their employees would give. Their ranking was 7, 6, 4, 8, 2, 3, 1, 5. Note that the employees stress satisfaction with the job itself. By contast, the managers thought employees would show little or no concern with getting credit for their work. How did your results compare?

In small groups, discuss your results. If a manager came to you and expressed the feeling that there was a motivational problem with employees, what would you tell him or her? Also discuss the following questions:

What do you want most from your job?

Why did you rate the areas the way you did?

Where are the largest gaps between employees' perceptions and those of their managers?

If you wanted to get managers and employees more in tune with each other how would you proceed?

What communications techniques would be most
  valuable for the 3000 employees?
What communications techniques would be the most
  valuable for the managers?

(*Source:* The survey results reported come from unpublished data from an organizational survey conducted in 1989 by Humber, Mundie, and McClary,
Milwaukee, WI.)

REFERENCES

Adler, N. J. (1991). *International dimensions of organizational behavior* (2nd ed.). Boston: Plus Kent.

Aldag, R. J., & Stearns, T. M. (1991). *Management.*
Cincinnati, OH: Southwestern.

Argyris, C. (1957). *Personality and organization.*
New York: Harper & Row.

Barnes, S., & Greller, L. M. (1994). Computer-mediated communication in the organization. *Commu-
nication-Education, 43*(2), 129–142.

Becker, H. S. (1982, Summer). Culture: A sociological view. *Yale Review,* 513–527.

Berlo, D. K. (1960). *The process of communication.*
New York: Holt, Rinehart & Winston.

Berrien, F. K. (1976). A general systems approach to
organizations. In M. D. Dunnette (Ed.), *Handbook of industrial and organizational psychology.*
Chicago: Rand McNally College Publishing Company.

Betts, C. A., & Halfhill, S. M. (1985). *Organization
culture: theory, definitions, and dimensions.* Presented at the National American Institute of Decision Sciences Conference, Las Vegas, November,
1985.

Campbell, D. (1995, May). *Some overall comments
about 360 degree assessment and feedback.* Workshop presented at the meeting of the Society for
Industrial Organizational Psychology, Orlando,
FL.

Corman, S. R., Banks, S. P., Bantz, C. R., & Mayer,
M. E. (1990). *Foundations of organization com-
munication: A reader.* New York and London:
Longman.

Davis, G. B., & Olson, M. H. (1985). *Management information systems: conceptual foundations, structure, and development* (2nd ed.). New York:
McGraw-Hill.

Davis, K. (1953). A method of studying communication patterns in organizations. *Personnel Psychology, 53,* 6, 301–312.

de Sola Pool, I., Frey, F. W., Schramm, W., Maccoby,
N., & Parker, E. B. (1973). *Handbook of Communication.* Chicago: Rand McNally.

Dubrovsky, V. J., Kiesler, S., & Sethna, B. N. (1991).
The equalization phenomenon: Status effects in
computer-mediated and face-to-face decision-making groups. *Human-Computer Interaction, 6*(2),
119–146.

Flesch, R. (1948). *The art of readable writing.* New
York: Harper & Row.

Fulk, J., & Boyd, B. (1991). Emerging theories of
communication in organizations. Special Issue:
Yearly review of management. *Journal of Management, 17*(2), 407–446.

Gerloff, E. A. (1985). *Organizational theory and design: A strategic approach for management.* New
York: McGraw-Hill.

Glaser, S. R., Zamanou, S., & Hacker, K. (1987,
November). Measuring and interpreting organi-
zational culture. *Management Communication
Quarterly,* 173–198.

Gordon, G. G., & Cummins, W. M. (1979). *Managing management climate.* Lexington, MA: Lexington Books.

Greenberg, J., & Baron, R. A., (1993). *Behavior in
organizations* (4th ed.). Boston: Allyn and Bacon.

Harris, T. E. (1993). *Applied organizational communication: Perspectives, principles, and pragmatics.*
Hillsdale, NJ: Lawrence Erlbaum.

Harrison, R. (1970). Nonverbal communication. In
J. H. Campbell and P. W. Harper (Eds.), *Dimensions in communication.* Belmont, CA: Wadsworth.

Haythornthwaite, C., Wellerman, B., & Mantei, M.
(1995). *Group Decision and Negotiation, 4*(3),
193–211.

Heath, R. L. (1994). *Management of corporate communication: From interpersonal contacts to external affairs.* Hillsdale, NJ: Lawrence Erlbaum.

Heyman, R. (1994). *Why didn't you say that in the
first place?* San Francisco: Jossey-Bass.

Janis, I. L. (1982). *Groupthink: Psychological studies
of policy decision and fiascos* (2nd ed.). Boston:
Houghton Mifflin.

Janis, I. L. (1989). *Crucial decisions.* New York: The
Free Press.

Katz, D., & Kahn, R. (1978). *The social psychology of organizations* (2nd ed.). New York: John Wiley and Sons.

Kelley, H. H. (1972). Attribution in social interaction. In E. Jones et al. (Eds.), *Attribution: Perceiving the causes of behavior.* Morristown, NJ: General Learning Press.

Knapp, M. L. (1972). *Nonverbal communication in human interaction.* New York: Holt, Rinehart & Winston.

Lawrence, P., & Lorsch, J. (1967). *Organization and environment: Managing differentiation and integration.* Cambridge, MA: Harvard University Press.

Likert, R. (1961). *New patterns of management.* New York: McGraw-Hill.

Likert, R. (1967). *The human organization.* New York: McGraw-Hill.

Loden, M., & Rosener, J. B. (1991). *Workforce America: Managing employee diversity as a vital resource.* Homewood, IL: Business One, Irwin.

Malloy, J. T. (1975). *Dress for success.* New York: Warner Books.

Matlin, M. W. (1994). *Cognition* (3rd ed.). Fort Worth, TX: Harcourt Brace.

McCaskey, M. B. (1979, November–December). The hidden messages managers send. *Harvard Business Review,* 135–148.

McGregor, D. (1960). *The human side of enterprise.* New York: McGraw-Hill.

Mehrabian, A. (1972). *Non-verbal communication.* Chicago: Aldine.

Miller, A. G., & Lawson, T. (1989, June). The effect of an informational option on the fundamental attribution error. *Personality and Social Psychology Bulletin, 15,* 194–204.

Miller, J. G. (1960). Information input, overload and psychopathology. *American Journal of Psychiatry, 116,* 367–386.

Myers, M. T., & Myers, G. E. (1982). *Managing by communication: An organizational approach.* New York: McGraw-Hill.

Nadler, G., & Hibino, S. (1990). *Breakthrough thinking.* Rocklin, CA: Prima.

Read, W. H. (1962). Upward communication in industrial hierarchies. *Human Relations, 15,* 3–15.

Robbins, S. P. (1996). *Organizational behavior* (7th ed.). Englewood Cliffs, NJ: Prentice Hall.

Rogers, E. M., & Argawala-Rogers, R. (1976). *Communication in organizations.* New York: The Free Press.

Ross, L. (1977). The intuitive psychologist and his shortcomings. In L. Berkowitz (Ed.), *Advances In Experimental Social Psychology, 10,* 174–220.

Schein, E. H. (1985). *Organizational Culture and Leadership.* San Francisco: Jossey-Bass.

Scott, W. G., & Mitchell, T. R. (1976). *Organization theory: A structural and behavioral analysis.* Homewood, IL: Richard D. Irwin.

Shaw, M. E. (1964). Communication networks. In L. Berkowitz (Ed.), *Advances in experimental social psychology.* New York: Academic Press.

Starbuck, W. H., & Nystrom, P. C. (1981). Why the world needs organizational design. *Journal of General Management, 6,* 317.

Straus, S. G., McGrath, J. E. (1994). Does the medium matter? The interaction of task type and technology on group performance and member reactions. *Journal of Applied Psychology. 79*(1), 87–97.

Taylor, F. W. (1947). *Scientific management.* New York: Harper.

Thach, L., & Woodman, R. W. (1994). Organizational change and information technology: Managing on the edge of cyberspace: *Organizational Dynamics, 23*(1), 30–46.

Weber, M. (1947). *The theory of social and economic organization,* Trans. A. M., Henderson and T. Parsons. New York: Oxford University Press.

Wilson Learning Corporation. (1982). *Connecting with people.* Eden Prairie, MN: Wilson Learning Corp.

Wilson Learning Corporation. (1990). *Social style series.* Eden Prairie, MN: Wilson Learning Corp.

Wilson Learning Corporation. (1992). *Social style series.* Eden Prairie, MN: Wilson Learning Corp.

Yoder, D., Heneman, Jr., H. G., Turnbull, J. G., & Stone, C. H. (1958). *Handbook of personnel management and labor relations.* New York: McGraw-Hill.

14

Leadership

Chapter Outline

n a *Wall Street Journal* article, Carley and Naj (1993) told of a General Electric (GE) executive who was fired after a fifteen-year management career. The executive, a vice-president for GE, joined GE in 1974. It was assumed that he had the qualities needed for a successful career in management, including an engineering degree and an MBA. He was handsome, energetic, and six feet tall and was generally considered to be good management material.

During his tenure as the vice-president of a GE division he increased division profits from 16.5 million dollars in 1986 to 70 million dollars in 1989. In 1990, profits dropped to 57 million dollars, and the executive was blamed for the loss. At this point he was characterized as lacking "middle American values," having poor work ethics, and drinking excessively. He was also accused of mismanaging his expense account. In addition, his personal life was criticized; he had divorced his wife and married one of his staff members, who was accused of meddling in management procedures.

Interestingly, when the trouble began, two supervisors were asked to characterize the executive. One characterized him as intelligent, hard-working, professional, warm, supportive, and caring. The second supervisor characterized him as insecure, lacking in strategic planning skills, a poor leader, paranoid, indecisive, and given to violent outbursts. After fifteen years as a successful manager, the executive was dismissed.

The executive initially exhibited the traits, behaviors, abilities, situational control, and interpersonal interaction skills that were assumed to be indicators of effective leadership. Toward the end of his tenure, however, he was no longer considered to be a good leader. Although he had initially shown great promise and some people still considered him effective, he was fired.

The various leadership dimensions, such as ability, personality, physical traits, situational expectations, and social interactions that this executive originally exhibited were interpreted as indicating that he had leadership abilities. Yet just before he was fired, there were mixed views about the executive's effectiveness. In a similar fashion, the existence

of multiple dimensions, all credited with being indicative of leadership ability, reflects the disagreements among researchers about what defines leadership. Yukl and Van Fleet (1992, p. 148) observed that "leadership has been defined in terms of individual traits, leader behavior, interaction patterns, role relationships, follower perceptions, influence over followers, influence on task goals, and influence on organizational culture."

This chapter begins with a definition of a leader and then reviews the trait, behavioral, situational, and cognitive theories of leadership. We will conclude with a discussion of additional variables considered in research on leadership.

LEADERSHIP RESEARCH

Leadership research has captured the interests of researchers and practitioners for centuries. Bass (1990) traced the roots of this interest to the time of early civilization. Research on what constitutes good leadership has been carried out with qualitative and quantitative methods and with a mix of both methods. Regardless of the approach, the goals of the research have been to identify the traits, behaviors, situations, leadership styles, and interactions that prove to be most indicative of a sound leader.

What is leadership? Researchers often make a distinction between a manager and a leader. The role of a manager is often characterized by knowledge, skills, abilities, and responsibilities, whereas a leader is defined by how he or she influences others to work toward goal achievement.

In their review of leadership theories, Yukl and Van Fleet (1992) discussed various definitions of leadership. They developed a broad definition that merges the notions of leader and manager. Yukl and Van Fleet (1992, p. 149) state that

leadership is defined broadly as a process that includes influencing task objectives and strategies, influencing commitment and compliance in task behavior to achieve these objectives, influencing group maintenance and identification, and influencing the culture of an organization.

Some leadership researchers are interested in answering the question "What is a leader?" Research in this area focuses on what traits, personalities, and behaviors differentiate leaders from nonleaders. A second line of research focuses on identifying leadership as a process of interaction among leaders, subordinates, and situations. These two lines of research are best summarized by Campbell, Dunnette, Lawler, and Weick's (1970) schematic model (see Figure 14.1). According to this model, factors that are associated with leaders and leadership are the person, the process, and the outcome. The **personal factor** includes the traits and characteristics necessary for effective leadership. **Process factors** include the actual job behaviors of an effective leader. Campbell et al. (1970) define job behavior as a function of the individual's ability, motivation, and organizational opportunities to apply effective leader behaviors (e.g., task structure, organ-

izational structure, and social psychological influences). The **product factor** is the result of effective leadership. Campbell et al. (1970, p. 13) introduced the importance of taking into account the "combination of organizational circumstances, personal characteristics, and behavior patterns that are likely to be perceived as effective [leadership]." The following section describes these factors as key components of several theories of leadership. We introduce them according to their historical development.

THEORIES OF LEADERSHIP

Trait Approach

The **trait approach** is based on the assumption that there are distinguishing features, or attributes, common among leaders. For example, Winston Churchill stated that "We are all worms, but I think that I am a glow worm" (Kets de Vries, 1994, p. 73). Trait theorists believed that

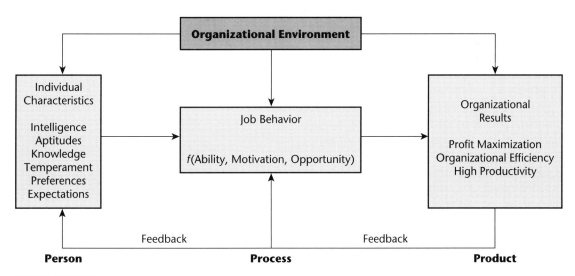

FIGURE 14.1   Determinants of managerial behavior.

Source: From *Managerial Behavior, Performance, and Effectiveness* (p. 11), by J. P. Campbell, M. D. Dunnette, E. E. Lawler III, and K. E. Weick, 1970, New York: McGraw-Hill Book Company. Copyright 1970 by McGraw-Hill Book Company. Reprinted with permission.

if a profile of an effective leader could be developed, it would improve the selection process, subsequent performance of subordinates, and the performance of the organization at large. Methods for collecting data concerning leadership traits have included observation, interviews of individuals holding leadership positions, analyses of historical data or biographical data, and correlational approaches.

Stodgill (1948) reviewed a series of studies that attempted to determine the traits associated with leadership, identifying the factors presented in Table 14.1 as being associated with leadership. A similar study by Lord, De Vader, and Alliger (1986) using validity generalization procedures, identified three traits that were significantly related to being a leader: intelligence, masculinity–femininity, and dominance.

These studies have emphasized traits or attributes that predispose an individual to being an effective leader. The characteristics of being sociable, intelligent, dominant, and adaptable may increase the likelihood that an individual will emerge as a leader. Even with these traits or attributes an individual may not behave as an effective leader. The process component discussed by Campbell et al. (1970) addresses the function of leader behavior as one of the components of a leader's traits. Another example is Stodgill's (1948) theory which referred to leader behavior as a function of the situation as defined by the task, the followers, and the objectives to be achieved. All these characteristics have been incorporated, either in part or in whole, by theorists who follow the trait approach. As intuitive as traits are as being related to leadership, research has found that traits alone are not enough to identify either current effectiveness of leaders or their potential.

Behavioral Approach

In the 1940s and 1950s research was taking place at two separate institutions investigating effective leadership. This research expanded the idea of leadership beyond the scope of personal traits. These studies focused on defining effective leader behaviors and their relationship to organizational outcomes, such as group effectiveness. The focus was with "what leaders *do* rather than in terms of what leaders *are*" (Blum & Naylor, 1968, p. 421). The factors that were identified in these studies were behavioral, not trait related.

Both groups of researchers developed several factors associated with effective leadership. The Michigan State studies were conducted on leaders working for the railroad and service industries. The initial study by Katz, Maccoby, and Morse (1950) was conducted on clerical employees and their supervisors. Katz et al. compared the leadership behaviors of supervisors of high- and low-producing employees. High-producing groups were differentiated from low-producing groups by specific supervisory behaviors. These included the following:

1. They were under less direct supervision.
2. Their supervisor placed less emphasis on production.
3. Their supervisor encouraged participation in decision making and was more focused on employee needs (Blum & Naylor 1968).

TABLE 14.1   Factors associated with leadership as identified by Stodgill (1948)

Factors	Definitions
Capacity	Intelligence, alertness, verbal facility, originality, judgment
Achievement	Scholarship, knowledge, athletic accomplishments
Responsibility	Dependability, initiative, persistence, aggressiveness, confidence, desire to excel
Participation	Activity, sociability, cooperation, adaptability, humor
Status	Socioeconomic status, popularity

The Michigan State research team identified four critical behaviors: leader support, interaction facilitation, goal emphasis, and work facilitation (Bowers & Seashore, 1966).

The studies that took place at Ohio State used industrial, military, and educational sites to examine leadership and group effectiveness. These studies (e.g., Fleishman, 1953; Hemphill, 1959, 1960) identified the factors of consideration and initiation of structure.

The research by Fleishman (1953), Fleishman and Harris (1962), and Fleishman and Peters (1962) at Ohio State became the basis for the development of a number of assessment instruments used to measure leader behavior. The research team developed over 1800 items that described leaders' behaviors. These items were sorted into ten different categories, which Fleishman and his colleagues assumed represented the multiple behavioral dimensions of effective leadership. Items were then selected from each category to develop a 150-item questionnaire. The questionnaire was administered in many different leader–group situations, and the results were factor analyzed. Fleishman and his colleagues discovered that the ten dimension categories were highly interrelated and could be grouped into two behavioral categories: consideration and initiating structure.

On the basis of these results the Ohio State research team developed the Leader Behavior Description Questionnaire (LBDQ), the Supervisory Behavior Description Questionnaire (SBDQ), and a shorter version of the LBDQ, the LBDQ–Form XII. The goal of these measures was to determine a leader's performance on the two dimensions of initiating structure and consideration. The dimensions were defined as follows (Fleishman & Peters, 1962):

Consideration: The extent to which a manager is likely to develop job relationships characterized by mutual trust, respect for subordinates' ideas, and concern for subordinates' feelings and needs.

Initiating structure: The extent to which a manager defines and structures the activities of his or her role and those of subordinates toward goal attainment.

A considerate leader is one who is oriented toward developing relationships or friendships with his or her group members. This type of relationship is often associated with increased employee satisfaction, self-esteem, and lower stress levels.

A leader who ranks high with respect to initiation of structure is described as production-oriented, deadline-oriented, and detail-oriented. In addition, both the Michigan State and Ohio State studies found that a structuring leadership style correlates with high self-esteem, high subordinate satisfaction, and high work group productivity.

In general, the Michigan State results initially supported the idea that an effective leader scored high either on task-related behaviors (initiation of structure) or on employee-related behaviors (consideration). The research team argued that a leader could not simultaneously exhibit both task- and employee-related behaviors. The Ohio State team disagreed and argued that the leader who exhibited *both* dimensions was most effective, depending on the interaction of the dimensions. For example, in their original study, Fleishman and Harris (1962) showed that supervisors who are moderate in consideration (see Figure 14.2 on page 486) have to exhibit a low amount of initiation of structure to have employees with low grievance rates. However, the combination of being moderate in consideration and high in structure relates to a high rate of grievances among employees.

The research at Ohio State and Michigan State provided researchers and practitioners with a starting point for recruiting, selecting, and training leaders. Later studies attempted to identify the critical levels of each of the behaviors associated with effective leadership. The additional data supported the conclusions that

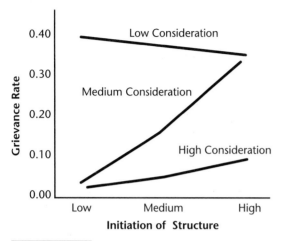

FIGURE 14.2   Interaction between the behavioral dimensions of consideration and initiation of structure.

Source: From "Patterns of Leadership Behavior Related to Employee Grievances and Turnover," by E. A. Fleishman, and E. F. Harris, 1962, *Personnel Psychology, 15,* 43–56, Durham, NC: Personnel Psychology, Inc. Copyright 1962 by Personnel Psychology, Inc. Reprinted with permission.

(a) the combination of these behaviors and their effectiveness could vary depending on the situation and (b) leadership behaviors are trainable, not inherited. With the accumulation of behavioral data, leadership research began to move away from the trait-only or behavior-only dichotomy and started to develop models that considered the interaction of traits, behaviors, and situations.

Situational Theories of Leadership

As examples of **situational theories,** we will discuss three theories that address the interaction between a leader and the leadership situation. The first is Fiedler's contingency model (1967), which focuses on matching a leader and a situation to maximize the leader's effectiveness and the subsequent organizational outcomes. The second theory is the path-goal theory (House, 1971; House & Mitchell, 1974), which emphasizes the leader's role in providing clear direc-

tion to subordinates toward goal achievement. This theory focuses on the leader's role in motivating employees and its relationship to organizational and subordinate outcomes. The third theory is the normative model developed by Vroom and Yetton (1973). This model is often referred to as the *decision tree theoretic model* because it requires the leader to define what level of subordinate involvement is appropriate in any particular situation. Underlying these theories is the belief that one leadership style is not necessarily effective in all situations. Rather, the effectiveness of the leader is contingent on both his or her abilities and the existing situational conditions.

The research on the situation as an additional component to be taken into account began in the late 1940s. The situational approach developed out of recognition that traits alone do not address the influence of the task and interpersonal context on the leader's behavior. Different traits and behaviors interact with different situations to produce effective leadership (Hollander & Offerman, 1990; Yukl & Van Fleet, 1992). Practice Perspective 14.1 shows how the situation can influence the way in which a leader is perceived. Bass (1990, p. 40) stated that theories of leadership "cannot be constructed for behavior in a vacuum. They must contain elements about the person as well as elements about the situation. Any theory must take into account the interplay between the situation and the individual."

Fiedler's Contingency Model

The **contingency model** of leadership addresses the interaction between a leader's style and situational contingencies. A leader's effectiveness is contingent on the unique combinations of the characteristics of the situation and his or her leadership style. According to Fiedler (1967), the contingency model assumes that **leader effectiveness** results from a positive match between the specific leadership style and the particular situation.

Leadership style is defined by the contingency model as a bipolar dimension ranging from relationship orientation to task orientation. A **relationship-oriented leader** exhibits behaviors similar to those described by the Ohio State studies' definition of consideration, that is, behaviors that emphasize relationships with the leader's subordinates. A **task-oriented leader** exhibits behaviors similar to those of the Ohio State's initiating structure leader, emphasizing subordinates' task accomplishment. To measure this bipolar leadership dimension, Fiedler developed the Least Preferred Coworker (LPC) Scale. Using the LPC Scale, a person is asked to select "the one coworker that they have been least able to work with." This **least preferred coworker** becomes the focus in completing the LPC Scale. The task is to describe this individual using adjectives such as those presented in Table 14.2 on page 488. The LPC Scale is an eight-point bipolar adjective scale composed of sixteen to twenty-four items. Subjects complete the scale by circling the number for each item that best describes how they feel about their least preferred coworker. The LPC score is obtained by summing the item values.

The lower the score subjects receive on the LPC Scale, the greater is their task orientation. The higher their score on the LPC Scale, the better is their relationship orientation (Rice, 1978). Leaders whose LPC scores represent a task orientation describe their least preferred coworker in terms of work behaviors rather than personality traits or attributes. An example of a task-oriented description would be "John Doe is always late for work and constantly misses his deadlines." Conversely, relationship-oriented leaders describe coworkers in terms of attributes, or personality, and not work behavior. For example, "Even though John Doe is late for work and misses deadlines, he is a very nice person."

The contingency model does not designate a preference for either leadership style but asserts that each style is most effective in certain situations. Hence, in addition to the leader's style, the contingency model recognizes the favorableness or unfavorableness of the situation.

A favorable situation is one in which leadership style and situational conditions match. There are three situational conditions to be taken into account: leader–member relations, task structure, and position power.

Leader–member relations involve the level of trust, acceptance, and loyalty that exists between a leader and group members (Fiedler, 1967). **Task structure** is defined according to four dimensions: decision verifiability, goal clarity, goal

---

TABLE 14.2 The Least Preferred Coworker Scale (LPC)

Think of the person with whom you can work least well. This person may be someone you work with now, or may be someone you knew in the past.

The person does not have to be the person you like least well, but should be the person with whom you had the most difficulty getting a job done. Describe the person as they appear to you.

Pleasant	8 7 6 5 4 3 2 1	Unpleasant
Friendly	8 7 6 5 4 3 2 1	Unfriendly
Rejecting	1 2 3 4 5 6 7 8	Accepting
Helpful	8 7 6 5 4 3 2 1	Frustrating
Unenthusiastic	1 2 3 4 5 6 7 8	Enthusiastic
Tense	1 2 3 4 5 6 7 8	Relaxed
Distant	1 2 3 4 5 6 7 8	Close
Cold	1 2 3 4 5 6 7 8	Warm
Cooperative	8 7 6 5 4 3 2 1	Uncooperative
Supportive	8 7 6 5 4 3 2 1	Hostile
Boring	1 2 3 4 5 6 7 8	Interesting
Quarrelsome	1 2 3 4 5 6 7 8	Harmonious
Self-assured	8 7 6 5 4 3 2 1	Hesitant
Efficient	8 7 6 5 4 3 2 1	Inefficient
Gloomy	1 2 3 4 5 6 7 8	Cheerful
Open	8 7 6 5 4 3 2 1	Guarded

Source: From *A theory of leadership effectiveness* (p. 41), by F. E. Fiedler, 1967, New York: McGraw-Hill. Copyright 1967 by McGraw-Hill. Current copyright held by F. E. Fiedler. Used by permission of F. E. Fiedler.

---

path multiplicity, and solution specificity. These four dimensions help to determine the extent to which a leader is able to control and supervise his or her subordinates. These four dimensions are briefly defined in Table 14.3.

Position power is defined along the lines of French and Raven's (1959) concepts of power. As can be seen in Historical Perspective 14.1, five types of power are identified: reward, coercive, legitimate, referent, and expert power. The type of power that a leader holds is related to the influence he or she has on subordinates and the leader's effectiveness in providing appropriate direction.

Situations are described along a dimension of favorability (see Table 14.4 on page 490), which indicates the degree of control the leader has on subordinates. Favorable situations are I, II, and III in Table 14.4. The most favorable situation is I, in which the leader–member relations are good, task structure is high, and position power is strong. Unfavorable situations are VII and VIII. In the most unfavorable situation (situation VIII), the leader–member relations are weak, task structure is low, and position power is weak. In the favorable situations, the leader monitors group performance to ensure that the tasks are completed. In the unfavorable situations, the leader must provide strong direction toward task accomplishment, not only using his or her task-oriented style, but engaging in position power as well.

In the moderate situations—IV, V, and VI— the leader with a relationship-oriented style is

TABLE 14.3   Dimensions defining task structure

Dimension	Definition
Decision verifiability	Extent to which a decision can be verified by reference to alternate documentation or similar situations, logic, or feedback available during task performance
Goal clarity	Clarity of task requirements to subordinates
Goal path multiplicity	Number of possible methods available for task completion
Solution specificity	Number of available correct task solutions

Source: From *A theory of leadership effectiveness* (p. 28), by F. E. Fiedler, 1967, New York, NY: McGraw- Hill. Copyright 1967 by McGraw-Hill. Current copyright held by F. E. Fiedler. Used by permission of F. E. Fiedler.

most effective. Moderate or mixed conditions require more interpersonal skill because the leader cannot influence task structure or group performance. Confronted with a moderate situation, a relationship-oriented leader tries to motivate group members and keep them goal-directed.

The contingency model and the LPC Scale have been critiqued by several researchers (e.g., Rice & Kastenbaum, 1983; Schriesheim, Bannister, & Money, 1979) and the meaning of the LPC Scale has been questioned (Vecchio, 1980). Specifically, researchers have not been able to

HISTORICAL PERSPECTIVE 14.1

The Bases of Social Power

In 1959, French and Raven proposed a way of examining leadership process based on the different types of power available to the leader and how that power is typically used. This framework became popular and has been the stimulus for a number of research studies.

The kinds of power that are commonly available to leaders were identified by French and Raven as the following:

Reward power, which is the power of a supervisor to control and dispense rewards to his or her subordinates.

Coercive power, or the power of a supervisor to control and dispense punishments to subordinates. This includes the power to fire.

Legitimate power, described as the right of a supervisor to influence subordinates and the accompanying obligation of the subordinate to accept that influence.

Referent power, which is the identification of the subordinate with his or her supervisor. That is, the individual accepts the supervisor's goals as his or her own.

Expert power, or power derived from the knowledge or expertise that a supervisor has.

An additional source of power was created by other investigators who combined referent power and expert power to define incremental power. Incremental power is the degree to which a leader has control over subordinates that cannot be explained simply by reward power or coercive power. It has also been called charisma.

Source: Based on material in French, J. R. P., Jr., & Raven, B. H. (1959). The bases of social power. In D. Cartwright (Ed.), *Studies in social power*. Ann Arbor: University of Michigan, Institute for Social Research. Copyright 1959 University of Michigan. Reprinted with permission.

TABLE 14.4	Fiedler's situational classifications		
Situation	Leader–Member Relation	Task Structure	Position Power
I	Good	High	Strong
II	Good	High	Weak
III	Good	Low	Strong
IV	Good	Low	Weak
V	Poor	High	Strong
VI	Poor	High	Weak
VII	Poor	Low	Strong
VIII	Poor	Low	Weak

Source: From *A theory of leadership effectiveness* (p. 142), by F. E. Fiedler, 1967, New York: McGraw-Hill. Copyright 1967 by McGraw-Hill. Current copyright held by F. E. Fiedler. Used by permission of F. E. Fiedler.

agree on the definition of the underlying construct of the LPC scale. In addition, concern has been raised about inconsistencies in the relationship between LPC scores and situational favorability and how the situation influences leader effectiveness (Rice, 1978). Recent research has shown that the inconsistency of these relationships may be a function of moderating variables, such as the extent to which social expectations influence leader behavior (Ayman & Chemers, 1991; Hughes, Ginnett, & Curphy, 1993). Regardless of the critiques, the contingency model continues to elicit research questions.

Path-Goal Theory

According to **path-goal theory,** leader effectiveness is defined by the leader's ability to supply subordinates with the necessary information (paths) to achieve valued rewards (goals) (Hughes et al., 1993):

Path	+	Goal	=	Outcomes
For example		*For example*		*For example*
task activities		productivity		satisfaction
environmental				motivation
demands				

Leadership styles are the basis of path-goal theory. House and Dessler (1974) claimed that the role of the leader is to improve the "psychological states" (p. 30) of subordinates to enhance their motivation to perform and to have higher job satisfaction. House and Mitchell (1974) identified the following behaviors that a leader can exhibit to enhance subordinate satisfaction and motivation:

1. Recognize what subordinates want and/or create subordinates' interest in and need for outcomes
2. Increase personal payoffs for work goal achieved
3. Make the path to these payoffs easier to travel by coaching and direction
4. Help subordinates to clarify expectancies
5. Reduce frustrating barriers
6. Increase opportunities for personal satisfaction contingent on effective performance

These leader behaviors involve leadership styles similar to those defined by the Ohio State and Michigan State studies (i.e., consideration versus initiation of structure). The theory formally defines four types of leadership styles:

directive, supportive, participative, and achievement-oriented (House & Mitchell, 1974). Directive leadership is similar to the Ohio definition of initiation of structure. The leader provides directives to his or her employees about the tasks they have to accomplish and the specific ways in which the tasks are to be achieved. The supportive leader is similar to the Ohio dimension of consideration. Concern and attention to employees' needs are the basis for the leader's behavior. A participative leader is one who encourages input from his or her employees and makes it part of decision making. An achievement-oriented leader establishes challenging goals for his or her employees. At the same time, such a leader supports and encourages subordinates in achieving these goals. The path-goal model is similar to Fiedler's contingency model in that a leader's effectiveness in applying different styles is determined by the situation in which that leader must function (Greene, 1979). The theory postulates two classifications of situational variables: subordinate characteristics and environmental pressures and demands on subordinates.

Subordinate characteristics include the subordinates' perceptions of the extent to which the leader's behavior is an immediate source of satisfaction or is associated with future satisfaction. The subordinates' perceptions of their own abilities to perform the task(s) also affect their interactions with the leader. For example, employees who believe that they are capable of performing a task are less likely to work well with a directive leader. They would be more satisfied and more motivated with a participative leader. **Environmental pressures and demands** include the subordinate's tasks, the organization's formal authority structure, and the subordinate's primary work group.

Each situational variable can serve as a motivator, constraint, or reinforcer of employee performance and satisfaction. The leader's role is to recognize the role of each situational variable and use this information to clarify subordinate path-goal relationships in a way that will maximize subordinate satisfaction and performance (Griffin, 1980). Figure 14.3 provides an example of the interactive effect of leader behavior and situational variables.

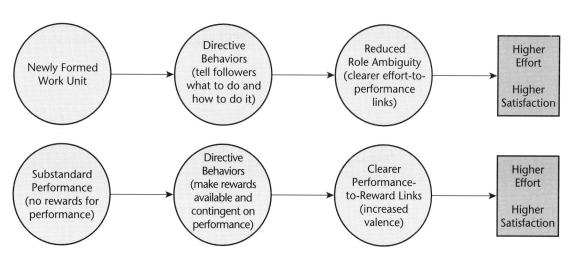

FIGURE 14.3 Interactive effect of leader behavior and situational variables.

Source: From *Leadership: Enhancing the Lessons of Experience* 2nd ed. (p. 513), by R. L. Hughes, R. C. Ginnett, and G. J. Curphy, 1996, Burr Ridge, IL: Irwin. Copyright © 1996 Irwin. Reprinted with permission.

A problem may occur if the leader attempts to clarify a path-goal relationship that is already clear to a subordinate. If so, the leader's behavior is seen as redundant and controlling (House & Mitchell, 1974). A problem can also occur when a leader does not provide enough direction. In either case the result is dissatisfied employees with the increased possibility of consequences such as resistance, sabotage, and conflict (Abdel-Halim, 1981).

The path-goal theory has been criticized for failing to recognize the effects of employee selection, training, and development (Yukl & Van Fleet, 1992). These skill-building variables can increase subordinate performance and satisfaction and are important considerations for any leader. The path-goal theory's primary focus is on improving performance and satisfaction by stressing employee motivation. Overall, the path-goal theory encourages leaders to use a long-term strategic focus to help employees cope with their environmental situations and thus maximize sub-ordinate effort, satisfaction, and rewards (House, Filley, & Kerr, 1971; House & Mitchell, 1974). It is similar to Fiedler's theory in the belief that effective leadership style is contingent on subordinate and environmental characteristics.

Normative Model

Vroom and Yetton (1973) developed the decision tree model, or **normative model.** The model proposes five levels of participation in decision making (Table 14.5), which vary according to the level of subordinate influence. The styles vary from autocratic to consultative to group decisions. Autocratic styles are unilateral; the leader makes decisions without first consulting with subordinates. The consultative approach occurs when the leader collects subordinates' reactions and ideas and takes them into account in making a decision. In group decision making, the leader and subordinates make decisions collectively.

Situational factors influence which decision-making style is to be used. The characteristics of

---

TABLE 14.5   Decision processes of the normative model

AI: You solve the problem or make the decision yourself, using the information available to you at the present time.

AII: You obtain any necessary information from subordinates, then decide on a solution to the problem yourself.

CI: You share the problem with the relevant subordinates individually, getting their ideas and suggestion without bringing them together as a group. You make the decision. This decision may not reflect the subordinates' influence.

CII: You share the problem with your subordinates in a group meeting. You obtain their ideas and suggestions. You make the decision. This decision may not reflect the subordinates' influence.

GII: You share the problem with your subordinates as a group. Together you generate and evaluate alternatives and attempt to reach agreement on a solution. The goal is to implement any solution that has the support of the entire group.

Source: From "On the Validity of the Vroom-Yetton Model" by V. H. Vroom and A. G. Jago, 1978, *Journal of Applied Psychology, 63*(2), 151–162. Copyright 1978 by American Psychological Association. Reprinted with permission.

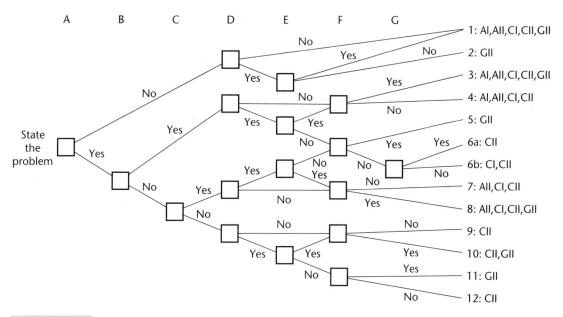

FIGURE 14.4   Vroom and Yetton's Normative Model of Leader Behavior.

Source: Reprinted from *Leadership and Decision Making* (p. 36), by Victor. H. Vroom and Philip W. Yetton, by permission of the University of Pittsburgh Press. Copyright © 1973 by University of Pittsburgh Press.

the situational factors lead to the following seven rules underlying the model: (a) the importance of the quality of the decision, (b) the extent to which the decision maker has the information necessary to make a decision, (c) the extent to which the problem is structured, (d) the extent to which subordinates' acceptance is important, (e) the probability that an autocratic decision will be accepted, (f) the extent to which subordinates are motivated to attain organizational goals, and (g) the extent to which subordinates are likely to disagree with proposed solutions (Jago & Vroom, 1980; Vroom & Jago, 1978).

As Figure 14.4 shows, the Vroom and Yetton model provides leaders with a series of questions to assist them in determining the level of subordinate participation that is required to make an effective managerial decision. The leader must take into account the issue at hand, current situational demands, and the extent to which employee participation will influence de-

cision quality. The outcome of this model is an understanding of the level of employee participation that is considered appropriate for the task or problem at hand.

The leader answers "yes" or "no" to each question. At each stage of the decision tree, each yes–no question pertains to one of the seven rules listed previously and serves to obtain one or more decision processes or a feasible set. A feasible set is a set of possible decision processes that, if implemented, will not affect the quality or subordinate acceptance of the decision (Field, 1982). The decision style that the leader selects from this feasible set is contingent on other situational factors such as time pressures or concern with subordinate development (Vroom & Jago, 1978). The result of this process is increased leader effectiveness and improved outcomes for the subordinate and the organization, including increased satisfaction, increased productivity, and reduced conflict (Crouch & Yetton, 1987).

Related to the normative decision model is the notion of participative leadership. Participative leadership is represented by the outcome GII of the normative model (see Figure 14.4). Participative leadership, as defined in Table 14.5, involves the sharing of a problem with subordinates as a group. Together, the leader and the subordinates generate and evaluate alternatives, attempting to reach agreement on a solution. The goal of participative leadership is to implement a solution that has the support of the entire group.

As surprising as it may seem, to date there is no direct empirical support for the advantages or disadvantages of participative leadership (Yukl & Van Fleet, 1992). However, Vroom and Yetton's model attempts to identify situations in which participation may be appropriate and lead to improved satisfaction and performance. According to Yukl and Van Fleet (1992), research in participative leadership could benefit from investigating the role of participation on leader effectiveness.

Transactional and Transformational Theories of Leadership

Some of the theories that have been reviewed to this point have focused on attempts to describe a leader according to traits and attributes. Others have demonstrated the interactional influences of situational variables and selected leadership styles on leader effectiveness. However, these theories do not take into account the negotiation that takes place between a leader and a subordinate as a part of the goal achievement process.

Transactional theories are based on the underlying concept that a job is not solely defined by the task domain; it also involves a relational domain. Transactional theories focus on the interaction of the task and relational domains that influence an employee's tenure, satisfaction, turnover, organizational functioning, and leader effectiveness (Graen, Liden, & Hoel, 1982; Graen, Novak, & Sommerkamp, 1982; Seers & Graen, 1984).

According to Deluga (1991), transactional leaders create a relationship with subordinates based on influence and bargaining power. In one situation, a leader may find himself or herself more dependent on a subordinate who has the special skills necessary for the completion of a particular task. In another situation, the subordinate may find himself or herself dependent on the leader, such as requesting time off during the work day.

In each situation, the influence and bargaining power of the leader and the subordinate is unequal, and either party member can use this to his or her own advantage. For example, suppose that the two scenarios mentioned above were combined in one situation. That is, suppose that the employee with special skills needs the time off, but the leader also needs that employee to accomplish an important work task. In this situation the leader and subordinate would bargain. The leader would promise the subordinate time off if the subordinate would promise to assist the leader with the task at hand.

Leader–Member Exchange Theory

One transactional model was described by Bass (1990) as a social exchange between the leader and his or her members. Here, the leader and subordinates negotiate subordinate roles and role expectations. Once roles are defined, the leader, who has control over reinforcements, shapes subordinate performance to ensure goal achievement. Accordingly, the leader places values on subordinates on the basis of their contribution to goal achievement. The value that is assigned to each subordinate influences the quality of the exchange that takes place between leader and subordinate. Subsequently, the type of exchange affects the quality of the subordinate's work experiences.

Scandura and Graen (1984) discuss how the value that a leader assigns to each subordinate contributes to the dichotomization of organizational groups. Work groups are dichotomized into low-quality leader–member exchange relations and high-quality leader–member exchange relations. The difference in groups is referred to as **in-group** versus **out-group** status. This differentiation occurs over time as a result of leaders developing different relations with different people. Being an in-group member leads to greater levels of satisfaction and commitment than does being a member of an out-group, because the leader provides in-group members with more latitude, more influence in decision making, more confidence in members, and greater support (Dansereau, Graen, & Haga, 1975; Greene, 1975; Scandura, Graen, & Novak, 1986).

Out-group members are not mistreated by the leader, but receive less challenge and support for individual interests and career development. The out-group members are able to perform their jobs, but do not share the additional relationship component with their leader, as do the in-group members. In-group members share more of a collegial relationship with the leader, maintaining a much more intimate working relationship.

In general, leader–member exchange theory addresses the need to understand the diverse relationships that exist between a leader and his or her work group. It is the nature of these relationships that influences productivity, satisfaction, commitment, and a range of outcomes for the organization and its subordinates. This theory allows leadership researchers to investigate issues of leadership at a dyadic level as well as at the larger group level.

A major criticism of leader–member exchange theory has been that it does not specify which situations are optimal for the various leader–member relations. Because of this, the theory is considered to be descriptive of leader effectiveness rather than providing prescriptive suggestions (Yukl, 1989).

In **leader–member exchange theory** the relationship between leader and subordinate is based on reward contingencies and performance feedback by the leader. The goal is to secure outcomes that are important to both individuals. In the next section the theory of transformational leadership will be reviewed. This theory states that the leader–subordinate relationship is more than just a negotiated exchange. Rather, the leader and the subordinate share a relationship that goes beyond transactions and involves behaviors that benefit the individuals involved as well as their organizations (Bass, 1981).

Transformational Theory of Leadership

Bass (1990, p. 53) defines a **transformational leader** as one who is able to

> ask followers to transcend their own self-interests for the good of the group, organization, or society; to consider their longer-term needs to develop themselves, rather than their needs of the moment; and to become aware of what is really important.

Outcomes of this type of relationship are a display of greater pride in and identification with the organization and the exertion of extra energy to achieve the organization's goals (Fullagar, McCoy, & Shull, 1992).

It has been demonstrated that transformational leadership augments or improves the outcomes of the leader–member interaction. For example, subordinates of transformational leaders have been shown to exert more effort than subordinates of transactional leaders (Ehrlich, Meindl, & Viellieu; 1990). Subordinates of transformational leaders express greater satisfaction and a preference for working with a transformational leader than subordinates of transactional leaders (Singer & Singer, 1990).

The difference between the leader–member exchange transactional theory and the transformational theory of leadership is that transactional leaders are presumed to exercise two general approaches to leading subordinates: management by exception and contingent rewards.

Management by exception occurs when managers provide subordinate feedback only when subordinate performance is inadequate, inappropriate, or deficient. When engaging in an interaction, transactional managers also make rewards or benefits for performance contingent on effective performance (**contingent reward**). The qualities that augment transactional leadership to create transformational leaders are charisma, intellectual stimulation, and individual consideration.

According to Yukl and Van Fleet (1992), transformational leaders empower their subordinates and elicit higher levels of performance. By identifying and considering individual group members' needs and goals, along with providing intellectual stimulation, the transformational leader affects subordinate attitude and organizational change by developing commitment and a feeling of organizational ownership. As predicted and consistent with previous research, Bycio, Hackett, and Allen (1995, p. 474) showed that, in general, the leader's effectiveness relates "positively to transformational leadership and negatively to management-by-exception." Specifically, their study indicated that transformational leadership relates moderately to decreases in employee intent to leave their organization. However, this exchange style also had a strong positive relationship to employees' emotional attachment to their organization.

Charismatic Leadership Theory

In 1977, House developed a theory that emphasizes the notion of charisma and **charismatic leadership**. House attempted to distinguish between charismatic and noncharismatic leaders. He explains that charismatic leaders capture employees' imaginations and inspire their devotion. In addition, charismatic leaders build follower commitment to task by creating a vision or ideological goal. They communicate high expectations to their followers and express constant confidence in subordinates' abilities and interests (House, 1977). Bass (1985) believes that charis-

matic characteristics are part of the transformational style of leadership.

Specifically, subordinates of charismatic leaders tend to place high levels of trust and respect in their leader. They demonstrate a tendency to "worship" a leader, whom they place in the position of an idol (Bass, 1985). This results in a strong obedience toward, and an unconditional acceptance of, the leader (House, 1977).

Transformational and charismatic theories of leadership have contributed to leadership research by demonstrating that leadership involves more than simply managing tasks. That is, leadership is affected by subordinate emotions, perceptions, the situation, and a leader's ability to manage his or her impressions (Yukl & Van Fleet, 1992). Transformational and charismatic leadership theories support the role of perception in leadership research. In the next section, we will discuss theories that specifically address the impact of perception and social cognition on leadership.

Cognitive Theories of Leadership

Cognitive theories developed out of an interest in understanding what effect, if any, the leader's perception of the subordinates' performance had on the leader's behavior. Cognition is defined as the ability to gain knowledge, to judge its meaning, and to discover its role in behavior. Green and Mitchell (1979) proposed the *attributional model of leadership* to explain that a leader's behavior is the result of the leader's perception of a subordinate's poor performance.

Attributional Model of Leadership

The **attributional model** suggests that a leader's perception is influenced by situational cues and the subordinate's performance history. Through experience with a subordinate the leader develops a schema that attempts to organize the employee's attributes in order to explain poor performance. Poor performance has been defined as low productivity, disruptive behavior, or missed deadlines (Bass, 1990). According to the attributional model, the leader perceives the employee's behaviors (the poor performance) and then attributes a cause to that behavior (the employee is lazy or unmotivated).

If a subordinate has a history of poor performance, his or her present poor performance will probably be attributed to personality, lack of ability, and/or low effort (Meindl, Erlich, & Dukerich, 1985). If the subordinate has a history of good performance, there is a higher probability that the leader will attribute the subordinate's present poor performance to external sources such as poor support, faulty machinery, and/or task difficulty (Mitchell, Green, & Wood, 1981).

Should the subordinate's poor performance be connected to internal attributes, the action that the supervisor takes may be more severe than the action that would be taken by a leader who perceived a subordinate's poor performance to be the result of external influences (Heerwagen, Beach, & Mitchell, 1985; Pence, Pendleton, Dobbins, & Sgro, 1982). The effect of such attribution on leader behavior is that some subordinates are relegated to an in-group and others to an out-group. Like the path-goal theory, the in-group receives more considerate and supportive treatment from the leader, along with greater delegation of responsibility. The out-group receives the opposite treatment and often reports lower levels of satisfaction and commitment. However, unlike the path-goal theory, in the attributional model the leader's behavior is driven by the leader's perception of a subordinate rather than by meeting needs via negotiation.

Perception is beginning to play an important role in leadership studies. It is an important factor in identifying the interactions between leaders and group members and in understanding why certain behaviors occur. Moreover, the process of understanding the consequences of those relationships is essential to organizational effectiveness.

Implicit Leadership Theory

Research on **implicit leadership theory** has focused on the *subordinate's* implicit concept of the leader. The interest is in identifying how the match between a subordinate's implicit leadership theory and a leader's actual leadership behavior affects outcomes such as subordinate satisfaction and leader performance. With implicit leadership, subordinates have a perception of what a leader should be and then evaluate the leader according to these perceptions. To do this, they use a cognitive representation or prototype of the individual or role that has been established on the basis of specific events, interactions, or situations involving an individual or a group (Markus, 1977).

A general observation that cognitive theorists make is that leadership is a social interaction in which the leader and the subordinate are both actors and observers (Ayman, 1993). Leader and subordinate behavior affect each other; that is, both the leader and the subordinate bring certain expectancies and assumptions to a social situation (such as the work context). These biased frames of reference constrain the flow of information, the way the information is processed, and the behaviors that are elicited (Heilman, Block, Martell, & Simon, 1989; Lord & Maher, 1993). Specifically, the implicit theory of leadership recognizes that the behavior that is elicited is mediated by a subordinate's perception of a leader and a leader's perception of a subordinate. It emphasizes the importance of a manager's awareness of how subordinates perceive managerial behavior.

The implicit theory shows that leadership ratings by followers are influenced by the fit between the leader's behavior and the followers' prototype of a leader (Fraser & Lord, 1988; Lord, Foti, & De Vader, 1984). Lord et al. (1984) reported that as the actual leader behaviors deviated from subordinates' prototypes of expected leader behavior, the subordinates' evaluation of their leader lowered. Additional research has shown that the consequence of a mismatch between a leader's actual behavior and the subordinate prototypes may affect trust, motivation, and performance (Eden & Leviathan, 1975; Lord & Maher, 1993).

Lord and Maher (1993), observed that implicit leadership research has been carried out primarily in laboratory settings. Future research needs to continue testing the theory in applied settings to validate its practical value. Another limitation is that many variables are involved in the concept of perception. As was noted earlier in this chapter, there are many definitions of leadership, so it is difficult to agree on a definition of a "prototypical leader."

Implicit leadership theory has received an increasing amount of attention from leadership researchers. It consolidates several areas of psychology, including social cognition, social psychology, and impression management research. Linking perception to performance provides organizations with additional perspectives on problem resolution that can lead to enhanced organizational performance.

The Operant Model of Leadership

The **operant model of leadership** is distinct from other leadership models in that it includes three critical elements that are frequently missing in the others: prescriptive statements of what the leader should do, direct observation of the team members' actions rather than simply the actions of isolated individuals, and the careful definition of interdependent tasks that require cooperation among the team members for successful completion. The operant model is described in detail in Komaki and Desselles's book, *Supervision Reexamined: The Role of Monitors and Consequences* (1990).

Two types of supervisory behavior are particularly important in the operant model: first, providing consequences by recognizing a job well done, noting corrections needed, and providing clear feedback; and second, monitoring the work by collecting performance information through samples of the work, asking for self-reports, or consulting a secondary source. Underlying the operant model are the theory and applications of operant conditioning (Frederikson, 1982; Komaki & Desselles, 1990; Skinner, 1974). Inferences from operant conditioning theory define an effective manager as one who regularly evaluates worker performance and on the basis of that performance, provides consequences such as feedback. An ineffective manager, in contrast, would not regularly assess performance of workers and only rarely provide feedback. As Komaki, Desselles, and Bowman (1989, p. 523) note:

> The potency of these categories has been demonstrated empirically in a series of investigations. Monitoring was found to distinguish between managers of different levels of effectiveness in one study (Komaki, 1986). Effective managers inquired about the work and examined actual output more often than their marginally effective counterparts. Consequences, when monitoring was sufficient, was the key difference between effective and marginally effective managers in another study (Jensen & Komaki, 1989). Effective managers recognized or corrected workers' performance. Thus, the operant model with its key behaviors of monitoring and consequences has an empirical as well as a theoretical basis.

The operant model of leadership has produced some exciting research. The study summarized in Scientific Perspective 14.1 is an example.

Substitute Leadership

Kerr and Jermier (1978) suggest that the formal leadership theories discussed in previous models may not always be necessary. These researchers focused on different types of subordinate characteristics, tasks, and the organization to reduce the need for a formal leadership structure. The substitutes that neutralize formal leadership have been defined as variables that make leadership either unnecessary or obsolete (Bass, 1990). That

SCIENTIFIC PERSPECTIVE 14.1

Definitely Not a Breeze

The Komaki and Desselles operant model of effective leadership identifies three critical elements of team leadership: prescriptive statements (what the leader should do), the actions of team members, and interdependent tasks (tasks that require cooperation among team members for successful completion). The model is important because it adds empirical evidence to the prescriptive statements and interdependent tasks to our understanding of team supervision. Komaki, Dresselles, and Bowman (1989) conducted a study to test and extend this operant model, identifying what team leaders ought to do to orchestrate optimal team performance. This is not simply a list of suggestions, but objective specification of leader actions that will improve their team's performance.

A sailboat regatta was arranged for research purposes. This capitalized on the facts that "sailboat racing has identifiable leaders; many of the maneuvers involve intense team efforts; and racing requires precisely timed orchestration among crew members" (Komaki et al., 1989, p. 524). The setting was a fleet racing competition; the subjects were a fleet of ten J-24 sailboats, nineteen skippers, thirty-six crew members, eleven observers, and four varsity coaches. During a series of six races, the Operant Supervisory Team Taxonomy (Komaki, Zlotnick, & Jensen, 1986) served as the measure of leader behavior. Events of interest were performance monitoring, performance consequences, antecedents, work-related nonperformance, and not interacting. The effectiveness of the teams and skippers was assessed by the series standings (actual performance outcome) and coaches' ratings and rankings of each skipper (a judgmental measure).

As was predicted by the operant model, leaders who collected performance information or gave feedback during the race were more likely to be successful in leading their crews to victory. Their series standings correlated significantly with the frequency with which those skippers stated performance consequences ($r = -.47$, $p < .05$) and monitored the performance of their crews ($r = -.51$, $p < .05$) during the races. No significance was found for the behaviors of skippers before the races. Providing consequences was also found to be significantly related to coach ratings and ranking of crew handling ($r = -.60$, $p < .05$). Monitoring, however, was not significantly related to the ratings and rankings ($r = -.42$, $p > .05$).

In this study, "leaders who finished ahead of their peers were more likely to oversee subordinates' efforts. Furthermore, skippers who let their crews know when they were doing things right or wrong were more likely to win races" (Komaki et al., 1989, p. 527). In contrast, those "aspects of monitoring and providing consequences especially concerned with the integration of team members" efforts were not found to be associated with skipper success" (Komaki et al., 1989, p. 528). The authors suggest that managerial candidates could be assessed in terms of their use of the behavioral categories and that management and leadership training could be based on objective skills that affect team performance rather than on armchair speculation.

Source: Adapted from Komaki, J. L., Desselles, M. L., & Bowman, E. D. (1989). Definitely not a breeze: Extending an operant model of effective supervision to teams. *Journal of Applied Psychology, 74,* 522–529.

is, substitutes, or **neutralizers,** replace the need for formal leadership and become the greater influence on subordinate satisfaction and performance (Bass, 1990). Table 14.6 on page 500

reviews several substitutes and shows how they may neutralize formal leadership.

An example of a substitute for formal leadership is the amount of experience a subordinate

| TABLE 14.6 | Substitutes for leadership |

	Will tend to neutralize	
Characteristic:	Relationship-oriented, supportive, people-centered leadership: consideration, support, and interaction facilitation	Task-orientated, instrumental, job-centered leadership: initiating structure, goal emphasis, and work facilitation
Of the subordinate		
1. Ability, experience, training, knowledge		X
2. Need for independence	X	X
3. "Professional" orientation	X	X
4. Indifference toward organizational rewards	X	X
Of the task		
5. Unambiguous and routine		X
6. Methodologically invariant		X
7. Provides its own feedback concerning accomplishment		X
8. Intrinsically satisfying	X	
Of the organization		
9. Formalization (explicit plans, goals, and areas of responsibility)		X
10. Inflexibility (rigid, unbending rules and procedures)		X
11. Highly specified and active advisory and staff functions		X
12. Closely knit, cohesive work groups	X	X
13. Organizational rewards not within the leader's control	X	X
14. Spatial distance between superior and subordinates	X	X

Source: From "Substitutes for Leadership: Their Meaning and Measurement," by S. Kerr and J. M. Jermier (1978). *Organizational Behavior and Human Performance, 22,* 375–403. Copyright 1978 by Academic Press. Reprinted with permission.

has with a specific task. If the subordinate has successfully completed the task a number of times on different occasions, there is no longer a need for formal instruction or direction by a leader. Kerr and Jermier (1978) claim that in such a case, formal instruction from a leader may have a negative impact because the subordinate may perceive the leader as not trusting the subordinate's ability.

Another example of a neutralizer would be an organization that has a democratic culture. The democratic culture neutralizes some of the powers leaders hold in a nondemocratic organization (Yukl & Van Fleet, 1992). For example, coercive power in a democratic organization may be neutralized because a democratic decision requires agreement rather than forced compliance.

Finding substitutes for leadership is an intriguing area of research that needs more empirical support (Yukl & Van Fleet, 1992). Specifically, Yukl and Van Fleet suggest that research is needed to explain the causal relationships among substitutes, neutralizers, and outcomes. They also recommend that more precise definitions of constructs be developed. It is important to be aware of the influences of substitutes, neutralizers, culture, and stereotypes on leaders and leadership. Most significant, however, is the recognition that leadership is more than simply a combination of situations and individuals. Rather, it is a mosaic of the interrelationship between multiple variables.

Gender Issues

The leadership theories discussed so far demonstrate the relevance of leadership to organizational outcomes, how the leader influences his or her subordinates to attain a common goal. More important is how the leader motivates and obtains subordinate commitment within the boundaries of organizational strategies and policies. In summary, a leader's effectiveness is influenced by his or her traits, the situations within which the leader operates, the quality of exchange with subordinates, and the mutual perceptions of the leader and his or her followers. However, there are additional moderating variables that can affect leader efficacy.

The traditional cultural premise in the United States has been that women typically do not hold high-status jobs. This is the result of gender differences in role expectations, which have been socialized throughout adolescence and adulthood via workplace policies, hierarchies, and informal networks. Research has consistently shown that the stereotype of a manager does not include physical or psychological characteristics that are considered feminine (Heilman et al., 1989; Schein, 1973, 1975).

Gender has received a substantial amount of research attention in the leadership area. Women often have been considered as not being able to successfully manage the work roles that have traditionally been played by men. A woman's behavior and her self-perception, self-expectations, and subsequent job performance were found to be influenced in situations in which she was the only female occupant, or one of a few, in her job category (Skrypnek & Snyder, 1982). An example is a token female in a group of male middle managers.

Stereotypes have been a major factor in perceived gender differences. According to Hoffman & Hurst, (1990, p. 207), "the interesting nature about gender stereotypes is not that a subset of the [target] category may indeed resemble the stereotype, but that the stereotype encompasses the category as a whole." That is, gender elicits the stereotypes and their related expectations (e.g., type of traits and behaviors and efficacy in various roles) for a member of that target category.

Women who have held traditionally male jobs have been referred to as "gender aliens" (Bailyn, 1987). Because women have historically been underrepresented in male-dominated positions (e.g., chief executive officer, comptroller, general manager), women's experiences in these roles and settings have been completely different from those of their male counterparts (Eagly & Steffen, 1984). Lower expectations have existed for women in the workplace, and these lower expectations have negatively affected advancement or career-related opportunities.

Heilman et al. (1989) initiated a study to determine whether men and women are perceived differently in leadership roles. Their study was based on a study by Schein (1973), which found that a leader was described in masculine terms.

Sixteen years later, Heilman et al. concluded that few, if any, changes had occurred in the traits used to describe leaders. Differential descriptions of men and women still persisted, the description of men being closer to the prototype of "successful manager." Qualities that were defined as central to successful leadership were repeatedly assigned to male managers and not to female managers. In general, Heilman et al. (1989, p. 941) stated that women who were perceived as successful managers were many times also described as "bitter, quarrelsome, [and] selfish."

Another study (Mansfield, Koch, Henderson, Vicary, Cohn, & Young, 1991) examined the relationship between job satisfaction and stress for women in blue-collar jobs. Mansfield and colleagues reported a number of critical issues that exist for women in nontraditional occupational roles. To be successful, women have had to endure high levels of sexual harassment and discrimination, and regardless of their level of competence, women have had to "overcome their gender." Women in nontraditional occupational roles reported that one of their worst problems is the degree to which they are isolated from the social networks to which men have access, networks that improve socialization, professional development, and the overall work experience.

Dreher and Cox (1996) found that women with MBAs were less likely than men with MBAs to establish a mentoring relationship with white men. A mentoring relationship is a developmental relationship between an individual (the protege) and a more senior and influential manager (the mentor). Such a relationship is important because it gives the protege access to information, visibility, and the chance to demonstrate competence. Dreher and Cox found that graduates who were able to establish mentoring relationships with white men achieved an average annual compensation advantage of $16,840 over those with mentors having other demographic profiles. They found no compensation differentials between women who established mentoring relationships with other women or with minority men and women who had not established any mentoring relationship.

Lyness and Thompson (1997) compared matched samples of female and male executives in terms of their career and work experiences. The study found more similarities than differences between the female executives and their male counterparts. The two did not differ significantly on the organizational outcomes of base salary or bonuses or on the developmental characteristics of developing new directions, high stakes, managing business diversity, job overload, or unfamiliar responsibilities. Important differences were found for women who had less authority, and received fewer stock options. Their career histories also reflected more interruptions than did those of the men. While both men and women expressed similar levels of interest in future international assignments, the interested women were significantly more likely than their male counterparts to indicate restrictions. Women at the highest executive levels reported more obstacles than did women at lower levels.

Although Lyness and Thompson did not find many of the gender disparities other studies have reported, they concluded that there were some important differences. Even in their carefully matched sample, they found that women's jobs had less authority than men's as measured by the number of subordinates managed. Women received fewer stock options than men even after the investigators controlled for level of education, performance rating, and management level. This suggests that in the organization where the study was completed, women are less valued than their male counterparts. Finally, Lyness and Thompson found variations in the subjective experiences reported by the male and female executives. The women reported experiencing more obstacles such as having to influence others without having clear authority in the situation. The senior women also reported significantly less satisfaction with their future career opportunities than did their male counterparts. This finding was particulary disappointing because the women were found to be comparable to the men on so many other factors. In general, the women expressed less satisfaction with their careers and their potential for promotion, both essential factors in overall job satisfaction.

Research also has attempted to assess directly the interplay of the multiple roles of women in society (Corse, 1990). Corse asked subjects to describe their impressions of two groups of women managers: those who were pregnant and those who were not. Two important findings emerged. First, both men and women held specific stereotypes for the behavior of a manager in general, a female manager, and a pregnant female manager. Not surprisingly, the manager role was described primarily in terms of masculine traits such as being aggressive and structured. The nonpregnant female manager was described as being closer to the manager stereotype than was the pregnant manager.

Expectations for the pregnant manager were that she would be more passive and nurturing than a nonpregnant manager. Pregnant managers were also described by subjects as rigid, mean, hostile, and aggressive. The roles of "pregnant woman" and "female manager" held different role expectations. When these expectations clashed, they influenced the work experience of the women in each role. An example of the conflicts this generates is described in Practice Perspective 14.2.

Women's self-confidence about success at work, when compared to that of men, is significantly related to external cues such as salary, support at home, and job networks (Bailyn, 1987). Bailyn also discovered that the characteristics of the task influenced the perception of whether a woman was successful, both on the job and outside of the work environment. In situations in which women's work and nonwork were similar, or at least not in conflict (e.g., nurse and mother versus nuclear engineer and mother), women reported higher levels of well-being and self-confidence. The ex-

---

PRACTICE PERSPECTIVE 14.2

A Day in the Life of Wendy L. Lewis: A Career Woman and Mother

"Long ago, I thought juggling work and family was like anything else in life: It would all work out if I tried hard enough.

"Several years and two babies later, I felt as though I had been hit from opposite directions by two speeding trains. My kids had experienced all sorts of day-care traumas, I had a bad case of burnout, and my career track through no fault of my employer looked like a dying man's cardiogram."

For most of us, a few days in the life of Wendy L. Lewis, for example, a 39-year-old single mother of three who is human resources manager for

the Chicago Cubs and studies weekends for an M. B. A., would feel like swinging a leaded bat before stepping up to the plate. Ms. Lewis trains like an athlete for her 19-hour days, watching her diet and often rising at 4 A.M. to work out.

planation for these results was that external support (e.g., family and friends) was available for both the work and nonwork roles (Bailyn, 1987).

A study by Rakowski (1987) further exemplifies the degree to which women experience different socialization, professional development, and overall work satisfaction. Rakowski demonstrated that lower expectations are held for women and that women are segregated into traditional gender roles. In interviews with female engineers working in the steel industry in Venezuela, women reported feeling that they were perceived first as women and then as engineers, that the negative performance of one woman was generalized to all women (while this was not the case for men), and that women intentionally lowered their productivity to the men's level as a way of reducing the animosity directed toward them by male coworkers. In addition, successful women were described by superiors and coworkers as exceptions. In this particular plant, differential treatment of men and women occurred at several levels, including within social networks, at the organizational policy level, and, surprisingly, in the area of accessibility to work tools (e.g., women were often given ill-fitting uniforms and helmets).

The female stereotype generally does not include holding a position of high status (e.g., doctor, manager), but often does include relatively traditional roles (e.g., nurse, secretary). In conclusion, the expectations for women, treatment of women, and expected level of managerial behavior for women may differ as a function of gender.

ORGANIZATIONAL CULTURE

According to Yukl and Van Fleet (1992, p. 148), "Leadership has been defined in terms of individual traits, leader behavior, interaction patterns, role relationships, follower perceptions,

influence over followers, influence on task goals, and influence on organizational culture." Up to this point in this chapter we have discussed the role of traits, interactions, and perceptions in leadership. This section discusses the impact of organizational culture on leaders and leadership.

Schein (1985; 1992), defined **organizational culture** as

> a pattern of basic assumptions—invented, discovered, or developed by a given group as it learns to cope with its problems of external adaptation and internal integration—that has worked well enough to be considered valid and, therefore, to be taught to new members as the correct way to perceive, think, and feel in relation to those problems. (Schein, 1985, p. 9)

A group develops standardized views in which specific patterns of values, thinking, perceiving, and reacting to situational factors exist. The outcome of such standardization is a reduction in uncertainty and anxiety (Schein, 1985). A leader's effectiveness is based, in part, on the match between his or her leadership style and the organizational culture.

Because culture has both overt and covert levels of operation, it is imperative that leaders be familiar with their work teams' covert assumptions, concerns, goals and the relationship of these factors to overt behavior. Greater understanding may provide the leader with a behavioral guide that he or she can use to maximize effectiveness. Reshaping the workplace (see Practice Perspective 14.3) is one way to change work team assumptions.

Organizational culture is a factor that influences transactions or exchanges that take place between a leader and a subordinate. Organizational culture is also a factor in the situational models because culture, in part, defines the situational contingencies that a leader faces. Finally, organizational culture influences the extent to which different leader traits, attitudes, values,

PRACTICE PERSPECTIVE 14.3

Hewlett Packard Keeps Trying to Reshape the Workplace to Help Family Life

On May 31, 1995 *The Wall Street Journal* reported a story about the Hewlett Packard Corporation defining parts of its cultural philosophy to incorporate the importance of a balance between family and work. To facilitate this balance, Hewlett Packard had introduced flex-time. Flex-time combines sick days and vacation days into one package so that employees have greater control over their time to meet their familial and personal needs.

Additional efforts include expanding child-care services. For example, Hewlett Packard restructured two jobs so that one job incumbent could care for children and the second could attend school. Another example is redesigning shifts for

rank-and-file employees to include three twelve-hour weekend shifts plus one eight-hour day on every other Thursday.

The article stated that Hewlett Packard's efforts to integrate work and family into its organizational culture serves as a tool to sustain productivity gains and not as "a batch of feel-good entitlements."

Source: Adapted from "Hewlett Packard Keeps Trying to Reshape Workplace to Help Family Life," *The Wall Street Journal,* May 31, 1995, p. B1. Reprinted by permission of The Wall Street Journal, © 1995 Dow Jones & Company, Inc. All Rights Reserved Worldwide.

and other characteristics are accepted and integrated into the workplace.

Leadership is part of an open system structure in which the organizational culture is influenced by the larger societal culture. The challenge for a leader is to understand how the larger societal culture is incorporated into the organizational culture. Organizational culture is an important issue today because of the global markets in which organizations must operate. Leaders are faced with increasingly complex organizational cultures and cross-cultural issues that significantly affect organizational operations and profitability.

The progression of research does not negate the importance of previous research. Past research has contributed to the awareness that leadership encompasses more than just an individual and a situation; it is symbiotic in its existence. That is, leadership is influenced by, and influences, the environment within which it takes place. This issue will continue to be the subject of future research efforts and perhaps gender-refined theories of leadership.

SUMMARY

The leadership theories reviewed in this chapter address the importance of understanding the multiple facets involved in leadership research. We have addressed the traits, personalities, and attributes associated with becoming a leader, as well as the situational factors that impact leader effectiveness.

As Yukl and Van Fleet noted, leadership has been defined in many ways. Definitions may involve individual traits, leader behavior, interaction patterns, role relationships, follower perceptions, influence over followers, influence on task goals, or influence on organizational culture. In general, three components that influence leadership are person, process, and outcome.

The chapter presents several different theories of leadership. The trait approach is based on the assumption that there are distinguishing features or attributes that are common among leaders. The situational approach is focused on defining effective leader behaviors and their relationship to organizational outcomes, such as group effectiveness. The basis of these theories is that a single leadership style is not necessarily effective in all situations. Rather, leader effectiveness is contingent on his or her abilities and situational conditions.

We also addressed the transactional and transformational approaches. Transactional theories take into account the negotiation that takes place between a leader and a subordinate as part of goal achievement. The transformational approach investigates the leaders whose relationship with their employees results in employees who display greater pride and identification with the organization, coupled with the exertion of extra energy to achieve the organization's greater goals.

The transformational approach provides an understanding of the cognitive aspect of leadership. That is, leadership is composed of more than a leader, a situation, and the leader's investment in the situation. Related to this concept is the implicit leadership approach, which aims to understand how the match between a subordinate's perception of what a leader is supposed to be and a leader's actual behavior can influence outcomes.

The remainder of the chapter discusses the theory of leadership substitutes. Substitutes, or neutralizers, replace the need for formal leadership and become the greater influence on subordinate satisfaction and performance. The chapter concludes with a discussion of the issues surrounding gender and organizational culture, both of which influence leader behavior and leader effectiveness.

KEY TERMS AND CONCEPTS

attributional model
charismatic leadership
consideration
contingency model
contingent reward
environmental pressures and
    demands
implicit leadership theory
in-group
initiating structure
leader effectiveness

leader–member exchange theory
leader–member relations
least preferred coworker
management by exception
neutralizers
normative model
operant model of leadership
organizational culture
out-group
path-goal theory
personal factor

position power
process factors
product factor
relationship-oriented leader
situational theories
subordinate characteristics
task-oriented leader
task structure
trait approach
transactional theories
transformational leader

RECOMMENDED READINGS

Graen, G. B., and Wakabayashi, M. (1994). Cross-cultural leadership making: Bridging American and Japanese diversity for team advantage. In M. D. Dunnette and L. M. Hough (Eds.), *Handbook of industrial and organizational psychology* (Vol. 4, pp. 415–446). Palo Alto, CA: Consulting Psychologists Press.

Lord, R. G., and Maher, K. J. 1990. Leadership perceptions and leadership performance: Two distinct but interdependent processes. In J. Carroll (Ed.), *Applied social psychology and organizational settings* (pp. 129–154). Hillsdale, NJ: Erlbaum.

Yukl, G., and Van Fleet (1992). Theory and research on leadership in organization. In M. D. Dunnette and L. M. Hough (Eds.), *Handbook of industrial and organizational psychology* (Vol. 3, pp. 147–197). Palo Alto, CA: Consulting Psychologists Press.

INTERNET RESOURCES

Style of Management and Leadership
A description of Manfred Davidmann's work on style in management and leadership. His theory includes a range of management styles and includes definitions of authority and responsibility. The full text of his paper and of some supporting studies is included.
http://www.demon.co.uk/solbaram/articles/clm2.html

Mind Tools
This page presents information on techniques for better thinking, planning and time management skills, and practical psychology.
http://www.mindtools.com

Leadership Development
This site describes the W. K. Kellogg Leadership Projects for innovation in community colleges.
http://www.league.org/leadinit.html

Leadership Strategies, Inc.—Leadership Coaching
This subscription site is designed to be a manager's personal leadership coach. It addresses topics such as creating vision, aligning a team, and personal leadership style.
http://www.leaderx.com/

Covey Leadership Center
This site is devoted to the Covey's seven habits and principle-centered leadership. The Covey Leadership Center provides products, materials, workshops, programs, and seminars that teach about personal, managerial, and organization leadership.
http://www.covey.com/

Centre for Innovative Leadership Home Page
The Centre for Innovative Leadership is dedicated to working in partnership with organizations and institutions that have the inspiration and ability to produce outstanding results. This site provides an information source for those organizations.
http://netlunx.netline.co.za/cil/

Center for Army Leadership
This site has the goal of leading the Army into the twenty-first century. Its intent is to be the U.S. Army's integrating center for current and emerging concepts and programs for developing leaders who embrace the Army's values and are able to train and lead in today's world. A related site is the Army HomePage Subject Area Index at http://www.army.mil/Subject/a.htm This site provides a master index to many Army-related sites, resources, and papers, including many important studies on leadership.
http://www-cgsc.army.mil/cal/index.htm

International Review of Women and Leadership
The home page for the *International Review of Women and Leadership,* a journal published by Edith Cowan University. The *International Review of Women and Leadership* is an applied interdisciplinary journal that considers leadership issues from women's perspective.
http://www.cowan.edu.au/dvc/irwl/welcome.htm

Center for Educational Leadership and Technology
CELT is a nonprofit educational service agency with the mission of integrating technology with educational reforms and research. This site provides valuable technology plan implementation kits to guide educational leaders in developing technology competencies and providing leadership in technological areas.
http://www.celt.org/

The Training Information Source, Inc.
This site provides corporations with up-to-date, non-biased training information that reduces the research time needed to locate professional training sources using the Internet. It accesses a comprehensive database of U.S. training and seminar vendors selected as "best in their class" by Fortune 500 firms with current lists of their course offerings.
http://www.training-info.com/

EXERCISE

Exercise 14.1

Diagnosing Problems in Leadership

You are the regional manager of an international management consulting company. You have a staff of six consultants reporting to you, each of whom enjoys a considerable amount of autonomy with the clients in the field.

Yesterday, you received a complaint from one of your major clients that the consultant you assigned to work on the contract was not doing his job effectively. The client was not very explicit about the nature of the problem, but it was clear that the client was dissatisfied and that something would have to be done if you were to restore the client's faith in your company.

The consultant who was assigned to work on the contract has been with your company for six years. A systems analyst, he is one of the best in his profession. For the first four or five years his performance was superb; he was a model for the junior consultants. However, recently he seems to have a chip on his shoulder; his previous identification with the company and its objectives has been replaced with indifference. His negative attitude has also been noticed by other consultants as well as other clients. This is not the first such complaint you have had from a client this year about his performance. One previous report to you indicated that the consultant had reported to work several times obviously suffering from a hangover.

It is important to get to the root of this problem quickly if you are to keep your client. The consultant obviously has the skills necessary to work with clients effectively—when he is willing to use them.

• Is it an individual or group problem?
• Apply the different leadership theories to help you explain how you (as a regional manager) would deal with this problem.

(*Source:* Adapted from *Organizational behavior: An experiential approach* (p. 354) by D. A. Kolb, I. M. Rubin, and J. M. Osland. Englewood Cliffs, NJ: Prentice-Hall. Copyright 1991 by Prentice-Hall. Reprinted by permission.)

REFERENCES

Abdel-Halim, A. A. (1981). Personality and task moderators of subordinate responses to perceived leader behavior. *Human Relations, 34*(1), 73–88.

Ayman, R. (1993). Leadership perception: The role of gender and culture. In R. Ayman & R. M. Chemers (Eds.), *The leadership theory and research: Perspectives and direction* (pp. 137–166). San Diego, CA: Academic Press.

Ayman, R., & Chemers, M. M. (1991). The effect of leadership match on subordinate satisfaction in Mexican organizations: Some moderating influences of self-monitoring. *Applied Psychology: An International Review, 40*(3), 299–314.

Bailyn, L. (1987). Experiencing technical work: A comparison of male and female engineers. *Human Relations, 40*(5), 299–312.

Bass, B. M. (1981). Individual capability, team response, and productivity. In E. A. Fleishman, & M. D. Dunnette (Eds.), *Human performance and productivity*. New York, NY: Erlbaum.

Bass, B. M. (1985). *Leadership and performance beyond expectations*. New York: Free Press.

Bass, B. M. (1990). *Bass & Stogdill's handbook of leadership: Theory, research, and managerial applications* (3rd ed.). New York: Free Press.

Blum, M. L., & Naylor, J. C. (1968). *Industrial psychology: Its theoretical and social foundations*. New York: Harper & Row.

Bowers, D. G., & Seashore, S. E. (1966). Predicting organizational effectiveness with a four-factor theory of leadership. *Administrative Science Quarterly, 11*, 238–263.

Bycio, P., Hackett, R. D., & Allen, J. S. (1995). Further assessments of Bass's (1985) conceptualization of transactional and transformational leadership. *Journal of Applied Psychology, 80*(4), 468–478.

Campbell, J. P., Dunnette, M. D., Lawler, E. E., III, and Weick, K. E. (1970). *Managerial behavior, performance, and effectiveness*. New York: McGraw-Hill Book Company.

Carley, W. M., & Naj, A. K. (November 23, 1993). End of the Road. *The Wall Street Journal, 75*(29), pp. A1, A8.

Corse, S. J. (1990). Pregnant managers and their subordinates: The effects of gender expectations on hierarchical relationships. *The Journal of Applied Behavioral Science, 26*(1), 35–47.

Crouch, A., & Yetton, P. (1987). Manager behavior, leadership style, and subordinate performance: An empirical extension of the Vroom-Yetton conflict rule. *Organizational Behavior and Human Decision Processes, 39*, 384–396.

Dansereau, F., Graen, G., & Haga, W. J. (1975). A vertical dyad linkage approach to leadership in formal organizations. *Organizational Behavior and Human Performance, 13*, 46–78.

Deluga, R. J. (1991). The relationship of upward-influencing behavior with subordinates-impression management characteristics. *Journal of Applied Social Psychology, 21*(14), 1145–1161.

Dreher, G. F., & Cox, T. H., Jr. (1996). Race, gender, and opportunity: A study of compensation attainment and the establishment of mentoring relationships. *Journal of Applied Psychology, 81*(3), 297–308.

Eagly, A. H., & Steffen, V. J. (1984). Gender stereotypes stem from the distribution of women and men into social roles. *Journal of Personality and Social Psychology, 46*(4), 735–754.

Eden, D., & Leviatan, U. (1975). Implicit leadership theory as a determinant of the factor structure underlying supervisory behavior scales. *Journal of Applied Psychology, 60,* 736–741.

Ehrlich, S. B., Meindl, J. R., & Viellieu, B. (1990). The charismatic appeal of a transformational leader: An empirical case study of a small, high-technology contractor. *Leadership Quarterly, 1*(4), pp. 229–247.

Fiedler, F. E. (1967). *A theory of leadership effectiveness.* New York: McGraw-Hill.

Field, R. H. G. (1982). A test of the Vroom-Yetton Normative Model of Leadership. *Journal of Applied Psychology, 67*(5), 523–532.

Fleishman, E. A. (1953). The description of supervisory behavior. *Journal of Applied Psychology, 37,* 1–6.

Fleishman, E. A., & Harris, E. F. (1962). Patterns of leadership behavior related to employee grievances and turnover. *Personnel Psychology, 15,* 43–56.

Fleishman, E. A., & Peters, D. A. (1962). Interpersonal values, leadership attitudes, and managerial success. *Personnel Psychology, 24,* 127–143.

Fraser, S. L., & Lord, R. G. (1988). Stimulus prototypicality and general leadership impressions: Their role in leadership and behavioral ratings. *Journal of Psychology, 122,* 291–303.

Frederikson, L. W. (1982). *Handbook of organizational behavior management.* New York: Wiley.

French, J. R. P., & Raven, B. (1959). The bases of social power. In D. Cartwright (Ed.), *Studies in social power.* Ann Arbor: University of Michigan, Institute for Social Research.

Fullager, C., McCoy, D., & Shull, C. (1992). The socialization of union loyalty. *Journal of Organizational Behavior, 13,* pp. 13–16.

Graen, G., Liden, R., & Hoel, W. (1982). Role of leadership in the employee withdrawal process. *Journal of Applied Psychology, 67,* 868–872.

Graen, G., Novak, M. A., & Sommerkamp, P. (1982). The effects of leadership-member exchange and job design on productivity and satisfaction: A dual attachment model. *Organizational Behavior and Human Performance, 30,* 109–131.

Green, S. G., & Mitchell, T. R. (1979). Attributional processes of leaders in leader-member interactions. *Organizational Behavior and Human Performance, 23,* 429–458.

Greene, C. N. (1975). The reciprocal nature of influence between leader and subordinate. *Journal of Applied Psychology, 60*(2), 187–193.

Greene, C. N. (1979). Questions of causation in the path-goal theory of leadership. *Academy of Management Review, 22*(1), 22–41.

Griffin, R. W. (1980). Relationships among individual, task design, and leader behavior variables. *Academy of Management Journal, 23*(4), 665–683.

Heerwagen, J. H., Beach, L. R., & Mitchell, T. K. (1985). Dealing with poor performance: Supervisor attributions and the cost of responding. *Journal of Applied Social Psychology, 15*(7), 638–655.

Heilman, M. E., Block, C. J., Martell, R. F., & Simon, M. C. (1989). Has anything changed? Current characterizations of men, women, and managers. *Journal of Applied Psychology, 74*(6), 935–942.

Hemphill, J. K. (1959). Job descriptions for executives. *Harvard Business Review, 37,* 55–67.

Hemphill, J. K. (1960). *Dimensions of Executive Positions* (Ohio Studies in Personnel, Research Monographs No. 98) Columbus, OH: Ohio State University, Bureau of Business Research.

Hoffman, C., & Hurst, N. (1990). Gender stereotypes: Perception or rationalization? *Journal of Personality and Social Psychology, 58*(2), 197–208.

Hollander, E. P., & Offermann, L. R. (1990). Power and leadership in organizations. *American Psychologist, 45*(2), 179–189.

House, R. J. (1971). A path-goal theory of leader effectiveness. *Administrative Science Quarterly, 16,* 321–338.

House, R. J. (1977). A 1976 theory of charismatic leadership. In J. G. Hunt and L. L. Larson (Eds.), *Leadership: The cutting edge.* Carbondale, IL: Southern Illinois University Press.

House, R. J., & Dessler, G. (1974). The path-goal theory of leadership: Some post hoc and a priori tests. In J. G. Hunt & L. L. Larsen (Eds.), *Contingency approaches to leadership.* Carbondale, IL: Southern Illinois University Press.

House, R. J., Filley, A. C., & Kerr, S. (1971). Relation of leader consideration and initiation structure to R and D subordinates' satisfaction. *Administrative Science Quarterly, 16,* 19–30.

House, R. J., & Mitchell, T. R. (1974). Path-goal theory of leadership. *Journal of Contemporary Business, 3*(4), 81–97.

Hughes, R. L., Ginnett, R. C., & Curphy, G. J. (1993). *Leadership: Enhancing the lessons of experience.* Homewood, IL: Irwin.

Hughes, R. L., Ginnett, R. C., & Curphy, G. J. (1996). *Leadership: Enhancing the lessons of experience.* (2nd ed.) Homewood, IL: Irwin.

Jago, A. G., & Vroom, V. H. (1980). An evaluation of two alternatives to the Vroom/Yetton Normative Model. *Academy of Management Journal, 23*(2), 347–355.

Katz, D., Maccoby, N., & Morse, N. C. (1950). *Productivity, supervision and morale in an office situation.* Ann Arbor: University of Michigan, Survey Research Center.

Kerr, S., & Jermier, J. M. (1978). Substitutes for leadership; Their meaning and measurement. *Organizational Behavior and Human Performance, 22,* 375–403.

Kets de Vries, M. F. R. (1994). The leadership mystique. *The Academy of Management Executive, 8*(3), 73–92.

Komaki, J. L. (1986). Toward effective supervision. *Journal of Applied Psychology, 71,* 270–279.

Komaki, J. L., & Desselles, M. L. (1990). *Supervision reexamined: The role of monitors and consequences.* Boston: Allyn & Unwin.

Komaki, J. L., Desselles, M. L., & Bowman, E. D. (1989). Definitely not a breeze: Extending an operant model of effective supervision to teams. *Journal of Applied Psychology, 74,* 522–529.

Komaki, J. L., Zlotnick, S., & Jensen, M. (1986). Development of an operant-based taxonomy and observational index of supervisory behavior. *Journal of Applied Psychology, 71,* 260–269.

Lord, R. G., DeVader, C. L., & Alliger, G. M. (1986). A meta-analysis of the relation between personality traits and leadership perceptions: An application of validity generalization procedures. *Journal of Applied Psychology, 71,* 402–410.

Lord, R. G., Foti, R. J., & De Vader, C. (1984). A test of leadership categorization theory: Internal structure, information processing, and leadership perceptions. *Organizational Behavior and Human Performance, 34,* 343–378.

Lord, R. G., & Maher, K. J. (1993). *Leadership and information processing: Linking perceptions and performance.* New York: Routledge.

Lyness, K. S., & Thompson, D. E. (1997). Above the glass ceiling? A comparison of matched samples of female and male executives. *Journal of Applied Psychology, 82*(3), 359–375.

Mansfield, P. K., Koch, P. B., Henderson, J., Vicary, J. R., Cohn, M., & Young, E. N. (1991). The job climate for women in traditionally male blue-collar occupations. *Sex Roles, 25*(1–2), 63–79.

Markus, H. (1977). Self-schemata and processing information about the self. *Personality and Social Psychology, 35*(2), 63–78.

Meindl, J. R., Ehrlich, S. B., & Dukerich, J. M. (1985). The romance of leadership. *Administrative Science Quarterly, 30,* pp. 78–102.

Mitchell, T. R., Green, S. G., & Wood, R. E. (1981). An attributional model of leadership and the poor performing subordinate: Development and validation. In B. M. Staw and L. L. Cummings (Eds.), *Research in organizational behavior.* Greenwich, CT: JAI Press.

Pence, E. C., Pendleton, W. C., Dobbins, G. H., & Sgro, J. A. (1982). Effects of causal explanations and sex variables on recommendations for corrective action following employee failure. *Organizational Behavior and Human Performance, 29,* 227–240.

Rakowski, C. A. (1987). Women in steel: The case of Ciudad Guayana, Venezuela. *Qualitative Sociology, 10*(1), 3–27.

Rice, R. W. (1978). Construct validity of the least preferred co-worker score. *Psychological Bulletin, 83*(6), 1199–1237.

Rice, R. W., & Kastenbaum, D. R. (1983). The contingency model of leadership: Some current issues. *Basic and Applied Social Psychology, 4,* 373–392.

Scandura, T. A., & Graen, G. B. (1984). Moderating effects of initial leader-member exchange status on the effects of a leadership intervention. Journal of Applied Psychology, 69(3), 428–436.

Scandura, T. A., Graen, G. B., & Novak, M. A. (1986). When managers decide not to decide autocratically: An investigation of leader-member exchange and decision influence. *Journal of Applied Psychology, 71*(4), 579–584.

Schein, E. H. (1985). *Organizational culture and leadership: A dynamic view.* San Francisco: Jossey-Bass.

Schein, E. H. (1992). *Organizational culture and leadership.* San Francisco, CA: Jossey-Bass.

Schein, V. E. (1973). The relationship between sex role stereotypes and requisite management characteristics. *Journal of Applied Psychology, 57*(2), 95–100.

Schein, V. E. (1975). The relationship between sex role stereotypes and requisite management characteristics among female managers. *Journal of Applied Psychology, 60,* 340–344.

Schriesheim, C. A., Bannister, B. D., & Money, W. H. (1979). Psychometric properties of the LPC scale: An extension of Rice's review. *Academy of Management Review, 4*(2), 287–290.

Skrypnek, B. J., & Snyder, M. (1982). On the self-perpetuating nature of stereotypes about women and men. *Journal of Experimental Social Psychology, 18,* 277–291.

Seers A., & Graen, G. B. (1984). The dual attachment concept: A longitudinal investigation of the combination of task characteristics and leader-member exchange. *Organizational Behavior and Human Performance, 33,* 283–306.

Singer, M. S., & Singer, A. E. (1990). Situational constraints on transformational versus transactional leadership behavior, subordinates' leadership preference, and satisfaction. *Journal of Social Psychology, 130*(3), 385–396.

Skinner, B. F. (1974). *About behaviorism.* New York: Knopf.

Stogdill, R. M. (1948). Personal factors associated with leadership: A survey of the literature. *Journal of Psychology, 25,* 35–71.

Vecchio, R. P. (1980). Alternatives to the least preferred coworker construct. *The Journal of Social Psychology, 112,* 261–269.

Vroom, V. H., & Jago, A. G. (1978). On the validity of the Vroom-Yetton Model. *Journal of Applied Psychology, 63*(2), 151–162.

Vroom, V. H., & Yetton, P. W. (1973). *Leadership and decision-making.* Pittsburgh, PA: University of Pittsburgh Press.

Yukl, G. A. (1989). *Leadership in organizations* (2nd ed.). Englewood Cliffs, NJ: Prentice Hall.

Yukl, G., & Van Fleet (1992). Theory and research on leadership in organization. In M. D. Dunnette and L. M. Hough (Eds.) *Handbook of industrial and organizational psychology* (Vol. 3, pp. 147–197). Palo Alto, CA: Consulting Psychologists Press.

Organizational Development, Group Influences, and Teams

H armony Hospitals, a Midwestern hospital holding company, is in the process of repositioning itself in its market. Strongly value driven, Harmony is proud of its record of providing first-class, community-oriented services in its hospitals. A recent merger created a situation in which one geographic area was served by three hospitals. Harmony decided to close one hospital and merge the remaining two into a single unit. Initially, this created friction and internal positioning as managers and staff tried to protect their jobs. An I/O psychologist was brought in to conduct team building with the new management team which consisted of members from the three hospitals.

A two-day retreat was held. The focus was on strategic planning and team building. Early in the session, the team identified a lack of a new vision as a single hospital replacing three separate facilities. Much of the first day was spent developing that vision and achieving consensus. Once that was accomplished, the team moved quickly into action planning, using their experience as managers to the fullest. By the end of the second day, much had been clarified; the team had a new vision, a clear statement of mission, and key objectives for the system and the units. The impact was significant and could be seen even a few days later as managers began to work together developing new, integrated patterns for using the facilities available to them in the three locations.

This chapter focuses on organizational performance and efficiency. In thinking about organizational performance, we must consider our perspective. We can think in terms of the individual, focusing on how a person interfaces with the organization. At the individual level, psychologists and researchers can study the interaction from either direction: how things that affect the individual employee (family pressures, personal stress, education, etc.) impact the organizations to which the person belongs, or how organizational factors (working conditions, policies, pay, benefits, etc.) affect the person. The individual perspective is rooted in the tradition of differential psychology, which we discussed as history in Chapter 1 and in application in Chapter 3. At the next level of analysis, researchers and practitioners study groups (usually small groups); this is the traditional focus of social psychology. We discussed some of this research in Chapter 13 ("Communication in Organizations"). We also covered elements important to OD group work in our chapters dealing with selection (Chapters 5, 7, and 8) and training and development (Chapter 9). The final and most challenging level of analysis considers the organizations themselves and how the application of the behavioral sciences can influence organizational change in the mission, goals, rewards, feedback, and support mechanisms. Change mechanisms can include systems, procedures, structure, jobs, roles, and even culture. Psychologists and researchers typically take one of these three basic perspectives.

Unfortunately, organizational development (OD) is an area in which the practice of organizational change has outstripped the research on organizational change. Most OD research has focused on individual and small-group behavior. Little research has explored the effectiveness of OD interventions. Fortunately, research on individual and small-group behavior is useful, because individual and small-group behavior are the basis for teamwork. Teamwork is rapidly becoming the preferred approach for improving organizational performance.

ORGANIZATIONAL DEVELOPMENT

Organizational development is a relatively new area of focus in industrial/organizational psychology. It studies planned, organizationwide efforts to increase organizational effectiveness and health through interventions using behavioral science knowledge (Beckhard, 1969; Beer & Huse, 1972). Burke (1991, pp. 950–960) summarized the objectives of organizational development as including the following:

1. Better use of human resources
2. Implementation of a new and different strategy that requires modification, at least in part, in the organization's culture
3. Design or redesign of structures and procedures to facilitate communication flow and decisions closer to information sources
4. The development of reward systems that relate more directly and effectively to performance and to the so-called higher-order needs in human motivation
5. Involvement of people in decisions that directly affect them
6. In general, creation of a more humanistically oriented work place

Organizational development makes unique contributions in studying and directing the relationships of organizational dimensions to social or human dimensions. A typical question that an OD practitioner or researcher addresses is: "How will the implementation of this new strategy affect the day-to-day work of the employees, and what will it take behaviorally to make this strategy work?" In addition, OD is an active collaboration between the client and the practitioner. In many ways, it is the full realization of the scientist-practitioner model: Interventions occur only after data collection and study; more than one intervention can be applied at the same time (multiple interventions are the rule rather than the exception in OD); and the behavioral science knowledge that is applied is drawn from many disciplines (e.g., biology, mechanics, industrial sociology, cultural anthropology, social psychology, clinical psychology, counseling psychology, industrial psychology).

Burke (1982) described three criteria to use in determining whether a behavioral science intervention in an organization is organizational development or simply an intervention. To be OD, an intervention must: (a) respond to the actual needs for change as experienced by organizational members, (b) involve the organization's members in the planning and implementation, and (c) lead to change in the organization's culture. Another way of classifying an intervention is to assess whether it applies one of the three methods historically associated with OD: sensitivity training, sociotechnical systems, or survey feedback. Our next section will describe these three foundations of OD practice.

Origins of OD

OD has its origins in three major change methodologies developed by researchers at three different institutions. These were sensitivity or T-group training, developed by the National Training Laboratories (known as NTL); the sociotechnical systems approach developed by the Tavistock Institute of London; and the survey feedback approach developed by the Institute for Social Research (ISR) at the University of Michigan.

Sensitivity Training

An outgrowth of the 1940s group dynamics research by Kurt Lewin, **sensitivity training** focuses on the interpersonal relations that exist in small groups in the organization. Using the behavior and feelings of the group members as the base, a practitioner of sensitivity training facilitates exchanges and feedback among the group members regarding their behavior in the group. This exchange is more candid and behaviorally based than is typical of day-to-day exchanges. It can be emotionally loaded as well.

Sensitivity training requires skilled facilitation and can have significant impact when done correctly. Originally applied to ad hoc teams of individuals working together, primarily to change their interpersonal behavior, sensitivity training methods became popular in the late 1950s and were often used with intact teams. This was the precursor for much of the team building that is done today.

Sociotechnical Systems

A famous coal mining experiment, described in Historical Perspective 15.1, became the basis for the **sociotechnical systems** approach. This ap-

proach describes change activities that consider technological requirements along with the social relationships of the employees working with the technology. At its heart, the sociotechnical systems method views every organization as both a technical system and a social system. The two are so intimately connected that neither can be ignored in organizational change efforts. Common sociotechnical systems today include job redesign, self-directed teams, autonomous work groups, cell assembly manufacturing, demand flow or just-in-time work design, and leading edge industrial engineering.

Survey Feedback

The University of Michigan's Institute for Social Research was the source for the OD methodology of using **survey feedback** to guide organizational change. Rensis Likert, Floyd Mann, and their associates extended existing survey techniques to include procedures in which survey re-

---

HISTORICAL PERSPECTIVE 15.1

Social and Psychological Consequences of the Long Wall Method of Coal Mining

The Tavistock Institute studies of coal mining (Trist & Bamforth, 1951) generated important information about the role of the work group by examining what happens when existing work groups are disassembled. In the mining method that existed at the beginning of the study, coal miners worked together in small groups of two to eight miners on their own small section of the mine. This approach was called *the short wall method* of removing coal. It was dangerous work that required a high level of interdependency and cohesiveness in these groups both on and off the job. As might be expected, this led to significant emotional closeness among the group members.

A technological advance, the invention of a machine called the continuous miner, dramatically

changed the nature of the work. The machine gouges out coal along a twenty-foot-wide face, pushing it to the rear, where it is loaded and transported out of the mine. This *long wall method* required that the existing groups be reformed into larger groups of forty to fifty workers. Considerable work interdependence was still present, but the interpersonal relationships on the job were severely disrupted. This quickly led to lower production and employee reports of feelings of indifference to, and alienation from, their work. Over a short time a new norm of low productivity developed that was attributed in part to the miners' efforts to cope with the emotional and technological difficulties they were experiencing.

sults were summarized and fed back to "family" units in the organizations (groups that worked together or that made up currently existing teams). Mann's (1951) process had the groups analyze the survey results from the perspective of their own group and its responsibilities, then plan for and resolve the problems identified in the surveys. Survey feedback is a common OD practice today.

Because OD is about changing organizations, many studies have focused on how to implement change in organizations and what is the nature of change in organizations. Often referred to as the OD consulting process, this is the topic of our next section.

The OD Consulting Process

Kurt Lewin, an early social psychologist, developed a simple but ubiquitous model conceptualizing the change process for groups and organizations. He saw change as the three step process of **unfreezing, moving,** and **refreezing.** To initiate change, it is necessary first to unfreeze the organization from its present state. This can be accomplished by confronting the organization with data that are stimulating, then challenging the managers and employees to action. Popular tools for accomplishing change are survey feedback about dysfunctional current operations and educational efforts, teaching the organization an exciting new method. Once the organization is unfrozen, it is ready to move. This is the process of making the necessary changes. Once the new procedures are in place, the final step is refreezing, in which appropriate rewards and support mechanisms are introduced to ensure that the new behaviors are maintained.

Several OD process models have become popular. One is Weisbord's six-box model (Weisbord, 1976). Conceptualized as a "radar screen" for observing fundamental relationships, Weisbord's model seeks to keep the practitioner from becoming fixated on one single aspect of an intervention. By asking the six key questions sum-

marized in Figure 15.1 on page 518, the practitioner can evaluate the gaps between the formal structure and aspects of the organization and its informal properties.

Beckhard and Harris (1987) use an even simpler conceptualization: a three stage model. They see organizational change in terms similar to Lewin's: as the actual present state of affairs, a transition state, and the desired state.

OD Research

As was mentioned earlier, OD is an area in which practice has outpaced research. One primary reason is that research on organizations is difficult to conduct. Even when a researcher or practitioner finds a company willing to participate, when the results are good, the sponsoring organization will often consider them proprietary and not want them published. Porras and Berg (1978) found and reviewed thirty-five studies of OD interventions. The results that were reported varied. Two important findings were that the changes had more impact on the outcomes than on the processes used and that they affected individuals more than groups. White and Mitchell (1979) believe that many of the successes of OD research may be attributable to the Hawthorne Effect. However, they did not conduct research to address that question. Eden (1986) drew a similar conclusion. He believes that OD interventions raise expectations for improved performance. This expectation, together with the OD practitioner as a catalyst, facilitates change (perhaps more than the specific method chosen). Terpstra (1981) reviewed fifty-two OD studies, evaluating each for the quality of the research and whether the results were positive, mixed, or negative. His disturbing conclusion was that the most positive results were reported by the studies that had been judged to have the lowest research quality and vice versa. Nicholas (1982) examined three classes of intervention. He found that technostructural approaches had a strong

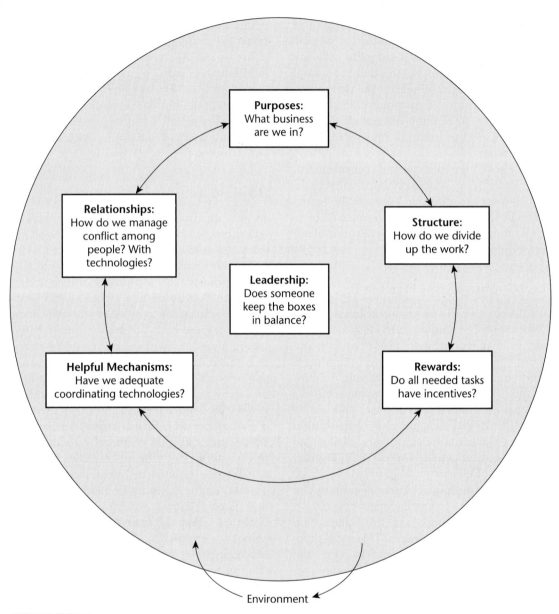

FIGURE 15.1   Weisbord's six-box model of organizations. The metaphor is a radar screen on which to observe relationships among the boxes and avoid fixation on one area or blip.

Source: From *Working with organizations and their people: A guide to human resources practice* (p. 111), Edited by D. W. Bray, 1991, New York: Guilford Press. Copyright 1991 by Guilford Press. Reprinted with permission.

impact on worker behavior but a limited impact on the organization. Human process interventions, which modify the interactions between worker and the work process, were effective for salaried workers, but less effective for others. Multifaceted interventions were most successful when they included all levels of the organization.

A second area of research has addressed the idea of organizational climate and its impact on organization members. **Organizational climate** has been described as the organization's "personality." Litwin and Stringer (1968) were early investigators of climate. They described climate as composed of six factors: structure, individual responsibility, rewards, risks and risk taking, warmth and support, and tolerance. Similar findings were reported in studies of climate by Kahn, Wolfe, Quinn, Snoek and Rosenthal (1964); Taguiri (1966); and Schneider and Bartlett (1968). Campbell, Dunnette, Lawler, and Weick (1970) reviewed this research on organizational climate and found five factors common to all the investigations:

- *Individual Autonomy:* The freedom of the individual to be his or her own boss, reserving considerable decision-making power for himself or herself. The individual does not have to be constantly accountable to higher management.
- *Degree of structure imposed upon the position*: The degree to which the objectives of, and methods for, the job are established and communicated to the individual by superiors.
- *Reward Orientation*: The feelings related to being confident of adequate and appropriate rewards—pay, praise, promotions, special dispensations, and/or general satisfaction—for doing a job well.
- *Consideration, warmth, and support*: The amount of management support that is expressed, including nurturance of subordinates, stimulation, and support.
- *Cooperativeness*: The honesty and openness of the organization toward interpersonal conflict, representing the type and quality of interpersonal relationships among peers.

Later studies, such as those of Sims and LaFollette (1975) and Muchinsky (1976), have found similar factors. In a study of training effects, Friedlander and Greenberg (1971) found

that the level of organizational supportiveness perceived by its members was the sole correlate of performance. They concluded that paying attention to climate was a way to improve training impact.

GROUP INFLUENCES ON INDIVIDUALS

In the next section we will describe and analyze how groups influence individuals in organizations. Group influences are powerful and have been the focus of much study in social psychology and industrial psychology. In Chapters 1 and 13, we described the Hawthorne studies (Roethlisberger & Dickson, 1939), which were designed to evaluate the impact of various working conditions (lighting, rest breaks, etc.) on productivity. The surprising result was that these objective working conditions had less influence than the strong group identity and group norms that developed during the study. In the Tavistock research on coal mining (Trist & Bamforth, 1951) described in this chapter (see Scientific Perspective 15.1 on page 520), the large, longwall groups experienced severe disruption in their existing interpersonal relationships. This disruption led to worker indifference and alienation. Productivity deteriorated, and a norm of low production developed.

Historical Perspective 15.2 on page 521 describes the classic study by Coch and French (1948), which found that when groups had direct participation in determining the changes in work practices, the group norms that developed supported high productivity. In this study, as in the Hawthorne and Tavistock studies, we can see how powerfully individual behavior is influenced by the group. The next research question is "Why?"

Hackman's Model

In two major reviews of group influences on individuals, Hackman (1976, 1992) describes a useful, heuristic model mapping the ways in

SCIENTIFIC PERSPECTIVE 15.1

An Experiment in Autonomous Working in an American Underground Coal Mine

Using the insights from the original Tavistock studies, Trist, Susman, and Brown (1977) applied the sociotechnical model to a U.S. coal mining operation. Working with the United Mine Workers, the U.S. Commission on Productivity and Work Quality, and a small independent deep coal mine, they designed a one-year experiment. Four basic conditions set the stage: All workers in the experimental group would be paid the same amount (this replaced the existing pay by job classification); normal grievance procedures were eliminated, being replaced by a joint worker-management council; workers in the groups were allowed to work in any of the different mining jobs; and the company delegated direction of the experimental crew members to the workers themselves. All participants were volunteers.

Major changes that the research team introduced included: changing the view of the mining process from one of production of coal to one of transporting coal, cross-training workers so that each had several different skills, giving groups day-to-day decision-making authority, providing performance feedback by section and in six-week intervals rather than by shift, and changing foremen to resource people rather than directors of the work. Work teams and researchers met to discuss progress every six weeks. In these meetings, goals were set for the next six-week period. Re-

searchers were on site in the mines twice a week, collecting information and reinforcing workers and foremen. Irregular meetings of the worker–management council handled grievances. All the foremen met regularly with the research team and management to discuss the experiments and their new role as resources to the teams.

The results were dramatic. Safety violations dropped from eighteen in the year before the study to seven the year of the study (control groups exhibited increased numbers of violations), the number of accidents remained about the same, with seven during the study compared to six the year before (control groups had significantly more accidents), absenteeism was equal to or lower than that of the control groups (2.5% in experimental groups versus 4.4% and 2.4% in the control groups), production remained about the same, and the attitudes of the experimental work groups improved.

Surprisingly, at the end of the study, the workers voted not to expand the experiment to the entire mine. The research team thought this decision was a result of some wage inequities, the fact that older workers were unhappy that most participants had been younger workers and apprentices, a fear that the method was an attempt to bust the union, and a belief that the experimental work groups were "elitist."

which groups control many of the stimuli to which individuals are exposed in the course of their organizational lives. The first dimension of the Hackman model categorizes stimuli into two types. **Ambient stimuli** are potentially available to all groups members. These stimuli are pervasive in the group and its environment; group members are normally exposed to them as a matter of course simply by being group mem-

bers. **Discretionary stimuli** are those which are transmitted or available to individuals on a differential or selective basis at the discretion of the other group members.

The second dimension of the Hackman model categorizes the influences of ambient and discretionary stimuli. Both kinds of stimuli can influence the **informational state,** or the individual's current beliefs and his or her accumulated

Overcoming Resistance to Change through Participative Goal Setting

Coch and French (1948) were interested in the impact of group participation in changing work practices. In a field study they structured an experiment in which changes were implemented in three ways: using direct participation by all affected employees in structuring the change and setting goals, using indirect participation (through a delegated representative), and using no participation or representation.

In all of the experimental groups, a Hawthorne Effect was observed. Being a part of the study and

experiencing the organizational changes heightened the employees' group identity. Group norms were created that decreased the variation of individual productivity within each of the groups.

The more important findings were that in the direct participation group, the norms were supportive of high productivity. In the nonparticipation group, the norms enforced low productivity. In the indirect participation group, there was an initial decline followed by a slow, steady increase in productivity.

job knowledge. Stimuli can influence an individual's **affective state,** or the person's attitudes and personal values. Finally, stimuli can influence a person's **behavioral state** (i.e., how the person acts or responds), by rewarding or punishing certain behaviors or by indirectly shaping what the person thinks or believes.

Ambient Stimuli

Informational State.   What is the cue value—the function of the cue in guiding behavior—of ambient stimuli? Hackman identifies two: cuing available outcomes, or the satisfactions that can be obtained from belonging to the group, and cuing behavior outcome expectancies, or knowing how to behave to achieve a selected personal satisfaction. For example, consider the ambient cues that are provided to a class of students and how they predict outcomes. A classroom in which chairs are lined up in rows, bolted to the floor, facing a front lectern or desk, fosters an entirely different set of behaviors than does a classroom in which the chairs are arranged in a large circle, with casters to provide easy movement, in a room with no clear front. In the former, a student may conclude that sitting quietly

and attentively, with face to the front, will result in no unpleasant exchanges with the instructor. In the latter, a student may conclude that interactions with others and high participation in the class are encouraged and that the instructor will be more a guide or facilitator than a lecturer.

Affective State.   What is the impact of ambient stimuli on group member attitudes, values, and emotions? Hackman describes two types of affective impact: arousing member's motive states and providing direct personal satisfactions. Ambient stimuli can alter the motivation of group members to seek certain outcomes. McClelland and his associates (Atkinson, 1954; McClelland, Atkinson, Clark, & Lowell, 1953) demonstrated how situational cues arouse and depress affective needs from their normal levels. In situations in which most of the members of a group share an experience, their motivations can be simultaneously and similarly influenced by the ambient stimuli that are present. For example, at a political convention, a hall decorated with posters and slogans; an audience equipped with signs, confetti, and noisemakers; and "warm-up" mini-celebrations are ambient stimuli that enhance group responses. When the candidate speaks, a "spontaneous" demonstration of support occurs.

Ambient stimuli can also be directly satisfying or frustrating. Many career counselors encourage people to trust their feelings and seek work that they love. This advice is based on the belief that the ambient stimuli that are present around things the person likes to do will enhance the person's affective responses to work related to those things.

Behavioral State. What is the direct impact of ambient stimuli on individual or social behavior? Hackman notes that ambient stimuli can impede behavioral change in groups by affecting social inertia. Ambient stimuli help to maintain stability in organizational groups. This can be a problem when change is needed. The reasons for this are threefold: Ambient stimuli are rarely noticed and discussed, and as a consequence, groups are usually unaware of their impact. Ambient stimuli become narrow and restricted over time; in stable groups, members tend to block certain stimuli from the group's collective attention. Finally, group members tend not to publicly test the inferences that they make privately from ambient stimuli.

Ambient stimuli can provide a mechanism for helping groups to overcome inertia. The group can alter ambient stimuli to help all members learn new behaviors. One example is the use of computer-assisted creative-thinking and decision-making tools to assist groups to become more participative and effective in working together. Ambient stimuli can be provided by a change agent or consultant through task and situational design. The primary elements that can be controlled are the people who make up the group, the situation itself, the environment within which the task is completed, and the task.

Discretionary Stimuli

Discretionary stimuli differ from ambient stimuli only in that they are under the direct control of the group and are administered on a contin-

gent basis. Groups have the following reasons for sending discretionary stimuli to members: to educate and socialize the members; to produce uniformity in procedures; to keep the group intact and functioning; and to produce diversity in role differentiation and division of labor for different classes of task activity. Individual members also seek out discretionary stimuli. People know what they want and seek it in their physical and social environments. The two most important reasons people will search for discretionary stimuli are to obtain information and to obtain group-controlled rewards or recognition.

Informational State. Discretionary stimuli can influence the individual's beliefs about the group and the environment. People want to know "how things are" and turn to others in the group for this information. This can create a **normative influence,** changing what the person says his or her beliefs are (regardless of what is privately believed), or an **informational influence,** changing what the person privately believes. Tajfel (1969) reviewed the research and found that social influence remains even when groups are manipulated to minimize the normative influences. He also found evidence that people are influenced by other group members even when they believe that their own responses are autonomous and when they are unaware that they are being influenced. Discretionary stimuli can increase the group member's job-relevant knowledge and skill. Groups assist their members in doing this through direct instruction, by providing feedback to members about their behavior, and by providing models of correct or appropriate behaviors.

Member Affective States. Groups have stronger influences on members' beliefs than on their attitudes. Studies of group effects on beliefs have demonstrated that subjects assume (often correctly) that their peers have more and better information about the world than they do. But attitudes and feelings are personal. If a group or other person advocates a certain belief, a given individual is less likely to accept that belief uncritically.

Discretionary stimuli can also affect the level of physiological arousal the group member experiences. Zajonc (1965) reviewed the research on social facilitation and proposed that the simple presence of other people increases the level of arousal and elevates performance. Further research has demonstrated that this occurs even when a person is doing his or her work privately but in the vicinity of others. There are also situations in which the group's effect is to provide comfort and support, reducing arousal and the person's level of anxiety.

Member Behavioral State. The last category of the Hackman model is concerned with how a person's behavior is directly affected by the discretionary stimuli controlled by fellow group members. This influence is accomplished by using behavioral norms. Norms are distinguished from other descriptors and features of groups in the following four ways (Hackman, 1992, pp. 235–236):

- Norms are structural characteristics of groups that summarize and simplify group influence processes.

- Norms apply only to behavior—not to private thoughts and feelings.

- Norms usually regulate only those behaviors that are viewed as important by group members.

- Norms usually develop gradually, but group members can choose to shortcut the norm development process.

Considerable research has been done in an effort to understand how norms operate. Understanding and applying this research to OD practice are challenging tasks. One model that organizes much of this research in a meaningful, useful way is the Jackson Return Potential Model.

The Jackson Return Potential Model

A powerful model that conceptualizes the structure and influences of group norms has been developed by Jackson (1960, 1965, 1966). The **Jackson Return Potential Model** (RPM) describes any situation in which a group norm is used to regulate individual member behavior. The ordinate plots the amount of approval or disapproval felt by the individual. High felt approval is plotted upward from the ordinate. Low felt approval is plotted downward from the ordinate. The abscissa plots the level of behavior exhibited. (See the example in Figure 15.2.)

If Figure 15.2 represents the operation of a norm about how much members talk during

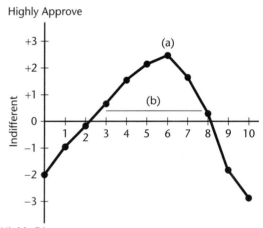

Note: The ordinate is an axis of evaluation; the abscissa is an axis of behavior.

FIGURE 15.2   The Jackson Return Potential Model (RPM), representing the relationship between the normative approval or disapproval expressed by a group for specified levels of behavior.

Source: From "Structural Characteristics of Norms," by J. Jackson, 1965. In I. D. Steiner and M. Fishbein (Eds.), *Current studies in social psychology* (p. 303). New York: Holt Rinehart and Winston. Copyright 1965 by J. Jackson. Reprinted by permission.

group meetings, we could discern that both talking too much and talking too little are disapproved by the group. Not talking at all (behavior rating = 0) is disapproved, with a rating of –2. Talking a little (behavior rating = 1) is disapproved with a rating of –1. In contrast, talking a lot (behavior rating = 10) is disapproved with a rating of –3. Further, the disapproval is stronger for talking too much (–3 maximum) than it is for not talking enough (–2 maximum).

Two additional dimensions influence the direct impact of norms: intensity and crystallization. **Intensity** is the overall strength of approval or disapproval associated with a norm-regulated behavior. **Crystallization** is the degree of consensus among group members about the amount of approval or disapproval associated with each point on the behavioral dimension. Research indicates that norms that are well crystallized and highly intense create greater compliance than do those that are not. A group with such norms is said to have **normative power** (Jackson, 1975). When the norm is highly crystallized but low in intensity, there is less compliance because the group members care less about the norm. This is called **vacuous consensus** (Jackson, 1975). Finally, a norm can be high in intensity but poorly crystallized. This is a state of **conflict potential** (Jackson, 1975) because people are concerned about the behavior but do not agree on what it should be.

....
TEAMS AND TEAM BUILDING

Scientific paradigms are the accepted current examples of actual scientific practice. When the laws, theories, applications, instrumentation, and models change significantly in a short period, we describe this as a *paradigm shift*. Such a paradigm shift is transforming organizations. Organizations are shifting from nineteenth century bureaucratic processes to new systems that can thrive in the rapidly changing world of the twenty-first century. Bureaucratic processes have

been in operation for a long time. Born shortly after the dawn of the industrial revolution, bureaucracy was successful because it created an organizational structure that was supportive of the new methods of manufacturing and new approaches for using labor that were hallmarks of the revolution. Bureaucracy achieves coordination by narrowly defining people's roles, usually to highly specific jobs, or even to portions of jobs. By using a bureaucratic approach, an organization gains considerable efficiency, since there is little argument about how something will be done. It will be done "the organizational way" following "standard procedures." Reporting relationships are clear because they are defined by "the chain of command." Employees know what to expect because the organization provides uniform rules—"the employee handbook" or "the union contract"—and because their career is one of "moving up the ladder." These elements were summarized by Max Weber (1946, 1947) in his classic description of a bureaucracy (Weber, 1947, p. 196)

> The fully developed bureaucratic mechanism compares with other organizations exactly as does the machine with non-mechanical modes of production. Precision, speed, unambiguity, knowledge of the files, continuity, discretion, unity, strict subordination, reduction of friction and of material and personal costs—these are raised to the optimum in the strictly bureaucratic administration.

Many elements of the bureaucratic system have been studied (see March & Simon, 1958). Some important criticisms have emerged from these studies: that bureaucracies are notoriously slow to change and that they do not deal well with exceptions and other deviations from the organizational norm. In spite of these problems, the bureaucratic system has persisted as the primary form of organizational structure for companies. But during the last decade, the pressures on organizations have become intense. Rapid information and cultural changes have been creating a new global workplace.

Organizational Change and Team Building

Hypercompetition, a competitive environment in which the competitive advantages of one firm are quickly adapted and implemented by its competitors, has replaced the "business as usual" world of only a few years ago.

Some of the changes that are affecting the nature of work include the following:

- The shift from unskilled labor to knowledge-based work
- The shift from jobs defined by routine, often repetitive tasks to jobs requiring initiative, flexibility, creativity, and caring
- The shift from work that requires individuals to be cogs in the wheel of production to work that relies on the power of teams to create total quality by examining the processes they use and changing them to work better
- The shift from work defined by a single skill or the function performed to work organized by projects, which often requires cross-functional teams and multiple skills
- The shift from bosses being the source of knowledge and direction to customers' wishes driving the organization and its priorities
- The shift from tight, hierarchical control from above to teamwork across the organization, both in developing the vision and mission and in coordinating the functions and business

This revolution is affecting all organizations. Whether large or small, the work in today's increasingly high-tech workplace requires very different responses from those dictated by the previous bureaucratic structure.

Today, change is everywhere in organizations. The new demands of a global marketplace have created revolutions in the way organizations operate. These include the quality movement (Deming, 1986; Juran, 1988; Scholtes, 1988),

reengineering (Hammer & Champy, 1993), high-performance teams (Buchholz & Roth, 1987), intelligent organizations (Pinchot & Pinchot, 1993), and organizational learning initiatives (Chawla & Renesch, 1995). We will not discuss these in detail, but at their core is a basic shift in the day-to-day control and feedback mechanisms from the previous hierarchical chain of command approach to an empowered, participative approach requiring collaboration within and among teams. Project teams, process improvement teams, "intrepreneurial" product development teams (skunk works), quality teams, cell assembly teams, and others are succeeding where bureaucracy has failed (for more information on these approaches, see Scholtes et al., 1988). In fact, teams are proving to be such a powerful force for empowerment, integration, and productivity that they form the basic building block of any "intelligent organization" (Pinchot & Pinchot, 1993). As we will see, given the right context, teams can generate the passion, engagement, and developmental speed that are needed to survive in the age of hypercompetition. An added benefit is that a team is something to belong to, a support group and political representative that gives its members more standing and power than they would attain as individuals. In the remainder of this chapter we will examine how teams work and why team learning has been called "the bridge to organizational learning" (Senge, 1990).

Teamwork skills play an integral role in organizational efficacy. This section focuses on the evolution of teams and the ways in which effective team building can lead to enhanced individual, group, and organizational performance. We will briefly review small-group and team research, discuss team skill training, and conclude with an overview of how to solve problems and resolve conflict within work groups.

In spite of its popularity, team building can be challenging. Most successful team building efforts are continuous processes that require considerable follow-up and ongoing evaluation.

Furthermore, much of the existing psychological research on team building is derived from small-group research or work conducted in experimental settings. This may be because team building can be messy from an experimental point of view. Numerous variables are involved in the process of creating work teams and combining the talents of a number of unique individuals. Specifically, research has been hampered by a lack of understanding or consensus among researchers with respect to how to analyze, define, measure, design, and evaluate team training and its many elements (Denson, 1981; Driskell & Salas, 1992; Dyer, 1984; Hall & Rizzo, 1975; Nieva, Fleishman, & Reick, 1978; Salas, Prince, Cannon-Bowers, Baker, Smith, & Hall, 1991).

In spite of these problems, team building has emerged as an effective means of increasing job satisfaction and is currently a popular area of concentration among I/O psychologists (Neuman, Edwards, & Raju, 1989). Considerable progress in understanding teams and how they form and function has been made as the result of a major investigative effort by the U.S. Navy's Training Systems Center. The recent book, *Teams, Their Training and Performance*, edited by Robert Swezey and Eduardo Salas (1992), describes much of this work.

According to the U.S. Naval Training Systems Center's research group on team training and performance (Salas, Dickinson, Converse, & Tannenbaum, 1992, p. 4):

> a team is a distinguishable set of two or more people who interact dynamically, interdependently, and adaptively. A team works toward a common goal/objective/mission. Team members are assigned specific roles or functions to be carried out over a limited period of time.

This definition is particularly strong because it contains elements that have been suggested by a number of investigators (e.g., Dyer, 1984; Hall & Rizzo, 1975; Modrick, 1986; Morgan, Glickman, Woodard, Blaiwes, & Salas, 1986; Nieva et al., 1978) and has a task completion focus

that is directly applicable to the work environment. Further, it stresses "a dynamic exchange of information and resources among team members, a coordination of task activities, constant adjustments to task elements, and organizational structuring of team members" (Salas et al., 1992, p. 4). This combination of task dependency and member interdependency provides the foundation for team formation and operation. It also is the basis for current theories describing teams and the way they operate.

Types of Teams

Teams exist across a continuum in a variety of forms. At one extreme are highly structured, independent teams; at the opposite extreme are teams characterized by little to no interaction among members, such as teams whose members perform distinctive, separate tasks within a group context. Teams can be further divided (within the broad continuum) into three specific types: functional, cross-functional, and multifunctional.

A **functional team** is composed of members who have the same skills and perform the same job functions. An example of a functional team is a computer assisted design (CAD) team, in which team members are grouped together to assist one another as needed and all perform the same tasks. A **cross-functional team** consists of individuals who have a variety of distinct skill requirements and functions and who all contribute to the same goal. Cross-functional teams have the advantage of connecting employees who understand an overall task and are able to break it into manageable parts and combine their skills to ensure its completion. A **multifunctional team** is made up of employees who are cross-trained in different functions, allowing for maximum flexibility in terms of members having the ability to perform each other's jobs as needed. Multifunctional teams create an environment that encourages shared problem solving and the development of a variety of personal skills.

Team Theory

The recent emphasis in business on using teams in many production situations has encouraged consultants and researchers to develop models attempting to explain the dynamics. These models are based on small-group research and basic categorization by the type of team being formed. Five major models have emerged: a team development model based on how teams evolve; a normative model focused on organizational context; a time and transition model focused on the dynamic nature of teams; a task effectiveness model based on how effectively a team accomplishes certain tasks; and a combination model, the team evolution and maturation model. We will discuss these in the following sections.

Small-Group Research

The topic of small groups has been of interest to behavioral scientists since the inception of psychology as a field of study. The focus of this interest has usually been theoretical. In a recent review of team-related research, Driskell and Salas (1992) concluded that most of the previous work was conducted to test theory rather than to investigate the application of theory to real-world settings. The authors indicated that although this focus is acceptable, it has resulted in several limitations. For instance, most research has been carried out in artificial laboratory environments and, therefore, cannot easily translate to the work environment. Also, most small-group research to date has been designed to test general theories rather than to investigate specific functions such as decision making or problem solving. Finally, past research often belabored the obvious, searching for small increments in knowledge about team behavior that had more theoretical than practical significance.

Team Development Model

There is a variety of theories regarding team building. Tuckman (1965; Tuckman & Jensen, 1977) devised a model, still popular today, that outlines team formation and operation. He de-

scribed the team maturation process in terms of its members gradually learning to cope with emotional and group pressures within the team construct. His model has four processes, or stages: forming, storming, norming, and performing.

Stage 1: Forming. The **forming stage** is also known as the initiation stage. Through this process, team members cautiously explore the boundaries of acceptable group behavior. Like hesitant swimmers, they stand by the edge of the pool and dip their toes in the water, testing its warmth but not yet ready to take the plunge. This stage signifies a transition from individual performer to member status, with members testing the team leader's ability to formally and informally guide the group.

Stage 2: Storming. The **storming stage** is the most difficult stage in the team-building process. Also known as the operation stage, it is as if team members abandon their hesitant poolside stance and take the plunge. Once committed, they feel as though they are going to drown, gulping for air and thrashing about. They realize that their task is more difficult than they had imagined and may become impatient, blameful, or overzealous. Because in this stage the group builds norms and attempts to define acceptable behaviors, members may argue over what actions the team should take. In an attempt to shape the team to meet their needs, they may rely on their own experience and expertise, often resisting collaborative efforts from other team members.

Stage 3: Norming. In the **norming stage**, team members start to reconcile competing loyalties and responsibilities, defining ground rules or norms. Also known as the maturation stage, this is where members begin to accept their roles within the team as well as the individuality of team members. Norming reduces the emotional conflict inherent in the storming stage, and previously competitive relationships become more cooperative. In other words, team members begin to realize that they are not going to drown and start helping each other to stay afloat.

Stage 4: Performing. In the **performing stage,** also known as the celebration stage, the team settles into its relationships and expectations. What was previously unknown is now accepted and familiar, and team members start to diagnose, problem solve, and implement change when needed. They accept each other's strengths and weaknesses and are now able to swim together.

Normative Model

Another useful model is Hackman's (1983) **normative model,** which emphasizes organizational context. Hackman believes that the organizational environment has an impact on team performance and so must be a primary consideration in any team-building effort. He suggests that individual effort, knowledge, skill, and performance strategies should be investigated to allow for a better understanding of how to motivate team members. In his normative model, which is summarized in Figure 15.3, Hackman diagrams the conditions necessary for effective team functioning and the process for creating those conditions.

Hackman believes that the manipulation of these key elements allowed for effective team structuring and management. As seen in Figure 15.3 Hackman's normative model provides methods for considering organizational context, group design, group synergy, group process, and material resources as factors determining group effectiveness.

The far left of the model includes organization context and group design. Hackman regards these two factors as the primary input variables that determine team functioning and affect the criteria team members use to evaluate team interaction. This process, in turn, influences the team quality and quantity of performance. Hackman theorizes that team process effectiveness is facilitated by group synergy, the

ability of the team members to work together over time. The far right side of the figure contains external factors such as the material resources allocated to the team. Hackman proposes that together, all these factors influence the ultimate level of team effectiveness as judged by its output, the ability of its members to combine efforts, and the satisfaction of its members.

Time and Transition Model

Gersick (1985, 1988) developed a **time and transition model** for work teams. By studying eight separate teams, she found only one common, observable behavioral pattern: Every team established a method of performing its given task during its first meeting. This initial method was maintained until midway through the task, when, without exception, the teams decided to implement a different task completion strategy. Gersick's emphasis on the dynamic nature of teams and her discovery that teams adapt their strategies at certain, predictable periods in their life cycle were important contributions to understanding team performance.

Task Effectiveness Model

Gladstein's (1984) **task effectiveness model** grew out of his work with large samples of employees in the work environment. He found that organizational context, open communication, degree of supportiveness, active leadership, experience, and training were all positively related to team members' ratings of group satisfaction and job performance. In his conclusions he emphasized the importance of process on team performance. The task the team performs governs the link between process and performance. This suggests that both the organizational situation and the broader organizational environment affect team success.

Team Evolution and Maturation Model

The **team evolution and maturation (TEAM) model** combined the findings of Gersick and

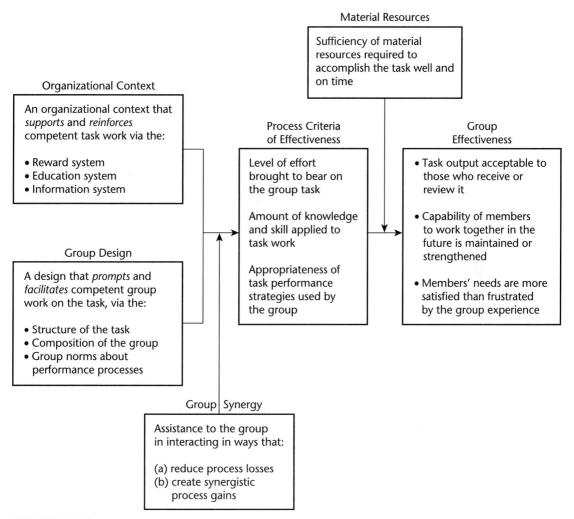

FIGURE 15.3   Hackman's normative model of group processes in organizational environments.

Source: From *Teams: Their training and performance* (p. 6), Edited by R. W. Swezey and E. Salas, 1992, Norwood, NJ: Ablex Publishing Corp. Copyright 1992 by Ablex Publishing Corporation. Reprinted with permission.

Original source: A normative model of work team effectiveness (Tech. Rep. No.2). By J. R. Hackman, 1983, New Haven, CT: Yale University.

Tuckman to create a model that predicts the stages teams go through before, during, and after completion of a task (Morgan et al., 1986).

This model describes a series of developmental phases through which teams evolve. Each phase represents a synthesis of elements previ-

ously identified by a variety of investigators (Bales & Strodtbeck, 1951; Bell, 1982; Bennis & Shepard, 1956; Caple, 1978; Gersick, 1985; Tuckman, 1965). The underlying framework for these hypothesized phases was derived from Tuckman's (1965; Tuckman & Jensen, 1977) classic description of the processes of forming, storming, norming, and performing, as well as from the findings of Gersick (1985). As was mentioned earlier, Gersick found that problem-solving groups experienced a transition, or "reforming" stage, about halfway through their life cycles. She also discovered that after this period of transition, teams concentrated their efforts on aspects of performance crucial to meeting final task requirements. Near the completion of a task, teams increased their efforts to produce outcomes that conformed to environmental demands (Gersick, 1985).

According to the TEAM model and consistent with Hackman's (1983) normative model, a work team is constantly influenced by the demands and constraints of the organizational context in which it operates. A team experiences specific interactions during the stages of forming, reforming, and conforming. The team receives its initial instructions during the forming stage. During the **reforming stage** the team reevaluates its responses to external demands. In the **conforming stage,** the team strives to ensure that its product matches the organizational goals and expectations. An illustration of this process is provided in Figure 15.4.

The TEAM model suggests the existence of two distinguishable activity tracks that occur across the phases of team development. The first track (represented by the upper row of linked circles in Figure 15.4) involves the **training-related activities** that are tied to a specific task performance. As Tuckman (1965) suggested, parts of the team's efforts are devoted to understanding task requirements, discovering the rules by which tasks are to be performed, establishing patterns of interaction with equipment, exchanging task-related information, and developing team problem-solving techniques. These activities comprise what Davis, Gaddy, and Turney (1985) refer to as **operational skills training** and encompass such areas as members' interaction with tools and machines, the technical aspects of the job, and other task-related activities.

The lower row of circles in Figure 15.4 represents the second track of team activity: relationships among group members. This track includes training for quality member interaction, interpersonal work relationships, affect, cooperation, and team coordination. It also addresses an initial testing of relationships (particularly the relationship between members and the team leader), intragroup conflict (if necessary), the establishment of individual roles, the acceptance of others within the group, the development of a cohesive work group, and the maintenance of the team structure.

TEAM PROCESSES

Problem solving in teams is a cognitive process. Unfortunately, teams often get caught up in the content of the problems and forget about using a systematic process to solve them. OD consultants help teams to get "unstuck" in problem solving by teaching them clearly defined processes that keep the content of the problem separate from the team process used to address it. In quality enhancement programs, a significant focus is on such team processes. Readers who are interested in step-by-step instructions for many team processes can find them in quality improvement manuals. We recommend *The Team Handbook* by Peter Scholtes (1988). Through the years, many such process interventions have been developed. We will briefly describe four of the most popular.

Nominal Group Technique

Nominal group technique is a group process in which team members individually assign point values to alternative solutions, rating the solutions in terms of importance. As a process, the nominal group technique is more structured than completing a series of votes or brainstorming. The term *nominal* comes from the fact that the group does not do as much interacting as might otherwise be the case.

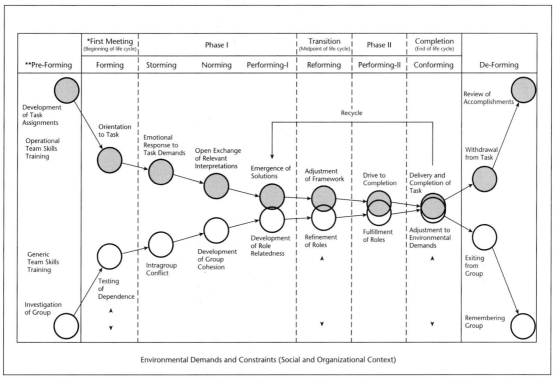

FIGURE 15.4   A generalized model of team evolution and maturation.

Source: From *Teams: Their training and performance* (p. 11), Edited by R. W. Swezey and E. Salas, 1992, Norwood, NJ: Ablex Publishing Corporation. Copyright 1992 by Ablex Publishing Corporation. Reprinted with permission.

The nominal group technique defines the following process steps: a formal brainstorming session to generate and clarify ideas and/or options, a vote on the importance of each item by each member of the group, and selection and ranking of alternatives based on the vote totals. After the process identifies the top choice, the team must then decide how to proceed.

To try out the nominal group technique, complete Exercise 15.1.

Root Causes

Teams often jump to conclusions without fully understanding the root causes of the problems they are addressing. This commonly leads to wasted time and unnecessary costs. The purpose of identifying root causes is to make certain everyone agrees with the definition of the problem to be solved before the team starts working on solutions.

The process of identification of root causes takes a team through the following steps:

1. Identify the potential causes of the problem.

2. Verify the cause with existing or freshly collected data.

3. Gather additional information if it is needed.

4. Check the conclusions about the cause by getting additional confirmation.
5. Take action to address the cause.

Affinity Diagrams

Brainstorming is a popular technique for generating many ideas in a short period of time. Affinity diagrams provide a quick way for organizing these thoughts comprehensively. Team members write their ideas on cards or sticky notes, with one idea per card or note. The entire team then assembles in front of a blank wall or bulletin board. Individual team members begin the process by posting their ideas on the board. Other team members add their ideas next to related items that have already been posted. Any team member can relocate any posted item or group of items if the person believes that the fit is better in some other place. This process continues until all items have been posted and the group is satisfied with the final organization.

The affinity diagram is documented by writing a sentence or paragraph that summarizes the thoughts. The affinity diagram process is used when a team needs to make a position statement or develop a common position. One frequent area of use is in the development of team mission statements.

....

TEAM TRAINING

The TEAM model suggests that as teams achieve optimum performance, task and group performance become separately enhanced and progressively focused. They ultimately converge, improving team viability and performance. Team training, then, should seek to improve the formal programming of task performance while enhancing the team's ability to communicate, relate, and interact (Salas, Dickinson, Converse, & Tannenbaum, 1992). Swezey and Salas (1992) stress the importance of this process in any teamwork or team skill training. That is,

team training techniques should be selected to obtain a specific outcome. Swezey and Salas organized their investigation around typical desired outcomes. In our discussion of their model we will apply their organization.

Team Mission and Goals

The **team mission statement** provides critical guidance for team members. The success of any team is determined by the description of the team's overall mission (Lewis, Hritz, & Roth, 1983), which sets the framework for creating specific team and individual goals. Goal specificity enhances team performance, feedback, and coordination; commitment to goals makes them more attainable (Helmreich, 1982; Ilgen, Shapiro, Salas, & Weiss, 1989). Therefore, in team training, it is important to clearly state, reiterate, and reinforce the team's mission, the team's goals, and individual goals to make sure the group is task-oriented and equipped to achieve success.

Environment and Operating Situation

In conducting team training, it is important to construct an environment that accurately simulates the setting, conditions, and constraints within which the team will perform (Dyer, 1984; Gaddy, 1987; McIntyre, Morgan, Salas, & Glickman, 1988). Team members must be made aware of, and exposed to, the external factors that could influence their performance on the job (Lewis et al., 1983). Because newly formed teams adapt more easily to simple conditions than to complex conditions (Dyer, 1984), it is helpful to simplify the initial situations within which teams will work.

Organization, Size, and Interaction

Team performance improves when training prepares individual members to recognize and smoothly execute the transitions between team members and team activities (Lewis et al., 1983). Team members need to understand how the team's interaction (both within the group and with external factors) can affect its overall performance. Members need to master the aspects of the team task that require adaptive, interdependent actions. These skills are supported by building trust within the group, which can be accomplished by providing opportunities for no-risk, cooperative interaction (Keller, 1986). For example, at a team meeting, all members could be encouraged to offer ideas with respect to task completion. The team leader could then praise members by highlighting the strong points of each suggestion. Such praise from the leader would let members know that their ideas had merit and that they were an important part of the team effort. Providing this type of safe, nonjudgmental setting could encourage participation from even the most recalcitrant members.

Optimum team size depends on the team task, specific individual abilities, and the difference between the team task and individual tasks (McIntyre et al., 1988). For instance, most problem-solving teams require only five or six members; production-oriented teams may need only two members (Bass, 1982). It is important to select an appropriate number of team members (usually two to six), clarify expectations for member interaction, instruct members on how their efforts will affect the team task, train members to appreciate other people's interaction styles, and teach them adaptive interaction skills.

Motivation, Attitude, and Cohesion

By delegating team tasks while holding individual members responsible for designing and directing major task-related activities, it is possible to increase motivation during team training (Ilgen et al., 1989). Doing so creates both a better understanding and a greater ownership by team members of the team's successes and failures. Inherent in this process is the use of positive reinforcers to reward successful performance and behaviors that are supportive of other team members (Morgan et al., 1986; Oser, McCallum, Salas, & Morgan, 1989). It is also important to mix homogeneous and heterogeneous groupings of team members to create teams that are representative of the larger employee population (Bass, 1982). An application of these principles to compensation for teams is described in Scientific Perspective 15.2 on page 534.

The following stages of team development for operational and generic teams (Glickman, Zimmer, Montero, Guerette, Campbell, Morgan, & Salas, 1987) show how to provide the practice, feedback, and coaching that are needed to increase motivation and cohesion among a team's members while taking into consideration the specificity of the assignment. Operational team skills are job specific. They can be linked directly to job and task analysis and to performance evaluation criteria. Examples of operational skills include information exchange, task assignment, strategy development, problem solving, and decision making. Generic team skills are the skills that have wide applicability. Examples of generic skills are; communications, feedback, influence, conflict resolution, and leadership.

For **operational skill development** in teams, the progression is as follows:

- Develop task assignments
- Orientate members to the task
- Check the emotional response to task demands
- Encourage an open exchange of relevant interpretations
- Encourage the emergence of solutions
- Adjust the framework if necessary
- Drive to completion
- Deliver and complete the task
- Withdraw from the task
- Evaluate performance

SCIENTIFIC PERSPECTIVE 15.2

Team Approaches to Rewards

I. Maintain individual performance management approach, but add features that enable teamwork and contribution to team to be a more important element of the appraisal and merit reward to individuals.

    A. Have teamwork as an explicit evaluation criterion on the performance appraisal form.

    B. Give the teamwork rating a weighting in the final rating so that managers can't choose to ignore it in their overall assessment.

    C. Collect input from teammates to help the manager make a more informed assessment of the impact of the individual on the team.

    D. Collect input from customers, suppliers and people who are supported by the individual.

    E. Create special awards for individuals who are judged by their peers to have contributed to team accomplishment.

    F. Eliminate forced distributions which cause people who must cooperate to compete with one another.

II. Tie together the fates of people who must work together to get the job done, but keep the individual as the focus of performance management.

    A. Joint accountabilities.

    B. Individual rating weighted by the performance of the team of which he/she is a member.

    C. Have regular performance feedback to team; provide regular time for team to decide how to improve its performance.

    D. Merit increase dependent on individual performance; performance bonus (not tied to base) dependent on accomplishment of team or unit performance.

III. Link the fates of people who must work together explicitly. Make the team a more explicit focus of performance management.

    A. Use salary as key lever:
Make merit pool dependent on team performance. Everyone gets similar raises, except for individuals who are clearly failing to contribute or those who have clearly contributed beyond the contributions of others in the team. In making these decisions, it is important that there be team input, and that people agree to the appropriateness of the action.

    B. The team becomes a central focus of the performance management process. Setting goals, determining who has what role, determining who needs what training and development, providing feedback to individuals, and deciding who, if anyone, is entitled to special awards (merit or bonus) is all done jointly by supervisor and team. Supervisor provides feedback and helps team develop. Overall increases in salary tied to team performance.

    (In the extreme, this is a self-managing team, where supervisor assumes a coaching and facilitating role; helps the team formulate goals; provides the team with the big picture; provides feedback to the team about team accomplishment; determines team salary action, but is not part of day-to-day task accomplishments decisions.)

Source: From *Team Approaches to Rewards* (p. 1–2), by S. A. Mohrman and A. M. Mohrman, Jr., 1993, Los Angeles: CA, Center for Effective Organizations. Copyright 1993 by Center for Effective Organizations. Reprinted with permission.

For **generic skill development** in teams, the progression is as follows:

- Investigate the nature of the work group
- Test the dependence of group members
- Address any intragroup conflict
- Develop group cohesion
- Develop role relatedness
- Refine roles

- Fulfill roles
- Adjust to environmental demands
- Exit from the group
- Remember the group

Individual members must receive specific, significant assignments that contribute to the team's overall performance. By positively rewarding task performance and supportive behaviors, a group leader stresses the connection of team assignments to team performance. It is this connection that positively affects the motivation and cohesion of the entire team.

Leadership

Successful team training includes clear discussions about what the team expects from its leader and what the leader expects from team members. This can be implemented by defining the criteria for leadership to determine whether the leader is performing effectively or ineffectively (Lewis et al., 1983). In other words, training should seek to improve the skills of the entire team, including the leader.

Leaders should be trained to verbalize plans (Helmreich, 1982), remain focused, and solicit ideas and discussion from team members (Franz, Prince, & Salas, 1990). Leaders need to specify the behaviors for team success, such as assertiveness (Foushee, 1984); initiating structure, (particularly with larger teams (Mullen, Symons, Hu, & Salas, 1989); and encouraging consideration of multiple viewpoints (McIntyre et al., 1988). It is also important that leaders provide feedback to the team. This can be straightforward, as in the example in Practice Perspective 15.1, or more subtle.

Communication

Team communication is essential to successful team performance. Any training effort is incomplete unless it addresses the development of communication skills (Davis et al., 1985). Major elements for team communication training include:

- The preferred communication format (Gaddy, 1987)
- The direction of communication (e.g., top-down, lateral) (Cream, 1978; Morgan et al., 1986)
- The frequency of communication (e.g., continuous or as needed, daily, weekly, monthly) (Foushee, 1984)

PRACTICE PERSPECTIVE 15.1

Cheering on the Team

If Harvard awarded MBAs to factory workers for their expertise, this team at General Mills cereal plant in Lodi, California, would graduate with honors. They do just about everything middle managers do, and do it well: Since General Mills introduced teams to the plant, productivity has risen up to 40%. Carmen Gomez, Ruby Liptack, and Bill Gesterner operate machinery to make cereal (Oatmeal Crisp). Denney Perak is a manager, but he doesn't supervise in the traditional sense.

He coaches the team on management techniques and serves as their link with headquarters. Donald Owen and William Walker help maintain the machinery, which Irma Hills operates. Team members like the added responsibility, but also feel more pressure. Says Owen: "I work a lot harder than I used to. You have to worry about the numbers."

Source: From "Cheering on The Team," *Fortune,* May 7, 1990, p. 52. Copyright 1990 by Time, Inc. Reprinted with permission.

- Key conditions requiring communication (McIntyre et al., 1988)
- How to handle communication involving criticism (Dyer, 1984; Gaddy, 1987; Hall & Rizzo, 1975; Morgan et al., 1986)

All communication, especially that of a critical nature, is best presented in a constructive, positive manner.

Adaptability

Teams need to be able to relate relevant information to the task at hand. They must be able to locate and correct errors, changing their methods of operation when necessary (Morgan et al., 1986). To achieve this end, team training is designed to progress from known tasks to unpredictable tasks, giving members the opportunity to practice adapting to unforseen circumstances (Gaddy, 1987). On completion of training, team members should demonstrate adaptability by being able to (a) recognize and list unexpected events and (b) describe the appropriate actions to take in response to an event that threatens to interfere with the team's purpose, structure, or interdependency (Lewis et al., 1983).

It is important to use examples throughout team training that reflect the possible real-life obstacles. Such examples can be presented by using simulations or videotaped samples. This focus moves team training from dealing with easily recognized errors to addressing the more complex, obscure situations that often occur in the work environment.

Knowledge and Skills

To be an effective member of any team, individuals need to possess several basic competencies. These abilities include, but are not limited to, a mastery of the details, skills that are specific to unique tasks, and facts relating to team performance (Guerette, Miller, Glickman, Morgan, & Salas, 1987). Differences in member profi-ciency often relate directly to the team's performance. Team training makes team members aware of the relationship between individual preparation and team success. Conversely, it is important that they also understand the connection between team performance and individual development and achievement (McIntyre et al., 1988).

Training should begin with a skills assessment to determine team members' readiness to contribute successfully to the team effort. This assessment uses criterion-based job performance skills and is conducted periodically throughout the team's lifetime. Successful leaders can apply the following steps to guide the team member selection process:

1. Thoroughly analyze job requirements before beginning the selection process.
2. Probe for objective evidence of an applicant's skills, knowledge, past successes and failures, dependability, and attitude toward work, coworkers, and supervisors.
3. Provide a description of teamwork to applicants and ask them to assess how they would work under team conditions.
4. Make certain each applicant understands the job requirements and expected standards of performance.
5. Evaluate facts carefully and avoid making premature conclusions or engaging in stereotyping.
6. Place selected team members in positions where there is potential for individual and team success.

Coordination and Cooperation

The skills of coordination and cooperation are integral to successful team performance. Members of coordinated teams can solicit information from other team members and are comfortable consulting with colleagues when they feel uncertain about some phase of the team goal.

Team members are considered to be cooperative when they willingly provide this type of information and assistance.

It is best to begin this training by first ensuring that individual members have mastered their specific duties. They then are trained to do the other jobs that are assigned to the team and work through those jobs. The cross-training and experience foster cooperation and active sharing.

Evaluation

The evaluation of leadership and team members provides a sense of direction, enhancing team performance through self-correction and development. The most effective evaluations are behaviorally based and address team development, turnover, interpersonal interaction, quality of work, and changes in member assignments and status.

The evaluation of the team leader typically includes a leader's self-assessment as well as an evaluation of his or her performance by team members (McIntyre et al., 1988). Often, team members assess their own performance, reviewing the effectiveness of their interactions with others.

Team-Training Situation

Team members' individual skill levels must be considered before, during, and after any team training. While effective team instruction involves all team members, the instructor should divide and train team members by task and specific assignment, moving from simple to complex tasks. In addition, team instructors need to identify real-life examples of preferred team behaviors before they can teach these behaviors to team members (McIntyre et al., 1988). Team leaders are prepared to provide specific examples, to play different roles, to appeal to a variety of individual learning styles, and to facilitate learning in various types of teams. They should

be knowledgeable about, and experienced in the many facets of team development, well informed about individual team members, and able to coach and guide individuals in their development. In addition, the leader functions primarily as a key team member rather than as a teacher or supervisor.

Assessment of Team Training

Teams are often assessed before training and after task completion. Both the pretraining and posttraining assessments include major outcome measures (such as program effectiveness) and measures of specific outcomes (such as criterion-referenced individual task performance).

Pretraining assessment based on program objectives provides information on the team's attitudes toward tasks, objectives, the team mission, the work environment, expectations of the training program, and how training can improve personal performance. The final assessment determines whether objectives were met, the validity of the program content, the impact of the program on individual trainees, the effect of the program on the operational environment, and can provide feedback to be used for program improvement (Cannon-Bowers, Prince, Salas, Owens, Morgan, & Gonos, 1989).

....

SPECIAL TEAM SITUATIONS

Special situations that may arise in organizations seem ready-made for the use of teams. In the following sections we will discuss several of the most common ones, including conflict resolution, problem solving, and high-performance teams.

Conflict Resolution

Because teams are comprised of employees with individual value systems and work ethics, it is essential to provide team members with skills to effectively resolve conflict. Conflict is a normal occurrence; it becomes unhealthy only when it is avoided or approached on a win/lose basis. The successful team leader will provide training at the onset of team formation rather than waiting for a conflict to arise, scrambling to react to an adverse situation that threatens to delay team production.

Differences in individual members' needs, objectives, and values can result in conflict. Differences in team members' perceptions of the motives, words, or actions of others can result in conflict. Unwillingness to work through issues, collaborate, or compromise can result in conflict. Therefore, it is critical that the team is prepared to handle conflict in a nonthreatening manner.

There are four major conflict resolution styles. The **avoidance style** is illustrated by the employee who ignores the problem and hopes that it simply will disappear with time. The employee who has the **accommodating style** avoids conflict by being extremely agreeable, often at the expense of personal or group goals. Both of these styles fail to address conflict and usually result in more significant conflict in the future as animosities build and ultimately explode.

The **win/lose style** is apparent when a team member is extremely attached to getting his or her own way. It is characterized by confrontational, assertive, or even aggressive behavior and by a lack of ability to consider multiple perspectives or differing points of view. Whenever there is a "winner," there is also a "loser," a result that undermines a sense of team morale and cohesion.

The **compromising style** recognizes that it is important for all participants to achieve their goals and to maintain positive working relationships. In this view, no one person or idea is perfect, and there is more than one solution to any problem. This approach is preferable to the previous styles, but participants can still be aggressive and may be clinging, even subconsciously, to a need to "win." For this reason the preferred conflict resolution style is the final style described—the problem-solving style.

The **problem-solving style** recognizes the legitimacy and importance of the needs of both parties. Similar to the compromising style, it assumes that a mutually beneficial solution can be reached by using compromise, respect for a variety of perspectives, and a supportive approach. The main characteristic of this method is that both parties are assertive (rather than aggressive) and cooperative. Because this is the preferred approach, the final section of this chapter provides an example of an effective problem-solving process.

Problem Solving

Sound group problem-solving techniques can contribute significantly to smooth team interactions. During the formation of a work team, it is important for team members to commit to finding the best possible solution to problems without focusing on their own exclusive views. This process is characterized by open communication, an absence of personal attack, and a task-oriented approach to problem solving. A task-oriented approach is characterized by communication that focuses on the task at hand rather than on the people performing the task.

The adage "two heads are better than one" is applicable when attempting to solve team problems. A group-formulated solution is often far more comprehensive and effective than subjective, individual suggestions. Following are some of the conditions that support effective group problem solving.

1. Team members should feel secure within the group. It is important that they feel free to readily contribute from their own experience and listen, without judgment, to the contributions of others.

2. Conflicts that arise from differing points of view should be considered helpful because they provide multiple perspectives and additional resources to aid in achieving team goals. Differences of opinion can be explored, discussed, and resolved with regard to the task at hand. It is important to recognize that while team members do not have to agree on every procedure or solution, they need to respect their colleagues' beliefs, suggestions, and feelings.

3. Team members should challenge suggestions that make them uncomfortable while avoiding arguments based on "winning."

4. Blocking behaviors should not be allowed to interfere with the team process. Team members are made aware of problem-solving communication skills during training and are on guard for behaviors that hinder the task-oriented approach to finding solutions. Blocking behaviors include, but are not limited to, switching topics to delay finding a solution, inappropriate humor, rationalizing, blaming or judging others, threatening others, and sarcasm.

Another basic problem-solving approach (Montebello, 1994) consists of seven simple steps and provides a framework within which to facilitate group problem solving. These seven steps are as follows:

Step 1: State what appears to be the problem. The real problem may not become apparent until the facts have been gathered and analyzed. Therefore, it is wise to start with a supposition of what appears to be the problem. This can be confirmed or corrected later.

Step 2: Gather facts, feelings, and opinions. What happened? When and where did it occur? What are its size, scope, and severity? Who or what is affected? Is it likely to happen again? Does it need correction? Time and expense may require that problem solvers assign priorities to the most critical elements of any problem.

Step 3: Restate the problem. The facts gathered in step 2 provide supporting data for this restatement, which may or may not be the same as stated in step 1.

Step 4: Identify alternative solutions. Generate ideas, or brainstorm and make a list of possible solutions. Do not eliminate any of the entries on the list until several suggestions have been discussed.

Step 5: Evaluate alternatives. Which alternative will provide the best solution? What risks are associated with this alternative? Are the costs inherent in implementing this solution in line with the perceived benefits? Will the solution create any new problems?

Step 6: Implement the decision. Who will be involved in its implementation? To what extent? How, when, and where will the solution be implemented? Who will be affected by this decision? What could go wrong? How will the proposed results be evaluated?

Step 7: Evaluate the results. Test the solution against the desired results and modify the solution if more effective results are needed.

High-Performance Teams

Most of us recognize that there are *teams* and there are *high-performance teams*. Teams work together well and are effective in their accomplishments; **high-performance teams** go beyond what is expected of them. In the world of teams, they are the stars. We recognize that there is something special about such teams that makes them stand out from others. At first, our inclination is to give credit to the team leader or coach. However, we soon see that as too simple an explanation. In these unique, high-performing teams, every member is a leader, inspired to give his or her best while working in close harmony with the other team members.

In 1987, Wilson Learning Corporation and Hughes Aircraft investigated such teams. Their study included a number of Fortune 100 companies which were surveyed to identify and examine peak team experiences. Focus interviews further helped to refine the definition of the specific characteristics of these high-performance teams. Out of this research developed a definition of the high-performance team, a method for creating high-performance teams, a process for employing such teams to solve business problems, and ideas about how to develop high-performance organizations based on high-performance teams.

Wilson Learning's research identified eight attributes that are typically present in teams that achieve high performance:

Participative leadership: creating an interdependency by empowering, freeing up, and serving others.

Shared responsibility: establishing an environment in which all team members feel as responsible as the manager for the performance of the work unit.

Alignment on purpose: having a sense of common purpose about why the team exists and the function it serves.

High communication: creating a climate of trust through open, honest communication.

Future focus: seeing change as an opportunity for growth.

Focus on task: keeping meetings focused on results.

Creative talents: applying individual talents and creativity.

Rapid response: identifying and acting on opportunities.

Because of the importance and usefulness of these attributes, we will discuss them in more detail.

Participative Leadership

In a high-performance team, the manager is one of the members. The manager focuses attention more on the group than on its individual members. In this one-to-group interaction, the man-

ager's goal is to empower individual members and the group itself by delegating responsibility, communicating the importance of team members, providing opportunities for the team and its members to contribute value to the effort, and enabling each team member to become an equal member of the team (Buchholz & Roth, 1987).

The manager works to provide team members with a level of empowerment that supports their efforts to optimize the use of individual talents, ideas, insights, and creativity in problem solving. Finally, the manager serves the team and its members by contributing to the growth of individuals. Serving others means finding ways to help them attain the money, respect, recognition, power, prestige, and other goals they have set for themselves. By helping each member to reach his or her own potential, the successful leader simultaneously secures a positive, productive team environment. As Robert Greenleaf pointed out in his book *Servant Leadership* (1977, p. 10):

> A fresh, critical look is being taken at the issues of power and authority, and people are beginning to learn, however haltingly, to relate to one another in less coercive and more creatively supporting ways. A new moral principle is emerging which holds that the only authority deserving one's allegiance is that which is freely and knowingly granted by the leader in response to, and in proportion to, the clearly evident servant stature of the leader. Those who choose to follow this principle will not casually accept the authority of existing institutions. *Rather, they will freely respond only to individuals who are chosen as leaders because they are proven and trusted as servants.*

These critical ideas were updated by Peter Block in his book, *Stewardship* (1993). In Block's conceptualization, the principle is stewardship, the willingness to be accountable for the well-being of the larger organization by operating in service rather than in control of those around us. It is accountability without control or compliance.

Shared Responsibility

The second characteristic of high performing teams is that they work in an environment in which each team member feels equally responsible for the performance of the work team/department (Buchholz & Roth, 1987).

In *Managing for Excellence* (1984), David Bradford and Allen Cohen describe a "heroic manager" as someone who tries to have all the answers, who accepts responsibility for performance of the work unit, who feels that he or she must be in control, coordinating and directing all efforts. Bradford and Cohen make the case that the heroic style is outdated and needs to be replaced. They suggest that a "post-heroic" manager is:

Someone who helps team members increase their sense of responsibility in the management of the unit or team.

Someone who facilitates team members' becoming more skilled in and committed to solving departmental or team problems.

Someone who involves team members in building the control and coordination they need for effective performance

Someone who finds satisfaction in the success of individual team members and in the development of a high-performing team or department

Alignment on Purpose

Purpose answers the question, "Why do we exist?" Wilson Learning's research found that in high-performance teams, all the team members shared the same purpose. Typically, the purpose was in the form of an overarching goal, something outside and apart from the existence and growth of the team itself. It defined the ongoing, general direction rather than a specific outcome. Charles Garfield described this in his book, *Peak Performers* (1986, p. 25): "Peak performance begins with a commitment to a mission. Peak performers want more than merely to win the next game. They see all the way to the championship. They have a long-range goal that inspires commitment and action."

One way to achieve alignment on purpose is to guide a team in creating its purpose statement. This process, as described by Buchholz and Roth (1987), includes the following:

1. Ask for input from team members. Have all team members participate in describing what they believe is the purpose of the work unit. They can consider the past performance of the team, its focus for the future, and what makes the team special.

2. Incubate the ideas. Once the ideas have been collected, allow the group some time to think about them.

3. Have subgroups of the team draft purpose statements and submit them to the team as a whole. Look for common themes in the statements; pull these together into a combined draft. Live with the draft for a while before refining it into a statement the team can accept as its vision for being.

4. Discuss the draft with team members. Ask for reactions, ideas, changes, and additions. Encourage all viewpoints. Work toward consensus, but do not give up inspiration. Bennis and Nanus (1985, p. 89) suggest that "a clearly articulated vision of the future (should be) at once simple, easily understood, clearly desirable, and energizing."

5. Write a final purpose statement that is built on the consensus of team members. There need not be 100 percent agreement, but it is best to have high general acceptance.

6. Ask all team members for a statement of commitment. These statements personalize the purpose statement for each team member

and demonstrate their alignment with the team's purpose.

High Communication

In the past, most communication in the work world was one-to-one and occurred from the manager down. Watson (1982) demonstrated that individuals in leadership roles were resistant when others in a group attempted to control the conversation. Furthermore, group members compliantly followed the manager's lead. Muchinsky (1977) examined the relationship between communication and satisfaction by correlating selected communication variables with measures of climate and job satisfaction. Employees who thought that communication was accurate and satisfactory were also satisfied with their work, their supervisors, and their coworkers. Employees who thought that communication was inaccurate or unsatisfactory were also unhappy with the organization, their supervisors, and relations with their coworkers.

Buchholz and Roth (1987, p. 70) summarized the research on satisfaction, frequency of communication and performance in the following table:

Satisfaction	Communication	Performance
High	High	Highest
Low	High	High
High	Low	Low
Low	Low	Lowest

From this, we can see how directly frequent communication is related to performance. From the high-performing team perspective the middle two sets of data are noteworthy. Employees who had low satisfaction but high communication performed better than highly satisfied employees who felt that communications were low.

Numerous books and articles have been published on increasing effectiveness of communications. One that provides a model of the key behaviors is J. R. Gibb's (1991) *Trust: A New View of Personal and Organizational Development*. In this book, Dr. Gibb identifies six behav-

ioral processes that encourage communication: description, equality, openness, problem orientation, positive intent, and empathy. He also identified six processes that hinder or stop communication: judging, superiority, certainty, controlling, manipulation, and indifference.

To create an atmosphere that is conducive to supporting a high-performing team, we need to reduce the behaviors that discourage communication while increasing those that encourage communication. The road map for a manager working to create a high communication environment can be succinctly outlined:

Decrease	Increase
Judging	Description
Superiority	Equality
Certainty	Openness
Controlling	Problem orientation
Manipulation	Positive intent
Indifference	Empathy

Future Focus

Being future focused is perceiving change as an opportunity for growth. Tregoe, Zimmerman, Smith, and Tobia (1989, p. 38) found that five major questions need to be answered for an organization's vision to be clear and focused:

1. What is the thrust or focus for future business development?
2. What is the scope of products and markets that will—and will not—be considered?
3. What is the future emphasis or priority and mix for products and markets that fall within that scope?
4. What key capabilities are required to make strategic vision happen?
5. What does this vision imply for growth and return expectations?

Focus on Task

Meetings are the primary setting in which one-to-group management skills are exercised. It is in meetings where these skills can have the greatest impact on the performance of a team.

Well-run meetings set the stage for high-performing teams. The rules for such meetings are straightforward: There is a clear sense of purpose, everyone participates, the discussion stays on target, and the meeting lasts only as long as is needed. In spite of this simplicity and the fact that these rules are well known, most of us have participated in meetings that were less than productive. In fact, it is probably safe to say there are more ineffective meetings than effective ones.

In their book *How to Make Meetings Work*, Michael Doyle and David Straus (1976) describe their "interaction method" for running meetings. This is summarized in their "Eighteen Steps to a Better Meeting" (Doyle & Straus, 1974, p. 289–290):

Before the Meeting:

1. Plan the meeting carefully; who, what, when, why, how many.
2. Prepare and send out an agenda in advance.
3. Come early and set up the meeting room.

At the Beginning of the Meeting:

4. Start on time.
5. Get participants to introduce themselves and state their expectations for the meeting.
6. Clearly define roles.
7. Review, revise, and order the agenda.
8. Set clear time limits.
9. Review action items from the previous meeting.

During the Meeting:

10. Focus on the same problem in the same way at the same time.

At the end of the Meeting:

11. Establish action items: who, what, when.
12. Review the group memory.
13. Set the date and place of the next meeting and develop a preliminary agenda.
14. Evaluate the meeting.
15. Close the meeting crisply and positively.
16. Clean up and rearrange the room.

After the Meeting:

17. Prepare the group memo.
18. Follow-up on action items and begin to plan the next meeting.

Creativity

Fostering the full use of a team's creative talents is easier said than done. The first step is to help the team break existing habit patterns to establish the kind of environment supportive of creative ideas. Some ways in which we limit our own thinking are habits, self-criticism, emotions, and patterns of thinking. Ways in which a team limits one another's participation include norms, rules, criticism of others, intimidation, and combining idea generation with idea evaluation.

Basadur, Graen, and Green (1982) developed and tested an approach for increasing the effectiveness of teams' creative problem solving. Their process is based on two major concepts, as illustrated in Figure 15.5 on page 544. First, it separates problem finding from problem solving and solution implementation. Second, it teaches an underlying fundamental process that is common to all three stages. This is the two-step process called *ideation-evaluation*. **Ideation** is idea generation without evaluation (putting aside judgment). Ideation is the divergent part of the process. **Evaluation** is the reverse, the convergent part of the process. It is the application of judgment to the ideas generated during ideation. The purpose of evaluation is to select the best ideas. Both the divergent and convergent aspects are considered essential to creativity (Farnham-Diggory, 1972).

Problem Finding: Ideation

1. Examine the problem as given. Write out the problem. Team members compare their definition.
2. Compare the different ways of viewing and conceptualizing the problem. Refine the team's understanding, using questions such as "What is the problem?" and "Who owns the problem?"

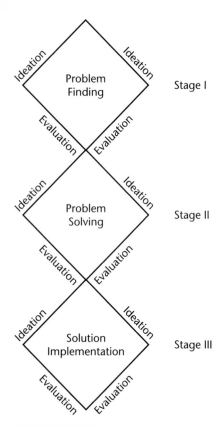

Stage I

Stage II

Stage III

FIGURE 15.5 Diagram of a complete creative problem-solving process emphasizing ideation-evaluation as a two-step process in each of three stages.

Source: From "Training in creative problem solving: Effects on ideation and problem finding and solving in an industrial research organization," by M. Basadur, G. B. Graen, and S. G. Green, 1982, *Organizational Behavior and Human Performance, 30,* 45. Copyright 1982 by Academic Press, Inc. Reprinted with permission.

3. Spark divergent, creative thinking. Ask questions such as "How might we broaden this perspective?" "How might we narrow it?" "How is this similar to other problems?" and "How is it different?"
4. Generate as many alternatives as possible.

Problem Finding: Evaluation

1. Review the definitions.
2. Select the definition that best reflects the problem.
3. Review the other definitions and borrow elements that refine the definition selected. Include those elements in the new definition.
4. Work to group consensus by reviewing and revising the problem definition.

Problem Solving: Ideation

1. Brainstorm possible solutions. Make no critical remarks.
2. Hitchhiking is legitimate. When you can improve on someone's idea do so.
3. Freewheeling is welcome. Wild ideas are encouraged, even if they seem absurd.
4. Quantity is welcome. The more ideas, the better.
5. Set a time limit. It motivates the group and keeps this part of the process from taking too much time.

Problem Solving: Evaluation

1. Conduct an open discussion to crystallize the solutions, choose between them, or combine them.
2. Combine and consolidate the creative ideas. This shortens the list and builds on the ideas that a majority of team members accept. This step can be done in subgroups, the results then being combined.
3. Identify and define the core solutions.
4. Rank or rate the possible solutions.
5. Select the solution to implement.

Solution Implementation: Ideation

1. Discuss the different ways of implementing the solution. Consider time, trust, commitment, and specificity of solution.
2. Consider the differences between problems that have multiple solutions (large problems with a variety of possible solutions) and those that have alternative solutions (problems with only two possible solutions).

3. Choose the criteria to be used in selecting which proposals to select or reject. Useful criteria include the following:

Contribution: How much the proposal will contribute to solving the problem.

Money: How much it will cost to implement the proposal.

Labor: How difficult it will be to find or allocate the labor or specialists needed to implement this proposal.

Commitment: How difficult it will be to find suitable people who will be committed to action on the proposal.

Resistance: How much resistance to the proposal can be expected from key people or others involved.

Problems: The degree to which implementing this proposal will create other problems. (Merry & Allerhand, 1977, p. 159)

4. Decide among the alternatives.

Solution Implementation: Evaluation

1. Project the solution into the future, anticipating and planning for the consequences of implementing it.
2. Improve the solution by reducing the disadvantages of putting it into action and increasing the advantages.
3. Discuss the problem-solving process and look for ways to improve the team process.
4. Follow up on the solution and its success. If necessary, revisit the problem solving and revise the solution if it is not proceeding as anticipated. Often, a team member is assigned this responsibility.

Rapid Response

High-performance teams are opportunistic. They identify opportunities for the organization on the basis of certain analyses and move to quickly exploit those opportunities. George Ainsworth-Land (1986) described this process as opportunity discovery. The Ainsworth-Land **opportunity discovery process** consists of seven steps:

1. State the desired outcome. State what you want to happen. Define a goal that can be measured.
2. Search for data. Assess current strengths and weaknesses. Do a complete SWOT (strengths, weaknesses, opportunities, and threats) analysis.
3. Identify characteristics. Think about the future. What characteristics and qualities will support achieving your goal? What will success look like for the team?
4. Compare characteristics to rank them in importance. Determine the priority of every characteristic.
5. Rate existing performance on each characteristic. On the basis of current performance, evaluate the team's performance on each aspect of the problem.
6. Graph the results on an opportunity map, such as that in Figure 15.6. Plotting priority or value on the *y*-axis and performance on the *x*-axis

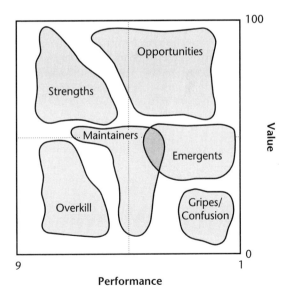

FIGURE 15.6   Example of classifications of problems using an opportunity map.

Source: From "The Innovator: Challenging People to Think," by Wilson Learning Corporation, 1989, *Learning Age, 2*, 1. Copyright 1989 by Wilson Learning Corporation. Reprinted with permission.

helps to identify areas for improvement. Characteristics that end up with a high value or priority and low existing performance are opportunities.

7. Create your action plan. Specify action steps for each opportunity. Most action plans include information on *what* is to be done, *who* will be responsible, *how* to proceed, *where* the action will occur, and by *when* it should be completed.

We have discussed how high-performance teams are superior to other teams in terms of eight basic attributes: participative leadership, shared responsibility, alignment on purpose, high communication, future focus, focus on task, use of creativity and talent, and rapid response. To create such teams requires that a leader focus on the future, identifying the positive outcomes that can be achieved while encouraging and enhancing the supportive relationships among people and facilitating group decision making and sharing of responsibilities. As can be seen in Scientific Perspective 15.3, the opposite can also

---

SCIENTIFIC PERSPECTIVE 15.3

Why Teams Don't Work

With all the emphasis these days on the use of teams in sales and marketing, it's somewhat surprising to find a study that decries their effectiveness. Yet that's the conclusion of a survey conducted by Wilson Learning Corp., an Eden Prairie, Minn., training and development firm.

The study of 4,500 teams from more than 50 organizations concluded that barriers to overall team effectiveness fall into two distinct categories—organizational and individual—both of which limit team performance. Beginning with the organizational barriers most frequently mentioned by survey respondents:

- Rewards and compensation. Fully 80% of survey participants said that most plans focus on individual performance and don't consider the team; therefore, there's little incentive to perform well.
- Personnel and HRD systems. The majority of respondents said their personal appraisal system doesn't consider team issues; only 10%–20% said team performance is considered in their appraisals.
- Information systems. Respondents in many organizations found access to pertinent information was hampered; they felt they were constantly having to "reinvent the wheel."
- Top management commitment. Most top management groups fear their staff can't handle team leadership responsibilities; but without their support, teams can't progress.

- Organizational alignment. Their organizational structure, said respondents, foments internal competition, limiting group effectiveness.

Respondents also cited the following individual factors as barriers to team productivity:

- Personal mind shift. Agendas of those unwilling to set aside position and power or unwilling to give up past practices make it hard for teams to be effective, said respondents.
- Individual abilities and characteristics. Since every team member may not have the ability, knowledge, or skill to contribute to the group, the workload may not be distributed equitably.
- Team membership factors. Members should contribute their unique viewpoints—despite the fact that what works for them individually may not work for the team.

The report suggests that the answer to team success may lie in "collaboration"—where there's strong commitment by top management to breaking down departmental and functional barriers and limiting competition. This, says Dr. Michael P. Leimbach, who analyzed the survey research, "facilitates a team's success, enabling [it] to become a positive driving force for the entire organization."

Source: From "Why Teams Don't Work," *Sales and Marketing Management,* April, 1993, p. 12. Copyright 1993 by Sales and Marketing Management. Reprinted with permission.

be true; teams that lack certain organizational and individual characteristics have limited performance, and often fail.

A carefully constructed team environment can generate an infectious effect. It can stimulate individuals to become stronger performers, a result that can benefit individual employees, teams, and ultimately the entire organization. Proper team training can solicit open communication among team members, which can lead to improved work methods. It can encourage those who are responsible for performing the work to contribute to goal construction. Employees and leaders alike can learn to commit to an environment of mutual concern and support. And team members can feel free to challenge their abilities, to articulate concerns, and to try out new ideas without fear of ridicule or rejection. All teams develop through predictable phases. Knowing these phases can be helpful to both the team and its leader. In addition to simple teams, there are high-performing teams which have special characteristics of their own.

SUMMARY

Research on organizations is conducted from one of three perspectives: individual, groups, and the organization as a whole. Organization development (OD) studies the organizationwide efforts to improve organizational effectiveness and productivity. There are three primary processes in OD work: sensitivity training which focuses on interpersonal relations among group members; sociotechnical systems which consider the impact of technological requirements on social relationships; and survey feedback which uses survey feedback in a structured way to guide organizational change.

Studies of the nature of organizations have found many dimensions that organizations have in common. Five that are frequently identified are: individual autonomy, degree of structure, reward orientation, consideration, and cooperativeness.

Small-group research has contributed to our understanding of organizations. Hackman's model summarizes this research by examining the two major stimuli—ambient and discretionary—and the ways in which these stimuli affect individuals. Hackman uses three states—informational, affective, and behavioral—to describe the different types of impact.

A classic framework, that of bureaucracy, has been the system of choice in many organizations. However, the world of work is changing, and organizations must adapt. Shifts to a more skilled work force, to more demanding jobs, to high-quality production, to cross-functional teams, to being customer driven, and to self-directed, empowered teams have created a need for new systems of organization. A major approach that is being used today is to increase the involvement of teams.

Teams consist of two or more people who interact to attain a common goal. Each member has specific roles or responsibilities within the team context. Most of the research on teams has been concerned with testing theory rather than with the application of theory. Consequently, it has been a challenge for I/O psychologists to generalize these findings to real-world work settings. In spite of this challenge, several theories have had significant impact on team building in today's work environment.

One widely accepted theory of team formation is Tuckman's theory of team development. He stated that a team undergoes four distinct phases. The first stage, forming, occurs at the onset of team formation and is characterized by members exploring the boundaries of acceptable group behavior. In stage two, storming, members start to realize that their tasks are more challenging than they had imagined. Norming, or stage three, occurs when members define the teams's ground rules and become more cooperative. In the final stage, performing, members actually begin completing tasks and operating as a team.

Other models of teams and team operation include Hackman's normative model which examines the impact of organizational environment on team performance; Gersick's time and transition model which is based on the dynamic nature of teams and their predictable adaptation of strategies; the Gladstein task effectiveness model which explains how the nature of the task the team performs governs process and performance; and the Team Evolution and Maturation (TEAM) model which predicts team stages before, during, and on completion of a task.

The TEAM model is a composite model that suggests the existence of two activity tracks throughout team development. The first track contains training-related activities that are tied to specific tasks. The second track addresses the interpersonal activities that affect the quality of team–member relationships.

The chapter concludes by summarizing the applied practice of team building. A carefully constructed team environment can have significant organizational effects. It can stimulate individuals and groups to become stronger performers. It can increase job satisfaction and longevity. It can inspire people to seek training and to apply their knowledge in creative, new ways. And it can encourage employees and leaders to make new commitments to their organizations. Even though organizational development and teaming have not been studied as much as other areas of I/O psychology, there is useful information in the data we have. That data can guide us to more effective application of organizational development, group influences, and teams in planning organizational change.

KEY TERMS AND CONCEPTS

accommodating style
affective state
alignment on purpose
ambient stimuli
avoidance style
behavioral state
compromising style
conflict potential
conforming stage
creative talents
cross-functional team
crystallization
discretionary stimuli
evaluation
focus on task
forming stage
functional team
future focus
generic skill development
generic teams
high communication
high-performance teams

hypercompetition
ideation
informational influence
informational state
intensity
Jackson Return Potential
    Model
moving
multifunctional team
nominal group technique
normative influence
normative model
normative power
norming stage
operational skills
    development
operational skills training
opportunity discovery
    process
organizational climate
organizational development
participative leadership

performing stage
problem-solving style
rapid response
reforming stage
refreezing
sensitivity training
shared responsibility
shortwall groups
six-box model
sociotechnical systems
storming stage
survey feedback
task effectiveness model
team evolution and
    maturation model
team mission statement
time and transition model
training-related activities
unfreezing
vacuous consensus
win/lose style

RECOMMENDED READINGS

Montebello, A. R., (1994). *Work teams that work: Skills for managing across the organization.* Minneapolis, MN: Best Sellers Publishing.

Orsburn, J. D., Moran, L., Musselwhite, E., & Zenger, J. H. (1990). *Self-directed work teams: The new American challenge.* Homewood, IL: Business One Irwin.

Reddy, W. B. (Ed.) (1988). *Team building: Blueprints for productivity and satisfaction.* San Diego, CA: NTL Institute for Applied Behavioral Science and Pfeiffer & Company.

Scholtes, P. R., with Joiner, B. L., Braswell, B., Finn, L., Hacquebord, H., Little, K., Reynard, S., Streibel, B., & Weiss, B. (1988). *The team handbook.* Madison, WI: Joiner Associates.

Swezey, R. W., & Salas, E. (Eds.) (1992). *Teams: Their training and performance.* Norwood, NJ: Ablex Publishing.

Tregoe, B. B., Zimmerman, J. W., Smith, R. A., & Tobia, P. M. (1989). *Vision in action: Putting a winning strategy to work.* New York: Simon and Schuster.

Wellins, R. S., Byham, W. C., & Dixon, G. R. (1994). *Inside teams: How 20 world-class organizations are winning through teamwork.* San Francisco, CA: Jossey-Bass.

Wellins, R. S., Byham, W. C., & Wilson, J. M. (1991). *Empowered teams: Creating self-directed work groups that improve quality, productivity, and participation.* San Francisco, CA: Jossey-Bass.

Zenger, J. H., Musselwhite, E., Hurson, K., & Perrin, C. (1994). *Leading teams: Mastering the new role.* Homewood, IL: Business One Irwin.

INTERNET RESOURCES

Teamwork on a Space Vehicle—7 Persons Working Together

> This site presents an interesting description of the experiences of people working together as a team to design a space vehicle. It also includes a number of photos of the team in action.

> **http://alberti.mit.edu/publications/designedmit7.html**

Joiner Associates, Inc.—Teamwork and Organizational Development

> Joiner Associates is an internationally known organization that provides materials and training for organizational improvement and team building. This site provides a full list of their materials and access to their free *Managing for Quality* newsletter.

> **http://www.joiner.com/**

Reengineering at Fort Stewart/Hunter Army Airfield

> This site is a detailed report of the reengineering initiative at Fort Stewart/Hunter. It provides a case example of organizational development and leadership applied in a demanding environment.

> **http://www.stewart.army.mil/ftsreeng.htm**

University of Paisley—Professional Practice and Leadership Module

> This site provides access to the resources list for the University of Paisley's BSC Health Studies Professional Practice and Leadership Module. Internet links are provided to the Leadership Forum, the Teamwork Search Tools, and to Leadership/Management Development. There are extensive book lists for Leadership and Teamwork Classics. Finally, there are sections on Aspects of Leadership and Educating for Multidisciplinary Teamwork.

> **http://202.40.17.1/lead.htm**

Group Performance Systems, Inc. Teamwork Resources on the Web and on the Net

> This site is a comprehensive list and set of links to teamwork resources. It is a convenient way to access many teamwork related sites.

> **http://www.gpsi.com/teamwork.html**

Journal of Managerial Psychology

This site presents full journal contents pages, abstracts, and articles to subscribers. A number of current articles on managerial teamwork are included.

http://www.mcb.co.uk/cgibin/mcb_serve/table1. txt&jmp&journal3.htm

. . . .

EXERCISES

Exercise 15.1

Job Redesign: Developing a Participatory Environment for Students

The academic environment is parallel to the world of work. Unfortunately, many innovations that have had an enriching and empowering effect in the work environment have not been applied in the academic setting. This exercise challenges you to form several teams of class members and to apply your knowledge from this chapter and from this book to the redesign of the academic workplace.

Steps in the process:

1. Review elements of participatory environments and work design. Think about how to best work together as a team. Plan your effort.
2. Collect additional information as necessary. Use specific examples of organizational development and team development techniques that you believe could be used.
3. Develop a process-activity map of the role of student.
4. Identify potential improvements. Multivote to select those with the most potential. (In multivoting, post your list, combine similar items, number the final list, and choose the top four to seven items to discuss as a team.)
5. Use nominal group technique to guide your discussion. Turn each item into a task-related question. Revise and clarify the question until everyone understands it. Generate ideas individually on a sheet of paper, then round table to pool ideas. Use brainstorming rules. Clarify and discuss each idea.
6. Compare lists and combine similar items, rewording as necessary to retain ideas. Where appropriate, identify ideas that qualify as subheadings. Continue this list laundering to reduce the number of items. For the remaining items, have

each member make selections and write them on separate cards or sticky notes. Also assign a value rating to each item (using an agreed-upon scale). Collect and tally the cards. Multiply values and points to get totals.

7. As a group, review and discuss the results and the members' reaction to the results. Display the results as a Pareto chart to see which items have the most votes and the greatest overall total. A Pareto chart is like a histogram. It is a series of bars with heights that represent the frequency or seriousness of problems. It differs from a histogram in that the bars are arranged in decreasing order of height from left to right. Categories of problems represented by the tall bars on the left are relatively more important than those represented by the shorter bars to the right. Pareto charts are helpful to teams that are trying to identify which problems are important enough to warrant attention and which ones they should attack first. Ask members to lobby for their favorites.
8. Working as a group, prepare a presentation of your results for the rest of the class.
9. Use the stages of team development to analyze your team's process and development. Identify key activities and behaviors in the following categories: initiating behaviors (getting the conversation going); gate-keeping behaviors (supporting and encouraging quiet members or discouraging or controlling dominant members); information-seeking behaviors (drawing out additional information or concerns from group members); and sharing feelings (sharing personal feelings and views or getting others to share theirs).
10. What three things went particularly well for your team?
11. What three things would you do differently? Why? How?

Exercise 15.2

Working with a Group to Improve Teamwork

Team development is often desired during times of crisis, periods of rapid growth, and other times of change. A starting point is to increase the trust, openness, mutual acceptance, and general communications in a group that is seeking to become a team.

Identify a group of which you are a member. Volunteer to act as a facilitator to help the group improve its teamwork. Conduct a brief problem-sensing session with the group.

Steps in the process:

1. Introduce yourself and the idea of dealing with problems during the first stages of their development. Remind people that it is at this stage that major feelings develop. Also, discuss the fact that the press of day-to-day activities often means that small problems get postponed rather than addressed.

2. Have the participants write down two or three problems. Have them provide full details. If it helps, define *problem* as a gap between the existing state and the desired state.

3. List the problems on a flipchart. Use the wording that the team members used. Write out the entire problem. Take one problem at a time from one person, going through the whole group several times to collect all the problem statements. Keep the group from discussing the problems during this phase.

4. Aided by the group, review and classify the problems. List the groupings on a fresh flipchart.

5. Using your work to this point conduct discussions of "What is hindering our effectiveness?" "Are we doing what we should be doing?" and "How can we improve our team functioning?"

....

REFERENCES

Ainsworth-Land, G. (1986). *The innovator family of group creative thinking tools: Facilitator's guide.* Eden Prairie, MN: Wilson Learning Corporation.

Atkinson, J. W. (1954). Explorations using imaginative thought to assess the strength of human motives. In M. R. Jones (Ed.), *Nebraska symposium on motivation: 1954.* Lincoln, NE: University of Nebraska Press.

Bales, R. F., & Strodtbeck, F. L. (1951). Phases in group problem solving. *Journal of Abnormal and Social Psychology, 46,* 485–495.

Basadur, M., Graen, G. B., & Green, S. G. (1982). Training in creative problem solving: Effects of ideation and problem finding and solving in an industrial research organization. *Organizational Behavior and Human Performance, 30,* 41–70.

Bass, B. (1982). Individual capability, team performance, and team productivity. In M. Dunnette & E. Fleischman (Eds.), *Human Performance and Productivity: Human Capability Assessment.* Hillsdale, NJ: Erlbaum.

Beckhard, R. (1969). *Organization development: strategies and models.* Reading, MA: Addison-Wesley.

Beckhard, R., & Harris, R. T. (1987). *Organizational transitions: Managing complex change.* Reading, MA: Addison-Wesley.

Beer, M., & Huse, E. F. (1972). A systems approach to organization development. *Journal of Applied Behavioral Science, 8,* 79–101.

Bell, M. A. (1982). Phases in group problem-solving. *Small Group Behavior, 13,* 475–495.

Bennis, W. G., & Nanus, B. (1985). *Leaders: The strategies for taking charge.* New York: Harper & Row.

Bennis, W. G., & Shepard, H. A. (1956). A theory of group development. *Human Relations, 9,* 470–477.

Block, P. (1993). *Stewardship.* San Francisco, CA: Berrett-Koehler.

Bradford, D., & Cohen, A. (1984). *Managing for excellence.* New York: Wiley.

Buchholz, S., & Roth, T. (1987). *Creating the high performance team.* New York: John Wiley & Sons.

Burke, W. W. (1982). *Organization development: Principles and practices.* Glenview, IL: Scott, Foresman.

Burke, W. W. (1991). Practicing organizational development. In Bray, D. W. (Ed.), *Working with organizations and their people: A guide to human resources practice* (pp. 93–130). New York: The Guilford Press.

Campbell, J. P., Dunnette, M. D., Lawler, E. E., & Weick, K. E. (1970). *Managerial behavior, performance, and effectiveness.* New York: McGraw-Hill.

Cannon-Bowers, J., Prince, C., Salas, E., Owens, J., Morgan, B., & Gonos, G. (1989). *Determining aircrew coordination training alternatives.* Paper presented at the 11th Interservice/Industry Training Systems Conference, Ft. Worth, TX.

Caple, R. B. (1978). The sequential stages of group development. *Small-Group Behavior, 9,* 470–477.

Chawla, S., & Renesch, J. (1995). *Learning organizations: Developing cultures for tomorrow's workplace.* Portland, OR: Productivity Press.

Coch, L., & French, J. R. P., Jr. (1948). Overcoming resistance to change. *Human Relations, 1,* 512–532.

Cream, B. W. (1978). A strategy for the development of training devices. *Human Factors, 20*(2), 145–148.

Davis, L. T., Gaddy, C. D., & Turney, J. R. (1985). *An approach to team skills training of nuclear power plant control room crews* (NUREG/CR-4258GP+R-123022). Columbia, MD: General Physics Corporation.

Deming, W. E. (1986). *Out of the crisis.* Cambridge, MA: MIT Center for Advanced Engineering Study.

Denson, R. W. (1981). *Team training: Literature review and annotated bibliography* (AFHRL-TR-80–40). Wright Patterson Air Force Base, OH: Logistics and Technical Training Division, Air Force Human Research Laboratory.

Doyle, M., & Straus, D. (1976). *How to make meetings work: The new interaction method.* San Francisco, CA: Wyden Books.

Driskell, J. E., & Salas, E. (1992). Collective behavior and team performance. *Human Factors, 34*(3), 277–388.

Dyer, J. (1984). Team research and team training: A state-of-the-art review. In F. Muckler (Ed.), *Human factors review* (pp. 285–323). Santa Monica, CA: Human Factors Society.

Eden, D. (1986). OD and self-fulfilling prophecy: Boosting productivity by raising expectations. *Journal of Applied Behavioral Science, 22,* 1–13.

Farnham-Diggory, S. (1972). *Cognitive processes in education.* New York: Harper & Row.

Foushee, C. (1984). Dyads and triads at 35,000 feet: Factors affecting group process and aircrew performance. *American Psychologist, 39*(8), 885–893.

Franz, T. M., Prince, C., & Salas, E. (1990). *Identification of aircrew coordination skills.* Paper presented at the 12th Annual Department of Defense Symposium, Colorado Springs, CO.

Friedlander, F., & Greenberg, S. (1971). Effect of job attitudes, training, and organization climate on performance of the hard-core unemployed. *Journal of Applied Psychology, 55*(4), 187–195.

Gaddy, C. (1987). *A practitioner's perspective on team skill training in industry.* Paper presented at the meeting of the American Psychological Association, New York.

Garfield, C. (1986). *Peak performers: The new heroes of American business.* New York: Avon.

Gersick, C. J. G. (1985). *Time and transition in work teams: Towards a new model of group development.* Unpublished Manuscript. Cited in Salas, E., Montero, R. C., & Morgan, B. B. (1987). *Group development, teamwork skills and training.* Unpublished manuscript, Naval Training Systems Center, Orlando.

Gersick, C. J. G. (1988). Time and transition in work teams: Towards a new model of group development. *Academy of Management Review, 31,* 9–41.

Gibb, J. R. (1991). *Trust: A new view of personal and organizational development.* North Hollywood, CA: New Castle.

Gladstein, D. L. (1984). Groups in context: A model of task group effectiveness. *Administrative Science Quarterly, 29,* 499–517.

Glickman, A. S., Zimmer, S., Montero, R. C., Guerette, P. J., Campbell, W. S., Morgan, B. B., Jr., & Salas, E. (1987). *The evolution of teamwork skills: An empirical assessment with implications for training* (Tech. Rep. No. 87–016). Orlando, FL: Naval Training Systems Command.

Greenleaf, R. K. (1977). *Servant leadership: A journey into the nature of legitimate power and greatness.* New York: The Paulist Press.

Guerette, P. J., Miller, D., Glickman, A., Morgan, B., & Salas, E. (1987). *Instructional processes and strategies in team training* (Tech. Rep. No. 87–016). Orlando, FL: Naval Training Systems Command.

Hackman, J. R. (1976). Group influences on individuals. In M. Dunnette (Ed.), *Handbook of industrial and organizational psychology* (1st ed., pp. 1455–1525). Chicago: Rand McNally.

Hackman, J. R. (1983). *A normative model of work team effectiveness* (Tech. Rep. No. 2). New Haven, CT: Yale University.

Hackman, J. R. (1992). Group influences on individuals in organizations. In M. D. Dunnette & L. M. Hough (Eds.), *Handbook of industrial and organizational psychology* (2nd ed., Vol. 3, pp. 199–267). Palo Alto, CA: Consulting Psychologists Press.

Hall, E., & Rizzo, W. (1975). *An assessment of U.S. Navy tactical team training* (TAEG Report No. 18). Orlando, FL: Training Analysis and Evaluation Group.

Hammer, M., & Champy, J. (1993). *Reengineering the corporation: A manifesto for business revolution.* New York: HarperCollins.

Helmreich, R. L. (1982). *Pilot selection and training.* Paper presented at the meeting of the American Psychological Association. Washington, DC.

Ilgen, D., Shapiro, J., Salas, E., & Weiss, H. (1989). *Functions of group goals; Possible generalizations from individuals to groups* (Tech. Rep. No. 87–022). Orlando, FL: Naval Training Systems Center.

Jackson, J. (1960). Structural characteristics of norms. In N. B. Henry (Ed.), *Dynamics of instructional groups: The fifty-ninth yearbook of the National Society for the Study of Education.* Chicago, IL: University of Chicago Press.

Jackson, J. (1965). Structural characteristics of norms. In I. D. Steiner & M. Fishbein (Eds.), *Current studies in social psychology.* New York: Holt, Rinehart and Winston.

Jackson, J. (1966). A conceptual and measurement model for norms and roles. *Pacific Sociological Review, 9,* 35–47.

Jackson, J. (1975). Normative power and conflict potential. *Sociological Methods and Research, 4,* 237–263.

Juran, J. M. (1988). *Juran on planning for quality.* New York: The Free Press.

Kahn, R. L., Wolfe, D. M., Quinn, R. P., Snoek, J. D., & Rosenthal, R. A. (1964). *Organizational stress: Studies in role conflict and ambiguity.* New York: Wiley.

Keller, R. T. (1986). Predictors of the performance of project groups in R&D organizations. *Academy of Management Journal, 29,* 715–726.

Lewis, C. M., Hritz, R. J., & Roth, J. T. (1983). *Understanding and improving teamwork: Identifying training requirements* (Report 4). Valencia, PA: Applied Science Associates.

Litwin, G. H., & Stringer, R. A. (1968). *Motivation and organizational change.* Boston: Division of Research, Graduate School of Business Administration, Harvard University.

Mann, F. (1951). Changing superior-subordinate relationships. *Journal of Social Issues, 7,* 56–63.

March, J. G., & Simon, H. A. (1958). *Organizations.* New York: Wiley.

McClelland, D. C., Atkinson, J. W., Clark, R. A., & Lowell, E. L. (1953). *The achievement motive.* New York: Appleton-Century-Crofts.

McIntyre, R. M., Morgan, B., Salas, E., & Glickman, A. (1988). *Teamwork from team training: New evidence for the development of teamwork skills during operational training.* Paper presented at the Interservice/Industry Training Systems Conference, Orlando, FL.

Merry, U., & Allerhand, M. E. (1977). *Developing teams and organizations: A practical handbook for managers and consultants.* Reading, MA: Addison-Wesley.

Modrick, J. A. (1986). Team performance and training. In J. Zeidner (Ed.), *Human productivity enhancement: Vol. 1. Training and human factors in systems design.* New York: Praeger Publishers.

Montebello, A. R. (1994) *Work teams that work: Skills for managing across the organization.* Minneapolis, MN: Best Sellers Publishing.

Morgan, B. B., Jr., & Salas, E. (1987). *The Evolution of Teamwork* (NAVTRASYSCEN TR 87–016). Orlando, FL: Naval Training Systems Center.

Morgan, G. B., Jr., Glickman, A. S., Woodard, E. A., Blaiwes, A., and Salas, E. (1986). *Measurement of team behavior in a Navy training environment,* (NAVTRASYSCEN TR 86–014). Orlando, FL: Naval Training Systems Center.

Muchinsky, P. M. (1976). An assessment of the Litwin and Stringer organization climate questionnaire:

An empirical and theoretical extension of the Sims and LaFollette study. *Personnel Psychology, 29,* 371–392.

Muchinsky, P. M. (1977). Organizational communication: Relationships to organizational climate and job satisfaction. *Academy of Management Journal, 20,* 592–607.

Mullen, B., Symons, C., Hu, L., & Salas, E. (1989). Group size, leadership behavior and subordinate satisfaction. *Journal of General Psychology, 116*(2), 155–169.

Neuman, G. A., Edwards, J. E., & Raju, N. S. (1989). Organizational development interventions: A meta-analysis of their effect in satisfaction and other attitudes. *Personnel Psychology, 42,* 461–490.

Nicholas, J. M. (1982). The comparative impact of organization development interventions on hard criteria measures. *Academy of Management Review, 7,* 531–542.

Nieva, V. F., Fleishman, E. A., & Reick, A. (1978). *Team dimensions: Their identity, their measurement and their relationships* (Contract No. DAHC19–78-C-0001). Washington, DC: Response Analysis Corporation.

Oser, R., McCallum, G. A., Salas, E., & Morgan, B. B., Jr. (1989). Toward a definition of teamwork: An analysis of critical team behaviors (NTSC Tech. Rep. 89–004). Orlando, FL: Naval Training Systems Center.

Pinchot, G., & Pinchot, E. (1993). *The end of bureaucracy and the rise of the intelligent organization.* San Francisco, CA: Berrett-Koehler.

Porras, J. I., & Berg, P. O. (1978). The impact of organizational development. *Academy of Management Review, 41*(2), 61–78.

Roethlisberger, F. J., & Dickson, W. J. (1939). *Management and the worker.* Cambridge, MA: Harvard University Press.

Salas, E., Dickinson, T. L., Converse, S. A., & Tannenbaum, S. I. (1992). Toward an understanding of team performance and training. In Swezey, R. W., & Salas, E. (Eds.), *Teams: Their training and performance* (pp. 3–29). Norwood, NJ: Ablex Publishing.

Salas, E., Prince, C., Cannon-Bowers, J., Baker, C., Smith, K., & Hall, J. (1991). *Skill training for teams: Ensuring success in interdependent tasks.* Workshop presented at the meeting of the Society for Industrial Organizational Psychology, St. Louis, MO.

Schneider, B., & Bartlett, C. J. (1968). Individual differences and organizational climate: I. The research plan and questionnaire development. *Personnel Psychology, 21,* 323–334.

Scholtes, P. R., with Joiner, B. L., Braswell, B., Finn, L., Hacquebord, H., Little, K., Reynard, S., Streibel, B., & Weiss, B. (1988). *The team handbook: How to use teams to improve quality.* Madison, WI: Joiner Associates.

Senge, P. M. (1990). *The fifth discipline: The art and practice of the learning organization.* New York: Doubleday/Currency.

Sims, H. P., & LaFollette, W. (1975). An assessment of the Litwin and Stringer organization climate questionnaire. *Personnel Psychology, 28,* 17–38.

Swezey, R. W., & Salas, E. (Eds.) (1992). *Teams: Their training and performance.* Norwood, NJ: Ablex.

Taguiri, R. (1966). *Comments on organizational climate.* Paper presented at a conference on organizational climate, Foundation for Research on Human Behavior, Ann Arbor, MI.

Tajfel, H. (1969). Social and cultural factors in perception. In G. Lindzey & E. Aronson (Eds.), *The handbook of social psychology* (2nd ed.). Reading, MA: Addison-Wesley.

Terpstra, D. E. (1981). Relationship between methodological rigor and reported outcomes in organization development evaluation research. *Journal of Applied Psychology, 66,* 541–543.

Tregoe, B. B., Zimmerman, J. W., Smith, R. A., & Tobia, P. M. (1989). *Vision in action: Putting a winning strategy to work.* New York: Simon and Schuster.

Trist, E. L., & Bamforth, K. W. (1951). Some social and psychological consequences of the long-wall method of coal getting. *Human Relations, 4,* 3–38.

Trist, E. L., Susman, G. I., & Brown, G. R. (1977). An experiment in autonomous working in an American underground coal mine. *Human Relations, 30,* 201–236.

Tuckman, B. W. (1965). Developmental sequences in small groups. *Psychological Bulletin, 63,* 384–399.

Tuckman, B. W., & Jensen, M. (1977). Stages of small group development revisited. *Group and Organizational Studies, 2,* 419–427.

Watson, K. M. (1982). An analysis of communication patterns: A method for discriminating leader and subordinate roles. *Academy of Management Journal, 25,* 107–120.

Weber, M. (1946). *Essays in sociology* (Trans. H. H. Gerth & C. W. Mills). Oxford, England: Oxford University Press.

Weber, M. (1947). *The theory of social and economic organization.* Oxford, England: Oxford University Press.

Weisbord, M. (1976). Organizational diagnosis: Six places to look for trouble with or without a theory. *Group and Organizational Studies, 1*(4), 1–8.

White, S., & Mitchell, T. (1979). Job enrichment versus social cues. *Journal of Applied Psychology, 64,* 1–9.

Wilson Learning Corporation. (1989). The Innovator: Challenging people to think. *Learning Age, 2,* 1. [Newsletter]. Eden Prairie, MN: Author.

Zajone, R. B. (1965). Social facilitation. *Science, 149,* 269–274.

International Perspectives

Chapter Outline

A British supervisor of a bridge-building project in Nigeria was shocked and confused when his team of Nigerian workers refused to continue the project. The problem started when he encouraged them to pick their own leader. He had known that his work team was a mixture of several tribes, but he did not suspect that tribal rivalry would be so significant that competition between the tribes for a leadership role would bring work on the bridge to a halt (Miller, 1994, p. 215).

Today, the world seems smaller than ever. Year by year, there are more and more international trade and communications. The speed with which events can be reported has never been faster. In fact, with news services such as CNN, events on the other side of the world are reported as they happen. Computer networking now includes the Internet with its easy access to worldwide resources. We are becoming what has been described as a "global village." This rapid access to other countries and cultures is also changing the ways we look at and conduct business. Included in these changes are major questions about I/O psychology and its theories about how management and leadership work.

Until recently, it was assumed that the organizational and management theories used in North America had universal applicability. MBA programs that were developed in other countries were often based on those in use in the United States. Organizational theories and processes sometimes were applied without consideration for the country or culture in which they originated or those in which they were used. Large multinational firms implemented corporatewide policies in locations around the world with little adaptation other than language translation. Through the years, psychologists and managers have learned the importance of completing a **back translation,** that is, translating something from one language to another and then having a different translator translate it back into the original language. This process has helped to ensure accurate translation of ideas rather than simply the translation of the words. Procedures such as back-translation improve the cross-cultural applicability of I/O theories and processes.

CRITERIA FOR CROSS-CULTURAL RESEARCH

I/O psychologists are becoming more aware of the impact of different cultures on the application of the core principles derived from our research. In the 1994 edition of the *Handbook of Industrial and Organizational Psychology,* Triandis noted (1994, p. 105):

Northwestern Europe and North America have been the centers of industrial development; more than 90 percent of the studies in industrial and organizational psychology have used data from these regions of the world. However, demographically speaking, such samples represent no greater than 15 percent of the world's population. Furthermore, it is a part of the world that highly values individualism. Individualism is a characteristic value structure of the European and, even more so, North American traditions. It is a philosophy that assumes that individuals have the right to "do their own thing," regardless of the needs or goals of family members, co-workers, fellow citizens, and other collectives, provided that what individuals do does not hurt others. As a result, contemporary psychological theories

underestimate the importance of groups, cultures, and other human-made entities outside of the individual. . . . While most [American] psychology reflects individualistic values and points of view, the majority of the people in the world (at least 70%) are socialized in collectivist cultures. Thus, the contrast between individualism and collectivism must be understood if psychology is to become a universal science.

These insights are also influencing the way organizations plan for the development of managers in the move toward globalization. Practice Perspective 16.1 summarizes one recent example of such a development plan. In this example,

PRACTICE PERSPECTIVE 16.1

Globalization as a Mindset

When Allen-Bradley made the decision to "globalize," it identified two key outcomes defining what that would mean for the company. These were: globalization is a mindset, and AB will be globalized when all the decisions of the company are made in the context of the global market.

To accomplish these objectives, AB decided that it would be necessary for all its managers and professionals to become globally aware. Defining this further, the company applied an adaptation of the 80/20 rule. Global awareness would be achieved when 80% of AB professionals and managers were "aware" and when 20% of the professionals and managers were "experienced."

To achieve global awareness for the 80% group AB committed itself to: (1) on-going training and development, at least one training or development experience each year directed specifically toward international and global awareness, (2) foreign language training encouraged for all employees, (3) continuous and "unrelenting" communication of globalization, and (4) including globalization objectives in each manager's annual objectives.

For the 20% group targeted to be considered "experienced," AB committed itself to: each year

having 5% of all professional and managerial positions filled by non-local nationals, hiring 5% of all new college employees non-locally nationally, and making rotating assignments such that 20% of all AB professionals and managers will have had significant experiences (2 + years) in international assignments. To support this last objective, the company committed itself to providing a safety net for expatriates. AB did not want people on international assignments to be "out of sight, out of mind." Each expatriate was assigned a home country mentor as well as an in-country mentor. The company established significant perks to encourage and support international assignments. Finally, it worked to counter the stereotypic assignment of returning expatriates to the "international" division. One element in this was reviewing all expatriates with the company's high potential managers once each year.

Source: From *Using human resource management to drive globalization.* Paper presented at the meeting of Division II of the Wisconsin Psychological Association, January, 1993, by W. J. Henderson. Milwaukee, WI: W. J. Henderson. Copyright 1993 by W. J. Henderson. Reprinted with permission.

a successful U.S. company, Allen-Bradley, examined its worldwide presence and realized that it had become a global company. Allen-Bradley then committed itself to changing its culture and U.S. mindset to be more supportive of its new business environment.

More than management recognition and planning is needed, however, for businesses to be successful globally. I/O psychology is currently contributing new internationally focused research to support globalization. We have learned that many factors need to be considered. Some are broad, general factors that appear to be present in all cultures. For example, Daab (1991) noted that in all societies the upper classes are more individualistic than the other societal classes; men are more individualistic than women; and residents of large, complex cities are more individualistic than people who live in simple rural environments.

There are also specific factors that illuminate subtleties within cultures. Triandis (1994) noted that even within individualistic cultures there are people who are more or less **idiocentric,** that is, they place their personal goals above the goals of their ingroups. We all know people who think first and foremost of themselves. Within U.S. culture these often are high achievers who set challenging personal goals that exceed those of the group in which they participate and who dedicate themselves to achieving those goals. In some situations, these are individuals who will be perceived as self-promoting; in other situations they may be called "stars" or "fast-trackers."

There are individuals who are **allocentric,** that is, they give more weight to the goals of their ingroups than to their own personal goals. These individuals may be particularly effective in teams. In the United States, we often describe such individuals as "team players." They are people who are good at building consensus and helping the group to commit to important company objectives. They may be group leaders in a formal sense or emergent leaders in informal groups.

Unfortunately,

> Inattention to social systems in organizations has led researchers to underestimate the importance of culture—shared norms, values, and assumptions—in how organizations function. Concepts for understanding culture in organizations have value only when they derive from observation of real behavior in organizations, when they make sense or organizational data, and when they are definable enough to generate further study. (Schein, 1996, p. 229)

Extending these insights and organizing the cultural information theoretically, Triandis (1994, p. 108) suggests that

> it is helpful to conceptualize *individuals* as belonging to different cultures, groups, organizations, and so on; *situations* as evoking different kinds of *behavior*; and a variety of constructs (such as habits, attitudes, and values) as linking consistencies in situations with consistencies in behavior. If individuals are grouped according to culture so that the within-group variance [differences between people from the same culture] on the constructs of interest is smaller than the between-groups variance [differences between people from different cultures], then culture has a useful role as an explanatory variable.

Cultural Syndromes

To make this a useful process, Triandis (1994) proposes that we identify cultural syndromes that distinguish one culture from another. **Cultural syndromes** are patterns of beliefs, attitudes, norms, values, and a characteristic self-concept that are associated with a particular culture.

Systematically linking cultural variables to behavior, Triandis (1977, 1980) developed a model that states that the probability of an act is a function of habits and behavioral intentions, moderated by facilitating conditions. The elements of culture enter his model in terms of how the behavior is defined, what is associated with the behavior, the form it takes, and the content of the various components. We will examine the major components of Triandis' model.

Behavioral intentions are self-instructions to do something. Three components play a part. The first, **social intention,** includes norms, roles, the person's self-concept, and interpersonal agreements. To illustrate, if I am an unskilled craftsperson and I decide to commit myself seriously to studying to prepare for an apprenticeship examination, I do so after considering the people I work with and how they will react. I also consider my family, my friends, how I feel about myself, the task of completing the necessary schooling, and any agreements I have with others (such as sharing child care with my spouse).

The second component of the model is **affective intention.** It includes emotions created by thoughts of the action. In our example, I might be proud of the encouragement and support of my fellow workers, yet be worried about the demands on my life and time, including my ability to be successful. I might also worry about my spouse's reaction and support.

The third component addresses the **consequences of actions.** It describes the personal usefulness of my actions defined as the sum of the products of the probability that each consequence will occur times the value of the consequence to me. In our example, as a craftsperson, I might conceptualize my choice of whether to study for the apprenticeship exam as a formal decision-making process. I could list all of the consequences I expect to occur, from having increased babysitting expenses, to cutting back on my bowling. Once I had the list completed, I could evaluate each outcome in terms of its value to me. Outcomes are rated on a point scale ranging from 1 to 100, higher scores corresponding to items of higher value. Then I could rate each outcome in terms of how likely it would be that the outcome would actually happen. This could be done simply by estimating the probability of occurrence and using that number as a decimal rating of likelihood. By mul-

tiplying these two ratings, I could calculate a consequence score for each outcome. A maximum value (100) times a maximum likelihood (1.0) would yield the maximum consequence score of 100. Adding all of the consequence scores would give me an overall score to use in evaluating my decision. The higher the total consequence score, the more likely it is that studying for the apprenticeship exam will be worth the effort for me in achieving outcomes that are important to me. If by doing these calculations I come up with an overall consequence score of 450 in favor of studying for my apprenticeship exam and a score of 675 in favor of not studying for it, I can conclude that my best decision is not to study for the exam.

Research has shown that in collectivist cultures (Hofstede, 1980a) the social component plays a greater role and has a larger weight (see Davidson, Jaccard, Triandis, Morales, and Diaz-Guerrero, 1976). For example, teams in Japan are notorious for taking a long time to reach decisions. One part of the reason is that in Japan individuals defer to the group to such an extent that it is uncomfortable for them to raise even important issues. In an effort to address this cultural reluctance to make critical comments, some Japanese companies have defined special meeting formats in which such criticism is encouraged and supported.

In individualistic cultures in which hedonism is respectable, the weight for the affective component is larger. In the United States, people are often encouraged to share their feelings about major issues facing the work team. There is a danger that, while such teams can reach a decision quickly, loud or emotional individuals will unduly influence the decision. This influence can cause serious problems.

There are factors that are not under the control of individuals. Classified as **facilitating conditions,** these are included as a component of Triandis's model. Facilitating conditions include physiological states such as arousal, ability, task difficulty, and the geographical location in which the behavior takes place, including the general cultural environment (Triandis, 1994).

Seeking Global Paradigms

Another way we can improve the application of I/O theories cross-culturally is to assume that the theories will be used globally. This means that we must abandon the simplistic view that the United States is a model for the rest of the world. We need to design studies with a clear expectation that the results will be applied internationally. Ten years ago, in a landmark review and position paper examining the pace of contemporary world development and the implications that had for research, Roberts and Boyacigiller (1984, p. 424) concluded it was "imperative for the social science of organizations to mature." To advance social science research, Roberts and Boyacigiller suggested eight criteria for cross-cultural organizational research. They argued that not all of their criteria can be met in every study, but that studies can overlap and support one another. Their criteria are as follows (Roberts and Boyacigiller (1984, pp. 428–432):

1. A good paradigm will either specify a definition of culture or replace it with a set of measurable variables. These variables together reflect potentially important factors in a cultural setting that affect organizations in that society.

2. An adequate paradigm will integrate multidisciplinary views of organizations in any single research project and/or in reviews of existing research.

3. Good research in this area will reflect agreement about sets of variables that should be studied.

4. An adequate paradigm will reflect agreement about appropriate strategies or methodologies for conducting research.

5. All organizational research needs to reduce reliance on rationalistic views of organizations.

6. Adequately designed cross-national organizational research will include the role of history.

7. Time must be accounted for in all organizational research.

8. Studies should build on one another so that a world view of organizations emerges.

The "Big Macs"

Roberts and Boyacigiller used their criteria to evaluate five major cross-cultural studies, which they identified as the **"Big Macs"** (multiattribute cultural studies). They found all these studies deficient in one way or another. Several failed to meet their own stated goals, either because the links between their constructs and their investigations were weak, or because their combinations of data and their analyses were so convoluted that the meanings were lost. Other studies exhibited weak conceptualizations and poor linkages from concepts to operations. Another severe problem was the way in which measures were obtained, aggregated, and analyzed. Finally, Roberts and Boyacigiller felt that the "Big Macs" failed to take advantage of the strengths of the basic social science disciplines from which the research questions originally emerged. Roberts and Boyacigiller identified three major problems that need to be addressed, which are more important in cross-national research than in single-nation research. These problems are as follows (Roberts and Boyacigiller, 1984, p. 462):

1. The tendency of cross-national research to focus specifically on environments in which organizations exist. This is often not true of single-nation organizational research.

2. The introduction of serious time problems. Time is used differently in different cultures. Researchers usually compound this problem by failing to specify theories of time underlying their work, gathering data over randomly se-

lected intervals, and measuring and relating variables over different time intervals.

3. Static studies that cannot assess the permeability of organizations by their environments.

The Peterson Study

A major cross-cultural study (Peterson, Smith, Akande, Ayestaran, Bochner, Callan, Cho, Jesuino, D'Amorim, Francois, Hofmann, Koopman, Leung, Lim, Mortazavi, Munene, Radford, Ropo, Savage, Setiadi, Sinha, Sorenson, & Viedge, 1995) demonstrates how carefully designed studies can provide meaningful insights. The Peterson et al. study examined role conflict, ambiguity, and overload reported by middle managers in twenty-one countries. Overload is a feeling of being overburdened by work events or the way the job is structured. The scores were related to national scores on **power distance** (the extent to which members of a culture accept inequality and perceive distance between those with power and those with little power), **individualism** (the extent to which people emphasize personal or group goals), **uncertainty avoidance** (the extent to which people accept or avoid uncertainty and the stress they feel as a result), and **masculinity** (the extent to which there is strong differentiation by sex). To achieve accurate, comparable measurement, Peterson et al. adapted earlier existing role stress scales and assessed the equivalence of those scales using factor analysis.

Peterson's collaborators all were experienced social researchers. Their role stress questionnaire was translated from English into each of twenty target languages by the collaborators or competent bilinguals under their supervision. These were checked by independent back-translations or parallel translations. The structure of the original role stress measures was evaluated on the data from each country to extract three factors: conflict, ambiguity, and overload. The results indicated that these factors were not measured in the same way by the different instruments in the different cultures. The consequence of this finding was that the researchers made the decision to reconstruct the measures.

Exploratory factor analysis on the results from each country identified items that formed reliable scales and gave similar factor structures across countries. Items that operated differently in different countries were eliminated. Next, three groups of countries (English, European languages, and all non-European languages) were examined. The results indicated that the thirteen role stress items retained their meaning in all countries. The role overload items had the most consistent factor structures, and the role conflict items the least consistent structures. Overall, the values of the fit indexes compared favorably to those found in the confirmatory factor analysis of the U.S. samples.

The Peterson et al. study found that role stress varies substantially more by country than by demographic and organizational factors. **Role stress** was defined as physiological stress created by the work role and the structure of the work role. The results showed greater differences in the stress that managers felt based on the country where the manager was located than based on demographic categories (e.g., level of management, age, and years as manager), the size of the organization, or the type of manufacturing done. There were some relationships that they expected to find but did not. For example, average role stress was not associated with high uncertainty avoidance, and role stress was not linked to masculinity. **Role overload** is the manager's feeling of not being able to cope with the demands of work events and the expectations connected with his or her role in the organization. Managers from countries where inequality and distance between managers and workers are accepted reported greater role overload than did managers from countries where inequality and distance between managers and workers are minor. This finding suggests that reducing ambiguity through establishing and supporting a hierarchy or standard operating rules can come at the cost of overload for the manager.

....

CULTURAL INFLUENCES

The Peterson et al. study demonstrates how important it is to consider divergent cultural influences in investigating or applying I/O principles internationally. In his recent review of cross-cultural industrial psychology, Triandis (1994) identified a number of ways in which culture influences behavior and the study of behavior in work environments in different countries. Some of the key influences are discussed next.

Culture and Perception/Cognition

The languages of separate cultures differ in the ways in which they allow people to categorize their experiences. Triandis (1994, p. 118) notes that "as far as we know, people in all cultures use the same cognitive processes . . . but the content of the categories, schemata, and values is different."

Triandis indicates that languages differ in the ways they allow people to categorize their experiences. Each culture groups together with a common term some experiences and stimuli that are observably distinct. For example, U.S. culture has one word for snow, while Inuit culture is said to have many words describing different types of snow. Categorization is one difference of significance in studying cultures. Another is the ways various cultures organize and link the categories they define. This process of organizing and linking creates the value structure and other schemas that are unique to a given culture.

There are two ways of organizing and linking. *Association* is made by informally linking functional relationships between psychological characteristics with the groups or categories that are used to identify and group the people in the culture. For example, in the United States

we associate a number of typical behaviors such as checking attendance, assigning work, checking quality, and mediating disputes with members of a group we call "supervisors." In contrast, *logical linking* is made by formally connecting the functional relationships with the groups or categories. For example, we can formally categorize someone by identifying who the person is in terms of sex, age, race, religion, tribe, ingroup, outgroup, or gang membership.

Triandis also observes that cultures vary in the specificity of the cognitive frameworks they use. Some cultures form *coherent-unitary cognitive frameworks*. These are cultural frameworks that are tightly tied together by a single supportive cultural and cognitive theme. For a long time in the United States there was such a cultural theme in the workplace. It was often referred to as "the Protestant work ethic." Tightly tied to it were themes of dedication to the job, hard work, pride in work well done, and job satisfaction stemming from productivity.

In contrast, there are cultures that use *differentiated-specific cognitive frameworks*. These are cultural frameworks that have distinctive, individually specific subgroups within the broader defined groups. For example, the current Chinese culture does not recognize the kind of hierarchy in supervision that is typical in the United States. A Chinese "worker" can be a worker, a first-level supervisor, a foreperson, or even a manager. In China, it is important to be explicit in communications because other communicators cannot rely on the cultural framework to fill in the gaps.

In **associative cultures,** people base communications on their own associations. They assume that the people with whom they are communicating use the same associations. In contrast, people in **abstractive cultures** tend to be much more explicit, defining terms and stating the implications of their communications.

The example that Triandis gives is that in all cultures the category "good supervisor" is associated with the category "considerate." But what it means to be considerate differs from culture to culture. A supervisor who talks with associates about a subordinate's personal problems when the person is absent is judged to be inconsiderate in Britain and the United States. That same behavior is judged to be considerate in the associative cultures of Hong Kong and Japan. In these associative cultures, people are concerned with saving face. Direct criticism is seen as inconsiderate, while indirect criticism is perceived as considerate.

Attributions

Studies sampling various cultures have found differences in the beliefs about the causes of some behaviors. Chandler, Shama, Wolf, and Planchard (1981) compared attributions for success and failure in India, Japan, South Africa, the United States, and Yugoslavia. Although there were many similarities, the Japanese used effort and luck to explain success more frequently than did the other countries. Kashima and Triandis (1986) found a Japanese sample that used luck and a U.S. sample that used ability to explain success. Smith and Whitehead (1984) found that U.S. students used ability and effort to explain promotions and demotions, whereas Indian students used matrimony, influence of friends, and corruption.

Intelligence

The concept of intelligence is interpreted variously by different cultures. In the United States, intelligence is associated with being quick, sharp, and correct; in Africa, it is associated with being able to behave correctly. In rural Africa an intelligent person is one who understands the situation in a manner that facilitates his or her responses. This can mean knowing another tribe's customs as well as those of one's own tribe, at least to the extent that doing so allows one to get along and avoid major social transgressions. As the education level of Africans increases, so does their use of an intelligence construct similar to the quick, sharp, and correct model standard in the United States (Price-Williams, 1985).

Cognitive Frames

Some cultures exercise coherent unitary frameworks for information processing (e.g., religious, spiritual, and political); other cultures apply differentiated-specific frameworks incorporating only the facts that are useful. For example, in Africa samples of sophisticated people use both scientific and spiritual explanations for events (e.g., Jahoda, 1969). Astrology is often used as a guide for business decisions in South and East Asia (Triandis, 1994).

Communication

Okabe (1983) studied U.S. and Japanese communication patterns and found that there are differences in both process and content. The U.S. sample used analysis, starting with what was said, and voting to resolve differences of opinion. Language conventions included "I–you," "yes," and "terrific." The Japanese sample used synthesis, intuition, concern for what was agreed, and how things were said. Participants worked toward consensus. The language used by the Japanese was group focused with terms such as "we," "maybe," "perhaps," and "slightly."

Culture and Norms

Exploring the variations among perceptions of correct behavior in specific situations is another way of understanding cultures. Mudd (1968) concluded that the severity with which a cultural group judges a deviation in behavior from that group's norm is a function of the degree of the deviation and the relevance of the norm. To illustrate, consider the simple gesture of waving good-bye to someone. In the United States we use the whole hand. In Niger this is an insulting gesture. In Belgium, Canada, Cyprus, Honduras, Hungary, Japan, and Malawi it means "stop." Waving good-bye in Canada is likely to be forgiven as ignorance of Canadian custom. Canadians will probably know that this does not mean "stop" and will overlook it as a minor mistake. They might even wave back, just to be friendly. In Niger, such behavior is regarded as a serious transgression of the cultural norm. A return wave will not be meant as friendly.

Culture and Motives

Klineberg (1954) studied the dependability of motives. He defined **highly dependable motives** as any motives that are physiological, universal, and exhibited by lower animals as well as humans. Klineberg thought that few motives were dependable. For example, in Maslow's hierarchy (Maslow, 1943), self-actualization was the ideal motive in individualistic cultures, while service to the group was the highest motive in collectivist cultures. In Maslow's terms, the highly dependable motives were the more basic ones.

Research evidence (Aram & Piraino, 1978; Hofstede, 1983; Nevis, 1983) suggests that humans can shift the importance of **less dependable motives.** For example, various cultures are likely to view different motives as being highest in their hierarchy. In the United States, esteem needs are high in the hierarchy; in Japan, love needs (the individual's desire to be accepted by others) are high. These findings indicate that Maslow's theory is culturally bound to the United States and similar cultures.

Culture and Values

Values differ in their level of abstraction. At a low level of specificity, the values are focused, feeling-oriented, and behavioral. For example, a person's attitude toward his or her job at a low level of abstraction could be that the job is in a "hot" area in which there will be many opportunities, that he or she likes the job, and that he or she is going to perform well on the job. At a high level of abstraction, values become more important, but the specificity is lower. For example, the value that equality is good can be strongly held, yet there are many goals and behaviors that can be seen or interpreted as consistent with that value (Triandis, 1994).

DIMENSIONS OF CULTURAL VARIATION

A number of theoretical frameworks have been developed to help understand cultural influences in the world of work. Within these models, about twenty key dimensions have been identified as being representative of cultural syndromes and showing potential as bases for further investigations. Triandis (1994, p. 133) believes that using

> dimensions of cultural variation, and using dimensions of value-difference, in particular, to classify empirical findings, and utilizing such dimensions as parameters of organizational theories (Triandis, 1982) seems desirable.

If I am working in a country where collectivism is an important value (the dimension of value difference), then my theory should tell me that my management style should emphasize teamwork, cooperation, consensus decision making, trust, and interdependence. Triandis would like us to be able to be even more specific as we develop our theories using dimensions of cultural variation. Going a step further, he believes that, "If we study the interactions of culture and personality with behavior, we will gain a deeper understanding of culture" (Triandis, 1994, p. 133).

Hofstede (1991) has also conducted major cross-cultural work. In one study, he analyzed 116,000 surveys completed by individuals from over sixty countries. All these people were IBM employees matched by occupation, age, and sex. Hofstede identified five possible dimensions of cultural variation in values. His five dimensions were power distance, uncertainty avoidance, individualism, masculinity, and truth versus virtue.

Power Distance

Power distance is the extent to which members of a culture accept inequality and whether they perceive much distance between people who have power (e.g., top management) and those who have little power (e.g., hourly workers). High-power-distance countries are the Philippines, Mexico, and Venezuela; low-power-distance countries are Austria, Israel, and Denmark. The United States is a relatively low-power-distance country.

Recent research efforts are finding power distance to be a very useful concept. Peterson et al. (1995) found power distance to be closely linked to the role conflict, role ambiguity, and role overload reported by middle managers from twenty-one countries. Perlaki (1994) studied power distance differences between Eastern European countries and the United States. He found fundamental differences between the social development of Eastern European culture and U.S. culture. For successful organizational development in Eastern European countries, Perlaki warns that interventions must be compatible with the culture and that we should be building a culture-specific organizational development theory.

Uncertainty Avoidance

Uncertainty avoidance is the extent to which there is an emphasis on ritual behavior, rules, and stable employment. The highest scores on this dimension are obtained in Greece, Portugal, Belgium, and Japan; the lowest scores are obtained in Singapore, Denmark, Sweden, and Hong Kong. The United States is low on this dimension.

Individualism

Individualism is the extent to which people emphasize personal or group goals. This is similar to the individualism versus collectivism concept (Triandis, McCusker, & Hui, 1990). Hofstede found that the most collectivistic countries are Venezuela, Colombia, and Pakistan; the most individualistic countries are the English-speaking countries including, at the top, the United States.

One area in which individualism is evident is the communication patterns of a given culture. Erez (1992) observed that the pattern of communication in Japanese corporations is shaped by the cultural values of traditional Japanese society. The low level of individualism has two important consequences: On the motivational level, sharing of common values makes for better consensus and commitment to those values; on the cognitive level, sharing of knowledge, ideas, and information enhances the level of productivity and innovation. Individualism has also been used to understand the resistance to affirmative action by some U.S. managers. Ozawa, Crosby, and Crosby (1996) illustrated that their Japanese sample was more collectivistic than their U.S. sample and that the Japanese endorsed an affirmative action solution more strongly than the Americans.

Masculinity

Masculinity is the extent to which societies differentiate primarily by sexual roles. Masculine societies emphasize job advancement; feminine societies emphasize quality of life. Hofstede found that the most masculine countries were Japan, Austria, and Venezuela; the most feminine were Sweden, Norway, and the Netherlands.

Truth versus Virtue

Truth versus virtue is the extent to which people in a culture emphasize empirical evidence ("truth") or moral excellence and beliefs ("virtue"). In the United States, the culture favors data and evaluates people's performance and worth on the basis of objective (or seemingly objective) measures. In Tibet, a high value is placed on belief, and while there are some signals that people have devoted themselves to their beliefs, these are not readily measured.

Recognizing cultural variations and using them are two very distinct skills. Even as some I/O psychologists are developing skills in recognizing and categorizing dimensions of variation such as power distance, uncertainty avoidance, individualism, masculinity, and truth versus virtue, other I/O psychologists are working to apply this knowledge in practice. One area in which the understanding of cultural variations is helpful is management practices.

Important Cross-Cultural Management Practices

In reviewing Hofstede's work, Triandis (1994) concluded that the most valuable conclusions drawn concerning managerial practices included the following:

- Self-interest is less valid in high-power-distance, low-individualism countries.
- Psychological theories based on self-actualization are less valid in low-individualism countries.
- The employer–employee relationship is calculative (based on the circumstances) in high-individualism countries and moral (based on cultural norms) in low-individualism countries.
- Task has a higher priority than relationship in high-individualism countries.
- Family involvement (nepotism) is acceptable in low-individualism countries.
- Harmony is more important in low-individualism countries.
- Paternalistic management is acceptable in high-power-distance countries.
- Status differences are more accepted in high-power-distance countries.

- Older individuals are more respected in high-power-distance countries.
- Channels for handling grievances are found only in low-power-distance countries.
- Management by objectives, the managerial grid, theory Y, and theory Z (which combines emphasis on production with emphasis on people) management styles do not work well in high-power-distance countries.
- Appraisal systems require low-power-distance, high-individualism cultures.
- High-masculinity cultures have a need for formal rules.
- Planning is more popular in low-uncertainty-avoidance countries.
- Time is more important in high-uncertainty-avoidance countries.
- Emotional expression is tolerated under certain conditions in high-uncertainty-avoidance countries.
- There is less tolerance for deviance in high-uncertainty-avoidance countries.
- High-masculinity countries emphasize competitiveness, equity, and sympathy for the strong.
- High-femininity countries emphasize solidarity, equality, and sympathy for the weak.
- Achievement motivation is high in high-masculinity countries and low in low-uncertainty-avoidance countries.
- A machismo style of management is acceptable in high-power-distance and high-masculinity cultures.
- Job differentiation according to sex role is rigid in high-masculinity cultures.

On the basis of these and other findings from his research, Hofstede (1980b) suggested that current theories of motivation, leadership, organization, and the current belief in the generality of quality of life values all need revision. In addition, he believes that his framework provides a basis for comparing and organizing other studies.

Nemetz and Christensen (1996) examined the value of using fundamental cultural beliefs to predict participants' reactions to diversity-training programs. They theorized that "ideal states of multiculturalism" can be defined and predicted by measuring individual beliefs on culturally selected polar opposites. Using such measures can help trainers to avoid negative reactions from participants in diversity-training programs. There is a growing body of research demonstrating that frameworks such as Hofstede's can be helpful in selecting and preparing people for work in "foreign" cultures.

SELECTION AND TRAINING

Most multinational or transnational companies provide some training or orientation for employees being sent to another country. This can include language training, orientation to the culture, business and economic principles, travel procedures, and health precautions. In most cases, however, there is not sufficient cross-cultural training to ensure that expatriates truly understand the cultures they are entering and that they will be able to function effectively in those cultures.

Cross-cultural problems are also experienced when people who have been working as expatriates return home after spending years in another country and culture. Essentially, what happens is that they learn the culture of the new country while forgetting their home country's culture or missing its evolution. Global companies experience special problems when they bring expatriates home. In these situations, it is also important to add updates on elements of the corporate culture to the equation because, just as the country's culture has evolved while the expatriate was gone, so has that of the corporation.

After studying the effects of expatriation, Mendenhall and Oddou (1985) identified four dimensions that they believe are important in employee selection and training for overseas work. These are self-orientation, other orientation, accurate perception, and cultural toughness.

Self-Orientation

Self-orientation is the expatriate's ability to substitute reinforcements provided in the new culture for those lost in the home culture because of the move. Self-orientation also includes the person's abilities to reduce stress and demonstrate technical competence. This can be a significant challenge in moving from individualistic cultures to collectivist cultures and vice versa. In the former, a more activist role often is judged to be the more professional and is how a person makes certain his or her ideas are heard and incorporated. In contrast, collectivist cultures judge this behavior to be disruptive and less productive. Many people do not find this kind of behavioral shift easy to make.

Other Orientation

Other orientation is the expatriate's ability to develop friendships, language skills, a positive attitude toward the host culture, and a desire to relate to that culture. It has been common for expatriates to congregate in limited, defined community groups in their host countries. These "ghettos" are, in a real sense, protective, becoming the expatriate's home away from home. When this tendency is taken to excess, an expatriate might avoid most contact with the host country's culture. There would still be situations in which contact with people from the host country would be unavoidable. The risk would be that the expatriate's lack of awareness could turn such contacts into negative experiences.

Accurate Perception

Accurate perception describes the expatriate's ability to make attributions about the behavior of the host that are fairly similar to those that the host makes about his or her own behavior. Included in this dimension are characteristics such as being nonjudgmental, having a high tolerance for ambiguity, and using broad categories in thinking about events. This is an expatriate's ability to put himself or herself in the host's shoes. It is understanding the host culture at a level that includes acceptance of behavior different from that in the expatriate's home country.

Cultural Toughness

Cultural toughness is the situation in which expatriates are more focused on getting obedience to their orders and their beliefs than on adapting to the host culture. The more insistent the expatriate, the greater is the distance that he or she is likely to experience from members of the host culture. Cultural toughness makes acceptance by the host difficult and increases the probability of a premature return home. A U.S. expatriate who steadfastly believes that the U.S. way is the only way will have difficulty winning acceptance in many situations. The stereotype of the "ugly American" stems from this pattern of thinking and behaving.

PRACTICAL APPLICATIONS OF CROSS-CULTURAL RESEARCH

To be truly successful in working across cultures requires an understanding of the cultures. Globalization of business has driven a number of research efforts that are designed to build the basic knowledge and understanding needed for practical applications such as communications and management. We will now review some research on cultural differences and influences.

Cultural Influences on Groups

The process of bridging two diverse cultures is referred to as **transculturation.** One of the objectives of transculturation is to assign culturally appropriate meanings to words, actions, proverbs, and concepts. A basic understanding

of these provides the foundation for a truer understanding of the other culture.

The most obvious example is that the same words mean different things in different cultures. Miller (1979, p. 44) cites the following example:

> To give a person a "Mickey" in the U.S. means that the person has been given knockout drops or some immobilizing drug. In England, giving a "Mickey" means you are joking ("pulling the person's leg"—another descriptive phase that would not be understood by many cultures).

The hardest ideas to communicate are abstract ones. A good example is the word *family*. The concept of what constitutes a family varies considerably from culture to culture. The hardest adjustment in transculturation is recognizing that when one uses an abstract term, such as *family,* there may be no common understanding among the cultures as to its meaning. For example, in the Chinese family the father's authority is absolute, as is his responsibility for the family welfare. The Japanese father's role is less omnipotent. Japanese fathers can admit uncertainty, share their family responsibilities, and share power with the mother. In the United States, there is often equality in the relationship between the father and the mother, although there may be some tendency for the father to give more of the task- and work-related guidance while the mother gives personal and supportive guidance. To bridge this gap, it becomes necessary to use active listening skills, and to ask many questions to test whether the person to whom you are talking understands your true meaning.

In the United States and many European cultures, the content of the message is usually explicit and to the point. In other cultures, such as Japan, China, and Iran, less information is contained in the verbal portion of the message. More of the meaning is in the context and the expression. The importance of understanding such subtleties can be illustrated by the process of

SCIENTIFIC PERSPECTIVE 16.1

Methodology for Distinguishing Culture from Personality

D'Andrade (see Shweder & LeVine, 1984) defined items of human learning as culture or personality depending on how they are positioned within a system of relationships and processes. For culture, the human learning involves adaptation to the environment; for personality, the learning is related to establishing consistency with the individual's motivational system.

Triandis, Bontempo, Leung, and Hui (1990) devised a method for defining and measuring D'Andrade's concept. They used groups of three people from the same language/time/place group (in Illinois or Hong Kong) and presented them with value-related stimuli selected as elements of either culture or personality. They timed the interval between the presentation of the stimulus and the point at which the small group was able to reach consensus that the value was important or unimportant.

They found a clear, systematic relationship between latency and values consensus. For some of the values, almost all of the three-person groups reached consensus in less than 6 seconds. For other values, consensus was more difficult, sometimes taking over 60 seconds. Because culture requires sharing of values, long response times imply that the elements requiring them are not cultural. Triandis et al. found that it was possible, using their methodology, to separate cultural differences from individual (personality) differences.

In Hong Kong, "persistence" was an extremely high value (all the triads agreed, with a mean time to consensus of 2.1 seconds). In Illinois, "opportunism" was a high value (all triads agreed, with a mean time to consensus of 4.2 seconds). An interesting contrast was the finding that the value "to have a high monthly income that allows me to live just the way I want to live" was considered unimportant by half the triads in both cultures. As a result this was judged to be a personality element, not a cultural one.

business contracting. In cultures such as Japan, China, and Iran, a person accepts responsibility for what has been agreed on without needing formal or legal contracts. Americans, who often do not understand this, may complain that the person they are doing business with never "gets to the point." They mean that this person is never specific about the contractual details the American wants to "get wrapped up." An American-style detailed specification of the business agreement seems impossible to obtain. Unfortunately, the detailed specification that the American wants is considered "too much explanation" in Japan, China, and Iran. For people in these countries it implies that the other person cannot think for himself or herself; this is considered an insult. An American businessperson who presses for a "normal" contractual agreement may be insulting the Asian customer out of cultural ignorance.

Researching cultural differences, as distinct from personality differences, has presented some significant challenges. One creative attempt is described in Scientific Perspective 16.1.

As a quick reference guide to significant cultural differences, Miller (1979) provides the chart in Figure 16.1 on page 572, which classifies eleven cultures, and rates them from high to low context.

Valuable guidance for companies on how to work with expatriates has emerged from I/O cross-cultural work. Triandis (1994) summarizes several fundamental areas of cross-cultural research that are relevant in selecting and training

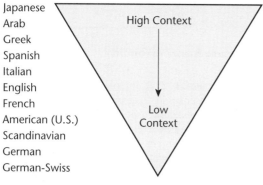

Japanese
Arab
Greek
Spanish
Italian
English
French
American (U.S.)
Scandinavian
German
German-Swiss

High Context

Low
Context

FIGURE 16.1   Cultural classification chart.

Source: From *The Guidebook for International Trainers in Business and Industry* (p. 45), by V. A. Miller, 1979. New York: Van Nostrand Reinhold Co. Copyright 1979 by The American Society for Training and Development, Madison, WI. Reprinted with permission.

people to work as expatriates. The areas that he identified and his conclusions include the following:

Leadership and group behavior are similar across cultures, but with shifts in emphasis. A principal finding is that leaders who are rated highly on production and/or performance (P) and maintenance (M) behaviors are rated as better by their subordinates than are leaders with different combinations of performance and maintenance behaviors. While the specific behaviors that define performance and maintenance vary across cultures, the impact of exhibiting the appropriate behaviors is consistently associated with leadership effectiveness. A leader who wants to be effective needs to ask, "For this cultural group, what do I need to do to be viewed as performance-oriented and a considerate leader?"

This is not an easy question to answer. The complexity and importance of cultural influences on leadership can be seen in the diverse ways in which nonverbal cues and actions are used. For example, in most cultures, when a leader moves his or her head from side to side, it is a nonverbal indication of disagreement; in India, it is a nonverbal indication that the person is in agreement. Practice Perspective 16.2 gives examples of gestures and actions that, while acceptable in one country, can be insulting in another. Such references can be invaluable to world travelers and to expatriates who have only a short time to prepare for their moves. Wise organizations will provide sufficient training to prepare individuals for such moves.

PRACTICE PERSPECTIVE 16.2

Table of Cultural Behaviors

Country	At a Meeting	Hands	Other Gestures
Argentina	Maintain eye contact.	Avoid gesticulation.	People generally stand close, sometimes finger a lapel or touch a shoulder.
Australia	Stand erect and use hands modestly.	A raised thumb with a clenched fist is a vulgar gesture.	Winking at women is improper.
Austria	Use a formal tone of voice.	Avoid talking with hands in pockets.	Do not chew gum during visits or in meetings.

PRACTICE PERSPECTIVE 16.2

Table of Cultural Behaviors *(continued)*

Country	At a Meeting	Hands	Other Gestures
Belgium	Posture is important.	Avoid snapping fingers or putting hands in pockets.	Touching another person while conversing is not as common as in other parts of Europe. Slapping the open palm over a cupped fist while snapping fingers is an obscene gesture.
Bolivia	Speak in a formal tone; maintain eye contact.	Fingers waved with hands down is a beckoning sign for children.	Use hands, eyes, and facial expressions to communicate. Patting on the shoulder is a sign of friendship.
Brazil	Use a formal tone of voice.	Avoid the U.S. "OK" sign; it has a vulgar meaning (substitute thumbs up).	Slapping the open palm over a cupped fist while snapping fingers is an obscene gesture.
Canada	Always direct remarks to the entire group.	Avoid gestures that use fingers.	A finger pointed to the side of the head indicates insanity. Do not stare into a woman's eyes.
Chile	Speak in a friendly, soft tone. Maintain eye contact. A story or joke is acceptable.	Avoid hand gestures; only waiters are beckoned with hand gestures.	Sit upright in a chair.
Colombia	Avoid discussions about politics.	People beckon others with the palm downward, waving the fingers or the whole hand.	Do not go barefoot. Do not put feet on furniture.
Costa Rica	Eye contact is not very important in speaking to groups.	When eating, both hands should be kept on the table.	Avoid clenched fist with thumb protruding between index and middle finger.
Ecuador	Avoid political references. Avoid moving the feet.	Avoid excessive hand movement.	It is best not to use the head to answer yes or no. Touching another person of the same sex is acceptable and shows friendly concern.

(continued)

PRACTICE PERSPECTIVE 16.2

Table of Cultural Behaviors (continued)

Country	At a Meeting	Hands	Other Gestures
El Salvador	Eye contact is important.	Natives use hands and head extensively to express feelings.	Do not point the fingers or feet at anyone. Only close friends are beckoned with a hand wave.
England	Avoid political references. A confidential, intimate, concerned mood gets best results. Start meetings on time.	Use hand gestures sparingly.	Extravagant gestures such as back slapping and arms around the shoulders should be avoided.
Fiji	Eye contact is appropriate when speaking to someone, but otherwise may be considered offensive. Folding the arms when talking to someone shows respect.	People are called by waving the whole hand, palm down.	It was once considered discourteous to touch a person's head, but this is changing.
Finland	The speaker stands erect. Avoid excessive joking. Look a person in the eyes when speaking.	Avoid excessive gestures.	Folding the arms is a sign of arrogance or pride.
France	Keep your hands out of your pockets while talking. Avoid political subjects.	The sign that means "OK" to Americans means zero to the French. Thumbs up is the French sign for "OK."	Snapping the fingers of both hands and slapping the palm over a closed fist have vulgar meanings.
Germany	Have a well-organized speech. Examples are not generally used to describe situations.	Keeping your hands in your pockets while talking is disrespectful.	Chewing gum is not appropriate during business meetings. Do not rest your feet on any desk, chair, or table.
Indonesia	Some people arrive late for meetings and appointments, but you should always be on time.	Do not use gestures to call someone unless it is a child or a *becak* driver. People generally do not put their hands in their pockets. It is disrespectful to give something with the left hand.	Even if he knows her well, a man does not touch a woman in public except to shake hands. It is not acceptable for foreigners to kiss in public.

PRACTICE PERSPECTIVE 16.2

Table of Cultural Behaviors *(continued)*

Country	At a Meeting	Hands	Other Gestures
Iran	Gestures are commonly used when talking. Make no reference to local females. Do not even hint at making fun of local customs.	Touching a woman may arouse suspicion or jealousy. Do not give something with the left hand; use the left hand as little as possible.	Putting an arm around a man's shoulder is a sign of affection. People tend to get very close and breathe on you when conversing.
Israel	One can be informal. Avoid general statements; be correct and selective in word usage. Converse in a low key.	It is acceptable to use gestures.	Good friends pat each other on the back or shoulder.
Italy	Begin meetings on time. Avoid references to your own culture.	It is best to gesture with one hand.	Shrugging the shoulders means "I don't care" or "I don't know." Persons of both sexes walk arm in arm with the same sex.
Japan	Posture is important while sitting or standing. Reserve and modesty are emphasized.	To beckon someone, the palm is turned down and the hand waved. The American "OK" sign is a symbol for money.	Erect posture while sitting with both feet on the floor is advisable.
Korea	Dark glasses (and often regular prescription glasses) are removed while talking.	Use both hands when handing something to another person.	Proper posture while sitting or standing is emphasized.
Lebanon	A few jokes are appropriate to arouse audience interest.	A handshake is appropriate on business occasions, usually accompanied by a slight nod of the head.	Gestures are used freely. Persons conversing with each other stand closer to each other than in the U.S.
Malaysia	Punctuality is expected.	Use two hands when giving or receiving gifts.	For beckoning people, the palm of the hand should be turned down and the whole hand waved downward.

(continued)

PRACTICE PERSPECTIVE 16.2

Table of Cultural Behaviors *(continued)*

Country	At a Meeting	Hands	Other Gestures
Mexico	Do not have excessive concern about time and schedules. Do not be condescending or too aggressive. Avoid political topics.	An animal's height is shown with the palm held flat. A person's height is shown with a raised index finger.	Beckon others with a downward waving motion of the palm. Keep both hands above the table when eating.
Netherlands	Close eye contact and facial expressions are important.	Signaling someone with the hands is normal practice. It is acceptable to wave to someone from a distance.	It is not customary to touch when talking to someone. Chewing gum or standing with your hands in your pockets is improper.
New Zealand	Meetings are expected to begin on time, but don't be surprised if they do not. New Zealanders have retained much of the characteristic reserve of the British.	Shaking hands is acceptable but not as popular as in the U.S. It is acceptable to wave to someone from a distance.	The American hitchhiking sign with the fist clenched and thumb horizontal and pointing in the direction of travel is considered vulgar.
Norway	Punctuality is important. All anecdotes should be universal and not related to America.	Normally, the handshake is used in formal situations or to show respect.	Physical contact is avoided in public.
Panama	You can expect scheduled meetings to begin about half an hour late. Don't state an exact time for the meeting to end. Eye contact is important.	Do not use the American "OK" sign. Waving the hands palm up motions a person to "come here."	Holding the arm low and bouncing the palm up is an impolite gesture. A nod and an *abrazo* are common greetings among friends; a handshake is appropriate for business meetings.
Paraguay	Promptness is often expected of North American visitors. Compliments about personality are given freely and expressively.	To beckon someone, the index finger is moved back and forth with the palm up; however, this is an intimate gesture. It is usually best to call a person's name.	Signs made with crossed fingers may be offensive. The "OK" sign should never be used.

PRACTICE PERSPECTIVE 16.2

Table of Cultural Behaviors *(continued)*

Country	At a Meeting	Hands	Other Gestures
Peru	It is best for a visitor to be prompt, even if others are not. Eye contact is important.	Taxis may be stopped by waving the hand. To beckon a person, the fingers are waved with the palm downward.	People stand close to converse, maintaining constant eye contact. Both men and women shake hands when departing.
The Philippines	One should not criticize a person or an institution, even jokingly; Filipinos may criticize each other but do not like outside criticism.	The everyday greeting for men and women friends is a handshake.	Most American customs are acceptable.
Portugal	Meetings are usually well organized and formal; the Portuguese do not stress punctuality in meetings, but a visitor should be prompt.	A warm, firm handshake is the best greeting. To call someone, extend the arm with palm down and wave the fingers.	The Portuguese do not use many gestures.
Samoa	Samoans take everything said quite literally. The authority of the speaker is important. Samoans often answer the way they think the other person expects them to answer. Samoans prize eloquent speech. Never refer to animals in talks.	Common American gesturing is not appropriate.	It is considered crude to stretch the legs in the presence of other people. Swaying from side to side indicates contempt.
Scotland	The speaker should perform in a rather formal manner. Do not discuss politics.	Use hand gestures sparingly.	The American hitch-hiking sign is a vulgar gesture in Scotland.

(continued)

PRACTICE PERSPECTIVE 16.2

Table of Cultural Behaviors *(continued)*

Country	At a Meeting	Hands	Other Gestures
Singapore	There is considerable English influence.	The handshake is the most common form of greeting, with the addition of a slight bow for orientals. Hitting the fist in the cupped hand is poor taste.	Avoid touching another person's head. Feet should not be pointed at anyone.
South Africa	Punctuality is expected. Stand erect when speaking. Avoid political topics.	Avoid making the "V" sign with the first two fingers. Avoid placing the thumb between the first two fingers.	Do not talk with your hands in your pockets.
Spain	Meetings start on time; a tie and jacket are customary dress at meetings. The Spanish feel it is their duty to correct errors as they see them.	To beckon someone, the fingers are waved with the palm down. Hands should not be concealed in pockets. In restaurants, waiters are called by raising the hand.	Arm and head gestures unique to Spanish culture are common.
Sweden	Maintain an erect posture. Keep gestures to a minimum. Eye contact is important. Swedes are proper and exact. Punctuality is important.	Hands should not be put in pockets.	Avoid excessive gestures.
Switzerland	Meetings should always start on time. A relaxed but composed posture is best.	A handshake is appropriate for both men and women.	Sitting sloppily shows bad manners.
Thailand	Before starting, there should be informal small talk or compliments on the country. Thais are reserved people. Do not speak loudly or show anger. Criticism of others is in poor taste. People have a habit of being late for meetings.	Most men shake hands; women do not. The traditional Thai greeting is a *wai*; the hands are placed together in a prayer position at the chest; the higher the hands are placed, the more respect is shown. People usually bow when making the *wai*; the lower the bow, the more respect.	Do not touch a person's head or pass objects over it. Never put your feet up on a desk or table where they would be pointing at another person's head.

Table of Cultural Behaviors (continued)

Country	At a Meeting	Hands	Other Gestures
U.S.	Meetings usually start on time; they sometimes last longer than scheduled, but no one is offended if an exact time is set for the meeting to end.	The thumb and forefinger together to form a circle, with the other three fingers extended, means "ok" or "all is right." Hands are used freely when speaking.	Americans are not "touch" people; extremely close contact is usually avoided.
Uruguay	Punctuality is not important. Meetings are expected to be well organized and formal. It is best not to mention politics or communism.	A firm handshake is the most common form of greeting.	Use the fork in the left hand when eating. Feet should be on the floor, not elevated.
Venezuela	Maintain continual eye contact.	A handshake is used.	Erect posture in chairs is advisable.

Source: From *The Guidebook for International Trainers in Business and Industry* (pp. 46–51), by V. A. Miller, 1979. New York: Van Nostrand Reinhold Co. Copyright 1979 by The American Society for Training and Development, Madison, WI. Reprinted with permission.

Organizational Cultures

Current research has emphasized the concept of culture more than that of climate. Although there have been a number of studies of culture, most have used definitions that are too abstract to be particularly helpful. Schneider's (1988) hypothesis that the organizational culture must be consistent with the national culture if the organization is to function well, has been an influential one. Schneider found this consistency to be important for the acceptance and implementation of most human resources practices such as career planning, performance appraisal, and compensation. One Milwaukee-based company recently opened a new plant in China. After one team did an outstanding job of increasing pro-

ductivity and quality, management decided to recognize and reward that team with jackets displaying the company logo. In collectivist China, this was not well received by the other workers. In only a matter of hours, the U.S. manager was approached by a delegation of workers who indicated that singling out this one team was highly inappropriate. To keep the peace and to make amends, the U.S. management team had to present jackets to all the workers in the plant.

Management

While management practices vary from organization to organization, there are similarities across organizations within the same country. Triandis (1994, p. 147) concluded that

> Japanese success seems related to collectivism and may be inspired by Confucian ethics. Collectivists commit themselves to in-groups for a long time, and it takes time to change ingroups, join ingroups, or change ingroup-outgroup perspectives.

Unfortunately, the existing data also indicate significant variations across organizations within the same country. For example, Erez (1986), working in Israel with first-level supervisors, found that the collectivism of a kibbutz was higher than that of a public or private organization. Triandis cites this example as a reason to be skeptical about linking management practices too closely to a national setting.

A different approach that has paid some dividends examines management values. Historical Perspective 16.1 describes an early international study by Haire, Ghiselli, and Porter (1966) that found differences between the beliefs and practices of managers. They also found that it is possible to cluster countries into cultural groups with similar responses.

Employee Control

Workers who feel that they are in control of their environment are likely to feel satisfied with their lives and work. Those who do not feel in control are likely to feel dissatisfied or even depressed. Marrow, Bowers, and Seashore (1967) described an example of a U.S. company doing business in Puerto Rico. The company decided to shift from the traditional directive style of management to a more participative approach. As soon as the managers started using the participative methods, many of their Puerto Rican employees quit. Exit interviews helped the company to discover that it had destroyed the workers' perceptions of management's competence. In effect, the workers thought, "If they have to ask us how to run this plant, they can't be that good." The workers quit to go to "better managed" plants where there was clear direction and authority.

In summarizing research on the sense of control one feels over one's work environment and its impact on motivation, we can see that culture is only one of many relevant variables. Because so many variables influence the impact of employee control, it does not appear to be a particularly helpful area for cross-cultural research.

HISTORICAL PERSPECTIVE 16.1

Gap between Management Beliefs and Practices

Haire, Ghiselli, and Porter (1966) surveyed 3,600 managers in fourteen countries. Their results identified a gap between the managers' beliefs about employees' capacity for initiative and leadership and the same managers' beliefs about participative management. The majority of managers who were surveyed believed in sharing information and encouraging subordinates to participate in the management process, but they also believed that the average individual preferred to be directed and wished to avoid responsibility.

In one of the first attempts to identify similarities in management beliefs in different countries, Haire, Ghiselli, and Porter also found that developing and traditional countries clustered together in managerial preferences and styles of behavior. The cultural clusters they identified included: Anglo-American, Latin or South European, North European, and Japanese.

Job Design

In 1980, Hackman and Oldham developed a theory of job design proposing that worker satisfaction increases with more variety, task identity, and feedback. This theory has been supported by research in Western countries (Karoly, 1982) and the Far East (Birnbaum, Farh, & Wong, 1986). In South Africa, however, it has been found only in Westernized samples (Orpen, 1983). In the design of jobs it is important to consider several types of matches: "the *skills* of the worker must match the *challenge* of the job . . . [and] . . . the *needs* of the worker must match the *values* of the culture that can be satisfied by the job" (Triandis, 1994, p. 154).

Organizational Development

Internationally, organizational development (OD) work has often focused on changing organizational cultures. This is in contrast to the more typical goal of organizational development, the creation of a new environment or culture that is defined through a consensus of the members. When culture is imposed, there are usually objections from most people.

By necessity, OD work across cultures is complex. Zeira and Adler (1980) developed a model for OD in which the parameters were described by a cube. One facet was the viewpoints of the parent culture, the second facet was the human components, and the third facet was the attributes of the environment.

A company that is planning OD work needs to consider who from the host country is participating, the social and economic factors related to the change, and the current state of the environment. In short, OD work has to be culture-specific.

Organizational Conflict

In organizational conflict situations, I/O psychology has identified some general patterns. For example, bargaining conducted by a desig-

nated representative leads to more rigid bargaining behavior than bargaining conducted by individuals who represent themselves (Davis & Triandis, 1970; Holmes, Ellard, & Lamm, 1985). There are also a large number of culture-specific patterns (e.g., that Japanese managers generally trust Americans who request mutual referral to a special problem-solving team for the resolution of disputes rather than Americans who propose binding arbitration). However, in his 1994 review, Triandis doubts that there will be consistent patterns between specific cultural patterns and optimal conflict resolution techniques.

The information and studies we have reviewed indicate that I/O psychology is developing an understanding of cultural differences. However, there is much work yet to be done. For example, there is no commonly accepted definition of the term *culture*. It is a fact, however, that a major economic evolution is under way. This is creating a global economic and sociopolitical system that is much different from that which has existed in even the recent past. Psychologists, particularly I/O psychologists, are likely to play an important role in helping businesses and organizations develop perspectives and approaches that will significantly extend our current understanding of work world behaviors and events. The research available to us today can help with some current problems and adjustments, but more important, it points to areas in which more investigation is needed. Next we will examine some specific applications of I/O psychology in Europe and Asia.

EUROPEAN INDUSTRIAL/ ORGANIZATIONAL PSYCHOLOGY

C. Lévy-Leboyer reviewed selection and assessment practices in Europe for Volume 4 of the *Handbook of Industrial and Organizational Psychology* (1994). In his chapter, he reported the results of several surveys of methods used for

| TABLE 16.1 | Table of management selection practices in Europe |

| | Survey | | | | |
Method	Bruchon-Schweitzer (1989: France) N = 102	Smith (1990; United Kingdom) N = 40	Beavan & Fryatt (1987; United Kingdom) N = 293	Schuler (1990; Germany) N = 88	Abramsen (1990; Norway) N= 61
Interviews	99	100	95	37	93
References	—	—	78	9	—
Vitae, application forms	—	—	91	90	—
Situational tests, work samples	7	—	32	16	—
Personality questionnaires	35	10	9	6	16
Cognitive & aptitude tests	31	5	5	15	25
Projective techniques	12	—	—	—	—
Assessment centers	—	10	—	9	3
Biodata	—	3	—	6	1
Graphology	93	2	5	6	2
Other methods*	15	0	—	—	1

Note: Figures represent the percentage of respondents who say they use the method.
—Indicates the question was not used in the survey.
*Other methods include astrology and morphopsychology.
Dates indicate when the survey was conducted, not published.

managerial selection in different European countries. His results are summarized in Table 16.1.

Lévy-Leboyer's data enable us to identify common trends and national differences. Use of interviews and analysis of resumes and/or of application forms are dominant everywhere. In contrast, references are widely used in the United Kingdom but less in Germany and even less in France, perhaps because French companies are reluctant to prepare or share written assessments about people who have worked with them.

Tests are used differently in the various countries. In the United States, situational tests and assessment centers have developed rapidly. These are also found in the United Kingdom, Germany, and the Netherlands. Personality, cognitive, and aptitude tests are used more frequently in France and Belgium than in Germany or the United Kingdom. The variations between the use of tests in Germany and in France are striking. Also, France uses graphology (handwriting analysis) widely, even though the low validity of this approach is known. Two reasons are given for the popularity of graphology in France: It is accepted by the applicants, and it is inexpensive. One does not need to personally see an applicant to use graphology; a handwritten letter of application is sufficient (Lévy-Leboyer, 1994).

Method	Survey			
	Lievens (1989; Belgium) N = 89	de Witte et al. (1991; Flanders) N = 53	Mabey SHL (1989; United Kingdom) N = 300	SHE (1992; France) N = 48
Interviews	100	98	100	90
References	73	59	—	—
Vitae, application forms	91	—	—	86
Situational tests, work samples	51	37	37	8
Personality questionnaires	42	63	47	39
Cognitive & aptitude tests	71	74	66	31
Projective techniques	42	6	—	6
Assessment centers	31	—	—	9
Biodata	—	—	—	—
Graphology	36	7	3	46
Other methods*	2	—	—	—

Source: Modified and reproduced by special permission of the Publisher, Consulting Psychologists Press, Inc., Palo Alto, CA 94303 from *Handbook of Industrial and Organizational Psychology, Volume 4*, by Harry C. Triandis, Marvin D. Dunnette, and Leaetta M. Hough. Copyright 1994 by Consulting Psychologists Press, Inc. All rights reserved. Further reproduction is prohibited without the Publisher's written consent.

While Lévy-Leboyer found that diverse methods are exercised in various European countries in dealing with different categories of people, he also found three broad patterns related to organizational size:

1. Large organizations often have personnel departments with at least one qualified psychologist.
2. Small organizations have a person in charge of personnel, but that person typically does not have training in psychology.
3. Some consulting firms have psychologists on staff; others do not.

Overall, Lévy-Leboyer found European work psychologists to be more concerned than U.S. psychologists about the need to protect individual privacy. The perception in Europe is that selection is a participative process that requires the involvement of both the individual and the organization. Also, there is greater emphasis on the overall management of the selection process. This leads to the European addition of **social validity** (Schuler, 1993) to the traditional U.S. predictive and content validity concerns. Social validity considers what is good for both the individual and the organization. Another important distinction is the fact that unemployment has long been an issue in Europe. The unemployment rate has been, and is, much higher in most European countries than in the United States.

In their article "Semantic Confusion and Attitudes to Work: Its Effect on Our Understanding of the Workplace," Toulson and Smith (1991) expressed concern that in talking and writing about attitudes, people often use different terminology. Because the definitions that are chosen are often culturally specific, Toulson and Smith believe that much of the work conducted in the area of job attitudes may not apply across nations. They propose "semantic integration and assimilation into national frameworks" (Toulson and Smith, 1991, p. 55). An example of such a framework that will advance international research is that of Buchholz (1976, 1977). As described in Table 16.2, the five dimensions defined in **Buchholz's Belief System** have been used in a number of cross-cultural studies.

Studies using Buchholz's framework with international populations have found the following (Dickson, 1982, 1983):

- A strong preference for the humanistic belief system and a rejection of both Marxist and work ethic systems in the United States (Buchholz, 1977).
- A strong commitment to the Marxist belief system among Iraqi managers (Ali and Schaupp, 1985).
- An inverse relationship between work ethic and representative participation, a positive relationship between humanistic beliefs and both representative and direct participation, and a positive relationship between Marxist beliefs and representative participation.

Toulson and Smith believe that Buchholz's conceptualization provides an imperfect but excellent starting point for developing a clear conceptual basis for discussion about work values and beliefs.

ASIAN INDUSTRIAL/ ORGANIZATIONAL PSYCHOLOGY

East Asia is usually thought of as including China, Japan, South Korea, Taiwan, Hong Kong, and Singapore. However, China and North Korea are difficult to represent adequately because of the lack of research and the strong state ideologies there. Redding, Norman, and Schlander (1994) reviewed individual attachment to organizations and noted that most cross-cultural work has focused on Japan. Studies that they found and reviewed examined whether the key variables were universal or culture-specific and compared commitment levels across cultures.

Organizational Commitment

Marsh and Mannari (1977) studied organizational commitment in relation to turnover. They concluded that the variables associated with commitment were not culture-specific. Luthans, McCaul, and Dodd (1985) studied age and tenure, finding both positively related to commitment in U.S., Japanese, and Korean workers. Putti, Aryee, and Liang (1989) extended this conclusion to all the values and to Asia in general. These results were challenged by Lincoln, Hanada, and Olsen (1981), who found that Japanese and Japanese-American workers place more value on **organizational paternalism,** in which the company provides protection for and control of workers, than did U.S. workers. However, they found no differences in the level of personal ties to associates. Near (1989) found that social interaction, fairness, and job content influence commitment across cultures, but that freedom on the job was more important in the United States and age was more important in Japan.

These results indicate that much is still to be learned about the psychological influences in East Asian countries. It appears that some of the variables operate in culture-specific ways, while

TABLE 16.2   Buchholz's Belief System definitions: Five major belief systems about the nature of work that capture unique assumptions about this kind of human activity.

The work ethic: Work is good in itself and bestows dignity on a person. Everyone should work, and people who do not are not useful members of society. By working hard, a person can overcome every obstacle that life presents and make his or her own way in the world. Success is thus directly linked to one's own efforts, and the material wealth a person accumulates is a measure of how much effort he or she has expended. Wealth should be wisely invested to earn still greater returns and not foolishly spent on personal consumption. Thrift and frugality are virtues to be practiced in the use of one's material possessions. (Clark, 1966; Green, 1959; Samuelsson, 1957; Tawney, 1926; Weber, 1958. All as cited in Buchholz, 1977.)

The organizational belief system: Work takes on meaning only as it affects the group or the organization for which one works and as it contributes to one's status and the rise in the organizational hierarchy. Work is not so much an end in itself as a means that is valued only for how it serves group interests and contributes to one's success in the organization. But, this success is more dependent on the ability to get along and "play the game" than it is on individual productivity. (Galbraith, 1967; Goodman, 1968; Mills, 1951; Packard, 1962, Whyte, 1956. All as cited in Buchholz, 1977.)

Marxist-related beliefs: Productive activity or work is basic to human fulfillment. Without work, people cannot provide for their physical needs nor can they maintain contact with the deepest part of themselves. Through work, people create the world and themselves and keep in touch with their fellow human beings. As currently organized, however, work in this country does not allow people to fulfill themselves as creative and social individuals. The work of the average person mainly benefits the ownership classes of society rather than the work-

ers themselves. Workers are exploited and alienated from their productive activity. They should have more of a say as to what goes on in corporations and exercise more control over the workplace. (Bottomore, 1963; Caute, 1967; Fromm, 1966; Israel, 1971; Meszaros, 1970. All as cited in Buchholz, 1977.)

The humanistic belief system: Work is to be taken seriously as the way in which people discover and fulfill themselves as human beings. Thus individual growth and development on the job is more important than the output of the work process. What happens to people in the workplace is more important than productivity. Work must be redesigned to allow people to become fully human and reach higher stages of development than fulfillment of material or lower-order needs and wants. Work is an indispensable human activity that cannot be eliminated. Therefore, work must be made meaningful and fulfilling for individuals and allow them to discover their potential as human beings. (Fromm, 1941, 1955, 1968; Hampden-Turner, 1970; Maslow, 1954. All as cited in Buchholz, 1977.)

The leisure ethic: Work has no meaning in itself but finds meaning only in leisure. Jobs cannot be made meaningful or fulfilling, but work is a human necessity to produce goods and services and enable one to earn the money to buy them. Human fulfillment is found in leisure activities in which people have choices regarding the use of their time and can find pleasure in pursuing activities of interest to them personally. This is where people can be creative and involved. Thus the less hours people can spend working and the more leisure time they have available, the better. (Bell, 1970; De Grazia, 1962; Poor, 1970; Roberts, 1970; Smigel, 1963. All as cited in Buchholz, 1977.)

Source: From "The Belief Structure of Managers Relative to Work Concepts Measured by a Factor Analytic Model," by R. A. Buchholz, 1977, *Personnel Psychology, 30,* pp. 567–587. Copyright 1977 by Personnel Psychology. Reprinted with permission.

others do not. The trends are not clear. One serendipitous finding, however, is that there are some significant cultural biases that affect the traditional measurement approaches used by I/O psychologists. Redding et al. (1994) note that when questionnaires and Likert scales are used with Japanese subjects, a cultural bias is created by the Japanese hesitance to make personal claims. This includes statements of expressed satisfaction. Redding et al. extended this observation as one explanation for the contradictory results that are often found in cross-cultural studies. At the very least, findings such as this one challenge I/O psychologists to develop new methods which can be effective in cross-cultural application.

Alston (1989) provided a succinct summary of the influences that affect managers who are working to develop systems and exercise power in order to increase cooperation and productivity. Alston (1989, p. 26) noted:

> In Japan, business relations operate within the context of *wa,* which stresses group harmony and social cohesion. In China, business behavior revolves around *guanxi* or personal relations. For Korea, activities involve concern for *inhwa,* or harmony based on respect of hierarchical relationships, including obedience to authority.

Redding et al. (1994) summarized their review of Asian psychology by suggesting adjustments that they believe U.S. I/O psychologists need to make in applying organizational theory, motivation theory, and leadership theory. Because such adjustments are becoming crucial, we will examine Redding et al.'s suggestions in more detail.

Organizational Theory Adjustments

In examining the structure of organizations, a serious question needs to be asked: "Do the underlying logics of current Western organization theory cover the nature of East Asian organization well enough to do justice to understanding

its real nature?" (Redding et al., 1994, p. 680). Redding et al. believe that four organizational characteristics are inadequately explained by current Western organization theory (Redding et al., 1994, pp. 680–681):

- The hierarchical ordering of high-power-distance cultures that provides an invisible, informal, structure which influences the nature of hierarchical structuring we look for in other cultures.

- The influence of reciprocity norms on the achievement of cooperation between leaders and subordinates; this includes the fact that Western organization theory does not easily handle the structural implications of Oriental paternalism.

- The influence of varying definitions of the *collectivity* to which a person belongs, that exist in collectivist cultures, and (especially in cases where this is a work group) the way in which coordination and cooperation are influenced by these varying definitions.

- The influence of interorganizational networking and the informal but powerful coupling of organizations on the definition of organizational boundaries; the understanding of variations in the clarity/diffuseness of what the organization actually is.

Motivation Theory Adjustments

Redding et al. also suggest that U.S. motivational theory may have a biased design. They believe that current motivational theory, when applied cross-culturally, has difficulty explaining the following (Redding et al., 1994, p. 681):

- The maintenance of face and similar manifestations of interpersonal sensitivity that influences behavior [in Asia]

- At a deeper level, the power of social embeddedness in mediating the connections between an individual's stimulus and response pattern

- The significance of different need structures for appropriate organizational responses when the body of managerial tradition visible in the literature derives from the fostering of self-actualization

Leadership Theory Adjustments

Redding et al. (1994) state that the common U.S. model of leadership, which is "research-based, positivist, fairly micro-level," like that typified by the Ohio State Leadership studies, assumes that its logic can be applied universally. In contrast, they note that the Asian leader–subordinate relationship is influenced by cultural factors such as the following (Redding et al., 1994, p. 681):

- Dependence needs, especially in Japan, which tend to widen the scope of leader–subordinate interaction and also provide it with an imported subliminal structure
- Strongly developed patterns of role compliance, buttressed by societally defined notions of authority, which prestructure many vertical relationships
- Ethics of paternalism, which, in the Confucian schema, stress responsibility for subordinate welfare as a source of legitimacy for power holders and have consequent implications for the behavior of leaders and the responses of subordinates

In a major study of the generality of leadership style measures across cultures, Smith, Misumi, Tayeb, Peterson, and Bond (1989) found that the characterizations of P (performance) and M (maintenance) leadership style had similar factor structures in different cultures. In addition, they found that the specific behaviors associated with the two styles varied markedly across cultures. The behaviors for each leadership style were understandable within the cultural norms for each of their studies. This finding supports **Misumi's PM Leadership Theory.**

Misumi's theory was developed in Japan thirty years ago and has been extensively validated there. Misumi believes that leadership can be understood in terms of the general (universal) structure of the behaviors (the way the leader's behaviors are interpreted) and their specific expression, including their cultural context (Misumi, 1985; Misumi & Peterson, 1985). A skillful leader needs to express certain specific leadership behaviors but in ways that vary to fit the specific situation.

The Smith et al. (1989) study examined responses to a measure of leader style using behavioral ratings completed by the leader's direct reports. Data were collected in four cultures: Britain, the United States, Hong Kong, and Japan. Subjects were shop floor work teams and their immediate supervisors. These teams demonstrated values about leadership characterized by individualism and collectivism.

Both the P and M factors were supported by the study. Factor analysis across the four cultures supported the two-factor solution. The authors also found evidence that the behaviors, as rated on the questionnaires, clustered in a different way within each of the four cultures. The pattern, however, included a weak general factor as well as a number of individual items that did not load on any of the extracted factors. Finally, Smith et al. (1989) found significant ($P < .001$) correlations for eight behaviors with M and for four behaviors with P.

A high M supervisor is seen as one who responds sympathetically to team members' personal difficulties, spends time discussing careers and plans, and is more likely to accept suggestions for work improvement. A high P supervisor, in contrast, is one who talks about progress in relation to the work schedule, shares information, and stays available.

CULTURAL ADAPTATION

Adapting behavior to approximate that of another culture has often been suggested as a way for expatriate managers to increase their effectiveness. Thomas and Ravlin (1995) tested this suggestion in a design varying culturally adaptive behavior, the level of participants' schematic complexity, and the importance of nationality to self-identity as the independent variables. They concluded that "simply teaching members of different cultures to behave like each other is an inadequate approach to improving intercultural interactions in business settings" (Thomas and Ravlin, 1995, p. 142). They found that, rather than consistently positive or negative, the responses of the subordinates depend on the attribution they made for the manager's behavior. Adaptation by the Japanese manager to behavior typical of U.S. managers resulted in higher levels of perceived similarity, higher perceived managerial effectiveness, and lower levels of attribution to internal causes. However, the adaptive behavior itself was often attributed to causes external to the manager.

Erez's Cross-Cultural Model

Miriam Erez (1994) has proposed a cross-cultural model for industrial/organizational psychology. She uses culture as "an important contextual factor that moderates the effects of managerial practices and motivational techniques on employees' behavior" (p. 557). Erez's cross-cultural model defines four major factors:

1. Cultural values and norms. Using a cognitive framework, the model defines culture "as a set of mental programs that affect individual responses in a given context" (Hofstede, 1980a, p. 586). Individuals can regulate their own behavior to achieve goals by self-monitoring (paying attention to their own behavior), self-evaluation (comparing their own behavior to goals or standards), and self-reaction (rewarding or punishing themselves for the success of goal-directed behavior). Through these processes, the self bridges the gaps among culture, management practice, and individual behavior.

2. Types of managerial practices and motivational techniques. Information about both is processed by the individual self. Managerial

practices such as participation in goal setting, effective job design, quality control circles, and appropriate reward allocation are seen to make a positive contribution. These practices are more likely to be accepted and to have a positive effect on employee behavior.

3. The self-regulating, self-interpreting managerial practices. As a person's mental representation of his or her own personality, the self is formed by experience and thought in the physical and social world (Kihlstrom et al., 1988). Self-regulatory processes work to create and maintain a positive representation of the self (as in positive self-worth and self-esteem). While "the structural and dynamic dimensions of the self are considered to be universal, the relative differentiation between self and others varies across cultures" (Erez, 1994, pp. 577). People from the same culture are likely to have similar values and cognitive representations. In Western cultures, individualistic values are crucial; emphasis is placed on being independent, unique, and self-reliant. In Eastern cultures, collectivistic values are central; value is placed on group coordination, harmony, conformity, obedience, and reliability.

4. The employee's work behavior. According to Erez (1994, p. 580),

> Cross-cultural studies on work values, work motivation, and human resource management clearly demonstrate that there are significant differences among cultures in collectivistic versus individualistic values and in values of power distance, which is the psychological distance between levels in the organizational hierarchy (Hofstede, 1980b; Triandis, 1989; Triandis et al., 1988).

Managerial techniques that agree with individual values—individual job enrichment, individual goal setting, and individual incentives—emerge and become effective in individualistic cultures. In contrast, the management practices that correspond to collectivistic, group-oriented values—quality circles, autonomous work groups, group goals, and participation in goal setting and decision making—predominate in more collectivistic cultures such as those in Scandinavia, Japan, China, and Israel (Earley, 1989, 1995; Erez, 1986, 1994; Erez & Earley, 1987; Matsui, Kakuyama, & Onglatco, 1987).

Criteria for Successful Global Competitiveness: Intraorganization Relations

Beyond interorganization effectiveness issues are matters of intraorganization relations. In a global economy it becomes important for individuals and organizations to broaden their thinking beyond the home country focus most have been using. Zaheer (1995) suggests a number of ways of overcoming the issue of foreignness. Bolt (1988, pp. 36–40) described the criteria for organizations to be successful global competitors. These include the following:

- Perceive themselves as multinational, understand the implication for their business, and are led by management that is comfortable in the world arena.
- Develop an integrated and innovative global strategy that makes it very difficult and costly for other companies to compete.
- Aggressively and effectively implement their worldwide strategy, and back it with large investments.
- Understand that technological innovation is no longer confined to the United States and have developed systems for tapping technological innovation abroad.
- Operate as though the world were one large market, not a series of individual countries.
- Have developed an organizational structure that is well thought out and unique.
- Have a system that keeps them informed of political changes abroad and their implications for their business.
- Recognize the need to make their management team international and have a system in place to accomplish that goal.

- Give their outside directors an active role in the affairs of the company.
- Are well managed.

SUMMARY

Industrial-organizational psychologists are faced with new challenges as the world shrinks in response to our increasingly global business environment. This is causing I/O psychology to re-examine its theories about how management and leadership work. What was formerly a U.S. or North American perspective is being extended and adapted to fit cultures in other countries. This includes realizing that the individualistic bias typical of the U.S., North American, and European cultures is the exception in the world, rather than the rule. Many more countries exhibit collectivistic cultures than individualistic ones. This must be considered in any research or process that will be applied internationally.

Triandis has proposed furthering the process of internationalizing I/O research by identifying the specific cultural syndromes that govern work behavior. These are patterns of beliefs, attitudes, norms, values, and the characteristic self-concepts associated with particular cultures.

Three major problems often affect cross-national research: the tendency for the researcher to focus more specifically on the environment within which the organization exists, the failure to account for differences in the way time is used in various cultures, and the interplay between the organization and its cultural environment.

One important area in which research is assisting day-to-day practice is in the preparation and support of expatriates. In multinational companies, expatriates experience a variety of problems. Most obvious are those related to the orientation of the expatriate to the host country culture. A self-oriented expatriate can substitute reinforcements lost in the home culture with new ones found in the host culture. Other-oriented expatriates demonstrate the ability to develop friendships, language skills, and a positive attitude toward the host culture. Also important is the expatriate's ability to accurately perceive and make attributions about the behavior of people in the host country. An expatriate who is focused on giving orders and getting obedience to his or her beliefs is likely to experience resistance. Cultural toughness of this variety compromises transculturation efforts.

Another area in which cross-cultural study is helpful is employment practice. Companies that do business internationally can improve their selection processes by understanding what are the established practices in various countries. For example, in Europe and the United Kingdom, the use of interviews, resumes, and application forms is common. References are most important in the United Kingdom, less common in Germany, and least common in France. Even larger differences occur in the use of tests. In the United States, the testing tradition is well established with tests being common. There are also situational tests and assessment centers. These are found in the United Kingdom, Germany, and the Netherlands as well. Personality, cognitive, and aptitude tests are used more often in France and Belgium than in Germany. Overall, an important difference between Europe and the United States is the European addition of social validity to predictive and content validity concerns. Social validity views selection as a participative process involving both the individual and the organization focused on considering what is good for both.

In the East Asian countries there are many subtleties that affect business relations. It is helpful to the international businessperson to understand the underlying concepts that are dominant in certain Asian countries. In Japan, the concept is *wa,* which stresses group harmony and social cohesion. In China, the concept is *guanxi,* which stresses personal relations. In Korea, the concept is *inhwa,* which focuses on respect of hierarchical relationships and obedience to authority.

Eventually, I/O psychology will have internationally based theories of management and leadership. An example of one such management theory that is culturally robust is Misumi's PM Leadership Theory. Misumi believes that leadership can be understood in terms of the general structure of the behaviors and their specific expression, including their cultural context. He found that P (performance) and M (maintenance) leadership styles have similar impacts in different cultures. His conclusion is that a skillful leader needs to express certain specific leadership behaviors, but in ways that fit the specific immediate cultural situation.

It appears that one of the major challenges facing I/O psychology is the need to adapt, and in many cases replace, existing theories and models that have emerged from our traditional North American and European roots with new theories and models more appropriate to our worldwide business and organizational focus. While the research in this chapter indicates places where I/O psychologists have begun this effort, it is also clear that we have a long way to go.

KEY TERMS AND CONCEPTS

abstractive cultures	Buchholz's Belief System	idiocentric
accurate perception	consequences of actions	individualism
affective intention	cultural syndromes	inhwa
allocentric	cultural toughness	less dependable motives
associative cultures	Erez's cross-cultural model	masculinity
back translation	facilitating conditions	Misumi's PM Leadership Theory
behavioral intentions	guanxi	organizational paternalism
"Big Macs"	highly dependable motives	other orientation

power distance

role overload

role stress

self-orientation

social intention

social validity

transculturation

truth versus virtue

uncertainty avoidance

wa

RECOMMENDED READINGS

Bond, M. H., & Hwang, K. K. (1986). The social psychology of Chinese people. In M. H. Bond (Ed.), *The psychology of the Chinese people.* Hong Kong: Oxford University Press.

Hofstede, G. (1991). *Cultures and organizations: Software of the mind.* London: McGraw-Hill.

Landis, D., & Bhagat, R. S. (Eds.). (1996). *Handbook of intercultural training* (2nd ed.). Thousand Oaks, CA: Sage.

Miller, V. A. (1994). *The guidebook for global trainers.* Amherst, MA: Human Resource Development Press.

Misumi, J., & Peterson, M. F. (1985). The Performance–Maintenance (PM) theory of leadership: Review of a Japanese research program. *Administrative Science Quarterly, 30,* 198–223.

Smith, P. B., & Peterson, M. F. (1988). *Leadership, organizations and culture.* London: Sage.

Triandis, H. C., Dunnette, M. D., & Hough, L. M. (Eds.). (1994). *Handbook of industrial and organizational psychology* (2nd ed., Vol. 4). Palo Alto, CA: Consulting Psychologists Press.

Triandis, H. C., & Lambert, W. W. (Eds.). (1980). *Handbook of cross-cultural psychology.* Boston: Allyn & Bacon.

INTERNET RESOURCES

International Association for Cross-Cultural Psychology (IACCP)

> The home page of the International Association for Cross-Cultural Psychology, this site provides a description of the International Association for Cross-Cultural Psychology including its publications, IACCP membership information, subscription information, and lists of officers, congresses, and conferences.
>
> **http://www.fit.edu/CampusLife/clubsorg/iaccp/ index.html**

Journal of Cross-Cultural Psychology

> This site provides info on the Journal of Cross-Cultural Psychology, which is published by Sage Publications for the Center for Cross-Cultural Research, Department of Psychology, Western Washington University in affiliation with The International Association for Cross-Cultural Psychology. It includes back issues and submission guidelines.
>
> **http://www.fit.edu/CampusLife/clubsorg/iaccp/ JCCP/jccp.html**

Resources for Psychology and Cognitive Sciences on the Internet

> This Japanese site is a collection of pointers that are related to psychology and cognitive sciences. Valuable links include those to directories of psychology and cognitive sciences, electronic journals and papers, and international associations.
>
> **http://sasuke.shinshu-u.ac.jp/psych/**

Cog & Psy Sci: Organizations & Conferences

> This site provides a comprehensive listing of organizations and conferences. The other sections at this site are Academic Programs, Journals & Magazines, Usenet Newsgroups, Discussion Lists, Announcement/Distribution Lists, Publishers, Software, Miscellany Acknowledgements, and What's New.
>
> **http://matia.stanford.edu/cogsci/org.html**

Applied Psychology/Psicologia Aplicada

> A comprehensive European resource site on applied psychology provided by the Dpto. Psicologia Diferencial y del Trabajo, Dpt. of Individual Dif-

ferences and Work Psychology. Among other things it provides links to the International Association of Applied Psychology, European Network of Work & Organizational Psychologists, Contem- porary Applied Psychology in Spain, WWW Pages of Psychology in Spain, and the Spanish Profes- sional Psychological Associations.

http://www.ucm.es/OTROS/Psyap/

EXERCISE

Exercise 16.1

Planning a Transition to Being an International Company

Assume that you are the director of training for a U.S. company that has recently acquired new plants in Japan and Germany. The president of your company has communicated a new vision for your now inter- national company. She sees the organization as a truly international one in which the products and ser- vices will be delivered globally to achieve economies of scale. She also recognizes that the products must remain competitive in the company's home markets.

Concerned that the local cultures may continue to dominate in the acquisitions, the president has de- cided to begin a major program to change the norms in the three plants from the current home-country focus to one that will be more international. As part of her vision, she sees managers in any location ulti- mately being interchangeable.

Rather than make the mistakes that other compa- nies have made in not preparing managers for expa- triate assignments, your president has asked you to assemble a team to design a training and develop- ment process which will prepare the company's man- agers for the new mindset and to function effectively in any plant. She has given you a one-year time frame in which to accomplish this objective.

Put together a team of four to six other students. Using what you know and any additional informa- tion you can uncover, develop the plan for your com- pany. You have been asked to plan for the following:

Communications

Recruiting of new managers and employees

Qualification and promotion of employees in part based on "international awareness"

Preparation for international assignments

Using international assignments as developmental ex- periences

General professional and management training

When you have finished your plan, prepare to present it and to offer supportive explanations to the president and other key managers in your company.

REFERENCES

Ali, A., & Schaupp, D. (1985). Iraqi managers' be- liefs about work. *The Journal of Social Psychol- ogy, 125*(2), 253–259.

Alston, J. P. (1989, March–April). *Wa, Guanxi,* and *Inhwa:* Managerial principles in Japan, China, and Korea. *Business Horizons*, 26–31.

Aram, J., & Piraino, T. (1978). The hierarchy of needs theory: An evaluation in Chile. *Interamerican Journal of Psychology, 12*, 179–188.

Birnbaum, P. H., Farh, J., & Wong, G. Y. Y. (1986). The job characteristics model in Hong Kong. *Journal of Applied Psychology, 71*, 598–605.

Bolt, J. (1988, January–February). Global competi- tors: Some criteria for success. *Business Horizons*, 34–41.

Buchholz, R. A. (1976). Measurement of beliefs. *Human Relations, 29*(12), 1177–1188.

Buchholz, R. A. (1977). The belief structure of man- agers relative to work concepts measured by a fac- tor analytic model. *Personnel Psychology, 30*, 567– 587.

Chandler, T. A., Shama, D. D., Wolf, F. M., & - Planchard, S. K. (1981). Multiattributional caus- ality for social affiliation across five cross- nation samples. *Journal of Psychology, 107*, 219– 229.

Daab, W. Z. (1991, July). *Changing perspectives on individualism.* Paper presented at the meeting of the International Society of Political Psychology, Helsinki.

Davidson, A. R., Jaccard, J. J., Triandis, H. C., Morales, M. L., & Diaz-Guerrero, R. (1976). Cross-cultural model testing: Toward a solution of the etic-emic dilemma. *International Journal of Psychology, 11,* 1–13.

Davis, E. E., & Triandis, H. C. (1970). An experimental study of white-black negotiations. *Journal of Applied Social Psychology, 1,* 240–262.

Dickson, J. W. (1982). Top managers' beliefs and rationales for participation. *Human Relations, 35*(3), 203–217.

Dickson, J. W. (1983). Beliefs about work and rationales for participation. *Human Relations, 36*(10), 911–932.

Earley, P. C. (1989). Social loafing and collectivism: A comparison of the United States and the People's Republic of China. *Administrative Science Quarterly, 34,* 565–581.

Earley, P. C. (1995). International and intercultural research: What's next? *The Academy of Management Journal, 38,* 327–340.

Erez, M. (1986). The congruence of goal setting strategies with socio-cultural values, and its effect on performance. *Journal of Management, 12,* 588–592.

Erez, M. (1992). Interpersonal communication systems in organisations, and their relationships to cultural values, productivity, and innovation: The case of Japanese corporations. *Applied Psychology, An International Review, 41*(1), 43–64.

Erez, M. (1994). Toward a model of cross-cultural industrial and organizational psychology. In Triandis, H. C., M. D. Dunnette, & L. M. Hough (Eds.), *Handbook of industrial and organizational psychology* (2nd ed., Vol. 2, pp. 559–607). Palo Alto, CA: Consulting Psychologists Press.

Erez, M., & Earley, P. C. (1987). Comparative analysis of goal-setting strategies across cultures. *Journal of Applied Psychology, 72,* 658–665.

Hackman, J. R., & Oldham, G. R. (1980). *Work redesign.* Reading, MA: Addison-Wesley.

Haire, M., Ghiselli, E. E., & Porter, L. W. (1966). *Managerial thinking: An international study.* New York: Wiley.

Hofstede, G. (1980a). *Culture's consequences: International differences in work related values.* Beverly Hills, CA: Academic Press.

Hofstede, G. (1980b) Motivation, leadership and organization: Do American theories apply abroad? *Organizational Dynamics, 8,* 42–63.

Hofstede, G. (1983). The cultural relativity of organizational practices and theories. *Journal of International Business Studies, 14,* 75–89.

Hofstede, G. (1991). *Cultures and organizations: Software of the mind.* London: McGraw-Hill.

Holmes, J. G., Ellard, J. H., & Lamm, H. (1985). Boundary roles and intergroup conflict. In S. Worchel & W. G. Austin (Eds.), *Psychology of intergroup relations* (pp. 343–363). Chicago: Nelson-Hall.

Jahoda, G. (1969). *The psychology of superstition.* London: Allen Lane.

Karoly, V. (1982). The control experiment of an industrial psychological model. *Magyar Pszichologiai Szemle, 39,* 383–403.

Kashima, Y., & Triandis, H. C. (1986). The self-serving bias in attributions as a coping strategy: A cross-cultural study. *Journal of Cross-Cultural Psychology, 17,* 225–248.

Kihlstrom, J. F., Cantor, N., Albright, J. S., Chew, B. R., Klein, S. B., & Niedenthal, P. M. (1988). Information processing and the study of self. *Advances in experimental social psychology* (Vol. 21, pp. 145–178). San Diego: Academic Press.

Klineberg, O. (1954). *Social psychology.* New York: Holt.

Lévy-Leboyer, C. (1994). Selection and assessment in Europe. In Triandis, H. C., M. D. Dunnette, & L. M. Hough (Eds.), *Handbook of industrial and organizational psychology* (2nd ed., Vol. 4, pp. 173–190). Palo Alto, CA: Consulting Psychologists Press.

Lincoln, J. R., Henada, M. R., & Olson, J. (1981). Cultural orientation and individual reactions to organizations: A study of employees of Japanese armed forces. *Administrative Science Quarterly, 26,* 93–115.

Luthens, F., McCaul, H. S., & Dodd, N. G. (1985). Organizational commitment: A comparison of American, Japanese and Korean employees. *Academy of Management Journal, 28,* 213–219.

Marrow, A. J., Bowers, D. G., & Seashore, S. E., (Eds.). (1967). *Management by participation.* New York: Harper & Row.

Marsh, R. J., & Mannari, H. (1977). Organizational commitment and turnover: A prediction study. *Administrative Science Quarterly, 22,* 57–75.

Maslow, A. H. (1943). A theory of human motivation. *Psychological Review, 50,* 370–396.

Matsui, T., Kakuyama, T., & Onglatco, M. L. (1987). Effects of goals and feedback on performance in groups. *Journal of Applied Psychology, 72,* 407–415.

Mendenhall, M., & Oddom, G. (1985). The dimensions of expatriate acculturation: A review. *Academy of Management Review, 10,* 39–47.

Miller, V. A. (1979). *The guidebook for international trainers in business and industry.* New York: Van Nostrand Reinhold.

Miller, V. A. (1994). *The guidebook for global trainers.* Amherst, MA: Human Resource Development Press.

Misumi, J. (1985). *The behavioral science of leadership: An interdisciplinary Japanese research program.* Ann Arbor, MI: University of Michigan Press.

Misumi, J., & Peterson, M. F. (1985). The performance-maintenance (PM) theory of leadership: Review of a Japanese research program. *Administrative Science Quarterly, 30,* 198–223.

Mudd, S. A. (1968). Group sanction severity as a function of degree of behavior deviation and relevance of norm. *Journal of Personality and Social Psychology, 8,* 258–260.

Near, J. P. (1989). Organizational commitment among Japanese and U.S. workers. *Organizational Studies, 10*(3), 281–300.

Nemetz, P. L., & Christensen, S. L. (1996). The challenge of cultural diversity: Harnessing a diversity of views to understand multiculturalism. *Academy of Management Review, 21*(2), 434–462.

Nevis, E. C. (1983). Using an American perspective in understanding another culture: Towards a hierarchy of needs for the People's Republic of China. *Journal of Applied Behavioral Science, 19,* 249–264.

Okabe, R. (1983). Cultural assumptions of East and West: Japan and the United States. In W. B. Gudyhkunst (Ed.), *Intercultural communications theory: Current perspectives.* Beverly Hills, CA: Sage.

Orpen, C. (1983). Westernization as a moderator of the effect of job attributes on employee satisfaction and performance. *Humanita: Journal of Research in the Human Sciences, 9,* 275–279.

Ozawa, K., Crosby, M., & Crosby, F. (1996). Individualism and resistance to affirmative action: A comparison of Japanese and American samples. *Journal of Applied Social Psychology, 26*(13), 1138–1152.

Perlaki, I. (1994). Organizational development in eastern Europe: Learning to build culture specific OD theories. *Journal of Applied Behavioral Science, 30*(3), 297–312.

Peterson, M. F., Smith, P. B., Akande, A., Ayestaran, S., Bochner, S., Callan, V., Cho, N. G., Jesuino, J. C., D'Amorim, M., Francois, P. H., Hofmann, K., Koopman, P., Leung, K., Lim, T. K., Mortazavi, S., Munene, J., Radford, M., Ropo, A., Savage, G., Setiadi, B., Sinha, T. N., Sorenson, R., & Viedge, C. (1995). Role conflict, ambiguity and overload: A 21-nation study. *The Academy of Management Journal, 38*(2), 429–452.

Price-Williams, D. R. (1985). Cultural psychology. In G. Lindzey & E. Aronson (Eds.), *Handbook of social psychology* (pp. 993–1037). New York: Random House.

Putti, J. M., Aryee, S., & Liang, T. K. (1989). Work values and organizational commitment: A study in the Asian context. *Human Relations, 42,* 275–288.

Redding, S. G., Norman, A., & Schlander, A. (1994). The nature of individual attachment to the organization: A review of East Asian variations. In H. C. Triandis, M. D. Dunnette, & L. M. Hough (Eds.), *Handbook of industrial and organizational psychology* (Vol. 4., 2nd ed., pp. 647–688). Palo Alto, CA: Consulting Psychologists Press.

Roberts, K. H., & Boyacigiller, N. A. (1984). Cross-national organizational research: The grasp of the blind men. *Research in Organizational Behavior, 6,* 423–475.

Schein, E. H. (1996). Culture: The missing concept in organizational studies. *Administrative Science Quarterly, 41,* 229–240.

Schneider, S. C., (1988). National vs. corporate culture: Implications for human resource management. *Human Resource Management, 27,* 231–246.

Schuler, H. (1993). Social validity of selection situations: A concept and some empirical results. In H. Schuler, J. L. Farr, & M. Smith (Eds.), *Personnel selection and assessment: Individual and organizational perspectives.* Hillsdale, NJ: LEA.

Shweder, R. A., & LeVine, R. A. (1984). *Culture theory: Essays on mind, self and emotion*. New York: Cambridge University Press.

Smith, P. B., Misumi, J., Tayeb, M., Peterson, M., & Bond, M. (1989). On the generality of leadership style measures across cultures. *Journal of Occupational Psychology, 62,* 97–109.

Smith, S. H., & Whitehead, G. T. (1984). Attributions for promotion and demotion in the U.S. and India. *Journal of Social Psychology, 124,* 27–34.

Thomas, D. C., & Ravlin, E. C. (1995). Responses of employees to cultural adaptation by a foreign manager. *Journal of Applied Psychology, 80*(1), 133–146.

Toulson, P. K., & Smith, M. C. (1991). Semantic confusion and attitudes to work: Its effect on our understanding of the workplace. *Applied Psychology: An International Review, 40*(1), 55–70.

Triandis, H. C. (1977). *Interpersonal behavior.* Monterey, CA: Brooks/Cole.

Triandis, H. C. (1980). Values, attitudes and interpersonal behavior. In H. E. Howe, Jr. & M. M. Page (Eds.), *Nebraska symposium on motivation,* 1979, Lincoln, NE: University of Nebraska Press.

Triandis, H. C. (1982). Dimensions of intercultural variation as parameters of organizational theories. *International Studies of Management and Organization, 12,* 139–169.

Triandis, H. C. (1989). The self and social behavior in differing cultural contexts. *Psychological Review, 96,* 506–520.

Triandis, H. C. (1994). Cross-cultural Industrial and Organizational Psychology. In H. C. Triandis, M. D. Dunnette, & L. M. Hough (Eds.), *Handbook of industrial and organizational psychology* (2nd ed., Vol. 4, pp. 103–172). Palo Alto, CA: Consulting Psychologists Press.

Triandis, H. C., Bontempo, R., Leung, K., & Hui, C. H. (1990). A method for determining cultural, demographic, and personal constructs. *Journal of Cross-Cultural Psychology, 21,* 302–318.

Triandis, H. C., Bontempo, R., Vilareal, M. J., Masaaki, K. A., & Lucca, N. (1988). Individualism and collectivism: Cross-cultural perspectives on self-ingroup relationships. *Journal of Personality and Social Psychology, 54,* 328–338.

Triandis, H. C., McCusker, C., & Hui, C. (1990). Multimethod probes of individualism and collectivism. *Journal of Personality and Social Psychology, 59,* 1006–1020.

Zaheer, S. (1995). Overcoming the liability of foreignness. *The Academy of Management Journal, 38,* 327–340.

Zeira, V., & Adler, S. (1980). International organizational development: Goals, problems and challenges. *Group and Organizational Studies, 5,* 295–309.

Index

Abilities and other characteristics
(AOs), 79, 95, 104
Ability tests
clerical, 217
mechanical, 215–216, 217
as predictors, 214–218
in selection process, 18, 19, 81,
83–84
sensory and physical, 217–218
Absence culture, 380
Absenteeism
involuntary, 381
job satisfaction and, 378–383
as performance criterion, 139–140,
141
Absolute frequency scale, 118
Abstractive cultures, 564
Acceptances, erroneous, 265
Accommodating style of conflict
resolution, 538
Accurate perception, 569–570
Achievement needs, 341–342
Achievement tests, 214–218
Action tendency scales, 385
Active listening, 456, 457
Activity analysis, 134
Activity sampling, 473
Actual criteria, 132, 133–134
Adams, H. L., 173
Adams, J. S., 349
Adaptation phase of systems
approach, 291
Additional allowance plan, 424
Adiar, J. G., 143
Adjective checklist method, 166, 169
Adler, N. J., 470–471
Adler, S., 581
Adult learning, 288–289

Adverse impact, 105–107,
272–273
Affective intention, 561
Affective state, 521–523
Affinity diagrams, 532
Affirmative action, 273–274
African-Americans, job satisfaction
of, 372–373
African culture, 565–566, 578
AGCT (Army General Classification
Test), 15
Age
job analysis and, 105–106
job satisfaction and, 371–372
Age Discrimination in Employment
Act of 1967, 105–106, 193, 404
Agents, 373
Agreeableness, 219
Ahlbom, A., 387
Ainsworth-Land, G., 545
Albemarle Paper Company v. *Moody*
(1975), 106, 273
Alderfer, C. P., 341
Alderfer's ERG theory, 341
Alexander, R. A., 151, 265
Alfredsson, A., 389
Algina, J., 233–234
Alignment on purpose, 540, 541–542
All-channel network, 446
Allen, J. S., 496
Allen-Bradley Co., 559–560
Alliger, G. M., 484
Allocentric individuals, 560
Allport, G. W., 218, 219
Alston, J. P., 586
Alternate form reliability, 211
Ambient stimuli, 520–522
Ambrose, M. L., 194

American Board of Professional
Psychology, 7
American College Testing
Corporation, 332
American Compensation Association,
403
American Psychological Association
(APA), 11, 16, 21–22, 106,
293
American Psychological Society
(APS), 21
American Society for Personnel
Administration, 403
Americans with Disabilities Act of
1990 (ADA), 249
American Telephone and Telegraph
Company (AT&T), 17
Amiable style, 464–466
Amirkahn, J., 273–274
Ammons, D. N., 179
Analytical style, 465, 466
Anastasi, A., 209, 211, 215
Anderson, B. R., 121
Andragogy, 288
Angarola, R. T., 223
Anhalt, R. L., 181
Antecedent variable, 35
Application blanks, 79, 224–225
Applied Motion Study (Gilbreth and
Gilbreth), 11, 13
*Applied Psychology—An International
Review* (journal), 23
Approximation, 457
Aptitude tests, 142, 209, 214–218,
228
Area Wage Survey, 411
Argawala-Rogers, R., 453
Argentinian culture, 572

Photo Credits